Accounting and Finance for Business Students

3rd Edition

Edited by Jill Hussey

Mike Bendrey, MSc, FCMA, FCCA
Roger Hussey, MSc, PhD, FCCA
Colston West, ACMA

Mike Bendrey is Principal Lecturer in Accounting and Finance at Bristol Business School
Roger Hussey is NWIS Professor of Financial Services at Bristol Business School
Colston West is a member of Bristol Business School and author of a number of accounting and computer texts

DP PUBLICATIONS LTD
Aldine Place
142/144 Uxbridge Road
Shepherds Bush Green
London W12 8AW

1995

Acknowledgements

We would like to thank all our colleagues at Bristol Business School who have used this book and whose valuable comments have been incorporated in this edition. We are also grateful to Dr David Dugdale and John Price for contributing to the questions in chapters 25 and 26, and to Jill Hussey for lending her editing skills.

ISBN 1 85805 075 8

A CIP catalogue record for this book is available from the British Library

First Edition 1989
Reprinted 1990
Second Edition 1992
Reprinted 1992
Third Edition 1994
Reprinted 1995

Printed in Great Britain by The Guernsey Press Co Ltd, Vale, Guernsey

Preface

Aim of the book

Accounting and Finance for Business Students is written for students on BTEC Higher National courses, foundation courses in Accounting and Finance, and first year degree courses in Business Studies. Students on other courses, such as engineering, hotel management and catering, Association of Accounting Technicians and a number of Royal Society of Arts and London Chamber of Commerce courses which include accounting and finance, will find this book a comprehensive introduction to the subject. Students studying on their own will also find the book an invaluable guide.

Nature of the book

This is not a traditional textbook. It is a combined ***textbook, workbook and course manual.***

- As a textbook it is aimed at the newcomer to accounting and finance. The style has been kept deliberately simple and there are plenty of examples with solutions in the text. Accounting terms are introduced gradually and explained in ordinary, everyday language.
- At the end of each chapter there are large number of student activities which enable the student to use it as a workbook.
- The book is divided into clearly defined chapters, making it ideal for use as a course manual. Lecturers can use it to plan lectures and assignments, and refer students to the appropriate chapter for the topic.

Structure of the book

Accounting and Finance for Business Students is divided into three parts:

Part I. Sources and Uses of Finance

Part II. Financial Accounting

Part III. Management Accounting

Each part contains a number of sections which cover all the major topics. Each section contains between two and six chapters, and an assignment.

Every chapter contains a set of objectives and an introduction, together with clear and simple text which includes many examples and solutions. At the end of each chapter there is a summary and a range of student activities. These include a balanced mixture of:

- tasks, which involve the student carrying out some research or looking in the text for information to complete the exercise;
- questions (without answers), which are problems to solve;
- objective tests, which will help students to assess how well they have understood the topic.

Effective use of the book

By students on a taught course:

- Your lecturer will tell you which chapter to read.
- Pay particular attention to the examples and solutions given in the text. Try to solve the problems given in the examples unaided and in writing before you read the solution.
- Attempt any student activities set by your lecturer. If you are not happy with your results, check your answers against those provided by the lecturer and try the activity again some time later.

By students studying on their own:

The text has been designed to be simple and easy to understand, even if you are studying without the assistance of a lecturer. Numerous examples and solutions are provided and you are advised to following the following guidelines:

- Attempt the examples when you come to them in the text unaided and in writing.
- Compare your answers with the solutions that follow.
- Attempt as many of the student activities as possible as they will progressively test your comprehension of the subject matter.

By the end of the book, you should have a good appreciation of the basic principles underlying the sources and uses of finance, and financial and management accounting.

By lecturers on a taught course:

There are many different ways in which this book may be used. A typical procedure might be:

- Using the contents page, select those chapters which are appropriate to the syllabus.
- Programme the coverage of chapters according to the weeks available for the course, allowing a few weeks for revision.
- In a lecture:
  Direct the students to the appropriate chapter.
  Explain the major principles.
  Exemplify the principles, using your own examples or those in the text.
  Set the directed learning, selected from the student activities at the end of each chapter.
- In a tutorial:
  Give guidance at the students' presentations of their work if possible, hand out photocopies of the answers (from the Lecturers' Supplement which is provided free).
- Select an assignment, if appropriate.

Coverage of the book

The number of topics which could be included in a book of this nature is extensive. Instead of attempting to include every topic briefly, only those we consider to be important, useful and interesting to business and management students have been included. This has allowed us to give more comprehensive explanations and more numerous examples and questions.

We have excluded bookkeeping. Some lecturers believe that this is a necessary preliminary to the study of financial accounting, even for business and management students. We do not subscribe to that view; it is not necessary to be a car mechanic in order to drive a car. The method of instruction employed in Part II of this book has proved successful over many years and saves students much time and tedium. Where the elements of bookkeeping are a necessary part of an accounting course, we believe that they should be taught after the principles and purposes of the profit and loss account and balance sheet have been mastered. We have found that this procedure is better for the students and they assimilate the principles of bookkeeping with greater speed, interest and comprehension.

At the end of any introductory accounting course, students should be able to give a financial description of a business, present information in such a way that the financial performance of a business can be appraised and controlled, and use and understand the accounting techniques that assist decision-making. We consider that this book not only satisfies these aims, but provides a sound foundation for students intending to study accounting at a more advanced level.

Lecturers' Supplement

Outline answers to all the questions and objective tests at the end of chapters and to assignments where appropriate are contained in the Lecturers' Supplement. This is available free from the publishers to lecturers adopting the book as a course text.

The 3rd Edition

Recent significant changes in financial reporting and the business environment have made it necessary to update certain chapters, in particular those concerned with limited liability companies (Chapters 20–22) and public sector financial statements (Chapter 25). We have also expanded the chapters on limited liability companies. In addition we have taken the opportunity of making some minor revisions and additions to the text throughout the book.

All this has been possible without altering any chapter numbers and the book retains the improved structure and presentation of the second edition. Therefore, both lecturers and students already familiar with the book will find it easy to move on to this latest edition.

We would like to thank our colleagues at the University of the West of England for their useful comments. Feedback obtained in this way confirms our view that students' enthusiasm for the learning activities offered in this book defies the old adage:

> *"Multiplication is vexation, division is as bad;*
> *the rule of three doth puzzle me, and Practice drives me mad."*
> *Anon*

Link with *Spreadsheets for Business Students*

For students learning spreadsheet applications (using Lotus 1-2-3 or compatible packages such As-Easy-As or VP-Planner), Colston West's ***Spreadsheets for Business Students*** (also published by DP Publications) makes an ideal companion to ***Accounting and Finance for Business Students***, as all the examples in ***Spreadsheets*** are lifted directly from this book. (Note: the examples are given in full in both books, so that they can be used equally effectively independently.)

Also ***Spreadsheets for Accountancy Students*** (by Colston West) incorporates the complete content of ***Spreadsheets for Business Students***, but, in addition, contains 21 modules, some interrelated, covering financial accounting, management accounting and financial management. The active construction of these additional models will help students to appreciate more fully the principles described in ***Accounting & Finance for Business Students*** as well as illustrating the potential of spreadsheets for solving 'what-if?' problems.

Both books are in the DP Publications 'Promoting Active Learning' series.

Mike Bendrey
Roger Hussey
Colston West

July 1994

Contents

Part 1

Sources and uses of finance

Personal finance

Introduction

This section (Chapters 1–5) is concerned with the various sources of personal finance and the uses to which it may be put. You will be introduced to many of the issues and calculations which appear again in subsequent sections.

In Chapter 1 we look at the main sources of personal finance and Chapter 2 concentrates on the system in the United Kingdom under which most people have taxation deducted from their earnings.

In Chapter 3 we briefly examine the other deductions which may be made from your pay before it is received and considers another form of taxation, Value Added Tax.

The decisions and calculations required when setting financial objectives are covered in Chapter 4.

Chapter 5, which examines cash planning and the construction of personal cash flows, completes this section on personal finance.

Chapter 1

Sources of personal finance

1.1 Objectives

At the end of this chapter you should be able to:

- explain what is meant by personal financial planning;
- carry out basic calculations of interest rates;
- identify the purposes and features of short-term finance;
- identify the purposes and features of long-term finance.

1.2 Personal financial planning

All forms of planning are concerned with:

- deciding what your present position is;
- setting objectives of where you wish to be within a certain time;
- deciding how you can achieve the objectives you have set;
- monitoring your actual performance against the objectives.

Personal financial planning is concerned with assessing your present and expected financial resources and deciding how they can be most effectively used to achieve objectives you have set. The three elements of personal financial planning are:

i) Determining what your present financial resources are such as:

   - savings you have made;
   - your earning power;
   - the amount of borrowing you can make.

   In other words, finding out your ***credit-worthiness.***

ii) Predicting future changes in your financial resources by:

   - examining the limitations and opportunities you are confronted with and determining what your realistic objectives can be within a certain period of time;
   - planning how your financial resources can best be used to achieve the objectives you have set.

iii) Monitoring your performance against your objectives.

In Chapter 4 we shall consider how financial objectives can be set and in Chapter 5 we shall examine the planning and control of receipts and payments of money. In this chapter we are concerned with explaining the various sources of personal finance.

1.3 Main sources of personal finance

The ***main sources*** of personal finance are ***savings, earnings*** and ***loans,*** both short and long-term. Not all of these sources are open to all individuals all the time. It is unfortunate, but the general rule is that the richer you are, the easier you will find it to borrow money. A person with a certain amount of savings and a good job will find that their ability to borrow is much higher than someone who is unemployed. The objective of personal financial planning is to use the various sources available sensibly and effectively whatever your financial status.

1.4 Savings

You might keep whatever ***savings*** you have as cash in an old teapot. In this way if you want to buy something, it is easy to take your savings from the teapot and make your purchase. However, such an approach is neither sensible nor effective.

It is not sensible because of the high risk involved. In the event of a fire or burglary you could lose your entire savings. It makes good sense to keep your savings in a safe place. For many people this may mean a bank or a building society. Both of these are very safe and could have the added advantage of paying you interest on the savings you have deposited. Your savings themselves are earning money and are therefore a source of finance.

But you also want your savings to be effective. In other words, you want to earn the best possible return on your savings in line with other objectives you may have. At first you may think that it is an easy matter to select the highest possible return from your savings and you need not worry about other considerations. But, if you reflect for a moment, you will realise that the position of say a student with savings of £300 with which he/she intends to buy a camera in 3 months' time is very different from that of a millionaire with £25,000 to invest.

Some matters may be very important to a student, but of less importance to the millionaire. For example, a student may want to know that his/her savings are safe and easily available in three months' time. The millionaire may not be too worried if the £25,000 is lost, but is probably looking for a really large return on the investment.

There are a number of other considerations which may have to be taken into account. All of these can be grouped under four specific headings, representing the four factors which every investor should consider:

i) The degree of ***risk*** involved in the investment
Some investments are very safe. If you put your money into a bank or a building society you have few fears that your savings will be lost. If you put your money into stocks and shares then you are aware that changes on the stock market could erode the value of your savings. The general rule is the higher the degree of risk associated with the investment the higher the return you would expect on your investment.

    The degree of risk you are willing to accept depends on your own character and the financial resources available to you. Some people may bet their last penny on an outsider in a horse race, whereas others may place their savings only in the safest of investments.

ii) The ***amount*** to be invested
Apart from personal characteristics, the amount of your savings also determines the degree of risk you will accept. Someone with life savings of a few thousand pounds would not be well advised to choose a risky investment, although a wealthy person with a range of investments may be quite happy to risk a certain amount on a speculative investment.

    The amount you have to invest not only helps to determine the risk you are willing to accept, but also helps establish the amount of return you enjoy. If you examine the amounts of interest offered by building societies, you will see that the greater the amount you deposit with the society the greater the amount of interest they pay you. There are a number of different investment opportunities where you must be willing to invest a certain sum.

iii) The ***access*** to the investment
The length of time you are willing to leave your money invested without taking any of it out can influence the amount of return you receive. This ability to withdraw your savings is known as access. Instant access or access on demand allows you to withdraw all your savings immediately. The interest on these types of investment are lower than where you have to give notice before making a withdrawal. The period of notice may range from seven days to a number of months. Because you are willing to commit your money for a certain period of time, the borrower is prepared to pay a higher rate of interest for the use of the money.

iv) The ***rate of return*** on the investment
This is the amount of interest you receive on your investment. It is a reward to you for sacrificing the opportunity to use your savings in some other way, such as spending them. Generally, the greater the sacrifice you are willing to make, the higher the rate of return you should expect. As we have seen, the rate of return is dependent upon the degree of risk, the amount of investment and the access required. Clearly you

will want the highest rate of return possible, but your decision will be influenced by the other three factors. The higher the rate of return you can obtain, the greater your savings will grow.

> *You should now be able to attempt Tasks 1.1 and 1.2 at the end of this chapter.*

1.5 Simple interest

Interest paid only on the ***principal*** (the amount invested) is known as ***simple interest***. We will consider the other form of interest, known as ***compound interest*** in the next section. The calculation of simple interest is very straightforward. To calculate the absolute amount you will receive from a given rate of interest the formula is:

$$\text{Amount received} = \text{Amount invested} \times \frac{\text{Interest rate}}{100} \times \text{period}$$

If you invest £250 for one year at an interest rate of 10% per annum payable at the end of the year, the amount of interest you would receive would be:

$$£250 \times \frac{10}{100} \times 1 \text{ year} = £25.$$

Example

If you invest £1,500 for one year at $8\frac{1}{2}$% per annum, payable at the end of the year, how much interest would you receive?

Solution

$$£1{,}500 \times \frac{8.5}{100} \times 1 \text{ year} = £127.50$$

Example

If you invest £5,000 for one year at 9% per annum, and this interest is added to your investment at the year end, how much will your investment be worth?

Solution

$$£5{,}000 + £5{,}000 \times \frac{9}{100} \times 1 \text{ year}$$

$$£5{,}000 + £450 = £5{,}450$$

Alternative calculation:

$$£5{,}000 \times 1.09 \times 1 \text{ year} = £5{,}450$$

Note: A percentage such as 9% can also be expressed as 0.09. Similarly, £1 invested at 9% for one year becomes £1.09.

Example

If you invest £10,000 for four years at 12% per annum, payable at the end of each year, how much interest would you receive in total?

Solution

$$£10{,}000 \times \frac{12}{100} \times 4 \text{ years} = £4{,}800$$

Example

If you invest £2,700 for six years at 7.5% per annum, payable at the end of each year, how much interest would you receive in total?

Solution

$$£27{,}000 \times \frac{7.5}{100} \times 6 \text{ years} = £12{,}150$$

You should now be able to attempt Questions 1.1–1.8 at the end of this chapter.

1.6 Compound interest

With some forms of investment the interest is not paid out but is automatically reinvested, and interest is paid not only on the principal (the original amount invested) but on the interest reinvested. This is known as ***compound interest.*** In this section we will only look at the basic principles of calculating compound interest. In Chapter 4 we will look at more complex calculations.

Many interest rates quoted are not easily compared because the interest may be paid out and reinvested more frequently with some forms of investment than with others. If an interest of 10% per annum on your £250 investment is paid not once a year but half-yearly, and the interest at the half year is immediately reinvested, the total amount of interest you will receive is:

$$\text{Interest for first six months} = £250 \times \frac{10}{100} \times \frac{6}{12} = £12.50$$

$$\text{Interest for second six months} = £262.50 \times \frac{10}{100} \times \frac{6}{12} = £13.125$$

The amount of interest received for the 12 months is £25.625

Alternative calculation:

(You may find it easier to convert the above fractions to decimals)

Interest for first six months = £250 × 0.10 × 0.5 = £12.50

Interest for second six months = £262.50 × 0.10 × 0.5 = £13.125

This may seem a small increase, but it is important if large sums of money are invested for long periods of time. The true rate of interest in the above example, where interest is paid half yearly, can be calculated as follows:

$$\text{True rate of interest} = \frac{£25.625}{£250} \times 100 = 10.25\%$$

Example

You invest £1,000 at 10% per annum. What is the total amount of interest you receive if the interest is paid and reinvested?

i) annually

ii) half yearly

iii) quarterly

Solution

i)	Whole year:	£1,000 × 0.10 =	£100.00
ii)	First 6 months:	£1,000 × 0.10 × 0.5 =	£50.00
	Second 6 months:	£1,050 × 0.10 × 0.5 =	£52.50
			£102.50
iii)	1st quarter:	£1,000 × 0.10 × 0.25 =	£25.000
	2nd quarter:	£1,025 × 0.10 × 0.25 =	£25.625
	3rd quarter:	£1,050.625 × 0.10 × 0.25 =	£26.266
	4th quarter:	£1,076.891 × 0.10 × 0.25 =	£26.922
			£103.813

Example

What are the true rates of interest for (i), (ii) and (iii) in the above example?

Solution

i) 10%

ii) $\frac{£102.50}{£1,000} \times 100 = 10.25\%$

iii) $\frac{£103,813}{£1,000} \times 100 = 10.3813\%$

You should now be able to attempt Questions 1.9–1.12 at the end of this chapter.

1.7 Types of investment

There are a number of different places where savings can be invested. The main ones are:

- ***Building societies,*** which offer many different schemes, all with low risk and clearly defined interest rates. Some accounts can be opened with only a small sum; many offer immediate access.
- ***Banks,*** where you can open a simple deposit account with as low an amount as you wish with immediate access. There are also term and fixed notice accounts which offer higher rates of interest.
- ***The Post Office,*** which offers very easy-to-operate schemes and competitive rates of interest through the National Savings Bank and National Savings Certificates.
- ***Stocks and shares,*** which are securities offered by public limited companies, local authorities, central government and other institutions for purchase by the public. In recent years there has been a significant increase in the number of people owning stocks and shares, but they not a recommended form of investment for those on a modest income.
- ***Unit trusts,*** which offer greater security against down-turns in the stock market, but are not recommended for those with modest savings requiring fast access. A unit trust is a fund held on behalf of the investors by trustees who are often banks, insurance companies or large financial institutions. The trustees employ fund managers who use the investors' money to buy and sell shares on their behalf.

> *You should now be able to attempt Task 1.3 at the end of this chapter.*

1.8 Earnings

For most people, the main source of personal finance is their ***earnings***. If you calculate the amount of money you hope to earn in your working life, it is likely to be a very large figure. Unfortunately, a proportion of your earnings are taken in taxation and other deductions before you even receive them. These are subjects to be dealt with in subsequent chapters.

To a great extent, the amount of your earnings determines your lifestyle, even if you are fortunate enough to have inherited wealth. Apart from those individuals on the lowest earnings, all of us are faced with the same major choice: Should we save or spend?

Although you may consider that your earnings are such that you can only afford the essentials, and have nothing spare to save, that is unlikely to be the case. We often make the decision to spend a certain amount and thereby exclude the possibility of saving. For example, we may choose to rent or buy a house because we find it pleasant or it is in a convenient area. In all probability cheaper accommodation would be available, but it would not be as pleasant or so convenient. We have therefore chosen to spend money on obtaining pleasant and convenient accommodation instead of saving.

We all know that giving up certain luxuries enables us to save for a particular item. Some people limit the number of social outings they have so that they can save for a summer holiday. Others may take sandwiches to work instead of eating out in order to save money. By selecting one course of action, we often have to give up the opportunity to do something else. This is a topic we shall return to in Chapter 4.

The amount of earnings we have depends on many factors: education, the types of skill we have, the demand in the local job market etc. But the amount of our earnings is not completely fixed. In the long-term we may seek higher paid employment by improving the skills we have to offer. In the short-term we may choose to increase our earnings by working harder. For many this means working longer hours, either through overtime or by taking additional part-time employment.

By working longer hours we increase our earnings, but we also have to make sacrifices. This may be a decrease in the amount of time we can spend with family and friends in sport and leisure activities. We may also be sacrificing our health if we work excessively long hours.

1.9 Loans

The final source of finance we are going to consider is ***loans***. Minors, those under the age of 18, are not legally bound by contracts for money borrowed. This means that in the case of non-repayment of the loan, the lender cannot bring a court action for the recovery of the money. Some financial institutions are willing to lend to a minor if parents or guardians sign an indemnity, accepting full liability for the debt.

No matter what the age of the borrower, the lender needs to be certain that the money will be repaid. In other words, the lender needs to ascertain the credit-worthiness of the borrower. The amount of money a person is able to borrow is usually limited by their perceived ability to repay the loan within a certain time. From the borrower's point of view, he or she is obtaining financial resources now, but promising to pay the interest and repay the loan out of future earnings.

There are two main forms of personal loans: short-term and long-term. Which is the most appropriate depends on the purpose for which the loan is required. It would not make sense to borrow money to buy a car and expect to repay the loan over 20 years. The general rule is that the repayment period should not exceed the length of time the specific purchase is expected to last. A 20-year-loan would be more suitable for the purchase of a house. A loan for a car is normally two to three years.

1.10 Short-term finance

Obtaining *short-term finance* serves a number of purposes:

- to fill the gap when earnings are temporarily lower than expenditure (for example, if you normally work overtime and this has temporarily ceased);
- to prevent the need to use savings which are not readily available; (perhaps you have invested them long-term to obtain a higher interest rate and do not have immediate access);
- to cover the cost of a purchase which can be met from future earnings (for example, buying clothes to start a new job);
- to cover the period when the expenditure takes place before the earnings are received (for example, buying materials to do a job for someone who will pay you later).

The commonest forms of short-term finance are:

- *Bank overdrafts*
  The borrower contacts the bank where they have a current account and a borrowing limit is agreed. This is the amount up to which the borrower is able to overdraw on his or her current account. The bank charges interest for this service which is usually calculated at a certain percentage above the bank's base rate. The base rate is a fixed rate set by the high street banks at intervals and is used by the banks as a basis for calculating their interest charges.
- *Credit cards*
  These cards, such as Access and Barclaycard, are issued by companies owned by the major banks. They can be used at various shops and outlets such as garages, restaurants and theatres. Some large retailers, for example Marks and Spencer, have their own credit cards which can only be used at their own store. The card issued to an individual has a maximum credit limit, usually based on salary level. Purchases are made by using the card instead of cash or a cheque. A monthly statement is sent to the cardholder showing the total purchases made and the total payment due. If payment is not made by the due date (normally 21 days from the date of the statement), interest at a high rate is charged. If payment is made before the due date, there is no interest payable and the cardholder enjoys free credit.
- *Credit accounts*
  With this form of finance the purchaser pays a regular monthly amount to the retailer. The account holder is able to make a purchase in excess of the total amount saved in the account at any time. The amount of credit is based upon the monthly sum saved and is usually approximately 30 times this amount. A person saving £2 per month would therefore be able to make purchases to the value of £60.

  Banks operate their own credit account system under a variety of names. The principles are the same as those run by retail outlets described above. The advantage with the banks' systems is that you are not tied to any one particular retailer when you make a purchase. It should be borne in mind that interest at quite a high rate is charged on any borrowings.

1.11 Long-term finance

Long-term finance is used to purchase those items which we cannot afford to buy outright from our earnings. The item is usually expensive and will last a relatively long time, for example a car, boat or house. The loan is repaid over a number of years. In the case of a mortgage on a house, this may be in excess of 20 years.

The commonest forms of long-term finance are:

- *Personal loans*
  A personal loan can be obtained from a bank or building society. This form of finance is normally used for the purchase of cars, boats, caravans, sports goods, photographic equipment etc. Features of a personal loan are:
  - It is for a fixed amount.
  - The interest rate is fixed for the period of the loan.

- The loan is for a fixed period of time.
- Repayments are by monthly instalments of a fixed amount.
- Repayment of the loan before the end of the period is usually not permitted without a fee being incurred.

- *Hire purchase*
  This is usually arranged by the retailer selling the goods. The retailer has an agreement with a finance house to supply the credit facilities and to complete the necessary paperwork when the goods are sold. Hire purchase is normally used to purchase specific items as with a personal loan, but unlike the personal loan, ownership of the goods does not pass to the purchaser until the final payment has been made.

- *Mortgage*
  A mortgage is most frequently used for the purchase of a house. It is a legal document which gives the lender legal rights over the property and the power to resell if the borrower is unable to maintain the repayments.

You should now be able to attempt Question 1.13 at the end of this chapter.

1.12 Annual percentage rate

The ***annual percentage rate (APR)*** allows borrowers to compare the cost of loans from different financial institutions. It is the total annual cost of the loan, including both interest and any fees the borrower may have to pay upon signing a credit agreement. The costs are expressed as a percentage of the amount borrowed.

As the APR may include fees, it is not an interest rate but a measure of the full cost. Even if fees are not payable, the calculation of the APR may show that the true cost of a loan is much higher than the interest rate may suggest. A loan of £500 at a fixed rate of 10% per annum over three years will cost £150. But the reality is that you will not borrow the total £500 for three years, as each month you will be paying back a part of it. In fact over a three year period, the average amount you will have borrowed is more like £250, and that is why the APR is usually about twice the flat rate of interest.

1.13 Summary

Personal financial planning is concerned with examining your present financial position, setting objectives and deciding how they may be achieved, and monitoring your performance against those objectives. The main sources of finance for individuals are ***savings, earnings*** and ***loans.***

- With ***savings*** you must take into consideration the degree of ***risk*** involved in the investment, the ***amount*** you have to invest, the ***access*** you require and the ***rate of return*** you would like to receive.
- ***Earnings*** are the main source of personal finance for most people. Over the entire length of your working life it will amount to a very large sum, but this will be subject to taxation.
- ***Loans*** may be short or long-term. There are many forms of borrowings and it is important to compare the costs of loans from different financial institutions by using the ***annual percentage rate.***

You should now be able to attempt the Objective Test at the end of this chapter.

Student activities

Task 1.1 A fellow student has inherited £1,000 and has written asking your advice on investing it. Write a reply listing all the questions you think your friend should ask him or herself before making a decision.

Task 1.2 A number of situations are described below. Explain whether you think those concerned could expect a very high rate of return on their investment or a lower rate of return. Before you come to your decision, you must consider the degree of risk, the amount involved and the access required.

i) A woman has won £100,000 and decides she is willing to risk £5,000 in investments.

ii) A young person is saving £20 per week for the purchase of a home computer which costs £800 and is desperately needed for his future studies.

iii) A number of work mates have formed a club and contribute £1 per week each. The contributions are invested and the members of the club choose the more speculative investments.

iv) A man has £1,500 to invest. He has saved the money to buy a second hand car and he is looking for one he likes.

v) An executive has savings of £8,000 and has decided to work abroad for three years. She wishes to invest her money whilst she is away.

Task 1.3 Look through newspapers and magazines, and collect as many advertisements as you can for different forms of investment. Compare them using rate of interest, degree of risk, access and minimum amount of investment required.

Question 1.1 If you invest £350 at 7.5% per annum, payable at the end of the year, how much interest will you receive?

Question 1.2 If you invest £6,000 at 11.25% per annum, payable at the end of the year, how much interest will you receive?

Question 1.3 If you invest £25,000 at 15.75% per annum, payable at the end of the year, how much interest will you receive?

Question 1.4 If you invest £7,000 at 8.75% per annum, and this interest is added to your investment at the year end, how much will your investment then be worth?

Question 1.5 If you invest £450 at 6% per annum, and this interest is added to your investment at the year end, how much will your investment then be worth?

Question 1.6 If you invest £120 at 16% per annum, and this interest is added to your investment at the year end, how much will your investment then be worth?

Question 1.7 All the following calculations are based on simple interest and the interest is added to the investment at the year end. Calculate the missing figures in the following table.

Principal invested	Interest rate per annum	Amount received at year end
£5,000	10%	?
£4,500	15%	?
£2,600	8%	?
£1,500	12%	?
£22,000	28%	?
£104,000	9.5%	?

Question 1.8 All the following calculations are based on simple interest and the interest is added to the investment at the year end. Calculate the missing figures in the following table.

Principal invested	Interest rate per annum	Period of years	Total interest received
£20,000	5%	12	?
£3,600	11%	4	?
£32,000	8.5%	7	?
£16,400	6%	15	?
£100,000	11.25%	20	?
£66,000	14.75%	12	?

Question 1.9 You invest £4,000. Interest, at a rate of 12% per annum, is added at the end of each quarter to the capital sum.

i) How much will the investment be worth at the end of the year?

ii) What is the true rate of interest?

Question 1.10 You invest £18,000. Interest at a rate of 7.5% per annum is added at the end of each quarter to the capital sum.

i) How much will the investment be worth at the end of the year?

ii) What is the true rate of interest?

Question 1.11 You invest £800. Interest at a rate of 16% per annum is added at the end of each quarter to the capital sum.

i) How much will the investment be worth at the end of the year?

ii) What is the true rate of interest?

Question 1.12 You invest £7,500. Interest at a rate of 10% per annum is added at the end of each quarter to the capital sum.

i) How much will the investment be worth at the end of the year?

ii) What is the true rate of interest?

Question 1.13 Are the following sources of finance long-term or short-term?

Mortgage	Long-term/short-term
Bank overdraft	Long-term/short-term
Access or Barclaycard	Long-term/short-term
Hire purchase	Long-term/short-term

Objective test *(tick the appropriate box)*

i) A student with savings of £500 which he may wish to draw upon in an emergency would be advised to invest this amount:

a) in the stock market ☐

b) in a bank current account ☐

c) in a building society account with instant access ☐

d) in an old teapot ☐

ii) If you invest £500 for one year at 5% per annum, with interest paid and reinvested annually, the investment at the end of two years will be worth:

a) £550.00 ☐

b) £551.25 ☐

c) £526.25 ☐

d) £555.00 ☐

iii) If you invest £2,000 for one year at 10% per annum, with interest paid and reinvested half-yearly, the true rate of interest is:

a) 10.20% ☐

b) 10.40% ☐

c) 11.025% ☐

d) 10.25% ☐

iv) If you invest £10,000 at 8% per annum, interest paid and reinvested quarterly, the amount which will have been added after 6 months will be:

a) £404 ☐

b) £1,664 ☐

c) £808 ☐

d). £800 ☐

v) If you require quick access to your savings, you should not invest in:

a) the Post Office Savings Bank ☐

b) bank current accounts ☐

c) buildings society share accounts ☐

d) unit trusts ☐

vi) The amount that an individual can borrow depends mainly on his or her:

a) salary ☐

b) investments ☐

c) social standing ☐

d) education ☐

vii) Bank overdrafts attract a rate of interest which is:

a) base rate set by high street banks ☐

b) base rate plus a premium ☐

c) related to building society mortgage rates ☐

d) determined by the Bank of England ☐

viii) APR stands for:

a) annual percentage rate ☐

b) average profit return ☐

c) actual percentage rate ☐

d) average percentage rate ☐

ix) The main source of personal finance for most people is:

a) savings ☐

b) earnings ☐

c) loans ☐

d) taxation ☐

x) The riskiest form of investment is:

a) Building societies ☐

b) Banks ☐

c) The Post Office ☐

d) Stocks and shares ☐

Chapter 2

Personal taxation

2.1 Objectives

At the end of this chapter you should be able to:

- explain the principles of personal taxation;
- identify the various forms and documents used;
- check a tax coding;
- calculate the tax payable by an individual.

2.2 Introduction

The payment of ***personal taxation*** is compulsory and is the Government's major source of revenue. Income tax is charged on income received by a person and this income includes pay, bonuses, tips, pensions, supplementary and unemployment benefit, and interest and benefits from investments, such as stocks and shares. Self-employed people have to pay income tax on the profits of their business. The income is calculated for the tax year which goes from 6 April one year to 5 April the following year. Fortunately, not all your income is taxed and you are entitled to certain ***allowances***, which reduce the income on which you have to pay tax. We will explain the main allowances later in this chapter.

Although it is legal to attempt to ***avoid*** full payment of tax by carefully arranging your affairs to reduce the total you have to pay, it is an offence to ***evade*** payment of tax, for example by not declaring all your earnings.

Individuals may receive their income in a variety of ways which affect the procedure for working out the amount of tax payable and how it should be paid. The main categories are:

- Earnings as an employee. In this case your employer will deduct the tax you have to pay from your weekly wage or monthly salary and pass it to the Inland Revenue.
- Earnings as a self-employed person. If you work for yourself you may ask an accountant to deal with your tax affairs or you may decide to do it yourself. You must inform the Inland Revenue of your income and outgoings and you will pay any tax in two instalments, in July and January.
- Unearned income from interest and dividends received from investments you have made.
- Income from property.

Taxation is a complex and specialised subject, but we will concentrate on the main principles and the system known as Pay As You Earn (PAYE), under which most people in the United Kingdom have taxation deducted from their earnings.

2.3 The PAYE system

The ***PAYE system*** began in 1944 and covers all employees paid on a regular basis. The main features of the system are:

- It is the employer's legal responsibility to deduct tax from the pay of employees.
- Employers must keep pay records and the Inland Revenue has legal powers to inspect them.
- Employees receive their pay after tax has been deducted by the employer. This is known as net pay.
- Taxpayers who are not self-employed are not included in the PAYE system.
- Tax rates relate to marginal income not to an employee's total income.

No one likes paying tax and there are many who would argue that the PAYE system should be abolished. In all probability they mean that taxation should be abolished. If you accept that taxation must be paid, the PAYE system has the following advantages:

- It is difficult for an employed person to avoid their tax liability.
- From the Government's point of view it is a cheap system as employers do all the work of collecting the tax.
- Tax is paid as the income is received which makes it a fair method for individuals.

However, there are also disadvantages:

- It is slow in operation so an employee may pay the wrong amount of tax for a considerable length of time.
- Employers must spend a considerable amount of time and effort collecting the tax and are not recompensed by the Inland Revenue.
- Employees are at a disadvantage compared with self-employed people who can often claim more expenses and pay their tax in two six-monthly instalments.

You should now be able to attempt Questions 2.1 and 2.2 at the end of this chapter.

2.4 Forms and documentation

To work effectively, the taxation system requires the completion of a number of ***forms and documents*** by individuals and employers. Some of these you may not see unless you are self-employed or your tax affairs are complex. It is important that all forms are completed correctly and copies are kept by you so that, if there is a query on your tax, you will have the information to sort it out. The various forms and documents in use are described in the following sections.

2.5 Tax return

A ***tax return*** is sent to individuals at their home address shortly after the end of the tax year and should be completed and returned within 30 days. These forms can be difficult to complete, but are essential to ensure that you pay the correct amount of tax.

To complete the form you must give details of all your income for the tax year including:

- Income from any trade, profession or vocation
- Income from employment
- Social security pensions, other pensions and benefits
- Income from property, i.e. rent
- Interest and dividends

As well as details of your income, you must give details of your ***outgoings*** and this information will be used to calculate the ***allowances*** to be set against your income. The sort of information includes:

- any expenses connected with your employment including fees or subscriptions to professional bodies;
- personal details on such matters as your marital status, children, dependent relatives, etc so that your ***personal allowances*** for the tax year can be calculated.

The Inland Revenue then uses the information to asses your tax liability for the year.

2.6 Notice of coding

Every employee is given an individual tax code. This is sent to you by the Inland Revenue each March on a small form headed ***PAYE Notice of Coding***. It shows how the Inland Revenue has calculated your code number and this number only will be sent to your employer so that the correct amount of tax will be deducted from your pay. It is up to you to check that the Notice of Coding is correct.

The code number consists of three numbers and a letter (for example, 382H). The letter tells your employer how to make adjustments to your coding automatically if there are changes for any reason during a tax year. The main letters are:

H The basic personal allowance plus the basic married couple's allowance

L The basic personal allowance

P Single pensioner

V Married pensioner

The numbers represent the ***allowances*** you are entitled to against your earnings. In other words, it sets the level of income you can enjoy without paying any tax. In our example of code number 382H, the person has received allowances of £3,825. This is the amount of income which can be earned in a tax year before any tax must be paid. For the purposes of the code number, the final number is dropped to give the code number 382.

The employer is informed of the code number and makes tax deductions from the employee's pay using tax tables and deduction sheets.

2.7 Tax tables

Employers have a duty to collect tax from their employees on behalf of the Inland Revenue. As well as informing the employer of the tax codes, the Inland Revenue will supply ***Tax Tables and Deduction Sheets.***

If we take the above example of the employee with a code number of 382H, it is easy to calculate how much tax that employee is liable for in a tax year if we know the gross pay, i.e. the pay before any stoppages. Let us assume that the employee with that code number earns £15,000 per annum gross. The calculation will be:

	£
Gross annual pay	15,000
Less personal allowances	3,825
Annual taxable pay	11,175

As an illustration, if the tax rate is 25% in the £, the total tax payable will be:

£11,175 × 25% = £2,793.75

The employer will not deduct the tax in one lump sum, but will deduct tax as you earn the income. This means that the employer must know the amount of tax to deduct each week if you are paid a weekly wage, or each month if you are paid a salary. The Inland Revenue supplies the employer with tax tables and deduction sheets which are known as Forms P11. These are of two types:

The ***Free Pay Table,*** known as Table A, show how much of an employee's income from the beginning of the tax year is free from tax for each week of the year and for every code number.

The ***Taxable Pay Table,*** known as Table B, shows how much tax is payable on the employee's taxable income since the beginning of the tax year.

2.8 Pay slip

An employer should provide each employee with a ***pay slip*** every time a payment of wage or salary is made. These take many forms and in larger companies are produced by computer. Whatever the design of the pay slip, the following information should be provided:

- gross pay for the week or month
- tax code

- National Insurance number
- amount of tax deducted
- amount of National Insurance deducted
- any other deductions
- net pay for the week or month
- total gross pay for the tax year to date
- total income tax deductions for the tax year to date
- total National Insurance deductions for the tax year to date

It is always best to check your pay slip each time you receive it. If you receive a regular income you need only satisfy yourself that your tax code is correct and the amounts are as they should be. If you work overtime or receive bonuses you may have to carry out a number of calculations to ensure the accuracy of the amounts given on your pay slip. Below is an example of a pay slip for a salaried employee.

There are different layouts for pay slips and the illustration below is just one example. Note that although the employee has gross pay of £1,465 for the month, the net pay is £1,082.10. This is the amount that the employee will actually receive and is often referred to as the 'take home pay'. This figure is crucial because it represents the amount you will have to live on if you have no other source of income. You have very little influence over the amounts which are deducted from your gross pay. In the following chapter we will discuss the deductions in addition to tax, such as superannuation and National Insurance, which may be made.

Example

PAY SLIP
for month ended 30 June 1989

Name of employee:	William Bolton	**National Insurance Number**
Address:	33, Shipside Street Lowestoft	ZY035455D
		Tax Code 413H
Pay reference	5106183	
Basic Pay	£1,465.00	
PAYE Income Tax	£228.75	
Superannuation	£58.05	
National Insurance	£96.10	
Total Deductions	£382.90	
Net Pay June 1988	£1,082.10	

Taxable pay this employment	£4,395.00
Tax this employment	£686.25
Superannuation	£174.15
National Insurance (Code D)	£288.30

You should now be able to attempt Question 2.3 at the end of this chapter.

2.9 Form P45

If you change employment it is important that your new employer knows your tax details so that the correct amount of tax can be deducted from your pay. For this to happen your existing employer will give you a form known as a *P45* to hand to your new employer. The P45 shows the cumulative amount for pay and tax up to the date that you change employment.

If you do not have a P45 or you lose it, your new employer will deduct tax on an emergency code. This means that you will only receive the basic allowances so you may be paying more tax than you need. The Inland Revenue will be contacted and your new employer given the correct details; you will receive a tax rebate if it is found that you have overpaid.

2.10 Form P60

At the end of each tax year the employer must provide each employee with a form known as a *P60* which should be kept in a safe place. The P60 resembles a pay slip and shows for each year ending 5 April:

- The total amount of pay received by the employee including overtime, bonuses etc for income tax purposes.
- The total tax deducted by the employer, less any refunds during the year.
- The total National Insurance contributions deducted by the employer during the course of the year.

The P60 allows you to check any tax assessment sent to you by the Inland Revenue and to check that the employer is making the correct deductions for National Insurance contributions.

You should now be able to attempt Questions 2.4 and 2.5 at the end of this chapter.

2.11 Personal allowances

Each year in the annual budget, the Chancellor of the Exchequer announces the ***personal allowances*** for the tax year. These are the amounts you can earn during the tax year on which no tax is payable. The personal allowances you are entitled to receive are deducted from your income to give the amount of your taxable income. The amount of tax you pay on your taxable income is calculated as a certain percentage, which is also announced by the Chancellor.

The types of personal allowances and the amounts allowed, and the tax rates are political and social decisions as well as economic ones. This is why the budget causes so much controversy. Not only does it determine the amount of tax we will pay, but it influences the type of society we live in.

If you are making any tax calculations, it is essential that you have the most recent allowances. As an indication of the types of allowances given in addition to the single person's allowance and the married man's allowance, some examples for the tax year 1993-94 are shown below. This is only a brief guide and other conditions may apply.

i) Single gifts to charity – If you make a single qualifying gift to a charity you get basic rate tax relief by giving less to the charity so no allowance is made in your code.

ii) Blind person's allowance – You can claim this if you or your wife is a registered blind person. This means a person who is so blind as to be unable to perform any work for which eyesight is essential.

iii) Personal Pension Plans – You can get basic tax relief on the contributions you pay to an approved personal pension scheme or to a scheme separate from your employer's pension scheme.

In addition to the personal allowances, you may receive other deductions from your income, depending on your personal circumstances. For an employee, the most likely allowances would be for expenses incurred in connection with their employment. This may includes fees or subscriptions to professional bodies.

You should now be able to attempt Tasks 2.1 and 2.2 at the end of this chapter.

2.12 Mortgage Interest Relief At Source (MIRAS)

There are not many people rich enough to purchase their own home outright. If you want to be a home owner, in all probability you will have to obtain a loan from a bank or a building society. This loan or *mortgage* will be over an extended period of time, often 20 years or more, and you will have to pay interest to the lender.

To encourage home ownership, it has been the practice in this country to allow tax relief to the borrower. All the interest paid on the first £30,000 of the loan attracts tax relief. If you borrow in excess of £30,000, you will not receive relief on the additional amount. This limit is set by the Chancellor of the Exchequer and may be changed in future budgets.

Repayments of the mortgage to the bank or the building society are made in a way which automatically takes care of the basic rate tax relief. This is then refunded to the building society or bank by the Inland Revenue through a system known as MIRAS.

2.13 Self-employed persons

Many people do not work for an employer – they are *self-employed*. They have the same responsibility to pay personal tax as an employed person, but the PAYE system cannot be used. Instead a self-employed person must inform the Inland Revenue of his/her earnings for the year. Certain deductions for expenses connected with the business can be made from the annual earnings before arriving at the amount which is assessable for tax purposes. When this has been determined the taxpayer will have to pay the total tax due for the year in two instalments in July and January.

The regulations concerning tax for a self-employed person are very complex and most people find that there is a great advantage in asking an accountant to deal with their tax affairs for them. Not only does this relieve the tax payer of the problems of completing all the paperwork, but ensures that the correct amount of tax is paid. To evade the payment of the correct amount of tax is a legal offence. To pay too much tax is foolish and an accountant will know how to avoid this.

You should now be able to attempt Task 2.3 at the end of this chapter.

2.14 Summary

Payment of ***personal taxation*** is compulsory and, although it is legal to attempt to avoid full payment of tax, it is an offence to evade payment.

The tax year is from the 6 April to the 5 April in the following year.

A number of ***forms and documents*** must be completed and kept by employers and individuals for the taxation system to work. Each employee should receive a regular ***payslip*** from their employer showing such information as the tax deducted from the gross pay. At the end of the tax year an employee should receive from the employer a ***P60*** showing the total amount of pay received in the tax year and the total tax and national insurance contributions deducted.

Each year the Chancellor announces in the annual budget the ***personal allowances*** for the tax year. These are amounts you can earn during the tax year on which no tax is payable

You should now be able to attempt the Objective Test at the end of this chapter.

Student activities

Task 2.1 Go to your library and look up the press reports following the last budget statement from the Chancellor. Do the newspapers express different opinions? If so, why do you think that is the case? What are your own views?

Task 2.2 Read through the newspapers for advertisements for Personal Pension Plans. Send for any information brochures on the subject that are offered. What are the main advantages claimed for Personal Pension Plans and why is personal taxation important in this respect?

Task 2.3 In a group, make a list of all the tax advantages you consider are enjoyed by self-employed people. Examples from friends or relatives who are self-employed may be helpful. Now discuss whether such advantages represent tax avoidance or tax evasion and whether it is fair that people paying tax under the PAYE system do not have the same allowances.

Question 2.1 Below are a number of situations. Decide whether you agree or disagree and explain why.

		Agree	Disagree
i)	A friend has got a job as a waitress for which she is paid £60 per week. In addition she receives approximately £40 per week in tips which she claims are not liable for tax.	☐	☐
ii)	You are about to start working for a large company. You have been told by a friend that you should save some of your wages to pay your tax at the end of the year.	☐	☐
iii)	You are already working full-time, but you do some gardening work for various neighbours on Sundays for which you receive about £15. You should tell the Inland Revenue about this income.	☐	☐
iv)	A colleague tells you that it is perfectly legal to evade tax as long as you do it only once in each tax year.	☐	☐
v)	In calculating your income for tax you must include all income for the year ending 31 December.	☐	☐
vi)	A relative has started his own business and argues that the Inland Revenue will ask him to pay a tax bill on 5 April of each year.	☐	☐

Question 2.2 Do you agree or disagree with the following statement? *The system of PAYE offers no advantages to employers and is nothing but a burden.* Give your views.

Question 2.3 Name five items of information you would normally expect to find on a pay slip.

Question 2.4 Explain the importance of a Form P60 and the type of information it provides.

Question 2.5 *Laurence Braithwaite* has been made redundant and has decided to start his own business and open a garden centre. He intends to employ two people to work in the gardens and one person to help him in the shop. A friend of his has told him that because he employs fewer than five people the employees will be responsible for paying their own tax. A quick telephone call to the Inland Revenue has convinced Mr Braithwaite that his friend is completely wrong and that as an employer he will have to deduct tax from his employees' pay and keep proper records.

Write a brief report to Mr Braithwaite explaining the PAYE system and the principal forms and documents used.

Objective test *(tick the appropriate box)*

i) Which one of the following activities is legal:

a) avoiding tax ☐

b) not declaring your income ☐

c) evading tax ☐

d) not declaring any earnings under £10 a week ☐

ii) The gross pay shown on a payslip is:

a) the amount of money you will take home ☐

b) the amount of tax you have to pay ☐

c) your contribution to the pension fund ☐

d) the amount of pay before any deductions ☐

iii) The personal allowances which are used to determine your taxable income are decided by:

a) your employer ☐

b) the Inland Revenue ☐

c) the Chancellor of the Exchequer ☐

d) yourself. ☐

iv) If the basic tax rate is 25%, a person with a taxable income of £16,000 per year will pay the following amount of tax:

a) nothing ☐

b) £8,000 ☐

c) £4,000 ☐

d) £16,000 ☐

v) If you are a self-employed person you will pay your tax:

a) at the end of each month ☐

b) on 5 April ☐

c) as you earn the money ☐

d) in July and January ☐

vi) If your personal circumstances change and you consider your tax code should be amended, you should:

a) tell your employer ☐

b) do nothing as it will automatically be adjusted ☐

c) inform the Inland Revenue ☐

d) write to your bank ☐

vii) You are already working, but have started doing a Saturday job for which you receive cash. You should:

a) do nothing as it is not taxable ☐

b) tell your full-time employer ☐

c) tell the Inland Revenue ☐

d) give 25% of the money back to the person paying you ☐

viii) When you change jobs you must give your new employer:

a) your notice of Coding ☐
b) your P45 ☐
c) your P60 ☐
d) your tax return ☐

ix) If you are purchasing a home on a mortgage you will:

a) be charged tax on the interest you pay ☐
b) receive tax relief on the interest you pay ☐
c) pay interest with no tax adjustment ☐
d) pay tax but no interest. ☐

x) A Notice of Coding will give an individual code number which an employer will use for each employee to:

a) calculate the gross pay ☐
b) work out mortgage repayments ☐
c) deduct the correct amount of tax ☐
d) decide the personal allowances ☐

Chapter 3

Deductions from pay and value added tax

3.1 Objectives

At the end of this chapter you should be able to:

- explain what is meant by national insurance;
- describe other deductions from gross pay;
- identify the main features of Value Added Tax;
- explain the operation of the Value Added Tax system;
- describe the accounting aspects of Value Added Tax.

3.2 Introduction

In this chapter we are going to look at other ***deductions,*** apart from personal tax, which are made before you receive your take home pay. Some of these stoppages offer you a direct and identifiable benefit and are easy to understand. But receiving your take home pay is not the end of the story as far as taxation is concerned. When you start spending your earnings you may be paying another tax – ***Value Added Tax (VAT).*** If you are not running a business and you are the final consumer of the purchase, you bear the burden of this tax.

If you refer to the example of a pay slip given in the last chapter, you will see that a number of deductions have been made from the gross pay before arriving at the figure of net pay. As already explained, income tax represents a significant figure, but there are also other deductions.

3.3 National Insurance

Most people who are employed or self-employed, and are between the ages of 16 and pensionable age, are liable to deductions from their pay for ***National Insurance.*** Your National Insurance Contribution (NIC) is taken from your wages or salary if you are an employee in the same way as PAYE is deducted. Employers must also make a contribution to National Insurance for all their employees earning above a certain amount.

By making these enforced contributions to the National Insurance Scheme people have qualified for such benefits as:

- **Invalidity benefit** which is made up of invalidity pension plus an invalidity allowance, if the illness began when you were still under 55 (women) and 60 (men).
- **Maternity allowance** which you may get if you are pregnant, but you are not entitled to statutory maternity pay.
- **Retirement pension** which is a taxable weekly benefit for women over 60 and men over 65 who have retired from work, even if they have not given up work completely. Women over 65 and men over 70 receive this benefit irrespective of the amount of work they do.
- **Sickness benefit** is payable for up to 28 weeks to people who are unable to work because of sickness or disability and do not qualify for statutory sick pay.
- **Unemployment benefit** is a weekly cash sum for those who are normally employed, but have lost their jobs.

- **Widows' benefits** – the main one is the widows' payment which is a lump sum payment for widows under 60 and for those over 60 whose husbands were not receiving a retirement pension when they died.

Everyone has their own National Insurance number and this is sent to you before you leave school. It is important to keep a record of your number as you will be required to give it to your employer or, if you are self-employed, to the Social Security office. This will ensure that your record of National Insurance contributions is kept up to date.

Not everyone pays the same amount and there are four classes of contribution as follows:

Class 1. If you are an employee and your earnings are at, or above, a certain figure you come into this class. There is an upper and lower figure in this class and the higher your pay between these two limits the more National Insurance you pay. Your employer will deduct the figure from your pay on a regular basis. Your employer also has to make contributions for all employees who earn at or above the set limit.

Class 3. If you are an employee and your pay is below the set limit, or you are unemployed, or you are self-employed with profits so low you are exempted from National Insurance, you can volunteer to make voluntary class 3 contributions. These are paid at a flat rate through your bank by direct debit. You may choose to make these payments to protect your retirement pension and widows' benefits.

Class 2. If you are self-employed you pay a flat rate contribution under class 2 unless your profits are so low that you have chosen to pay under class 3. Payment can be made through a bank, or a Giro account.

Class 4. If you are self-employed and your profits or gains are above a certain amount you may have to pay class 4 contributions in addition to the flat rate contributions under class 2. Class 4 contributions are related to your level of profit and you pay them direct to the Inland Revenue when you pay your income tax.

You should now be able to attempt Question 3.3 at the end of this chapter.

3.4 Pension schemes

There are several different types of pension scheme in the UK including the following:

- The ***basic state pension*** which is for everyone who has been in employment and is earned by paying basic national insurance contributions.
- The ***State Earnings Related Pension Scheme (SERPS)*** which provides an additional pension based on earnings since 1978 on which increased national insurance contributions have been paid. When SERPS was introduced employers were allowed to leave the state scheme if they could offer an alternative scheme. This could be done by setting up an occupational scheme (see below) which was acceptable to the Inland Revenue.
- ***Occupational schemes*** should provide greater benefits for employees than SERPS. The employer usually contributes a certain amount to the scheme (often known as superannuation) and the employee also make a contribution which is deducted from gross pay. There are two main types of scheme. In a ***final salary scheme*** the amount of pension is based on the employee's final salary. This may be the annual salary the last year of employment or an average of any three consecutive years. For example, an employee with 40 years' service might receive two-thirds of his or her final salary. The second method is a money purchase scheme which creates an individual pension account for each employee.
- ***Personal Pension Plans (PPPs)*** have been available since 1 July 1988 and are operated by banks, insurance companies and building societies. Premiums are paid directly by the individual and are invested in an investment plan until retirement, when the proceeds are used to purchase a pension from an insurance company. PPPs are of particular benefit to self-employed people or those in non-pensionable employment.

The choice of pension scheme depends on the particular circumstances of the individual, but usually a good occupational pension scheme is the best.

You should now be able to attempt Task 3.1 at the end of this chapter.

3.5 Membership fees and other deductions

It may be that you are already a member of a union or will join when you start work. You may pay your ***membership fees*** directly to the union, or the company you work for may operate a ***check-off system***. Under this arrangement, the employer deducts trade union contributions from the wages or salaries of trade union members in their employment and pays them to the union or unions concerned.

In addition to the stoppages listed above, there are other deductions which may take place. For example, if your company has a sports or social club you can agree that the membership fees, if any, are deducted directly from your pay.

On a more sober note, it may be that for some reason a court has determined that deductions must be made from your pay to meet some legal responsibility. In this case the employer will deduct the amount required and pay it directly to the court.

You should now be able to attempt Task 3.2 at the end of this chapter.

3.6 Value Added Tax

Value Added Tax (VAT) is a tax which involves all businesses with a turnover of over a certain amount set by the government. It is administered by HM Customs and Excise. All sole traders, partnerships, limited companies, associations, clubs, charities etc with a turnover greater than the specified limit must register for VAT and will be given a VAT number.

Certain items and services when made by VAT registered business must have VAT added to them at the standard rate which is currently 17.5%. The technical term for the sales is the output and the VAT added is known as the output tax. But as well as adding VAT to their sales many businesses will be paying VAT when they purchase goods or services subject to value added tax from another business which is registered for VAT. The VAT that the businesses have to pay on these purchases is known as the input tax. The following example shows the impact of input and output tax.

Example

Lesley Marshfield, who is registered for VAT, purchases 50 boxes of plumbing fittings at £10 per box from a business which is also registered. Mr Marshfield later sells these fittings at £12 per box. What is the input and output tax?

Solution

Description of items	Amount	Vat at 17.5%	Total
	£	£	£
Sale of 50 boxes at £12 per box	600.00	105.00	705.00
Purchase of 50 boxes at £10 per box	500.00	87.50	587.50

Output tax = £105.00
Input tax = £87.50

In the above example we can see that Mr Marshfield had to pay £87.50 in VAT on the purchases he made and charged £105.00 in VAT on his sales. Mr Marshfield owes the output tax of £105.00 to the Customs and Excise, but he is owed £87.50 by the Customs and Excise for the input tax he has already paid. The easiest way to settle this is for Mr Marshfield to send a payment for the difference of £17.50 to the Customs and Excise.

You should now be able to attempt Questions 3.4 and 3.5 at the end of this chapter.

3.7 VAT records

Every business that is registered for VAT must maintain proper ***records*** of all payments of VAT made and all collections of VAT. At the end of each quarter, the business must send a VAT return to HM Customs and Excise. This will show details of outputs and output tax, and inputs and input tax. Where the output tax is greater than the input tax, payment of the difference must be made. When the input tax is greater than the output tax, a position that can arise, the Customs and Excise will refund the difference.

It is essential that records are maintained of transactions which show the gross amount paid or received, the VAT and the net amount. When a business is calculating its profit or loss for a period, it is the net amounts which must be used i.e. excluding any VAT.

Example

Jean Lansdown purchases 20 gold bracelets for £20 each on which VAT is charged. She later sells them for £35 each. What are the figures for input and output tax, and what figures will be used to calculate the profit?

Solution

		Net	VAT	Gross
		£	£	£
Sales	20 bracelets @ £35 each	700.00	122.50	822.50
Purchases	20 bracelets @ £20 each	400.00	70.00	470.00

The input tax is £70 and the output tax is £122.50. The difference of £52.50 must be paid to HM Customs and Excise. It is the net figures of sales of £700 and purchases of £400 which will be used to calculate the profit.

You should now be able to attempt Questions 3.6 and 3.7 at the end of this chapter.

3.8 Cash transactions

In some businesses where ***cash*** is used for the transactions, such as in a shop, no separate record is kept of the output tax. All the receipts of cash are recorded inclusive of VAT. A shop which shows that its takings are £1410 has included VAT in the amount and a separate calculation must be carried out to find the appropriate amount of output tax.

If the figure of £1,410 includes VAT at 17.5%, then £1,410 = 117.5%. The output tax will therefore be:

$$\frac{£1{,}410 \times 17.5}{117.5} = £210$$

The output (sales) figure must therefore be £1,200.
This calculation can be checked by adding 17.5% onto £1,200 and this gives £1,410.

You should now be able to attempt Questions 3.8 to 3.10 and Task 3.3 at the end of this chapter.

3.9 Further considerations

We have looked at the main principles and calculations of VAT, but in reality it is a very complex tax with many variations and exemptions. In our examples we have assumed that the rate is always 17.5%. In practice, some business add output tax at a special rate i.e. zero on some or all of the outputs. There is a fairly long list of items which are zero-rated. Businesses with zero-rated outputs can reclaim the input tax from HM Customs and Excise.

As well as zero-rated items, some items are exempt and no VAT is added when they are sold. Once again, there is a long list, but the important feature is that businesses selling exempted items cannot recover any input tax borne on inputs which relate to the exempted items.

As illustrated in all the examples, the consumer who finally purchases the item is paying the full VAT to the seller. The VAT will then be paid to HM Customs and Excise by the seller, who is in fact acting as a collector of taxes.

3.10 Summary

In addition to Income Tax, there are a number of stoppages made from gross pay. ***National Insurance*** is a compulsory deduction which may qualify you for such benefits as ***maternity allowances, retirement pension, sickness benefits***. In the UK there are several different types of ***pension schemes***. For employees in ***SERPS*** or ***occupational pension schemes***, the premiums are deducted by the employer from their gross pay. However, an individual with a ***personal pension plan*** is responsible for paying his or her own premiums to the financial institution.

Value added tax is a tax which involves all businesses with a certain level of turnover. It is administered by HM Customs and Excise and the current rate is 17.5%. Every business that is registered for VAT must maintain proper records of all payments and collections of VAT made by them.

VAT is very complex, with many variations and exemptions. Some items are ***zero-rated*** and businesses with zero-rated outputs can reclaim the input tax. If an item is ***exempt*** from VAT, a business selling it cannot reclaim the input tax.

You should now be able to attempt the Objective Test at the end of this chapter.

Student activities

Task 3.1 Look through the financial pages of newpapers for advertisements about Personal Pension Plans. Send off for any publicity material and compare the claimed advantages of the different schemes.

Task 3.2 Obtain as many different pay slips as you can from friends and relations. Calculate what percentage the total stoppages figure is of the gross pay. Calculate what percentage the largest item deducted is of gross pay. Calculate the average percentage for all the pay slips you have.

Task 3.3 Keep a record of all the payments you make during a month which include VAT. Compare your list with other class members and analyse how the pattern of an individual's expenditure may account for any differences.

Question 3.1 Describe five benefits which people may be entitled to through National Insurance contributions.

Question 3.2 *Mr Bathford* purchases 100 kilos of fertilizer at £5 per kilo on which VAT is charged. He later sells this for £8 per kilo. What is the output tax, the input tax and the amount due to HM Customs and Excise?

Question 3.3 *Mrs Widcombe* purchases 250 boxes of plain listing paper at £2 per box on which VAT is charged. She later sells them for £2.60 per box. What is the output tax, the input tax and the amount due to HM Customs and Excise?

Question 3.4 *Robert Burnham* is a trader in chemical compounds and purchases 750 kilos at £2.20 per kilo. The chemicals are later sold at £3.00 per kilo. What are the figures for input and output tax and what figures will be used to calculate the profit?

Question 3.5 *John Laycock* has a mail order business and buys 3,000 car alarms at £12 each. These are later sold at £18.50 each. What are the figures for input and output tax and what figures will be used to calculate the profit?

Question 3.6 Using the following figures of gross takings, calculate the output tax:

i) £470.00

ii) £58.75

iii) £82.25

iv) £1,116.25

v) £38,070.00

Question 3.7 The Chancellor of the Exchequer has decided to increase the rate of VAT from 17.5% to 20%. *Mrs Jupiter* runs a small stationary shop and last year her turnover was £80,000 excluding VAT. When the rate of VAT was 17.5% the amount she paid to HM Customs & Excise was £3,500. Calculate the following figures for last year for Mrs Jupiter's business:

i) the output tax

ii) the input tax

iii) the profit of the business based on the figures you have

Assuming that Mrs Jupiter maintains the same level of turnover and profit when the rate of VAT is increased to 20%, calculate the following figures:

iv) the output tax

v) the input tax

vi) the amount due to HM Customs & Excise

Question 3.8 *Bob Dithers* has become very confused over the VAT transactions associated with his business. All transactions have been for cash and although VAT has been charged at the correct rate of 17.5%, no separate records have been maintained of the output tax. During the course of the year the total takings, including VAT, were £35,250. No records were kept of purchases or input tax, but Bob believes that he took £10,000 cash out of the business after paying for all his purchases.

On the basis of this information, calculate the following figures:

i) the sales figure excluding VAT

ii) the amount of purchases excluding VAT

iii) the input tax

iv) the amount which should have been paid to HM Customs & Excise

Objective test *(tick the appropriate box)*

i) If you are unemployed and wish to volunteer to make National Insurance contributions you would pay under:

a) Class 1 ☐

b) Class 2 ☐

c) Class 3 ☐

d) Class 4 ☐

ii) If you are a man, you are entitled to receive a state retirement pension, if you are:

a) over 60 but still working ☐

b) over 65 but not retired ☐

c) under 60 but not working ☐

d) over 70 but still working ☐

iii) If you are registered for VAT you pay to the Customs and Excise:

a) the output tax ☐

b) the input tax ☐

c) the output tax less the input tax ☐

d) the input tax less the output tax ☐

iv) A shop has takings, including 17.5% VAT of £2,604.50. The output tax is:

a) £327.30 ☐

b) £750.00 ☐

c) £387.90 ☐

d) £115.15 ☐

v) A business has sales of £1,380 and purchases of £1,035, all including VAT at 17.5%. Assuming there are no stocks involved and these are the only activities of the business, the profit to the nearest £ will be:

a) £345 ☐

b) £294 ☐

c) £480 ☐

d) £165 ☐

Chapter 4

Financial objectives and opportunity costs

4.1 Objectives

At the end of this chapter you should be able to:

- explain the different financial decisions;
- describe the process of setting financial objectives;
- calculate various aspects of interest rates in the context of financial objectives;
- explain the importance of opportunity costs.

4.2 Introduction

Most of us, if asked what our ***financial objectives*** are, would immediately reply: to have lots of money. After thought we might expand on this, but even then it is doubtful whether we have clear financial objectives. What we will have expressed are some general financial desires. Financial objectives should be defined as precisely as possible. By making them precise we can state how we are best able to achieve those financial objectives and can monitor and control progress towards their achievement.

If we are going to be more precise about the general financial desire to have lots of money we need to state:

- how much money we want;
- the date we want it by.

When these objectives have been established, we can determine how we might best achieve them. Usually in achieving our financial objectives we have to make sacrifices in other directions. The costs of making these sacrifices are known as ***opportunity costs*** and, as explained later in this chapter, need to be considered when making decisions.

4.3 The financial decisions

Financial decisions are concerned with the amount of income we receive, the way we spend our money and the amount of money we save. We can improve our income by seeking a higher paid job, working overtime or taking on part-time work. We can also improve our income by saving part of it, and receiving an income in the form of interest on our savings.

Even on a very low income we will have to make a number of financial decisions on the way we spend it. Some of these may be at the level of deciding which brand of cereal we can afford for breakfast. Often we have to decide how to allocate our income over the many claims made on it. This means deciding how much rent we can afford, whether to have a car, what clothes to buy and other aspects of how we live on a day-to-day basis. When making these decisions we also have to consider whether we should save part of our income.

The prime decisions are whether to:

- Spend all our income as it is received – such a decision would mean we would be living a 'hand to mouth' existence. This may be a very enjoyable and even luxurious existence, but there is no planning for future needs.

- Save part of our income to meet unknown future needs or wishes – there is no defined requirement for the savings, no decision has been made as to what the total amount to be finally saved should be and by which date. A decision must be made, therefore, on what proportion of the regular income should be saved and where it should be invested. The amount to be saved will be decided by personal attitudes. For example, some people enjoy an extravagant lifestyle and will save a minimum amount, whereas others will be frugal to the point of meanness.
- Save part of our income to meet a future known need or wish – if we have a specific need which we cannot meet from our present financial resources, we may decide to save for it. By saving part of our income we can earn interest towards the amount required for the future purchase. But this means that we must sacrifice part of our current consumption and suffer the delay in purchasing the item.
- Borrow to purchase now and repay interest in the future – if we decide to borrow we will have the immediate use of the item we require, but will have to repay the loan, plus interest, from our future income. Many of us will do this at some stage in our life, either for a large item, such as a car, or for smaller items, such as cameras, stereos or clothes. There is the danger that if we become unemployed or our income reduces because we fall sick, we could get in arrears with the repayments.

You should now be able to attempt Task 4.1 at the end of this chapter.

4.4 Investment and financial objectives

In our society it is normal practice to set aside a proportion of our income, if possible, to form the basis of regular savings for ***investment***. There are a number of reasons for this, apart from some vague moral notion that to deprive ourselves of immediate consumption is good for the soul.

One of the benefits to the individual is the ***return*** he or she will receive. Money buried in a hole in the garden brings no return and can be stolen and devalued by inflation. Money invested in a bank or a building society will show a return in the form of interest. This is a reward given to investors to compensate them for sacrificing the use of their money for a period of time.

So we may save for a number of reasons, but there are specific financial objectives we will want to set in respect of our investment. These are:

- the amount we are going to invest;
- the length of time we are going to invest it for;
- the percentage return we want on our investment;
- the total amount we want after a certain period of time.

To set these financial objectives, we have to carry out certain calculations. In Chapter 1 we looked at interest rate calculations and we can now take this a stage further and relate the calculations to setting specific financial objectives.

You should now be able to attempt Task 4.2 at the end of this chapter.

4.5 Simple interest calculations

It is important that investors obtain the best return on their savings as this represents their future purchasing power. Investors will therefore wish to know the amount of interest they will receive if they invest a certain sum at a specific interest rate for a given period of time. As we explained in Chapter 1, interest may be calculated as follows:

$$\text{Amount of interest} = \text{Amount invested} \times \frac{\text{interest rate}}{100} \times \text{number of years}$$

The amount invested is known as the principal and the above calculation can be expressed in the form of a formula

$$I = \frac{P \times R \times N}{100}$$

where

I means amount of interest
P means principal
R means rate of interest
N means the number of years

When we apply this formula, we are assuming that interest is only paid on the principal and is not reinvested. This is known as ***simple interest***. Where the interest is reinvested and interest is also paid on that, we have to apply the formula for ***compound interest*** calculations.

Example

What is the simple interest on £10,000 invested for 5 years at a rate of interest of 9% per annum?

Solution

$$\frac{£10{,}000 \times 9 \times 5}{100} = £4{,}500$$

You should now be able to attempt Question 4.1 at the end of this chapter.

4.6 Simple interest problems

In setting financial objectives, the investor may well require answers to questions other than the total amount of interest. Such questions may be:

1. What rate of interest must I earn on an investment of £1,000 to have received a total of £200 interest in 4 years time?
2. For how long must I invest £2,000 at 10% per annum to receive £800 interest?
3. How much must I invest now at 10% per annum if I want to have received £500 interest in 5 years time?

All these questions are concerned with different aspects of the formula we used to calculate the amount of interest.

Question 1 is concerned with the rate of interest (R).

Question 2 is concerned with the number of years (N).

Question 3 is concerned with the amount to be invested (P).

To answer each of these questions, and similar questions, we can rearrange the formula to obtain the missing figure.

Example

What rate of interest must I earn on an investment of £1,000 to have received £200 interest in 4 years time?

Solution

The formula $I = \frac{P \times R \times N}{100}$ can be rearranged to give $R = \frac{100 \times I}{P \times N}$

Substituting the figures we obtain $R = \frac{100 \times 200}{1{,}000 \times 4}$

The rate of interest required is therefore 5%.

Example

For how long must I invest £2,000 at 10% per annum to have received £800 interest?

Solution

The formula $I = \frac{P \times R \times N}{100}$ can be rearranged to give $N = \frac{100 \times I}{P \times R}$

Substituting the figures we obtain $N = \frac{100 \times 800}{2{,}000 \times 10}$

The length of time is 4 years.

Example

How much must I invest now at 10% per annum if I want to have received £500 interest in 5 years time?

Solution

The formula $I = \frac{P \times R \times N}{100}$ can be rearranged to give $P = \frac{100 \times I}{R \times N}$

Substituting the figures we obtain $P = \frac{100 \times 500}{10 \times 5}$

The amount to be invested is £1,000

You should now be able to attempt Questions 4.2 to 4.5 at the end of this chapter.

4.7 Compound interest calculations

When you invest money the most common form of interest is ***compound interest***. This is used by building societies, banks and pension funds. With this method, the interest obtained at the end of a financial period is automatically reinvested. In the next financial period, the interest is calculated not only on the principal (the original sum) but on the interest which has been reinvested. As explained in Chapter 1, the frequency with which the interest is calculated, e.g. annually, quarterly, monthly, is critical in determining the total amount, that is principal and interest due to you at the end of a period of time.

The above calculation can be expressed in the form of a formula:

$$A = P(1 + r)^n$$

where A means amount of principal plus interest or the final amount

P means principal

r means rate of interest expressed as a decimal eg 10% = 0.10

n means period of time in years

Example

What will a principal of £10,000 invested at 12% compound interest amount to in 3 years' time?

Solution

$A = £10,000\ (1.12)^3$

$A = £10,000\ (1.12 \times 1.12 \times 1.12)$

$A = £10,000 \times 1.4049$

The answer is £14,049 to the nearest £.

You should now be able to attempt Questions 4.6 and 4.7 at the end of this chapter.

4.8 Comparing interest rates

When ***comparing interest rates*** it is most important to ensure how they are being quoted. The following terms are used:

Gross – This means that the interest rate is being calculated before any deduction of tax. If you are liable to pay tax this could make a substantial difference to the amount of money you end up with. If the gross amount of interest you receive is £100 but you pay tax at 25%, you must pay the Inland Revenue £25 and will have £75 to enjoy yourself.

Net – Some institutions, pay interest after deduction of tax, i.e. net. The institution pays the tax due to the Inland Revenue and the amount you receive is after the tax has been deducted, i.e. the net amount. If the interest rate is quoted at say 7.4% net per annum, you will receive an amount of £7.40 if you invest £100 for one year.

Compounded Annual Rate – One complication in comparing interest rates is that some institutions pay interest annually, some twice a year, and others monthly. To allow comparisons, the banks and building societies carry out a calculation to show what would have happened if you had reinvested your interest as it was received and therefore earned interest on your interest. This calculation is known as the Compounded Annual Rate and can make a significant difference. For example, imagine you have £1,000 net to invest. Two institutions are paying 10% net, but one pays interest annually and the other monthly. In the first institution you will receive £100 interest at the end of the year. In the second institution, because of the monthly interest payments, the Compounded Annual Rate is 10.47%, so you receive £104.70.

4.9 Interest rates and inflation

The word ***inflation*** is widely used and it is important to appreciate the impact of inflation on interest rates. For example, if you have £1,000 at the beginning of the year and the inflation rate is 4% per annum, you would need £1,040 at the end of the year to be in the same financial position. If you have not invested your money for a return which is greater than 4% per annum, you will be worse off at the end of the year!

If we want to look at the effectiveness of our investments we have to make a calculation for the impact of inflation. The real interest rate in a time of inflation is the actual interest rate less the inflation rate. If the actual interest rate is 8% and inflation is 3%, the real rate of interest is 5%. This is the rate at which your money is growing in value.

If the rate of inflation is higher than the actual interest rate, the real interest rate will be negative. In other words your savings are declining in value. What we need to do is to ensure that we invest our savings so that we have a positive real interest rate.

You should now be able to attempt Task 4.3 at the end of this chapter.

4.10 Saving or borrowing

If you wish to purchase a specific item, you will have to decide whether to ***save*** the money and purchase at some future date or to ***borrow*** the money now and repay the loan and interest in the future.

If you decide to save, you are going to reduce your present consumption and delay your purchase until you have enough money. However, there are some advantages to these sacrifices. By investing wisely, you will not have to save the total purchase price because of the interest you will earn on your investment. You must ensure that you take into consideration the rate of inflation and possible changes in the price and availability of your intended purchase.

If you decide to borrow, you have the pleasure and immediate use of your purchase. But you will be financially penalised by your action. Not only will you have to repay the loan out of future earnings, but you will have to pay interest.

Sometimes the decision must be made without reference to the financial implications. If you need transport to get to your place of work because there is no public transport, you may borrow to buy a car if you do not have sufficient savings. But even with this decision there may be alternatives for which the figures are available and can be considered. You may decide to change your place of work or even to move home. You may find someone willing to give you a lift if you share the cost of the petrol.

You should now be able to attempt Task 4.4 at the end of this chapter.

4.11 Opportunity costs

When you are making financial decisions regarding saving money or borrowing, it is most important that you take every factor into account. One factor is that of ***opportunity cost,*** which can be regarded as the value of the alternative that has been sacrificed in order to pursue a certain course of action. This is best explained by means of the following example.

Example

David Dundry commutes regularly to London. At the moment he purchases a monthly rail ticket from his salary and the cost is £88, making his total rail costs £1,056 per annum. The cost for an annual ticket would be £1,000, representing a saving of £56. Mr Dundry has this amount saved in the building society and receives 7.5% net per annum. What should he do?

Solution

Although a straight comparison of the cost of the tickets suggest a saving of £56 per annum, we must take into account that Mr Dundry would have to forgo the interest of £75 he receives on his savings if he buys an annual ticket. The real cost to him of the annual ticket is therefore £1,075 – the £1,000 cost of the ticket and the £75 interest he sacrifices.

You should now be able to attempt Question 4.8 at the end of this chapter.

4.12 Summary

We have to make ***financial decisions*** concerning the amount of income we receive, the way we spend our income, the amount of money we save and where we invest it.

In making an ***investment*** we set financial objectives concerning the amount we intend to invest, the length of time we will invest it for, the percentage return we want on our investment and the total amount we require after a certain period of time. By carrying out ***simple*** and ***compound interest*** calculations we can obtain answers to many of the questions concerning our investment objectives.

Where interest is paid on the principal and not reinvested, this is known as ***simple interest***. Where the interest is reinvested and interest is also paid on that, it is known as ***compound interest***.

To obtain a realistic picture of the effectiveness of our investments, we should make a calculation for the impact of inflation. If the rate of inflation is higher than the actual interest rate, the real interest rate will be negative.

In deciding whether to save, spend or borrow, a number of factors must be taken into account. One factor is that of ***opportunity cost***, which can be regarded as the value of the alternative that has been sacrificed in order to pursue a certain course of action.

You should now be able to attempt the Objective Test at the end of this chapter.

Student activities

Task 4.1 Use the following guide to determine how much you can theoretically save in a year:

A. ***Income*** £

Student grant or earnings for the year
Any part-time earnings
Any interest received
Any other income

Total income

B. ***Fixed spending*** (These are items you cannot change quickly.)

Rent or mortgage £
Rates
Insurance
Heating and lighting bills
Car expenses (tax, insurance, running costs)

Telephone
Television hire, licence
Subscriptions
Travelling costs
Hire purchase repayments
Other loan repayments
Other uncontrollable payments

Total fixed spending

C. *Essential spending* (These are items you must purchase, but you have some control in the short term on how much you spend.) £

Food
Repairs and decorating
Medicines
Cleaning materials
Clothes and shoes
Haircuts and toiletries
Any other

Total essential spending

D. *Controllable spending* (You may disagree that some of these items are controllable, but make certain you include everything.) £

Drinks
Cigarettes
Presents
Holidays
Cinema, theatre, concerts etc.
All other items.

Total controllable spending

Now add up the totals for B,C, and D, your expenditure, and deduct that figure from A, your income. If your income is higher than your expenditure the difference is the minimum amount you should be able to save. If your expenditure is higher than your income you have severe financial problems and you must control your 'controllable spending'.

Task 4.2 What are the benefits to the individual and society at large by a person making regular savings even when there is no specific future need or desire to be met in the future?

Task 4.3 Visit your local building societies and obtain leaflets on their rates of interest on different deposit accounts. Draw up a table to show which is best and how this is affected by the amount you have to invest and the degree of access you enjoy.

Task 4.4 *Gerry Slade* lives in a small village and the nearest town is 5 miles away. She has just obtained a job in the town, but there is no public transport. A friend has a car for sale for £2,500 but G Slade has no savings. She is thinking of obtaining a bank loan to purchase the car. What other alternatives and factors should she take into consideration and what figures would she need to know to make the best decision?

Question 4.1 In the following questions calculate the amount of simple interest if the principal is invested at the rate stated for the specified period of time:

i) Principal of £800 at 5% per annum for 8 years

ii) Principal of £2,000 at 4.5% per annum for 3 years

iii) Principal of £150 at 12% per annum for 6 years

iv) Principal of £25,000 at 6.75% per annum for 5 years

v) Principal of £12,400 at 8.25% per annum for 4 years

vi) Principal of £1,500 at 5% per annum for 2.5 years

vii) Principal of £2,500 at 6% per annum for 3.25 years

viii) Principal of £15,000 at 7.25% per annum for 6.5 years

ix) Principal of £20,000 at 8.75% per annum for 3.75 years

Question 4.2 Identify the rates of simple interest required from the following information:

i) Principal £500 to obtain £60 interest in 2 years time

ii) Principal £12,000 to obtain £9,360 interest in 6 years time

iii) Principal £750 to obtain £240 interest in 8 years time

iv) Principal £6,000 to obtain £2,250 interest in 5 years time

Question 4.3 Identify the length of time the money must be invested from the following information based on simple interest.

i) Principal of £3,000 at 10% per annum to obtain interest of £900

ii) Principal of £4,500 at 12% per annum to obtain interest of £2,160

iii) Principal of £3,700 at 15% per annum to obtain interest of £1,665

iv). Principal of £24,000 at 8.25% per annum to obtain interest of £12,870

Question 4.4 Identify the principal to be invested from the following information based on simple interest:

i) Invested at 10% to obtain interest of £1,500 in 2 years time

ii) Invested at 9% to obtain interest of £288 in 4 years time

iii) Invested at 8.75% to obtain interest of £1,050 in 10 years time

iv) Invested at 7.25% to obtain interest of £290 in 8 years time

Question 4.5 All the following calculations are based on simple interest. Insert the missing figures in the following table:

Principal invested	Interest rate per annum	Number of years	Total interest received
£17,500	15.5%	6	?
?	7.2%	11	£396
£2,400	?	20	£6,528
£3,300	11.7%	?	£3,861
£4,730	?	4	£1,419
?	9.5%	8	£5,054

Question 4.6 In the following questions calculate the amount due to the nearest £ if the principal is invested at the compound interest rate stated for the specified period of time:

i) Principal of £1,000 at 5% per annum for 4 years

ii) Principal of £2,000 at 4.5% per annum for 3 years

iii) Principal of £250 at 12% per annum for 5 years

iv) Principal of £25,000 at 6.75% per annum for 3 years

v) Principal of £12,400 at 8.25% per annum for 4 years

Question 4.7 All the following questions are based on compound interest and the interest is added annually. Insert the missing figures in the following table:

Principal invested	Interest rate per annum	Number of years	Total interest received
£4,000	10%	?	£5,324
£6,600	?	2	£8,279
?	14.5%	4	£4,297
£12,150	6.5%	3	?
£15,000	?	5	£22,040

Question 4.8 *Nicola Boscastle* has just started her first new job and the office is situated next to a prestige health club. Most of the office staff belong to the health club and have suggested that Nicola also joins. They go to the health club on average twice per week for 48 weeks of the year.

The annual membership fee of the club is £450 per annum, but it is possible instead to pay £5 per visit as long as you are signed in by an existing member. Nicola's friends have said that they would be willing to sign her in each time if she does not want to pay the annual membership. Nicola has £1,000 invested in the building society which is paying net interest of 8.25% per annum. What are the financial implications of the alternatives and what other factors do you think Nicola should take into account?

Objective test *(tick the appropriate box)*

i) If you are setting personal financial objectives for the forthcoming year, which one of the following would you not need to know?

a) the savings you currently have ☐

b) the rate of inflation two years ago ☐

c) your expected income ☐

d) your anticipated expenditure ☐

ii) Which one of the following items would you not classify as controllable spending?

a) cigarettes ☐

b) meals out ☐

c) visits to the theatre ☐

d) car tax ☐

iii) The amount of money which is invested is known as the:

a) principal ☐

b) compound ☐

c) borrowings ☐

d) interest rate ☐

iv) If you invest £10,000 at 4% per annum, interest paid and reinvested quarterly, the amount which will have been added after 6 months is:

a) £400 ☐

b) £201 ☐

c) £104 ☐

d) £402 ☐

v) The interest rate quoted by banks and building societies to show what happens if interest is reinvested and earns further interest is known as the:

a) gross equivalent to basic rate tax payer ☐

b) compounded annual rate ☐

c) simple interest ☐

d) annual percentage rate ☐

Chapter 5

Cash planning and personal cash flow

5.1 Objectives

At the end of this chapter, you should be able to:

- explain the purposes and importance of a cash flow forecast;
- define the terms positive cash flow, negative cash flow and net cash flow;
- construct a cash flow forecast for an individual or his business.

5.2 Introduction

For individuals and companies, the control of ***cash*** is a most important activity. In Chapter 15 we shall look at the difference between cash and profit. In this section we shall concentrate on cash. By cash we mean coins, notes, cheques, i.e. money which is held either as cash in the safe (or elsewhere) or as a balance in the bank.

Cash flows in and out of an organisation. Cash flowing in, known as ***positive cash flow***, is cash received, e.g. from debtors, or from customers paying cash. Cash flowing out, known as ***negative cash flow***, is cash paid out, e.g. to suppliers or for wages. The difference between cash flowing in and cash flowing out is known as the net cash flow. This may be a surplus (more cash in than out), or a deficit (more cash out than in). Never refer to these as a profit or loss.

Individuals and organisations need to plan and control cash flows. This allows them to:

- ensure that they have sufficient cash to carry out their planned activities;
- ensure that the cash coming in is sufficient to cover the cash going out;
- ensure that they do not run out of cash, and that they receive early warning that a bank overdraft or other loan is required;
- enable decisions to be made about the investment of any cash surplus.

You should now be able to attempt Question 5.1 at the end of this chapter.

Example

At the end of December ***B. Bristol*** decides that he wants to go on holiday at the beginning of July. He has savings of £250, but knows that he must have £500 available by the end of June to be able to afford this holiday.

He expects to receive a net salary pay of £700 per month, and predicts that his monthly cash flows will be as follows:

Rates:	£320 per annum, payable in two instalments in April and October
Rent:	£200 per month, payable monthly at the start of each month
Electricity:	£180 per quarter, payable at the end of each quarter
Travel:	£50 per month, payable each month

Insurances: £10 per month, payable each month, with extra premiums due for payment: £30 in February and £120 in April
Sundries: £120 per month, payable monthly
Food: £150 per month, payable monthly
Holiday: £500 payable in June

Solution

We can draw up a simple statement to show the movements of cash flow for the six month period. This statement is known as a *cash flow forecast.*

B. Bristol Cash Flow Forecast
for the six month period January - June

	Jan	Feb	Mar	Apr	May	Jun	Total
	£	£	£	£	£	£	£
Cash inflows							
Salary	700	700	700	700	700	700	4,200
Total Inflows (A)	700	700	700	700	700	700	4,200
Cash outflows							
Rates	–	–	–	160	–	–	160
Rent	200	200	200	200	200	200	1,200
Electricity	–	–	180	–	–	180	360
Travel	50	50	50	50	50	50	300
Insurances	10	40	10	130	10	10	210
Sundries	120	120	120	120	120	120	720
Food	150	150	150	150	150	150	900
Holiday	–	–	–	–	–	500	500
Total Outflows (B)	530	560	710	810	530	1,210	4,350
Net cash flow (A – B)	170	140	(10)	(110)	170	(510)	(150)
Balances:							
Start of month	250*	420	560	550	440	610	250*
End of month	420	560	550	440	610	100	100

* Savings at 1st January

Notes

- This layout shows the difference between cash coming in and going out for each month (the net cash flow). It shows also the cumulative cash position (the total amount of cash which B. Bristol has at the end of each month). The June and total columns both show that B. Bristol should have £100 in hand at the end of June, and that the other monthly columns show that there is adequate cash in hand.
- Note how the cumulative cash flow is calculated. If the difference for the net cash flow is negative, you should put brackets around the figure. In calculating the cumulative figure, follow the usual rules of arithmetic, i.e. add a positive net cash flow to a positive net cash flow, deduct a negative from a positive and add a negative to a negative.
- If B. Bristol has drawn up his cash flow forecast and finds that he should have adequate cash in hand at the end of June after paying for his holiday, he has carried out a valuable planning exercise. But as he has only predicted the cash flows, it is rather unlikely that the actual cash flows will be exactly as forecast. To ensure control, B. Bristol should record the actual cash flows each month and compare them with his plan. If at the

end of any month there are significant differences between the plan and what actually happened, he can decide what action is necessary to improve the situation.

5.3 Procedure for constructing a cash flow forecast

An easy way to construct a ***cash flow forecast*** is to adopt the following procedure:

- Predict the amounts of cash coming in and going out.
- Identify the timing of these cash flows.
- Draw up a cash flow forecast and enter the appropriate headings.
- Enter the cash balance for the start of the period. (In the example above, this was £250, entered against 'start of month' under 'June'.)
- Enter all inflows of cash and subtotal.
- Enter all outflows of cash and subtotal.
- Deduct the subtotal of outflows from the subtotal of inflows, and enter the monthly difference, i.e. the net cash flow.
- Add the net cash flow for the month to any balance brought forward from the previous month to give the cumulative figure.
- Carry forward the cumulative figure at the end of one month to the beginning of the next month.

Example

Below is shown the cash flow forecast form for ***B. Bristol***, and the figures for the first three months are now the ***actual*** cash flows. You will see that Mr Bristol, at the end of March, has only £430 actual cash instead of the planned figure of £550.

	Actual			*Revised forecast*			
	Jan	Feb	Mar	Apr	May	Jun	Total
	£	£	£	£	£	£	£
Cash inflows							
Salary	700	700	700				
Total Inflows (A)	700	700	700				
Cash outflows							
Rates	–	–	–				
Rent	200	200	200				
Electricity	–	–	220				
Travel	50	60	60				
Insurances	10	60	10				
Sundries	120	150	130				
Food	150	150	150				
Holiday	–	–	–				
Total Outflows (B)	530	620	770				
Net cash flow (A – B)	170	80	(70)				
Balances:							
Start of month	250	420	500				
End of month	420	500	430				

The original forecast was to have £100 cash at the end of June after paying for his holiday, but the actual cash outflows have exceeded the forecast figures by £120 (£60 in February and £60 in March). This would mean that even if the forecast is strictly adhered to during April, May and June, B. Bristol would be £20 overdrawn at the end of June.

B. Bristol, being somewhat overweight, therefore decides to cut his food bill by £40 per month, i.e. by £120 for the next three months, and to try to keep to the original budget for his other items of expenditure. This means that he should still have £100 cash at the end of June, after paying for his holiday.

Fill in the revised forecast figures in the the above table, and then compare your figures with the table below.

Solution

B. Bristol

	Actual			Revised forecast			
	Jan	Feb	Mar	Apr	May	Jun	Total
	£	£	£	£	£	£	£
Cash inflows							
Salary	700	700	700	700	700	700	4,200
Total Inflows (A)	700	700	700	700	700	700	4,200
Cash outflows							
Rates	–	–	–	160	–	–	160
Rent	200	200	200	200	200	200	1,200
Electricity	–	–	220	–	–	180	400
Travel	50	60	60	50	50	50	320
Insurances	10	60	10	130	10	10	230
Sundries	120	150	130	120	120	120	760
Food	150	150	150	110	110	110	780
Holiday	–	–	–	–	–	500	500
Total Outflows (B)	530	620	770	770	490	1,170	4,350
Net cash flow (A – B)	170	80	(70)	(70)	210	(470)	(150)
Balances:							
Start of month	250	420	500	430	360	570	250
End of month	420	500	430	360	570	100	100

You should now be able to attempt Task 5.1 at the end of this chapter.

5.4 Cash planning and the new business

It is essential for individuals thinking of starting a ***new business*** to prepare a cash flow forecast as it allows them:

- to see if the business will generate sufficient cash – as we will see in a later chapter, a business may make a profit, but still not have sufficient cash to meet its needs;
- to decide upon the timing of cash inflows and outflows – as a general rule in a business, you want the cash to come in as quickly as possible and the cash to go out as slowly as possible. A business with a cash shortage may attempt to achieve this by collecting in the money it is owed as soon as it can, but delay any payments it has to make;
- to calculate the amount of capital (ie cash) they should invest in the business;

- to ascertain what additional funds they may require – the owners of a new business may be able to provide some cash of their own, but a cash flow forecast will show if they should be trying to obtain a loan from outside sources such as a bank.

You should now be able to attempt Task 5.2 at the end of this chapter.

Example

C. Cardiff sets up as a manufacturer of sports equipment. He has £25,000 which he pays into a business bank account on 1st July.

He budgets as follows:

- Machinery to be purchased on 1st July for £30,000, and this will have to be paid for by the end of the month.
- Wages: £3,000 per month.
- Rent of factory: £48,000 per annum, payable in monthly instalments at the start of each month.
- Other costs incurred in the running of the business (excluding material purchases): £15,000 per month, payable (on average) in the month following the month in which the costs are incurred.
- Materials: Mr Cardiff has arranged one month's credit from his suppliers, i.e. materials purchased in July will have to be paid for by the end of August.
- Sales: he expects half of his sales will be for cash, and the remaining half will be on credit. Although his quoted terms are to be 'net monthly account', he is realistic enough to budget for two months' credit being taken, an average, by his credit customers, i.e. credit sales in July will not be settled by them until September.
- After careful market research, he expects a steady but rapid expansion in his business, and his forecast for sales and purchases of materials is as follows:-

	Sales	Purchases
	£	£
July	40,000	16,000
August	60,000	24,000
September	80,000	32,000
October	100,000	40,000
November	120,000	48,000
December	140,000	56,000

Required

Prepare a monthly cash flow forecast for Mr Cardiff for the six months from July to December.

Solution

C. Cardiff

Monthly Cash Flow Forecast for 6 months ending 31st December (£'000)

	Jul	Aug	Sep	Oct	Nov	Dec	Total
	£	£	£	£	£	£	£
Cash inflows							
Capital introduced	25	–	–	–	–	–	25
Cash sales	20	30	40	50	60	70	270
Credit Sales	–	–	20	30	40	50	140
Total Inflows (A)	45	30	60	80	100	120	435
Cash outlfows							
Machinery	30	–	–	–	–	–	30
Wages	3	3	3	3	3	3	18
Rent	4	4	4	4	4	4	24
Other costs	–	15	15	15	15	15	75
Materials	–	16	24	32	40	48	160
Total Outflows (B)	37	38	46	54	62	70	307
Net cash flow(A – B)	8	(8)	14	26	38	50	128
Balances:							
Start of month	nil	8	–	14	40	78	nil
End of month	8	–	14	40	78	128	128

5.5 Planning capital requirements

Some problems present you with the amounts of cash coming in and going out, and you are asked to calculate the amount of cash required at the start of the financial period to ensure that the individual does not require an overdraft (it may be that this is not obtainable).

The way to tackle this kind of problem is to draw up a cash flow forecast, using the figures supplied but leaving the opening cash balance (or the amount to be inserted for ***Capital introduced***) as a blank item. Proceed with all the calculations as usual. Then the highest cumulative figure of ***negative*** cash in the period (the bottom line of the layouts used so far) will be the sum required at the start to ensure that there is not a cash deficit (e.g. overdraft) at any time.

This will be illustrated in the example and solution which follows. You are advised to work this example, before reading the solution.

Example

G. Glasgow plans to start a business on 1st January manufacturing and selling haggis. His plans include the following:

Equipment: This will cost £20,000 and will be purchased and paid for on 1st January.

Rent of factory: £500 per month, payable monthly at the start of each month.

Overheads: Estimated at £1,000 per month, payable monthly during the month in which they are incurred.

Sales: Estimated at £6,000 per month for the first three months, then increasing to £7,500 per month from April onwards. Mr Glasgow, perhaps realistically, budgets to give all his customers two months' credit, i.e. receipts from January sales will materialise in March.

Materials: These are estimated at one-third of sales value, and friendly suppliers have reluctantly agreed to give Mr Glasgow one month's credit.

Loan: Mr Glasgow's bank has agree to grant him a loan of £10,000 from 1st January. Interest will be charged at 20% per annum, and charged to his bank account at the end of each quarter, i.e. at the end of March, June, September and December.

Required

a) Prepare a monthly cash flow forecast for the six months to June, ignoring any capital which Mr Glasgow may have to introduce.

b) How much capital will this have have to be in order to ensure that Mr Glasgow does not incur a cash deficit during the first six months' trading?

Solution

Cash Flow Forecast for Mr G Glasgow
for the six months ending 30th June

	Jan £	Feb £	Mar £	Apr £	May £	Jun £	Total £
Cash inflows							
Capital	[ ]						[ ]
Loan	10,000						10,000
Sales	–	–	6,000	6,000	6,000	7,500	25,000
Total Inflows (A)	10,000	–	6,000	6,000	6,000	7,500	35,500
Cash outflows							
Equipment	20,000	–	–	–	–	–	20,000
Rent	500	500	500	500	500	500	3,000
Overheads	1,000	1,000	1,000	1,000	1,000	1,000	6,000
Materials	–	2,000	2,000	2,000	2,500	2,500	11,000
Interest on loan	–	–	500	–	–	500	1,000
Total Outflows (B)	21,500	3,500	4,000	3,500	4,000	4,500	41,000
Net cash flow (A – B)	(11,500)	(3,500)	2,000	2,500	2,000	3,000	(5,500)
Balances:							
Start of month	–	(11,500)	(15,000)	(13,000)	(10,500)	(8,500)	–
End of month	(11,500)	(15,000)	(13,000)	(10,500)	(8,500)	(5,500)	(5,500)

£15,000 is the amount of capital which would have to be introduced by Mr Glasgow in order to eliminate the highest cash deficit which is at the end of February.

You should now be able to attempt Questions 5.2 to 5.6 at the end of this chapter.

5.6 Summary

A ***cash flow forecast*** is a financial statement showing movements of cash in and out. It is an essential statement for planning and decision making. By regularly comparing the planned flow of cash with the actual flow, control can be achieved.

To draw up a cash flow forecast, you must know the ***amounts*** of the cash and the ***timings*** of the flows.

The most common mistakes made by students are:

- entering the correct cash flow in the incorrect month;
- incorrectly calculating the cumulative cash figures.

You should now be able to attempt Task 5.3 and the Objective Test at the end of this chapter.

Student activities

Task 5.1 Using your own bank statement or one belonging to a friend, use the figures to construct a cash flow as in ***B. Bristol*** in Section 5.3.

Task 5.2 Visit your local bank and ask if they can give you a proforma cash flow forecast. Most banks have a supply of these for customers wishing to apply for a business loan. Compare the layout of the cash flow from the bank with the examples we have given in this chapter

Task 5.3 In groups, select a business you would like to start. It may be a hairdressing salon, a restaurant, a windsurfing school, sports centre or any other type of business. Make a list of the information you would require and where you would obtain it in order to construct a cash flow forecast.

Question 5.1 Give the reasons why individuals and organisations should plan and control their cash flows.

Question 5.2 Recalculate the cash flow forecast for ***Mr Glasgow*** in Section 5.4, entering the inflow of capital of £15,000 between the square brackets.

Question 5.3 If ***Mr Glasgow*** in Section 5.4 did not have sufficient capital to introduce to prevent the cash deficits, what do you suggest he does apart from obtaining a further loan.

Question 5.4 ***W. Wellington*** is a boot manufacturer who has been in business for several years. He is thinking of expanding his business in three months' time, and wishes to know how this will affect his cash flow for the next six months, April to September. His budget figures for this period are as follows:

Cash sales: £10,000 per month, for the first three months, and £20,000 per month from 1st July onwards.

Credit sales of £55,000 per month have been achieved during the January – March period this year, and this is likely to continue until the end of June, after which it is hoped that credit sales will double. Mr Wellington allows his customers two months' credit.

Material purchases: These have been £10,000 per month for the last few months, and this is likely to be the pattern until 30th June, after which they will double. Mr Wellington's suppliers allow him one month's credit.

Wages: £15,000 per month until 30th June, after which they will double.

Overheads: £20,000 per month until 30th June, after which they are expected to increase to £35,000 per month.

Machinery: In order to achieve the increased production, new machinery will have to be purchased in June, and payment of £100,000 made in July.

Factory extension: A new building will also be necessary, which will be built during April and May, and payment of £150,000 will be due in July.

Bank balance: On 31st March, Mr Wellington has a credit balance on his business bank account of £140,000.

Mr Wellington can foresee a cash flow problem in July, and has an appointment to see his friendly bank manager, who, as well as listening, wants to see Mr Wellington's cash flow forecast for the next six months.

Required

Prepare this cash flow forecast for Mr Wellington, and append a few brief but relevant comments.

Question 5.5 In December 1991 ***Joan Norton*** plans to take a summer holiday abroad the following July. She has savings of £150 but the holiday she has chosen costs £500 and she will have to pay for it on 1st July 1992. Her net salary per month is £800 and she predicts that her cash flows for 1992 will be as follows:

Rent:	£300 per month payable at the beginning of each month
Electricity:	£230 per quarter payable at the end of each quarter
Travel:	£50 per month
Insurance:	£10 per month with additional premiums of £30 in February and £50 in April
Food:	£200 per month
Clothes and entertainment:	£70 per month
Endowment policy:	£30 per month

Required

Construct a cash flow forecast for the period January to June 1992 for Joan Norton. If Joan does not have sufficient cash to go on holiday, what action would you advise her to take so that she does have the required sum by 1st July?

Question 5.6 ***Tom Cherry*** is planning to start a business manufacturing wet suits for water sports. He has carried out a market survey and has found that at a retail price of £125 each he can expect to sell the following numbers of wet suits:

Month	**Number of wet suits**
January	10
February	20
March	30
April	60
May	80
June	80
July	60
August	50
September	50
October	40
November	40
December	30

He expects that half his customers will pay cash and the other half take one month's credit. He has found suitable premises with a workroom and a showroom in a seaside town. The rent is £10,000 per annum payable at the beginning of each quarter. Overheads such as heat and light are expected to be £400 per month payable in the month following the month in which they are incurred. He estimates other costs as follows:

Telephone:	£250 per quarter payable in the first month of the following quarter
Printing and stationery:	£50 per month payable in the month following the month in which they are incurred
Insurance:	£300 per quarter payable at the beginning of each quarter
Advertising:	Regular advertising will cost £60 per month, but extra advertising will be needed in April, May and June. This will cost an additional £500 which will be paid in two instalments in March and July.

The cost of materials for making each wet suit is £65 and the suppliers of the materials will allow two months' credit. Packaging will cost £3 per wet suit sold and the supplier is prepared to allow one month's credit. A friend of Tom's has agreed to cut out the wet suits for £5 per suit and he will be paid monthly. Tom plans to make 50 wet suits per month. The cost of the equipment for making the wet suits is £16,000 which will have to be paid for in January. The equipment will be depreciated over five years. The cost of fitting out the showroom is estimated at £3,500 and must be paid for by 31st March.

Required

i) Draw up a cash flow forecast for Tom Cherry for the 12 months January to December.

ii) How much capital does he require to make his business financially viable?

Objective test *(tick the appropriate box)*

i) Positive cash flow is:

a) cash flowing into an organisation ☐

b) cash flowing out of an organisation ☐

c) payments made to suppliers ☐

d) money taken out of the business by the owner ☐

ii) If more cash has come in than has gone out, this is known as :

a) profit ☐

b) cash deficit ☐

c) negative cash flow ☐

d) cash surplus ☐

iii) Constructing a cash flow forecast is a:

a) method for ensuring control ☐

b) valuable planning exercise ☐

c) way of recording a business's debts ☐

d) check on statements issued by the bank ☐

iv) If a business anticipates a cash deficit it can improve the position by:

a) not collecting any money from its customers ☐

b) making all payments as soon as possible ☐

c) withdrawing any money it has in the bank ☐

d) delaying any payments it has to make. ☐

v) If you are trading on credit you should enter the money owed by your customers on the cash flow forecast:

a) as soon as the sale is made ☐

b) when the customer first places the order ☐

c) when you expect the customers to pay ☐

d) two weeks after each sale is made ☐

Assignment A

An investigation for a loan

Context

Your cousin has recently inherited £5,000 and has been approached by *L. Corsham*, a local businessman, who has requested a loan of £2,000 to cover "some cash shortages of a temporary nature over the next few months." L. Corsham offers to pay interest of 18% per annum on the loan, to be paid to your cousin in cash each month. Your cousin is uncertain whether to loan the money to the businessman, or deposit the money in a building society and has sought your advice. Your cousin, who is in a well paid job, explains to you that she has no immediate need for the money and would like to invest it for at least 6 months and obtain a good return.

The only figures that L. Corsham has proffered to support his request for a loan are as follows.

List of Assets and Liabilities

	31 August 19X4	31 August 19X5
	£	£
Premises	10,000	10,000
Stock	5,000	5,500
Creditors	2,500	2,750
Bank	1,000	1,250
Vehicles	3,000	4,000
Debtors	3,000	3,750

Forecast income and expenditure for the period 1 September 19X5 to 28 February 19X6 :

- Sales all on credit of £5,000 per month. Cash from credit sales will be received in the month following the date of sale.
- Purchases will be paid for in the month following the date of sale. It is expected that the purchases will average £3,750 per month.
- Expenses to be paid in the month in which they are incurred are as follows:

  General expenses £150 per month

  Advertising £280 per month

  Rent £2,400 per annum to be paid monthly

  Heating and lighting £150 per month.
- Cash of £300 per month will be withdrawn from the business by Mr Corsham for his own use.
- In December of 19X5 it is intended to buy a delivery van of £3,200. The agreement with the garage supplying the van is that cash will be paid.

Student activities

i) Draw up a cash flow forecast for the period 1 September 19X5 to 28 February 1986 assuming that your cousin makes the loan of £2,000 on 1 September 19X5.

ii) Draw up a cash flow forecast for the period 1 September 19X5 to 28 February 1986 assuming that your cousin does not make the loan.

iii) Compare the two cash flow forecasts and make some conclusions on the financial viability of Mr Corsham's business.

iv) Conduct a survey of building society interest rates and determines which appears most favourable to your cousin. Your survey should include at least 3 different building societies.

v) Compare the advantages and disadvantages of your cousin making a loan to L. Corsham or investing the money in a building society.

Format

A report is required addressed to your cousin which shows:

- the two cash flows for L. Corsham;
- an assessment of the financial viability of the company and the wisdom of loaning money to it, based on the financial information you have;
- a brief review of the various building society interest rates and a recommendation of the most favourable one for your cousin. The report should contain a newspaper clipping, explanatory leaflet or advertisement giving details of the particular building society and the form of the deposit you recommend;
- a final recommendation as to whether your cousin should loan the money to Mr Corsham or deposit it in a building society.

Objectives

In this assignment the student will appreciate the use of cash flow forecasts in analysing business problems, and experience the advantages and problems of collecting and collating information from external sources in order to make a decision.

References

Chapters 1, 4 and 5 are of particular value to this assignment.

Business finance

This section (Chapters 6-9) is concerned with business organisations, their sources of finance and the disclosure of financial information by such organisations.

In Chapter 6 we consider the different types of structures which may be used in forming business organisations. This is important when examining different sources of finance and the financial responsibilities of the owners.

In Chapter 7 we look at different sources of external and internal finance for the various types of organisations.

In Chapter 8 we discuss the role of the accountant and look at an overview of the accounting profession and of accountancy as a career.

In Chapter 9 we look at the potential users of financial information, the sources available to them and the uses to which the information may be put.

Chapter 6

Different organisational structures

6.1 Objectives

At the end of this chapter you should be able to:

- define the different organisational forms;
- describe the main features of different organisational forms;
- explain the significant differences between the organisational forms;
- list the advantages and disadvantages of different organisational forms;
- indicate the main reporting requirements of the different organisational forms.

6.2 Introduction

Business organisations in the UK take a number of different forms and these are defined by legislation. The way in which a business is managed, conducts its affairs, borrows money, the type of financial information it generates and the people who receive such information are to a great extent matters related to the legal structure of the organisation. We will examine the different ***organisational structures*** and their features in detail later in this chapter. For our purposes, the most important are:

- The sole trader: one person running the business for his or her own exclusive benefit.
- The partnership: two or more people own the business.
- Companies limited by shares, also known as limited liability companies: these may be owned by many people who have no part in the day to day management of the company.
- Public sector organisations: for example, local authorities, public corporations such as British Rail, and health authorities.
- Social organisations: for example, tennis clubs or angling clubs. Although such organisations are run by the members for the purpose of promoting their particular interest, proper accounts should be kept.

Choosing the most suitable organisational structure for a business depends on a number of factors. The main ones are:

- The nature of the activity: To take an extreme example, it is evident that running a nuclear power station will require greater resources and administration than having a window cleaning business.
- The number of people involved: Two or more people could not launch a business as a sole trader.
- The amount of money needed to start the business: Few people are rich enough to launch a large business venture with their own money alone.
- The amount of financial risk involved: If a venture is very risky there is a good argument for spreading the possibility of financial failure.

In deciding which is the most appropriate organisational form for a particular business, it is important to consider both the nature of the proposed business and the wishes of the owners. The different organisational forms have their own particular advantages and disadvantages and these are considered in the sections which follow.

You should now be able to attempt Question 6.1 at the end of this chapter.

6.3 Sole traders

A *sole trader* can be defined as one person trading alone with a view to making a profit. The business may simply be in the name of the person or may have a business name such as 'Quickclean Windows'. The business trading name does not have to be registered, but if one is used the owner's name should appear on all letterheads etc.

If you start a business as a sole trader you are the owner of that business, taking all the profits but also suffering any losses. You are totally responsible for the business, although you may decide to employ people to do some of the work or to manage the business for you. But they will be employees; you are the person with the final responsibility.

When starting the business you will have to provide all the finance. If you are unable to do this from your own savings, you will have to borrow the money from other people. You will be responsible for paying them back, even if the business is unsuccessful. Banks and other financial institutions, if asked to lend money, usually want to see detailed plans of the proposed business.

If the business runs into financial problems, you will be called upon to resolve them. This means that if the business ends up owing money, then you will be personally responsible for paying the debts, even if this means selling your house, car and any other possessions of value you may have. In the worse possible circumstances, if you cannot pay all the debts you may be declared legally bankrupt.

The ***advantages*** of being a sole trader are:

- It is very simple to start the business; there are no legal formalities.
- You make all the decisions without having to consult any other person.
- You enjoy all the profits.
- You have total control over the business.

The ***disadvantages*** of being a sole trader are:

- You may not have sufficient money to start the business and you may not be able to borrow what you need.
- If the business makes a loss, you will suffer all of it.
- You will have to provide all the management expertise, unless you can afford to employ other people.
- You are personally responsible for the debts of the business, which means you can be made legally bankrupt if you are unable to pay.
- As explained in Chapter 2, you are liable to pay tax on the profits of the business.

6.4 Partnerships

A ***partnership*** can be defined as two or more people carrying on a business with a view to profit. The maximum number of partners allowed is 20, apart from professional firms such as accountants and solicitors who can exceed this number. Partnerships are very common, although you may not appreciate that many of the businesses with which you come into contact have this organisational form. It is quite usual for professional people such as dentists, doctors, solicitors and accountants to offer services not by themselves but with two or more colleagues. In other words, they are trading their services as a partnership. In addition, estate agents, barbers, shops and other small businesses offering a range of services from painting and decorating to catering for a wedding, may be owned by two or more people; they have formed a partnership.

The partners are all owners of the business; they jointly share in the decisions and the running of the business. As in the case of a sole trader, they may operate under a business name which does not have to be registered and need not include any wording to show it is a partnership. For example, The Daw and Jakes Partnership is clearly a partnership, but 'Quickclean Windows', the name we used as an illustration for a sole trader could also be a partnership; you cannot tell from the name. However under the ***Business Names Act 1985*** the names of the partners must appear on the firm's stationery.

It may be easier to raise the finance to start a business as a partnership because each of the partners may be able to contribute a sum of money. All the partners will expect a share of any profit the business earns, but they must also take a share of any losses. Partners normally ask a solicitor to draw up a legal agreement showing the proportions in which they will share any profit or loss and other matters.

It may be that because one partner spends more time in the business than the others, he or she is entitled to a larger share of the profit, or even a salary. This should be stated in the Partnership Agreement. If the partners fail to draw up an agreement, the rules of the ***Partnership Act 1890*** apply. This can be very important in the event of a dispute between partners and in Chapter 23 we look at these rules more closely.

As in the case of a sole trader, the owners of the business, i.e. the partners, are personally responsible for the debts of the business. This may cause great hardship because should one partner disappear to South America, the remaining partner(s) is/are personally liable for all the debts of the business.

The ***advantages*** of a partnership are:

- More capital can be raised to start the business.
- The pressures of running and controlling the business are shared.
- Legal requirements are few (but remember the Partnership Act 1890 applies if the partners fail to draw up an agreement).
- If the business makes a loss it is shared amongst the partners.

The ***disadvantages*** of a partnership are:

- You do not have sole control and the other partners may overrule your decisions.
- You do not enjoy all the profits but have to share them.
- If the business runs into financial problems, you will be personally responsible for the debts of the partnership.

You should now be able to attempt Question 6.2 at the end of this chapter.

6.5 Limited liability companies

A ***limited liability company*** (often just referred to as a limited company) can be defined as a 'legal person' and is separate from the owners. This feature is so distinctive and important that we will discuss it now before we consider any other feature of limited companies.

In the case of a sole trader or a partnership, the people are the business even though, for example, John Smith may trade under the name of Futuristic Events; he and the business are one and the same. If you want to take legal action you will be suing John Smith and he will be responsible. It is the same with a partnership. But matters are very different with a limited company. If you and two of your friends decide to form a small limited company called 'Threesome Limited', from a legal point of view there will be four of you: the three shareholders, i.e. you and your two friends, and a fourth legal person, the limited company.

Because a limited company is regarded as being separate from its owners, it is often referred to as a ***legal entity***. The most important consequence of this is that the company is responsible for the debts incurred in trading. If the business is unable to pay its debts, then the company can be sued in its own name. The owners of the company (the ***shareholders***) are responsible for the amount of money they have invested and/or agreed to invest in the company, but their liability is limited to that amount.

If the company is unable to pay its debts, it may go into liquidation and have to stop trading. This will not affect the shareholders. Although they may lose the amount they have agreed to invest in the company they will not be expected to sell their personal possessions. If you look back at the personal responsibilities of small traders and partnerships, you will appreciate the crucial difference.

All shareholders in limited companies have a great advantage over sole traders and partnerships. By forming a limited company they have reduced the risk of losing money, as they are only liable for the amount they have invested or agreed to invest. Because of this great benefit there are a number of legal burdens placed on limited companies.

On the formation of the company certain documents must be registered with the ***Registrar of Companies*** which is a part of the Department of Trade and Industry. In addition, every year a limited company must send certain financial information to all its shareholders and register certain information with the Registrar. As any person may consult the files of the Registrar, the data submitted by the companies become public documents.

As well as having a legal personality and existence separate from its owners, the identity of the company is not affected by changes of ownership and the company can enter into contracts without necessarily having to refer to its owners. The owners of a limited company, particularly the larger ones, do not run it on a day-to-day basis themselves but appoint directors to do it for them.

Companies limited by shares are the most important form of business organisation, not because of their number, but because of their size. All the major organisations in the private sector are companies limited by shares. Companies whose shares can be offered to the public are known as ***public limited companies (plc)*** and these words must appear after the name. You will find that most major organisations such as the high street banks, Boots, Sainsburys, Marks and Spencers, are public limited companies, although in conversations and in press reports the words 'public limited company' may not be added to the name.

As well as public limited companies, there are ***private limited companies*** whose shares may not be offered to the public. Private companies must put the word 'limited' in their name. A public company can choose to offer its shares to the public through the *Stock Exchange*; a private company can not do this.

The ***advantage***s of limited companies are:

- The liability of the owners (also known as members) of a company for the debts it incurs is limited to the amount they have agreed to subscribe for shares.
- It can be easier to raise large sums of money.
- The company can be professionally managed by directors.
- Owners can sell their shares in a public limited company if they wish to relinquish their ownership because the Stock Exchange is a market place for dealing in shares.

The ***disadvantages*** of limited companies are:

- It is more expensive to start business as a limited company than as a partnership or sole trader. (Although it is possible to form a limited company for approximately £100.)
- Any decisions you make about the company may be vetoed by other shareholders.
- There are considerable legal requirements to be fulfilled.
- Some of the financial affairs of a limited company become public property.

You should now be able to attempt Task 6.1 and Question 6.3 at the end of this chapter.

6.6 Public sector organisations

A large number of organisations are controlled by the Government. Such organisations include British Rail, Defence, the BBC and the Post Office which are held in public ownership to serve our needs. These various bodies make up the public sector and can be classified as follows:

- Public corporations: for example, British Broadcasting Corporation, British Rail
- Health authorities
- Local authorities responsible for the provision of such services as fire services, education, libraries and recreational facilities

- ❐ Central Government departments: for example, the departments of Social Security, Environment, Defence

All these organisations are accountable to the public and issue financial statements. They are there to serve the public and to spend public funds as efficiently as possible. There are some business activities where it is clear that the only way to organise them is through the public sector. Defence, for example, must be organised on a national basis with each member of the population contributing to it. Whether we should spend so much or even anything on defence is a political and moral argument outside the scope of this book.

Some of the organisations in the ***public sector*** provide a service which would be difficult or impossible to undertake by ***private sector*** organisations. Even if it were practical to make some of these organisations into limited companies, it raises questions about whether we want natural resources or important services to be in private hands.

There are some who argue that a number of organisations in the public sector are inefficient. By allowing them to be privatised, i.e. become public limited companies owned by shareholders, a better and cheaper service would be provided. Others argue that there is no proof that they would be more efficient and may overcharge for their services to make large profits. There are also some activities which are run at a loss in the public sector because the organisation has a social duty to provide a particular service.

These political and efficiency arguments are important and have some bearing on the financial operations of some organisations in the public sector. Some public corporations, in their operations, can be compared with public limited companies in the private sector. They have financial targets and other measures of performance, and the financial statements that they make available to the public are very similar.

6.7 Social organisations

Some organisations are formed not with the objective of making a profit, but to serve other purposes their members. Examples are tennis clubs, drama clubs, angling societies and other organisations formed to arrange and promote activities for members' interest and benefit.

Such organisations are financed by the members and although car boot sales and barn dances may raise money to swell the club's funds, it is not the main purpose of the organisation to be pursuing profit.

However, there are some organisations involved in social activities which are run with the intention of making a profit. This is particularly true of activities concerned with leisure and exercise which can be run by a sole trader, a partnership or even a limited company selling services to the club members in order to make a profit. Such organisations are not social organisations, which are run for the benefit of members by the members themselves, normally through a committee.

Some ***social organisations*** are quite large and raise and spend considerable sums of money. Even a Parent Teacher Association or Rugby Club can raise over £10,000 a year. Therefore it is vital that all social organisations ensure that proper accounting records are maintained and that members are informed of the club's financial position.

6.8 Reporting requirements

In this chapter we have looked at the essential features of different organisational structures. At this stage it is useful to examine the difference in the types of information which they must disclose. In subsequent chapters we will deal with this more thoroughly and in the following sections only the main legal requirements are considered

6.9 Sole traders

A sole trader has very few legal requirements to fulfil. The most important ones are:

- ❐ If the value of the taxable supplies of the sole trader is over a certain sum per annum, the business must be registered with H M Customs and Excise for Value Added Tax purposes. The Chancellor of the Exchequer sets this figure each year in his annual budget. It is a legal requirement that businesses registered for VAT maintain accurate records and the operation of VAT is explained in an earlier chapter.

- The Inland Revenue collects tax from a profitable business. It is not necessary for a sole trader to ask an accountant to attend to the tax affairs, but many consider it wise to do so. To ensure that the correct amount of tax is paid, proper accounting records should be maintained.
- A sole trader may well be interested in the amount of profit the business has made in the year, but there is no legal requirement to produce a statement showing this. (The Inland Revenue will expect to see one or it may not believe the amount of tax the sole trader thinks should be paid). Where the sole trader does produce a financial statement showing the profit of the business for the year, this remains confidential information and need not be shown to any other person without the sole trader's permission.
- The *Business Names Act 1985* applies to sole traders (and partnerships) carrying on a business under a name which does not consist solely of their name (with or without their initials or forenames). This is designed to prevent a person carrying on a business using a name which gives the impression that the business in connected to the government or any local authority, or uses certain words or expressions which are prohibited under the Act. If the Act applies the name and address of the owner must be displayed on all business premises and stationery.

6.10 Partnerships

The comments relating to VAT, the Business Names Act and the Inland Revenue for sole traders are also pertinent to partnerships. In addition, the *Partnership Act 1890* lays down the following:

- Proper books of accounts must be kept.
- Capital must be distinguished from profits and losses.
- A record must be kept of profit shares and drawings.
- Partners are bound to render true accounts and full information of all things affecting the partnership to any partner or his legal representative.

The requirements placed on partnerships are therefore more onerous and in Chapter 23 we will study these in detail. It is important to stress that the partnership is not legally required to make any financial information about itself available to the general public. This is very different from limited companies, as we will see in the next section.

You should now be able to attempt Question 6.6 at the end of this chapter.

6.11 Limited liability companies

The legal reporting requirements surrounding limited companies are complex and are contained in the *Companies Act 1985*. This was not the first companies act. A number of different acts have been passed from the middle of the last century, but all limited companies are now regulated by the provisions of the 1985 Act. This Act has now been amended and added to by the *Companies Act 1989*. You will find, however, that people still refer to the Companies Act 1985 and it is implied that they mean "as amended by the Companies Act 1989".

There are variations depending on the type of company and its size but the main general provisions are:

- Every limited company must keep accounting records to show and explain the company's transactions.
- At the end of each financial year every limited company must prepare final accounts which comprise:
  - the profit and loss account
  - the balance sheet
  - the auditor's report
  - the directors' report

- These final accounts are given to each shareholder, debenture holder and any persons entitled to attend the Annual General Meeting of the company, prior to the date of such a meeting. The accounts should also be lodged with the Registrar of Companies. In this way they become public documents and for a small fee anyone can obtain a copy of them.

In addition to the Companies Act 1985, limited liability companies are regulated by ***Statements of Standard Accounting Practices (SSAPs)***. These are statements of guidance issued by the professional accounting bodies in the UK. These statements do not have the force of law, but are recommendations as to how certain accounting matters should be dealt with by limited companies and how the information should be disclosed in their accounts.

If a public limited company wishes to be listed (i.e. for its shares to be traded) on the Stock Exchange then it must also comply with the specific rules that the Stock Exchange has concerning disclosure of information.

There are a number of terms and phrases above that you may be encountering for the first time. We will explain them fully in later chapters. At this stage it is only important to appreciate that limited liability companies have to comply with strict legislation concerning their financial activities and certain information will be publicly available.

You should now be able to attempt Question 6.5 at the end of this chapter.

6.12 Public sector finance

If we look at the finances of central Government there are two aspects. One is the spending of money on our behalf and the other is raising the money from us. Most people know about some of the ways in which the money is raised because it receives lots of attention in the Chancellor's annual budget. This is announced late in the calendar year, debated in Parliament and then appears in a subsequent Finance Act. There are a number of sources that the central Government has for raising finance. These are:

- Taxes on incomes and capital, the main one being income tax
- Taxes on expenditure through such taxes as VAT
- National Insurance contributions
- Short-term loans
- Through the issue of gilts on the Stock Exchange
- Privatisation
- Public savings in schemes such as National Savings Certificates

The deliberations on the spending side start some 12 months before the budget. Officials from the Treasury and other central Government departments draw up the Public Expenditure survey showing the money to be spent by central and local Government bodies, nationalised industries and public corporations. These estimates are passed to the Treasury before the Budget so that the amount of money to be raised is known.

The term ***local authority*** includes County Councils, Borough or District Councils and Parish Councils. These bodies do not aim to make a profit, but are responsible for expenditure on such services as social services, fire and public protection, libraries and leisure facilities.

There are a number of sources of finance for local authorities. These are:

- Central government grants
- Receipts from the rates
- Charges for services

- ❒ Loans
- ❒ Sale of capital stock
- ❒ Gifts and bequests
- ❒ Business enterprises

There are strict financial controls placed on local authorities and they must endeavour to give value for money. An annual report giving the financial information is published by each local authority and this is available in town halls and public libraries as well as copies being sent to interested groups. Local authorities also send brief financial information to all people liable to pay rates or some other form of community charge.

You should now be able to attempt Tasks 6.2 and 6.3 at the end of this chapter.

6.13 Summary

In this chapter we have considered the various forms of organisational structures and their reporting requirements.

A ***sole trader*** is a person trading alone with a view to making a profit. This is a very easy way to start a business and gives the owner complete control. The sole trader is personally responsible for all the debts of the business. The sole trader does not have to make any financial information about the business publicly available.

A ***partnership*** is two or more people carrying on a business with a view to profit. The Partnership Act 1890 applies to partnerships in the absence of any other agreement. Partnerships do not have to make any financial information publicly available, but partners are individually liable for the debts of the partnership.

A ***limited liability company*** is a legal person as distinct from the owners. The financial responsibilty of the owners is limited to the amount they have invested or agreed to invest in the company. There are very strict disclosure of information regulations applied to all limited liability companies through the Companies Act 1985.

Public sector organisations such as public corporations, public utilities, health authorities and local authorities are controlled by the government. The financing of these organisations has a considerable impact on all our lives.

Social organisations such as tennis clubs, angling societies etc are formed notwith the the objective of making a profit, but to serve other purposes of the members. Such organisations should maintain suitable accounting records and keep their members informed of the financial position.

Student activities

Task 6.1 Make a list of different limited companies whose products or services you use in one day. Some of the companies you may know already as plc's. With other companies you will find the words (usually in very small print) on the label of their products or stationery.

Task 6.2 From a ratepayer, such as your parents or a relative or neighbour, obtain a copy of the brief financial information sent by the local authority. How does the local authority obtain its finance and how much does it spend on each of the activities it undertakes?

Task 6.3 You have decided to start a business with two friends delivering sandwiches to office workers. One of your friends argues that you should form a limited company and the other believes that you should form a partnership. Bearing in mind the type of business you are envisaging, write a letter to your friends giving your opinion and explaining the reasons.

Question 6.1 Select the correct response to the following statements:

	True	False
i) It only needs one person to start a partnership.	☐	☐
ii) A limited company is the simplest way for an individual to start a small business.	☐	☐
iii) The amount of money required to start a business is important in determining the most appropriate organisational form.	☐	☐
iv) A sole trader is a business owned by one person.	☐	☐

Question 6.2 Select the correct response to the following statements:

	True	False
i) All sole traders must call their business by a different name from their own.	☐	☐
ii) A sole trader is personally responsible for all debts incurred by the business.	☐	☐
iii) A sole trader does not have to pay tax on the profits of the business.	☐	☐
iv) If two or more persons own a business they must include the word 'partnership' in its name.	☐	☐
v) If partners do not make an agreement on the share of profit the rules of the Partnership Act 1890 apply.	☐	☐
vi) Only partners who receive a salary from the partnership must contribute to any debts incurred by the business.	☐	☐

Question 6.3 Select the correct response to the following statements:

	True	False
i) All shareholders are personally responsible for all debts incurred by the limited company in which they have invested.	☐	☐
ii) A private limited company is exactly the same as a partnership.	☐	☐
iii) In the event of one of the shareholders dying, a limited company would have to cease business.	☐	☐
iv) Only a public limited company can offer its shares to the public.	☐	☐
v) By forming a private limited company, all its financial affairs can be kept secret.	☐	☐

Question 6.4 Which of the following statements refer to sole traders, which to partnerships, and which to both?

i) If the turnover of the business is above a certain figure it must be registered for VAT.

ii) No financial information about the business has to be made publicly available.

iii) Apart from tax responsiblities, there are no legal requirements stating what financial records the business must maintain.

iv) It is important to distinguish between capital and profit shares and drawings.

Question 6.5 Complete the missing items in the following statement:

All limited companies are regulated by the Companies Act _____. This requires companies to prepare __________ at the end of each financial year. Both private limited companies and __________ must deposit certain information with the __________ and it thus becomes public.

Objective test *(tick the appropriate box)*

i) To form a business as a sole trader you must:

a) have a bank loan ☐

b) register your name with the Department of Trade and Industry ☐

c) be willing to take all the financial risks by yourself ☐

d) make public your financial results ☐

ii) To form a partnership you must:

a) have at least four partners ☐

b) register the business name with the Department of Trade and Industry ☐

c) have at least two partners ☐

d) make public your financial results ☐

iii) A limited company offers the advantage of:

a) being very easy to establish ☐

b) complete financial secrecy ☐

c) no legal formalities to meet ☐

d) limited financial risk to its owners ☐

iv) The Companies Act 1985 applies only to:

a) all limited companies ☐

b) all partnerships ☐

c) all public limited companies ☐

d) all private limited companies ☐

v) When the government privatises an organisation such as British Steel, the money thus raised goes to:

a) the London Stock Exchange ☐

b) the Government ☐

c) the new shareholders ☐

d) the company itself ☐

Chapter 7

External and internal sources of finance

7.1 Objectives

At the end of this chapter you should be able to:

- list the various sources of finance;
- describe the different types of finance;
- explain the advantages and disadvantages of different types of finance;
- describe the contents of a business plan;
- recommend the appropriate sources of finance in given circumstances.

7.2 Introduction

In Chapter 1 we looked at the issues and decisions to be made when borrowing money. In this chapter we are going to look at business organisations. A business can attempt to obtain finance from external sources, such as banks, or from internal sources, for example where one company in a group seeks funds from the holding company.

Finance may be required for the following reasons:

- to start up a completely new business;
- to expand an existing business: this may be by such means as expanding the factory or work premises or by seeking funds to allow you to hold more items in stock. It may mean launching an entirely new product or seeking markets in other parts of the world;
- to deal with unexpected problems in an existing business: for example, crucial repairs on machinery or the advent of a postal strike which delays the receipt of money owed;
- to deal with a special situation: for example, an order from a new client may require the purchase of certain new tools or raw materials.

Even when a business can raise the finance from internal sources, there will be a need to justify on financial grounds the reason for the decision. When a business is seeking external finance the prospective lender will expect to see evidence that the loan will be safe and that there is a very high probability that it will be repaid, with interest, on the appointed date. This evidence will be prepared in an essential document known as a business plan.

7.3 The business plan

Planning is an essential function of management. At all stages in the life of a business, plans will be constructed to ensure the effective operation of business activity. If an organisation requires finance it must draw up a particular type of plan known as a ***business plan***. This is a document designed to provide answers in a understandable and comprehensive fashion to all the questions a prospective lender may ask. There are four crucial questions which the business plan must answer:

- the purposes for which the loan is required;
- how the loan will be spent;
- how large a loan is required;

- when and how the loan will be repaid.

The essential reason for a business plan is to enable the business to obtain the loan. The business plan will therefore put forward the advantages of the proposal in the most attractive way. Any weaknesses must also be included, as the plan must be realistic, otherwise the prospective lender will not treat it seriously. But as well as being designed to obtain the loan, a business plan has other uses, even when internal finance is being sought. The plan will:

- clearly set out the targets to be achieved including the level of sales to be achieved and the planned profit;
- show the actions to be followed to achieve the targets, thus becoming an action document as well as a planning document;
- show possible weaknesses in the proposed scheme so that decisions can be taken regarding the best ways in which to overcome them;
- demonstrate to the potential lender and other people that the owners of the business know what they are doing.

A business plan requires a considerable amount of effort and time to construct. After drawing up a plan, a company may decide that the project is not viable after all or requires improvement before a loan can be sought. But without a realistic and credible business plan it will be impossible to apply for a loan.

You should now be able to attempt Task 7.1 at the end of this chapter.

7.4 Contents of a business plan

What goes into a business plan depends on the nature of the proposal and the type of finance being sought. However, the structure of the document and the principal information it contains is common to most business plans and should include the following:

- ***Background to the proposal***
  This will include a description of the experience, qualifications and business successes of the people concerned with the proposal, as well as an indication of the general nature of the proposal.
- ***Details of the proposal***
  This section will include detailed information about the proposal. For instance, if you plan to manufacture a new product, you would give a detailed description of the product and the manufacturing process.
- ***The market***
  No matter how good or new the product or service you intend to offer, the prospective lender will want to be assured that there is someone who wants to buy it. Details of the number of potential customers and competitors, and your advantages over them, must be given.
- ***The financial forecasts***
  Having convinced the recipient of the document that your product or service that is eagerly desired by many people, you arrive at the heart of the business plan, the financial forecasts. These forecasts must show that the business is financially viable, the size of loan required, when it is needed and when it will be repaid. One key financial statement will be the ***cash flow forecast*** which we looked at in Chapter 5.

You should now be able to attempt Question 7.1 at the end of this chapter.

7.5 Types of finance

Having constructed a business plan, you know how much money you need to borrow and for how long. For limited liability companies a major source of finance is through the issue of shares or debentures. We will look at these particular forms in chapters 20-22 and concentrate on other sources of finance in this chapter. The type of finance can be classified according to the length of time the loan is required:

- *Long-term finance* is used when the loan is expected to be for about 20 years, for example a mortgage.
- *Medium-term finance* is used when the loan is required for a number of years, for example when purchasing such items as machinery.
- *Short-term finance* is used when the loan is to be repaid in weeks or months, for example a bank overdraft.

Selecting the appropriate type of finance is most important, as it determines the best source of that finance and also affects the interest you will have to pay and therefore the cost of the loan. The table below shows the types of finance and some examples of the purposes for which they may be required.

Long-term finance

Type of finance	Purpose
Mortgage	New business premises
Venture capital	New machinery, investment in new technology

Medium-term finance

Type of finance	Purpose
Hire purchase	Purchase of cars
Leasing	Purchase of plant and machinery
Loan Finance	Improvements to premises

Short-term finance

Type of finance	Purpose
Short term loan	Purchase of machinery with a short life, increasing stocks
Factoring	Raising finance against debtors
Overdraft	Short term cash deficit

You should now be able to attempt Question 7.2 at the end of this chapter.

7.6 Sources of finance

Financial institutions, such as banks and building societies, advertise in the newspapers and on the television the availability of funds for borrowers. You should not be misled by the advertising into thinking that loans are easily obtainable. To obtain loans can be difficult for individuals and businesses. Although the financial institutions wish to lend money, they will do so only if they believe that there is a very high probability that the loan will be repaid. Identifying sources where loans may be obtained is not the same as stating that you will be able to obtain a loan in all circumstances.

7.7 Banks

For most small businesses, the high street banks are the main source of finance. You will probably know from seeing television advertisements that they run a number of different schemes each with their own advantages. The main types of finance offered by the banks are:

- *Long-term loans*
  Banks lend money over a long period of time for the purchase of items such as business premises. The bank normally wants some form of security for a long-term loan and the usual method is by a mortgage.

- *Medium-term loans*
  The bank makes a commitment to lend the money to the business for a specified period of time and the loan is repaid by instalment. The bank may agree that the instalments need not commence until the project starts earning money; repayments may be monthly, quarterly or even half yearly.
- *Overdrafts*
  These are usually the cheapest and easiest to arrange form of loan. However, overdrafts are not granted as a form of medium or long-term loan and the bank can ask you to repay the overdraft at very short notice.

You should now be able to attempt Task 7.2 at the end of this chapter.

7.8 Hire purchase

This is widely used by individuals to buy cars, home computers, furniture and electrical goods. However, hire purchase is also used by many businesses, as it allows them to obtain an item and use it to generate sufficient profits to repay the hire purchase, thus paying for itself.

7.9 Factoring

A factoring organisation is able to take over the debts owed to you by your customers for goods or services. It invoices your customers, collects the money and pursues any bad debts. Even if the factoring organisation has not collected the money from the customers, it will still pay you the amount owing on the agreed date. It is possible to receive up to 80 per cent of the money still owed by customers.

Factoring allows a business to be certain about the dates on which it will be receiving money in the future and relieves it of the paperwork in invoicing and collecting money from customers. Many factoring organisations are operated by the main banks, so they are highly reputable; details of the service offered can be obtained from the bank or from advertisements in the financial press.

Of course, the factoring organisation makes a charge to the company for its services. The exact amount will depend on the level of business, but is usually calculated at between 0.5 and 3 per cent of turnover. If you decide that you want money from the factoring organisation before your customers pay up, there will be a further charge which is approximately 3 per cent over the current bank base rate.

There is some argument that by factoring you lose contact with your customers, who may be concerned about your company's financial position because you use factoring. However, this method is becoming more widely used and therefore more acceptable.

7.10 Venture capital

If you are looking for a loan in excess of £100,000, a venture capitalist may be an appropriate source. Finance is offered to businesses in the form of ordinary shares, preference shares and loans. To obtain venture capital your business plan must be very sound and offer a very high return. The exact amount of return depends on the risk involved, but most venture capitalists expect a return of at least 25 per cent.

In addition, the venture capitalist normally expects to withdraw his investment from the business after three years. This means that someone else must be found to take over the loan and ways must be found of attracting other shareholders.

7.11 Shares

A limited liability company can issue shares to obtain finance. If a company quoted on the Stock Exchange wishes to expand and therefore requires finance, it can offer shares to the public. The public is able to subscribe for the shares, paying the amount due, and in this way the company raises the money it requires.

Shareholders are unlikely to be attracted to buy the shares unless the company is doing well or has plans which look very solid indeed. The advantage to the company is that it does not have to pay back the money thus raised. Neither does it have to pay regular interest to the shareholders, but only a dividend when it makes a profit. These matters will be explained more fully in Chapter 21.

A sole trader or a partnership cannot offer shares as neither is a limited company. However, a sole trader or partnership can become a limited company. Because of the expense involved, it is not usual to start off as a public limited company able to offer shares to the public, but as a private limited company. This allows members of the family and friends to buy shares in the company, thereby raising money. This has the advantage that the shareholders limit the risk of losing any money except their investment and they do not interfere with the day-to-day running of the company.

7.12 Government assistance

A number of different schemes are run by central and local Government to help small businesses. These include the availability of work premises at a modest rent or the payment of a weekly amount until the business has got on its feet.

There are a great many different schemes and they are always changing. Fortunately, there are a number of organisations which provide up-to-date information and guidance on such schemes.

Most of the schemes entail satisfying certain criteria which have nothing to do with the soundness of your business plan. For example, you may have to have been unemployed for a certain period of time or be living in a particular area to qualify for Government assistance. No matter what other criteria you have to comply with, you will be expected to produce a sound and well constructed business plan.

You should now be able to attempt Questions 7.3 and 7.4 at the end of this chapter.

7.13 Internal finance

Most of the comments we have made so far have been concerned with attracting external finance for the business. In this last section we look at internal finance. Where a business has been operating successfully, the owners may have decided not to pay all of the profits out, but to reinvest some in the business. These retained profits form the major source of internal finance to be used for future expansion.

A department, division or a subsidiary company in a group of companies may require additional finance for any number of reasons. Instead of going outside the organisation for the finance, it is often best to see whether the finance is available elsewhere in the organisation; there is little sense in paying interest to a bank if the funds are readily available internally.

The reasons for requiring additional finance are:

- to expand existing business activities;
- to launch a new product or service;
- to improve existing efficiency;
- to improve safety standards or working conditions.

If the company is obliged to improve safety standards, the major decision will be to ascertain whether there are sufficient funds within the company. If not, application must be made to external sources.

If a part of the company is hoping to launch a new product, improve existing efficiency or expand existing business activities, criteria must be used to determine whether it is worthwhile. It may even be that there are a number of divisions within the company, all with their pet schemes, and if funds are limited, some way must be found to rank the proposals to select the best.

Which scheme is the best? All parts of the company must put forward a convincing proposal for their own scheme. As with the business plan, this will include detailed information about the new product or service, the likely level of sales and the position of competitors. However, the financial information will be somewhat different. The person within the company responsible for deciding whether the funds will be made available, is not so interested in whether the loan will be repaid with a set figure of interest as in the profitability of the scheme. In other words, does it use the company's financial and other resources efficiently? The company will want to earn the greatest amount of profit possible for every £ spent and that will be the main criterion for deciding on funding a project internally.

The amount of profit (the return) is normally expressed as a ratio. If a proposal does not promise to reach this target, it is very doubtful that this proposal will be funded. The methods we use to measure the profitability of a specific project, i.e. the rate of return we can expect from the investment, fall under the heading of Capital Investment Appraisal or Project Appraisal. This is the subject of Chapters 36–39 in this book.

It is no easier to obtain internal finance than external finance, in some cases much harder. There may be some willingness to be sympathetic to riskier projects, but the rate of return expected from internally financed projects is usually substantially higher than the interest charges from external sources.

You should now be able to attempt Task 7.3 at the end of this chapter.

7.14 Presenting the case

Whether the proposal for finance is being made internally or externally, a sound and convincing case must be made. The steps to be followed are:

- ❐ assemble all the information to be included in the business plan or application for internal finance;
- ❐ decide on the structure of the proposal and organise the information into this order;
- ❐ write the proposal, questioning any assumptions and making the necessary revisions;
- ❐ avoid jargon in the proposal, but make certain that it is realistic;
- ❐ include or refer to independent evidence, e.g. market surveys, to support your case where appropriate;
- ❐ include any risks and problems in your proposals and how you intend to resolve them;
- ❐ get the plan typed and bound with an index;
- ❐ prepare for the interview with the lender of the money. Even with applications for internal funding you may be called to a meeting to explain your proposal. With external funding an interview is certain; for large amounts there will be a number of interviews.

If you are successful with your application for funding, do not throw away the business plan; it is even more important now. The lender of the money will expect you to achieve the plan or be able to explain why you have not done so. This means that the business plan can be used to monitor and control your performance.

7.15 Summary

In this chapter we have looked at the reasons why ***finance*** may be required by a business. It may be wanted to start a new business, expand an existing business, to deal with unexpected problems or with special situations. Finance can be classified into ***long-term, medium-term*** and ***short-term***. It is essential to select the appropriate type as this will affect the interest you have to pay.

For most small businesses ***banks*** are a main source of finance, but ***hire purchase, factoring*** and other sources may be appropriate. In attempting to obtain finance it is essential to prepare a ***business plan***. At the heart of the business plan are the financial forecasts and the most crucial financial statement is the ***cash flow forecast***.

You should now be able to attempt the Objective Test at the end of this chapter.

Student activities

Task 7.1 Imagine that a friend wants to start a small business selling computer software and has asked you for a loan of £2,000. Make a list of the most important questions you would ask.

Task 7.2 Collect leaflets on loan facilities from a number of various banks and compare the different arrangements and terms which are offered.

Task 7.3 Look through the financial press for the advertisements offering sources of finance. Cut them out and classify them into long, medium and short-term finance.

Question 7.1 Select the correct response to the following statements:

		True	False
i)	A business plan is essential for a business to obtain a loan.	☐	☐
ii)	Any possible weakness in a business plan should be omitted so as not to worry the prospective lender.	☐	☐
iii)	It is best not to include information in a business plan about the predicted level of sales.	☐	☐
iv)	The most crucial statement in the business plan is the cash flow forecast.	☐	☐

Question 7.2 Identify the type of finance which may be required for the following:

i) purchase of new car

ii) acquisition of business premises

iii) extending credit to customers

iv) increasing the amount of raw materials held

v) covering a short-term cash deficit

vi) repainting business premises

Question 7.3 Match the type of finance with its relevant characteristic in the following list:

a) Mortgage	i) Only available to limited companies
b) Hire purchase	ii) Suitable for purchase of premises
c) Factoring	iii) Useful for short-term cash problems
d) Overdraft	iv) Item is not owned until last payment
e) Share issue	v) For collecting debts from customers

Question 7.4 Look again at Question 5.6 in Chapter 5. Assuming that ***Tom Cherry*** has only £15,000 of his own money available to start his business with, what sources of finance do you consider might be suitable to cover the shortfall?

Objective test *(tick the appropriate box)*

i) If you required a business loan to cover a short-term cash problem you would:

a) raise a mortgage ☐

b) issue shares ☐

c) obtain an overdraft ☐

d) obtain hire purchase ☐

ii) When drawing up a business plan you should make it:

a) as realistic as possible ☐

b) as cautious as possible ☐

c) as optimistic as possible ☐

d) as vague as possible ☐

iii) The crucial part of the business plan is the:

a) educational details of the potential borrower ☐

b) the names of all the likely competitors ☐

c) the financial statements ☐

d) the publicity details for the business ☐

iv) A factoring organisation offers the service of:

a) taking over the debtors of a company ☐

b) paying off the loans of a company ☐

c) paying the creditors of a company ☐

d) negotiating a bank loan ☐

v) For a partnership wishing to buy new premises the most appropriate way to raise money would be:

a) issue shares to the public ☐

b) obtain a mortgage ☐

c) obtain a bank overdraft ☐

d) use a factoring organisation ☐

Chapter 8

The role of the accountant

8.1 Objectives

At the end of this chapter you should be able to:

- explain what is meant by the term accounting;
- describe the structure of the accounting profession;
- explain the role of the accountant;
- compare the main forms of accounting;
- describe the various areas of accounting work.

8.2 Introduction

The words ***accounting*** and ***accountant*** are frequently used by people without any understanding of what the terms convey. Accounting in its broadest sense is concerned with the measuring, recording and communicating of the financial aspects of business activities and accountants are the people who carry out these tasks. This description gives some impression of the subject, but in this chapter we will examine the various subdivisions of accounting and the different types of accountants and the tasks they carry out.

There are two main forms of accounting and accountants will often refer to their own work in this way. There are a number of subdivisions and variations, but the two main forms are ***financial accounting*** and ***management accounting.***

8.3 Financial accounting

Financial accounting is concerned with classifying and measuring the transactions of a business and recording them. At the end of a period of time, usually a year but possibly more frequently, a ***profit and loss statement*** is prepared to show financial performance over that period of time and a ***balance sheet*** to show the financial position of the business at the end of the period. The preparation of these two financial statements at the end of the period is for the benefit of the owners of the business, although other people may also be interested in them.

Financial accounting is concerned with giving a ***true and fair view*** of the business. To ensure this, considerable attention is paid to any ***accounting conventions and concepts*** which influence the preparation of financial accounts. In the case of limited companies, attention will be paid to the legal requirements of the ***Companies Act 1985*** as amended by the ***Companies Act 1989*** and the requirements of ***Statements of Standard Accounting Practice.*** If a company is listed on the Stock Exchange, the reporting ***regulations of the Stock Exchange*** must also be complied with.

Financial accounting can be divided into a number of specific activities, such as auditing, taxation advice, insolvency and bookkeeping. We will look at some of these more closely later in the chapter but we will concentrate on bookkeeping at this stage.

Bookkeeping is concerned with the recording of business transactions. It is an essential business activity and modern bookkeeping was developed in Italy in the 14th and 15th centuries. The records kept by bookkeepers were originally in handwritten ledgers, although many businesses now use computers. Although bookkeeping is a crucial aspect of accounting in a business, the skills and knowledge of a highly qualified accountant are not required for the work. It is normal therefore for a business to employ someone who is not able to carry out all accounting functions, but has sufficient knowledge and experience to be able to carry out bookkeeping competently.

If you look in the local Press under 'situations vacant' you will find jobs advertised for bookkeepers. These will often state that the applicant should be experienced to trial balance. This is the stage of accounting before the preparation of a profit and loss account, but where all the records have been summarised at the end of a period.

8.4 Management accounting

The main function of ***management accounting*** is to provide financial information to managers. Such information will be needed by the managers so that they can plan the progress of the business, control the activities and see the financial implications of any decisions they may have to take.

A financial accountant needs to ensure that the information complies with established conventions, concepts and legal requirements. A management accountant, however, needs to ensure that the information is of value to managers. Management accounting uses a range of techniques and methods to provide the information. We will consider these in Part III of this book. The main point to remember is that management accounting is concerned with identifying why the information is required so that the most appropriate technique can be used to supply information to managers which will be of value to them.

You should now be able to attempt Question 8.1 at the end of this chapter.

8.5 The structure of the accounting profession

What do we mean when we speak about a person being a qualified accountant? A number of people know something about accounting and may have a BTEC qualification in Business and Finance or a Degree in Accounting, but are not regarded as being qualified. To become a qualified accountant you must pass the examinations and become a member of a ***recognised professional body***. When you have done this you can put designatory letters after your name.

There are a number of accounting bodies, but the major professional bodies of accountants are shown on the following list, together with recent figures of members and students. The numbers are given as an indication of size only and all of the professional bodies are experiencing significant growth.

Institution	Membership 1990	Number of students 1990	Designatory letters
Institute of Chartered Accountants in England and Wales (ICAEW)	92,000	17,000	FCA, ACA
Institute of Chartered Accountants in Ireland (ICAI)	5,500	2,000	FCA, ACA
Institute of Chartered Accountants in Scotland (ICAS)	12,000	1,700	CA
Chartered Association of Certified Accountants (CACA)	34,000	82,000	FCCA, ACCA
Chartered Institute of Management Accountants (CIMA)	29,000	48,000	FCMA, ACMA
Chartered Institute of Public Finance and Accountancy (CIPFA)	10,000	3,000	IPFA

Source: *Certified Accountant*, November 1991

None of these professional bodies is better than another. The members of all of them are considered as qualified accountants. If you wish to become an accountant, the professional body you choose will depend on the way you wish to train and the type of work you wish to do when you are qualified.

The first three professional bodies used to require their students to train with professional firms in practice although these rules are now being relaxed. This means that you will be working for a firm of accountants. The firm can be just one accountant – a sole practitioner – or a large partnership employing a few thousand people. Once you are qualified you may choose to remain working in the profession, i.e. working as a sole practitioner or for a firm of accountants. Approximately half of the members of the first three bodies work in professional practices.

Members of the ***Chartered Association of Certified Accountants*** can choose to train in the profession or in industry or commerce, i.e. working for a company. Some of the largest organisations such as British Rail, Rolls Royce, CEGB. run special training schemes. On qualifying, approximately 25 per cent of ***Certified Accountants*** choose to work in practice, 15 per cent in financial and public administration, and the remainder in industry.

Members of the ***Chartered Institute of Management Accountants*** do their training in industry and commerce and usually continue to work there when they are qualified. Members of the ***Chartered Institute of Public Finance and Accountancy*** work in local authorities, the National Health Service, and other similar public bodies.

You should now be able to attempt Task 8.1 at the end of this chapter.

8.6 The nature of accountancy work

The accountant, whether in practice or working in industry, commerce or the public sector, has an important role in collating, recording and communicating financial information. As well as communicating the implications of financial information, accountants are expected to give advice on a wide range of matters which will include the following:

- How financial affairs can be best arranged so that the lowest amount of tax may be paid. This could be for an individual with a small income or a very large company.
- The best way to borrow money for a specific project. This could range from an individual building an extension to their home or a company building a complete factory.
- The costs of offering a new product or service.
- The financial benefits of introducing new technology.
- The total costs of a pay offer to be put to the trade unions.
- The profit to be made from organising a huge pop concert.

The above list gives only a few examples. Wherever there is a need for financial information and advice, the accountant has a key role. Because of the very different types of work there are, accountants tend to specialise in particular areas.

It is impossible to list the many areas of activity in which a management accountant in industry is involved as they are so varied and different. The primary task is to assist the other managers in their work. This involves examining alternative courses of action and determining the future activities of the company; measuring the activities of the company and comparing with the plans so that control can be maintained; analysing the financial consequences of taking certain decisions.

With financial accounting there are some activities which can be identified, although these only give an indication of the types of work undertaken. The main areas of work concerning the financial accountant are:

Accounts preparation

This is a large area of activity, both for financial accountants working in industry or commerce and for accountants working in practice. Limited companies are obliged under the ***Companies Act 1985*** to keep proper books of account and produce certain financial statements. Most limited companies will employ an accountant to carry out this task. In large companies there will be many qualified accountants.

Even sole traders and partnerships will have to declare their profits to the Inland Revenue. If the business is so small that there is insufficient work to employ an accountant, then the proprietor will go to an accountant working in the profession to get the work done.

Auditing

The law provides that the accounts of a limited company must be subject to audit by a registered accountant. An audit is a thorough examination of the financial records of the company to confirm that the profit and loss account and balance sheet which are prepared from these records give a true and fair view.

An audit can be conducted on any financial statement, not only the annual accounts of a limited company. However, the audit of the limited companies accounts is required by legislation and the law states clearly who is qualified to conduct the audit. Only those who are properly supervised and appropriately qualified can be appointed as company auditors. The audits must be carried out properly, with integrity and with a proper degree of independence.

Taxation

If you are an employee of a company and that is your only source of income, you have little opportunity to adjust the amount of tax you pay. However, people who are self-employed and enjoy a significant income will need an accountant to handle their tax affairs. The accountant will attempt to arrange the individual's financial affairs in such a way that the lowest amount of tax possible is paid, although, of course, what is legally due to the Inland Revenue must be paid.

Limited companies are subject to corporation tax and this is a complex area needing the knowledge of an accountant to ensure that the correct amount of tax is paid.

You should now be able to attempt Task 8.2 at the end of this chapter.

8.7 Becoming an accountant

Becoming a member of any of the professional bodies of accountants mentioned in this chapter takes a considerable time and lots of effort. As well as doing accountancy work, you will have to take a number of rigorous examinations. The failure rate in the examinations is very high and even a student with an accounting degree, who passes all the examinations the first time, can expect to take three years to qualify. For many students the period will be five to six years.

The rewards, both financially and in terms of job satisfaction, are very high for qualified accountants. The work can be as varied as resolving someone's taxation problems in the Bahamas, calculating the cost of building a road in Africa or auditing the books of a small company in an English country town. It is these opportunities that makes accounting an exciting career and the general requirements for two of the professional bodies are shown below.

To become a ***chartered accountant*** you must train with a firm of chartered accountants for 3 or 4 years by entering into a training contract. This will allow you to gain practical experience as well as preparing to take the professional examinations. Normally candidates should hold a degree or have successfully completed a foundation course in accountancy. The Institute of Chartered Acccountants has introduced a scheme allowing students to qualify in industry.

Certified accountants can train and work in industry, commerce, local and central government, nationalised industries and practice. Although students must be doing recognised accounting work, the Association allows moves between different sectors of employment during the training period.

The prospective student may be a graduate of any discipline and holders of Higher National Diplomas are considered. The student must have sound O level mathematics and be highly motivated. There is a wide choice of ways to study for the examinations. Students may have day or block release at college, go to evening classes or take a correspondence course.

You should now be able to attempt Questions 8.2 and 8.3 at the end of this chapter.

8.8 Summary

In this chapter we have looked at the two main forms of accounting. ***Financial accounting*** is concerned with classifying, measuring and recording the transactions of a business. ***Management accounting*** is concerned with providing financial information which is useful to managers.

Accountancy work is very broad in its nature and accountants have an important role in industry, commerce and the public sector, as well as in practice.

You should now be able to attempt Task 8.3 and the Objective Test at the end of this chapter.

Student activities

Task 8.1 Read through the situations vacant columns of national newspapers and collect all the advertisements for accountants. Analyse these to see if there is a pattern between the type of work and the accountancy qualification required.

Task 8.2 Look at the advertisements for accountants in the financial Press. Make a list of the various types of work specified and attempt to classify them into either financial or management accounting.

Task 8.3 Conduct a survey in your college to ascertain how many students intend to pursue a career as an accountant and if so which professional body they are going to choose. Ask them for their reasons for choosing a career in accounting.

Question 8.1 Classify the following activities into those which are financial accounting and those which are management accounting:

i) Keeping the financial records of a company.

ii) Providing financial information to be used by managers.

iii) Ensuring compliance with the Companies Act 1985.

iv) Preparing the profit and loss account and balance sheet at the year end.

v) Analysing the financial implications of management decisions.

vi) Managing the tax affairs of a company.

vii) Auditing the books of a company.

Question 8.2 Select the correct response for the following statements:

	True	False
i) Bookkeeping is the most technical activity a qualified accountant undertakes.	☐	☐
ii) Under the Companies Act 1985 limited companies are obliged to maintain proper books of account.	☐	☐
iii) To become a qualified accountant you must train with a firm of accountants working in practice.	☐	☐

	True	False
iv) Management accounting is primarily concerned with producing financial information which is valuable to managers.	☐	☐
v) To pass all the examinations of any of the main professional bodies of accountants normally takes at least two years.	☐	☐

Question 8.3 *Nick Adams* has just finished his first year's training as a painter and decorator. He has been operating as a sole trader and his wife, June, who has a BTEC qualification, has been keeping his accounts. Nick's brother asks him if he can join the business, but Nick refuses saying that as a partnership they would have to have a properly qualified account to audit the books and that would be very expensive.

Required

Write a letter to Nick explaining the legal position on auditing. Identify any advantages there may be for Nick in employing a qualified accountant instead of June and explain the different types of accounting qualifications.

Objective test *(tick the appropriate box)*

i) Management accounting is mainly concerned with:

a) providing financial information to managers ☐

b) recording information for tax purposes ☐

c) communicating financial information to shareholders ☐

d) auditing the accounts of a company ☐

ii) An audit is a:

a) method of recording financial information ☐

b) examination of the financial records of an organisation ☐

c) process of constructing a profit statement ☐

d) statement issued by the professional bodies of accountants ☐

iii) The two main forms of accounting are:

a) bookkeeping and auditing ☐

b) taxation and investment appraisal ☐

c) financial and management accounting ☐

d) profit statement and balance sheet ☐

iv) If you wished to pursue a career in local government the most appropriate accounting qualification would be:

a) Institute of Chartered Accountants ☐

b) Chartered Association of Certified Accountants ☐

c) Chartered Institute of Management Accountants ☐

d) Institute of Public Finance and Accountancy ☐

v) It is a legal requirement that an audit is carried out on the financial records of:

a) a sole trader ☐

b) a partnership ☐

c) a limited liability company ☐

d) none of these ☐

Chapter 9

Potential users of financial information

9.1 Objectives

At the end of this chapter you should be able to:

- identify the potential users of financial information;
- explain the types of decisions they make;
- identify the types of information they require.

9.2 Introduction

In this chapter we are concerned with the ***potential users of financial information*** about a business. The owners of shares will be interested in the financial performance and stability of the business, but so may other groups such as trade unions, creditors, employees, financial analysts etc. Managers can be regarded as a special group which we will consider in Part III of this book.

There are a number of ***sources of financial information*** and we will discuss the main ones and the type of information they contain.

9.3 Sources of financial information

Certain people and organisations have no difficulty in obtaining any financial information they require about a particular company. Managers inside the company often receive very detailed information to allow them to do their job properly. The Inland Revenue and HM Customs and Excise have extensive powers to demand information from a company. But there are various other groups of people, such as prospective shareholders, creditors and trade unions, who are not in such a favourable position. These groups depend on the information that the company makes publicly available.

Sole traders and partnerships do not have to make any of their financial information publicly available, but limited companies are required to make certain financial information available to each of their shareholders and the public. This chapter is concerned with that information and its potential users.

The most useful and important financial document for those outside the company is the ***annual report*** and ***accounts***. This is sent to each shareholder of the company and to the Registrar of Companies. In Chapter 20 we will take a closer look at this document. However, there are many other sources of information, many of them freely available from your local library. Some contain scant financial information, but give details of the company's products, markets, structure and even the proper address which will help you to investigate further.

It would be impossible to list all potential sources of information, but the following is a selection of the better known sources and the type of information provided. You should be able to find most of these publications in your library.

The Financial Times
This is the most important daily source of financial information. As well as giving extensive and excellent news of general business and commercial topics, it provides comprehensive coverage of UK and international companies' activities and their finances.

Investors Chronicle
This is a weekly guide to the activities of the City and financial news. It also provides valuable reviews of selected companies and industries.

Kompass
This guide is published annually in two volumes. Volume 1 is a classified catalogue of products and services, giving the names of manufacturers, wholesalers and distributors. Volume 2 contains information on over 30,000 companies, including the names of directors, details of share capital, turnover, number of employees, nature of business and product group.

Kelly's Manufacturers and Merchants Directory
This is an annual directory covering some 90,000 UK manufacturers, merchants and wholesalers. The firms are listed with addresses, telephone and telex numbers and telegraphic addresses.

The Stock Exchange Official Year Book
This is the only reference book giving authorative information about what is bought and sold on the Stock Exchange. It is the prime source of information about the operation of the London Stock Exchange and gives information on the companies' directors, capital, accounts and dividends.

Who Owns Whom
This is an annual directory in two volumes. The parent companies and their subsidiaries are listed in Volume 1 and the second volume is an index of subsidiaries and associate companies showing their parent companies.

Extel Cards
These are sometimes available in the business section of libraries. There are a number of different Extel Card Services, each providing comprehensive financial information on certain types of companies. For example, the UK Listed Companies Service covers every company listed on the London and Irish Stock Exchanges.

CD Rom
Many libraries now have databases of corporate and stock exchange information stored on CD Rom computer disks. These disks are regularly updated with information and their advantage over book-based information sources is that they are easily accessed with the aid of computer terminals by setting up an individual's own search strategy. Examples are Datastream and Fame (Financial Analysis made Easy).

You should now be able to attempt Task 9.1 at the end of this chapter.

9.4 Potential users of financial information

There are a number of ***potential users of financial information.*** We say potential users because the extent to which they use company financial information and the value it is to them is not fully known. It is possible to suggest why and how they might use such information, but insufficient research has been conducted to know if the potential users do this. The main groups of potential users are:

- shareholders
- lenders
- trade unions and employees
- business contacts
- analysts and advisers

9.5 Shareholders

The rights of ***shareholders*** to information about a company arise from the direct financial relationship between them. The amount of information required by a shareholder depends to some extent on the size of the shareholding and whether the investor is a private shareholder or a financial institution employing professional investors.

The number of individual shareholders has steadily risen in this country in recent years. However, many of these new investors have very modest shareholdings, often in one company. They do not actively trade on the stock market by regularly buying and selling shares, but keep their original holding until they decide to sell. Possibly, one of the main reasons they choose to sell their shares is that they require the money for other purposes, e.g. a holiday or to buy a new car.

There are some individual shareholders who take a great interest in the stock market and have sizable holdings. These investors often rely on the services of a professional adviser such as a broker. Because of the size of their investment, their need for information may be greater than the individual who has acquired only a few hundred shares in a single company.

Approximately 75 per cent of all UK equities is held by institutional investors such as pension funds, unit trusts and insurance companies. They employ people to invest funds on the stock market. These professional investors are dealing with huge sums of money which do not belong to them but to their employer. Although the professional investor has no personal stake in the share transactions, the decisions made by him or her affects the success of the financial institution which employs them. The professional investor, therefore, has the motivation and the time to conduct detailed research on a company.

Whatever type of shareholder we are considering, there are three basic decisions to be taken by investors:

- to buy more shares;
- to hold on to the shares already owned;
- to sell all or part of the shares owned.

The way these decisions are made depends on the investor's view of the prospects of the stock market as a whole, the particular company in which the investment is made, and the industry in which the company operates. The important thing to stress is that the investor is interested in the future. What has happened in the past will be of value only in so far as it helps to predict what is likely to happen in the future.

By attempting to predict the future, investors hold one or both of two main objectives: to secure a regular and attractive income from the investment in the form of a dividend paid by the company and/or to achieve capital growth. The latter will be achieved if the market value of the shareholding increases. In other words, if the shares can be sold for a higher price than that paid, the investor will make a capital gain.

The shareholder may place far greater emphasis on one of these objectives and than the other. A retired person, for example, may want a regular and secure income and have no interest in capital growth, apart from keeping pace with inflation. A professional investor may buy shares in the belief that they will rapidly increase in price and a profit can be made by selling them and not be concerned much with dividends.

Whatever the objectives of the shareholder and the decisions to be made, financial information is required. Although the financial information will not forecast the future, it will enable conclusions to be drawn about the past and present financial performance of a company. This assists in judging what is likely to happen in the future.

You should now be able to attempt Question 9.1 at the end of this chapter.

9.6 Lenders

A business may have a number of sources from which it has borrowed money. One of the main sources is likely to be a bank. The loan from the bank may be long-term, for a period of, say, over five years, or short-term, such as an overdraft which is repayable on demand. In addition, most businesses transact their trade on credit; goods are supplied but payment is not made until some weeks later.

If a *lender* has made a long-term loan to a company or has been asked to do so, a number of financial judgements must be made. The lender will wish to assess the long-term economic stability of the company. There is no sense in making a long-term loan to a company that is likely to go out of business in a few months.

The lender will also want to ensure that there is every prospect of the loan being repaid and the degree of risk involved. If the worst should happen and the organisation goes out of business, the lender will want to know the possibility of the loan being repaid out of the proceeds of the sale.

Short-term lenders and ***trade creditors*** are interested in the company's cash and near cash position and how they are likely to change in the future. They will want to estimate the risk and consequences of the organisation not being able to pay any outstanding debt.

9.7 Trade unions and employees

Individual ***employees*** and ***trade unions*** are also interested in the finances of a company. The future livelihood and prospects of employees depend on the financial stability and success of the company that employs them. An employee may wish to assess the security of employment and will be interested in any indications of the position, progress and prospects of the company. Employees may not only wish to avoid the risks of redundancy, but may be seeking to ascertain career prospects.

It is also natural that an employee, who spends a large part of the day working for an organisation, has a general interest in its financial performance. A large number of organisations realise this and produce simplified financial accounts for employees and sometimes show employees videos giving financial information.

Trade unions representing employees in a particular organisation require financial information for the same reasons as employees. The trade unions are interested in security of employment and the prospects of the business. Financial information is also required for the purposes of collective bargaining when the trade union attempts to negotiate improvements in the pay and conditions of its members.

However, trade unions are more likely to take a broader view of the organisation than an individual employee. They are also more likely to have the resources and knowledge to enable them to conduct a more detailed financial analysis. A number of trade unions employ research officers, who are qualified accountants and skilled at analysing financial information. In addition to requiring the same type of information needed by investors and lenders, trade unions need information for the following reasons:

- to estimate the future prospects of the organisation, particularly its ability to make wage increases;
- to predict future levels of employment and changes in skill demands in the company;
- to evaluate managerial performance, efficiency and objectives;
- to assess the prospects of individual factories and other parts of a large organisation or group of companies.

To some extent, trade unions are in a more favourable legal position than other groups of users. If a trade union requires financial information from a company for the purposes of collective bargaining, it is possible that it may be able to obtain this information under the provisions of the ***Employment Protection Act 1975***. This legislation permits a recognised trade union to obtain information in certain circumstances.

You should now be able to attempt Task 9.2 at the end of this chapter.

9.8 Business contacts

An organisation has a large number of ***business contacts***. Suppliers of goods and services to the organisation rely on it for the success of their own businesses. The customers may be dependent on it if there are few or no other organisations offering the same goods or services. Its competitors may be interested in takeovers or mergers and may also wish to make comparisons of efficiencies, market share and new products. All these business contacts require ***financial information.***

Suppliers of goods and services require information on the business's ability to pay. Suppliers are also be interested in its long-term prospects. If it appears that the business is highly successful and likely to expand, suppliers may wish to improve their own production capacity or make other significant changes in order to benefit from the opportunities offered.

Customers also want information about the products and services offered. In particular, customers are interested in details of prices, product specifications, delivery dates and likely product improvements. If the customer is relying on the organisation for continuing supplies or its ability to complete a long term contract, a longer term view will be taken. Information on the financial position of the organisation and its profitability may help customers to make decisions.

Competitors may seek financial information because they wish to invest in the business or launch a takeover bid. In this case the competitor will require the same information as the professional investor. In addition, competitors often require information so that they can make comparisons and therefore judge their own efficiencies. If a similar business in the same industry is much more profitable, there is a need to examine where improvements can be made.

Competitors are interested in all aspects of an organisation's affairs, including information about pricing and marketing policies, production methods, research and development initiatives, investment plans and overall profitability. Some of this information will be confidential, but some will be publicly available.

9.9 Financial analysts and advisers

There are a large number of ***financial analysts and advisers*** in the industry. The financial Press carries many articles which analyse in depth the financial affairs of particular companies and industries. Stockbrokers use their own analysts so that they can advise their clients. Companies, trade unions, the Government and other institutions all employ analysts and advisers.

The information needs of the analysts and advisers are similar to the needs of the client for whom they are working. For example, stockbrokers need information to advise their clients on the investments they should make and therefore seek the same financial information as the investor. A researcher working for a trade union will require financial information relating to pay, prospects and job security.

Analysts and advisers are likely to need more complex information and, in turn, will produce sophisticated and highly informed observations on the activities of companies. A considerable amount of the information used will come from the annual report and accounts published by companies. We will discuss this in detail in Chapter 20. To interpret this information, accounting ratios will be used and these will be discussed in Chapter 22.

You should now be able to attempt Question 9.2 and Task 9.3 at the end of this chapter.

9.10 Disclosure and confidentiality

Limited companies are legally obliged to make available certain information to their shareholders and register this with the Registrar of Companies thus making it a public document. Public limited companies which are quoted on the Stock Exchange will provide more information than legally required and the annual report and accounts is, to some extent, a public relations document designed to promote the name and image of the company.

However, there are certain types of information a company would be unwilling to give. The reason for this is known as commercial confidentiality. Put quite simply, this means that it might cause harm to the company if this information was disclosed. For example, if a company had invented a new product, it would not want its competitors to know all the details. Similarly, a company would not want its customers to know all its costs and the profit made on each product.

This commercially confidential information is often the very information that the potential users would like to receive. If we knew that a major drugs company had just discovered a wonder drug that would cure every disease, it would be very useful information. It would be even more useful if we knew this before others, because we could buy the company's shares. When the news of the drug became common knowledge, there would be a demand for the company's shares, because investors would consider the company had a successful future. This demand for shares would push up the price and we could sell our holding and make a profit.

If we had bought the shares because we had carefully examined information which was public, and through our general knowledge had predicted there was the possibility of a new drug being discovered, there is no problem. However, if the chief chemist of the company had told us in private, we would be in receipt of privileged information. If we had bought shares on this basis, we would be guilty of insider dealing, which is an offence.

9.11 Summary

In this chapter we have considered the main sources of readily available information on ***limited companies. Sole traders*** and ***partnerships*** do not have to make financial information publicly available.

We have identified the main potential users of such information. ***Shareholders*** have a legal right to receive certain financial information and will require such information to make decisions on their investments. ***Trade unions*** and ***employees*** rely on the financial stability and success of the company for their future livelihood and future prospects. They require information to assess these matters, but employees may have also a general interest in the financial welfare of their employer. ***Business contacts,*** whether they be lenders, suppliers, customers or competitors, are interested in the financial information of a company. ***Financial analysts and advisers*** interpret the financial information and comment on its significance.

Although limited liability companies must disclose certain information, there may be concerns over ***confidentiality***. A company may believe that the disclosure of some types of information might cause it harm.

You should now be able to attempt the Objective Test at the end of this chapter.

Student activities

Task 9.1 Choose one very well known company with a household name and a small local company. Go to your library and by using the various reference books and papers see how much information you can obtain on each of them.

Task 9.2 See if you can obtain any copies of financial reports which have been produced by companies specifically for employees. You may find working relatives may receive them. Business libraries sometimes have copies and well known companies will often send a copy if you write to them. Compare the information in the report for employees with the annual report for shareholders which companies are legally obliged to publish. What are the similarities and differences in the contents and the way the information is presented?

Task 9.3 Using a well known company name as an example, draw up a list of the information you would like if you were a supplier to the company. Ask a friend draw up a list as a customer of that company. Compare your lists and attempt to explain any differences in the type of information you require.

Question 9.1 Select the correct response to the following statements:

	True	False
i) Partnerships have to disclose financial information to the public if requested to do so.	☐	☐
ii) Only limited companies quoted on the Stock Exchange have to produce an annual report and accounts.	☐	☐
iii) If you know the correct name of a subsidiary company it is possible to find out the name of the holding company.	☐	☐
iv) Shareholders are only interested in buying shares in companies which pay large dividends.	☐	☐
v) If an investor sells shares for a higher price than was originally paid a capital gain has been made.	☐	☐

Question 9.2 Match the potential users of information with the purpose for which they may require it in the list below:

a) Customers	i) To ensure that a loan will be repaid
b) Trade unions	ii) For dealing in shares
c) Lenders	iii) To evaluate products and services

d) Employees — iv) For producing highly informed observations
e) Investors — v) To negotiate improvements in pay
f) Analysts — vi) To assess security of employment

Question 9.3 Which of the following types of information would you normally expect to find in the annual report and accounts of a public limited company?

i) A profit and loss account
ii) The current share price
iii) The names of the directors
iv) The name of the chairman
v) The name of the auditors
vi) A cash flow forecast

Objective test *(tick the appropriate box)*

i) The best source of financial information about a company is:

a) the Financial Times ☐
b) the Stock Exchange Official Year Book ☐
c) the annual report and accounts ☐
d) the Investor's Chronicle ☐

ii) If a bank makes a short-term loan to a company, the most important information for the bank would be:

a) the balance sheet for the last five years ☐
b) the predicted cash position ☐
c) the share price of the company ☐
d) the profit for the last five years ☐

iii) A creditor of a company is someone who:

a) is owed money by the company ☐
b) owes money to the company ☐
c) wants to buy shares in the company ☐
d) wants to sell shares in the company ☐

iv) A company's annual report and accounts must legally be sent:

a) to the bank ☐
b) only to institutional investors ☐
c) only to shareholders with over 500 shares ☐
d) to all shareholders ☐

v) Insider dealing is when you buy shares because:

a) the share price is going down ☐
b) you are in possession of privileged information ☐
c) you have loaned money to the company ☐
d) you are an employee of the company ☐

Assignment B

Starting a business

Context

A local school has recently introduced a scheme designed to improve sixth form pupils' understanding of business. The pupils are divided into groups of four and they have to examine the problems and advantages of setting up their own business. To make the project realistic, each group has to decide on the type of business it would like to run and construct a Business Plan.

To assist the pupils, the school arranges for a series of outside speakers to come and talk on relevant topics. You have been asked if you would give a talk on different forms of business organisations and the various sources of finance available, with particular reference to the local situation. The school has asked you to make the talk as relevant as possible to the types of business proposed by the pupils and these are:

- ❒ hairdressing salon
- ❒ car valeting service
- ❒ fish and chip van
- ❒ job agency for Saturday staff
- ❒ wedding photography

Student activities

i) Conduct research into local sources of finance and advice for small businesses.

ii) Draw up a list of recommendations for appropriate organisational structures for the proposed businesses.

iii) Prepare an outline of the presentation you will give to the pupils.

iv) Prepare overhead transparencies or flip charts to be used during your presentation.

v) Prepare a handout for the pupils covering the main points in your presentation and provide a list of addresses from which they can obtain further advice and information.

Format

You should assemble the material for the presentation which should include:

- ❒ notes for your speech;
- ❒ handout for the pupils;
- ❒ visual material you intend to use.

Objectives

In this assignment the student will experience the process of conducting research and will gain knowledge of the local position in respect of sources of finance and advice for small businesses. The student will also understand the value of organising and structuring material for a presentation.

References

Chapters 6 and 7 are of particular value to this assignment.

Part 2

Financial accounting

Sole Traders

This section (Chapters 10-15) is concerned with the accounts of sole traders. In Chapter 10 we shall look at a financial statement known as the profit and loss account.

In Chapter 11 we look at another document which is closely related to the profit and loss account, the balance sheet.

Chapter 12 examines the presentation of accounts, particularly the vertical format, and also some of the principles employed in preparing accounts.

In Chapter 13, we look at the concept of depreciation, and in Chapter 14 bad debts and provision for them is explained.

In the final chapter of this section, Chapter 15, we recall Chapter 5 and relate cash flow forecasts, profit and loss accounts and balance sheets.

Chapter 10

Sole traders – profit and loss account

10.1 Objectives

At the end of this chapter you should be able to:

- explain what is meant by a trading account;
- explain what is meant by a profit and loss account;
- define such terms as realisation convention and matching convention;
- construct a simple trading account and profit and loss account for a sole trader.

10.2 Introduction

In this chapter we shall be looking closely at a financial statement known as a ***profit and loss account***. A profit and loss account measures ***performance over a period***, and shows at the end of the period what ***profit*** has been achieved.

Profit is not an easy concept to describe. It normally has very little to do with ***cash***, except in very simple circumstances. If you bought an article yesterday for £2, paying cash for it, and then sell it today for £3, also for cash, then you will have £1 cash more today than you had yesterday. Also, you will have made a profit of £1.

If, however, you did not pay cash yesterday, but bought the article on credit, and today you sell the article, not for cash, but to someone who says he will pay you next month, i.e. also on credit, then no cash has changed hands. But, in accounting terms, you will still have made a profit of £1.

The position, whether or not any cash has changed hands, is that:

the *sale* is	£3
the *cost of sale* is	£2
	—
and the *profit* is	£1
	═

Profit can therefore be described as ***sales*** less the ***cost of sales***.

We shall now look at the ***profit and loss account*** in more detail, and look at the various accounting conventions which are employed in the calculation of ***profit***.

10.3 The profit and loss account

Strictly speaking, the full name for this account is the ***trading and profit and loss account***. A simple account would look something like this:

Example

		£
Trading account	Sales	10,000
	Less Cost of goods sold	4,000
	= Gross profit	6,000
Profit and loss account	*Less* Expenses	5,000
	= Net profit	1,000

10.4 Trading account

The following example and solution will help illustrate various principles and accounting conventions.

Example

Thomas Tenby, trading as ***Tenby & Company***, owns a business which sells a standard computer to educational establishments. He buys these at £700 each and sells them for £1,000 each.

1. At the start of January 19X9, Thomas had 25 computers in stock.
2. During January he bought 60 computers from his supplier.
3. On 25th January he paid his supplier for the 70 computers which he had bought in the previous month of December.
4. During January he sold 75 computers to various educational establishments.
5. During January he received payment for 45 computers which he had sold in December.
6. On 25th February he paid his suppliers for the 60 computers which he bought during January.
7. During February he received payment for 55 of the 75 computers which he sold in January.

Required

Calculate how much gross profit Thomas Tenby has made, during the month of January.

Solution

To the uninitiated, this must seem an awful mess. Accountants, however, have developed a set of rules or conventions which make it easier to sort the wheat from the chaff.

Anything to do with cash payments or cash receipts is *irrelevant* in calculating profit (or loss). Therefore items 3, 5, 6 and 7 are irrelevant (though this information would be essential for producing cash flow statements, balance sheets, and managing the business).

This leaves items 1, 2 and 4 which are relevant.

We can express the computer position as follows:

Item 1 Stock at 1st January	25
Item 2 *Add* Purchases during January	60
	85
Item 4 *Less* Sales during January	75
= stock at 31st January	10

We can produce a trading account as follows:

Trading Account for Tenby & Company
for the month ending 31st January 19X9

	£
Sales of computers 75 @ £1,000	75,000
Less Cost of computers sold 75 @ £700	52,500
= Gross profit	22,500

The account on the previous page is now shown in greater detail.

a) *Trading Account for Tenby & Company*
b) for the month ending 31st January 19X9

			£	£
c)	Sales of computers	75 @ £1,000 =		75,000
d)	*Less* Cost of sales:			
e)	Opening stock	25 @ £700 =	17,500	
f)	*Add* Purchases	60 @ £700 =	42,000	
g)	available for sale	85 @ £700 =	59,500	
h)	*Less* Closing stock	10 @ £700 =	7,000	
i)	(Therefore cost of sales is)	75 @ £700 =		52,500
j)	= Gross profit			22,500

Notes

There are a number of important points to notice, and reference will be made to the letter at the start of each line of the detailed trading account above.

a) Always give an account a title which includes the name of the business. In this case it is Tenby & Company, a business entity which is accounted for separately from T. Tenby himself.

b) Always give the period to which the account relates. In this case we show that we are not interested in December or February.

c) Sales of computers. This recognises the ***realisation convention***. Accountants only recognise a profit ***when goods are sold***, i.e. when the goods pass to a customer who is 'invoiced' for them, irrespective of when that customer is likely to pay for them.

d) Cost of sales. This is a heading which precedes the calculation in lines (e), (f), (g) and (h). Line (i) is the result of the calculation. In the answer, we have tried to make this clear by repeating the heading: (Therefore cost of sales is), though this is usually omitted.

i) The cost of sales means the cost of the number of computers sold. This recognises the ***matching convention*** which requires that the costs of sales should be ***matched*** with the sales (or revenue) for the period covered by the statement. This ***matching convention*** applies not only to the ***trading account*** (cost of goods sold), but also to the ***profit and loss account*** (expenses for the period), and we shall look at this in more detail later on.

   In the above example we have shown the detailed calculations required to obtain the total amount eg 75 computers at £1,000 = £75,000. This is for illustrative purposes only and normally you would only show the full amounts.

You should now be able to attempt Question 10.1 at the end of this chapter.

10.5 Profit and loss account

In the previous example we saw that Thomas Tenby made a ***gross*** or ***trading profit*** of £22,500. Unfortunately for Thomas, that is not the end of the story. In operating his computer business, he will have costs or expenses other than buying computers from his suppliers.

These expenses might include:

- Rent of premises
- Business Rates (if not included in rent)
- Electricity for lighting and power
- Gas for heating
- Telephone
- Stationery
- Cleaning costs
- Insurances
- Accountancy and legal fees
- Delivery van expenses
- Depreciation of delivery van
- Depreciation of equipment
- Bad debts and provision for doubtful debts
- Interest on loans and / or bank overdraft
- Salaries of sales and technical staff

All these expenses effectively reduce his ***gross profit*** to a ***net profit,*** out of which he will have to pay tax and draw his living expenses. These terms may be new to you and some of them are explained more fully in later chapters (e.g. depreciation and bad debts), but it is necessary now to go through this list, item by item, to show you how an appropriate amount is calculated for inclusion under the heading 'Expenses' for ***one month only,*** so that we can arrive at Thomas Tenby's ***net profit.***

Rent of premises
Thomas rents premises where he can demonstrate computers to prospective customers and keep his stock of computers. The rent is £12,000 per annum, payable quarterly in advance. On January 2nd he paid £3,000 for the January-March quarter. Would he therefore include £3,000 in his expenses for January? Answer: ***no***! Remember that in the example we ignored cash payments and applied the ***matching convention.*** Here we ignore the cash payment of £3,000, and match the cost of rent against the period of the account: January. Assuming for practical purposes that each month is one-twelfth of a year, the cost of rent for January is £1,000 (The fact that Thomas paid £3,000 in January means that he has pre-paid £2,000 in respect of February and March. This will be important when we look at balance sheets.)

Business Rates (not included in rent)
These are charges by local authorities and usually cover the 12-month period April – March. Many authorities require payment in two instalments, April – September (payable in advance in April) and October – March (payable in advance in October). Some authorities allow payment of one-tenth, payable from, say, March to January. Thomas paid £3,000 last year (19X8), for the period October to March. The matching convention requires that we include one-sixth of this in the expenses for January, i.e. £500.

Electricity
Thomas receives a quarterly account from the electricity board, who sent him a bill for £450 on January 5th relating to electricity used for the quarter October – December. Thomas paid this on January 30th. What can we include for electricity for January? Unless Thomas has read his own meter on January 31st, he will not know the actual cost. However, we can estimate the cost at £150, using the last quarter's bill as a basis for the estimate.

Gas for heating
The situation is similar to that for electricity, and we estimate £50, based on previous bills.

Telephone
Thomas finds it easier to pay British Telecom £300 per month by direct debit. Last year, this, in fact, resulted in only a slight overpayment, so we shall include £300 in January's expenses. In this case the cash payment (by direct debit) does correspond with the amount to be included in expenses.

Stationery and postage etc
This is quite difficult to estimate. In the calendar year 19X8, the total amount spent on stationery etc. was £8,476, but costs are likely to increase this year because Thomas is hoping to embark on a mail-shot campaign, costing about £3,500. It would seem reasonable to estimate £1,000 for January.

Cleaning costs
This heading includes for two cleaners costing currently £9,770 per annum, and materials which last year cost £1,848. Allowing for inflation this year, it would seem reasonable to include £1,100 for January.

Insurances
Payment for these can be complicated. Most policies require payment annually in advance, but where, for example, the premium is expressed as a percentage of wages paid, a balancing premium is often payable after the year-end, when the amount of wages paid is known. In the case of Thomas, the insurance brokers estimate that the premiums for 19X9 are £7,200, i.e £600 per month.

Accountancy and legal fees
These again are irregular payments. However, an estimate for 19X9 can be made on the basis of costs in 19X8, and, allowing for likely increases in 19X9, we estimate £500 per month in 19X9, and include this amount for January.

Delivery van expenses
These can be divided under two headings:

a) Those which are paid at long or irregular intervals, e.g. road tax, insurance, servicing and repairs. These are best totalled for a year; a monthly estimate can then be included in the monthly expenses, e.g.

	£
Road tax, paid August 19X8:	100
Insurance, paid August 19X8	450
Servicing and repairs, 19X8	370
	920

Therefore include for January 19X9 (£920/12) say £80.

b) Petrol and oil, i.e. continuous costs. Thomas pays for these by cash as needed. Therefore there is no reason why the actual payments for January 19X9 should not be regarded as the actual costs: £70

Depreciation of van
Depreciation will be discussed in detail in chapter 13, and we shall include for January £90.

Depreciation of equipment
Again we shall discuss this aspect in chapter 13, and include for January: £120.

Bad debts and provision for doubtful debts
We shall discuss this in detail in chapter 14, and we shall include for January: £125 as a provision for a doubtful debt.

Interest on loans and/or overdraft
Thomas has an overdraft. The bank charges interest which appears quarterly on his bank statement. On his bank statement for December 19X8 appeared:

18 Dec Charges to 4 Dec £470.28

This does not help much with what the charges will be during January, but an estimate can be made by multiplying the average overdraft figures for January by the interest rate, say, £170.

Salaries of sales and technical staff
Thomas employs two staff, and their gross pay plus employer's National Insurance for January was £1,250.

Example

We will now look again at Tenby & Company, and using the above data concerning Thomas's expenses prepare a trading and profit and loss account for the month of January.

Solution

Tenby & Company
Trading and profit & loss account
for the month ending 31st January 19X9

	£	£
Trading account		
Sales:		75,000
Less Cost of sales:		
Opening stock	17,500	
Add Purchases	42,000	
	59,500	
Less Closing stock	7,000	
		52,500
Gross profit		22,500
Profit & loss account		
Less Expenses:		
Rent of premises	1,000	
Rates	500	
Electricity	150	
Gas	50	
Telephone	300	
Stationery	1,000	
Cleaning	1,100	
Insurances	600	
Accountancy and legal fees	500	
Delivery van expenses	150	
Depreciation of van	90	
Depreciation of equipment	120	
Doubtful debt provision	125	
Interest on overdraft	170	
Staff salaries	1,250	
		7,105
Net profit		15,395

Some students are surprised at all this estimating. They say that they have always assumed that accountants are very precise, and that the accounts prepared by them are correct to the penny. Bookkeeping is precise. Cash paid or received is recorded meticulously. An invoice for £99.99 is for £99.99, no more, no less. Bookkeeping records all the monetary transactions of a business entity. Accounting inevitably requires some estimating.

For example, in the profit and loss account for the year to 31st December 19X4, electricity charges to 31st November 19X4 may be known and recorded. But if the accounts are prepared on 17th January 19X5, and the electricity meters have not been read on 31st December 19X4, then the quarterly charge for the period 1st December 19X4 to 28th February 19X5 will not be known, and an estimate of the charges for December 19X4 will have to be made and added to the known expenses for the year to 31st December 19X4, in order to conform with the matching convention, i.e. the matching of expenses to the period covered by the accounts.

What usually happens, very roughly, in the preparation of accounts such as the profit and loss account and the balance sheet, is as follows. The accurate figures resulting from bookkeeping are extracted from the accurately kept records, and are listed down the left-hand side of a large piece of paper. This is known as the ***trial balance***. In the middle section of the paper, all kinds of adjustments are made in order to conform with the ***matching convention***, and it is here that some estimates have to be made. On the right-hand side of the paper, the accountant, taking the adjustments in the middle section into account, produces the profit and loss account for the period under consideration, and the balance sheet as at the date at the end of that period. This working paper is called an ***extended trial balance***.

It is the ***matching convention*** which necessitates the estimating. However, in the long run, any over- or under-estimates cancel out, and ultimately (for example when the business is wound up) complete accuracy is (or should be) restored.

You should now be able to attempt Questions 10.2 and 10.3 at the end of this chapter.

10.6 Summary

Sales (or sales revenue) are recognised when the goods are transferred to the customers, irrespective of when payment is made for them. This is known as the ***realisation convention***. Trading profit is calculated as sales less cost of sales. Cost of sales is opening stock plus purchases less closing stock. This conforms to the ***matching convention*** – the matching of sales with the cost of sales.

Net profit is trading (or gross) profit less expenses. Expenses are those costs which are incurred during the period covered by the profit and loss account, irrespective of when payment is made for them. This also conforms to the ***matching convention*** – the matching of expenses with the period covered by the account.

Bookkeeping is a precise process but accounting inevitably requires some estimating.

You should now be able to attempt Tasks 10.1, 10.2, 10.3 and the Objective Test at the end of this chapter.

Student activities

Task 10.1 Make a list of the various types of expenses which you think a small business would incur. Tick those which you consider you would know with certainty by the year end. Explain why you would have to do some estimating with the others, and how you would do this.

Task 10.2 The Confederation of British Industry wishes to find out the extent to which sole traders understand the profit and loss account. A self-completion questionnaire will be used for the survey. Construct three questions to be included in the questionnaire which you consider would test the understanding of the sole traders.

Task 10.3 You have been asked by a local school to give a speech to sixth formers on the importance of calculating the profit for a business. Write notes for your speech.

Question 10.1 This question follows on from the example of ***Tenby & Company*** given in this chapter.

During February, Thomas purchases 100 computers, but the price has decreased to £650 per computer. Thomas had been aware that the price decrease was imminent, and had accordingly kept his stocks low. He has informed his customers that his selling price would drop to £950 per computer in February. During February he sold 90 computers. He values his closing stock at the revised purchase price.

Required

Calculate how much gross profit Thomas has made and set out the trading account in a proper format.

Question 10.2 Mr Milford Haven, trading as the ***Pembroke Croquet Company***, has for several years sold medium-priced croquet sets by mail order. For the second quarter (April to June) of 19X9, the following details of his business are available:

Opening stock (1st April 19X9): 50 sets valued at cost £4,900

Purchases: 200 sets @ £102 each £20,400

Sales, inclusive of postage and packing: 190 sets @ £149 each £28,310

Closing stock is valued at £102 per set

Postage £950

Packing materials £660

Rent of premises (which includes rates) is £3,200 per annum, payable quarterly at the start of each quarter.

Advertising: advertisements are placed regularly in monthly magazines and occasionally in Sunday newspapers. The cost of advertising for the quarter was £1,000

Insurances: these are payable annually early in January, and £840 was paid to insurance brokers on 17th January.

Electricity: Milford pays £50 monthly by direct debit to the Electricity Board. Last year this system resulted in a slight overpayment for the whole year.

Depreciation of office equipment: this is £480 per annum.

Part-time wages (clerical and packing): amounted to £500

Stationery: costs last year were £500 and are expected to be £60 more this year.

Telephone: a telephone bill received on July 4th recorded:

quarterly charge 1st July – 30th September: £39.20p

metered units 28th March – 24th June: 3200 units @ 4.40pence: £140.80p

Required

Prepare a trading and profit and loss account for Mr. Milford Haven's business for the three months ending 30th June 19X9. All items in this account should be rounded to the nearest £1.

Question 10.3 Mike Mumbles owns a small concern trading as ***Llanelli Language Courses*** which has developed a popular language course in the Welsh language for English-speaking people. The course consists of a set of cassette tapes, tutorial book and dictionary, a small personal stereo cassette player, all attractively packaged. He buys the package from a manufacturer and sells it by mail order in response to advertisements in selected journals.

Last year (ending 31st December 19X2) Mike sold 2,900 packs at £89 each. He started the year with 350 packs, valued at £19,250 and ended the year with a stock of 600 packs. During the year he received 3,150 packs from his manufacturer, who charged him £59 per pack; this price is the figure which Mike uses to value his closing stock.

Mike employs part-time staff, and their salaries and wages totalled £14,500. Postages worked out at £2 per pack sold, and packing at 50 pence per pack sold. Mike rented a small warehouse at £1,000 per month.

Advertising bills totalled £15,000 and an invoice for a further £500 is still awaited.

Insurance premiums paid were £3,500, but of this amount £650 refers to the current year, 19X3.

Bills for power, light and heat have been received for £2,900, with a further bill for the last quarter of 19X2 expected to be approximately £500.

Mike uses a computer for administrative and customer records, and this, together with word-processing equipment, cost £4,000 in 19X0. Mike reckons this equipment will last about five years, so he allows £800 per annum in his accounts for depreciation. In addition to this, his stationery bill totalled £1,350.

During 19X2, he received four telephone bills, totalling £3,500, of which £200 relates to rental in advance for 19X3. In the previous year (19X1) rental in advance of £150 (relating to the first quarter of 19X2) had been deducted from the bills for 19X1 in arriving at the expenses for 19X1.

Mike also spent £5,100 on research and development of his product, which resulted in minor improvements to his language pack, with work well advanced on a new edition of the pack, planned for 19X4. Mike's policy on research and development is to write off all expenditure in the year in which it is incurred; he feels this is prudent, since research work may not prove to be productive.

Mike's accountants are very busy, and are not expected to produce figures for 19X2 until next month. Mike asks you to give him an idea of his profit for 19X2.

Required

Prepare a trading and profit and loss account for Llanelli Language Courses for the year ending 31st December 19X2.

Objective test *(tick the appropriate box)*

i) The trading account of a business shows:

a) the cash left after sales less cost of sales ☐

b) the gross profit of a business ☐

c) the net profit of a business ☐

d) none of these ☐

ii) Cost of goods sold requires, for its correct calculation, inclusion of:

a) all expenses, suitably matched for the period ☐

b) all expenses, suitably matched for the period, but excluding depreciation ☐

c) all expenses, suitably matched for the period, but excluding depreciation, plus the cost of goods purchased ☐

d) closing stock of goods ☐

iii) The realisation convention in the trading account means that profit is only realised when:

a) cash is received and paid ☐

b) goods are paid for ☐

c) goods are sold ☐

d) expenses are correctly matched ☐

iv) The matching convention requires that for any specified period:

a) revenues should be matched with associated costs ☐

b) cash receipts and payments should refer only to that period ☐

c) expenses paid should relate to the appropriate revenues ☐

d) all costs for that period should relate only to the purchases for that period ☐

v) For company X, electricity charges for the period April 19X8 to March 19X9 were £2,743. At the end of April 19X9, no account has been received. The meter has not been read, and the Electricity Board has stated that charges are to be increased by 5% as from 1st April 19X9. Consumption of electricity does not fluctuate significantly from month to month. The amount to be included as an expense in the profit and loss account for the month of April 19X9 is:

a) £ 228 ☐

b) £ 342 ☐

c) £ 240 ☐

d) £ 230 ☐

Chapter 11

Sole traders – balance sheet

11.1 Objectives

At the end of this chapter, you should be able to:

- explain what is meant by the accounting equation;
- define such terms as assets and liabilities;
- describe the purpose of a balance sheet;
- construct a simple balance sheet for a sole trader.

11.2 Introduction

For any business to operate, it needs ***resources*** which may include the following:

- the ***premises*** which the business owns and from which it operates;
- ***equipment, plant*** and ***machinery***, so that production and / or trading can take place;
- ***desks, telephones*** and other ***furniture*** and ***equipment***, so that administration, selling and distribution departments can operate;
- ***stocks*** of ***raw materials*** will be required by a manufacturer, so that these can be turned into finished goods for resale;
- ***stocks*** of ***goods*** for sale will be required by a trader, whether wholesaler or retailer;
- ***cash*** will be needed to buy any of the above items.

11.3 The accounting equation

All the above ***resources*** are known as ***assets***. For a new business to acquire ***assets***, it will have to obtain some money. Usually, it is the ***owner*** of the business who is the main source of such money.

The money supplied by the owner is known as the business ***capital***, and the ***business*** will owe this ***capital*** to the ***owner***. ***Capital*** is therefore a ***liability*** of the business, i.e. something for which the business is liable to the owner who supplied it. If no person, other than the owner, has supplied funds to the business, then:

Assets = Capital

In addition to the owner, other people may lend money to the business. For example:

- a bank may approve a ***loan*** or agree to an ***overdraft***;
- suppliers of ***raw materials*** or ***goods for resale*** may supply goods but grant credit arrangements whereby the business does not have to pay until some agreed date. Until payment is made, these suppliers are known as ***creditors***.

These sources of funds are known generally as ***liabilities***.

At any one point in time, all the ***assets*** owned by the business will exactly equal the amount of the ***capital*** supplied by the owner plus all these other outstanding ***liabilities***. This relationship is known as the ***accounting equation*** and can be expressed thus:

Assets = Capital + Liabilities

This *accounting equation* always holds true. If we know any two of the three items in the accounting equation, we can calculate the third.

> *You should now be able to attempt Questions 11.1 and 11.2 at the end of this chapter.*

A business cannot increase its total ***assets*** without increasing its total of ***capital*** and ***liabilities***. An ***individual*** asset can increase (for example, stocks can increase), but only if capital or a liability also increases, or if another asset decreases by a similar amount. This principle is known as the ***dual nature of transactions*** and can be illustrated by the following example.

Example

Complete the columns below to show the effect of the following transactions for the business known as *Pier Supplies*, owned by Mr B. Brighton.

You should enter the names of the asset or liability which you think are affected by the transaction in the appropriate column, showing whether it has increased or decreased. We have done the first one for you.

	Transaction	Assets	Capital	Liabilities
a)	Pier Supplies buys a delivery van on credit	+ Van		+ Creditors
b)	Pier Supplies repays a loan paying cash			
c)	Pier Supplies buys stock, paying by cheque			
d)	B. Brighton takes some cash out of the business for a holiday			

Solution

	Assets	Capital	Liabilities
a)	+ Van		+ Creditors
b)	– Cash		– Loan
c)	+ Stock – Bank		
d)	– Cash	– Capital	

> *You should now be able to attempt Question 11.3 at the end of this chapter.*

11.4 The balance sheet

A balance sheet:

- is a statement of the financial position of a business at ***one point in time;***
- shows in greater detail the financial relationship expressed by the ***accounting equation;***
- details the ***assets*** owned by the business and its ***capital*** and ***liabilities.***

In this chapter we shall use the ***horizontal format*** of presentation, i.e ***assets*** on the left-hand side, and ***capital*** and ***liabilities*** on the right-hand side.

There are other formats for presenting the balance sheet, but we shall leave these until Chapter 22.

The ***horizontal format*** is easy to understand at this stage, because it reflects the ***accounting equation.***

The following worked example will consolidate what you have learned so far, and illustrate how ***balance sheets*** can be presented to show the day-to-day progress of the business.

Example

1. William Worthing starts a business known as ***Worthing & Company*** on the 1st January 19X8 with £10,000.

   If we describe the business by using the accounting equation, we can see that the business will have an asset (cash) of £10,000 which will equal the capital supplied by the owner. On the balance sheet this will be shown as follows:

Worthing & Company
Balance sheet as at 1st January 19X8

	£		£
Cash	10,000	*Capital*	10,000

2. On the 2nd January, the business purchases fixtures for £5,500 and stock of goods for £3,500.

	£	£		£
Fixed assets			***Capital***	10,000
Fixtures		5,500		
Current assets				
Stock	3,500			
Cash	1,000			
		4,500		
		10,000		10,000

Note that the assets have been classified into:

- ***fixed assets,*** i.e. those resources which the business means to keep in the long-term, and
- ***current assets,*** e.g. stock and cash, which are items which are part of the trading cycle, and which will be used up in the day-to-day activities.

3. On the 3rd January, the business buys a further £1,000 of stock, but does not pay the supplier, and therefore incurs the liability of having a trade creditor

Worthing & Company
Balance sheet as at 3rd January 19X8

	£	£		£
Fixed assets			***Capital***	10,000
Fixtures		5,500		
Current assets			***Current liabilities***	
Stock	4,500		Trade creditors	1,000
Cash	1,000			
		5,500		
		11,000		11,000

4. On the 4th January, the business sells for £3,000 in cash stock which it purchased for £2,500.

Worthing & Company
Balance sheet as at 4th January 19X8

	£	£		£
Fixed assets			***Capital***	10,000
Fixtures		5,500	Profit	500
Current assets			***Current liabilities***	
Stock	2,000		Trade creditors	1,000
Cash	4,000			
		6,000		
		11,500		11,500

Note that the profit of £500 earned on the stock (sales £3,000 less cost of sales £2,500) belongs to the owner of the business, and as we are dealing with the accounts of a sole trader, the amount of profit is shown as an addition to his capital. In other words, the business (Worthing and Company) now has a new liability of profit, which it owes to the owner, Mr. William Worthing.

5. On the 5th January, the business purchases equipment of £1,000 for cash, and a further £4,500 of stock on credit.

Worthing & Company
Balance sheet as at 5th January 19X8

	£	£		£
Fixed assets			***Capital***	10,000
Fixtures	5,500		Profit	500
Equipment	1,000			
		6,500		
Current assets			***Current liabilities***	
Stock	6,500		Trade creditors	5,500
Cash	3,000			
		9,500		
		16,000		16,000

6. On 6th January:

a) the owner of the business, Mr. Worthing, withdraws £200 cash for his own use, and

b) the business sells £3,000 worth of stock for £4,000 to customers on credit, i.e. these customers are expected to pay the amount they owe in one month's time. Until they pay, they are known as debtors to the business.

Worthing & Company
Balance sheet as at 6th January 19X8

	£	£		£	£
Fixed assets			***Capital***		10,000
Fixtures	5,500		Previous profit	500	
Equipment	1,000		New profit	1,000	
		6,500			1,500
Current assets					11,500
Stock	3,500				
Debtors	4,000		*Less:* Drawings		200
Cash	2,800				
		10,300			11,300
			Current liabilities		
			Trade creditors		5,500
		16,800			16,800

11.5 Procedure for constructing a balance sheet for a sole trader

1. Identify and list all the assets of the business.
2. Identify and list all the capital and liabilities of the business.
3. Ensure that the total of assets = capital + liabilities.
4. Head up paper with name of the business *and* "Balance Sheet as at ......", ensuring that you put in the correct date.

5. On the ***left-hand side*** of the balance sheet:
   - Divide the assets into ***fixed*** and ***current***.
   - List the assets within each group in the order of permanence, i.e. start with the most permanent asset (for example, land) and finish with the least permanent asset, usually cash.
   - It is usual to show a sub-total for each group.
6. On the ***right-hand side*** of the balance sheet:
   - Show the amount of ***capital***. Add any profit and deduct any drawings.
   - Next, show any long-term liabilities, e.g. bank loans for over one year.
   - Finally, list current liabilities under the appropriate headings, and sub-total them.
7. Total both sides of the balance sheet on the same line, even if this means leaving a space on one side.
8. Ensure that the totals agree.

Example

Draw up a balance sheet for *N. Newhaven* as at 31st March 19X8, from the following information:

	£
Capital	16,000
Machinery	10,500
Creditors	1,150
Stock	2,150
Debtors	620
Bank balance	6,840
Loan from S. Seaford	2,960

Solution

N. Newhaven
Balance sheet as at 31st March 19X8

	£	£		£
Fixed assets			*Capital*	16,000
Machinery		10,500		
Current assets			*Loan*	2,960
Stock	2,150			
Debtors	620		*Current liabilities*	
Bank	6,840		Creditors	1,150
		9,610		
		20,110		20,110

11.6 Deducing the amount of capital

If the figure of capital is not given in the question, the procedure is as follows:

1. List all the assets of the business, and total.
2. List all the liabilities of the business, and total.
3. Remembering the accounting equation, deduct the liabilities from the assets, and the balance will represent the capital.

Example

E. Eastbourne sets himself up in a new business.

Before starting trading, he buys:	Motor lorries:	£30,000
	Premises:	£60,000
	Stock:	£8,000

He still owes £3,000 in respect of the above stock purchase.

He has borrowed £25,000 from P. Pevensey.

After these events, and before starting trading, he has £1,000 cash in hand, and £9,000 cash at his bank.

Required

Calculate the amount of Eastbourne's capital at the start of trading.

Solution

E. Eastbourne
Balance sheet as at start of trading

	£	£		£
Fixed assets			*Capital*	X
Premises	60,000			
Motor lorries	30,000		*Loan*	25,000
		90,000		
Current assets			*Current liabilities*	
Stock	8,000		Creditors	3,000
Bank	9,000			
Cash	1,000			
		18,000		
		108,000		X + 28,000

As capital + liabilities = assets, X + £28,000 = £108,000

Therefore X (capital) = £80,000.

You should now be able to attempt Question 11.4 at the end of this chapter.

11.7 The impact of transactions

A balance sheet reflects the financial position of a business ***at one point in time***. The next transaction undertaken by the business will alter the previous balance sheet.

Example

In this question, you are given the balance sheet for *H. Hastings* at 30th June 19X8. There follows a list of transactions.

You are required to draw up a new balance sheet after each transaction, i.e. five balance sheets in all.

H. Hastings
Balance sheet as at 30th June 19X8

	£	£		£
Fixed assets			***Capital***	146,000
Buildings	65,000			
Vehicles	35,000		***Loan***	24,000
		100,000		
Current assets			***Current liabilities***	
Stock	22,000		Creditors	10,000
Debtors	38,000			
Bank	20,000			
		80,000		
		180,000		180,000

The following transactions take place:

a) 2 July Hastings pays £4,000 to a creditor.

b) 4 July Hastings buys some more stock, on credit, for £9,000.

c) 6 July Hastings buys Office Equipment for £8,000, by cheque.

d) 8 July A debtor pays Hastings £3,000 by cheque.

e) 10 July Hastings pays off £10,000 of the loan, by cheque.

Solution

H. Hastings
Balance sheet as at 2nd July 19X8

	£	£		£
Fixed assets			***Capital***	146,000
Buildings	65,000			
Vehicles	35,000		***Loan***	24,000
		100,000		
Current assets			***Current liabilities***	
Stock	22,000		Creditors	6,000
Debtors	38,000			
Bank	16,000			
		76,000		
		176,000		176,000

H. Hastings
Balance sheet as at 4th July 19X8

	£	£		£
Fixed assets			***Capital***	146,000
Buildings	65,000			
Vehicles	35,000		***Loan***	24,000
		100,000		
Current assets			***Current liabilities***	
Stock	31,000		Creditors	15,000
Debtors	38,000			
Bank	16,000			
		85,000		
		185,000		185,000

H. Hastings
Balance sheet as at 6th July 19X8

	£	£		£
Fixed assets			***Capital***	146,000
Buildings	65,000			
Vehicles	35,000		***Loan***	24,000
Office equipment	8,000			
		108,000		
Current assets			***Current liabilities***	
Stock	31,000		Creditors	15,000
Debtors	38,000			
Bank	8,000			
		77,000		
		185,000		185,000

H. Hastings
Balance sheet as at 8th July 19X8

	£	£		£
Fixed assets			***Capital***	146,000
Buildings	65,000			
Vehicles	35,000		***Loan***	24,000
Office equipment	8,000			
		108,000		
Current assets			***Current liabilities***	
Stock	31,000		Creditors	15,000
Debtors	35,000			
Bank	11,000			
		77,000		
		185,000		185,000

H. Hastings
Balance sheet as at 10th July 19X8

	£	£		£
Fixed assets			***Capital***	146,000
Buildings	65,000			
Vehicles	35,000		***Loan***	14,000
Office equipment	8,000			
		108,000		
Current assets			***Current liabilities***	
Stock	31,000		Creditors	15,000
Debtors	35,000			
Bank	1,000			
		67,000		
		175,000		175,000

Notes

Instead of drawing up a balance sheet after each transaction, you could make pencil adjustments to the original balance sheet for each of the items affected.

Note that *two* adjustments are required for each transaction. This method would show the ***cumulative*** effect of all the transactions on every item upon the balance sheet. For example, in the above example, the bank figure changes like this:

			£
	Bank at 30th June		20,000
2 July	Cheque paid to creditor	(deduct)	4,000
			16,000
4 July	No change		–
			16,000
6 July	Cheque paid for office equipment	(deduct)	8,000
			8,000
8 July	Payment received from debtor	(add)	3,000
			11,000
10 July	Cheque paid to reduce loan	(deduct)	10,000
			1,000

The final figure of £1,000 is the same as your figure on the final balance sheet.

You could have pencilled in these changes against the item of Bank on the original balance sheet, like this:

20,000 – 4,000 – 8,000 + 3,000 – 10,000 = 1,000.

You should now be able to attempt Questions 11.5 and 11.6 and Task 11.3 at the end of this chapter.

11.8 Summary

Assets are resources which the business owns or has use of. ***Capital*** is money invested in the business by the owner. ***Liabilities*** are monies owed by the business. The ***accounting equation*** demonstrates the relationship between assets, capital and liabilities:

Assets = Capital + Liabilities

A balance sheet is a statement of the financial position of the business at any ***one point in time.***

The most common mistakes made by students are:

- not heading up the balance sheet with owner's name or the name of the business, and the date of the balance sheet;
- not correctly identifying assets and liabilities;
- forgetting how to calculate the capital figure, if this is not given;
- not listing the assets and liabilities correctly within their respective groups.

You should now be able to attempt Tasks 11.1, 11.2 and the Objective Test at the end of this chapter.

Student activities

Task 11.1 The following advertisement has appeared in an accounting magazine:

Grand Christmas Competition

Write a poem

The writer of the best poem concerned with balance sheets will receive a prize of a leather-bound cash book. All entries should be received by 5th April. The judges' assessment will be final. The winner last year was Mr Mike Blunder, with the following entry:

A naughty accountant called Roger
With balance sheets – he was a bodger;
If his books didn't agree,
He cooked them , you see;
Hence they called him old Roger the dodger.

Required

Submit your entry (not necessarily a limerick) to the competition.

Task 11.2 At a recent meeting, the Chief Accountant of the company you work for referred to the balance sheet as "a financial snapshot of the business". One of the marketing managers asked you after the meeting what this phrase meant. Send him a memorandum giving a clear explanation.

Task 11.3 You work for a training company which is developing an open learning course for students. One unit is an introduction to balance sheets. Construct a glossary of the main terms found on the balance sheet for inclusion in the unit.

Question 11.1 Complete the gaps in the following table. The answers to (a) and (b) have been placed in square brackets to show you the idea.

	Assets	Capital	Liabilities
	£	£	£
a)	13,000	[8,000]	5,000
b)	15,500	7,500	[8,000]
c)	8,000		2,700
d)	9,700	2,800	
e)		11,900	6,400
f)	42,000		19,700
g)	119,400	43,900	
h)		15,632	14,739

Question 11.2 Classify the following business items into assets, capital and liabilities by ticking the appropriate column:

	Assets	Capital	Liabilities
Motor vehicles			
Loan from bank			
Cash at bank			
Fixtures and fittings			
Cash in hand			
Overdraft			
Creditors			
Machinery			
Stock of raw materials			
Owner's stake in the business			
Loan from owner's brother			

Question 11.3 Complete the columns below to show the effect of the following transactions for a business owned by *Mr H. Hove,* who runs an ice-cream van business known as Ideal Ice-cream. Follow the same instructions as for B. Brighton in Section 11.3.

	Assets	Capital	Liabilities
a) H. Hove increases the capital of his business by paying £1,000 of his own money into Ideal Ice-cream's bank account.			
b) Ideal Ice-cream sells an old van for cash.			
c) Ideal Ice-cream buys a supply of cornets on credit.			
d) H. Hove takes home some ice- cream for his daughter's birthday party.			
e) Ideal Ice-cream pays by cheque the supplier who provided the cornets in (c) above.			

Question 11.4 Draw up the balance sheet of *B. Bexhill* at 31st December 19X8, from the following items:

	£		£
Lorries	47,000	Buildings	50,000
Loan (long-term)	32,000	Balance at bank	6,000
Stocks	17,000	Creditors	15,000
Cash in hand	2,000	Debtors	21,000

You will have to deduce the amount of capital.

Question 11.5 *R. Rye* has the following items in his balance sheet as at 31st March 19X8:

	£
Capital	85,000
Creditors	5,000
Loan from W. Winchelsea	15,000
Fixtures and fittings	45,000
Stocks	24,000
Debtors	17,000
Bank balance	19,000

During the first week of April, R. Rye did the following:

- Bought more stock on credit for £7,000.
- Repaid W. Winchelsea all he owed him.
- Collected a cheque for £7,000 from a debtor.
- Bought more fixtures and fittings, paying £5,000 for them by cheque.
- Paid one of his creditors £3,000 by cheque.

Required

Draw up the balance sheet for R. Rye as at 7th April, after all the above transactions have been taken into account.

Question 11.6 *Denis Dymchurch* is a wholesaler trader in railway memorabilia. At the 30th June 19X7, he had a balance sheet which showed the following items:

	£
Capital	100,000
Long-term loan from D. Dungeness	20,000
Overdraft at bank	2,000
Trade and other creditors	18,000
Debtors	17,000
Stocks	9,000
Delivery van (at book value)	12,000
Fixtures and fittings	8,000
Warehouse and offices	94,000

During the three months ending 30th September, the following transactions were recorded:

- Purchased £63,000 worth of stock on credit.
- Sold £55,000 worth of stock to his credit customers for £86,000.
- Received £83,000 from his credit customers, all of which he paid into the bank.
- Paid off £5,000 of his long-term loan from D. Dungeness.
- Paid his trade creditors £59,000.
- Bought (and paid for) some new fixtures and fittings for £4,000.
- Traded in his old van for its book value and bought a new van for £15,000, paying the balance by cheque.
- Paid out £11,000 in expenses, all of which were chargeable against profits.

Required

Draw up the balance sheet for Denis Dymchurch's business as at the 30th September 19X7, after all the above transactions have been taken into account.

Objective test *(tick the appropriate box)*

i) On a horizontal-style balance sheet, the figure of capital will appear:

a) at the top on the left-hand side ☐

b) under fixed assets ☐

c) under current liabilities ☐

d) at the top on the right-hand side ☐

ii) The horizontal-style balance sheet shows:

a) assets on the right-hand side ☐

b) capital and liabilities on the right-hand side ☐

c) capital and liabilities on the left-hand side ☐

d) assets and capital on the left-hand side ☐

iii) Those items which a business owns or has use of in the long-term are known as:

a) current assets ☐

b) capital ☐

c) current liabilities ☐

d) fixed assets ☐

iv) If a company purchases a motor van (which it intends to use in the business) on credit, the van will be classified as a:

a) current liability ☐

b) current asset ☐

c) fixed asset ☐

d) long-term liability ☐

v) A company buys equipment for £5,000 on credit. The effect of this transaction will be to:

a) increase assets and decrease liabilities ☐

b) increase assets and increase liabilities ☐

c) decrease assets and decrease liabilities ☐

d) decrease assets and increase liabilities ☐

vi) A company sells part of its factory premises, and is paid £5,000. The effect of this transaction will be to:

a) decrease fixed assets and decrease capital ☐

b) decrease fixed assets and increase cash ☐

c) decrease fixed assets and decrease cash ☐

d) increase fixed assets and increase capital ☐

vii) If the figure of capital is missing in a question, it may be found by:

a) adding fixed assets and current assets ☐

b) deducting liabilities from total assets ☐

c) adding liabilities to total assets ☐

d) deducting liabilities from current assets ☐

viii) A company has assets of £15,000 and liabilities of £8,000. The capital is therefore:

a) £23,000 ☐

b) £7,000 ☐

c) £8,000 ☐

d) £15,000 ☐

ix) A company has fixed assets valued at £5,000, current liabilities of £4,000 and current assets of £3,000. Its capital will be:

a) £12,000 ☐

b) £4,000 ☐

c) £6,000 ☐

d) £7,000 ☐

x) A company has capital of £12,200, fixed assets of £8,050 and current liabilities of £2,250. The value of the company's current assets is:

a) £4,150 ☐

b) £14,450 ☐

c) £6,400 ☐

d) £5,800 ☐

Chapter 12

Presentation and principles

12.1 Objectives

At the end of this chapter you should be able to:

- understand and prepare a balance sheet in vertical format for a sole trader;
- differentiate between accruals and prepayments, and incorporate them correctly in the accounts of a sole trader;
- prepare trading and profit and loss accounts and balance sheets, including the correct treatment of:
  - bank balances;
  - carriage inwards and carriage outwards;
  - drawings;
  - discounts allowed and discounts received;
  - returns inwards and returns outwards;
  - rents receivable.

12.2 Introduction

In Chapter 11, we presented the balance sheet of a sole trader in what is known as the ***horizontal format***, i.e assets in a column on the left and liabilities on the right. In this chapter we shall look at the ***vertical format*** where all items, both ***assets*** and ***liabilities***, are set out according to accepted conventions in columnar form ***down*** the page.

We shall also consider other principles which are important to an understanding of profit and loss accounts and balance sheets.

12.3 Vertical format of the balance sheet

We said in the previous chapter that the horizontal format of the balance sheet had the advantage of reflecting the ***accounting equation***. However, sometimes we may wish to communicate clearly other important facts on the balance sheet. We may wish to show how much money has, in total, been invested in the fixed assets combined with the working capital (current assets less current liabilities). This cannot be found immediately on a horizontal type of balance sheet without calculation, i.e. deducting the current liabilities on the right-hand side from the total assets on the left-hand side. Many businesses now use the vertical format of balance sheet because it is possible to provide this information more easily than in the horizontal format.

In Chapter 11, we considered the balance sheets of Worthing & Company. Here is the balance sheet as at 6th January 19X8, in ***horizontal format***:

Example

Worthing & Company
Balance sheet as at 6th January 19X8

	£	£		£	£
Fixed assets			*Capital*		10,000
Fixtures	5,500		Previous profit	500	
Equipment	1,000		New profit	1,000	
		6,500			1,500
Current assets					
Stock	3,500				11,500
Debtors	4,000		*Less* Drawings		200
Cash	2,800				
		10,300			11,300
			Current liabilities		
			Trade Creditors		5,500
		16,800			16,800

Now we shall re-present it in ***vertical format***:

Example

Worthing & Company
Balance sheet as at 6th January 19X8

	£	£	£
Fixed assets			
Fixtures		5,500	
Equipment		1,000	6,500
Current assets			
Stock	3,500		
Debtors	4,000		
Cash	2,800	10,300	
Less Current liabilities			
Trade creditors		5,500	
Working capital (or ***net current assets***)			4,800
Capital employed			11,300
Represented by (or financed by):			
Capital			10,000
Add Previous profit		500	
New profit		1,000	
		1,500	
Less Drawings		200	1,300
			11,300

The changes in format from ***horizontal*** to ***vertical*** can be represented diagrammatically and are shown below. Compare this diagram with the figures for Worthing & Company above. You should notice the following differences between the two formats:

Horizontal	Vertical
i) The total of the left-hand side shows the ***total assets*** (***fixed*** plus ***current***). The total of the right-hand side shows ***total liabilities*** (***long-term*** plus ***current***).	i) The total of the top half shows the ***capital employed*** (***total assets*** less ***current liabilities***). The total of the bottom half shows the ***owner's worth*** (which is the same figure as ***capital employed***).
ii) ***Working capital*** (also known as ***net current assets***) is ***not*** shown. (You would have to work it out by deducting ***current liabilities*** from ***current assets***.)	ii) ***Working capital*** is shown as a deduction of ***current liabilities*** from ***current assets***.
iii) Offset figures (to show sub-totals clearly) are not as pronounced as in the vertical format.	iii) Offset figures are employed to the extent of using three (or even four) columns. For example: ***Current assets*** are listed in the third column from the right, with a sub-total in the second column from the right. This enables the sub-total for ***current liabilities*** to be deducted from that for current assets and the result shown in the last column. This result (the ***working capital***) can then be added to the total for ***fixed assets***, to give the ***capital employed***.

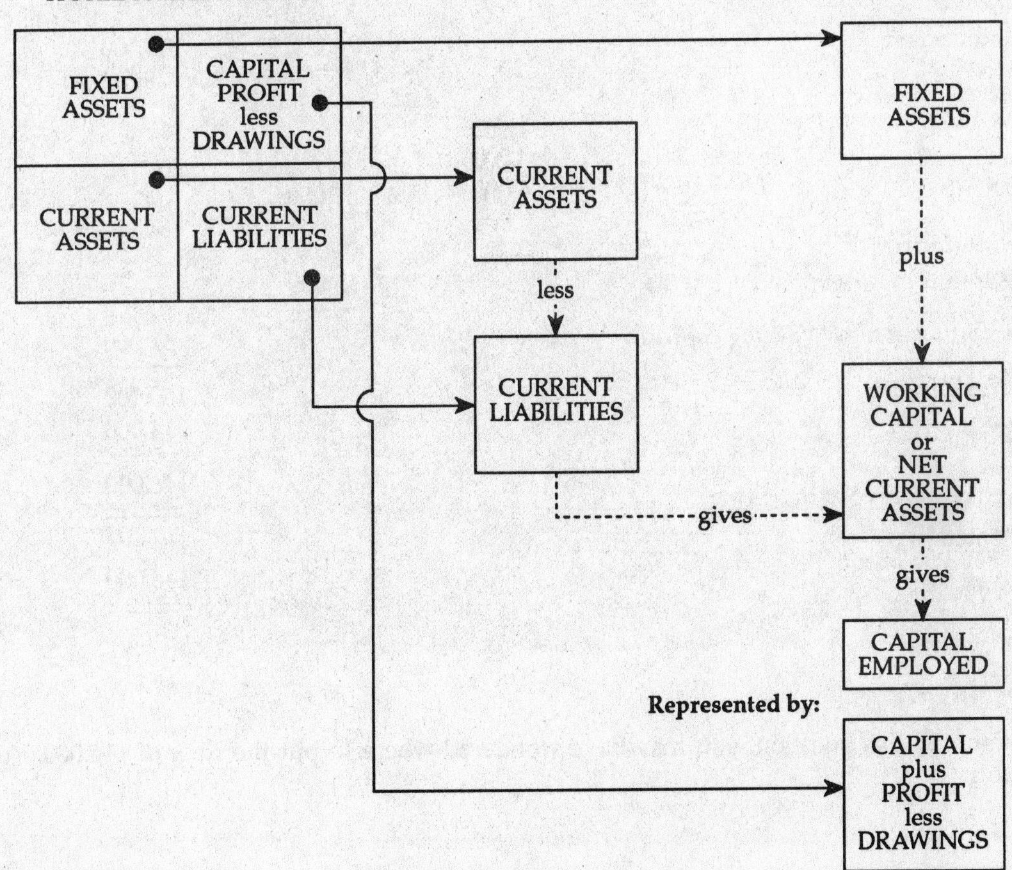

Example

In Chapter 11 the balance sheet for H. Hastings on the 10th July 19X8 was as follows:

H. Hastings
Balance sheet as at 10th July 19X8

	£	£		£
Fixed assets			*Capital*	146,000
Buildings	65,000			
Vehicles	35,000		*Loan*	14,000
Office equipment	8,000			
		108,000		
Current assets			*Current liabilities*	
Stock	31,000		Creditors	15,000
Debtors	35,000			
Bank	1,000			
		67,000		
		175,000		175,000

Represent this balance sheet in vertical format.

Solution

H. Hastings
Balance sheet as at 10th July 19X8

	£	£	£
Fixed assets			
Buildings		65,000	
Vehicles		35,000	
Office equipment		8,000	108,000
Current assets			
Stock	31,000		
Debtors	35,000		
Bank	1,000	67,000	
Current liabilities			
Creditors		15,000	
Net current assets (or *Working capital*)			52,000
Capital employed			160,000
Less Loan			14,000
			146,000
Represented by:			
Capital			146,000

12.4 Loans

When you attempted this question, you may have wondered where to put the ***loan*** of £14,000. You may have shown it like this:

	£	£
Capital employed		160,000
Represented by:		
Capital	146,000	
Loan	14,000	160,000

It may seem that this is is a satisfactory presentation since it shows the calculation of capital employed (fixed assets plus working capital), and how it has been financed (capital plus loans). However, the presentation in the answer is the one which conforms with commonly accepted practice. You will see that the first figure of £146,000 is the capital employed *less* the loan, and the second figure of £146,000 is the capital. The idea of this is to show the *inside* financing of the business, i.e. what the owner of the business has provided (*capital*) and the retained profit which has accrued to that capital. The *loan* is *outside* financing, i.e. what has been provided by a party other than the owner, for example by a bank or finance house. Thus the second total of £146,000 shows what the owner is worth, and the first figure of £146,000 shows all the assets less all the liabilities, both short-term (current liabilities) and long-term (loans).

You will note that *creditors* are classified as a current liability, whereas the *loan* is a long-term liability. The distinction between the two is that:

- *current liabilities* represent *creditors*: amounts due within one year;
- *long-term liabilities* represent *creditors*: amounts due after more than one year.

In fact, in the reports and accounts issued annually by public limited companies to their shareholders, these definitions are very often printed, rather than the shorter titles of current liabilities and long-term liabilities. When we consider the balance sheets of public limited companies later, we shall use the longer titles to conform with accepted practice.

In this chapter we are dealing with the accounts of sole traders. But there is no reason why we should not conform with what is now considered to be customary formats of presentation.

You should now be able to attempt Question 12.1 and Task 12.1 at the end of this chapter.

12.5 Capital and revenue expenditure

It is important to distinguish between *capital expenditure* and *revenue expenditure. Capital expenditure* relates mainly to *fixed assets,* i.e.assets which are not completely used within a financial year. For example, machinery: the cost of buying it, transporting it in, installing it and subsequently modifying or improving it. This type of expenditure appears on the *balance sheet*, under the heading of *fixed assets*.

Revenue expenditure relates to day-to-day running costs, such as wages and salaries, rent and rates, insurances, heating and lighting, etc. For example, machinery: running costs, maintenance and repairs. This type of expenditure appears in the *trading* and *profit and loss account*. Further details are given in Chapter 27.

12.6 Drawings

Drawings are an appropriation of the owner's profit. They represent what the owner has drawn out of the business *for his or her own personal use,* both cash and other assets such as stock. They, therefore, represent a reduction of capital, just as profit represents an addition to capital. They are shown on the balance sheet as a deduction from the opening capital, to which may have been added any net profit for the period covered by the profit and loss account.

For an example of presentation, look back at the balance sheet of Worthing & Company as at 6th January 19X8 earlier in this chapter.

12.7 Accruals

Accruals arise as a result of the ***matching convention*** discussed in Chapter 10.

Example

Accounts are prepared to the 31st December 19X5. The last invoice received for electricity was for the period to the 30th November 19X5. Estimated electricity cost for December is £500.

Profit & Loss Account: Add £500 to the expense of electricity.

Balance Sheet: Show £500 as an accrual under current liabilities.

Sometimes accruals are grouped together with creditors as creditors and accruals.

12.8 Prepayments

Prepayments also arise as a result of the ***matching convention*** discussed in Chapter 10.

Example

Accounts are prepared to the 31st December 19X5. Rates for the period 1st October 19X5 to 31st March 19X6 were paid on 6th October 19X5, in the sum of £2,000. Since £1,000 of this sum refers to the period 1st January 19X6 to 31st March 19X6:

Profit & Loss Account: Deduct £1,000 from the expense of rates.

Balance Sheet: Show £1,000 as a prepayment under current assets.

Sometimes prepayments are grouped together with debtors as debtors and prepayments.

12.9 Bank balance

If there is money in the bank, show this as ***bank*** under current assets on the balance sheet. If there is an overdraft, show this as a current liability. An overdraft, which can be recalled at any time, is usually shown as a current liability, even if in practice the facility is available for more than one year. Loans are usually secured on the assets of the business, and are usually for periods in excess of one year, in which case they are treated as long-term, and deducted from the capital employed as described earlier in this chapter.

12.10 Stock valuation

The general rule Statement of Standard Accounting Practice (SSAP) 9 is that closing stock values should be shown on the profit and loss account and in the balance sheet at the lower of cost or net realisable value. Cost is the amount incurred in bringing the stock to the state and condition existing at the date of the stock valuation. Net realisable value is the income the stocks will generate if sold less any costs in getting the stock to the cutomers.

Usually the net realisable value will be higher than the cost because the business hopes to sell its goods at a profit, but sometimes the net realisable value may be lower. For example, a trader may have bought some toys at £15 each, hoping to sell them for £20 each. The demand for toys drops dramatically by the time the trader is preparing the profit and loss account and balance sheet and he considers that he could sell the toys for £12 each. This is their net realisable value and, as it is lower than the cost of £15 each, it will form the basis for the closing stock values to be shown on the profit and loss account and balance sheet.

Determining the cost of stock can prove a problem if prices are fluctuating. Assume that a trader buys 10 items at £5 each from his wholesaler in May. In June a further 8 items are purchased, but the price has now increased to £6 for each item. If the trader then sells 15 of the items the question arises as top what is the cost of the three items unsold for calculating the stock values. Is the correct figure for the stock values 3 items at £5 each or 3 items at £6 each? There are a number of approaches accountants use to resolve this dilemma, including the calculation of an 'average' cost. In the UK we tend to use a method known as First In, First Out (FIFO). We assume that the items purchased first will be the ones sold first. Any unsold items will therefore be the last ones we bought and in our example the stock value would be 3 items at £6 each = £18.

In the examples we have used we have concentrated on the business of a trader; the buying and selling of goods. The problems of stock valuation at the end of a financial period become more difficult if we look at a manufacturing organisation. At the year end there will be not only finished goods waiting to be sold, but raw materials waiting manufacture into the finished product, and also work-in-progress where the manufacturing process is only part complete. For example, a car manufacturer will have a stock of partly finished cars which require engines, wheels, or electrics to complete them. Although stock valuation in these circumstances is complex, the general rule of of valuing stock at the lower of cost or net realisable value must be applied.

12.11 Profit and loss account items

There are a number of items which need to be shown on the ***profit and loss account*** in a particular way. It is not possible to give a list of everything you might meet, but listed below are the most common ones.

- ***Carriage outwards***
  This represents the cost of delivery of finished goods to customers. Show as an expense in the profit and loss account.
- ***Carriage inwards***
  This represents the cost of bringing in goods, raw materials etc. Add to the cost of purchases in the trading account.
- ***Discounts allowed***
  These are discounts allowed to debtors. They are deducted by customers from the balances due for sales when paying their accounts. Show as an expense in the profit and loss account.
- ***Discounts received***
  These are discounts which a business has deducted from balances payable for purchases, effectively reducing the cost of those purchases. Add to the gross profit in the trading account.
- ***Returns inwards***
  These are goods which have been returned by customers for various reasons. For example, they may be faulty or unsuitable. They can therefore be regarded as a reduction of sales. Deduct from sales in the trading account.
- ***Returns outwards***
  These are goods which a business returns to suppliers for various reasons. For example, they may be faulty or unsuitable. They can therefore be regarded as a reduction of purchases. Deduct from purchases in the trading account.
- ***Rents receivable***
  A business may let some of its premises to a third party. Such rent is not part of normal manufacturing or trading income. It should not therefore be shown as sales income. Add to gross profit in the trading account.
- ***Depreciation***
  This deserves separate consideration and is discussed in Chapter 13.
- ***Bad debts and provision for doubtful debts***
  These also deserve separate consideration and are discussed in Chapter 14.

Example

Bessie Bangor owns a bookshop, ***Bangor's Bookshop*** and the following figures have been extracted from her bookkeeping records at 31st December 19X2.

	£
Sales	151,500
Purchases	103,500
Salaries and wages	18,700
Office expenses	2,500
Insurances	1,100
Electricity	600
Stationery	2,400
Advertising	3,500
Telephone	800
Rates	3,000
Discounts allowed	100
Discounts received	200
Rent received for spare room	2,000
Returns inwards	1,500
Returns outwards	3,500
Opening stock (as at 1.1.19X2)	46,000
Premises	80,000
Fixtures and fittings	5,000
Debtors	4,800
Cash in hand	200
Creditors	7,500
Overdraft at bank	12,000
Capital at 1.1.19X2	111,000
Drawings during year	14,000

In addition, the following information is available:

Stock at 31st December 19X2 valued at £41,000
Insurance paid in advance at 31st December 19X2: £400
Electricity accrued at 31st December 19X2: £300
Advertising expenses accrued at 31st December19X2: £200
Rates prepaid at 31st December 19X2: £600

Prepare a trading and profit and loss account for the year ending 31st December 19X2, and a balance sheet as at that date, in vertical format.

Solution

Bangor's Bookshop
Trading and profit & loss account for the year ending 31st December 19X2

	£	£	£
Sales		151,500	
Less Returns inwards		1,500	
			150,000
Less Cost of sales			
Opening stock		46,000	
Add Purchases	103,500		
Less Returns outwards	3,500		
		100,000	
		146,000	

	£	£	£
Less Closing stock		41,000	
			105,000
Gross profit			45,000
Add Rents receivable		2,000	
Add Discounts received		200	
			2,200
			47,200
Less Expenses			
Salaries and wages		18,700	
Office expenses		2,500	
Insurances	1,100		
Less prepaid	400		
		700	
Electricity	600		
Add accrued	300		
		900	
Stationery		2,400	
Advertising	3,500		
	£	£	£
Add accrued	200		
		3,700	
Telephone		800	
Rates	3,000		
Less prepaid	600		
		2,400	
Discounts allowed		100	
			32,200
Net profit			15,000

Note: Details of accruals and prepayments against individual items of expense would not normally be shown, and are included here to demonstrate the calculations.

Bangor's Bookshop

Balance sheet as at 31st December 19X2

	£	£	£	£
Fixed assets				
Premises			80,000	
Fixtures and Fittings			5,000	
				85,000
Current assets				
Stocks		41,000		
Debtors	4,800			
Add Prepayments (400 + 600)	1,000			
		5,800		
Cash		200	47,000	

Current liabilities				
Creditors	7,500			
Add Accruals (300 + 200)	500			
		8,000		
Overdraft		12,000		
			20,000	
Net current assets (working capital)				27,000
Capital employed				112,000
Represented by:				
Capital at start of year			111,000	
Add Profit for year			15,000	
			126,000	
Less Drawings			14,000	
Owner's worth				112,000

You should now be able to attempt Questions 12.2 and 12.3 at the end of this chapter.

12.12 Summary

A ***balance sheet*** may be shown in ***vertical or horizontal format***. In either case it will balance, although the totals differ from one format to another because of the way in which the figures are presented and calculated.

There are a number of items, such as ***capital*** and ***revenue expenditure, drawings*** and ***stock values,*** which must be treated correctly on the ***profit and loss account***. Other items, such as discounts and returns, must be shown in a particular way when arriving at the figures of gross and net profit.

Balance sheets

a) Horizontal format: Assets on the left; liabilities on the right.

b) Vertical format:

	£	£
Fixed assets		X
Current assets	X	
Less Current liabilities	X	
Net current assets		X
Total net assets		X
Less Long-term loans		X
Owner's worth		X

	£	£
Opening capital	X	
Add Net profit for year	X	
	X	
Less Drawings	X	
Owner's worth		X

You should now be able to attempt Tasks 12.2 and 12.3 and the Objective Test at the end of this chapter.

Student activities

Task 12.1 Obtain a vertical balance sheet of a business from the published accounts of a public limited company and convert it into a horizontal format.

Task 12.2 Your aunt has a small business and has given you the following example of a balance sheet she has drawn up for her business.

	£		£
Stock	1,000	What I owe suppliers	5,000
Car	5,000	Less What I am owed (debtors)	3,000
Land	5,000		
Buildings	6,000		
	17,000		2,000
Less Profit	3,000	Capital I invested in the business	12,000
	14,000		14,000

Required

Redraft the balance sheet in a more conventional form and write a letter to your aunt explaining what you have done and why.

Task 12.3 Conduct a survey amongst members of your class to find out which balance sheet format is preferred by most students and why.

Question 12.1 *Mr H Holyhead* has been in business for several years as a manufacturer of fishing nets. At the 31st December 19X7, you find that his assets and liabilities are as follows:

	£'000
Stocks	29
Creditors	12
Premises	90
Overdraft	14
Capital at 1st January 19X7	150
Profit for year to 31st December 19X7	21
Debtors	24
Vehicles	27
Drawings for year to 31st December 19X7	16
Plant	30
Long-term loan	20
Cash in hand	1

Prepare a balance sheet for Mr Holyhead as at 31st December 19X7, setting it out in vertical format, in good style and presentation.

Question 12.2 Brian Barmouth is a sole trader, and one of his businesses trades as ***Barmouth & Company***. At the 30th June 19X9, you have extracted the following balances from his books:

	£
Sales	47,600
Purchases	22,850
Office expenses	1,900
Insurances	700
Wages	7,900
Rates	2,800
Heating, lighting	1,200
Telephone	650
Discounts allowed	1,150
Opening stock at 1st July 19X8	500
Returns inwards	200
Returns outwards	150
Premises	40,000
Plant and machinery	5,000
Motor vehicles	12,000
Debtors	12,500
Bank balance (in credit)	7,800
Creditors	3,400
Long-term loan	10,000
Capital	60,000
Drawings for the year	4,000

In addition, the following information is available, as at 30th June 19X9:

	£
i) Stock is valued at	550
ii) Heating, lighting costs accrued	300
iii) Insurances prepaid	150
iv) Rates prepaid	700

Prepare a trading and profit and loss account for the year ending 30th June 19X9, and a balance sheet as at that date for Barmouth & Company, in vertical format.

Question 12.3 David Dolgellau owns the ***Dolgellau Camping Equipment Company***, which has been operating successfully for a number of years. The following figures are available from the bookkeeping records as at 31st March 19X5.

	£
Sales	378,500
Discounts received	2,400
Rent received for sub-let of warehouse	7,500
Returns outwards	7,700
Creditors	18,700
Overdraft at bank	30,000
Capital at 1st April, 19X4	287,500
Purchases	261,700
Salaries and wages	45,700
Office expenses	8,400
Insurance premiums	3,100
Electricity	1,600
Stationery	6,200
Advertising	8,400
Telephone	2,100
Business rates	7,500
Discounts allowed	600
Returns inwards	4,100

	£
Opening stock at 1st April, 19X4	120,600
Warehouse, shop and office	210,000
Fixtures and fittings	12,800
Debtors	13,000
Cash in till and petty cash	500
Drawings during the year	26,000

In addition, the following information is available:

Stock at 31st March 19X5 is valued at:	£102,500
Electricity charges accrued at 31st March 19X5:	£700
Advertising expenses accrued at 31st March 19X5:	£500
Insurance premiums paid in advance at 31st March 19X5:	£900
Business rates prepaid at 31st March 19X5:	£1,500

Required

Prepare a trading and profit and loss account for the year ending 31st March 19X5, and a balance sheet as at that date in vertical format for the Dolgellau Camping Equipment Company.

Objective test *(tick the appropriate box)*

i) On a vertical style of balance sheet, capital employed represents:

a) net current assets plus long-term liabilities ☐

b) fixed assets plus working capital ☐

c) current assets plus fixed assets ☐

d) the total of all assets and liabilities ☐

ii) On a vertical format style of balance sheet, without further calculation, it is not possible to find the figure for:

a) net current assets ☐

b) capital employed ☐

c) working capital ☐

d) total assets ☐

iii) Drawings, for a sole trader, are shown:

a) as an expense in the profit and loss account ☐

b) as a current asset on the balance sheet ☐

c) as a deduction from capital and profit on the balance sheet ☐

d) as an accrual under current liabilities on the balance sheet ☐

iv) Carriage outwards is shown:

a) as an expense in the profit and loss account ☐

b) as an addition to purchases in the trading account ☐

c) as an addition to gross profit in the trading account ☐

d) as a deduction from purchases in the trading account ☐

v) Discounts allowed are shown:

a) as an addition to purchases in the trading account ☐

b) as a deduction from debtors on the balance sheet ☐

c) as an addition to gross profit in the trading account ☐

d) as an expense in the profit and loss account ☐

vi) Rents receivable are best treated in the accounts:

a) as an addition to sales in the trading account ☐

b) as an expense in the profit and loss account ☐

c) as an addition to gross profit in the trading account ☐

d) as a current asset on the balance sheet ☐

vii) Returns inwards are shown:

a) as a deduction from sales in the trading account ☐

b) as a deduction from purchases in the trading account ☐

c) as a deduction from debtors on the balance sheet ☐

d) as an expense in the profit and loss account ☐

viii) An accrual is dealt with in the accounts by:

a) adding the amount to the appropriate expense in the profit and loss account ☐

b) including the amount under current liabilities in the balance sheet ☐

c) both (a) and (b) ☐

d) none of these ☐

ix) A prepayment is dealt with in the accounts by:

a) including the amount under current liabilities in the balance sheet ☐

b) adding the amount to the appropriate expense in the profit and loss account ☐

c) both (a) and (b) ☐

d) none of these ☐

x) Amounts which fall due after more than one year include:

a) overdrafts ☐

b) bank balances ☐

c) long-term loans ☐

d) none of these ☐

Chapter 13

Depreciation

13.1 Objectives

At the end of this chapter, you should be able to:

- understand the concept of depreciation;
- calculate depreciation using the straight-line method, and the reducing balance method;
- prepare accounts incorporating depreciation into the profit and loss account, and the balance sheet.

13.2 Introduction

Depreciation is a concept which is frequently misunderstood. We saw in Chapter 10 that when a business incurs costs such as electricity, telephone, wages etc, these costs are matched to the period to which the profit and loss account relates, i.e. matched to the period in which the benefits arise from these costs.

A problem arises, however, with the cost of purchasing an asset such as a van. If a business buys a van in year 1 for £10,000, it would not be observing the matching convention if it set the whole cost of the van as an expense against the profits for year 1.

Suppose the van is likely to have fairly heavy use, and estimate that it will be sold in four years time for about £2,000. This means that the van will have cost £8,000 over the next four years. If we apportion the cost evenly over those four years, we could say that the cost of the van is £8,000 ÷ 4 years = £2,000 per annum. There are various ways of looking at this:

- We could say that the benefits are spread over the four years.
- We could say that the business uses up the fixed asset over the period of four years, and that this using up is therefore a ***cost*** or ***expense***.
- We could also say that the £2,000 per annum we propose to charge to expenses is a charge for the use of the van.
- We could say that the £2,000 per annum is an attempt to spread the expenditure incurred in acquiring the asset over its useful life.
- We could say that the van is wearing out and therefore dropping in value over the four years. This is rather more difficult to justify, because at the end of year 1, we are saying that the van has dropped in value by £2,000 (from £10,000 to £8,000), whereas it is common for new vehicles to drop in value much more in their first year than in second and subsequent years. However, the future is always uncertain, and the principle still holds good even if the figures prove to be somewhat unrealistic.

The term used by accountants for all these five descriptions is ***depreciation***. There are two main methods of calculating depreciation: the ***straight line method*** and the ***reducing balance method***.

13.3 Straight line method of depreciation

This is the method used above concerning the van.

The calculation is as follows:

$$\frac{\textit{Original cost less estimated scrap value}}{\textit{Number of years of expected use}} = \text{Annual depreciation charge}$$

For the van described above, this gives:

$$\frac{£10{,}000 - £2{,}000}{4 \text{ years}} = £2{,}000 \text{ per annum}$$

Entries in the profit and loss accounts and the balance sheets for the four years would be:

	Profit and loss accounts charged to Expenses under Depreciation of vans	**Balance sheets** at year ends shown under ***Fixed assets: Vans***			
		Fixed assets at cost	*less*	Accumulated depreciation	= Net book value (NBV)
Year	£	£		£	£
1	2,000	10,000		2,000	8,000
2	2,000	10,000		4,000	6,000
3	2,000	10,000		6,000	4,000
4	2,000	10,000		8,000	2,000

Note: On the balance sheet, fixed assets are required to be shown at cost less ***accumulated*** depreciation to the date of the balance sheet.

It is the ***net book value,*** sometimes known as the net book amount (NBA) or ***written down value (WDV)*** which is the figure used to balance the balance sheet. The other figures (cost and accumulated depreciation) are, in a sense, only notes to show how the net book value has been calculated.

Example

Brian Blackpool bought a generator on 1st January, 19X5 for £6,000. He expects this to last 5 years at the end of which time he hopes to sell it for £1,000. He uses the straight-line method of depreciation.

Show the entries relevant to depreciation for his profit and loss account for the year ending 31st December 19X6, and his balance sheet as at that date.

Solution

Profit & loss account for the year ending 31st December 19X6 (Extract)

Expenses:	
Depreciation of generator	£1,000

Balance sheet as at 31st December 19X6 (Extract)

Fixed assets	**Cost**	**Accumulated depreciation**	**Net book value**
Generator	£6,000	£2,000	£4,000

You should now be able to attempt Question 13.1 at the end of this chapter.

13.4 Disposals

It is not proposed in this book to describe the bookkeeping entries for the ***disposals*** of fixed assets, but you should understand what happens. Suppose that the van described earlier in this chapter is sold at the start of year 5 for £1,500, i.e before additional depreciation for year 5 has been incurred. Then it could be said that there has been an apparent loss of £500, because, at the date of the sale, the net book value is still £2,000. This £500 would be shown as "Loss on sale of van: £500" under expenses in the profit and loss account for year 5.

Similarly, if the van is sold for £2,500 instead of £1,500, then the profit of £500 could be shown as a negative expense under expenses. Alternatively, the profit on sale of van could be shown at the end of the trading account, as an addition to gross profit, i.e. before the listing of expenses.

There would, of course, be no entry on the balance sheet at the end of year 5, since the asset would no longer be owned by the business.

13.5 Reducing balance method of depreciation

This is an alternative method of calculation. A fixed percentage rate is applied to the ***net book value*** (not the cost) at the end of each period. As a very rough rule of thumb, the percentage required is nearly double that required for the straight line method. The following example is based on the van.

Example

Cost £10,000

Depreciation rate: 40% per annum on the reducing balance.

Year		Profit and loss account	Balance Sheet		
		Depreciation	Cost	Accumulated depreciation	Net book value
		£	£	£	£
1	40% of £10,000	4,000	10,000	4,000	6,000
2	40% of £6,000	2,400	10,000	6,400	3,600
3	40% of £3,600	1,440	10,000	7,840	2,160
4	40% of £2,160	864	10,000	8,704	1,296

Another way of presenting this is as follows:

	£
Original cost	10,000
Year 1 depreciation	4,000
Reduced balance	6,000
Year 2 depreciation	2,400
Reduced balance	3,600
Year 3 depreciation	1,440
Reduced balance	2,160
Year 4 depreciation	864
Reduced balance	1,296

The reduced balance at the end of year 4 is £1,296 compared with £2,000 using the straight-line method. This shows that our rough rule of thumb of doubling the rate results in rather more depreciation being applied to the asset over the 4 years (£8,704 compared with £8,000).

In order to obtain the exact rate, which under the reducing balance method would result in a scrap value of £2,000, we could use the following formula:

$$r = 1 - \sqrt[t]{\frac{s}{c}}$$

where:

r = rate of depreciation required

t = time (number of years)

s = scrap value

c = cost of the asset

$$\text{e.g. } r = 1 - \sqrt[4]{\frac{2{,}000}{10{,}000}} = 1 - \sqrt[4]{0.2} = 1 - 0.6687403 = 0.3312597 = 33.12597\%$$

Therefore:

	£
Original cost	10,000.00
Year 1 depreciation	3,312.60
Reduced balance	6,687.40
Year 2 depreciation	2,215.27
Reduced balance	4,472.13
Year 3 depreciation	1,481.44
Reduced balance	2,990.69
Year 4 depreciation	990.69
Reduced balance	2,000.00

This degree of accuracy is not normally required and the above has been demonstrated purely for illustrative purposes.

In practice, if a scrap value of £2,000 is required after 4 years, a depreciation rate of 33% would result in a reduced balance of £2,015, which is near enough.

13.6 Which method?

The straight line method is popular because it is simple to understand and calculate. Those who favour the reducing balance method argue that it produces high depreciation in the early years and lower depreciation in the later years and that:

- it relates more accurately to normal experience, e.g. new cars usually drop in value heavily in the first year;
- it offsets low maintenance costs in the early years and higher maintenance costs in the later years.

Those who favour the straightline method would reply that:

- apportioning depreciation unequally over a period of time fails to conform with the matching convention, which requires that the charge for the use of the asset should be spread evenly over the period during which the asset is being used;
- offsetting high maintenance costs in the later years with low depreciation tends to obscure the true factual high level of maintenance costs.

Example

Using the data from the ***Brian Blackpool*** example we used earlier, what would the answer be if B. Blackpool employed the reducing balance method of depreciation, with a depreciation rate of 30% on the reduced balance?

Solution

Calculation:

	£
Original cost	6,000
Depreciation 19X5	1,800
Reduced balance 31st December 19X5	4,200
Depreciation 19X6	1,260
Reduced balance 31st December 19X6	2,940

Profit & loss account
for the year ending 31st December 19X6 (Extract)

Expenses:	
Depreciation of generator	£1,260

Balance sheet
as at 31st December 19X6 (Extract)

Fixed assets	£ Cost	£ Accumulated Depreciation	£ Net Book Value
Generator	6,000	3,060	2,940

You should now be able to attempt Question 13.2 at the end of this chapter.

Example

The following example includes the calculation of depreciation and its incorporation into the accounting documents. This example also calls upon skills learnt in previous chapters of this book.

On 31st December 19X8, the accountant of ***Bolton Bakeries*** produced a balance sheet which included the following information:

	£	
Stocks	4,400	
Bank balance	2,800	
Creditors	4,000	
Debtors	2,200	
Fixed assets, at net book value, were:		
Motor vehicles	£40,000	(original cost £50,000)
Plant & equipment	£22,500	(original cost £30,000)

During the year 19X9, Bolton Bakeries purchased another vehicle for £15,000 and new plant and equipment for £16,000. At the end of 19X9, the books and other records showed the following:

- Customers owed £2,600
- Suppliers were owed £4,500
- Stocks were valued at £3,700
- The cash book showed a bank balance of £9,400

Bolton Bakeries adopt the following principles in calculating depreciation:

- Depreciation is charged on the straight-line basis at a rate of 20% of original cost for vehicles and 25% of original cost for plant and equipment.
- Depreciation for a full year is charged on all assets purchased during a year, irrespective of the date of purchase.

Calculate the capital of Bolton Bakeries as at 31st December 19X8

Prepare a balance sheet for Bolton Bakeries as at 31st December 19X9.

Solution

	£	£	£
			NBV
Fixed assets			
Motor vehicles			40,000
Plant and equipment			22,500
			62,500
Current assets			
Stocks	4,400		
Debtors	2,200		
Bank	2,800		
		9,400	
Less Current liabilities			
Creditors		4,000	
Net current assets (Working capital)			5,400
Therefore *Capital* at 31st December 19X8 was			67,900

Bolton Bakeries

Balance sheet as at 31st December 19X9

	£	£	£
Fixed assets	Cost	Acc.Dep'n	NBV
Motor vehicles	50,000	20,000	30,000
Add New vehicles	15,000	3,000	12,000
	65,000	23,000	42,000
Plant & equipment	30,000	15,000	15,000
Add New plant and equipment	16,000	4,000	12,000
	46,000	19,000	27,000
Total fixed assets	111,000	42,000	69,000
Current assets:			
Stocks	3,700		
Debtors	2,600		
Bank	9,400		
		15,700	
Less Current liabilities			
Creditors		4,500	
Working capital (Net current assets)			11,200
Capital employed			80,200
Represented by:			
Capital as at 31st December 19X8		67,900	
Add Profit for year ending 31st December 19X9		12,300 *	
Capital as at 31st December 19X9			80,200

*This is the balancing figure

You should now be able to attempt Question 13.3 at the end of this chapter.

13.7 Summary

Depreciation is a charge for the use of an asset over the period of its useful life. There are two methods of calculation. The ***straight line method*** uses the following formula to calculate the annual depreciation charge:

$$\text{Annual depreciation charge} = \frac{\text{Original cost} - \text{Estimated scrap value}}{\text{Number of years of expected life}}$$

The ***reducing balance method*** calculates the annual depreciation charge by applying a fixed percentage to the previous net book value.

The ***annual depreciation charge*** is shown as an expense in the profit and loss account and is added to the accumulated depreciation charge at the beginning of the year in the balance sheet. The total accumulated depreciation at the year end is deducted from the original cost of the asset in the balance sheet to give the ***net book value.***

You should now be able to attempt Tasks 13.1, 13.2 and 13.3 and the Objective Test at the end of this chapter.

Student activities

Task 13.1 As a group, make a list of the fixed assets which a business may own. Individually, decide what you think would be a reasonable life for each asset. Compare your answers and where there are any significant differences discuss why these have arisen.

Task 13.2 Obtain the published reports and accounts of a number of companies. Look for the section on their accounting policies and write down their depreciation policies for each class of asset. Do any of the companies you have chosen have a very different policy from the others? If so, have they explained why in the report and accounts?

Task 13.3 Construct line graphs to illustrate the differences between the straight line method and the reducing balance method of depreciation. You can use your own figures or those given in this chapter.

Question 13.1 ***Harry Heysham*** bought a ferry on 1st January 19X1, and the cost was £500,000. Anticipated life of the boat is 10 years, at the end of which time it is hoped that the boat can be sold for £100,000. The straight line method of depreciation is employed for calculations.

Required

Show the entries relevant to depreciation for Harry's business profit and loss account for the year ending 31st December 19X5, and the balance sheet as at that date.

Question 13.2 Using the data from the previous question, what would the answer be if ***H. Heysham*** employed the reducing balance method of depreciation, with a depreciation rate of 20% on the reduced balance?

Question 13.3 Peter Preston started a business on 1st January 19X1, trading as the ***Preston Packaging Company***. He started with a capital of £120,000 and made a profit during the first year of trading of £23,300.

Buildings cost £100,000 on 1st January 19X1, and Peter's policy is not to allow for depreciation in his accounts. Fixtures and fittings cost £40,000 on 1st January 19X1, and Peter decided to depreciate them on a reducing balance basis, using a 20% rate on the written-down value at the end of each year. The net book value at the end of 19X1 was therefore £32,000.

Motor vehicles cost £30,000 on 1st January 19X1, and Peter decided to write them off over four years on a straight-line basis. The net book value on 31st December 19X1 was therefore £22,500. On 2nd February 19X2, a new vehicle was purchased for £12,000, and Peter decided to apply a whole year's depreciation to this vehicle for the year ending 31st December 19X2.

Figures for the year to 31st December 19X2 were as follows:

	£	£
Salaries and wages		19,600
Office expenses		3,500
Heating and lighting		1,800
Telephone		1,400
Rates		3,600
Premises		100,000
Fixtures and fittings (NBV)		32,000
Motor vehicles – original (NBV)		22,500
Motor vehicles – new		12,000
Stock at 1st January 19X2		20,000
Sales		307,000
Purchases		247,400
Debtors		40,000
Bank balance (in credit)		8,000
Creditors		21,000
Loan (long-term)		50,000
Capital at 1st January 19X1	120,000	
Add profit for year to 31st December 19X1	23,300	
		143,300
Drawings for year ended 31st December 19X2		9,500

Additional information relative to 31st December 19X2:

Stocks:	£30,000
Heating and lighting accrued:	£300
Rates prepaid:	£900

Required

Prepare a trading and profit and loss account for Peter Preston for the year ending 31st December 19X2, and a balance sheet as at that date, relating to the business of the Preston Packaging Company.

Question 13.4 *Mary Morecambe* owns a fashion shop which she bought in 19X4. She started trading in April 19X4 and has built up what she considers to be a successful business. The following figures are available from the bookeeping records as at the 31st March 19X7:

	£
Sales	147,900
Creditors	14,300
Capital at 1st April 19X6	201,790
Purchases	89,600

	£
Salaries and wages	18,500
Administrative and general expenses	3,400
Insurance premiums	1,400
Light and heat	720
Stationery and postages	840
Advertising	1,530
Telephone	900
Business rates	6,500
Opening stock at 1st April 19X6	19,400
Shop premises	150,000
Fixtures and fittings	32,000
Estate car	10,800
Debtors	1,400
Cash at bank	13,560
Cash in till and petty cash	240
Drawings during the year	13,200

In addition, the following information is available:

Stock at 31st March 19X7 is valued at: £21,500

Electricity charges accrued at 31st March 19X7: £270

Insurance premiums paid in advance at 31st March 19X7: £200

Business rates prepaid at 31st March 19X7: £1,300

The value of the shop premises (£150,000) is the original cost when purchased in 19X4, and Mary's policy is not to allow for depreciation in the accounts.

The fixtures and fittings of the shop cost £40,000 in April 19X4, and Mary decided to depreciate them on a straight line basis over ten years. The written-down value at 1st April 19X6 was therefore £32,000, after allowing for 2 years of depreciation.

Mary bought an estate car in April 19X4 which cost £18,000 and has used it for collecting and delivering goods. She decided to depreciate it over 5 years on a straight line basis, ignoring any scrap or resale value it might have at the end of the five years. The written-down value at 1st April 19X6 was therefore £10,800, after allowing for 2 years' depreciation.

Required

Prepare a trading and profit and loss account for the year ending 31st March 19X7 and a balance sheet as at that date in vertical format, for Mary Morecambe's fashion shop.

Question 13.5 *Mary Morecambe*, whom we met in the previous question, is not happy with her depreciation policy for fixtures and fittings and her estate car. She feels that the fixtures and fittings will not last the ten years originally planned, because a new look to her shop may become essential within a shorter period of time; however, she considers that the original items will still have a good resale value when she decides to replace them. Also, concerning the estate car, she feels that five years is the time after which she will need to replace the car, but that it will have some resale value.

As a result she has asked you to make theoretical calculations which will show the figures which would have resulted if the following depreciation policies had been followed from the beginning, i.e. April, 19X4:

Fixtures and fittings: 20% per annum on a reducing balance basis (instead of 10% straight line)

Estate car: 20% per annum on a reducing balance basis (instead of 20% on a straight line basis)

Required

i) Prepare a table which compares the original (straight line) and suggested (reducing balance) calculations for depreciation of Mary's fixtures and fittings, and (separately) her estate car, for the three separate years ending 31st March 19X7. The table should show the depreciation charge against profits for each year and also the reduced balance or written down value at the end of each year.

ii) Calculate how much more (or less) depreciation the suggested revised policy would have been charged against profit in the first two years, i.e. the years ending 31st March 19X5 and 19X6.

iii) Calculate the revised figure for Mary's opening capital at 1st April 19X6 (which at present is £201,790), assuming the revised policy had been applied from April 19X4.

iv) Calculate the revised figure for net profit for the year ending 31st March 19X7, again assuming the revised policy had been applied from April 19X4.

v) Calculate the revised figure for "Owner's Worth" at 31st March 19X7, again assuming the revised policy had been applied from April 19X4.

vi) Which depreciation policy would you have recommended to Mary in April 19X4?

vii) What would you advise now, concerning the accounts for the third year ending 31st March 19X7, assuming that the accounts for the first two years cannot now be altered?

Objective test *(tick the appropriate box)*

i) A machine is purchased at the start of year 1 for £12,000 and is depreciated over 5 years on a straight-line basis. At the end of year 3, the net book value (or written-down value) is:

a) £6,000 ☐

b) £7,200 ☐

c) £4,800 ☐

d) £3,600 ☐

ii) Another machine is purchased at the start of year 1 for £30,000, and is depreciated on the reducing balance method, applying each year a depreciation rate of 12% on the written-down value. At the end of year 3 the written-down value is (to the nearest £):

a) £23,232 ☐

b) £20,444 ☐

c) £17,991 ☐

d) £19,200 ☐

iii) Office furniture is purchased at the start of year 1 for £15,000, and is depreciated on a straight line basis over 6 years. The accumulated depreciation at the end of year 4 is:

a) £10,000 ☐

b) £12,000 ☐

c) £ 7,500 ☐

d) £ 5,000 ☐

iv) The net book value of a motor vehicle at the end of three years (from date of purchase) is £10,000. If the depreciation each year is £2,500, calculated on a straight line basis, the original cost was:

- **a) £12,500** ☐
- **b) £20,000** ☐
- **c) £15,000** ☐
- **d) £17,500** ☐

v) A baker's oven, during the second year of its life, has been depreciated by £855, and its written-down value at the end of this second year is £7,695. Depreciation has been calculated on the reducing balance method by applying each year a percentage of 10% to the reduced balance: The oven originally cost:

- **a) £9,618** ☐
- **b) £9,405** ☐
- **c) £9,500** ☐
- **d) £9,310** ☐

Chapter 14

Bad debts and provision for doubtful debts

14.1 Objectives

At the end of this chapter you should be able to:

- understand what is meant by bad debts;
- understand what is meant by a provision for doubtful debts;
- distinguish between them;
- apply the principles to a set of accounts for a sole trader.

14.2 Introduction

Whenever a sale is made ***on credit***, the effect is that ***sales*** increase in the profit and loss account and ***debtors*** increase on the balance sheet.

What happens if:

a) a debtor fails to pay up, or

b) at the time of the preparation of the balance sheet, it appears that a debtor or debtors are unlikely to pay up?

The answer to (a) is that a ***bad debt*** is created. The answer to (b) is that a ***provision for doubtful debts*** is created.

The difference between a) and b) is sometimes the cause of confusion and it is best if they are regarded as separate items. Some text books sometimes refer to provisions for bad debts but we prefer to use the term provision for doubtful debts to emphasise the difference between the two items.

14.3 Bad debts and provision for doubtful debts

Bad debts represent monies that are irrecoverable. It may be that a debtor has become bankrupt, or a business has gone into liquidation with an indication that amounts owing to their creditors are unlikely to be paid. In this case, the amount of the irrecoverable debt is charged to the profit and loss account as a business expense, and deducted from the previous total of debtors on the balance sheet.

In Chapter 10, we discussed the matching convention. The treatment of bad debts above, i.e. charging the bad debts to the profit and loss account an an expense for the period in which the sale took place, conforms with the matching convention. However, quite often it is not possible to ascertain whether a debt is irrecoverable until after the accounting period in which the sale took place.

It is therefore prudent to make what is known as a ***provision,*** in an accounting period, for the estimated expense for debts which may ultimately prove to be irrecoverable or bad. Obviously, this provision can never be more than a prudent estimate. Such estimates can be made in various ways:

- A list can be made of debtors who can be regarded as doubtful. In fact, sometimes the provision is called ***provision for doubtful debts*** or ***provision for bad and doubtful debts.***
- Where this is difficult, some accountants simply apply a percentage to the amount for debtors outstanding at balance sheet date, this percentage being based on past experience, adjusted up or down depending on the state of the economy at the time.
- A more realistic method, an extension of the above, is to prepare an ***ageing schedule*** where the debtors are analysed according to the length of time that the debt has been outstanding, and to apply percentages increasing with the age of the debt.

Example

Period debts outstanding	Amounts totalling	Estimated percentage bad	Provision for doubtful debts
	£	%	£
Less than one month	100,000	0	NIL
1 – 3 months	50,000	2	1,000
4 – 6 months	30,000	3	900
6 – 12 months	20,000	5	1,000
over 12 months	10,000	50	5,000
	210,000		7,900

Using these figures as an illustration, they would appear in the accounts as follows:

In the *profit and loss account* (under expenses)

		£
Provision for doubtful debts		£7,900

In the *balance sheet* (under current assets)

	£	£
Debtors	210,000	
Less Provision for doubtful debts	7,900	
		202,100

14.4 Changes in provision for doubtful debts

Provision for doubtful debts is similar in concept to provision for depreciation, in that it is ***cumulative***. The following table illustrates this.

Example

Year	Provision for doubtful debts charged to profit & loss account		Cumulative amount of provision to be deducted from debtors on the balance sheet
	£		£
1	1,000		1,000
2	500	(increase)	1,500
3	500	(increase)	2,000
4	(200)	(decrease)	1,800
5	700	(increase)	2,500

In the case of year 4, it was obviously felt that the £2,000 cumulative provision brought forward from year 3 was too much for the position at the end of year 4. Hence a reduction of £200 to £1,800 was applied. This reduction of £200 would be shown under expenses in the Profit & Loss Account as a negative (bracketed) amount, or possibly as an addition to gross profit at the end of the Trading Account, before deducting expenses.

Example

Keith Kendal manufactures and sells mint cake. During the year ending 31st December 19X5 his sales totalled £96,000, and his debtors at the end of the year amounted to one month's sales. This was after allowing for two of his debtors who had gone 'bad'. One of these had become bankrupt, owing Keith £300, and other, who had owed him £550, had given a fictitious address and was untraceable.

Last year (ending 31st December 19X4), Keith had made a provision for doubtful debts in his accounts of £400, and now feels, in view of experience, that this provision should be increased to £1,000 for this year.

Required

Show the relevant entries in Keith Kendal's accounts for the year ending 31st December 19X5.

Solution

Keith Kendal

Profit & loss account for year ending 31st December 19X5 (extract)

	£	£
Sales		96,000
Expenses:		
Bad debts	850	
Increase in provision for doubtful debts	600	

Balance Sheet as at 31st December 19X5 (extract)

	£	£
Current assets		
Debtors	8,000	
Less Provision for doubtful debts (£400 + £600)	1,000	
		7,000

You should now be able to attempt Question 14.1 at the end of this chapter.

The following example illustrates the accounts of a sole trader, and covers aspects of this and previous chapters.

Example

William Whitehaven, a local commercial photographer, is thinking of joining forces with a friend who is also a photographer. This friend has asked to see William's balance sheet, and William has asked you to prepare one for him. William has provided you with the following information as at 30th April 19X9:

	£
Photography equipment, original cost	20,000
Estate car, original cost	12,000
Stocks of materials	2,000
Balance at bank (in credit)	4,300
Debtors	5,000
Creditors	2,400
Drawings during the past year	12,000
Long-term loan	5,000

Additional information provided is:

- ❒ Both the photographic equipment and the car were purchased on the 1st May 19X8, and are depreciated on a straight-line basis. The photography equipment has an expected life of 5 years, and the car 4 years, with insignificant scrap or resale value.
- ❒ William owes rent of £400 in respect of the past year.
- ❒ Included in debtors is a client who has owed £500 for over 11 months, and seems very unlikely to pay.

You have prepared a profit and loss account for William, allowing for the above adjustments, and the net profit for the past year amounted to £15,000.

Required

Prepare a balance sheet, in vertical format, as at 30th April 19X9, for William's photographic business.

Solution

William Whitehaven – Photographic Business
Balance sheet as at 30th April 19X9

	£	£ Cost	£ Acc.Dep'n	£ NBV
Fixed assets				
Photography equipment		20,000	4,000	16,000
Estate car		12,000	3,000	9,000
		32,000	7,000	25,000
Current assets				
Stocks		2,000		
Debtors	5,000			
Less Provision for doubtful debt	500			
		4,500		
Bank		4,300		
			10,800	
Current liabilities				
Creditors		2,400		
Rent accrued		400		
			2,800	
				8,000
				33,000
Less Long-term loan				5,000
				28,000
Financed by:				
Opening capital (1st May 19X8) *			25,000	
Add Net profit for year			15,000	
			40,000	
Less Drawings			12,000	
				28,000

* William's opening capital has to be deduced from the other figures, i.e. it is the balancing figure.

You should now be able to attempt Questions 14.2 and 14.3 and Task 14.3 at the end of this chapter.

14.5 Summary

Sales are shown in the profit and loss account in total, regardless of the amount of cash received. This raises the problem of customers who may not pay. ***Bad debts*** are shown as an expense in the profit and loss account and represent money which is known to be irrecoverable.

Provision for doubtful debts is an estimate of the amount of money owed by debtors which may not be recovered. Only the increase or decrease in the cumulative provision for doubtful debts is shown in the ***profit and loss account***. The cumulative figure is shown as a deduction from debtors in the ***balance sheet.***

You should now be able to attempt Tasks 14.1, 14.2 and the Objective Test at the end of this chapter.

Student activities

Task 14.1 You work for a company where your representatives make sales without worrying about the credit-worthiness of the customers. Write a circular which explains how the company is affected by bad debts.

Task 14.2 You have just started to work for a small company where the practice has been to make a provision for doubtful debts at the year end as a percentage of outstanding debtors. Write a memorandum to the managing director stating which other methods can be used, and the one you recommend.

Task 14.3 Your friend works in an American company. The accountant there has a sign on his desk saying *Sales are a gift until the cash comes in.* Explain to your friend what principles are involved in this statement.

Question 14.1 Bert Barrow manufactures and sells furnaces, trading as *Barrow & Company.* During the year ending 31st March 19X7, he incurred bad debts totalling £8,500. His sales for the year totalled £2,500,000.

At the end of the previous year (ended 31st March 19X6), his cumulative provision for doubtful debts was £12,000. At 31st March 19X7, the position of his debtors was as shown in the following ageing schedule:

Period debt outstanding	Debtors	Estimated bad debts
	£	%
Less than one month	250,000	0
1 – 3 months	120,000	3
4 – 6 months	50,000	4
6 – 12 months	10,000	5
over 12 months	6,000	75
	436,000	

Required

Show the relevant entries in the accounts for Barrow & Company for the year ended 31st March 19X7.

Question 14.2 *W Workington & Company* is a trading business owned by Wilhelmina Workington. Her books show the following figures at 30th June 19X4:

	£	£
Buildings at cost	55,000	
Fixtures at cost	14,000	
Provision for depreciation of fixtures		5,600
Debtors	17,000	
Creditors		12,650
Cash at bank	1,850	
Stock at 1.7.19X3	42,250	
Purchases	84,750	
Sales		130,500
Delivery expenses	1,350	
Discounts allowed	270	
Interest on loan	3,800	
Salaries and wages	16,500	
Office expenses	2,470	
Insurances	5,300	
Bad debts	1,610	
Provision for doubtful debts		3,000
Long-term loan		42,000
W. Workington: Capital at 1.7.19X3		52,400
	246,150	246,150

At 30th June 19X4, the following information is also available:

- Stock is valued at £55,300.
- Wages unpaid amount to £350.
- Office expenses accrued are £130.
- Insurances prepaid are £400.
- The provision for doubtful debts is to be reduced to 10% of debtors.
- Depreciation of fixtures is to continue on a straight-line basis at the rate of 10% on cost. Buildings are not depreciated.

Required

Prepare for W. Workington & Company, in vertical format:

i) a profit statement (profit and loss account) for the year to 30th June 19X4;

ii) a balance sheet as at 30th June 19X4.

Question 14.3 George Green, who trades as ***Gretna Trading***, started business on 1st January 19X5 buying and selling sports equipment. George has asked you to prepare some accounts for him for the year to 31st December 19X5. He has left the following message on your answering machine:

"Aunt Gertie left me £5,000 in her will, and this formed my initial capital in my Gretna Trading account at my bank. A friend also loaned me £2,000 at ten per cent per annum interest. He gave me a cheque which I also banked. I bought an estate car to help with my collection and delivery of stock, and I made £500 profit on this car deal. The salesman wanted £1,700 for the car but I beat him down to £1,200, and I paid him by cheque. I reckon the car is good for 4 years before it goes to the scrapyard.

I rent a garage to keep my stock in, and this costs me £400 per annum. I've paid £500 so far (by cheque) as the owner insists on quarterly payments in advance.

My first bit of trading was to buy 3,000 pairs of trainers for £9,000. I've paid a cheque to the supplier for £6,000, and shall have to pay the balance soon. I've sold 2,500 pairs so far for £9,500 cash, and am owed £500. Twenty per cent of this is dodgy, but the rest should be collectable. I've banked all the cash received so far.

Then I bought some trampolines – a job lot of 200 for £4,000 (by cheque). I've sold 180 of these for £5,400 cash, but the remainder are faulty, and I've found someone who says he can repair them, and will take them off my hands for £100.

I also do a good line in track-suits. 300 of them cost me only £1,500. I haven't paid for them yet, since a number of them appear to have faulty stitching. I've complained to the supplier who says he will reduce the price to £900. I think I'll agree, since I know someone who will look them all over and repair as necessary for £2 a track-suit. I can sell them for £10 each, and make a profit of £1,500, if my maths is right.

The cash I got for the trampolines I've used to pay some bills: petrol for the estate car came to £500, and electricity for the garage £200. I've also spent £4,500 on myself; after all, a man has to eat!

I also had a holiday in August, which cost £700, but I paid for that by cheque from the Gretna account. I must also pay the first year's interest on the loan soon, I suppose."

Required

Prepare a trading and profit and loss account for Gretna Trading for the year ending 31st December 19X5, and a balance sheet as at that date. Show the cash and bank balances separately on the balance sheet, and present the figures in vertical format.

Objective test *(tick the appropriate box)*

i) Bad debts are dealt with in the accounts of a trader by:

a) showing them as a deduction from debtors on the balance sheet ☐

b) increasing the provision for bad debts ☐

c) charging them as an expense in the profit and loss account ☐

d) both (a) and (c) above ☐

ii) A provision for doubtful debts is dealt with in the accounts of a trader by:

a) charging the current year's adjustment of the provision as an expense in the profit and loss account ☐

b) deducting the provision from debtors on the balance sheet ☐

c) adjusting the gross profit in the profit and loss account ☐

d) both (a) and (b) above ☐

iii) In the accounts of a sole trader, last year's provision for doubtful debts amounted to £800. This year, debtors are £7,000 and the provision is to be 10% of debtors. The following is true:

a) £1,500 is shown as a provision for doubtful debts in the profit and loss account ☐

b) £100 is deducted from debtors on the balance sheet with the heading "less provision for doubtful debts" ☐

c) The profit and loss account shows "reduction in provision for doubtful debts: £100" ☐

d) £700 is charged to the profit and loss account as "provision for bad debts" ☐

iv) The ageing schedule of XYZ Company is as follows:

Period debt outstanding	**Debtors**	**Estimated bad debts**
	£	%
less than one month	9,000	0
1 – 3 months	4,000	5
4 – 6 months	2,000	10
over 6 months	1,000	15

Select the correct response to the following statements:

a) The profit and loss account is charged with £550 bad debts. ☐

b) £550 is added to last year's doubtful debts provision. ☐

c) Debtors are reduced by 10% on the balance sheet. ☐

d) None of these. ☐

v) Using the ageing schedule in Question (iv), if the provision for doubtful debts last year was £600, the provision this year should be:

a) increased by £550 ☐

b) increased by £50 ☐

c) decreased by £50 ☐

d) none of these ☐

Chapter 15

The relationship between financial statements

15.1 Objectives

At the end of this chapter you should be able to:

- appreciate the relationship between budgeted cash flow forecasts, profit and loss accounts and balance sheets;
- construct these inter-related documents using budgeted data;
- appreciate the difference between budgeted profits and budgeted cash flows.

15.2 Introduction

In this section we have been looking at the accounts of a sole trader, particularly the ***profit and loss account*** and the ***balance sheet***. We have been looking at these documents as records of what has actually happened in the past. In this chapter we shall be looking at the future, i.e. ***forecast*** or ***budgeted profit and loss accounts*** and ***balance sheets***, and seeing how they relate to a document we considered in chapter 5: the ***cash flow forecast***. If you have forgotten how to prepare a cash flow forecast, you would be well advised to revise Chapter 5 at this stage.

15.3 The relationship between cash flow forecasts and the budgeted profit and loss accounts and budgeted balance sheets

Example

Peter Pontefract has inherited £30,000, and plans to commence a confectionery business trading as *Pontefract* on 1st April 19X1.

His plans include the following:

- Equipment costing £16,000 will be bought and paid for on 1st April. Further equipment will be bought and paid for on 1st July, costing £8,000. Peter estimates that this equipment will last 10 years with no scrap value, and he will charge depreciation in his accounts from the date of purchase on a straight-line basis.
- Wages will be £2,000 per month for the first 3 months, and £3,000 per month thereafter.
- Selling and administration costs are expected to be £1,200 per month for the first 3 months, rising to £1,400 per month thereafter, payable in the month when the costs are incurred.
- Premises will be rented at £7,200 per annum, payable quarterly in advance starting on 1st April 19X1.
- Selling price of goods is calculated at purchase price plus 50%.
- Terms of trade are for customers to pay in the month following receipt of goods, and Peter has arranged with his suppliers for payment to be made two months after the month of purchase.

❒ Peter's planned sales and purchases are:

	Sales (£'000)	Purchases (£'000)
April	12	30
May	16	24
June	20	20
July	24	20
August	24	20
September	24	20
	120	134

Required

Prepare the following ***budgeted*** documents for Pontefract:

i) Cash flow forecast for the first 6 months' of trading, showing the expected bank balances at the end of each month.

ii) Trading and profit and loss account for the 6 months to 30th September 19X1.

iii) Balance sheet as at 30th September 19X1.

iv) A brief report on the viability of the project.

Solution

Workings:

i)

	Sales (£'000)		Purchases (£'000)	
	Invoiced	Cash received	Invoiced	Paid
April	12		30	
May	16	12	24	
June	20	16	20	30
July	24	20	20	24
August	24	24	20	20
September	24	24	20	20
Totals	120	96	134	94
	Debtors	24	Creditors	40
		120		134

ii) Depreciation of equipment:

£16,000 × 10% p.a. = £1,600 pa ∴ 6 months = £800
£8,000 × 10% p.a. = £800 pa ∴ 3 months = £200
£1,000

iii) Stock: See Trading Account. This is calculated as follows:

Sales are £120,000 (data) which is 50% on cost of sales. Cost of sales is therefore two-thirds of sales value, i.e. £80,000. Stock is therefore the difference between purchases of £134,000 (data) and cost of sales of £80,000.

i)

Pontefract

Cash flow forecast for the first six months of trading

	April	May	June	July	Aug	Sept	Total
	£	£	£	£	£	£	£
Receipts							
Capital	30,000						30,000
Sales		12,000	16,000	20,000	24,000	24,000	96,000
Total (A)	30,000	12,000	16,000	20,000	24,000	24,000	126,000
Payments							
Purchases			30,000	24,000	20,000	20,000	94,000
Wages	2,000	2,000	2,000	3,000	3,000	3,000	15,000
Selling/Admin	1,200	1,200	1,200	1,400	1,400	1,400	7,800
Rent	1,800			1,800			3,600
Equipment	16,000			8,000			24,000
Total (B)	21,000	3,200	33,200	38,200	24,400	24,400	144,400
Net cash flow (A–B)	9,000	8,800	(17,200)	(18,200)	(400)	(400)	(18,400)
Balances:							
Start of month	nil	9,000	17,800	600	(17,600)	(18,000)	nil
End of month	9,000	17,800	600	(17,600)	(18,000)	(18,400)	(18,400)

ii)

Pontefract

Budgeted trading and profit & loss account for the 6 months ending 30th September 19X1

	£	£
Sales		120,000
Less Cost of sales:		
Purchases	134,000	
Less Closing stock	54,000	
		80,000
Gross Profit		40,000
Less Expenses:		
Wages	15,000	
Selling & administration expenses	7,800	
Rent	3,600	
Depreciation of equipment	1,000	
		27,400
Net profit		12,600

iii)

Pontefract

Budgeted balance sheet as at 30th September 19X1

	£ Cost	£ Acc.Dep'n	£ NBV
Fixed assets			
Equipment	24,000	1,000	23,000
Current assets			
Stock	54,000		
Debtors	24,000		
		78,000	
Current liabilities			
Creditors	40,000		
Overdraft	18,400		
		58,400	
Net current assets			19,600
Capital employed			42,600
Represented by:			
Capital		30,000	
Profit for six months		12,600	
			42,600

iv) Report:

- Net profit is £12,600, which is nearly 30% of the capital employed (at 30th September 19X1) of £42,600. This would seem to be a reasonable return. It is also 42% of the initial capital of £30,000.
- The cash flow forecast reveals that the business will experience a cash flow deficit during July, August and September. It will therefore be necessary to arrange finance, e.g. an overdraft with the bank. This might require security (e.g. Peter's home). Otherwise Peter will have to obtain a loan, or raise money by some other means. It may be necessary to prepare a further cash flow forecast for the six months to 31st March 19X2, to see if the money required is likely to increase or decrease. For example, a full year's forecast might show that an overdraft or loan was only necessary until, say, December, in which case the finance needed would only be temporary. Another possibility would be to lease the equipment, rather than buy it. This would obviate the need for the extra finance, at least in the short term.
- Note that although the budgeted profit is £12,600, the cash position deteriorates from £30,000 at the start to an overdraft of £18,400 at the end of the six months. Why is there such a discrepancy?

	£
Starting with cash of	30,000
and making a net profit of	12,600
you might expect to end up with	42,600
instead of an overdraft of	(18,400)
which is a difference of	61,000

The balance sheet (which was a blank to start with) reveals:

Equipment purchased	24,000
Debtors funded	24,000
Stock purchased	54,000
	102,000

	£
but creditors have provided financing of	40,000
	62,000
and the depreciation fund has been built up by	1,000
which explains the difference of	61,000

This explanation is, in fact, a simple cash flow statement, which is another of the documents to be found in published accounts.

❐ It is always useful to reconcile the key figures on your three financial statements. For example, you will see that from the trading and profit and loss account, your total sales for the period are £120,000. The cash flow forecast shows that the total cash you expect to receive is £96,000. The difference must be debtors of £24,000 which appear in the balance sheet. These calculations could be shown like this:

	£
Level of sales achieved as per profit and loss account	120,000
Less cash received as per cash flow forecast	96,000
Figure of debtors for the balance sheet	24,000

The same kind of reconciliation could be carried out for purchases/creditors. By doing this you are less likely to make a mistake.

When preparing these statements, do not confuse cash flow with profit. All sales, whether for cash or on credit, are shown on the ***profit and loss account***. Receipts from sales or debtors are shown on the ***cash flow forecast***. The difference between sales and receipts (debtors) appears on the ***balance sheet***.

Never include depreciation in the cash flow forecast. The cash flow occurs when the asset is purchased. However, do remember to include the purchase price of the asset in the cash flow forecast in the month in which the asset is paid for.

You should now be able to attempt Questions 15.1, 15.2 and 15.3 at the end of this chapter.

15.4 Summary

Budgeted statements such as ***cash flow forecasts, profit and loss accounts*** and ***balance sheets*** enable managers to look into the future and see the possible financial consequences of their plans. They may indicate poor profits, in which case plans should be revised by adjusting selling prices, controlling expenses etc. Cash flow problems may be highlighted, in which case timings of cash flows should be examined and extra funding arranged if necessary. Ratios should be examined (see Chapter 22) if balance sheets are unsatisfactory and plans revised accordingly.

You should now be able to attempt Tasks 15.1, 15.2, 15.3 and the Objective Test at the end of this chapter.

Student activities

Task 15.1 Students on an accounting course are going to hold a "Brains Quiz". Devise five questions for the panel to answer, which will demonstrate their understanding of the relationship between financial statements.

Task 15.2 Divide the group into pairs. One member of each pair should prepare a simple question on the relationship between financial statements (Question 15.1 The Grimsby Company is a good example) which the other member should try to answer.

Task 15.3 Construct a diagram to show the relationship between a cash flow forecast, a profit and loss account and a balance sheet.

Question 15.1 Gill Grimsby, trading as ***The Grimsby Company***, starts a business on 1st July 19X2 with a capital of £50,000, some of which she immediately spends on fixed assets, costing £20,000. Budgeted figures for the first six months are:

	£'000
Sales	420
Cost of materials actually sold	170
Labour	126
Overheads (including depreciation for 6 months in the sum of £2,000)	98
Materials purchased	190

Payments for labour and overheads can be regarded as evenly spread over the six month period.

	Receipts from debtors £'000	Payments to creditors £'000
July	35	35
August	42	35
September	49	28
October	56	14
November	70	14
December	84	14
	336	140

Required

Tabulate the budgeted figures into:

i) a cash flow forecast for the first six months;

ii) a budgeted profit & loss statement for the period to 31st December 19X2;

iii) a budgeted balance sheet as at that date.

Question 15.2 ***Middlesbrough Marinas*** is a privately owned business, which is being planned early in December 19X2, with the main purpose of trading in holiday pleasure craft. Initial capital is £100,000, to be banked in the business bank account during December 19X2.

The owner proposes to commence trading on 1st January 19X3. During December 19X2, fixed assets costing £40,000 will be installed and paid for. Sales are estimated to be:

- £12,000 in January 19X3
- £20,000 in February 19X3
- £40,000 per month thereafter.

Gross profit (i.e. sales price less the purchase price of the boats) is expected to run at a uniform rate of 25% of the sales price.

Customers will be required to pay for boats by the last day of the second month after that in which the boats were collected by them, e.g. sales in January should be paid for by 31st March. Purchasing is to be so arranged that initially, and at the end of every month, the stock will be exactly sufficient (and no more) to supply all the expected sales in the following month. Trade creditors are to be paid on the last day of the month after that in which the boats were purchased.

It is expected that wages and salaries will amount to £2,000 in each month and paid during the month in which they are incurred. Similarly for general expenses of £3,000 per month. Any temporary excess of payments over receipts is to be financed by a bank overdraft and a bank has agreed to this.

Required

Prepare the following financial statements for ***Middlesbrough Marinas***,

i) a budgeted cash flow forecast for the seven months to 30th June 19X3, showing the expected bank balances at the end of each of the six months ending 30th June;

ii) a simple budgeted trading and profit and loss account for the seven months ending 30th June 19X3;

iii) a balance sheet as at that date;

iv) a brief report commenting on the benefits to be gained from preparing such budgeted statements.

Question 15.3 Sid Scarborough has owned several businesses which he has built up and then sold. As a result, he has accumulated capital of £125,000 which he plans to invest in a new business, trading in sports equipment to be called ***Sid's Sports Equipment and Accessories***. He decides to commence trading on 1st April 19X9.

He intends to rent a warehouse at a cost of £30,000 per annum, payable quarterly in advance, starting on 1st April 19X9. He will need storage and handling equipment which will cost £64,000, and this will have to be paid for on 1st April. Life expectancy of this equipment is 10 years, with no scrap value. Sid favours the straight line method of depreciation.

Wages are budgeted for at £8,500 per month, rising to £10,000 per month from 1st July. Selling, administration and distribution costs are expected to be £5,000 per month for the first 3 months, rising to £6,000 per month thereafter, payable in the month in which they are incurred.

The selling price of goods is expected to average the purchase price plus 60%. Terms of trade are for customers to pay in the month follwing receipt of goods, and the same terms have been arranged with Sid's suppliers. Planned sales and purchases for the first six months are:

	Sales	Purchases
	£	£
April	50,000	60,000
May	70,000	60,000
June	80,000	60,000
July	90,000	60,000
August	100,000	60,000
September	90,000	60,000
	480,000	360,000

Required

Prepare the following for Sid's Sports Equipment and Accessories:

i) a monthly cash flow forecast for the six months ending 30th September 19X9;

ii) a budgeted profit and loss statement for the same period;

iii) a budgeted balance sheet as at 30th September 19X9;

iv) a brief report commenting on the budgeted plans and giving Sid any advice which you consider to be appropriate.

Objective test *(tick the appropriate box)*

i) Depreciation of a particular asset for the year ending 31st December 19X4 is calculated as being £500. This will have the effect of:

a) increasing the working capital on the balance sheet by £500 ☐

b) reducing the cash flow for the year by £500 ☐

c) decreasing the profit shown by the profit and loss account by £500 ☐

d) increasing the net current assets by £500 ☐

ii) A company borrows £10,000 from its bank on 1st January as a five-year loan. The interest is 15% per annum, payable at the end of each quarter. Select the correct response to the following statements:

a) The loan will be shown on the balance sheet as £8,500 at 31st December. ☐

b) The cash flow forecast will show £375 under receipts during the month of March. ☐

c) The half-yearly accounts will show £1,500 as bank interest under expenses in the profit and loss account. ☐

d) None of these ☐

iii) The following budget information is available for a company in respect of next year:

Cost of sales	£70,000
Purchases	£80,000
Payments for materials	£60,000

Select the correct response to the following statements:

a) Stock at the year end will be worth £20,000. ☐

b) Creditors at the year end will be £20,000. ☐

c) Sales for the year will be £50,000. ☐

d) Gross Loss for the year will be £10,000. ☐

iv) In the example of Pontefract in this chapter the minimum amount needed to be introduced (either as a loan or as additional capital) during April to avoid an overdraft at any time during the 6 months ending 30th September 19X1 would be:

a) £18,400 ☐

b) £17,800 ☐

c) £ 9,000 ☐

d) £17,600 ☐

v) There are other ways of avoiding the overdraft referred to in (iv) above. One possible adequate method might be:

a) to lease the equipment rather than buying it ☐

b) to delay paying creditors for a further two weeks ☐

c) to allow only two weeks rather than one month's credit ☐

d) to pay all wages monthly rather than weekly ☐

Assignment C

Sam Shanklin

Context

You have recently received the following letter from your uncle, Sam Shanklin:

28th November, 19X5

Dear Jo,

I hear you are on a course in business studies, and I wonder if you can help me.

I am thinking of setting up a business retailing carpets. As you know, I have worked for many years in a carpet store, and understand the market fairly well. Since becoming redundant, I must obviously find some way of making a living.

If you think the project is viable, I shall go to an accountant to get his professional advice, but I have no experience of accounts and things like that, and, if you could analyse my proposals, this would help me a lot.

I have found suitable shop premises which I can occupy at a quarterly rental of £1,000 payable in advance on the first day of each quarter, starting on 1st January, 19X6.

I shall have to buy some shop fittings, for which I have been quoted £13,800. I expect they will last about ten years, before I have to scrap them and buy new.

I shall, of course, be working full-time, but I shall need an assistant. Your cousin, Fred, says he would help, and his wages, National Insurance and so on will cost about £500 per month. I'll pay him monthly.

You could allow for heating and lighting of the shop at, say, £600 per month, starting on 1st January, payable monthly at the end of each month. Telephone charges will be about £200 per quarter, payable at the end of each quarter.

I have arranged with carpet manufacturers to pay for purchases at the end of the month following month of purchase. I expect these to be £1,000 per month, except that, for the first three and last three months of the year (winter being slightly busier than the summer), they will be £100 more per month. I should have one month's purchases in stock at any one time.

Sales, I expect, will be £3,600 per month for the first three months, increasing to £4,000 per month for the following six months, and then dropping back to £3,600 per month for the last three months of the year. Half of these sales will be for cash, the remainder, of necessity, being on credit. Of my credit customers, if past experience is anything to go by, half will pay on time, i.e. in the month following month of sale, and the other half in the month following that. I doubt if any credit customers will go 'bad' during the year, but you could allow a 10% reserve at the year end if you think that would be prudent.

Many customers will require their carpets to be fitted, and I shall sub-contract this work. I estimate this sub-contract work will cost £150 per month, payable one month after completion of the work.

My brother has offered me a loan of £5,000 on 1st January. He suggests 12% (cheaper than the bank) per annum interest, payable half-yearly on 30th June and 31st December. He wants his money back within the next three years. I'll accept his offer, and aim to pay him back in about two years' time.

I'll have to be careful during the first year, but I should make enough money to draw, say, £500 per month out of the business to live on.

I've had a preliminary chat with my bank manager about an overdraft. He says no go, not unless he gets an accountant's report on the project, with a cash flow forecast, whatever that may be, and also he would want my house as security. So he can get lost. I've decided to finance it myself out of my redundancy lump sum and savings which total £12,500. Do you think this will be enough? I'll aim to keep at least £250 in credit at the bank.

Any figures and advice and so on would be helpful. What do you want for Christmas (within reason!)?

Yours as ever,

Uncle Sam

Student activities

Reply to your Uncle Sam, showing him how professional a student you can be. Surprise him. You should include the following in or with your letter:

i) a cash flow forecast for the year to 31st December 19X6, showing the initial capital your uncle will need to introduce into the business;

ii) a forecast trading and profit and loss account for the year ending 31st December 19X6;

iii) a forecast balance sheet as at 31st December 19X6;

iv) comments on the foregoing three statements, which you consider need explanation, bearing in mind that your uncle, though intelligent, is not experienced in accounting terminology;

v) any other comments and advice which you consider would be helpful to your uncle.

Format

A letter to your uncle with statements and comments suitably appended.

Objectives

In this assignment, the student should show an appreciation and understanding of:

- ❐ cash planning and personal cash flow;
- ❐ the role of the accountant in giving advice on personal finance;
- ❐ simple final accounts;
- ❐ planning the financial needs of an organisation or project.

References

Chapters 5, 10–15.

Concepts and control

This section (Chapters 16-19) is concerned with the different types of records which are maintained by businesses and the accounting concepts used.

Chapter 16 looks at situations where a business has either not maintained adequate accounting records or some of the records have been lost or destroyed. Methods for deducing missing figures are explained and as well as introducing new material, this chapter serves as a useful reinforcement for understanding the trading and profit and loss account and balance sheet.

In Chapter 17 we examine some of the source documents supporting business transactions and Chapter 18 is concerned with the proper recording of cash transactions.

The final chapter in this section, Chapter 19, discusses accounting concepts and conventions. This provides a valuable framework and draws together many of the issues introduced in earlier chapters.

Chapter 16

Incomplete records

16.1 Objectives

At the end of this chapter you should be able to:

- explain what is meant by single entry bookkeeping;
- draw up a statement of affairs;
- make adjustments to cash records for accruals and prepayments;
- apply formal layouts and percentage calculations to deduce missing figures;
- construct a trading and profit and loss account and balance sheet from incomplete records.

16.2 Introduction

Although large businesses keep sophisticated ***records***, many small businesses do not have the time or expertise to do this. The owners may rely on bank records, odd slips of paper and what they can remember to keep control of the business. This presents a problem at the end of the year when a trading and profit and loss account and a balance sheet are required. The information from the business will be ***incomplete*** and the accountant will have to make adjustments to the original records to obtain the correct figures.

This process of constructing full accounts from incomplete records is a favourite topic for examiners. Sometimes it is referred to as ***single entry bookkeeping***, because the business has not maintained a system of ***double entry bookkeeping*** which would have provided all the information required. Usually the main information available is a cash record and bank statement with notes on amounts owed to and owing by the company at the beginning and end of the financial year.

Both in the examination room and in practice, incomplete records problems are not confined to small businesses. A company may maintain a good accounting system, but an event such as a fire, computer breakdown, or theft may mean that some information is missing at the year end. This will entail making many adjustments to arrive at the correct figures for the trading and profit and loss account and balance sheet.

In this chapter we examine problems concerned with incomplete records. This involves some of the topics which were introduced in Chapter 12 and you may wish to revise that chapter first.

16.3 Typical problems

At the heart of most incomplete records examination questions is the fact that profit and cash are not the same thing. It is easiest to demonstrate this by looking at the first year of a new business. Later in the chapter we will consider the adjustments made for a continuing business.

Let us assume that a trader in his first year of business receives £9,000 cash for ***sales*** he has made during the year, but is still owed £2,000 by customers at the year end. The sales figure for the profit and loss account is £11,000. This is calculated by adding the £2,000 that is owed to the £9,000 already received. In the balance sheet it will be shown that debtors owe the business £2,000.

The adjustments are similar in respect of ***purchases*** made by the company. If a business has made cash payments to its suppliers totalling £29,000, but still owes £2,500 at the year end for goods it has received, the total figure for purchases in the trading and profit and loss account is £31,500. On the balance sheet there will be a figure of £2,500 for trade creditors.

> *You should now be able to attempt Question 16.1 at the end of this chapter.*

16.4 Prepayments

As well as the purchase and sale of goods, a business incurs other expenses. Some of these are not paid completely by the end of the year. Some expenses have been paid in advance and are known as ***prepayments***. A good example of an expense paid in advance is rates. The date on which the business has to pay its rate demand may not coincide with the year end of the company so there will be a prepayment. The amount of the prepayment will have to be deducted from the total paid by the business to obtain the correct figure of expense for the profit statement. The prepayment will be shown under current assets on the balance sheet.

Example

L. Frome in her first year of trading pays a cheque of £30,000 for business rates. This payment covers the 12 months of the current financial year and the first three months of the next year.

Required

What amount should be shown in the profit and loss account and balance sheet?

Solution

The correct amount to put in the profit and loss account is:

$$\frac{\text{£30,000}}{\text{15 months}} \times 12 \text{ months} = \text{£24,000 for the year}$$

The figure of £24,000 is put on the profit and loss account and a figure of £6,000 is shown under current assets as a prepayment in the balance sheet. This is an asset because it represents something that the business has paid for, but from which it has not yet received the benefit.

16.5 Accruals

If a business has not paid for all the expenses it has incurred during the year the amounts still owing at the year end are known as ***accruals***. These have to be added to the cash or cheque payments made during the year to obtain the total cost incurred for the profit and loss account. The amounts outstanding will be shown on the balance sheet under current liabilities with the heading of Accruals.

Example

The cash record of a business shows that it has paid motor vehicle repairs of £3,600, but there is an invoice outstanding at the year end for £500.

Required

What is the amount of vehicle repairs to be put in the profit and loss account for the year and what entry will be made in the balance sheet?

Solution

The total expense incurred to be put in the profit and loss account is £4,100. This is the amount of cash paid of £3,600 plus the invoice outstanding of £500. In the balance sheet an amount of £500 will be shown as an accrual under current liabilities as this represents something the business owes at the end of the year.

You should now be able to attempt Question 16.2 at the end of this chapter.

16.6 Adjustments in a continuing business

In the above examples we saw that where there is an amount owed by the business at the year end and we know the amount of cash paid during the year, the figures must be added to obtain the correct amount to enter on the trading and profit and loss account of the business. The amount owed at the year end will appear on the balance sheet.

The position for a business which has been trading for some years previously is very similar, but you may have to make ***adjustments*** to allow for items in respect of the previous financial year. The rule is to ensure that you always look at the balance sheet at the end of the previous financial year.

16.7 Trade creditors and accruals

When dealing with ***trade creditors*** and ***accruals*** you must remember that any cash payment made during the current financial year will first be used to pay amounts showing as liabilities at the end of the previous financial year. An adjustment must then be made for amounts owing at the end of the current financial year to obtain the correct figure for the profit and loss account.

Example

On the 31 December 19X6 *Jane Kingston* owed £500 for rent. During 19X7 she paid cash of £1,250 in respect of rent, but at the end of that year still owed £600.

Required

What is the figure for rent to be included in the trading and profit and loss account for the year ended 31 December 19X7?

Solution

The calculation is as follows:	£
Cash paid in 19X7	1,250
Less due on 31 December 19X6	500
	750
Add amount due on 31 December 19X7	600
Correct figure for year ended 31st December 19X7	1,350

The above layout is very suitable for calculating the amount to be entered in the trading and profit and loss account.

You should now be able to attempt Questions 16.3 at the end of this chapter.

16.8 Finding the missing figure

In some examination questions you may be given the figure for the trading and profit and loss account, but some other figure is missing; for example the amount still owing at the year end. This can easily be calculated by using the format above as in the following example.

Example

At the 31 December 19X7 the trade creditors amounted to £500. The trading and profit and loss account for the year ended 31 December 19X8 showed a figure for purchases of £900 and our records showed that we paid our creditors £1,000 cash in that year.

Required

What did we owe our creditors at the 31 December 19X8?

Solution

If we use the above layout, inserting the figures we know, we get:

	£
Cash paid in 19X8	1,000
Less due on 31 December 19X7	500
	500
Add amount due on 31 December 19X8	x
Amount in profit and loss account	900

The missing figure must be £400 and this is the amount we owe our trade creditors on 31 December 19X8.

You should now be able to attempt Question 16.4 at the end of this chapter.

16.9 Trade debtors and prepayments

Debtors should cause few problems as we are only doing the reverse of the calculations we did above for creditors.

Example

A business is owed £600 at the end of 19X2. During 19X3 it receives cash of £2,000 from its customers and is owed £500 at the year end.

Required

What is the figure of sales to be shown on the trading and profit and loss account?

Solution

Modifying the above layout slightly, the known figures can be inserted:

	£
Cash received in 19X3	2,000
Less owed on 31 December 19X2	600
	1,400
Add amount owed on 31 December 19X3	500
Amount for sales in profit and loss account	1,900

Sometimes students experience difficulties when dealing with ***prepayments***. If you refer to the previous section on prepayments you will see that we deducted the prepayment at the end of the current financial year from the cash paid in the year. The resulting figure was the correct amount to be shown on the profit and loss account. We can simply extend this approach to account for any prepayments made in the previous financial year.

Example

A company had made a prepayment of £600 in respect of insurance as at the 31 December 19X5. During the year ended 31 December 19X6 cash payments for insurance of £4,000 were made. This amount included £1,000 in respect of 19X7.

Required

What is the correct figure for insurance to be entered in the profit and loss account?

Solution

The main point to remember is that the prepayment at 31 December 19X5 of £600 is part of our total liability for the year ended 31 December 19X6. The layout is:

	£
Prepayment at the 31 December 19X5	600
Add cash paid in 19X6	4,000
	4,600
Less prepayment at the 31 December 19X6	1,000
Amount for profit statement for 19X6	3,600

16.10 Using layouts

In some problems key figures are missing and a certain degree of ingenuity is required to calculate the missing figure. It may be possible by using the ***standard layout*** or ***format*** for a profit and loss account or balance sheet to calculate the missing figure by deduction. In some instances relationships between figures can be expressed in ***percentage terms*** and you need to apply these to calculate the figures. This may require, in addition, the use of a standard layout to arrive at the missing figure.

This is very simple as long as you remember the standard layout for the specific financial statement needed. If you still have difficulty remembering the items you would normally find on a profit and loss account and balance sheet, work through the examples in earlier chapters. The following example illustrates the use of layouts.

Example

A business has made a gross profit of £10,000 on sales of £50,000. At the beginning of the year it had an opening stock of £4,000 and made purchases during the year of £42,000.

Required

What is the figure of closing stock?

Solution

To solve this you must draw up a standard format for the trading and profit and loss account, leaving a blank for the missing figure

Trading and Profit and Loss Account

	£	£
Sales		50,000
Less Cost of sales		
Opening stock	4,000	
Purchases	42,000	
	46,000	
Less Closing stock	x	y
Gross Profit		10,000

The missing figures can now be inserted. The cost of sales (y) must be £40,000 to give the gross profit of £10,000. This means that a closing stock figure(x) of £6,000 must be inserted as the figure to be subtracted from the £46,000. The completed layout looks like this:

Trading and Profit and Loss Account

	£	£
Sales		50,000
Less Cost of sales		
Opening stock	4,000	
Purchases	42,000	
	46,000	
Less Closing stock	6,000	40,000
Gross profit		10,000

The similar approach to the use of layout can be applied if there is a missing figure on the balance sheet. A typical examination problem is for the amount of profits to be omitted and there is insufficient information to construct a profit and loss account. The answer is to use a balance sheet layout to calculate the missing profit figure as in the example below. The same approach can be used to ascertain the amount of drawings.

Example

A sole trader starts his business with £10,000 capital. The closing capital of the business is £15,000 and the owner has made drawings of £8,500.

Required

What was the figure of profit for the year?

Solution

We start by drawing up the part of the balance sheet concerned with showing the capital of a sole trader.

Balance Sheet (Extract)

	£	£
Opening capital	10,000	
Add Profit	x	
	y	
Less Drawings	8,500	
Closing capital		15,000

We can now insert the missing figures. To obtain the closing capital of £15,000 after deducting from y the drawings of £8,500, it means that y must be £23,500. To get the figure of £23,000 a profit of £13,500 must be added to the opening capital. With the figures inserted the balance sheet is:

Balance Sheet (Extract)

	£	£
Opening capital	10,000	
Add Profit	13,500	
	23,500	
Less Drawings	8,500	
Closing capital		15,000

16.11 Using percentages

Some figures may be available for the profit and loss account, but the cost of sales figure or the sales figure may be missing. However, in such examples the ***gross profit percentage*** will be given and from this it is possible to calculate the missing figures.

The gross profit can be expressed either as a percentage of cost of sales and is known as the ***gross profit mark up,*** or as a percentage of sales and is known as the ***gross profit margin.***

$$\text{Gross profit mark up} = \frac{\text{Gross profit}}{\text{Cost of sales}} \times 100$$

$$\text{Gross profit margin} = \frac{\text{Gross profit}}{\text{Sales}} \times 100$$

Using the figures : Sales £5,000; Cost of sales £4,000; Gross profit £1,000, the calculations are:

$$\text{Gross profit mark up} = \frac{£1{,}000}{£4{,}000} \times 100 = 25\%$$

$$\text{Gross profit margin} = \frac{£1{,}000}{£5{,}000} \times 100 = 20\%$$

The procedure for calculating the missing figure where the gross profit percentage is given is as follows:

1. If the gross profit percentage is the margin, then make sales equal 100%.
2. If the gross profit percentage is the mark up, make cost of sales equal 100%.
3. Enter gross profit as a percentage of 100.
4. Calculate the missing figure.

In the following examples various problems are explained. You should work through these very carefully before tackling the relevant questions at the end of the chapter.

Example

Tom Wrington makes an average gross profit margin of 25%. For the year the cost of sales figure is £15,000.

Required

What are the figures for sales and gross profit?

Solution

First enter the figures which are known:

	£	
Sales	x	
Cost of sales	15,000	
Gross profit	y	25%

As the gross profit margin is 25%, we make sales 100%. Therefore the cost of sales is 75%:

	£	
Sales	x	100%
Cost of sales	15,000	75%
Gross profit	y	25%

The missing figures can now be added because if cost of sales of £15,000 equals 75% then:

$$\text{Sales} = £15{,}000 \times \frac{100}{75} = £20{,}000$$

The completed figures are:

	£	
Sales	20,000	100%
Cost of sales	15,000	75%
Gross profit	£5,000	25%

Example

Sarah Priddy operates a business where the gross profit mark up is 25% on cost of sales. Cost of sales is £4,000.

Required

What is the figure for sales and gross profit?

Solution

First enter the figures which are known:

	£	
Sales	x	
Cost of sales	4,000	
Gross profit	y	25%

As the gross profit mark up is 25%, we make cost of sales 100% and sales are therefore 125%:

	£	
Sales	x	125%
Cost of sales	4,000	100%
Gross profit	y	25%

The missing figures can now be added because if cost of sales of £4,000 equals 100% then:

$$\text{Sales} = £4{,}000 \times \frac{125}{100} = £5{,}000$$

The completed figures are:

	£	
Sales	5,000	125%
Cost of sales	4,000	100%
Gross profit	1,000	25%

Example

Nigel Clutton has a business where the gross profit margin is 10% and the figure for sales is £55,000.

Required

What is the figure for cost of sales and gross profit?

Solution

First enter the figures which are known:

	£	
Sales	55,000	
Cost of sales	x	
Gross profit	y	10%

As the gross profit margin is 10%,we make sales 100% and cost of sales is therefore 90%:

	£	
Sales	55,000	100%
Cost of sales	x	90%
Gross profit	y	10%

The missing figures can now be added because if sales of £55,000 equals 100% then:

$$\text{Cost of sales} = £55{,}000 \times \frac{90}{100} = £49{,}500$$

The completed figures are:

	£	
Sales	55,000	100%
Cost of sales	49,500	90%
Gross profit	5,500	10%

Example

Fred Paulton has a garden centre where the average gross profit mark up is 50% on cost of sales and the sales value is £60,000.

Required

What is the value for cost of sales and gross profit?

Solution

First enter the figures which are known:

	£	
Sales	60,000	
Cost of sales	x	
Gross profit	y	50%

As the gross profit mark up is 50%, we make cost of sales 100% and sales are therefore 150%:

	£	
Sales	60,000	150%
Cost of sales	x	100%
Gross profit	y	50%

The missing figures can now be added because if sales of £60,000 equals 100% then:

$$\text{Cost of sales} = £60{,}000 \times \frac{100}{150} = £40{,}000$$

The completed figures are:

	£	
Sales	60,000	150%
Cost of sales	40,000	100%
Gross profit	20,000	50%

You should now be able to attempt Question 16.5 and Task 16.1 at the end of this chapter.

16.12 Combining layouts and percentages

In some questions a considerable amount of information may be missing and you will have to use your knowledge of layouts and percentages to calculate the missing figures. You should have no problems if you tackle the question methodically. The following simple procedure will help you:

1. Draw up a standard layout naming all the items you would expect to find in it.
2. Insert any figures which are given in the question.
3. Identify which figures are missing.
4. Calculate the missing figures as a separate working.
5. Complete your layout using the figures you have calculated.

Example

The following figures for a financial year are available:

Sales	£30,000
Opening stock	£4,000
Purchases	£25,000
Gross profit margin	20%

Required

What is the gross profit and cost of sales?

Solution

The first step is to draw up the standard layout for a profit statement, inserting any figures we know:

Profit statement for the year ended ———

	£	£
Sales		30,000
Less Cost of sales		
Opening stock	4,000	
Add Purchases	25,000	
	29,000	
Less Closing stock	a	b
Gross profit		c

The figures we have missing are:

a) closing stock

b) cost of sales

c) gross profit

We cannot work out the closing stock figure until we have the gross profit and cost of sales and these can be calculated as follows:

	Known figures £	%	Missing figures £
Sales	30,000	100	
Cost of sales	b	80	24,000
Gross profit	c	20	6,000

As we have calculated that the cost of sales figure is £24,000, the closing stock figure must be £5,000 (£29,000 – £24,000). We can now complete the layout.

Profit statement for the year ended ———

	£	£
Sales		30,000
Less Cost of sales		
Opening Stock	4,000	
Add Purchases	25,000	
	29,000	
Less Closing stock	5,000	24,000
Gross profit		6,000

You should now be able to attempt Question 16.6 at the end of this chapter.

16.13 Incomplete records and a new business

We have examined the various problems which can arise where a business has incomplete records and the various techniques which may be used to calculate any missing figures. We can now put this knowledge together to draw up a trading and profit and loss account and a balance sheet for a business.

Question 16.7 at the end of this chapter concerns a ***new business*** which has not maintained proper records and has now completed the first year of trading. You should make reference to the earlier parts of the chapter if you have difficulties. You will find that when you come to complete the balance sheet at 31 December 19X8 there is no figure given for the cash held on that date. You will have to calculate this by drawing up a simple cash statement showing the cash coming in to the business, the cash going out and the balance in hand at the end of the year.

You should now be able to attempt Question 16.7 and Task 16.3 at the end of this chapter.

16.14 Incomplete records and the established business

If you have been able to draw up the profit statement and balance sheet from the incomplete records of a new business, you should not experience many problems with an ***established business***. One new feature is that some questions ask you to draw up a ***statement of affairs*** at the beginning of the financial year. This statement is nothing more than a simple balance sheet which serves to arrange the information in a convenient order and allows the calculation of the capital.

Example

Magna Company, manufacturers of stone ornaments for the garden, has supplied you with the following financial information of the business as at 1 January 19X3:

	£
Premises	30,000
Machinery	15,000
Stock	15,000
Debtors	10,000
Insurance prepaid	500
Creditors	7,000
Cash	2,000
Accrual for maintenance charge	400

Required

Draw up a statement of affairs as at 1 January 19X3.

Solution

Magna Company
Statement of affairs
as at 1 January 19X3

	£	£
Assets		
Premises		30,000
Machinery		15,000
Stock		15,000
Debtors		10,000
Prepayments		500
Cash		2,000
Total assets		72,500
Liabilities		
Creditors	7,000	
Accruals	400	
Total liabilities		7,400
Capital		65,100

Having given a financial structure to the business, it is now possible to deal with any further problems. In Question 16.8 at the end of the chapter the above Statement of Affairs is the start of the financial year. Use it, with the additional information given, to prepare a profit and loss account and balance sheet.

You should now be able to attempt Question 16.8 and Task 16.2 at the end of this chapter.

16.15 Summary

If a business has not maintained proper accounting records, it will be necessary to make ***adjustments*** to the information available to construct a ***profit and loss account*** and ***balance sheet***. The most common problem is where a record has been kept only of ***cash*** transactions.

Where key figures are missing in an ***incomplete records*** question, it is normally possible to calculate them by using ***layouts*** and ***percentages***. With an established business it may be necessary to draw up a ***statement of affairs***.

You should now be able to attempt the Objective Test at the end of this chapter.

Student activities

Task 16.1 Collect a number of advertisements of sales bargains from the newspapers. Using the appropriate layouts for margins and mark ups, calculate the relevant figures.

Task 16.2 Take your bank statement for the last three months and draw up a profit and loss account for the period. This will mean that you will have to make adjustments to the bank entries for accruals and prepayments at the beginning and end of the period.

Task 16.3 Your cousin has been in business for almost a year, but has not kept proper accounting records. Write her a letter explaining the step-by-step procedure to draw up a trading and profit and loss account and balance sheet.

Question 16.1 In the following questions assume it is the first year of trading for the company.

i) ***A. Radstock*** banks £12,000 from his customers during the year and is still owed £2,500 at the year end. What are the correct figures for:

a) sales on the profit and loss account;

b) trade debtors on the balance sheet.

ii) ***M. Shepton's*** records showed that he paid £24,600 to his suppliers by cheque during the course of the year and £3,200 by cash. At the end of the year he still owes £5,300. What are the correct figures for:

a) purchases on the profit and loss account

b) trade creditors on the balance sheet

iii) Extracts from ***A. Mallet's*** bank and cash records show:

Received	**£**	**Paid**	**£**
Cheques for sales	27,000	Suppliers by cheque	22,000
Cash for sales	4,600	Suppliers by cash	1,900

At the end of the year the business owes £4,600 to its suppliers and the debtors stand at £5,400. What are the correct figures for:

a) sales on the profit and loss account

b) trade debtors on the balance sheet

c) purchases on the profit and loss account

d) trade creditors on the balance sheet

Question 16.2 In the following questions assume it is the first year of trading for the company.

i) ***A. Drew*** pays a cheque for electricity charges for £8,400 and has an unpaid invoice for £1,200 at the end of the year. What are the correct figures to show for:

a) electricity expenses in the trading and profit and loss account

b) accruals in the balance sheet

ii) A business in its first year of business pays cash to its landlord of £6,000 in respect of the rent for the first 18 months. What are the correct figures to show for:

a) as rent in the trading and profit and loss account

b) under prepayments in the balance sheet?

iii) The bank statement of a business shows that the following payments have been made in its first year of trading:

Electricity:	£4,000
Insurance:	£2,400
Repairs:	£3,900
Rates:	£3,000

Investigations reveal that an electricity invoice for £450 has still not been paid and £330 is owed in respect of repairs. Of the amount paid for insurance, £195 represents an advance payment. The payment for rates includes an amount for the first three months of the following year. What are the correct figures to show:

a) for each item on the trading and profit and loss account

b) as accruals on the balance sheet

c) as prepayments on the balance sheet

Question 16.3 i) The amount due for electricity for the previous financial year was £200. During the current financial year cash was paid of £800, but there was still £430 owing at the year end. What is the correct figure to be entered in the trading and profit and loss account?

ii) During the current financial year an amount of £500 cash was paid for stationery and a further £250 was still outstanding at the year end. An amount of £150 was outstanding from the previous year. What is the correct figure to be entered in the trading and profit and loss account?

iii) At the end of 19X5 an amount of £3,000 was owing to trade creditors. During the financial year ended 31 December 19X6 we paid cash of £12,500 to trade creditors, but still owed £1,600 at the year end. What is the figure for purchases to be entered on the trading and profit and loss account for the year ended 31 December 19X6.

Question 16.4 In the following questions you have been given certain figures. Calculate the missing figures.

Amount owing to creditors at end of previous financial year	Cash paid to creditors in current year	Amount owing to creditors at end of current year	Amount in profit and loss account in current year
£	£	£	£
200	800	300	?
500	750	800	?
500	2,000	?	1,750
400	1,750	?	1,800
700	?	900	1,000
400	?	600	700
?	1,000	200	1,100
?	650	250	850

Question 16.5 i) A business sells its goods at cost plus 20%. The gross profit is £5,000. What are the sales and cost of sales?

ii) A gross profit margin of 25% is made on sales. The cost of sales figure is £60,000. What are the figures for sales and gross profit?

iii) The value of sales for the year is £11,000. The gross profit mark up is 10%. What are the gross profit and cost of sales?

iv) On cost of sales of £108,000 there is a gross profit mark up of 25%. What is the gross profit and sales?

v) A company makes a gross profit margin of 25% on its sales. The cost of sales is £108,000. What is the sales and the gross profit?

Question 16.6 *Lewis Harptree* has been running a successful business printing calendars for a number of years. At the end of the current financial year it has made sales of £60,000 and started the year with an opening stock of £8,000. During the year it made purchases of £50,000.

Unfortunately, a fire at the end of the year means that no figure is available for the stock at the year end. However, the company knows that it makes a gross profit mark up of 25%.

What are the following figures:

i) closing stock at the year end;

ii) the cost of sales for the year;

iii) the gross profit for the year?

Question 16.7 *Louise Litton* started a mail order business selling dog baskets with £12,000 capital. During the year to 31 December 19X8 £10,000 was received from customers and at the year end an amount of £3,000 was still owing. Goods had been purchased to the value of £5,000, but only £4,000 had been paid to suppliers at the end of the year. During the year machinery had been purchased for cash to the value of £6,000. It is estimated that this machinery will last 6 years and will have no scrap value. Louise has decided to depreciate the machinery using the straight line method.

A part-time assistant has been employed and paid £2,500 in wages. Rent had been paid of £1,000, but there was still £500 owing at the year end.

Insurance had been paid of £1,250 which included an amount of £250 for 19X9. Other expenses of the business for the year to the 31 December 19X8 amounted to £3,500 and these had been paid in full. On the 31 December 19X9 the closing stock was valued at £2,500.

Required

Draw up a trading and profit and loss account for the year ended 31 December 19X8 and a balance sheet as at 31 December 19X8.

Question 16.8 To answer this question you will need to use the data from the example in Section 16.14. During the course of 19X3 *Magna Company* received £85,000 from customers and at the end of the year was owed £5,000. Suppliers were paid £62,000, but £10,000 remained owing at the 31 December 19X3. The following cash payments were also made during the year:

Wages:	£6,000
Motor expenses:	£1,900
Insurance:	£850

You find that of the amount paid for insurance £250 was in respect of the period 1 January 19X4 to 30 June 19X4. You also discover at the end of 19X3 there is still an unpaid bill for maintenance charges of £250. Further investigation reveals that the value of stock at the 31 December 19X3 is £25,000

The owner of Magna Company informs you that £5,000 had been drawn out in cash during 19X3 for his own use.

After consideration you decide that the machinery should be depreciated by £2,000 for the year.

Required

Draw up a trading and profit and loss account for the year ended 31 December 19X3 and a balance sheet as at 31 December 19X3.

Objective test *(tick the appropriate box)*

i) Prepayments are shown on the balance sheet as a:

a) current liability ☐

b) fixed asset ☐

c) capital amount ☐

d) current asset ☐

ii) Accruals are shown on the trading and profit and loss account as:

a) an addition to sales ☐

b) an addition to the appropriate expenses ☐

c) a deduction from the appropriate expenses ☐

d) a deduction from purchases ☐

iii) If a company has debtors at the beginning of the year of £3,000, receives £20,000 from customers during the year and is owed £5,000 at the year end, the sales figure for the profit statement is:

a) £28,000 ☐

b) £22,000 ☐

c) £18,000 ☐

d) £12,000 ☐

iv) If a gross profit is shown as a mark up, it has been calculated as a percentage of:

a) cost of sales ☐

b) purchases ☐

c) sales ☐

d) closing stock ☐

v) If a gross profit is shown as a margin, it has been calculated as a percentage of:

a) purchases ☐

b) cost of sales ☐

c) opening stock ☐

d) sales ☐

vi) If cost of sales are £5,000 and gross profit is £1,000, the gross profit mark up will be:

a) 20% ☐

b) 16.7% ☐

c) 25% ☐

d) 5% ☐

vii) If sales are £50,000 and gross profit £5,000, the gross profit margin will be:

a) 9.09% ☐

b) 20% ☐

c) 10% ☐

d) 11.1% ☐

viii) If a business has a capital of £10,000, a profit for the year of £18,000 and closing capital of £22,000, the figure for drawings will be:

a) £30,000 ☐

b) £14,000 ☐

c) £28,000 ☐

d) £6,000 ☐

ix) If the opening capital is £4,000, drawings £12,000 and closing capital £18,000 the net profit is:

a) £26,000 ☐

b) £16,000 ☐

c) £2,000 ☐

d) £22,000 ☐

x) A statement of affairs can be described as a:

a) simple profit statement ☐

b) simple balance sheet ☐

c) method of single entry bookkeeping ☐

d) figure of gross profit ☐

Chapter 17

Source documents

17.1 Objectives

At the end of this chapter you should be able to:

- explain the importance of source documents;
- identify the purpose and features of specific documents;
- prepare a document for a specific purpose;
- construct a flow diagram for source documents.

17.2 Introduction

In earlier chapters we looked at the various transactions carried out by organisations, such as buying and selling goods, and the way in which financial statements are prepared to show the performance of the business and its financial position. In this chapter we are going to look more closely at the transactions and the documents needed.

Organisations carry out many of the transactions between themselves on credit. If a manufacturing company sells goods to a retailer, payment is not always made in cash or by cheque immediately, but a period of credit is taken. The manufacturer must therefore issue an ***invoice*** to obtain the payment. This is a ***source document***.

When purchasing goods a business usually sends an ***order*** specifying the exact goods required, when they are required, and the address to which they should be sent. The sending and receipt of the goods needs both of the organisations concerned to issue a number of documents.

As well as requiring documents to record external transactions, a system of documentation is set up by most businesses for internal planning and control. For example, it may be necessary to record the amount of time that a worker has spent on a particular job or the amount of raw materials used in a manufacturing process. The documents used to measure these activities form the source from which the financial records of the organisation are drawn up.

All the documents used by a business are designed for its own needs and purposes. However, there will be a great similarity between the documents used by different businessess. There is certain information which must be included on an invoice, such as the date and the amount due, although the business name, invoice design and colour of paper and print may vary. Even with internal documents there are likely to be many similarities between one organisation and another because the need to record certain types of information is common.

In this chapter we will look at the main source documents used, explain their purposes and the procedures adopted for issuing and controlling the documents. We will use standard formats for the documents and you should take the opportunity, wherever possible, to examine documents issued by various organisations to see the individual differences in practice.

You should now be able to attempt Task 17.1 at the end of this chapter.

17.3 Purchasing goods

When an organisation purchases goods on credit a number of documents are raised by both the business buying the goods and the business selling the goods. The following flow diagram shows the documents which may be issued by a large organisation and the internal records maintained.

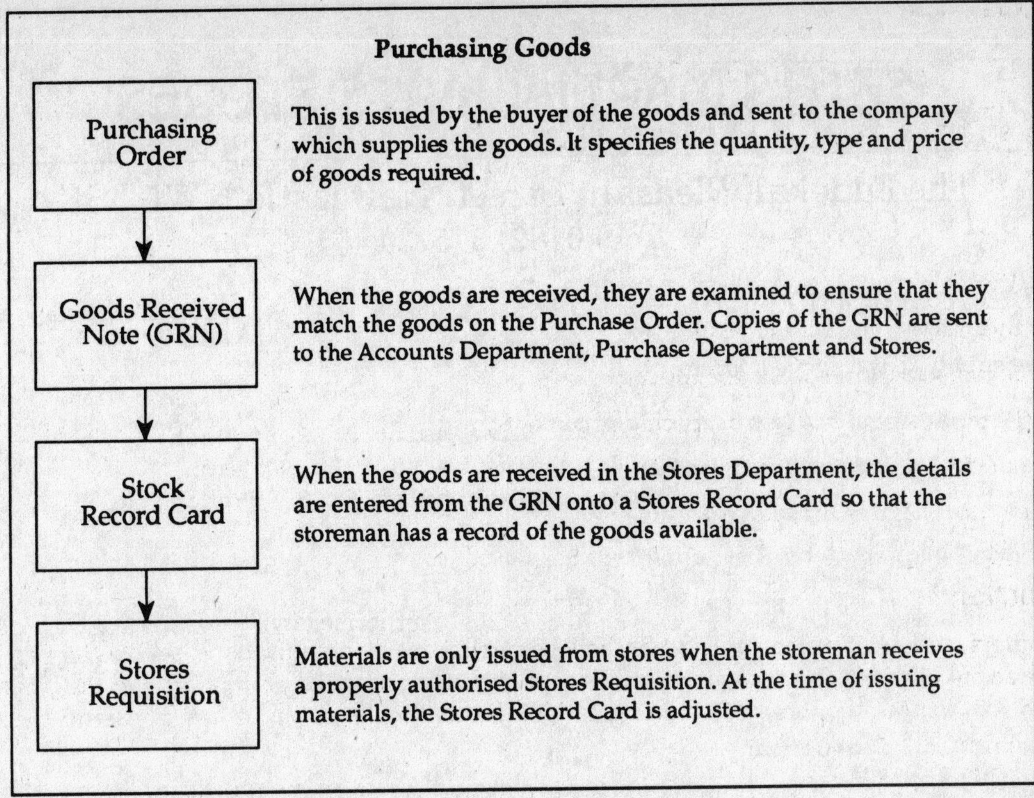

The document which starts off this chain is the ***purchase order***. The essential information which must appear on the purchase order is:

- The name of the business buying the goods and the address to which the goods are to be delivered
- The name and address of the supplier of the goods
- Description of the goods, the quantity required and the price
- Date of the purchase order, a reference number and the signature of the person in the company responsible for ordering the goods

On the following page is an example of a purchase order for ***Seth's Martial Arts Stores.***

Having sent this order the next stage in the transaction for Seth's Martial Arts Stores is the receipt of the goods. If Seth's Stores is large with goods being delivered from a number of suppliers, a record of the receipt of the goods is made. The layout and information used for the internal documents such as the goods received note and stores requisition depends on the system maintained by the company. However, the essential details to be given on all such documents are:

- Date and reference number
- Description and quantity of goods
- Signature of person authorising the document

You should now be able to attempt Task 17.2 at the end of this chapter.

17.4 Selling goods

On receipt of an order the seller sends the goods to the buyer and ensures that payment will be received by issuing an invoice. The main documents which may be issued by a large organisation are shown in the flow diagram on the following page.

SETH'S MARTIAL ARTS STORES

The Judokai, Pleasant Street, Newcastle NW5 3SR
Tel: (0782) 315234

PURCHASE ORDER NO: 9011 Date: 10th May 19X5

Please supply to the above address:

250	Size 4	Colour White belts @ £2.60 each
160	Size 6	Colour Blue belts @ £2.90 each
120	Size 6	Colour Black belts @ £3.05 each

Delivery required by 1st June 19X5

Authorised by: ....
Chief Buyer

To:
Eastern Clothing Company
135, Blissford Avenue
LONDON EC2 4ER

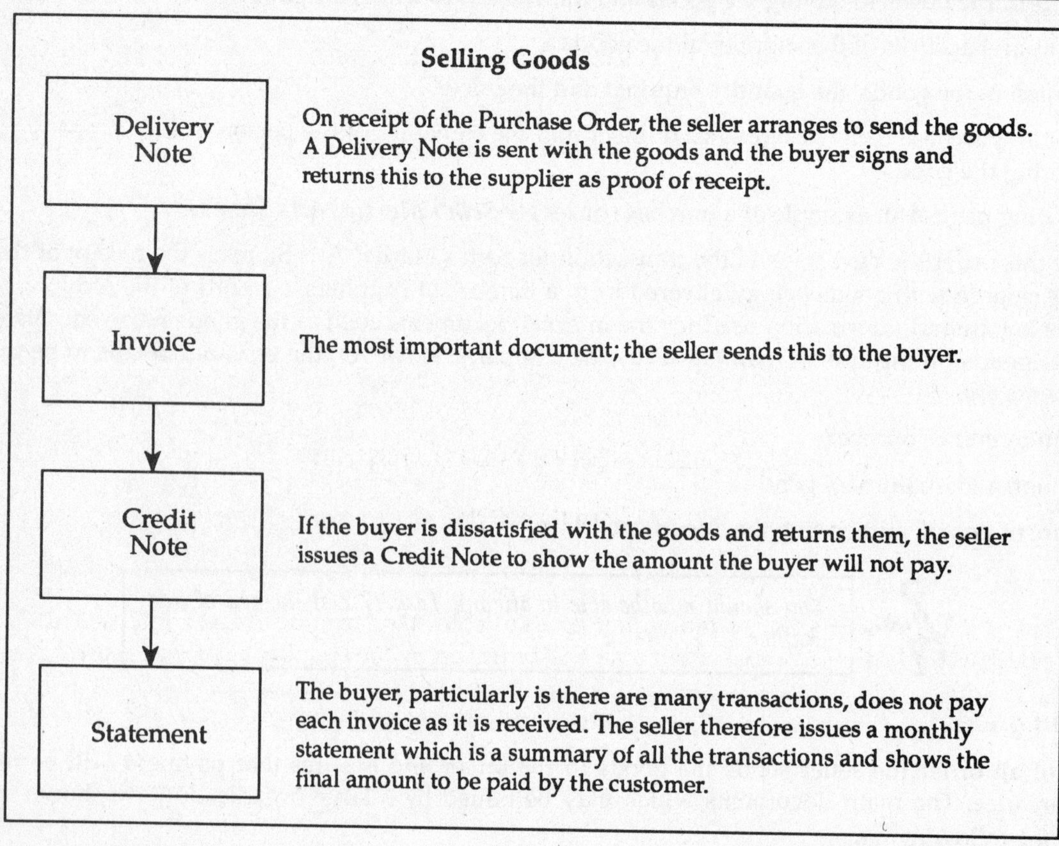

The *invoice* issued by the seller is a most important document and contains a considerable amount of information as follows:

- Name and address of seller
- Name and address of buyer
- Reference number and date
- Details of goods supplied and purchase order number
- Date by which payment is required and if a cash discount is given for prompt payment
- The total net price of the goods
- The amount of Value Added Tax (if any)
- Total amount due from customer including Value Added Tax

The following example is a suitable design for an invoice.

INVOICE

From:
Eastern Clothing Company
135, Blissford Avenue
LONDON EC2 4ER
Tel: 01 352 8101

Tax point/Date	10th June 19X5
Invoice No	2876A
Purchase Order No	9011

Quantity	Description		Unit Price	Amount
250	Size 4	Colour White belts	£2.60 each	£650.00
160	Size 6	Colour Blue belts	£2.90 each	£464.00
120	Size 6	Colour Black belts	£3.05 each	£366.00
			Sub Total	£1,480.00
			Value Added Tax (17.5%)	£259.00
			Invoice Total	£1,739.00

To:
Seth's Martial Arts Stores
The Judokai
Pleasant Street
Newcastle NW5 3SR

Payment due within thirty days of invoice date

VAT Reg No: 860 1856 40

Should the buyer decide the goods are faulty, not of a suitable standard, incorrectly despatched or otherwise unacceptable they will be returned and a credit note will be issued by the supplier as in the following example.

You should now be able to attempt Question 17.1 at the end of this chapter.

CREDIT NOTE

From: Eastern Clothing Company
135, Blissford Avenue
LONDON EC2 4ER
Tel: 01 352 8101

Credit Note No 331C
Tax point/Date 22nd June 19X5
Invoice No 2876A
Purchase Order No 9011

Quantity	Description		Unit Price	Amount
6	Size 4	Colour White belts	£2.60 each	£15.60
2	Size 6	Colour Blue belts	£2.90 each	£5.80
		Sub Total		£21.40
		Value Added Tax (17.5%)		£3.75
		Invoice Total		£25.15

Goods returned due to colour staining

To: Seth's Martial Arts Stores
The Judokai, Pleasant Street
Newcastle NW5 3SR

VAT Reg No: 860 1856 40

17.5 Statements

The buyer does not pay on each invoice as it is received, but waits until a ***statement*** has been received from the supplier. The statement sent by the seller is a summary of the transactions with a particular purchaser over a period of time (usually a month). The main information shown is:

- Names and addresses of seller and purchaser
- Invoices and credit notes sent and any payments received
- Date and reference number
- Balance due from purchaser as with invoices, the design of a statement may vary, but the following is an example showing the information which should be given as a minimum.

As with invoices, the design of a statement may vary, but the following is an example showing the information which should be given as a minimum.

STATEMENT

From: Eastern Clothing Company
135, Blissford Avenue
LONDON EC2 4ER
Tel: 01 352 8101

Number 565S
Date 30th June 19X5

Date	Reference	Amount
10 June	Invoice No 2876A	£1,739.00
22 June	Credit Note 331C	£25.15
		£1,713.85

To: Seth's Martial Arts Stores
The Judokai, Pleasant Street
Newcastle NW5 3SR

VAT Reg No: 860 1856 40

You should now be able to attempt Question 17.2 at the end of this chapter.

17.6 Recording labour

Wages paid to the workforce are an important item of expenditure, particularly in a manufacturing organisation. For many companies this represents a very large proportion of their annual expenditure and it is important that the business controls every aspect of this activity and properly records it. In a large organisation with well established systems, the procedures which are established will show:

- The actual number of hours spent by workers on the factory premises. This may mean the recording of hours by each worker having an individual clock number and using a clock card in a machine at the factory entrance to print starting and leaving times.
- The actual hours spent by the workers on specific production activities. It should be possible to reconcile this figure with the actual hours spent on the factory premises.

In addition to the above information, details will be maintained in the wages office of each individual worker. These show the remuneration of each employee, including rates, allowances, tax codes and statutory deductions.

You should now be able to attempt Task 17.3 at the end of this chapter.

17.7 Time sheets and job cards

To record the actual time spent on specific production activities either a system of ***time sheets*** or ***job cards*** is used. Time sheets are completed on a weekly or daily basis by the employees themselves and countersigned by their supervisor. The time sheet shows how much time has been spent on a particular job for a client. Accountants working in professional offices complete time sheets so that they may charge their clients correctly for the time spent on their affairs. Job cards are for a specific job and each employee completes the time spent on that particular job so that a record is built up of the total hours it has taken to complete all the work.

17.8 The wages office

A ***payroll*** is prepared which shows the details of each employee's pay. The clock cards, which show the attendance time of the employees, are reconciled to the job cards, which show the amount of time recorded on each job. The total labour cost is calculated and the wages paid and the labour costs analysed for entry into the cost records. The following diagram illustrates the procedure.

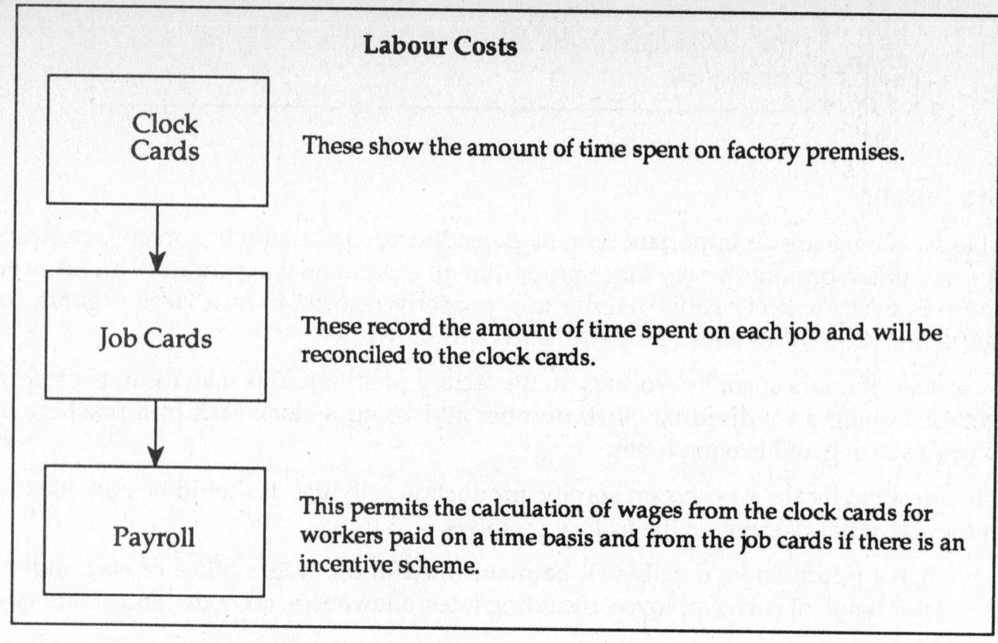

You should now be able to attempt Question 17.3 at the end of this chapter.

17.9 The role of the accountant

In a very large organisation the system and procedures for source documents are very complex. It is essential that the system is efficient. If there are deficiencies in the system, the business may fail to collect the money due to it; pay for goods which were not received or were faulty; fail to pay the correct wages; run out of their stock of goods. These are only some of the problems. In addition there is always the danger of fraud. If the system or controlling and recording the transactions is weak, there is a possibility that some unscrupulous employee will exploit it to their own advantage.

The responsibility for establishing good systems and procedures and ensuring that they are operated efficiently is that of the accountant. In a small company the external auditors ensure, as part of their regular examination, that there are no deficiencies. If there are, they bring this to the notice of the directors of the company.

In a large company there is frequently an internal audit department. This employs accountants whose task is to conduct investigations into the systems and procedures of the company, to ensure that if there are any weaknesses, corrective action is taken to remedy them.

You should now be able to attempt Questions 17.4 and 17.5 at the end of this chapter.

17.10 Summary

Organisations carry out many business transactions on ***credit***. It is essential that there are the proper documents to support these transactions. When a company buys goods it normally sends an ***order*** to the supplier. When the supplier sends the goods to the buyer a ***delivery note*** is sent with them. To obtain payment the supplier sends an ***invoice*** to the buyer and may also send a ***statement*** at the end of the month .

As well as completing the correct documents for external transactions, a business must maintain procedures for recording and controlling internal activities. One important item of expenditure in many organisations, particularly if they are manufacturers, is ***wages***. It may be necessary to record the time spent by workers on certain jobs through the use of ***time sheets*** and ***job cards***.

You should now be able to attempt Objective Test at the end of this chapter.

Student activities

Task 17.1 Collect a selection of invoices from companies. Draw up a table to illustrate the differences and similarities. Analyse the design of the invoice separately from the contents.

Task 17.2 Design an appropriate goods received note for seth's martial arts stores. As it as a document which is only used inside the company, it should be plain and simple, but contain the essential information.

Task 17.3 Design a purchase order and an invoice for a television company which wishes to promote a glossy, dynamic image on all its business documents.

Question 17.1 Select the correct response to the following statements:

	True	False
i) A company will always issue an invoice when a cash payment has been made.	☐	☐
ii) When a company orders goods it normally sends a delivery note to the supplier.	☐	☐
iii) A company selling goods on credit will always send an invoice to the purchaser.	☐	☐
iv) If goods are returned by a buyer because they are unacceptable, the seller will usually issue a credit note.	☐	☐
v) A credit note must be paid in full by the buyer.	☐	☐
vi) A goods received note will show the quantity and description of the goods which the buyer has received.	☐	☐
vii) Buyers will not compare the goods received note with a copy of their original purchase order.	☐	☐

Question 17.2 Tick the items on the following list that you might normally expect to see on an invoice:

i) the name and address of buyer
ii) the profit made by the seller
iii) the amount of Value Added Tax, if any
iv) the total net price of the goods
v) details of the goods supplied
vi) details of credit notes issued in the previous month
vii) goods received note reference
viii) purchase order number

Question 17.3 Match the appropriate documents with their descriptions in the lists below:

Document	Description
a) Time sheet	i) A summary of sales transactions for a period of time
b) Invoice	ii) A request for goods of a particular type and quantity
c) Purchase order	iii) A record of how much time an employee has spent on a particular job
d) Goods received note	iv) A request for payment showing the amount due
e) Statement	v) A notification to the purchaser of amounts not due for payment
f) Credit note	vi) A record of the goods actually received by the purchaser

Question 17.4 List some of the difficulties that can arise if an organisation does not have a proper system of source documents.

Question 17.5 *Natalie Hodges* has a thriving business which employs ten people to sell high quality silk clothing by mail order. After six months' trading, she is concerned that the profit is not as high as expected and she suspects that theft is taking place. At the end of the six months she has 425 garments in stock.

Required

Write a brief report to Natalie Hodges explaining which documents she can use and how they can help her calculate how many garments should be in stock.

Objective test *(tick the appropriate box)*

i) A company wishing to buy goods from another company on credit would send:

a) a delivery note ☐

b) a purchase order ☐

c) a goods received note ☐

d) a credit note ☐

ii) Which of the following information would not be shown on a purchase order:

a) the quantity of items required ☐

b) the price of each item ☐

c) the value added tax to be paid ☐

d) the delivery address ☐

iii) What information is shown on a clock card:

a) the income tax to be paid by an employee ☐

b) the number of hours the employee has spent on the premises ☐

c) the number of hours the employee has spent on a particular job ☐

d) the National Insurance to be paid by an employee ☐

iv) Which of the following information will not be shown on a statement issued by a company:

a) any payments received from the customer ☐

b) credit notes issued to the customer ☐

c) goods received notes issued by the customer ☐

d) invoices issued to the customer ☐

v) A stock record card will be used by a company so that it knows:

a) the price of goods it sells ☐

b) the amount of goods it has available ☐

c) the amount of VAT it has to pay ☐

d) the number of orders it has received ☐

Chapter 18

Documents for cash control

18.1 Objectives

At the end of this chapter you should be able to:

- explain the importance of cash control;
- describe the procedures for cash control;
- compare a cash book and a petty cash book;
- record cash receipts and payments in the correct manner.

18.2 Introduction

Whatever the size of a business, the ***control of cash*** is critical. In this context the word ***cash*** means cash itself as well as cheques, postal orders and other means of transferring money from one person or organisation to another. Both a large multinational company and the newspaper seller on the street corner are deeply interested in cash. Without adequate amounts of cash they would not be able to pay their bills and would therefore go out of business.

Businesses often obtain bank loans and overdrafts to help them pay their bills, but these loans have to be paid back at some stage. Although a loan may be useful as a temporary measure, over a long period of time a business must ensure that it has more cash coming in than it pays out. If it is unable to do this it will go out of business. In Chapter 5 we saw how organisations use cash flow forecasts to enable them to predict and control their cash flows

Because of the critical importance of cash, businesses pay particular attention to recording the amounts of cash coming into and going out of the business. Regular checks are made to ensure that the actual amount of cash held at any one time agrees with the records. It is obvious that cash must be kept in a safe place as carelessness in doing so could lead to theft.

18.3 Procedure for recording cash

In most organisations it is normal to give one person the responsibility for maintaining the ***cash records***. This person is known as the ***cashier***. In a very large organisation the task may require more than one person. If there are payments made of small amounts, a petty cashier will be appointed to record them.

The main responsibilities of the cashier are:

- to record receipts of cash and cheques;
- to pay cash and cheques received into the bank;
- to make cash payments and record them;
- to prepare cheques for signature and record them;
- to keep safely any amounts of actual cash (known as cash floats);
- to ensure the petty cashier has sufficient cash;
- to reconcile the cash records maintained with bank statements.

18.4 Cash book

The recording of cash is carried out in a ***cash book***. This may be maintained on a computer, or be a standard book which can be obtained from any stationers, or be designed for the company's own particular needs. A page of a typical cash book is shown below with notes explaining its features.

Example

Cash book

Receipts					Payments				
Date	Details	Ref	Cash	Bank	Date	Details	Ref	Cash	Bank
			£	£				£	£

All receipts are shown on the left hand side and payments on the right hand side. Actual cash received and paid is recorded in the cash column whereas receipts and payments by cheques are shown in the bank column. The details column shows the type of transaction and often includes a reference, e.g. the cheque number or receipt number. Where cash is drawn out of the bank for cash payments to be made or where actual cash received is paid into the bank, this is known as a ***contra entry***. This means that both parts of the transaction are shown in the same book. We have omitted VAT for the purposes of simplicity and you should refer to Chapter 3 to see how this would be dealt with in the records of the business.

Example

A. Sodbury has just started in business and the following are the transactions for the first week.

June 1 A. Sodbury pays £2,000 into bank account
June 1 Paid office rent of £250 by cheque
June 2 Took £250 cash from bank for business use
June 2 Bought stationery for £50 cash
June 2 Bought design materials for £175 cash
June 3 Received £300 cheque from client
June 3 Paid cheque of £125 for promotional material
June 4 Received £200 cash from client
June 5 Paid £150 cash into bank

You are the cashier of the company and must enter up the cash book.

Solution

Cash book

Receipts				Payments			
Date	Details	Cash	Bank	Date	Details	Cash	Bank
		£	£			£	£
June 1	Capital		2,000	June 1	Rent		250
June 2	Bank (contra)	250		June 2	Cash (contra)		250
June 3	Sales		300	June 2	Stationery	50	
June 4	Sales	200		June 2	Design material	175	
June 5	Cash (contra)		150	June 3	Promotional material		125
				June 5	Bank (contra)	150	

You should now be able to attempt Task 18.1 at the end of this chapter.

18.5 Balancing the cash book

At the end of the week Mr Sodbury may wish to know how much actual cash he has available and how much money he has in the bank. To find this out we will ***balance the cash book***. This is done at least monthly.

Example

1. Add up all the columns putting the totals in pencil. For Mr Sodbury these pencil totals are:

Cash book

Receipts				**Payments**			
Date	**Details**	**Cash**	**Bank**	**Date**	**Details**	**Cash**	**Bank**
		£	£			£	£
		450	2,450			375	625

2. Enter the difference between the two cash column figures and the difference between the two bank column on the lowest side so that both cash columns and both bank columns now total the same. In this case the figures will be £75 for cash and £1,825 for bank. These will both be entered on the right hand side of the page with the words "balances carried down" put in the details column.

Cash book

Receipts				**Payments**			
Date	**Details**	**Cash**	**Bank**	**Date**	**Details**	**Cash**	**Bank**
		£	£			£	£
				June 5	Balances c/d	75	1,825

3. The final stage is to add both sides and rule them off. The balances you have entered are then shown as the opening balances on the opposite side. In the description column you write the words "Balances brought down". The cash book now looks like this:

Cash book

Receipts				**Payments**			
Date	**Details**	**Cash**	**Bank**	**Date**	**Details**	**Cash**	**Bank**
		£	£			£	£
June 1	Capital		2,000	June 1	Rent		250
June 2	Bank (contra)	250		June 2	Cash (contra)		250
June 3	Sales		300	June 2	Stationery	50	
June 4	Sales	200		June 2	Design materials	175	
June 5	Cash (contra)		150	June 3	Promotional material		125
				June 5	Bank (contra)	150	
				June 5	Balances c/d	75	1,825
		450	2,450			450	2,450
June 6	Balances b/d	75	1,825				

Just a final word on the balances before you attempt a question. By transferring the closing balances on the 5 June to the opposite side of the cash book as the opening balances on the 6 June, we are showing Mr Sodbury's position. On the 6 June, he has £75 cash and this can be checked by counting it. He also has £1,825 in the bank and this can be checked by telephoning the bank or requesting a bank statement. Later in this chapter we will discuss what happens if the figures on the bank statement and the cash book do not agree and have to be reconciled.

In this example the closing balances were on the right hand side and were transferred to the left hand side to show how much money Mr Sodbury has. It is possible at the end of the period that the closing bank figure will be on the left hand side and will be brought down as an opening balance on the right hand side. This shows that the business has no money in the bank of its own and must have an overdraft.

You should now be able to attempt Question 18.1 at the end of this chapter.

18.6 Cash discounts

In business a ***cash discount*** is given sometimes to encourage customers to pay early. For example, goods may have been sold to the value of £100 and the customer is told that a cash discount of 5% will be given if payment is made within 30 days. If the customer pays on time, an amount of £95 only will be paid. To record this, a third column may be added to the cash book to show all the cash discounts received and allowed by the company. The amount of cash paid or received is entered in the appropriate cash or bank column.

Recording transactions would continue in the same fashion until it was decided to balance the cash book. The bank and cash columns are balanced in the way we explained earlier in the chapter. The discount columns would be individually totalled - they are not balanced. The total of each of the discount columns is then transferred to another ledger and appear in the trading and profit and loss accounts.

It is important to remember that only ***cash*** discounts are recorded and not ***trade*** discounts.

Example

David Corsham has the following transactions:

Jan 1 Received £195 cheque from a customer, a discount of £5 having been allowed.

Jan 2 Customer sent cheque for £390 having deducted £10 discount.

Jan 4 Paid cheque for £192 having taken a £8 discount.

Required

Prepare the cash book showing the cash discount received and allowed by the company.

Solution

Cash book

Receipts					**Payments**				
Date	**Details**	**Discount**	**Cash**	**Bank**	**Date**	**Details**	**Discount**	**Cash**	**Bank**
		£	£	£			£	£	£
Jan 1	Sales	5		195	Jan 4	Goods	8		192
Jan 2	Sales	10		390					

You should now be able to attempt Question 18.2 at the end of this chapter.

18.7 The petty cash book

All businesses are called on to make numerous small payments. These may be for such things as postage, purchasing a small amount of stationery, bus or taxi fares etc. It is not appropriate to write cheques for such amounts and cash payments are made. However, such transactions may be quite numerous and the main cash book is a record of great importance and should not include the details of insignificant amounts. As a record must be kept of all cash payments, it is normal to use a ***petty cash book*** to enter items of small expenditure.

The method of making entries in the petty cash book is the same as the cash book and a typical layout is as follows. You will see that we have added a column for the separate recording of value added tax. This topic is dealt with more fully in Chapter 3.

Petty cash book

Receipts			Payments				
Date	Details	Total	Date	Details	Total	VAT	Net
		£			£	£	£

In some businesses the payments made by petty cash are analysed into separate columns in the petty cash book so that they can be easily incorporated into the accounting system. If at the end of the period the totals for each column of analysed expenditure are added, the amount should agree with the main total column. This is known as cross casting and ensures the arithmetical accuracy of your workings and that the same amount is entered in the total column as well as the analysed column.

You should now be able to attempt Question 18.3 at the end of this chapter.

18.8 The imprest system

In some businesses the petty cashier will ask the main cashier for more cash when it is needed. The system most commonly used, however, is known as the ***imprest system,*** This allows better control of cash and the procedure is as follows:

1. The cashier gives the petty cashier a starting sum of cash known as the float or the imprest.
2. The petty cashier makes payments when a properly authorised petty cash voucher is submitted.
3. Periodically, say every month, the cashier checks the accuracy of the petty cash book. If everything is correct the cashier reimburses the petty cashier for all payments made. This returns the imprest to the original amount.
4. At intervals a senior member of staff checks the petty cash book. The total of the current petty cash vouchers held by the petty cashier and the amount of cash held should agree with the original imprest amount.

Example

A petty cashier is given an imprest of £50.00 on 1 January. On 15 January the petty cashier holds vouchers for £18.60. On 31 January the amount of cash held by the petty cashier is £4.60.

i) What was the balance of cash held by the cashier on 15 January?

ii) What sum needs to be reimbursed by the cashier to restore the imprest to its original sum?

Solution

		£
i)	Original impress amount	50.00
	Cash paid against vouchers	18.60
	Cash held on 15 January	31.40
ii)	Original impress amount	50.00
	Cash held on 31 January	£4.60
	Amount required to restore imprest	45.40

You should now be able to attempt Question 18.4 at the end of this chapter.

18.9 Bank reconciliation

When you get to the end of a financial period and have calculated your closing balances, the figures in the cash book should be checked. The actual cash held should be counted and should agree with the cash column. Differences can be due to the following:

- Incorrect recording in the cash book
- Theft or loss of cash
- Incorrect additions
- Omission of entries in the cash book

Any differences should be investigated and action taken to rectify them. However, the position is not so straightforward with the bank column in the cash book. A number of differences may arise and the reasons may be:

- The bank has made a mistake
- A mistake has been made in the cash book
- Items are shown in the cash book but not on the bank statement
- Items are shown on the bank statement, but not in the cash book
- There are timing differences

The first two reasons for the differences, if they arise, should be investigated and put right.

Point 3 can occur for a number of reasons. One frequent cause is that a cheque has been received and entered into the cash book, but has been subsequently dishonoured (bounced) and is not on the bank statement.

Point 4 may be due to a variety of reasons. Although the business is informed of transactions it may have forgotten to put them in the cash book. Examples are standing orders, direct debits, cash point withdrawals and bank interest and charges.

Point 5 is the most common cause and it is normal to prepare a bank reconciliation to show that the difference in the cash and bank figures arise from timing differences. These differences are due to two main reasons:

- The business has sent out a cheque which has been entered in the cash book, but the recipient has not paid it into their account by the end of the period.
- The business has received money which it has shown in the cash book as being paid into the bank, but it has not yet been entered on the bank statement. There is usually only a day or two delay.

The procedure for carrying out a ***bank reconciliation*** is as follows:

1. Tick all the entries in the cash book against those made on the bank statement.
2. If no mistake has been made by the bank then correct the cash book for those entries which should be shown.
3. Total the cash book to give the new correct balance.
4. Identify the differences between the bank statement and cash book which are due to timing differences only.
5. Draw up a bank reconciliation statement proving that the cash book and bank statement agree apart from the transactions involving timing differences.

Example

John Westbury finds that his cash book and bank statement do not agree. He adjusts his cash book for errors and obtains a new balance of £227. The balance shown on the bank statement is £271 and John notices that £52 he had paid into the bank on the last day of the period has not yet been shown in his account. Further investigation reveals that the last two cheques drawn for £96 in total have not yet been presented to their bankers by the recipients. Draw up a bank reconciliation.

Solution

Bank reconciliation statement

	£
Balance on the bank statement	271
Add Deposits not yet cleared	52
	323
Less Cheques not yet presented	96
Balance as per cash book	227

Note: Details of the deposits not yet cleared and the cheques unpresented would be shown. The cash figure shown at the bottom of the reconciliation statement of £227 is the figure which would appear in the balance sheet and not the bank statement figure.

You should now be able to attempt Question 18.5 at the end of this chapter.

18.10 Summary

The control of cash is critical in all organisations. The person responsible for recording transactions is known as the ***cashier***. All cash and cheque receipts and payments are recorded in a ***cash book***. The cash book is balanced at regular intervals and checks made to ensure that the correct amounts are held either in immediate cash or at the bank. Where small cash payments are made, they are recorded in a ***petty cash book***. This is normally controlled on the ***imprest system***.

If the balance in the bank column of the cash book does not agree with the bank statement, a ***bank reconciliation*** is drawn up. This shows the reasons for the differences and adjustments are made to the cash book if errors need correcting.

You should now be able to attempt Task 18.3 and the Objective Test at the end of this chapter.

Student activities

Task 18.1 Visit a good stationery shop and examine the cash books on display. Note the differences in format and compare them with the examples we have used in this chapter.

Task 18.2 Draw up a cash book for your own receipts and expenditures as they occur during the next month. At the end of the month obtain a bank statement and prepare a bank reconciliation.

Task 18.3 Design a standard form which might be used in a small business for carrying out monthly bank reconciliations.

Question 18.1 You have been appointed as cashier to Warminster and Sons. The cash book on January 1 has the following balances:

Cash book

Receipts				Payments			
Date	Details	Cash	Bank	Date	Details	Cash	Bank
		£	£			£	£
Jan 1	Balances b/d	450	2,185				

During the month of January the following transactions take place:

January 2 Paid cheque of £1,250 for materials

January 3 Paid cheque of £500 for rent

January 6 Received £200 cash for sales

January 8 Paid delivery charges of £150 cash

January 9 Bought packaging materials for £185 cash

January 12 Received £1,000 cheque from customer

January 16 Paid cash of £115 for advertising

January 19 Customer paid £650 cheque

January 20 Drew £200 from bank for business use

January 24 Paid cheque of £3,000 for machinery

January 27 Paid electricity bill of £135 in cash

January 29 Cheque of £500 from customer

Required

Draw up the cash book for January showing the opening balances for 1 February.

Question 18.2

i) A company buys goods for £250 cash. What would the entry in the cash book be?

ii) At the end of a month the cash book shows cash receipts of £425 and cash payments of £297. What entries would be needed to balance the cash book?

iii) Cash of £350 is drawn from the bank for business purposes. What entries should be made in the cash book?

iv) An amount of £3,250 has to be inserted in the left hand bank column so that the two totals agree at the end of the month. Does this represent money that the business has in the bank or an overdraft?

v) A supplier offers you a trade discount of 5% if you purchase goods to the value of £1,000. What figures should be entered in the cash book if you pay by cheque?

vi) If a cash book showed an opening balance in the cash column on the right hand side, what would you conclude?

vii) What is a contra entry?

Question 18.3 The following transactions need to be analysed in the petty cash book. The first two transactions have been entered. Complete the entries and total the columns. Cross cast your analysed columns at the end to ensure that there are no errors. Note that only the payments side of the petty cash book is given and VAT has been ignored.

July 1	Bought envelopes for £12.00
July 1	Rail fare to Nottingham £16.20
July 1	Meal purchased at station £3.60
July 2	Writing paper and envelopes £5.20
July 2	Taxi fare to attend meeting £2.45
July 3	Coffee and milk for office £1.35
July 3	Postage of parcel £4.45
July 4	Paper clips, drawing pins and pens £6.55
July 4	Rail fare to Leicester £6.20
July 5	Postage stamps £3.80
July 5	Window cleaner £2.40
July 6	Biscuits for office £1.10

Petty cash book

Payments					
Date	Details	Total	Postage & stationery	Travelling expenses	Misc
		£	£	£	£
July 1	Envelopes	12.00	12.00		
July 1	Rail fare	16.20		16.20	

Question 18.4 David Stroud is responsible for the petty cash book. On the first of September an imprest of £50 is given to David. During that month the following amounts are paid by David.

September 1	Rail Fare £4.25
September 2	Tea and coffee for the office £1.80
September 3	Taxi fare for client's meeting £2.25
September 6	Envelopes and paper £3.45
September 7	Recorded delivery parcel £1.65
September 7	Cleaning cloths and disinfectant for office £2.65
September 10	Postage stamps £1.90
September 12	Special inking pen £1.05
September 14	Bus fares £0.40

September 16	Milk for office £2.20
September 17	Taxi fare £2.20
September 17	Recorded delivery parcel £3.00
September 18	Printer ribbon £1.80
September 21	Postage stamps £1.90
September 22	Manilla envelopes £3.00
September 24	Receipt book £1.00
September 24	Tea and coffee for office £1.80
September 24	Polish and cleaners £2.80
September 26	Bus fares £0.75
September 28	Rail fare £3.20
September 28	Meal £3.60

Required

Draw up the petty cash for the month analysing the expenditure into

- ❐ Postage and stationery
- ❐ Travelling expenses
- ❐ Miscellaneous

Give the entry on 1 October restoring the imprest.

Question 18.5 *Bob Chipping* has a pet shop. At the 30 June his cash book balance was £332, but when the bank statement was received it showed a balance in his favour of £607. On investigation Bob finds that cheques have been entered in to the cash book for £539 and sent to suppliers, but had still not been presented to the bank. On 30 June Bob had paid £264 into his bank account. This had been recorded in his cash book, but did not appear on his bank statement until 2 July. Prepare a bank reconciliation statement as at 30 June.

Objective test *(tick the appropriate box)*

i) *David Bowood* has received an invoice for £280 and pays this promptly in order to obtain the cash discount of 2.5%. What is the actual amount David pays:

a) £7.00 ☐

b) £287.00 ☐

c) £273.00 ☐

d) £277.50 ☐

ii) If at the end of a financial period you have £5.60 in the petty cash, you would expect to see this figure in the petty cash book as:

a) the closing balance on the right hand side ☐

b) the opening balance on the right hand side ☐

c) a total figure on the left hand side ☐

d) a total figure on the right hand side ☐

iii) If a company receives a trade discount, the cash book would:

a) show it on the left hand side ☐

b) show it on the right hand side ☐

c) not show it ☐

d) show it on both sides ☐

iv) The imprest system is a method whereby at the end of a period the petty cash is:

a) restored to its original amount ☐

b) put in the company bank account ☐

c) used to buy stationery ☐

d) counted three times ☐

v) Cheques which have been drawn but not yet presented are cheques which have been:

a) paid into the bank, but are not yet cleared. ☐

b) paid to suppliers, but are not yet on the bank statement ☐

c) received from debtors, but not yet paid into the bank ☐

d) none of these ☐

Chapter 19

Accounting concepts and conventions

19.1 Objectives

At the end of this chapter you should be able to:

- explain the importance of accounting concepts and conventions;
- describe the main concepts and conventions;
- explain the limitations of financial statements;
- calculate the impact on profit if a company is inconsistent in its accounting policies.

19.2 Introduction

So far in this book we have told you how you should carry out certain accounting activities. Some of you will have wondered why these activities are dealt with in one particular way when another method would seem to be just as good. You may have also found yourself wondering what you should do when you come up against a problem for which we have not given you specific guidance.

With accounting in the workplace it is not possible to have a huge text book which supplies answers to all the difficulties which are likely to arise. What you require is some help in deciding what is the best thing to do in certain circumstances. This often means wanting to know what other accountants would do and why. You require a framework in which to make your decision and this framework is the ***accounting concepts***. These give the assumptions that accountants make and the conventions that they use.

Some text books separate ***concepts*** from ***conventions*** and may also refer to generally accepted ***accounting principles***. The precise terms do not matter. What this chapter examines are the rules used in preparing financial statements.

19.3 Money measurement convention

Financial statements are prepared by measuring items in ***monetary values***. For example, if a business sells 500 tins of baked beans in a year and 250 bags of sugar, we can record the information in this way. But if we wish to prepare financial statements, these transactions must be recorded in terms of money so that we have a sales figure for the profit statement.

A business may look at its fixed assets at the end of the year in terms of being 5,000 square metres of office space, 5 cars and 15 personal computers. If we are to summarise these items on a balance sheet a common unit of measurement must be used. This unit is monetary value and can be expressed in any currency, such as pounds sterling, yen or francs, as long as we do not mix the different currencies in the same financial statements.

Unfortunately, there are a number of serious disadvantages with the ***money measurement concept***. Items which cannot be measured in money terms are ignored. A company may have very loyal and creative employees, but this will not be shown in any of the financial statements. Another company may have a large number of highly dissatisfied customers, but this will not be shown in the financial statements.

It is true that in the long-term one would expect that the company with loyal employees would prosper and the company with dissatisfied customers would go out of business. These are some of the reasons for the success or failure of the business, but these reasons are not shown anywhere on the financial statements only the consequences measured in monetary terms.

Another difficulty with using money as a measure is that it is not stable due to inflation. If you measure your desk and it is one metre long, you would expect it to be one metre long next year, and the year after. If you replaced your desk with another which is one metre long, you would be very surprised if you put the two side by side and one was longer than the other. However, if your desk originally cost £150 two years ago and you wished to replace it,you would expect, possibly, to pay more because of inflation. The same desk may now cost £165. The type of desk has not changed, but the money measure is different.

If you consider the balance sheet, the fixed assets will all be shown at cost less their cumulative depreciation to give their written down value. If the fixed assets have been bought at different times, then the money measure of cost will be different. A company may have identical computers, but if they were bought in different years the cost will not be the same and this fact will not be evident from the balance sheet. The written down values which are shown on the balance sheet may not be a good guide as to what the items are now worth and there will be no information given as to how much it would cost if they were to be replaced.

Despite the severe drawbacks to the money measurement concept, it is in universal use. A number of proposals have been made for adjusting financial statements to show the effects of inflation. These have not been successful so far but the issue is constantly being considered by accountants and alternatives sought.

You should now be able to attempt Task 19.1 and Question 19.1 at the end of this chapter.

19.4 Business entity convention

Financial statements describe the business as if it were entirely separate from its owner. If Josie Stamen owns a flower shop and we prepare the financial statements for the shop, we regard the shop as being a ***separate entity***, i.e. a thing with a real existence. When we produce a profit and loss account, the profit will have been "earned" by the business and it will be shown on the balance sheet as a liability which the business owes to Josie.

This view is a very artificial one because Josie runs the flower shop, but it is very helpful. When we are preparing financial statements, we have to draw some boundaries on what we are going to describe. Josie, as well as owning the flower shop, may also run a keep fit class two nights a week for which she is paid, be restoring a yacht, and may inherit £5,000 from her grandmother which she is using for speculating on the Stock Exchange. These are important activities for Josie and the people who know her, but if we set out to prepare financial statements for her flower shop, we need to concentrate on the activities which are related to that business. This task is made easier is we regard the business as a separate entity.

You will remember from Chapter 6 that an important feature of a limited company is that it is regarded as a distinct legal entity. This is of crucial importance in determining the financial liabilities of the owners of the business.

19.5 Going concern concept

A profit and loss statement and balance sheet are prepared for a business on the assumption that it will continue trading in the foreseeable future, in other words that it is a ***going concern***. In the vast majority of cases this is true and there is no intention to close the business or reduce any of its activities significantly.

If the business is not a going concern, the financial statements can be very misleading. Some of the assets owned by the business may have a very different value placed on them from that shown in the balance sheet. For example, an aeroplane manufacturer will have very specialised factories and equipment shown in the balance sheet at written down values. If the business were to close, it is very doubtful if there would be many buyers, apart from other aeroplane manufacturers, of the fixed assets and they may not sell for the figures shown on the balance sheet.

Because of the going concern basis, financial statements can mislead and the possible consequences of closure are not shown. Apart from fixed asset valuation, there are other items which are not revealed. For example, when a business is wound up, it will have to pay redundancy to its employees, and this information is not shown.

> *You should now be able to attempt Task 19.2 and Question 19.2 at the end of this chapter.*

19.6 Matching concept

We have met this before in Chapters 10 and 12 and it is an essential concept in the preparation of financial statements. It means that there must be a matching exercise so that expenses and revenues both refer to the same goods and the same financial period. Thus the receipt and payment of cash are not the only information required for the preparation of financial statements and accruals and prepayments must be taken into account.

Some writers divide the matching convention into a number of topics or show some of the implications under different headings. These are:

The period concept which means that a profit and loss account and balance sheet must be prepared at regular time intervals, for example each year. Unfortunately, business activities do not divide neatly into these periods and there are difficulties in dealing with this. For example, fixed assets last for a number of financial periods and business activity may not always correspond with the financial period selected.

The realisation concept is concerned with ensuring that when a transaction occurs it is recorded in the correct financial period. This is particularly relevant to sales. With cash sales there are no problems, but imagine that a shipbuilder has received an order for a luxury yacht which will take two years to build and will require further finishing after the owner has used it for six months. It is important to determine when the sale takes place and when the costs are incurred so that the correct figure of profit can be shown for a particular financial period.

19.7 Consistency concept

This means simply that once a particular method of accounting treatment has been selected it should be used to account for similar transactions and in subsequent financial periods. Failure to do this would mean that the financial results would be distorted and comparisons over a period of time would be impossible.

The importance of the ***consistency concept*** can be illustrated by a simple example. Imagine that a business has reported that it made a profit of £3,000 each year in the first two years of trading. Upon investigation you find that the business bought fixed assets of £50,000 in the first year. In year one the business decided to depreciate on a straight line basis with a life of five years and a nil scrap value. In year two it changed to the reducing balance method over a different estimated life to give a depreciation charge of £8,000 for the year.

In year one the depreciation charge would have been £10,000, but by changing its method and the life, the depreciation charge in year two is reduced by £2,000. If we are consistent and use the straight line method, the profit in year two is only £1,000.

> *You should now be able to attempt Task 19.3 at the end of this chapter.*

19.8 Prudence concept

This concept means that when you are preparing financial statements you should be a pessimist and not an optimist. Do not include revenues or profits unless you are certain that they will be realised.

On the other hand, all known liabilities should be included, even when the amount is not known with certainty and a best estimate has to be made. Thus on the profit and loss account accruals should be made for all expenses incurred, even if the invoice has not been received and the actual amount is not known. Similarly, a provision for bad debts will be made and deducted from the debtors on the balance sheet if we are not confident that all the money will be received.

Another example of accountants using the ***concept of prudence*** is in the valuation of stock held by a business. Stock at the year end will be valued at the lower of cost or net realisable value. Net realisable value can be taken as the estimated proceeds of selling the stock less all the costs required to put it into a marketable condition less all the costs to be incurred in marketing, selling and distributing the stock.

You should now be able to attempt Question 19.3 at the end of this chapter.

19.9 Summary

Accounting has a number of ***concepts*** and ***conventions*** which are used in maintaining accounting records and preparing financial statements. The concepts and conventions provide a ***framework*** and are essential in accounting. As well as providing a common basis for understanding accounts, the concepts and conventions also set some limitations on the usefulness of financial information.

You should now be able to attempt the Objective Test at the end of this chapter.

Student activities

Task 19.1 Consider a business such as an advertising agency or a hairdressing salon. Which aspects of the business do you think are important, but do not show on the financial statements?

Task 19.2 Make a list of local businesses and decide where there may be differences in the valuation of fixed assets as shown on the balance sheet under a going concern basis and the actual amounts which may be received if the businesses close. Do not worry about trying to get the figures, merely identify the major items.

Task 19.3 Make a list of the various transactions of a business which, if not dealt with in a consistent manner, would affect the financial statements.

Question 19.1 State the main disadvantages of using money as a unit of measurement to record business transactions.

Question 19.2 Select the correct response to the following statements:

	True	False
i) The value of items shown in the balance sheet is a good guide to what it would cost to replace them.	☐	☐
ii) Items which cannot be measured in monetary terms are omitted from financial statements.	☐	☐
iii) A sole trader's business is a separate legal entity.	☐	☐
iv) Businesses with very specialised assets do not have to produce financial statements on a going concern basis.	☐	☐
v) Inflation has no effect on the values of assets shown in the balance sheet.	☐	☐

Question 19.3 ***Keith Wilson*** trades in furniture. During the year he bought 80 coffee tables for £25 each and sold 60 of them for £27. At the year end he sees that a competitor is selling the tables for £24 each. Keith decides that his remaining tables require polishing, which will cost £1.50 each, and that he will have to advertise in the papers, which will cost £60, if he wishes to sell the remaining stock. What would be the stock valuation of the tables in the balance sheet at the year end?

Objective test *(tick the appropriate box)*

i) A profit and loss account and balance sheet are usually prepared for a business on the assumption that:

a) it will close the next day ☐

b) it is a going concern ☐

c) it will continue for only one year ☐

d) it will continue for only one month ☐

ii) If fixed assets are shown on the balance sheet at cost it means that:

a) this is the cost of replacing them now ☐

b) this is the cost if you wished to buy them ☐

c) this is the original cost at which the business bought them ☐

d) this is the cost of keeping them maintained ☐

iii) A major advantage of using money as a unit of measurement is that:

a) it is not stable due to inflation ☐

b) it allows a value to be put on employees' loyalty ☐

c) fixed assets are shown on the balance sheet at current values ☐

d) it allows different activities to be summarised in the accounts ☐

iv) When valuing the stock held by a business, an accountant will use:

a) the selling price ☐

b) the lower of cost or net realisable value ☐

c) the lower of cost or the selling price ☐

d) the replacement price ☐

v) If the owner of a business changed the method of depreciating fixed assets, it would be contrary to the:

a) matching concept ☐

b) prudence concept ☐

c) going concern concept ☐

d) consistency concept ☐

Assignment D

A problem with the bank

Context

You have received the following letters and papers from a friend:

SHIRES AGENCY
Import and Export
35A Alexander Buildings
Nottingham
Tel: 0335 216243

10 November 19X8

Dear Emma,

I wonder if you can help me. I have received the enclosed letter from the Bank Manager who is getting a bit shirty. I'm unable to understand why the overdraft is so high as I charge a mark up of 75% on the goods I trade in, which I think is fair enough.

Last year an accountant did some figures for me, but I have lost these. As there was some unpleasantness over non-payment of his fees, I am reluctant to go back to him. However, I have listed at the bottom of this letter the only figures I have been able to find that he did.

Would you please prepare the statements the Bank want? During the year to 30 June 19X8 I made sales of £84,700 on credit and I purchased £49,000 of goods from my suppliers. I've lost my bank statements and I don't want to ask for copies from the bank at the moment, but I have drawn up a list of all the money I have received and paid during the year.

Payments:	
Suppliers	£47,810
Wages	£9,500
Rates	£2,500
Carriage out	£96
Administrative expenses	£9,200
Insurance	£240
Car expenses	£3,500
Postage	£400
Telephone	£600
Electricity	£520
Receipts:	
Customers	£83,479

I still have to pay my last electricity bill for the year which amounts to £300, and of the amount for insurance, 50% of it refers to the next financial year. On the 30 June 19X8 I had stock worth £3,200.

Perhaps I had better explain about the loan. It is from my father, free of interest, and he does not want to be repaid until I have sorted myself out a bit.

I had better explain about the car as well. I think it is important to have a prestige vehicle like the Rolls. It does cost a lot to run and as there has been some misunderstanding over repair bills, the garage now makes me pay before they will let me have the car back and I think their charges are steep. The last accountant said it was best to depreciate the car at 20% on cost and I am happy to go on doing that, although I don't know what it means.

One problem is that I don't know how much money I've taken out of the business during the year for my own needs. Perhaps there is some way you can work this out for me?

By the way, I expect the manager will ask me some pretty shrewd questions and I want to show him I am on the ball when it comes to finance. Could you please tell me briefly what a profit and loss account and a balance sheet is and what they show me? If you have any comments or advice on my accounts could you please include them m your reply.

I know you will not expect a fee for your help, but I will take you out for a meal next time I see you.

Your sincerely

Figures from last accountant

Balances as at 30 June 19X7

Owned:	£
Premises at cost	40,000
Car (cost £40,000) net book value	32,000
Stock	2,600
Debtors	2,000
Bank	1,126
	77,726
Liabilities:	
Trade creditors	1,500
Loan from father	10,000
	11,500

The Forest Bank

Baytree Road, Nottingham
Tel: 0335 212788

26 September 19X8

T Shires, Esq.,
35A Alexander Buildings
Nottingham

Dear Mr Shires,

I am surprised to note that despite my previous letters you have taken no action to reduce your business overdraft which stood at £4,761 on 30 June 19X8. Although I have asked you to make an appointment to see me on a number of occasions, you have failed to do so. I must therefore ask you to attend a meeting at my offices on 7 December 19X8. You must bring your most recent trading and profit and loss account and balance sheet with you.

If you fail to attend the meeting I will have no alternative but to stop all payments from this account and take legal action for the recovery of the money due to the bank.

Yours faithfully,

G Sherriff

G Sherriff
Branch Manager

Student activities

i) Construct a balance sheet as at 30 June 19X7.

ii) Prepare a trading and profit and loss account for the year ended 30 June 19X8.

iii) Construct a balance sheet as at 30 June 19X8.

iv) Analyse the results of the business in the light of the information given in the two letters.

Format

A letter is required addressed to your friend which includes:

- ❒ A trading and profit and loss account for the year ended 30 June 19X8.
- ❒ A balance sheet as at 30 June 19X8.
- ❒ Recommendations as to the action your friend should take to resolve his financial problems.

Objectives

In this assignment the student will apply and appreciate the techniques for preparing financial statements where the information is not presented in a straightforward manner and appreciate the implications of the financial statements in a specific business context.

References

Chapter 16 will be of particular use.

Limited liability companies

This section (Chapters 20-22) is concerned with limited liability companies.

In Chapter 20 we considered the regulatory framework of limited liability companies. We look at the main statements made publicly available by limited liability companies, the main regulations affecting the information published by them, and the information contained in the annual report and accounts.

Chapter 21 looks at various aspects of the profit and loss account and balance sheet of limited liability companies and compares them with the accounts of sole traders.

In Chapter 22 we consider various aspects of the interpretation of company accounts, particularly some accounting ratios, together with trend analysis and inter-firm comparisons.

Chapter 20

The regulatory framework

20.1 Objectives

At the end of this chapter you should be able to:

- identify the main documents made publicly available by limited companies;
- explain the main regulations affecting the information published by limited companies;
- describe the information contained in an annual report and accounts;
- examine critically the information contained in an annual report and accounts.

20.2 Main features of limited liability companies

In Chapter 6 we examined different organisational structures and looked at their main characteristics. Before we proceed we will review the main features of limited liability companies:

- The company is a legal entity; it has a legal identity separate from that of its owners.
- The liability of the shareholders in the company is limited to the amount that they have agreed to invest.
- A company must have at least two shareholders.
- The rights of management are frequently delegated to directors.

There are two types of companies limited by shares. A ***public limited company*** must be registered as such and is able to offer shares to the public. Such companies must include the words ***public limited company*** or the abbreviation ***plc*** after the company's name, or the Welsh equivalent if the company's registered office is in Wales. Public limited companies are often listed on the ***Stock Exchange***. This means that their shares can be bought and sold by the public there. However, they do not have to be listed.

Any company that is not a public limited company is a ***private limited company***. Such companies must include the word ***Limited*** or the abbreviation ***Ltd*** after the company's name, or the Welsh equivalent if the company's registered office is in Wales. Private limited companies cannot offer shares to the public.

You should now be able to attempt Question 20.1 at the end of this chapter.

20.3 Main documents published by limited companies

All limited companies must be registered with the ***Registrar of Companies*** at Companies House which is under the control of the Department of Trade and Industry. There are a number of legal requirements to be met when a limited liability company is first formed, including filing certain documents with the Registrar. The principal documents required on registration, which we will examine, are the ***memorandum of association*** and the ***articles of association***.

The most useful document published by a limited liability company is the annual report and accounts. All limited liability companies have to send every shareholder a copy of the company's annual report and accounts and file a copy with the Registrar of Companies. As anyone can visit Companies House and obtain a copy for a modest fee, the ***annual report and accounts*** is a public document.

Public limited companies which are listed on the Stock Exchange make their annual report and accounts freely available. If you read the financial pages in the Press you will find that they carry announcements by public limited companies of their financial results for the year and an address from which to obtain a copy of their annual report and accounts.

Because of the importance of the annual report and accounts to those who are interested in the company, most of this chapter is concerned with the contents of such documents and the legislation which affects them. But first we will consider the memorandum of association and the articles of association which are submitted to the Registrar when a company is first formed.

20.4 Memorandum and articles of association

The ***memorandum of association*** defines the company's constitution and the objects. This means the purpose for which it is trading. The ***articles of association*** are the internal regulations of the company. As these documents are filed with the Registrar of Companies, they are open to public inspection, although only those people who are deeply interested in the affairs of a company would wish to refer to them. The documents are of great importance in defining the way that the company conducts its affairs. If the directors of the company wish to implement significant changes in the rules of the company, it may be necessary to obtain permission of the shareholders to make the necessary changes in the memorandum or articles of association

The main information provided in the ***memorandum of association*** is:

- ❒ the name of the company;
- ❒ whether it is a public limited company;
- ❒ the country where the registered office is situated;
- ❒ the objects of the company (this may merely state that the object is to carry on business as a general commercial company);
- ❒ a statement that the liability of the members (shareholders) is limited;
- ❒ the amount of share capital with which the company proposes to be registered, and its division of shares into a fixed amount;
- ❒ a formal statement that the subscribers are desirous of being formed into a company.

The ***articles of association*** must be printed and divided into numbered paragraphs, bear a deed stamp, and be signed by the subscribers to the memorandum with the signature of one witness. They deal with such matters as:

- ❒ share and loan capital and the holders' rights;
- ❒ meetings and voting rights;
- ❒ the power, duties, appointment and removal of directors;
- ❒ accounts and audit.

Alteration of the Articles requires a special resolution of the members, with twenty-one days' notice to them and a three-quarters' majority of votes cast at the meeting.

You should now be able to attempt Task 20.1 and Question 20.2 at the end of this chapter.

20.5 The regulatory framework

By ***regulatory framework*** for limited companies, we mean the legislation that controls their financial reporting and accounting, and other regulations which have been set by the ***Stock Exchange*** or the ***Accounting Standards Board.***

The purpose of the regulatory framework is to ensure that those who have an interest in a company can obtain financial information which gives a ***true and fair view*** of the company's affairs. However, this is not easy. Companies may not wish to disclose certain financial information for a number of very goods reasons. For example, if confidential information got into the hands of a company's competitors it could cause damage to the company and its shareholders and employees. Occasionally companies may not wish to disclose financial information for the wrong reasons. If you look at major company scandals, many of them are concerned with the information the company did or did not disclose.

20.6 Companies Acts

The first ***Companies Act*** was passed in 1844. This allowed companies to be incorporated by legislation instead of by special Act of Parliament or Royal Charter. There have been a number of Companies Acts since that date imposing further responsibilities and requirements on companies. The most recent act is the ***Companies Act 1989***.

The legislation and other regulations are very lengthy and complex. If you decide to become an accountant, you will have to study them in great detail. However for students of most financial and business courses it is sufficient to know only the main requirements.

The most recent UK legislation has introduced requirements which have been designed to harmonise company accounting throughout the European Community (EC). This process of harmonisation is set by directives issued by the ***Council of the European Communities***. The aim is not to eliminate all differences throughout the EC, but to narrow them and establish some minimum standards.

The ***Companies Act 1989*** makes changes to the law principally to introduce the requirements of the ***Seventh Directive*** on group accounts and the ***Eighth Directive*** on regulation of auditors. The Act has been written so that it replaces, amends or adds sections and schedules to the ***Companies Act 1985***, which therefore remains a major piece of legislation in the UK. For this reason, most text books on accounting still refer to the Companies Act 1985, meaning as amended by the Companies Act 1989.

The main requirements of this legislation are applicable to all limited companies, but there are some exemptions given to private limited companies. these are designed to relive them of some of the administrative burdens. For the purposes of this book, the most important requirements are:

❐ to keep accounting records sufficient to show and explain the company's transactions;

❐ to prepare final accounts which will comprise:

  a profit and loss account;

  a balance sheet;

  an auditor's report;

  a directors' report.

The final accounts are laid before the ***shareholders*** (often referred to as the ***members***) at a general meeting. They are circulated before the meeting to all members and debenture holders and delivered to the Registrar of Companies.

The formats, the way the final accounts should be presented, are given in Schedule 4 of the Companies Act 1985. Examples of some of these are given in the following chapters, but the main points are:

❐ The balance sheet has two alternative formats. Format 1 is a vertical layout with the current liabilities deducted from the current assets. Format 2 has the same contents, but in two blocks headed ***assets*** and ***liabilities***, current assets and current liabilities not being netted off. The blocks can be placed in a vertical or a horizontal layout.

❐ The profit and loss account has four formats. In format 1 the items are vertically arranged according to function, for example administration costs, distribution expenses. Format 3 arranges the same information in two blocks headed "***charges*** and ***income***" and these may be presented horizontally. Format 2 classifies costs according to their nature, for example raw materials, wages, depreciation, in a vertical format. Format 4 is a two block version of format 2.

20.7 The Accounting Standards Board

Although company legislation is complex, it has not been enough by itself to control adequately all the accounting activities of companies. At the end of the 1960s there were some highly publicised events which brought accounting into disrepute. In response to this, the Institute of Chartered Accountants in England and Wales set up the ***Accounting Standards Committee (ASC)*** at the beginning of the 1970s and the other accounting bodies soon joined. The ASC was formed to narrow the areas of difference and variation in accounting practices by issuing ***Statements of Accounting Practice (SSAPs)***. The ASC issued a total of 25 SSAPs before it was disbanded in 1990.

The ASC had done much to improve accounting in the UK, but the Committee found it increasingly difficult to obtain acceptance by companies of regulations on controversial topics. Some commentators suggested that a tougher enforcement regime was required. In 1987 an independent review of the standard-setting process was carried out and proposals for a new structure and system were issued in 1988 and came into being in 1990. The following diagram shows the new standard-setting structure.

The accounting standards-setting structure

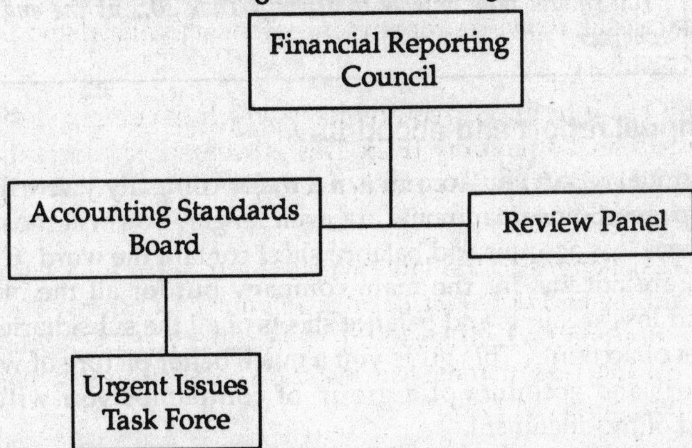

The ***Financial Reporting Council*** is responsible for guiding the Accounting Standards Board on its work programme and on broad matters of policy. The ***Accounting Standards Board (ASB)*** has a full-time chairman and a full-time technical director, as well as part-time members. The ASB is responsible for issuing new standards and has adopted the SSAPs issued by the ASC. The new standards are known as ***Financial Reporting Standards (FRSs)***. The ones issued by the ASB so far have had a significant impact on the accounts of companies. Financial Reporting Standard 1 requires companies to publish a Cash Flow Statement. Financial Reporting Standard 3 – Reporting Financial Performance has introduced significant changes to the profit and loss account by requiring companies to give information on any significant activities which have been discontinued.

The ***Review Panel*** is responsible for the investigation of any departures from accounting standards by companies and the ***Urgent Issues Task Force*** tackles issues not already covered by accounting standards but which require immediate action. The Urgent Issues task Force has issued a number of pronouncements (known as Abstracts) on a range of important topics.

The strength of the new standard-setting structure has been increased by legislation. Companies must state whether their accounts have been prepared in accordance with accounting standards and give information if they have not done so. If the Secretary of State or the Review Panel are dissatisfied with the published accounts of a company, they can apply to the courts and the company concerned may be required to prepare revised accounts which do give a true and fair view.

20.8 The London Stock Exchange

If a company chooses to be listed on the ***London Stock Exchange***, that is for its shares to be traded there, it must comply with additional reporting requirements. In addition to the annual report and accounts required by the ***Companies Act 1985***, a company must prepare a half-yearly report on its activities and profit and loss during the first six months of each financial year. This is known as an ***interim report*** and it must be sent to the holders of its listed securities or inserted as a paid advertisement in one national daily newspaper.

Stock Exchange regulations require that the annual report and accounts provides significantly more information than that required by the Companies Act 1985. The following short list includes some of the items required:

- A statement by the directors giving the reasons for any significant departures from applicable standard accounting practices.
- A geographic analysis of net turnover and of contribution to trading results of those trading operations carried on outside the UK and Ireland.
- The following particulars regarding each company in which the group interest exceeds 20% of equity capital:

  the principal country of operation;

  particulars of its issued capital and debt securities;

  the percentage of each class of debt securities attributable to the company's interest.
- A statement of the amount of interest capitalised during the year, together with an indication of the amount and treatment of any related tax relief.

You should now be able to attempt Task 20.2 at the end of this chapter.

20.9 Information in the annual report and accounts

If you obtain the published annual report and accounts of a major company you will find that it may comprise of anything between 40 and 70 pages. Some documents are even longer. You will most likely find that the financial statements such as the profit and loss account and balance sheet contain the word 'Consolidated' in their heading. This is because the accounts are not just for the main company but for all the other companies it owns ie its subsidiaries. All the profit and loss accounts and balance sheets of all the subsidiaries have been brought together and 'consolidated' into one set of accounts. This gives you a much better picture of what is happening in the entire group. If you have the report and accounts of a group of companies you will find a list of the principle subsidiaries usually at the end of the document.

Because most of the published reports and accounts which are readily obtainable refer to groups of companies, we will concentrate on these. The information in the report and accounts can be divided approximately into two main sections. The first half of the document is mainly information that the company chooses to give. The second part of the document is information the company is obliged to give under the regulatory framework. This second part is often printed on a different type or coloured paper. We will concentrate on this section first.

The regulatory framework section

Under the Companies Act 1985, accounting standards and, for a listed company, Stock Exchange regulations the following are the main items of information which should be provided:

- Profit and loss account. This is required by the Companies Act 1985 but will also show certain information on new aquisitions and discontinued activities as required by Financial Reporting Standard 3.
- Balance sheet. This is required by the Companies Act 1985 and the vertical format as discussed in Chapter 12 is the most common form of presentation.
- Cash flow statement. This is required by Financial Reporting Standard 1 and will show the cash flow for the financial period under the following five headings

  Operating activites

  Returns on investments and servicing of finance

  Taxation

  Investing activities

  Financing
- Statement of total recognised gains and losses. This is a primary financial statement required by Financial Reporting Standard 3. Not all aspects of a companiy's financial performance will go through the profit and loss account and the purpose of this new statement is to highlight those other gains and losses which are recognised in a period and increase or decrease sharholders' funds. Examples are unrealised deficits or

surpluses on revaluation of investment properties, unrealised losses or gains on trade investments, and foreign exchange translation differences.

- Directors' report. This is addressed to the members or shareholders and provides a range of information which is usually quite technical. You will also find information on such matters as any political or charitable donations and the employment of disabled persons.
- Auditors' report
- Notes to the accounts

In the following sections we discuss the auditors' report and the notes to the accounts in more detail.

The review section

The first section of the annual report and accounts is a type of review and may even be published as a separate document with that title. Although some of the information in this section will be provided because it is required or 'encouraged as good practice' under the regulatory framework, much of the information will be voluntary. The types of information will vary from company to company, but the following list is an indication of the types of information you may find.

- Chairman's statement. It would be highly unusual not to find a statement by the Chairman of the Company. This will provide an overview of the company's performance and any major events. Not surprisingly the Chairman will want to give the most favorable picture to the shareholders.
- Highlights of the main financial results. This is often just one page concentrating on the main financial results such as the profit figure and the dividends.
- Review of the company's activities. This section will tend to be more factual and detailed than the Chairman's Statement. Often the main parts of the business and their financial performance and business operations will be discussed. The Accounting Standards Board is encouraging companies to give an Operating and Financial Review which interprets the financial data, discusses the business, its risks and the structure of its finance.
- Corporate Governance statement. Following some of the major financial scandals in the 1980's the financial and business community became very concerned over the ethics of business and the way it was governed. A committee was established to consider the problem and a series of recommendations were issued under the title of the Cadbury Report. Companies listed on the Stock Exchange should disclose the extent to which they comply with the Cadbury Recommendations. A number of companies discuss their approach at some length and you may find a section entitled corporate governance.
- Historical summaries. Most companies provide a statement of their main financial results for the last five or ten years. This is a useful source of information when you wish to draw up accounting ratios as discussed in Chapter 22.
- Environmental issues. As corporate governance became an important topic in annual reports and accounts so has the environment. A number of companies make statements on their environmental policies and in some industries which have a high environmental profile you may find lengthy discussion on their activities and policies.

In this section we have not been able to refer to all items of information you might find. There will certainly be a profusion of photographs and diagrams. You will also find information on topics such as visits to the company by royal personages, charitable and community activities and sporting and scholastic achievements by employees.

You should now be able to attempt Task 20.3 and Question 20.3 at the end of this chapter.

20.10 The auditors' report

All limited companies in the UK are required by law to have their accounts ***audited*** by a professional accountant qualified under the Companies Act to do so. The auditor must be registered and supervised by the accounting bodies. The annual report and accounts must include a report from the auditors. Although it is brief, it is an essential piece of information in the annual report and accounts and will alert you to any problems that the auditors may believe affect the financial statements.

The auditor's report will be addressed to the members of the company, this means the shareholders. There will be an introductory paragraph in which the auditors make clear to which pages of the annual report and accounts they are referring. You will find that these pages will be in the second part of the document which we called the regulatory framework section.

The second paragraph of the auditors' report will state that it is the Directors' responsibility to prepare the financial statements and that it is the auditors' responsibility to form an opinion on those financial statements and report upon them. The next section of the auditors' report will be headed 'Basis of Opinion' and the auditor will refer to the manner in which they conducted the audit.

The final paragraph is the actual opinion of the auditors and the important phrase is whether the auditors consider that the financial statements give a 'true and fair' view. If this is not the case any reader of the financial statements should take considerable care in drawing any conclusion or making any interpretations.

You should now be able to attempt Task 20.4 at the end of this chapter.

20.11 Notes to the accounts

The financial statements are supported by notes to the accounts which will take up a considerable number of pages. Some of the notes will provide explanations or further information on certain figures in the financial statements. Other notes will provide new information.

The notes are important as they help you to better understand the financial statements and provide more detailed information. It would be impossible to get all the informationin the financial statements themselves. On the face of the profit and loss account, balance sheet and cash flow statement will be given the appropriate note number for the separate items.

The nature type and detail of the notes will vary depending on the company and the activities in which it is engaged. There are, however, some important notes which are common to most companies and you should be able to find examples of these in your annual report and accounts.

- Accounting Policies. This is a most important note and will either be note number 1 or 2 or may even be on a separate page before the numbered notes. Companies are required to publish their policies in respect of certain accounting treatments. Although these can be very technical they are important as they describe items which are significant in determining the profit and financial position of the company. You should find statements such as depreciation, goodwill, foreign exchange, pensions and research and development.
- Segmental information. Large companies will give a breakdown by class of business and geographical area of their turnover and profit. This is most useful in ascertaining the most profitable areas of the company and where it seems to be experiencing risks or problems. This information can be used for constructing accounting ratios as discussed in Chapter 22.
- Directors' emoluments. In its broadest sense this means the pay of directors and this note usually receives great attention from the press. You will find the pay of the Chairman or the highest paid director if it is not the chairman. You will also find the emoluments of the other directors grouped in bands of £5,000.
- Employee information. Companies are obliged to disclose information on the numbers of employees and the staff costs. The number of employees is one way of measuring the relative size of a company and you can work out the turnover and profit per employee and compare these figures to other companies to find out which company has the most 'profitable' employees.
- Tangible fixed assets. There are the resources such as buildings, machinery, cars and equipment. Although the assets are grouped under main headings, the note will be very comprehensive and give not only the original cost or value of the items, but additions and disposals as well as the cumulative depreciation and the net book values.

You should now be able to attempt Task 20.5 and Question 20.4 at the end of this chapter.

Summary

Limited liability companies are either ***public limited companies,*** able to offer their shares to the public, or ***private limited companies,*** which are not permitted to do so. All limited companies must register with the ***Registrar of Companies*** and file an ***annual report and accounts*** which thus becomes a public document. All companies must also file a ***memorandum of association,*** which defines the company's constitution and objects, and ***articles of association,*** which contain the internal regulations of the company.

The activities of limited liability companies are controlled within a ***regulatory framework.*** This comprises legistation in the form of the ***Companies Acts,*** pronouncements of the ***Accounting Standards Board*** and, for ***listed companies,*** the requirements of the ***London Stock Exchange.***

The annual report and accounts is the most useful document issued by limited companies. The annual report and accounts of a public limited company is readily available and discloses information required by the regulatory framework and also information on other issues.

Student activities

Task 20.1 Read the financial Press and find any announcements on meetings being held by companies to pass a resolution to amend the company's articles or memorandum of association. What is the most frequent reason for the change?

Task 20.2 Search the financial Press for the announcement of the interim results of a well known company. Read a number of financial newspapers and collect the comments made on the interim results. Do different newspapers make similar statements or do they vary?

Task 20.3 On which pages of your annual report and accounts is the following information:

- ❒ Notice of the annual general meeting
- ❒ Auditors' report
- ❒ Chairman's statement
- ❒ Directors' report
- ❒ Profit and loss account
- ❒ Balance sheet
- ❒ Five or ten year summary of results

Task 20.4 Answer the following questions using the information in your annual report and accounts:

i) Who are the auditors?
ii) Which Statements of Standard Accounting Practice (if any) are noted in the auditors' report?
iii) On what date did the auditors sign their report?
iv) What fee was charged by the auditors for their services?

Task 20.5 Examine the notes in your annual report and accounts and answer the following questions:

i) What was the issued share capital of the company at the year end?
ii) How many authorised shares are there?
iii) What was the emolument (salary) of the chairman?
iv) What was the total value of stocks at the year end?
v) What was the total of wages and salaries?

Question 20.1 Select the correct response to the following statements:

		True	False
i)	Only public limited companies are quoted on the Stock Exchange.	☐	☐
ii)	There are no limits to the number of shareholders there can be in a limited company.	☐	☐
iii)	You cannot take legal action against a limited company.	☐	☐
iv)	All limited companies must put the letters plc after their names.	☐	☐
v)	The share prices of private limited companies are published each day in the Financial Times.	☐	☐
vi)	If a private limited company is unable to pay all its debts, the shareholders are responsible for them.	☐	☐

Question 20.2 Tick the items in the following list which should appear in a limited liability company's memorandum of association:

i) Objects of the company

ii) Profit and loss account

iii) Name of the company

iv) Statement that the liability of the members is limited

v) Auditors' report

vi) Whether it is a public limited company

vii) Voting rights

Question 20.3 List the main types of information you would expect to find in the annual report and accounts of a public limited company.

Question 20.4 Insert the missing word or phrase in the following statements:

i) An auditors' report should normally state that the accounts give a .... view.

ii) The Companies Act 1989 mainly introduced requirements on the regulation of auditors and ....

iii) A company which can offer its shares to the public is known as a ....

iv) The .... is responsible for issuing accounting standards.

v) The regulatory framework consists of three elements: company legislation, ... and ....

Objective test *(tick the appropriate box)*

i) A limited liability company:

a) must have at least three shareholders ☐

b) is quoted on the Stock Exchange ☐

c) must have the letters plc written after its name ☐

d) is a company where the liability of its shareholders is limited to the amount that they have agreed to invest ☐

ii) The memorandum of association provides information concerning:

a) accounts and audit ☐

b) meetings and voting rights ☐

c) the objects of the company ☐

d) the powers, duties and removal of directors ☐

iii) A limited liability company is required to circulate shareholders with copies of its final accounts by:

a) a Statement of Standard Accounting Practice (SSAP) ☐

b) the Companies Act 1985 ☐

c) a Statement Of Recommended Practice (SORP) ☐

d) the articles of association ☐

iv) The Companies Act 1985 gives the format for the appropriate presentation of the balance sheet. The format must be:

a) in vertical format ☐

b) in horizontal format ☐

c) in blocks of assets and liabilities either in vertical format or horizontal format ☐

d) any of these ☐

v) In addition to the requirements of the Companies Acts, the Stock Exchange requires a listed company to produce:

a) a statement by the directors giving reasons for significant departures from SSAPs ☐

b) an auditors' report ☐

c) a directors' report ☐

d) all of these ☐

Chapter 21

Profit and loss accounts and balance sheets

21.1 Objectives

At the end of this chapter you should be able to:

- appreciate the major differences between the accounts of a sole trader and the accounts of a limited liability company;
- understand the meanings of the terms:

  share capital

  dividends

  preference and ordinary shares

  authorised and issued shares

  appropriation account

  transfers to reserves

  provisions for taxation;
- examine the accounts for limited liability companies incorporating the above.

21.2 Introduction

In Chapter 20 we looked at the ***regulatory framework*** of ***limited liability companies*** and in Chapters 10–15 you gained practice in preparing the ***accounts*** of a ***sole trader***. The accounts of a limited liability company incorporate many of the principles used in the accounts of a sole trader, but there are a number of important differences between them.

One major factor to note is that a limited liability company's business is usually much larger and more complex than a sole trader's. Consequently, the accounts contain much more detail. In addition to preparing a full profit and loss account and balance sheet for internal use, a limited liability company is obliged to publish statutory accounts. The latter do not contain the same amount of detail as those produced for internal use.

First we will look at the major ***differences*** between the accounts of a sole trader and those of a limited liability company. Then you will be introduced to some of the terms needed to understand company accounts. Next we will examine the internal profit and loss account and balance sheet produced by limited liability companies and then at the structure and content of the published statutory accounts. In doing this we will concentrate on the published accounts of a group of companies, ie Consolidated accounts, as these are the type you will most likely encounter.

21.3 Major differences

The major ***differences*** between the accounts of a ***sole trader*** and those of a ***limited liability company*** can be summarised as follows:

Sole trader	*Limited liability company*
Capital is the sum introduced by the owner at the start.	***Share capital*** is the amount invested by the shareholders whose liability is limited to their shareholding (or if a share is only partly paid, also to the amount owing on the shares).
It is increased by ***profit***	***Profit*** belongs to the share- holders but is not part of the share capital. It is part of the shareholders' worth.
and decreased by ***drawings***, which are usually shown as a deduction from ***capital*** plus ***profit*** on the balance sheet.	***Dividends*** are recommended by the directors and if approved by the shareholders are paid to the shareholders. Dividends are an ***appropriation*** of the profit.
Loans are made by banks, other financial institutions or individuals.	***Debentures*** represent loans made to the company. They are bonds issued by the company.

21.4 Financial terminology

The above summary of the differences between the accounts of a sole trader and those of a limited liability company introduces some new terms with which you may not be familiar and it will be helpful if these are explained before we proceed.

- ***Share capital***

  Shares can be of various denominations; 25p is fairly common. If you look at the London Share Service page of the Financial Times, this is the default value. Other denominations are 1p, 5p, 10p, 50p, £1.

- ***Dividends***

  Directors decide on the amount of dividend to be recommended for approval at the ***annual general meeting (AGM)***. The amount depends on the profits. Dividend policy is too complicated to be discussed here, but usually some profit is retained and perhaps transferred to reserves (kept back for use in the business). Shareholders cannot propose a dividend higher than that recommended by the directors, though they can (unusually) propose a reduction in the dividend if they feel that it would be more advantageous for the company to retain profits, perhaps to improve the cash (liquidity) position.

  It is common practice to express the dividend for preference shares and those for ordinary shares as pence per share, or as a percentage as shown in the following examples for ordinary shares.

	Example 1	*Example 2*
Number of shares	100,000	1,000,000
Denomination	25p	£1
Share capital	£25,000	£1,000,000
Dividend (%)	10%	5%
Dividend (pence)	2.5p	5p
Total amount of dividend	£2,500	£50,000
Sample shareholding of	1,000 shares	1,000 shares
gives a dividend of	£25	£50

- ***Debentures***

  These are long-term loans, sometimes held by banks. They are usually secured on specific assets such as property or on all or some of the assets (called a ***floating charge***). Interest paid on debentures, like interest charged on overdrafts, is charged as an expense in the profit and loss account. Debentures are not part of the share capital and debenture holders are not members of the company unless they also hold shares.

- ***Preference shares***

  Preference shareholders are entitled to a specified percentage rate of dividend and are paid before ordinary shareholders. There are two main categories of preference shares:

  Cumulative preference shares: If there are insufficient profits for any dividend to be paid in one year, the arrears have to be paid to cumulative preference shareholders before any other class of share is paid in any subsequent year.

  Non-cumulative preference shares: Arrears are not accumulated.

- ***Ordinary shares***

  These are the most common form of share capital and usually carry voting rights. Whereas preference shareholders are entitled to specific rate of dividend, ordinary shareholders only receive dividends after preference shareholders have been paid. Dividends are proposed at the discretion of the directors. Therefore ordinary shares are often described as ***risk capital*** or ***equity***.

- ***Authorised share capital***

  This is the amount of share capital a company is allowed to issue. The issued share capital may be less than the authorised share capital. The authorised share capital is shown as a *note* on (or to) the balance sheet and is not part of the figures needed to balance.

- ***Called-up capital***

  This is a proportion of the issued shares for which payment has been demanded and paid for. It is not unusual for companies to issue shares with part of the amount due paid initially and the balance at some later date.

Example

Sunderland Ltd was formed with a right to issue 500,000 ordinary shares of £1 each, but to date only 400,000 shares have been issued. None of the shares issued has been fully paid and only 60p per share has been called. On 1,000 of the shares, no payment has been received; on another 2,000 the full amount of £1 per share had been paid.

Required

Quantify the following:

i) Authorised share capital

ii) Issued share capital

iii) Called-up capital

iv) Calls in arrears

v) Calls in advance

vi) Paid-up capital

Solution

i) 500,000 shares of £1 each = £500,000

ii) 400,000 shares of £1 each = £400,000

iii) 400,000 shares × 60p = £240,000

iv) 1,000 shares × 60p = £600

v) 2,000 shares × 40p = £800

vi) £240,000 – £600 = £239,400

❐ ***Minority interests***

The holding company of a group of companies may not own all the shares of its subsidiaries. They may be owned by outside shareholders whose shareholding is known as a minority interest. When the results of all the separate companies in the group are consolidated, it is important to show the amount belonging to minority interests.

❐ ***Exceptional and extraordinary items***

One reason for looking at a profit and loss account is to find out what profit a company makes from its business activities. But what if the company has suffered a large loss through fire and it was not insured or perhaps a war led to the loss of its overseas assets? If these events are significant, it is important for the company to identify them separately in its accounts. There is considerable argument among accountants as to which events are exceptional and which are extraordinary, and how they should be shown in the accounts. Under FRS 3 extraordinary items are now very rare.

❐ ***Corporation tax charge***

At the time of the preparation of the accounts, it is unlikely that the liability to corporation tax will have been agreed. Therefore an estimate is made and a suitable amount provided for.

Taxation is a large and complicated subject. In the questions which follow later in this chapter, in order to keep things simple, estimated liability for tax is shown under ***Creditors: amounts due within one year*** on the balance sheet.

❐ ***Transfers to reserves***

When the directors of a company transfer profits to reserves, it is simply an indication that they do not intend to distribute the amount transferred as a dividend in that particular year. Reserves are also shown on the balance sheet in the ***Financed by*** or ***Represented by*** section.

❐ ***Proposed dividends***

Assuming there are adequate profits remaining after the previous two items, a dividend is shown as already described. Many companies issue an interim statement during a financial year, reporting on profits, usually for the first six months of the year. At the same time, if interim profits are adequate, they declare and pay an ***interim dividend***. This interim dividend is usually shown in the final accounts for the year as follows.

Example

	£	£
Interim dividend paid	4,000	
Proposed final dividend	8,000	
		12,000

Proposed dividends are shown on the balance sheet under ***Creditors: amounts due within one year.***

After the above appropriations, there is almost always a balance of unappropriated profit. This is transferred to the profit and loss account balance in the balance sheet as part of the shareholders' equity.

21.5 The appropriation account

In the profit and loss account of a sole trader the net profit before tax is transferred to the capital section of the balance sheet. However, it is not quite so simple with a limited liability company as it is necessary to show what happens to the net profit. An ***appropriation account*** is used for this. It is shown at the bottom of the ***profit and loss account*** and starts with the figure of ***net profit*** before tax.

The items entered in the appropriation account vary according to the size and complexity of the company and what the directors decide to do. Typical entries include:

- ❐ Corporation tax charge
- ❐ Dividends paid and proposed

- Transfers to reserves
- Additions to the profit and loss account balance

The following is an example of an appropriation account containing the above items.

Example

	£	£
Net profit before tax (this year)		60,000
Corporation tax charge		20,000
Profit for the year available to shareholders		40,000
Dividends, interim, paid	4,000	
Proposed, final	8,000	12,000
		28,000
Profit and loss account balance brought forward from previous year		5,000
		33,000
Transfer to reserves		30,000
Profit and loss account balance carried forward to next year		3,000

We will now work through an example of a profit and loss account and balance sheet for a limited company. We have simplified this example but remember that you will not see all this detail when you look at the published accounts which are available to the public.

Example

The books of ***Hartlepool plc*** showed the following figures at 31st December 19X2:

	£'000	£'000
Sales		1,250
Opening stock at 1st January 19X2	50	
Purchases	610	
Wages and salaries	250	
Rates	20	
Insurance	15	
Light and heat	10	
Office expenses	30	
Miscellaneous expenses	50	
Buildings	280	
Plant and equipment	200	
Cumulative provision for depreciation on plant and equipment		80
Motor vehicles	120	
Cumulative provision for depreciation on motor vehicles		30
Debtors	130	
Bank (in credit)	116	
Creditors		50

	£'000	£'000
Share capital:		
8% Preference shares (100,000 authorised)		
Issued 50,000 of £1 each		50
Ordinary shares (500,000 authorised)		
Issued 400,000 of £1 each		400
Reserves brought forward at 1st January 19X2		15
Profit and loss account balance		
brought forward at 1st January 19X2		6
	1,881	1,881

The following additional information is provided as at 31st December 19X2:

Stocks are valued at	£60,000
Accruals:	
Wages and salaries	£10,000
Light and heat	£3,000
Prepayments:	
Rates	£5,000
Insurance	£3,000
Depreciation for the year:	
Buildings	Nil
Plant and equipment	20% of cost
Motor vehicles	25% of cost
Proposed dividends:	
Preference shares	pay full dividend
Ordinary shares	15p per share
Provide for corporation tax	£70,000
Transfer reserve is	£60,000

Required

Prepare a trading and profit and loss account with an appropriation account for Hartlepool plc for the year ending 31st December 19X2 and a balance sheet as at the same date presented in vertical format.

Solution

Hartlepool plc
Trading and profit and loss account
for the year ending 31st December 19X2

	£'000	£'000
Sales		1,250
Less Cost of sales:		
Opening stock	50	
Add Purchases	610	
	660	
Less Closing stock	60	
		600
Gross profit		650
Less Expenses:		
Wages and salaries (£250 + £10)	260	
Rates (£20 – £5)	15	
Insurance (£15 – £3)	12	
Light and heat (£10 + £3)	13	
Office expenses	30	

	£'000	£'000
Depreciation of plant and machinery	40	
Depreciation of motor vehicles	30	
Miscellaneous expenses	50	
	—	450
Net profit		200
Corporation tax charge		70
Profit for the year available for appropriation		130
Proposed dividends		
Preference dividend of 8%	4	
Ordinary dividend of 15p per share	60	
	—	64
		66
Profit and loss account balance brought forward from previous year		6
		72
Transfer to reserves		60
Profit and loss account balance carried forward to next year		12

Hartlepool plc

Balance sheet as at 31st December 19X2

	Cost £'000	Accumulated depreciation £'000	Net book value £'000
Fixed assets			
Buildings	280	–	280
Plant and equipment	200	120	80
Motor vehicles	120	60	60
	600	180	420
Current assets			
Stock	60		
Debtors	130		
Prepayments	8		
Bank	116		
	—	314	
Creditors: amounts due within one year			
Creditors	50		
Accruals	13		
Proposed dividends	64		
Current taxation	70		
	—	197	
Net current assets (Working capital)			117
Capital employed			537

	£'000	£'000
Financed by:		
Share capital		
Authorised:		
8% Preference shares		
100,000 of £1 each (£100,000)		
Ordinary shares		
500,000 of £1 each (£500,000)		
Issued and fully paid:		
8% Preference shares 50,000 of £1 each	50	
Ordinary shares 400,000 of £1 each	400	
		450
Reserves brought forward	15	
Add Transferred from profit and loss account	60	
		75
Profit and loss account balance at 31st December 19X2		12
		537

You should now be able to attempt Questions 21.1, 21.2 and 21.3 at the end of this chapter.

21.6 Published accounts

As explained earlier in this chapter, limited liability companies are not obliged to publish all the details in their profit and loss account and balance sheet. What they do have to publish, and therefore make publicly available, is determined by legislation and the regulatory framework, although certain companies are exempt from these requirements. These are mainly small and medium-sized companies and in this section we will only be looking at the ***consolidated published accounts*** of large companies. You will find it useful to have a copy of the published accounts of a large company as you work through this chapter.

The key financial statements published are the ***profit and loss account*** and the ***balance sheet***. Under the *Companies Act 1985* a company must use one of four different formats for the former and one of two for the latter. Each company can choose which formats to adopt. As well as giving the financial results for the current financial year, the figures for the previous financial year must also be shown.

If you look at the published profit and loss account and balance sheet in a company's accounts, you will see that normally they occupy one page each. However, at the side of these two statements are many items referring to note numbers. The ***notes*** are also included in the document and take up many pages.

The reason why companies use notes is because the regulatory framework requires certain information to be given and it is impossible to include it all in the financial statement itself. The notes are therefore used to explain and expand on items in the profit and loss account and balance sheet. For simplicity we have not given the notes or the previous year's figures in the examples which follow in the next section.

21.7 The published profit and loss account

The *Companies Act 1985* gives no less than four alternative ***formats*** for the presentation of the published ***profit and loss account***. Two are ***vertical*** and two are ***horizontal***. You will find that most UK companies use one of the two vertical formats. Of these, one analyses expenses by their purpose or function and the other by type. The following example illustrates the format which analyses expenses by their purpose.

Example

Colerne plc
Consolidated profit and loss account
for the year ended 31 December 19X2

	19X2
	£'000
Turnover	40,000
Cost of sales	(33,000)
Gross profit	7,000
Distribution costs	(3,400)
Administrative expenses	(2,200)
Operating profit	1,400
Other income receivable and similar income	50
Interest payable and similar charges	(420)
Profit on ordinary activities before taxation	1,030
Tax on profit on ordinary activities	(400)
	630
Minority interests	(20)
Profit on ordinary activities attributable to the members of Colerne plc	610
Extraordinary items	80
Profit for the financial year	690
Dividends paid and proposed	(350)
Profit retained, transferred to reserves	340

The above illustration may not be exactly the same as the example you have obtained, the main difference being the requirements of FRS 3 and disclosure of discontinued activities. However, the main points are:

- We are looking at a consolidated profit and loss account because we are dealing with a group of companies. All the profit and loss accounts of the separate companies in the group have been ***consolidated*** into one account.
- In reality the figures for the previous year would also be given.
- Similarly, many of the items would make reference to the notes to the accounts on a later page where more information and explanation would be given.

You should now be able to attempt Tasks 21.1 and 21.2 at the end of this chapter.

21.8 The published balance sheet

The ***Companies Act 1985*** gives two alternative formats for the balance sheet. Format 1 is essentially a ***vertical format***, deducting liabilities from assets. Format 2 is a ***horizontal format*** with all the assets on one side and all the liabilities on the other. The following example uses format 1, which is commonly adopted by UK companies.

Example

Colerne plc

Consolidated balance sheet as at 31 December 19X2

	19X2 £'000	£'000
Fixed assets		
Intangible assets	300	
Tangible assets	5,550	5,850
Current assets		
Stock	6,300	
Debtors	4,850	
Cash at bank and in hand	2,050	
	13,200	
Creditors: Amounts falling due within one year		
Bank loans and overdrafts	1,300	
Trade creditors	2,100	
Other creditors including taxation and social security	1,300	
Proposed dividend	200	
Accruals and deferred income	320	
	5,220	7,980
Total assets less current liabilities		13,830
Creditors: Amounts falling due after more than one year		(1,850)
Provisions for liabilities and charges		(660)
Minority interests		(200)
		11,120
Capital and reserves		
Called up share capital		8,000
Share premium account		950
Reserves		900
Profit and loss account		1,270
		11,120

The above illustration may not be exactly the same as the example you have obtained and you may need to refer the section 21.4 for explanations of some of the terminology used. Do not worry if you do not fully understand every item. It is more important that you understand the structure of the statement and the main information it contains.

21.9 Summary

There are a number of differences between the profit and loss account and balance sheet of a ***sole trader*** and those of a ***limited liability company***. These give rise to new terminology and an ***appropriation account***, which is used to show what happens to the ***net profit***.

As well as preparing a ***profit and loss account*** and ***balance sheet*** for its own purposes, a limited company is legally required to publish these financial statements. However, the published financial statements do not include as much information as those prepared for internal purposes.

You should now be able to attempt Task 21.3 and the Objective Test at the end of this chapter.

Student activities

Task 21.1 The Institute of Directors intends to publish a simple guide to published accounts. Write a suitable preface and contents page for the proposed publication.

Task 21.2 Obtain the published accounts of three different companies and compare their balance sheets. Attempt to explain any differences in their form and contents.

Task 21.3 Your uncle has recently had his ironmongery business changed into a limited liability company. He is confused by some of the terms which his accountant is now using and tells you:

"For example, my accountant is now talking of dividends instead of drawings."

Draw up a list of items where the terms used for a limited liability company are different from those used for a sole trader. List them in two columns with brief but simple explanations which your uncle will be able to understand.

Question 21.1 The balance sheet of ***Aldeburgh plc*** revealed the following balances as at 31st December 19X3:

	£'000
Fixed assets at cost:	
Land and buildings	6,791
Plant and equipment	13,887
Motor vehicles	1,953
Accumulated depreciation of fixed assets:	
Land and buildings	1,939
Plant and equipment	7,308
Motor vehicles	1,036
Stocks	11,278
Creditors	9,387
Debtors	9,099
Investments	2,261
Cash at bank and deposits	3,801
Bank overdraft	2,888
Debentures	9,509
Profit and loss account	544
Current taxation	1,022
Reserves	13,876
Proposed dividends	469
Ordinary share capital	793
Preference share capital	299

Required

Complete the following form, grouping the above balances as single figures under suitable headings:

Aldeburgh plc

Balance sheet as at 31st December 19X3

	£'000	£'000	£'000
Fixed assets			
Tangible assets		....	
Investments		....	....
Current assets			
Stocks	....		
Debtors	....		
Cash and deposits	....	....	
Creditors: Amounts due within one year			
Bank overdraft	....		
Trade creditors	....		
Taxation	....		
Dividends proposed	....	....	
Net current assets			....
Total assets less current liabilities			....
Creditors: Amounts due after more than one year			
Loans			....
Financed by:			
Capital and reserves			
Called up share capital			....
Reserves		....	
Profit and loss account		....	....

Question 21.2 You have received the following memorandum from your managing director.

Memorandum

It is planned to form a new company called *Lowestoft Transport Limited.* We intend to start operations on 1st October 19X6 and therefore the first financial year will end on 30th

September 19X7. Plans are well advanced for a start on 1st October.

We have bought a garage and office premises for £50,000, four lorries at £50,000 each, and plant and equipment for £40,000. I suggest depreciation rates of 4% per annum for the premises and 12.5% per annum for the lorries and plant and equipment, all starting from 1st October 19X6.

Operating expenses are estimated as follows for the first year:

Drivers' wages	£29,000
Manager and office staff	£21,000
Fuel oil	£8,000
Maintenance and repairs	£7,000
Rates	£4,000
Insurances	£6,000
Miscellaneous expenses	£3,000
Administration expenses	£9,000

We propose that the capital of Lowestoft Transport Ltd will be 200,000 ordinary shares of £1 each. There will be a five-year bank loan of £60,000 with interest at 10% per annum. Sales turnover is estimated at £150,000 for the first year.

As a matter of policy, we will allow for debtors at two months of sales turnover, and for the fuel oil, maintenance and repairs and miscellaneous expenses, we will allow for one month's credit.

Insurance and rates will be for a full year, so there will be no need to allow for prepayments at the year-end. We can also ignore stocks, taxation and dividends. You may assume that both costs and sales occur evenly throughout the year.

The cash flow forecast shows that the above proposals result in a balance at bank of £3,500 at 30th September 19X7. Please prepare a budgeted profit and loss account for this first year together with a budgeted balance sheet at the year end.

Managing Director

Required

Prepare the budgeted accounts for the year to 30th September 19X7 as requested by your managing director. These should be in vertical format.

Question 21.3 The books of *Colchester plc* reveal the following figures as at 31st December 19X4:

	£'000	£'000
Sales		87,100
Sales returns	85	
Opening stock at 1st January 19X4	2,375	
Purchases	63,450	
Purchases returns		120
Rent received		1,050
Office expenses	1,685	
Insurances	175	
Wages	3,820	
Rents	2,000	
Rates	1,650	
Bad debts written off	2,150	
Provision for bad debts at 1st January 19X4		1,000
Profit and loss account balance at 1st January 19X4		85
Reserves		101,500
Premises	131,000	
Equipment	6,000	
Provision for depreciation of equipment		1,600
Debtors	23,500	
Bank and deposits	11,125	
Creditors		26,560
Share capital, authorised and issued:		
5,000,000 7% preference shares of £1 each		5,000
100,000,000 ordinary shares of 25 pence each		25,000
	249,015	249,015

The following additional information is provided as at 31st December 19X4:

	£'000
Wages accrued:	130
Prepayments:	
Insurance:	25
Rent payable:	550
Rent receivable for 19X4, but unpaid as at 31st December 19X4:	180
Stock at 31st December 19X4:	2,625

Depreciation should be provided on the equipment using the straight line basis. Expected life is five years, with scrap value at the end of that time of £2,000,000.

The provision for bad debts is to be increased by	250
Transfer to reserves:	3,500
Provision for Corporation tax:	4,750

Proposed dividends:

Pay the preference dividend

Pay a dividend on the ordinary shares of 18% (4.5p per share)

Required

Prepare a trading and profit and loss account (with appropriation account) for the year ending 31st December 19X4 and a balance sheet as at that date for Colchester plc, presented in vertical format.

Objective test *(tick the appropriate box)*

i) The share capital of a limited liability company consists of:

a) Authorised shares plus profit retained ☐

b) Issued share capital plus profit retained ☐

c) Issued share capital plus profit brought forward from last year, less appropriations ☐

d) None of these ☐

ii) For private limited liability companies, the number of shareholders can be:

a) Minimum 30 ☐

b) Maximum 30 ☐

c) Minimum 2, maximum 30 ☐

d) None of these ☐

iii) If number of shares = 50,000
denomination of each share = 25p
dividend proposed = 15%
then the total amount of the proposed dividend is:

a) £750 ☐

b) £7,500 ☐

c) £1,875 ☐

d) £187.50 ☐

iv) If number of shares = 63,000
denomination of each share = 50p
dividend per share proposed = 13p
shareholding of Mr Salisbury = 1,500 shares
then Mr Salisbury will receive (if proposal approved by shareholders at the AGM):

a) £195 ☐

b) £97.50 ☐

c) £4,095 ☐

d) £9.75 ☐

v) If net profit this year = £9,876
net profit brought forward from last year = £1,234
transfer to reserves = £3,654
provision for Corporation tax = £3,456
proposed dividend = £1,432
then the net balance on the profit and loss account carried forward to next year will be:

a) £100 ☐

b) £2,568 ☐

c) £19,652 ☐

d) £5,432 ☐

Chapter 22

Accounting ratios

22.1 Objectives

At the end of this chapter you should be able to:

- understand the meaning of accounting ratios;
- calculate four performance ratios and three liquidity ratios;
- appreciate the value of trend analysis and inter-firm comparisons.

22.2 Introduction

In this and previous chapters, we have described and constructed ***profit and loss accounts*** and ***balance sheets***. The profit and loss account shows how much profit has been made and how much has been appropriated. The balance sheet gives a snapshot of the business at one moment in time which shows:

- how the business has been financed by ***internal finance***: share capital, retained profits and ***external finance***: loans, debentures etc. By ***internal*** we mean the capital provided by shareholders, and all retained profits belonging to them. By ***external*** we mean finance provided by parties (other than shareholders) with no financial interest in the business other than the finance provided by them;
- how that finance has been used, on ***fixed assets*** and ***working capital*** (current assets less current liabilities).

This is all interesting information, but can we answer questions such as:

- Is the profit satisfactory?
- Is the liquidity position satisfactory?
- How do the results compare with previous years?
- How does this company compare with others in the same type of business?

We can apply various analytical techniques to the accounts in an attempt to answer such questions. These are:

- ***Performance ratios*** (sometimes called profitability ratios)
- ***Liquidity ratios*** (sometimes called solvency ratios)
- ***Trend analysis***
- ***Inter-firm comparison***

There are a large number of ratios in common use. We shall look at the main ones. Others are chiefly refinements or ratios which are sub-analyses of those described here. Unfortunately, there is little agreement on definitions of terms such as ***profit*** when used in ratio analysis. The important point is ***consistency***. Data drawn from different sources or different years should be as comparable as possible. With published accounts you may not find the figures you require and may have to make adjustments or use alternative figures.

22.3 Performance ratios

The term ***profit before interest and tax (PBIT)*** needs to be explained since it is used in the ratios under this heading. Interest on loans (including debentures) and bank overdraft interest can be found under expenses in the profit and loss account. In other words, interest is charged against profit ***before*** the figure of net profit is arrived at. However, interest can be regarded as a return on ***external finance*** – a reward to the lender of the money, in the same way as dividends are a reward to shareholders for ***internal finance***.

Example

Form of finance	Type	Amount	Rate of return	Amount of return
		£		£
Share capital	Internal	100,000	20% dividend *	20,000
Loan	External	50,000	15% interest	7,500

* Usually expressed as 20 pence on a £1 share etc.

Both the £20,000 and £7,500 are ***returns*** on the financing of the business.

The proposed dividend is shown on the profit and loss account as an appropriation of net profit. But interest on loans etc. is deducted before the calculation of net profit. Therefore, in order to calculate PBIT (profit before interest and tax), we have to take net profit, and ***add back*** the loan interest. The resulting PBIT reflects the profit made by the business before any of it is appropriated for lenders, shareholders or the taxman.

The logic is that the manager of the business is given ***finance*** in order to make ***profit***. It is irrelevant where this finance comes from, internal or external. The manager's efficiency is measured by the amount of profit he makes on the resources with which he has been entrusted.

22.4 Prime ratio (Ratio A)

This measures the percentage ***return on capital employed (ROCE)***.

$$\frac{\text{PBIT}}{\text{Capital employed}} \times 100$$

Capital employed is either:

Share capital + Reserves + Loans (long-term or debentures)

or Fixed assets + Working capital (net current assets)

i.e. Fixed assets + Current assets - Creditors: amounts due within one year

The figure used for capital employed is usually the figure in the balance sheet at the end of the year, since this is the balance sheet which is published with the profit and loss account for the year ending on that date. This is the figure used in the analyses in this chapter. Be careful to find the correct figure on the balance sheet. Remember that long-term loans (creditors: amounts due after more than one year) are deducted from capital employed on a vertical format balance sheet.

Other figures for capital employed are sometimes used, e.g. the figure at the start of the year, which is in theory better, since that is the capital employed which generated the profit made in the following year.

22.5 Profit margin ratio (Ratio B)

This measures the percentage ***return on sales (ROS)***. It is designed to focus attention on the profit margin arising from business activities.

$$\frac{\text{PBIT}}{\text{Sales}} \times 100$$

22.6 Capital turnover ratio (Ratio C)

$$\frac{\text{Sales}}{\text{Capital employed}}$$

It is usually expressed as a ratio i.e. number of times or as number of times : 1

These three ratios are inter-related.

If we multiply ratio B by ratio C we obtain ratio A. i.e.

$$\frac{\text{PBIT}}{\text{Sales}} \times \frac{\text{Sales}}{\text{Capital employed}} = \frac{\text{PBIT}}{\text{Capital employed}}$$

For example, we can work out the ratios for two companies and compare them.

Example

	Company X	Company Y
	£	£
PBIT	10,000	20,000
Capital employed	50,000	100,000
Sales turnover for year	500,000	200,000

Ratio A. Prime ratio

	Company X	Company Y
$\frac{\text{PBIT}}{\text{Capital employed}}$	$\frac{10{,}000}{50{,}000} = 20\%$	$\frac{20{,}000}{100{,}000} = 20\%$

Ratio B. Profit margin ratio

	Company X	Company Y
$\frac{\text{PBIT}}{\text{Sales}}$	$\frac{10{,}000}{500{,}000} = 2\%$	$\frac{20{,}000}{200{,}000} = 10\%$

Ratio C. Capital turnover ratio

	Company X	Company Y
$\frac{\text{Sales}}{\text{Capital employed}}$	$\frac{500{,}000}{50{,}000}$ = 10 times	$\frac{200{,}000}{100{,}000}$ = 2 times
B × C = A	2% × 10 = 20%	10% × 2 = 20%

Both Company X and Company Y make the same ROCE but they make it in different ways. Company X (maybe a food store) makes 2% net profit on sales, but its capital turnover is 10 times a year. Company Y (maybe a furniture store) makes 10% net profit on sales, but its capital turnover is only twice a year.

A business can improve its ROCE ratio by:

- reducing costs and/or raising prices, which will improve its profit margin;
- increasing sales volume and/or reducing capital employed, which will improve its capital turnover.

The *prime ratio* (Ratio A) indicates the return on the money invested in the business. It could be compared with the returns available elsewhere, e.g. on deposit in a building society. The amount of return expected should reflect the risk involved in investing the money in an entrepreneurial business rather than, say, in a building society. The more risky the business, the higher should be the expected return.

Further comments can be found below under Section 22.13 *Trend analysis* and Section 22.14 *Inter-firm comparison*.

22.7 Gross profit percentage (Ratio D)

This ratio expresses *gross profit* as a percentage of sales.

$$\frac{\text{Gross profit}}{\text{Sales}} \times 100$$

Example

	Company X		Company Y	
	£		£	
Gross profit	25,000		40,000	
Sales for year	500,000		200,000	

$$\frac{\text{Gross profit}}{\text{Sales}} \qquad \frac{25{,}000}{500{,}000} = 5\% \qquad \frac{40{,}000}{200{,}000} = 20\%$$

Here again, trends and inter-firm comparisons are useful.

22.8 Liquidity ratios

These ratios are concerned with liquidity rather than profit and are described in Sections 22.9 – 22.11.

22.9 Current test ratio (Ratio E)

This is also known as the ***working capital ratio***. This ratio is usually expressed as a ratio of x : 1 (i.e. number of times), rather than as a percentage.

$$\frac{\text{Current assets}}{\text{Creditors: Amounts due within one year}}$$

Working capital (current assets less creditors: amounts due within one year) is important to all organisations, since a healthy circulation of working capital enables the business to finance its day-to-day activities. Stock is sold to debtors who pay cash which is used to pay the creditors who supply the stock. Thus the ratio could be expressed:

$$\frac{\text{Stock + Debtors + Bank (Cash)}}{\text{Creditors + Overdraft (if any)}}$$

Example

Stock	£8,000
Debtors	£12,000
Bank	£10,000
Creditors	£15,000

The current test ratio would be:

$$\frac{£8{,}000 + £12{,}000 + £10{,}000}{£15{,}000} = 2:1$$

What is a good current test ratio? The answer depends on the type of business. There should be enough current assets to cover current liabilities. In the above example, there is not enough cash at bank to pay the creditors immediately, but there is more than enough when debtors pay up. For many businesses, a ratio between 2 : 1 and 1.5 : 1 could be considered satisfactory. Below 1.5 : 1 could indicate illiquidity. Above 2 : 1 could indicate current assets which are not paying their way. For example, it could indicate too high a level of stocks, debtors or cash, or too low a level of creditors (who may be being paid more quickly than their credit terms require). For other businesses, a ratio lower than 1.5 : 1 may not be unreasonable. Some businesses, by their very nature, do not hold stocks (e.g. by getting their suppliers to deliver direct to the customers). Other businesses have few or no debtors (e.g. cash only businesses such as food stores etc.). More important is the trend of the ratio from period to period, and comparison of the ratio with that of other businesses in the same type of business.

22.10 Acid test ratio (Ratio F)

This is also known as the ***quick ratio*** or the ***liquid capital ratio***. This is a more stringent test than the current test ratio.

$$\frac{\text{Current assets} - \text{Stock}}{\text{Creditors: Amounts due within one year}} \quad \text{i.e.} \quad \frac{\text{Debtors} + \text{Bank (Cash)}}{\text{Creditors: Amounts due within one year}}$$

Example

(Using the figures from Ratio E above):

$$\frac{£12{,}000 + £10{,}000}{£15{,}000} = 1.47{:}1$$

Stocks (raw material, work-in-progress, and finished goods stock) are excluded from current assets, because they are less liquid than debtors or cash-at-bank. A rough rule of thumb is that this ratio should not normally be less than 1 : 1, though this generalisation would not apply to all types of business. For example some trades collect from debtors weekly, but pay creditors monthly. Here again, trends and inter-firm comparisons are useful in interpreting the ratio.

22.11 Debt collection period (Ratio G)

$$\frac{\text{Trade debtors} \times 365}{\text{Sales for year}}$$

This ratio measures the ***average*** time (in days) that debtors take to pay.

Example

$$\frac{\text{Debtors (at balance sheet date)} \times 365}{\text{Sales for year}} = \frac{£12{,}000 \times 365}{£144{,}000} = 30.4 \text{ days}$$

If, instead of multiplying by 365, we multiply by 12, the answer will be in months:

$$\frac{£12{,}000 \times 12}{£144{,}000} = 1 \text{ month}$$

Similarly:

$$\frac{£12{,}000 \times 52}{£144{,}000} = 4.33 \text{ weeks}$$

Changes in cash sales/credit sales mix can distort this ratio.

You may need to know what the average collection period is for a business which exclusively offers the term of 'net monthly account'. Net monthly account means that sales throughout, say, April are invoiced throughout April, and normally included on a statement made up to 30th April. These statements are sent to customers as soon as possible after the month end. Customers are expected to pay by the end of May. Therefore the customers will obtain credit for a period, on average, of from mid-way through April until the end of May, i.e 15 days (April) plus 31 days (May) = 46 days or about 1.5 months or 6.5 weeks. If the average collection period exceeds this, then the matter should be investigated. Here again, trends and inter-firm comparisons are important.

22.12 Other ratios

There are numerous other ratios which could be calculated, most of which are refinements of the above. For example, the ***current test ratio*** could generate further ratios:

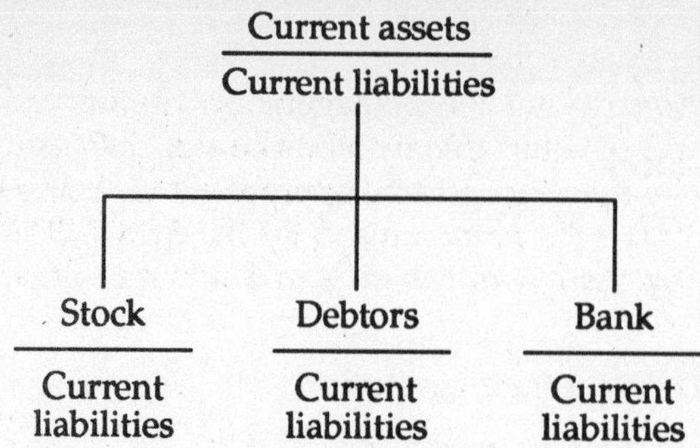

The above seven ratios (A–G) have been selected because they are important ratios of fairly universal application.

22.13 Trend analysis

We have mentioned above the importance of trend analysis. The following example illustrates this.

Example

The following are figures extracted from the accounts of ***Lincoln Ltd*** for the last three years:

	19X6	19X7	19X8
	£	£	£
Profit before interest and tax	15,000	16,000	17,000
Sales	125,000	123,000	122,000
Capital employed	75,000	88,000	113,000

Required

Calculate the prime, profit margin and capital turnover ratios, and comment on the trends.

Solution

Ratio A. (Prime Ratio)	$\frac{\text{PBIT}}{\text{Capital employed}}$	20.0%	18.2%	15.0%
Ratio B. (Profit Margin)	$\frac{\text{PBIT}}{\text{Sales}}$	12.0%	13.0%	13.9%
Ratio C. (Capital Turnover)	$\frac{\text{Sales}}{\text{CE}}$	1.67 times	1.40 times	1.08 times

Ratio B (profit margin) is steadily improving over the three years, but this should be offset against the downward trend of ratio C (capital turnover).

Ratio B × Ratio C = Ratio A.

Ratio A, the prime ratio, measures return on capital employed (ROCE), and shows a downward trend over the three years. The effect of the improvement in profit margin has been more than wiped out by the drop in capital turnover.

It could be that the effort of management to improve profit margins has had an adverse effect on sales turnover, and company policy in this matter should be further investigated.

22.14 Inter-firm comparison

Although trends are important, they do not tell management whether any particular ratio is good or bad, compared with what should or could be attainable by a business of their particular type. To help ascertain this, many businesses join an ***inter-firm comparison*** scheme appropriate to their own particular type of industry. For example, a printing firm might join a scheme organised by the British Printing Industries Federation. Other industries and trades are served by their own schemes and schemes organised by the Centre for Interfirm Comparison. Such schemes:

- provide detailed definitions of terms used in the ratios;
- establish principles of valuation to ensure uniformity;
- collect the appropriate figures from participating firms;
- examine the figures for consistency and possible errors;
- calculate the ratios and tabulate them;
- circulate the results in a form which protects the participating members from identification;
- help the members interpret the ratios.

All firms, however seemingly efficient, can benefit from such schemes. There is always room for improvement. It only needs one ratio which is below par to be identified, and the attention of management is drawn to an area where investigation may reveal inefficiencies which need remedial action.

You should now be able to attempt Task 22.1 at the end of this chapter.

Example

Skegness Ltd is a wholesale trading company. Abbreviated results for the last two years are given below:

Profit and loss accounts

Years to	31st December 19X3		31st December 19X4	
	£'000	£'000	£'000	£'000
Sales		350		560
Cost of sales		280		462
Gross profit		70		98
Administration costs	35		42	
Selling & distribution costs	14		14	
		49		56
Net profit		21		42
Retained profits brought forward		84		91
		105		133
Proposed dividends		14		35
Retained profits carried forward		91		98

Balance sheets

As at	31st December 19X3			31st December 19X4		
	£'000	£'000	£'000	£'000	£'000	£'000
Fixed assets						
Buildings			35			105
Equipment			70			161
			105			266
Current assets						
Stocks	56			98		
Debtors	35			84		
Bank	84			63		
		175			245	
Creditors: amounts due within one year						
Creditors	35			28		
Dividends	14			35		
		49			63	
			126			182
			231			448
Represented by:						
£1 Ordinary shares			140			350
Retained profits			91			98
			231			448

Required

i) Calculate for Skegness Ltd the seven ratios described in this chapter for each of the years 19X3 and 19X4.

ii) Comment briefly on the ratios.

Solution

i)

Type of ratio	Method of calculation	Ratios 19X3	Ratios 19X4
Performance:			
Prime	$\frac{\text{PBIT}}{\text{Capital employed}}$	$\frac{21}{231} = 9.1\%$	$\frac{42}{448} = 9.4\%$
Profit margin	$\frac{\text{PBIT}}{\text{Sales}}$	$\frac{21}{350} = 6.0\%$	$\frac{42}{560} = 7.5\%$
Capital turnover	$\frac{\text{Sales}}{\text{Capital employed}}$	$\frac{350}{231} = 1.52$ times	$\frac{560}{448} = 1.25$ times
Gross profit	$\frac{\text{Gross profit}}{\text{Sales}}$	$\frac{70}{350} = 20.0\%$	$\frac{98}{560} = 17.5\%$

Liquidity:

Current test	$\frac{\text{Current assets}}{\text{Current liabilities}}$	$\frac{175}{49} = 3.6$ to 1	$\frac{245}{63} = 3.9$ to 1
Acid test	$\frac{\text{Current assets} - \text{Stocks}}{\text{Current liabilities}}$	$\frac{119}{49} = 2.4$ to 1	$\frac{147}{63} = 2.3$ to 1
Debt collection period	$\frac{\text{Debtors} \times 365}{\text{Sales}}$	$\frac{35 \times 365}{350} = 36.5$ days	$\frac{84 \times 365}{560} = 54.8$ days

ii) **Comments**

Performance:
The prime ratio has increased slightly, despite the fact that the capital employed has nearly doubled (£k231 to £k448) due to the increase in share capital. The capital turnover ratio has dropped, but the increase in the profit margin has more than made up for this. (Ratio C × Ratio B = Ratio A)

Liquidity:
The current test ratio has increased slightly, but the acid test ratio has dropped slightly, indicating an increase in stocks. Both ratios are rather high, which would prompt an investigation into the composition of current assets: Balance at bank could indicate an idle asset, though the amount has dropped between the two years. Debtors have increased and the reason for the increase in debt collection period should be ascertained.

You should now be able to attempt Questions 22.1, 22.2 and 22.3 at the end of this chapter.

22.15 Summary

Ratio analysis is a technique for interpreting the financial statements of companies. Ratios can be used to assess the performance of a company and its solvency. To aid the assessment, ***comparisons*** must be made over time, inter-company or with industry averages. Caution must be taken over the definition of ratios to ensure consistency of approach. The main ratios are:

Performance ratios:

Prime ratio (Ratio A) $\frac{\text{PBIT}}{\text{Capital employed}} \times 100 = \%$

Profit margin ratio (Ratio B) $\frac{\text{PBIT}}{\text{Sales}} \times 100 = \%$

Capital turnover ratio (Ratio C) $\frac{\text{Sales}}{\text{Capital employed}} = \text{times}$

Ratio B × C = A

Gross profit percentage (Ratio D) $\frac{\text{Gross profit}}{\text{Sales}} \times 100 = \%$

Liquidity (solvency) ratios:

Current test ratio (Ratio E)
(Working capital)

$$\frac{\text{Current assets}}{\text{Current liabilities}} = \text{times}$$

Acid test ratio (Ratio F)
(Quick, or liquid capital)

$$\frac{\text{Debtors + Bank (Cash)}}{\text{Current liabilities}} = \text{times}$$

Debt collection period (Ratio G)

$$\frac{\text{Trade debtors}}{\text{Sales for year}} \times 365 = \text{days}$$

$$\frac{\text{Trade debtors}}{\text{Sales for year}} \times 52 = \text{weeks}$$

$$\frac{\text{Trade debtors}}{\text{Sales for year}} \times 12 = \text{months}$$

Current liabilities = Creditors: amounts due within one year.

You should now be able to attempt Tasks 22.2 and 22.3 and the Objective Test at the end of this chapter.

Student activities

Task 22.1 Obtain an annual report and accounts of a company in an industry which interests you. Turn to the financial statements and find:

- the profit and loss account or the consolidated profit and loss account;
- the consolidated balance sheet or the balance sheet of the company.

The latter is probably that of the holding company, showing mainly (as assets) the investment in the subsidiary companies of the group. Ignore this balance sheet. Choose the consolidated or group balance sheet, which means that it is the combined balance sheet of all the companies in the group.

Try to find the items you need to calculate all the ratios described in this chapter. You may need to look up the notes to the accounts to find some of them.

Calculate the ratios for the current year and last year. Comparative figures for last year are usually provided. Look for the changes between this year and last year. Which are good and which are bad? Is there anything in the reports, notes etc. which indicate reasons for any of these changes?

Is there any ratio which you cannot work out because the figures are not provided?

Task 22.2 Invent an imaginary company, and compose its accounts for the last two years. The accounts need only be in sufficient detail for the seven ratios described in this chapter to be calculated from them. Try to arrive at figures such that three or four of the ratios show favourable changes and the other ratios show unfavourable changes. Pencils and rubbers are recommended for your rough workings! Present your final accounts and ratios in an acceptable format, and append your comments on the causes of the favourable/unfavourable changes.

Task 22.3 Read the financial pages of the newspaper and extract any items which refer to ratios.

i) Compare them with the ratios examined in this chapter.

ii) Construct a frequency table to illustrate the most quoted ratios.

Question 22.1 The following information is available in respect of *Norwich Ltd* for the year ending 31st December 19X4:

Debtors amount to £33,600, and the debt collection period is one month.

Gross profit is 25% of sales.

Net profit is 5% of sales.

Sales: WDV (written down value) of fixed assets is a ratio of 2 : 1.

Purchases totalled £336,000.

Creditors are equal to one month's purchases.

Opening stock at 1st January 19X4 was £28,000.

Expenses are the difference between gross and net profits.

Share capital is 239,120 shares of £1 each.

Dividends proposed are half of the net profit.

The current test ratio is 2 : 1 at 31st December 19X4.

Bank overdraft is £9,520 at 31st December 19X4.

Required

Prepare for Norwich Ltd a trading and profit and loss account for the year ending 31st December 19X4, and a balance sheet as at that date, in as much detail as possible, taking into account all the above information.

Hint: Prepare a blank set of accounts, fill in any given figures, calculate other figures from them using any ratios provided, and then any missing figures can be calculated from them.

Question 22.2 Your managing director has asked you to analyse the last three years' accounts of a competitor, *Ipswich Ltd*. There is a rumour that this company is experiencing serious financial problems, and he wonders if your analysis will confirm this. The figures for Ipswich Ltd for the three years in question are as follows:

	19X5 £'000	19X6 £'000	19X7 £'000
Sales turnover	92,727	99,161	133,911
Gross profit	28,745	29,579	35,464
Profit before interest and tax	9,467	9,635	11,112
Profit after tax	7,458	8,771	8,211
Capital employed	52,303	55,854	70,890
Current assets	36,742	36,939	51,236
Creditors: amounts due within one year	24,333	26,125	39,061
Stocks	10,298	8,953	9,426
Debtors	13,420	14,158	20,258
Balances at bank and cash	13,024	13,828	21,552

Required

Prepare a memorandum concerning the accounts of Ipswich Ltd for your managing director giving:

i) the calculation of seven different accounting ratios in respect of each of the three year periods;

ii) an explanation of what each ratio indicates;

iii) an interpretation of the ratios you have calculated, paying particular attention to trends, with comment on whether they confirm the rumour concerning Ipswich Ltd.

Question 22.3 Various types of trade or industry will have balance sheets which differ widely from each other in respect of the relative sizes of their assets and liabilities.

Given below are the assets and liabilities of five different companies engaged in five different kinds of trade or industry. The figures given are ***percentages of capital employed.*** This should help you compare and contrast the relative sizes of the various components of the balance sheets.

Company	A	B	C	D	E
	%	%	%	%	%
Fixed assets					
Buildings	18	25	76	21	51
Plant & Machinery	9	60	1	47	8
Office equipment	5	4	4	5	15
Vehicles	72	3	2	5	10
Current assets					
Stocks	4	8	8	37	45
Debtors	1	25	17	26	1
Current liabilities	(9)	(25)	(8)	(41)	(30)
Capital employed	100	100	100	100	100

The industries represented above are as follows:

i) A commercial vehicle manufacturer

ii) A bus company

iii) A general engineering company

iv) A chain of food stores

v) A hotel and leisure group

Required

Match the numbers of the industries against the letter of the company.

Company	Industry
A	____
B	____
C	____
D	____
E	____

Hint: A cash business will have relatively low debtors; an engineering company will have a relatively high investment in plant and machinery.

Objective test *(tick the appropriate box)*

i) Capital employed is calculated by:

a) Adding fixed and current assets ☐

b) Adding back interest on loans ☐

c) Adding fixed assets and net current assets ☐

d) Adding fixed assets and net current assets and deducting long-term loans ☐

ii) Profit before interest and tax is included in the calculation of the:

a) Capital turnover ratio ☐

b) Current test ratio ☐

c) Gross profit margin ratio ☐

d) Prime ratio ☐

Use the following data to answer (iii) – (vii) below

	£'000
Gross profit	243
Profit before interest and tax	77
Capital employed	804
Sales	1,320
Current assets	642
Creditors: amounts due within one year	285
Stocks	208
Debtors	131

iii) The current test ratio is:

a) 2.25 : 1 ☐

b) 1.52 : 1 ☐

c) 3.09 : 1 ☐

d) None of these ☐

iv) The acid test ratio is:

a) 2.25 : 1 ☐

b) 1.52 : 1 ☐

c) 3.09 : 1 ☐

d) None of these ☐

v) The debt collection period is:

a) 36 months ☐

b) 36 days ☐

c) 36 weeks ☐

d) None of these ☐

vi) The capital turnover ratio is:

a) 1.64 times ☐

b) 1.52 times ☐

c) 2.25 times ☐

d) 3.09 times ☐

vii) The profit margin ratio is:

a) 58.3% ☐

b) 18.4% ☐

c) 1.84% ☐

d) 5.83% ☐

viii) The prime ratio results from multiplying:

a) Profit before interest and tax by capital employed ☐

b) The gross profit ratio by the capital turnover ratio ☐

c) The profit margin ratio by the capital turnover ratio ☐

d) The capital turnover ratio by the current test ratio ☐

ix) The ratio $\frac{\text{Stock + Debtors + Bank}}{\text{Creditors + Overdraft}}$ is called the:

a) Quick ratio ☐

b) Acid Test ratio ☐

c) Current ratio ☐

d) Turnover ratio ☐

x) If debtors are £20,000, creditors are £7,000, stocks are £6,000 and overdraft is £6,000, then:

a) The current test ratio is 1.54 : 1 ☐

b) The current test ratio is 2.25 : 1 ☐

c) The acid test ratio is 1.54 : 1 ☐

d) The acid test ratio is 2.00 : 1 ☐

Assignment E

A simple guide to the balance sheet

Context

Your local Chamber of Commerce has become increasingly concerned about the standard of financial knowledge particularly among its junior managers in the locality. It has decided to launch a series of conferences, seminars and publications to improve basic financial knowledge.

As part of this programme, it has asked you to prepare a draft of a small booklet to be entitled 'A Simple Guide to the Balance Sheet'.

The aim of the guide is to provide managers with a simple, clear and concise:

- ❒ description of what a balance sheet is;
- ❒ explanation of the basic concepts underlying a balance sheet;
- ❒ description of what the principle components of a balance sheet signify;
- ❒ exposition of how a balance sheet can be analysed and interpreted.

To this end, it has suggested that you obtain an actual example of a balance sheet, taken from a published report and accounts of a public limited company, and include a copy of it in your booklet, suitably annotated and explained.

Student activities

i) Obtain from a friend, relation, library or company, a number of published Report and Accounts. Find the balance sheets in them. There may be several. Choose the one which is headed 'group' or 'consolidated'. Select the balance sheet which is well presented, in vertical format, and with clear, simple headings. More important, choose one from an industry which interests you. Obviously, you will have to take a photocopy of the balance sheet page if you have to return or not deface the original.

ii) Decide on the plan of your booklet, in order to cover the points which the local Chamber of Commerce requires.

iii) Decide what you are going to do with the balance sheet, for example

- ❒ leave it unmarked, and include it as one of the pages;
- ❒ put reference numbers or symbols on it to which you can refer in your text;
- ❒ write your actual annotations on it; in which case, it could be in the form of a large pull-out or fold-out chart, with the copy of your balance sheet in the middle, perhaps.
- ❒ choose another way of presenting it which is an improvement on the three previous suggestions.

iv) Write the draft guide, bearing in mind that it should be in a format which is suitable for printing by professional printers.

Format

A booklet, any suitable size, with a title page, introduction, simple, clear and concise text, containing the balance sheet in a form as suggested in activity (iii) above, and with diagrams, graphs, etc. which you consider to be appropriate. It should not be more than the equivalent of 12 A4-size pages, including title page, diagrams etc. and the balance sheet itself.

Hints

The guide should be interesting to someone who probably will not want to devote more than, say, half-an-hour to reading it. Avoid too much detail: keep to the major items which have been explained in this book. There will inevitably be a number of items in the published accounts which you will not understand unless you read a more advanced text than this present book. Ignore these items.

Read through all the notes to the accounts, chairman's report etc. in the published Report and Accounts; you are bound to come across something of interest which will help you explain, interpret or comment upon the items on the balance sheet.

Objectives

In this assignment, the student should show an appreciation and understanding of:

- the uses and limitations of accounting concepts as they affect the recording of financial data;
- simple final accounts;
- interpretation of financial information in order to measure performance against the perceived objectives of the organisation.

References

Chapters 19-22 and earlier chapters.

Other organisations

This section (Chapters 23 – 26) considers the other types of organisations for which accounts are prepared. We have already looked at the accounts of sole traders and limited liability companies. This section shows how adaptable finance and accounting is required to be in order to be useful to a variety of other quite different organisations.

In Chapter 23 we look at the accounts of partnerships. A partnership is really the next stage of expansion from a sole trader and the introduction of additional owners of a business results in changes in the accounting requirements.

Chapter 24 is concerned with the accounts of clubs, societies and other organisations which are not trading for profit but are formed mainly for recreational purposes. We look at the alternative statements which might be presented to members of such clubs and the way in which one of those statements, the receipts and payments account, can be converted into an income and expenditure account.

In Chapter 25 we look at accounting in the public sector. Some organisations in this part of the economy use the same accounting techniques and statements as sole traders, partnerships and limited companies. Others use techniques which are more akin to cash flow accounting. Accounting for local authorities is included in this chapter.

The final chapter in this section, Chapter 26, examines a financial statement known as a manufacturing account which is produced by manufacturing organisations. This additional statement records the transactions of such organisations more adequately than the trading, profit and loss account alone.

Chapter 23

Partnership accounts

23.1 Objectives

At the end of this chapter you should be able to:

- appreciate the reasons for the formation of partnerships;
- understand some of the legal aspects which apply to partnerships;
- prepare a partnership profit and loss account;
- prepare a partnership balance sheet.

23.2 Introduction

In Chapters 10-15 consideration was given to the preparation of the accounts of small traders. One drawback to this form of business is that the availability of capital is restricted to the amount which the sole trader either has, or is capable of raising either by borrowing or by generating profit. This is a major reason why sole traders tend to be small businesses.

One way of increasing the amount of capital available to the business, and therefore increasing its size, is to form a partnership. Capital can then be made available to the business based on the ability of all the partners to raise funds, whilst at the same time increasing the range of skills available to the business.

23.3 Definition

A ***partnership*** is a form of business organisation in which two or more persons join together to carry on a business, with the object of making profits. There are several important characteristics of partnerships

- A partnership, unlike a limited company, does not enjoy a legal status which is separate from its owners. All individual partners are liable for all the activities, and ultimately the debts, of the partnership. Thus, if a creditor cannot obtain payment from the partnership for a genuine debt, any of the partners can be required to pay in full.
- A partnership is limited to a maximum of 20 persons, with the exception of professional firms such as accountants and solicitors, where there is no upper limit.
- Under the ***Limited Partnership Act 1907*** a partnership may have partners whose liability is limited to the amount of capital they have agreed to subscribe, but the limited partners may not take part in the management of the business.

23.4 Other legal requirements

The major legislation which governs the operation of partnerships is the ***Partnership Act 1890***, and amongst its requirements for accounting and reporting are:

- Proper books of account must be kept.
- Capitals must be distinguished from profits and losses.
- A record must be kept of partners' shares of profit and drawings.
- There may be loans by the partners to the business, in addition to their capital and profits.

- Partners are bound to render true accounts and full information of all aspects affecting the partnership to any partner or his legal representative.

23.5 The partnership agreement

Partners are well advised to draw up a ***partnership agreement*** when they form a partnership so that the relationship between the partners is clearly defined. Some aspects of any partnership agreement will affect the profit and loss account and balance sheet of the partnership, examples of these are:

- The amount of capital to be contributed or subscribed by each partner.
- The proportion in which profits and losses are to be shared or borne.
- The rate of interest, if any, to be paid on capital contributed by the partners.
- The rate of interest, if any, to be paid on loans to the partnership by the partners.
- The rate of interest, if any, to be charged on partners' drawings.
- The salaries, if any, to be paid to the partners.

In the absence of alternative agreements made between the partners about these matters, the following rules apply to the partnership, based on the ***Partnership Act 1890***:

- **Profits and losses**

  All partners are entitled to share equally in the capital gains and profits, and must contribute equally towards the losses, whether capital losses or otherwise, incurred by the firm.

- **Interest on capital**

  Partners are not entitled to any interest on capital, and therefore such interest cannot be deducted in ascertaining the profits of the business.

- **Interest on loans**

  Partners are entitled to interest at 5% per annum on any loan capital contributed in excess of the agreed capital subscribed.

- **Salaries**

  Every partner is entitled to take part in the management of the business, but no partner is entitled to any remuneration for acting in the business of the partnership.

You should now be able to attempt Task 23.1 at the end of this chapter.

23.6 Final accounts preparation

All the basic rules covered so far with regard to the preparation of the ***final accounts*** of sole traders (see Chapters 10 and 11) apply also to the preparation of profit and loss accounts and balance sheets of partnerships. However, certain changes are required in order to adjust to the particular requirements of partnerships. The major changes are to the profit and loss account which is expanded into two sections. The additional section is known as the ***profit and loss appropriation account***, or ***appropriation section.***

The appropriation account, although not necessarily headed as such, follows on directly from the main profit and loss account. It commences with the the amount available for appropriation. This is determined by the gross profit less operating expenses, which is a normal feature of a profit and loss account of a sole trader, where it is described as the net profit.

The other entries in the appropriation account are those which represent the transactions between the partnership and the individual partners, as partners. These transactions include salaries, interest on capital, interest on drawings and interest on loans.

23.7 Salaries

Salaries paid to partners are not deductible in ascertaining profits of the partnership as they are rather like drawings, therefore they may not be shown in the main profit and loss account as an expense. However, any salaries paid or due to the partners is bound to affect the amount remaining to be shared amongst the partners as profit or loss.

Example

James, Curtis and Matlock are in partnership with profits being shared 50%, 25%, and 25% respectively. James is credited with an annual salary of £30,000, and Curtis and Matlock receive £20,000 each. The profit available for appropriation is £190,000.

Required

Write up the entries in the profit and loss account appropriation account for the year ended 31st December 19X1.

Solution

James, Curtis and Matlock

Profit and loss appropriation account for the year ended 31st December 19X1.

			£	£
Net profit available for appropriation				190,000
Salaries:	James		30,000	
	Curtis		20,000	
	Matlock		20,000	70,000
Balance of profits to be shared:				120,000
	James	50%	60,000	
	Curtis	25%	30,000	
	Matlock	25%	30,000	120,000

23.8 Interest on capital

Interest paid on the ***agreed capital*** contributed by each partner is a charge against the profits available for appropriation and therefore, like salaries, reduces the amount of profit remaining to be shared amongst the partners.

Example

James, Curtis and Matlock (see previous example) contribute agreed capitals of £100,000, £150,000 and £170,000 respectively, and their partnership agreement allows for interest at 10% on their capitals to be credited to the partners.

Required

Redraft the appropriation account shown in the example in Section 23.7 to include interest on capitals.

Solution

James, Curtis and Matlock
Profit and loss appropriation account for the year ended 31st December 19X1

			£	£	£
Net profit available for appropriation					190,000
Interest on capital:	James		10,000		
	Curtis		15,000		
	Matlock		17,000	42,000	
Salaries:	James		30,000		
	Curtis		20,000		
	Matlock		20,000	70,000	112,000
Balance of profits to be shared:					78,000
	James	50%	39,000		
	Curtis	25%	19,500		
	Matlock	25%	19,500		78,000

23.9 Interest on drawings

In order to avoid cash flow problems which might be caused if partners draw substantial amounts in anticipation of profits, there is often an agreement whereby ***interest*** may be charged by the business on ***partners' drawings***. This encourages partners not to make drawings until profits are calculated.

In such cases, interest is charged from the dates on which the drawings are made to the date when the accounts are closed, or alternatively, to some mutually agreed date. Where interest is charged, the amounts received by the business are credited to the profit and loss appropriation account as income to the business.

Example

James, Curtis and Matlock (see previous examples) regularly make drawings in anticipation of profits. For the current year the interest charged by the business on those drawings was £1,000, £2,000 and £1,000 respectively.

Required

Redraft the appropriation account shown in the example in paragraph 23.8 to include the interest on drawings.

Solution

James, Curtis and Matlock
Profit and loss appropriation account for the year ended 31st December 19X1

		£	£	£
Net profit available for appropriation				190,000
Add				
Interest on drawings	James	1,000		
	Curtis	2,000		
	Matlock	1,000		4,000
				194,000

Less			£	£	£
Interest on capital:	James		10,000		
	Curtis		15,000		
	Matlock		17,000	42,000	
Salaries:	James		30,000		
	Curtis		20,000		
	Matlock		20,000	70,000	112,000
Balance of profits to be shared:					82,000
	James	50%	41,000		
	Curtis	25%	20,500		
	Matlock	25%	20,500		82,000

You should now be able to attempt Task 23.2 at the end of this chapter.

23.10 Interest on loans

Interest paid on loans provided by the partners in excess of their agreed capitals, unlike interest on partners' capitals, represents a normal business expense. The fact that the loans are provided by the partners is incidental; loans could equally be provided by outsiders to the partnership, in which case the interest paid would be deductible from the normal trading profits. Interest on loans provided by the partners are treated in the same way, thus reducing the net profit available for appropriation, which is always the opening line in the appropriation account. Interest paid on partners' loans, therefore, should be shown as an expense in the profit and loss account, and not in the profit and loss appropriation account.

Capital accounts

A capital account is opened for each partner and an entry made showing the amounts of the agreed capitals when contributed by the partners.

Current accounts

A current account is opened for each partner and the transactions between the partnership and the partners, other than changes in capital, are passed through this account.

To ensure a clear distinction between fixed capitals, of which no part may be withdrawn without agreement, and the transactions arising through the profit and loss appropriation account, it is normal to show interest on capital, salaries, interest on drawings and share of profits in the partners' individual current accounts.

In addition, the actual drawings made by the partners should be passed through the partners' current accounts.

Example

The amounts which were shown as owing to the partners, *James, Curtis and Matlock,* at the beginning of the year were:

	£
James	7,000
Curtis	4,000
Matlock	10,000

During the year, the partners' drawings amounted to:

	£
James	90,000
Curtis	40,000
Matlock	57,000

Required

Refer to the examples in Sections 23.7, 23.8 and 23.9, and use the information which is summarised in the solution in Section 23.9 to record the entries in the current accounts of each partner for the year.

Solution

Current account – James

	£	£
Opening balance due to James	7,000	
Salaries	30,000	
Interest on capital	10,000	
Share of profit	41,000	88,000
Interest on drawings	1,000	
Drawings	90,000	91,000
Closing balance due from James		3,000

Current account – Curtis

	£	£
Opening balance due to Curtis	4,000	
Salaries	20,000	
Interest on capital	15,000	
Share of profit	20,500	59,500
Interest on drawings	2,000	
Drawings	40,000	42,000
Closing balance due to Curtis		17,500

Current account – Matlock

	£	£
Opening balance due to Matlock	10,000	
Salaries	20,000	
Interest on capital	17,000	
Share of profit	20,500	67,500
Interest on drawings	1,000	
Drawings	57,000	58,000
Closing balance due to Matlock		9,500

Notes

Of the three closing balances, James owes the partnership £3,000 because he has effectively overdrawn the balances due to him. The other partners are owed money by the partnership at the year end.

If salaries are paid in cash then it is possible that no entries in respect of this item may appear in the current accounts. If, however, salaries are credited to the partners periodically to be drawn on a different date, then entries in respect of salaries will appear in the current accounts. This is because the current account balances represent the amounts due to or from the partners, and if the payment of salaries has been made as and when due, then no entry in the current account may be necessary.

You should now be able to attempt Questions 23.1 and 23.2 at the end of this chapter.

23.11 Balance sheets

The ***balance sheets*** of partnerships are drawn up in a way similar to those of sole traders, but with the following exceptions.

Capital accounts

A capital account is shown in the balance sheets for each partner, the balance on the account representing the agreed fixed capitals invested in the business by each partner. The fixed capitals change only when additional capital is introduced, or alternatively, some capital is withdrawn by agreement. Unlike sole traders, profits or losses for the period do not adjust the capital accounts of the owners, but adjust the current accounts of the partners.

Current accounts

A current account for each partner is shown in the balance sheet, the balance on the account representing the amounts due to or from the partner at the date of the balance sheet

Example

Bond and Riddles are in partnership sharing profits 60% and 40% respectively. A summarised list of transactions drawn up from the partnership books as at 31st March is as follows:

	£	£
Buildings (cost £150,000)	120,000	
Plant & machinery (cost £30,000)	21,000	
Trade debtors	89,772	
Trade creditors		18,375
Stock at beginning of the year	49,075	
Purchases and sales	119,768	269,580
Carriage inwards	1,688	
Cariage outwards	2,040	
Administration expenses	19,050	
Wages	33,375	
Bad debts	593	
Provision for doubtful debts		630
Capital accounts: Bond		135,000
Riddles		60,000
Current accounts: Bond		3,930
Riddles		3,060
Drawings: Bond	18,900	
Riddles	13,800	
Bank	1,514	
	490,575	490,575

The following information is also available:

- Stock at 31st March was £72,365.
- Depreciation on buildings is at 2% per annum based on the reducing balance method, and on plant at 10% per annum straight line.
- Administration expenses accrued due amount to £780 and carriage inwards £70.
- The provision for doubtful debts is to be set at £510.
- Partners are to be credited with salaries of £18,000 each.
- Interest on capital is allowed at 10% per annum.

Required

i) Prepare a partnership trading, profit and loss account, including an appropriation section, for the year ended 31st March.

ii) Prepare a partnership balance sheet for the year ended 31st March.

iii) Show the movements on the current accounts for the year, and the balances outstanding at the end of the year.

Solution

Bond and Riddles

Trading, profit and loss account for the year ended 31st March

		£	£	£
Sales				269,580
Opening stock			49,075	
Purchases		119,768		
Carriage inwards		1,758	121,526	
			170,601	
Less Closing stock			72,365	98,236
Gross profit				171,344
Depreciation:	Buildings		2,400	
	Plant		3,000	
Administration			19,830	
Carriage outwards			2,040	
Wages			33,375	
Bad debts written off		593		
Provision (630 – 510)		(120)	473	61,118
Net profit available for appropriation				110,226
Salaries:	Bond	18,000		
	Riddles	18,000	36,000	
Interest on capital:	Bond	13,500		
	Riddles	6,000	19,500	
Share of profits:	Bond	32,836		
	Riddles	21,890	54,726	110,226

Current accounts:	Bond	Riddles
	£	£
Opening balance due to partners	3,930	3,060
Interest on capital	13,500	6,000
Salaries	18,000	18,000
Share of profits	32,836	21,890
	68,266	48,950
Less Drawings	18,900	13,800
Closing balance due to partners	49,366	35,150

Bond & Riddles
Balance sheet as at 31st March

	£	£	£
Fixed assets	**Cost**	**Accumulated depreciation**	**Net book Value**
Buildings	150,000	32,400	117,600
Plant	30,000	12,000	18,000
	180,000	44,400	135,600
Current assets			
Stock	72,365		
Debtors (£89,772 – £510)	89,262		
Cash	1,514	163,141	
Creditors due within one year			
Creditors	18,375		
Accruals	850	19,225	143,916
			279,516
	Bond	**Riddles**	**Total**
Capital accounts	135,000	60,000	195,000
Current accounts	49,366	35,150	84,516
			279,516

You should now be able to attempt Task 23.3 and Questions 23.3 and 23.4 at the end of this chapter.

23.12 Summary

Partnership accounts are in many ways similar to those of sole traders with the following exceptions:

- The profit and loss account includes an ***appropriation account*** in which the transactions which affect profits between the partners as partners and the partnership are shown.
- ***Separate accounts*** are shown for each partner's capital and current balances, the former being fixed except where capital is either introduced or withdrawn. Profits or losses and other transactions between the partners and the partnership adjust current accounts only.

Partnership agreements determine relationships between the partners, otherwise the ***Partnership Act 1890*** applies.

You should now be able to attempt the Objective Test at the end of this chapter.

Student activities

Task 23.1 Choose a partner or partners from your group with a view to forming a partnership to carry on a business of your choice. All partners should draw up a draft partnership agreement to cover all the aspects of the business relationship between the partners. All partners should now discuss the draft partnership agreements, and incorporate all the agreed clauses into a final document. How easy was it to agree a final document?

Task 23.2 List all the advantages and disadvantages you can recall which accrue to a business which trades as a partnership compared to those of (a) a sole trader, and (b) a private limited company. You may wish to refer to earlier chapters in this book to carry out this task.

Task 23.3 ***James, Curtis and Matlock*** are unable to understand the profit and loss appropriation account (see section 23.9) and have asked you to present the information in the form of a diagram.

Hint: You may find a pie chart or a segmented bar chart is the best type of diagram.

Question 23.1 The following information refers to the partnership of ***Smith and Jones*** for the year ended 31st December 19X1:

The net profit available for appropriation for the year amounted to £47,500.

Smith is credited with a salary of £25,000 for the year.

Interest is allowed on Capitals at 5% per annum.

Capital invested by the partners:

Smith	£10,000
Jones	£30,000

Drawings by the partners during the year:

Smith	£7,500
Jones	£6,000

Interest is charged on drawings as:

Smith	£750
Jones	£400

Profits are shared:

Smith	60%
Jones	40%

Required

i) Prepare the profit and loss appropriation account for the year.

ii) Prepare the current accounts of Smith and Jones for the year.

Question 23.2 ***Stanier, Collett and Hughes*** **share profits and losses equally. The partnership made a net profit available for appropriation of £99,189 for the year ended 31st December 19X1. At the beginning of the year, the balances due to the partners on their current and capital accounts were as follows:**

	Stanier	Collett	Hughes
	£	£	£
Capital accounts	54,000	54,000	36,000
Current accounts	6,660	5,130	3,528
Drawings by the partners during the year were:	40,860	34,650	15,750
Interest is charged on drawings by the partners of:	1,944	1,449	1,296
Salaries are to be credited to the partners:	22,500	16,200	–
Interest is allowed on capital accounts at a rate of 10% per annum.			

Required

i) **Prepare the profit and loss appropriation account for the year.**

ii) **Prepare the current accounts for the partners for the year.**

Question 23.3 The following is a summarised list of transactions which was taken from the books of the partnership of ***Stirling, Drummond and Webb*** as at 30th June 19X2.

		£	£
Sales			381,690
Purchases		243,222	
Returns in and out		6,450	10,800
Stock at 1st July 19X1		54,630	
Discounts allowed and received		4,728	4,131
Wages		48,675	
Bad debts		1,419	
Electricity		1,895	
General expenses		1,263	
Postage and stationery		3,563	
Fixtures (cost)		24,000	
Fixtures – accumulated depreciation			12,000
Creditors			33,247
Debtors		77,170	
Bank overdraft			3,197
Rates		1,000	
Drawings: Stirling		24,030	
Drummond		18,135	
Webb		18,375	
Current accounts:	Stirling		4,035
(as at 1.7.19X1)	Drummond (overdrawn)	1,875	
	Webb (overdrawn)	1,170	
Capital accounts:	Stirling		37,500
	Drummond		22,500
	Webb		22,500
		531,600	531,600

The following information is also available:

Closing stock at 30th June 19X2 was valued at £44,025.

A provision of £750 for doubtful debts is to be made.

At the end of the year amounts accrued due for electricity and general expenses were £375 and £60 respectively.

An amount of £750 has been paid in advance for rates at the year end.

Depreciation on fixtures is to be charged at 25% per annum on cost.

Interest is to be charged on drawings: Stirling £1,125, Drummond £950, and Webb £500.

Interest is to be allowed on capital at 10% per annum.

Profits are to be shared: Stirling 40%, Drummond 40% and Webb 20%.

Required

i) Prepare the profit and loss account (including the appropriation section) of Stirling, Drummond and Webb for the year ended 30th June 19X2, and a partnership balance sheet as at that date.

ii) Show the entries in each partner's current account for the year.

Question 23.4 *Churchwood, Dean and Collett* agree to share profits in the ratio 3:2:1. The partnership agreement states that the partners are entitled to receive interest on capitals at 10% per annum, that Collett is entitled to a salary of £5,000 per annum, and that 10% per annum interest is charged on drawings. In addition, Churchward has guaranteed Dean a minimum total income of £30,000 for the year.

The agreed balances at the beginning of the year were:

	Capital Accounts	Current Accounts
	£	£
Churchward	50,000	6,500
Dean	50,000	1,000
Collett	20,000	(3,000)

Note that Collett's current account is overdrawn.

The net profit for the year available for appropriation was £71,500, and the partners' total drawings for the year were:

Churchward	£25,000
Dean	£15,000
Collett	£15,000

Required

Draw up the profit and loss appropriation account for the year, and the entries in the current accounts of the three partners.

Objective test *(tick the appropriate box)*

i) A partnership:

a) is limited to a maximum of 50 persons ☐

b) enjoys legal status separate from its owners ☐

c) must distinguish capitals from shares of profits and drawings ☐

d) is governed by the Companies Act 1985 ☐

ii) One of the requirements of the Partnership Act 1890 is that, for accounting and reporting:

a) balance sheets should be in vertical format ☐

b) proper books of account must be kept ☐

c) interest on capital must be clearly shown ☐

d) capital must be increased by profits and reduced by drawings ☐

iii) If a partnership agreement is not drawn up, then the rules of the Partnership Act 1890 apply, which state that:

a) partners must share profits in proportion to their capitals ☐

b) partners are entitled to interest at 5% on their capitals ☐

c) working partners are entitled to a fair salary ☐

d) partners share equally in capital gains and profits ☐

iv) In partnership accounts, the profit and loss appropriation account:

a) must not show salaries, which are deducted as an expense before arriving at net profit ☐

b) must not include interest on capital, which is deducted as an expense before arriving at net profit ☐

c) should include interest on loans provided by the partners in excess of their agreed capitals ☐

d) none of these ☐

v) The current accounts of partners do not include:

a) interest on loans ☐

b) interest on capital ☐

c) salaries of partners when paid as and when due ☐

d) drawings ☐

Chapter 24

Club and society accounts

24.1 Objectives

At the end of this chapter you should be able to:

- draw up accounts appropriate to clubs or societies;
- understand differences between the accounts of trading-for-profit and not-for-profit organisations;
- convert receipts and payments accounts into income and expenditure accounts;
- construct and interpret balance sheets of clubs and societies.

24.2 Introduction

The principles of preparing ***accounts of clubs and societies*** are similar to those used for the preparation of sole traders, with some adjustments to make the accounts appropriate to this kind of non profit-making organisation.

You will see that many club accounts are produced as receipts and payments accounts, simply being a summary of the cash and bank entries for the period. Other accounts take into consideration the principles of capital and revenue and accruals and prepayments. It would be helpful, therefore, if you revised these topics, particularly in Chapter 16 where we considered the effects of accruals and prepayments at the beginning and end of accounting periods.

24.3 Definition of clubs and societies

A ***club*** is an organisation formed by a number of persons joining together in order to pursue a purpose which is mainly non profit-making and usually of a recreational nature. Examples of such clubs are small local sports clubs for rugby, cricket, football and judo, or other recreational pursuits such as winemaking, theatregoing, and societies for the appreciation of music or art.

Some clubs and societies are formed for purposes which are not entirely recreational and have more far-reaching objects. For example, Tottenham Hotspur Football Club is listed on the London Stock Exchange, and most of the clubs in the Football League are professional organisations. Similarly, building societies are subject to special legislation and nowadays operate in a similar way to many banks. Such clubs and societies are organisations which are outside the scope of this chapter.

24.4 Club organisation

The ***organisation*** of clubs or societies may range from the very formal where there are clear rules agreed by the members about the club's objects, election of officers and operations, to the very informal where such questions are resolved as and when they arise.

It is usual for club members to elect annually at the ***annual general meeting (AGM)*** the ***club officers*** and the ***club committee***. The officers are usually the chairman, sometimes called the chairperson or chair, the secretary, who is responsible for the administrative aspects of running the club, and the treasurer, who is responsible for the financial affairs of the club or society.

The ***treasurer*** is responsible for collecting club subscriptions from the members, paying the expenses which the club incurs, and maintaining the accounting records of the club. The treasurer usually presents an accounting statement to the club members at the AGM which shows them a financial summary of the the club's financial transactions over the period being considered by the AGM, normally a year. A statement showing the club's financial position at the end of the year is also presented. The precise form of the annual financial statement presented to the membership will depend upon the type of financial records kept, and the skill of the treasurer in accounting for the club's transactions.

24.5 Financial records

The elected treasurer is often a person who may have very limited accounting knowledge. Consequently, in these circumstances the treasurer will keep the books of the club in the simplest way possible. This will probably mean simply recording in a ***cash book*** the cash receipts and the cash payments of the club for the period. Payments and receipts by cheque which have to be passed through the club's bank account are also regarded as cash transactions for this purpose, indeed, the statements received by the treasurer from the bank from time to time can be of great assistance to him in keeping the cash book.

Example

Cash book

Receipts			Payments			Balance
Date	Details	£	Date	Details	£	£

In some cases a cash book with analysis columns is used so that the total amounts of each transaction can be placed in the appropriate column. For example, on the receipts side separate columns may be used for subscriptions, bank interest, fees and other income, and on the payments side separate columns may be used for, say, room rentals, refreshments, ground fees and heating.

24.6 Receipts and payments account

Where a receipts and payment account is the statement which is presented to the membership at the AGM, it represents a summary of the entries which will have been recorded in the cash book for the year.

The receipts and payments account will show:

- ❒ The balance of cash in hand and/or at the bank at the beginning of the period.
- ❒ An analysis of the cash receipts which have been received by the club during the period.
- ❒ An analysis of the cash payments which have been made by the club during the period.
- ❒ The balance of cash in hand and/or at the bank at the end of the period.

Example

The Grace Cricket Club

Receipts & Payments Account for the year ended 31st December

			£	£
+	Receipts:	Subscriptions received	X	
		Match fees	X	
		Net receipts from bar	X	
		Net receipts from raffles	X	
		Net receipts from socials	X	
		Other receipts	X	X
			—	

			£	£
–	Payments:	Purchase of equipment	X	
		Repairs to pavilion	X	
		Catering costs	X	
		League fees	X	
		Groundsman's wages	X	
		Umpires' expenses	X	
		Other expenses	X	X
=	Excess of receipts over payments			X
+	Opening balance of cash/bank			X
=	Closing balance of cash/bank			X

Notes

All the items are recorded on a cash basis, therefore no adjustment is made for either outstanding expenses for the period due to be paid after the period end, or for income due for the period but not received by the period end. You will recall from chapter 10 that where such adjustments are made the accounts are said to be prepared on an accruals basis. A receipts and payments account is therefore not prepared on an accruals basis.

There is no attempt to differentiate between expenditure on items which have an extended life, such as equipment, and expenditure on items where the benefits arise almost immediately, such as league fees. We have seen in Chapter 15 that the former are regarded as capital expenditure items and the latter as revenue expenditure. A receipts and payments account treats these items in an identical manner by treating them as simply payments.

Where a receipts and payments account is produced, then it is not possible to produce also a balance sheet of the society or club at the period end without substantial adjustments to the figures to convert them to an accruals basis. The financial position of the club is shown simply by the balance of cash and/or bank at the period end.

Because of such drawbacks in using a receipts and payments account, therefore, some club or society treasurers prepare statements for the members which give a more comprehensive and informative picture of the club's surplus or deficit for the period, together with its state of affairs at the end of the period.

The statements which are produced to show this improved picture are ***income and expenditure accounts*** and ***balance sheets***, and are prepared along similar lines to those accounts prepared for sole traders.

24.7 The club's accumulated or general fund

Unlike sole traders or partnerships, clubs and societies do not have capitals as such, as they do not trade for profit. Instead they have what is known as an ***accumulated fund*** or ***general fund***, and instead of revealing a profit or loss for a period they record a ***surplus*** or ***deficit***. A surplus is where income for the period exceeds expenditure, and a deficit is where expenditure exceeds income.

Any surplus or deficit for a period made by a club is treated in a way similar to a profit or loss made by a sole trader; a surplus is credited or added to the accumulated fund and a deficit is debited to or charged against the accumulated fund.

The value of the accumulated fund can be calculated at any time by valuing the net assets of the club. This will be equal to the accumulated fund. The net assets are made up of the assets less the liabilities, and you may remember that a similar technique was used to calculate the value of the owner's capital when dealing with the accounts of sole traders in Chapter 16.

Example

The Coarse Rugby Club wishes to value its accumulated fund at the beginning of the season on 1st September 19X1. It owns a clubhouse which is valued at £25,000 in which the fixtures and fittings are worth £2,000 and the bar stock is valued at £900. £10,500 remains outstanding on a loan which was obtained from the brewery four years ago to finance the construction of the clubhouse.

The stock of shirts, shorts, etc is worth £200, and the rugby equipment valued at £100. The club owes six month's rent to 31st August 19X1 for the pitch, which is rented at a rate of £500 per annum. Club members owe ten annual subscriptions at £10 each, and a delivery of beer valued at £300 on 31st August 19X1 has not been paid for and remains outstanding. The bank balance stands at £1,250.

Required

Calculate the Club's accumulated fund as at 1st September 19X1.

Solution

The recommended approach to this problem is to draw up a statement of assets and liabilities of the club at the date of the valuation of the accumulated fund. This statement is known as a ***statement of affairs.***

The Coarse Rugby Club

Statement of affairs as at 1st September 19X1

		£	£
Assets:	Clubhouse	25,000	
	Fixtures & fittings	2,000	
	Rugby equipment	100	
	Rugby kit	200	
	Bar stock	900	
	Bank Balance	1,250	
	Subscriptions (10 x £10)	100	29,550
Less Liabilities:	Loan	10,500	
	Creditors:		
	Beer	300	
	Rent payable	250	11,050
Valuation of accumulated fund			18,500

Note that the calculation of the accumulated fund enables a balance sheet to be constructed which can provide the basis for recording the club transactions on double entry lines, thus enabling accruals and prepayments to be taken into consideration when preparing club ***income and expenditure accounts.*** The balance sheet in vertical form may appear as follows:

The Coarse Rugby Club

Balance sheet as at 1st September 19X1

Capital employed:		£	£
Fixed assets:	Clubhouse	25,000	
	Fixtures & fittings	2,000	
	Rugby equipment	100	
	Rugby kit	200	27,300
Current assets:	Bar stock	900	
	Subscriptions (10 x £10)	100	
	Bank	1,250	
		2,250	

	£	£
Less		
Current liabilities:		
Creditors:		
Beer	300	
Rent payable	250	
	550	
Net current assets		1,700
Net assets		29,000
Financed by:		
Accumulated fund		18,500
Loan from Brewery		10,500
		29,000

You should now be able to attempt Question 24.1 at the end of this chapter.

24.8 Conversion of a receipts and payment account to an income and expenditure account

An *income and expenditure* account is really the profit and loss account of a *non-trading organisation,* and like a profit and loss account it contains only the revenue items of income and expenditure for the period to which it refers. You will remember from Chapter 16 that whether or not those revenue items are actually received or paid within that period, they are included as income and expenditure for the period.

In comparing the characteristics of an income and expenditure account with those of a receipts and payments account, the main differences are as follows:

Income and expenditure account

- Includes items outstanding and unpaid for the period (accruals), items due but not received, and items paid in advance (prepayments).
- Excludes capital receipts and capital payments.
- Includes depreciation charges.
- The balance represents the surplus or deficit for the period.

Receipts and payments account

- Includes cash transactions only made in the period.
- This may include payments and receipts of items of a capital and revenue nature.
- The balance represents the cash and/or bank balance at the end of the period.

In order to convert a receipts and payments account to an income and expenditure account, the following steps should be made:

1. Identify the revenue items in the receipts and payments account and treat the revenue receipts as income and the revenue payments as expenditure.
2. Draw up a statement of affairs of assets and liabilities at the commencement of the period, but clearly showing the accuals, prepayments and stocks in respect of the revenue items which appear in the income and expenditure account.

3. Identify the accruals, prepayments and stocks at the end of the period in respect of the revenue items which appear in the income and expenditure account.
4. Adjust the items in (1) above so that the accruals, prepayments and stocks in (2) and (3) create the income and expenditure appropriate to the period for which the accounts are prepared.
5. Any capital items of expenditure which appear in the receipts and payments account must be added to the capital items taken from the statement of affairs at the commencement. Suitable adjustments for any sales of assets should be made, to take into consideration the profits and losses on their disposal which are credited to the income and expenditure account.
6. Any other capital payments, such as the repayment of a loan, should be deducted from the liability in the balance sheet.
7. The balance of the income and expenditure account for the year is then transferred to the opening accumulated fund balance which was calculated from the statement of affairs. A surplus is added to the accumulated fund (assuming that the fund is in credit), and any deficit for the year is deducted from the accumulated fund.
8. The balance sheet may then be constructed in the normal way, bringing into the balance sheet the assets and liabilities and accruals and prepayments from the statement of affairs adjusted by the transactions in (3) and (5) above.

Example

Refer to the example in Section 24.7. Having prepared the opening balance sheet, the *Coarse Rugby Club* treasurer wishes to produce the income and expenditure account for the year to 31st August 19X2. He has already produced a receipts and payments account, as follows:

	£	£
Receipts:		
Subscriptions received	600	
Match fees	250	
Net receipts from bar	3,100	
Net receipts from raffles	920	
Net receipts from socials	540	
Other receipts	30	5,440
Payments:		
Purchase of tables for clubhouse	510	
Repairs to clubhouse	1,220	
Loan repayment	1,000	
Interest on Loan	1,050	
Rugby equipment	100	
Rugby kit	100	
Rent of pitch	250	
Bank charges	100	4,330
Excess of receipts over payments		1,110
Opening balance of cash/bank		1,250
Closing balance of cash/bank		2,360

At the end of the year:

Amounts due amounted to:	Rent	£500
	Beer for bar	£700
	Subscriptions	4 members
	Band for social	£140

Bar stock was valued at £500

It is club policy to depreciate fixed assets using the diminishing balance method as follows:

Rugby equipment	25% per annum
Rugby kit	50% per annum
Fixtures and fittings	20% per annum
Clubhouse	10% per annum

Required

Draw up the club's income and expenditure account for the year, and the balance sheet as at 31st August 19X2.

Solution

The Coarse Rugby Club

Income & expenditure account for the year ended 31st August 19X2

		£	£
Income:			
Subscriptions (£600 – £100 + £40)		540	
Match fees		250	
Bar profits (£3,100 Stock – £900 + £500 Creditors +£300 – £700)		2,300	
Raffle profits		920	
Social profits (£540 – £140)		400	
Other income		30	4,440
Expenditure:			
Repairs to clubhouse		1,220	
Interest on loan		1,050	
Rent of pitch (£250 – £250 + £500)		500	
Bank charges		100	
Depreciation:	£		
Rugby equipment 25% (£100 + £100)	50		
Rugby kit 50% (£200 + £100)	150		
Fixtures & fittings 20% (£2,000 + £510)	502		
Clubhouse 10% (£25,000)	2,500	3,202	6,072
Deficit of expenditure over income			1,632

The Coarse Rugby Club
Balance sheet as at 31st August 19X2

Capital employed:	£	£
Fixed assets:		
Clubhouse (£25,000 – £2,500)	22,500	
Fixtures & fittings (£2,000 + £510 – £502)	2,008	
Rugby equipment (£100 + £100 – £50)	150	
Rugby kit (£200 + £100 – £150)	150	24,808
Current assets:		
Bar stock	500	
Subscriptions (4 × £10)	40	
Bank	2,360	
	2,900	
Less		
Current liabilities:		
Creditors:		
Beer	700	
Band for social	140	
Rent payable	500	
	1,340	
Net current assets		1,560
Net assets		26,368
Financed by:		
Accumulated fund	18,500	
Less deficit for the year	1,632	16,868
Loan from Brewery (£10,500 – £1,000)		9,500
		26,368

You should now be able to attempt Task 24.3 and Questions 24.2 and 24.3 at the end of this chapter.

24.9 Summary

The accounts of clubs and societies are often in the form of ***receipts and payments accounts***, which are nothing more than summaries of the cash and/or bank transactions which have taken place over the period. An alternative presentation, the ***income and expenditure account***, takes into consideration both the accruals and prepayments and the different natures of capital and revenue expenditure in determining the club's income and expenditure for the period.

Clubs or societies do not trade for profit, therefore the excess of income over expenditure for the period is known as a ***surplus***. Any excess of expenditure over income is known as a ***deficit***. The surplus or deficit adjusts the club's ***accumulated fund*** in the balance sheet. The accumulated fund replaces the capital account normally found in the accounts of businesses which trade for profit such as sole traders.

> *You should now be able to attempt the Objective Test at the end of this chapter.*

Student activities

Task 24.1 There are many people who act as honorary (unpaid) treasurers of such clubs or societies considered in this chapter. Discuss with a club treasurer the way in which he keeps the financial records, the books, of the club. Consider the following questions.

i) Is a complete set of books maintained or simply a cash book?

ii) Does the treasurer produce a receipts and payments account or an income and expenditure account at the year end?

iii) If a receipts and payments account only is produced, can you help the treasurer produce an income and expenditure account for the period?

iv) Is an annual balance sheet produced? If not, can you help the treasurer produce an opening statement of affairs and a closing balance sheet?

Task 24.2 Now you know how to keep the financial records of a club or society, the next time the club of which you are a member requires a treasurer, volunteer to put yourself up for election to that position. If you are elected, maintain the records in such a way as to enable a club income and expenditure account and a club balance sheet to be prepared when you present the financial report to the members at the AGM.

Task 24.3 Imagine you are the treasurer of the Coarse Rugby Club (see section 24.8). You are expected to present the income and expenditure account and balance sheet at the AGM which is held in the club bar. Prepare a speech which you consider will be appropriate for the members of the club attending.

Question 24.1 *The Mozart Music Club* has the following assets and liabilities at 30th September 19X2:

Subscriptions overdue from members: £45
Affiliation fee overdue to Music Club Associates: £25
Compact disc player (at cost): £1,080
Record and disc library (at valuation): £560
Rent of premises prepaid: £60
Printing costs of September magazine not yet paid: £100
Fixtures and fittings (at cost): £800
Electricity for September quarter not yet paid: £40
Cash at bank: £222
Cash in hand: £48

The disc player was purchased two years ago and has an anticipated life of five years, with an estimated sale value of £80 at the end of that time. The fixtures and fittings were installed four years ago and are being depreciated over ten years with no residual value. The straight line method of depreciation is used.

Required

Draw up a statement of affairs and determine the value of the accumulated fund on 30th September 19X2.

Question 24.2 *Adelaide Vintage Car Club* is preparing its accounts for the year to 31st December 19X2 for the annual general meeting. The treasurer cannot decide whether to produce a receipts and payments account or an income and expenditure account, so he decides to produce both. The information available is as follows:

- The balance at bank on 1st January 19X2 was £900.
- During the year subscriptions were received of £1,600, of which £50 represented amounts overdue at the beginning of the year, and £100 paid in advance. £75 of subscriptions were outstanding at 31st December 19X2.
- A summary of the other cash/bank entries is as follows:

Receipts	£	Payments	£
Interest received	70	Bank charges	62
Sales of parts	1,250	Rent of premises	400
Raffles (Net)	261	Purchase of parts	642
		Socials (net)	124
		Electricity	105
		Printing & Stationery	206
		Furniture	420
		Books	160

- Other information:

Parts for resale:
Stocks at 1st January 19X2: £50
31st December 19X2: £80
Amounts due to suppliers on 1st January 19X2: £144
31st December 19X2: £300
Printing costs for raffle tickets outstanding on 31st December 19X2: £56
Electricity outstanding for December quarter 19X2: £25
Stationery:
Stock at: 1st January 19X2: £24
31st December 19X2: £46
Amount due to supplier at 31st December 19X2: £25

- Other assets at the beginning of the year were:

Vintage Rolls Royce (at cost): £4,000
Furniture (at valuation): £1,280
Library (at valuation): £340

Library and furniture should be depreciated at 20% on the value in the accounts at the year end. The Rolls Royce is not depreciated.

Required

i) Prepare a statement of affairs at 1st January 19X2

ii) Prepare a receipts and payments account for the year ended 31st December 19X2.

iii) Prepare an income and expenditure account for the year ended 31st December 19X2.

iv) Prepare a balance sheet as at 31st December 19X2.

Question 24.3 The following opening balances were taken from the books of *Viney Green Golf Club* on 1st January 19X1:

Golf course at cost: £100,000
Clubhouse at cost: £50,000
Investment in building society: £12,000
Subscriptions in advance: £800
in arrears: £1,200
Bar stock: £9,700
Equipment at cost: £7,000
Cash in hand and at bank: £2,500

Analysis of the bank statements and cash book for the year revealed the following transactions:

Receipts:	£	Payments:	£
Subscriptions	52,000	Course maintenance	34,100
Green fees	1,000	Bar wages	6,000
Sale of equipment	100	General expenses	14,100
Bar takings	46,200	Cost of professional	4,000
Interest received	980	Purchase of equipment	2,400
		Bar purchases	25,180

- Outstanding balances at 31st December 19X1 were:

  Creditors for bar supplies: £2,000
  Subscriptions in advance (19X2): £1,800
  in arrears (19X1): £700

- Bar stocks at 31st December 19X1 were £8,650
- Insurance paid in advance (included in general expenses) £1,200
- Depreciation on equipment and the clubhouse (a temporary one) is to be provided at 20% per annum on cost at the year end.
- The equipment sold originally cost £500.

Required

Prepare an income and expenditure account for the club for the year ended 31st December 19X1, and a balance sheet as at that date.

Objective test *(tick the appropriate box)*

i) The receipts and payment account represents a summary of:

a) the bank account ☐

b) the cash account ☐

c) both ☐

d) neither ☐

ii) The receipts and payments account fails to differentiate between:

a) capital and revenue expenditure ☐

b) accruals and prepayments ☐

c) income and expenditure ☐

d) cash and non-cash items ☐

iii) The statement of affairs is drawn up primarily to establish, at the beginning of the period,:

a) total fixed assets ☐

b) value of the accumulated fund ☐

c) total current liabilities ☐

d) total assets ☐

iv) Subscriptions received in cash are £1,125. This includes £25 outstanding at the beginning of the year when £40 was prepaid, and at the end of the year £60 was prepaid and £50 was overdue. The subscription income for the year to be included in the income & expenditure account was:

a) £1,250 ☐

b) £1,130 ☐

c) £1,135 ☐

d) £1,265 ☐

v) Net cash received from bar sales less payments amounted to £2,161 for the year. The opening stock was £440, and the closing stock was £280. The final delivery last year of £920 was unpaid at the end of that year, and this year £640 of deliveries remains unpaid. A private social had been supplied with drinks amounting to £600, and this amount remains unpaid at the end of this year. The bar net income for the year was:

a) £2,881 ☐

b) £4,781 ☐

c) £1,711 ☐

d) £3,471 ☐

Chapter 25

Public sector financial statements

25.1 Objectives

At the end of this chapter you should be able to:

- understand how public sector accounts differ from those of private commercial organisations;
- understand how the public sector is financed and controlled;
- understand the layout of some public sector final accounts;
- understand how capital expenditure is accounted for in local authority and other public sector accounts.

25.2 Introduction

The ***public sector*** in the United Kingdom represents a substantial proportion of the economy. However, it cannot be regarded as a single entity as it is made up of a variety of different organisations including the following.

Central government is responsible for determining how the funds which are raised through taxation and other sources are spent. Examples of the nation's services are employment, defence, the law and other sectors of activity which are either partly or completely nationalised, such as education, health, transport and social services.

Local government is responsible for local services, some of which are shared with Central Government, such as education, policing, housing, social services and transport.

Nationalised industries and public corporations include organisations such as British Rail, British Coal, the Post Office, the Bank of England and the British Broadcasting Corporation (BBC).

The National Health Service is really a section of central government. It is generally subdivided into regional and district health authorities, but individual hospitals and hospital groups now have the legal right to opt out of these authorities and form independent trusts under the National Health Service.

Although much of the expenditure on ***primary and secondary education***, for children up to the age of 18, is under the control of the local authorities, the Government's introduction of the ***Local Management of Schools (LMS)*** initiative has allowed many schools to opt out of their care and become responsible for controlling their own expenditure budgets.

Higher education in the United Kingdom is primarily made up of the university sector, but there are also many non-university institutions. The Further and Higher Education Act 1992, together with associated legislation for Scotland and Wales, gave university status to polytechnics and many colleges of higher education, and by 1993 the university sector in the United Kingdom comprised 90 institutions. Higher education in the public sector in the UK is funded by the government using four funding councils, the largest being the ***Higher Education Funding Council for England (HEFCE)***. The other funding councils are the ***Welsh Funding Council***, the ***Scottish Higher Education Funding Council (SHEFC)*** and the ***Northern Ireland Higher Education Council (NIHEC)***.

25.3 Characteristics of public sector organisations

Public sector organisations differ from those of the private commercial sector in the following ways:

- There is usually no specific ownership of such organisations and therefore no capital or share capital held by owners; they are state controlled.
- They are often set up by a specific act of Parliament.

- They usually operate within a strict legal framework set by that specific act of Parliament.
- They are mainly not-for-profit organisations, with the exception of certain organisations such as British Rail and British Coal which are set financial targets by the Government. In the case of not-for-profit organisations, they are mainly controlled by government-imposed cash limits. In the case of profit-making organisations, they are controlled by a combination of financial targets and cash limits.
- The decisions made by such organisations are often made on political, rather than financial or commercial, grounds.
- Each organisation is required by law to produce accounts. The precise requirements as to content and to whom to report vary according to the act of Parliament under which they were set up.

25.4 Funding

The *funding* of much of the public sector is voted by Parliament out of the ***Consolidated Fund*** into which taxes are paid by the Inland Revenue and the Customs & Excise departments. The payments from the Consolidated Fund are of two types:

- Standing Service Payments, such as payments of interest on the national debt or judges' salaries, for which no annual vote is required;
- Supply Service Payments, such as expenditure subject to annual votes of Parliament to finance government expenditure.

Expenditure is audited by the ***Auditor and Comptroller General***. He is independent of Parliament and reports to the Public Accounts Committee, a committee of the House of Commons. Any special emergency expenditure is not met from the Consolidated Fund but is taken from the ***Contingencies Fund***. Such amounts are approved retrospectively by Parliament.

Although the taxes raised are paid into the Consolidated Fund, there may be circumstances where the public spending which is met from the Consolidated Fund exceeds the amount raised. Under these circumstances the deficit is financed by borrowings, where the government of the day applies to the market to raise the required funds by issuing government gilt-edged securities at an interest rate ruling at the time of issue. The funds thus raised are paid into the ***National Loans Fund***, which are then used to finance deficits in the Consolidated Fund and to repay the lenders. The funds raised are part of the ***Public Sector Borrowing Requirement (PSBR)***.

25.5 Control of public expenditure

Public expenditure is controlled in a number of ways. In not-for-profit organisations it is carried out mainly by:

- ***Cash limits*** which are set for many government departments and local authorities. Control of the latter is achieved by restricting the revenue support grant which central government uses to part-finance some of the activities of the local authorities such as education.
- The Treasury monitors expenditure through the ***Financial Information System (FIS)*** on a regular monthly basis. The data transmitted to the Treasury within ten working days of the month end enables remedial action to be taken at government level if this proves necessary.

25.6 Supply services

The accounts of central government which deal with the actual receipts and payments of ***supply services*** are known as ***appropriation accounts.*** Although they differentiate between the payments on capital items and those which may be classified as revenue, there is no attempt to capitalise such expenditure in a balance sheet as a private commercial business might.

All payments are recorded against income (that is, income received from taxation) as and when made, and therefore no capital items are carried forward year after year to be depreciated as happens in the private sector.

25.7 Trading activities

In cases where ***trading activities*** take place, income and expenditure accounts are used rather than a receipts and payments basis. (See Chapter 24 for an explanation of the differences between these two statements.) In these cases a commercial-like accruals basis of accounting is used where an allowance is made for accruals and prepayments and capital and revenue expenditure in the normal way.

25.8 Local government authorities

Local government authorities, also known as councils, may be of two types: ***county councils*** and ***district councils.*** Each authority sub-divides its income and expenditure into capital and revenue and into various funds and accounts. The major funds/accounts are:

❐ Operational:	General/county Fund Housing Revenue Account
❐ Trading:	Theatres, Restaurants and Abattoirs Direct Labour Organisations Direct Service Organisations
❐ Internal or Special:	Loans Pool Insurance Reserve Superannuation Fund
❐ Collection Fund:	Council Tax

The income for each fund/account comes from a number of sources. The main sources are central government grants, council tax and business rates, and charges for services provided.

Each year a local authority must publish a summary ***revenue account*** for each main fund, together with a ***consolidated balance sheet*** for all the pools and accounts combined, excluding superannuation, trust and collection funds.

The methods of raising funds locally from the populations of district and county council areas to finance local government expenditure have undergone changes in recent years. From raising funds through a levy or tax on householders and businesses known as rates, it was changed to a community charge system designed to require all inhabitants to make a contribution to the funding of local authorities. Businesses continued to pay a business rate, but since April 1993 individuals are required to pay a tax called the council tax.

25.9 Capital expenditure accounting

Capital expenditure in local authorities is usually financed by borrowing. The authority is required to charge interest to the relevant account and make a minimum revenue provision, as required by legislation, for the repayment of ***debt principal***. You will remember that the principal on a loan is the amount borrowed.

These charges of principal and interest are called ***debt charges*** and notionally replace the depreciation which would have been charged if normal commercial accounting practices were adopted by local authorities. Local authorities currently only charge normal depreciation when dealing with trading activities such as direct labour and service organisations. These are organisations which local authorities have been required by central government to set up to compete on a commercial basis with outside businesses for the services which are provided by local councils, such as street cleaning, house repairs and refuse collection. This will change in 1994 with a new system of capital accounting with depreciation based on current market values being charged.

Capital expenditure may also be financed by capital receipts or grants, or contributions from the Revenue Account.

Example

A local authority's revenue account

Last Year Net Expenditure £		This year Gross Expenditure £	Income £	Net Expenditure £
	Committee:			
	Development Services			
	Educational Services			
	Leisure Services			
	Management Services			
	Social Services			
———		———	———	———
	Interest on Internal Balances			
	Surplus on Trading Organisations			
———				———
	Revenue Support Grant			
	Net Receipts from Collection Fund			
	Surplus/(Deficit) for year			
———				———
	Balance on Revenue Fund:			
	At beginning of year			
	Surplus/(Deficit) for year			
	Balance at the end of year			
═══				═══

Example

A local authority's capital spending account

	This year	Last year
	£	£
Gross capital spending by		
Development Services Committee		
Educational Services Committee		
Housing Services Committee		
Management Committee		
Social Services Committee		
Total		
Spent on		
Acquisition of land and existing		
Buildings and works		
New constructions		
Vehicles, plant and machinery		
Grants and advances		
Total		
Paid for by		
Borrowings		
Capital Receipts		
Revenue Funds		
Government Funds		
Special Reserves		
Total		

Notice that in both the ***revenue expenditure*** and the ***capital spending accounts*** much of the expenditure is analysed by committee. This reflects the way in which local authorities are organised. The elected members of the council serve on various committees which incur specific costs of carrying out the services for which they are responsible.

Local authorities are required to produce a balance sheet to indicate the financial state of the organisation at the end of the period of report in the same way as organisations in the private sector. The following example is a typical balance sheet of a district local authority.

Example

A local authority's consolidated balance sheet

	This Year	Last Year
	£	£
Net fixed assets		
Council dwellings		
Other land and buildings		
Vehicles, plant, furniture and equipment		
Deferred charges		
Investments		
Long-term debtors		
Housing Act advances		
Housing Association loans		
Mortgages on houses sold		
Current assets		
Stocks and work in progress		
Debtors		
Temporary investments		
Bank		
Less **Current liabilities**		
Creditors		
Temporary borrowings		
Bank overdraft		
Net assets		
Financed by		
Long-term borrowing		
Deferred capital receipts		
Capital receipts unapplied		
Provision for credit liabilities		
Fund balances and reserves		
Total financing		

25.10 Nationalised industries

Nationalised industries' accounts and operations vary according to the acts which set them up and govern their operations. Typical examples include British Rail, which has a virtual monopoly in the operation of rail transport in the United Kingdom, and British Coal, which owns the bulk of the coal mines. Financial control is exercised by central government by setting financial targets such as:

- return on net assets;
- profit as a percentage of turnover;
- a specified percentage of self-financing from the industry's own resources; for example, retained surplus or profit and depreciation provisions.

(See Chapter 22 for a full description of the use of accounting ratios.)

The ***accounting methods*** in nationalised industries are similar to those used in commercial private businesses. Capital and revenue expenditure are clearly differentiated. Capital expenditure is capitalised in being charged in the balance sheet and depreciated in the normal way, as opposed to the debt financing approach of the local authorities.

25.11 The National Health Service

The majority of the funds used in the ***National Health Service (NHS)*** are provided directly from central government raised through taxation. Relatively small but significant amounts are raised from charges and donations from individuals and organisations.

Extensive changes have taken place in the organisation of the NHS in recent years with the introduction of a market for health care provision. These changes are reflected in the accounts prepared within the service.

The internal market means that the roles of purchaser and provider of services have been split so as to create some element of competition between providers within the NHS. The purchasers and providers are:

PURCHASERS	PROVIDERS
District Health Authorities	NHS Hospital Trusts
General Practice Fundholders	Non Trust Hospitals
	Private Hospitals

The government provides cash limited funds to the purchasers, through Regional Health Authorities, and the purchasers agree contracts with the providers of healthcare for health services to the population of the district which the purchasers serve.

District Health Authorities and NHS Trusts both prepare annual accounts which are subject to audit. The main statements in both sets of accounts are income and expenditure account, cash flow statement and balance sheet. The income and expenditure account is prepared using fundamental accounting concepts and principles such as accruals and prudence. The statements also reflect the purchaser/provider roles of the District Health Authorities and NHS Hospital Trusts.

Example

District Health Authority
Income and Expenditure Account

	This Year £	Last Year £
Income		
Allocations from central government		
Expenditure		
Health care purchased from providers		
Administrative expenses		
Surplus/deficit for the year		

Example

NHS Trust Hospital
Income and Expenditure Account

	This Year £	Last Year £
Income from		
District Health Authorities		
General Practitioner Fundholders		
Private patients		
Operating Expenses		
Staff wages		
Supplies and services		
Depreciation		
Interest payable		
Interest receivable	( )	( )
Net expenditure		
Surplus/(deficit)		

Balance sheets provided by trusts are very similar to those produced for a company. However, fixed assets must be valued at current cost rather than historic cost.

Example

NHS Trust Hospital
Summarised Balance Sheet

	This Year	Last Year
	£	£
Fixed Assets		
Current Assets		
less Creditors		
	______	______
Total Assets Employed		
	______	______
Financed by:		
Public Dividend Capital		
Long Term Loans		
Income and Expenditure Account		
	______	______
	______	______

Like other commercial organisations, NHS trusts generate their own finance from retained profits, depreciation, long term loans and sales of assets. NHS trusts remain in the public sector but have been the subject of much controversy. If you are interested in this area, most trusts will supply copies of their annual accounts on request.

25.12 Higher and further education

The higher education sector has been through a considerable process of reorganisation in recent years. The hitherto 30-strong polytechnic sector has disappeared with the government's policy of enabling polytechnics to assume university status, bringing the number of UK universities to 90 institutions. In addition there are a number of non-university higher education colleges all funded by the appropriate funding councils of England, Scotland, Wales and Northern Ireland.

The further education colleges which were responsible to local authorities have now been given independent status and therefore are responsible for their own affairs. In general, independent universities and colleges are financed from student fees and appropriate funding council grants. They maintain their own accounting records and financial controls, and produce their own annual financial statements.

The professional accounting bodies in the guise of the Accounting Standards Committee (ASC) issued a number of Statements of Recommended Practice (SORPs). Although the ASC has been superceded by the Accounting Standards Board (ASB), a SORP on Accounting in UK Universities is still in operation, although in 1993 consideration was being given to its revision. The following is a proposed layout of final accounts for the university sector.

Example

University Sector
Proposed Consolidated Income and Expenditure Account

	This Year	Last Year
	£	£
Income		
Funding Council Grants		
Academic Fees and Support Grants		
Research Grants and Contracts		
Other Operating Income		
Endowment Income		
Interest Receivable		
	______	______
Total Income		
	______	______

	This Year £	Last Year £
Expenditure		
Staff Costs		
Depreciation		
Other Operating Expenses		
Interest Payable		
Total Expenditure		
Surplus/(Deficit) before Tax		
Taxation		
Surplus/(Deficit) after Tax		
Net Release from Revaluation Reserves		
Surplus/(Deficit) before Transfers		
Transfers (to)/from Reserves		
Retained Surplus for Year		

A more detailed analysis of many of the figures which make up the ***income statement*** of a higher education corporation is normally given in ***notes***. These form an integral part of the accounts.

The ***balance sheet*** of such an organisation is very similar to balance sheets which are drawn up by a commercial organisation with the exception that there is no share capital. The funds which finance the net assets of the organisation are made up of ***reserves***, which may be specific reserves, such as asset replacement reserve, or other reserves, such as capital reserve or general reserve.

The higher education sector in the United Kingdom is made up of 90 universities who are allowed to confer their own degrees and other qualifications and many higher education colleges, some of which are members of the Consortium of Independent Colleges and Research Institutions. In addition there are many institutions in the further education sector which do not normally confer degrees but carry out technical, business and commercial education and confer diplomas and other qualifications of such bodies as the Business and Technical Education Council.

25.13 Summary

The ***public sector*** is a large element of the economy of the UK. It includes a variety of different organisations ranging from central government itself to trading organisations such as British Rail or British Coal.

Each type of organisation in the public sector has an accounting system which is appropriate to its own particular circumstances. The trading organisations mainly adopt systems which are similar to other commercial enterprises. They produce either ***income and expenditure accounts*** or ***profit and loss accounts***, which discriminate between ***accruals and prepayments*** and ***capital and revenue*** expenditure.

Local authorities have a special way of treating capital expenditure in that the ***debt charges*** and not depreciation are charged against each fund.

Health authorities have their own way of classifying capital expenditure. They also do not depreciate fixed assets. They account for ***income and expenditure***, whether capital or revenue, on what is virtually a cash basis.

Higher education universities and colleges are also required to produce ***income and expenditure accounts*** and ***balance sheets*** annually in a format similar to commercial enterprises, but without share capital forming a part of the source of finance.

You should now be able to attempt Tasks, Case Study and Objective Test at the end of this chapter.

Student activities

Task 25.1 Your local authority is legally obliged to make a copy of its accounts available at the council offices. Although you may not be allowed to take a copy away, go to the council offices with a copy of the report and accounts of a well-known public limited company of your choice (write to the company secretary at the company's registered office and ask for a free copy) and inspect the council's accounts, making notes of the following:

i) List ways in which the council's revenue accounts differ from the profit and loss accounts of the limited company.

ii) Make a note of how the various activities of the council are accounted for.

iii) List ways in which the balance sheets of the two organisations differ.

Task 25.2 Collect a copy of the accounts of as many different public sector organisations as possible. They should include the accounts of a trading organisation or company such as British Rail or British Coal, a health authority, a university and a local authority. Compare and contrast the accounts of each organisation by listing the major ways in which they are similar to and different from each other.

Task 25.3 You have been asked by the full council of the local authority to present some of the important financial information contained in the annual report in a way which will enable the information to be more easily understood by the counsellors. From a copy of your local council's report, prepare such statements, charts, graphs and diagrams which you consider necessary to comply with their request.

Question 25.1 ***Budgeting in higher education***

A university has adopted a faculty structure with the intention of ensuring that each faculty will act as a budget centre. The faculty direct costs are chargeable to each faculty, together with an equitable share of the support services of the institution. The budgeted direct costs of each faculty for the year, together with the personnel numbers, are as follows:

Faculty	Numbers of staff		Costs	
	Lecturers	Administration	Staff	Other*
			£m	£m
Business School	70	20	1.90	0.25
Science	50	13	1.40	0.25
Engineering	40	5	1.25	0.30
Mathematics	23	7	0.70	0.15
Social Sciences	41	14	1.33	0.20
Art & Design	10	4	0.35	0.10
Surveying	12	6	0.30	0.12
Nursing & Health	11	5	0.32	0.15

* Other costs are those non-staff costs which can be directly attributed to the individual faculties. They include such costs as staff development, research, stationery, photocopying and depreciation of equipment.

The budget for the university's support services is as follows:

	£m
Management & Administration	0.95
Registry	0.45
Library	1.40
Information Systems	1.00
Sites & Buildings	2.26
Personnel	0.25

Each faculty earns income based on the number of students accepted by that faculty, and the value per student is credited to each faculty on the following basis:

	Funding rate per student £ pa
Business School/Social Science	2,700
Science/Engineering	3,600
Mathematics	3,000
Art & Design/Nursing & Health/Surveying	3,200

The operating statistics for the year are as follows:

Faculty	Student numbers Existing (years 2/3/4)	Intake (1)	Staff numbers	Space occupied ('000 sq m)	Use of information systems (%)
Business School	750	350	90	100	10
Science	350	200	63	120	10
Engineering	160	100	45	100	15
Mathematics	140	80	30	50	15
Social Sciences	600	300	55	70	8
Art & Design	40	30	14	20	3
Surveying	100	50	18	20	3
Nursing & Health	60	30	16	30	6
Support					
Management & Administration			35	3	5
Registry			20	1	5
Library			48	50	15
Information Systems			15	2	–
Sites & Buildings			8	1	–
Personnel			18	1	5

The Business School student intake is expected to comprise 700 full-time students and 1,000 part-time students rated at 0.4 full-time equivalents (FTE) each.

Required

The director of the university has asked you, the financial manager, to write a brief report which considers the following questions:

i) Will the university pay its way next year?

ii) Which faculties will make a surplus and which are in deficit?

iii) Which faculties should be expanded and which closed down?

iv) What are the financial implications of your proposals?

Question 25.2 This question follows on from Question 25.1. The director is considering whether to allow parts of the university to engage part-time staff and expand certain faculties' activities. He has asked you to write a further report on the following topics:

i) Which faculties should be permitted to engage part-time staff at £20 per hour? Give reasons.

ii) Should any faculty be allowed to increase the number of its full-time personnel? Give reasons.

iii) How should the university respond to a wage claim of 10% by the lecturing staff? What are the financial implications of such a claim in a full year by faculty?

Question 25.3 Refer to the data in Question 25.1 also for this question. The director has asked your views on the following problems. Write him a brief report giving your reasons. Work to three decimal places of £m in your calculations.

i) How might the effectiveness of each of the support services be measured?

ii) What is the importance of choosing equitable bases of apportionment to ensure that each faculty bears a fair share of the support departments' costs.

iii) How should the university respond to increasing labour turnover in registry and information systems where salaries are 20% below private sector rates?

iv) What guidelines can be set for lecturer teaching loads in each faculty?

Objective Test *(tick the appropriate box)*

i) Public sector organisations are:

a) public limited companies ☐

b) private limited companies ☐

c) a variety of state-controlled organisations ☐

d) large organisations such as British Rail and the BBC ☐

ii) Central government controls public expenditure by:

a) setting cash limits ☐

b) setting financial targets ☐

c) none of these ☐

d) both of these ☐

iii) The way in which capital expenditure is accounted for in business is to charge such expenditure to fixed assets and depreciate over its useful life. In which of the following organisations is this generally not done?

a) British Rail ☐

b) local authorities ☐

c) health authorities ☐

d) universities ☐

iv) Local authorities do not depreciate fixed assets, they:

a) charge them against a particular fund as and when purchased ☐

b) capitalise them, and charge interest charges thereon to a fund ☐

c) capitalise them, and charge instalments of principal to a fund ☐

d) a combination of (b) and (c) ☐

v) The following generally use the normal business accounting techniques of distinguishing between capital and revenue expenditure, and bringing in accruals and prepayments:

a) British Rail ☐

b) local authorities ☐

c) health authorities ☐

d) universities ☐

Chapter 26

Manufacturing organisations

26.1 Objectives

At the end of this chapter you should be able to:

- appreciate the link between manufacturing accounts and trading, profit and loss accounts;
- understand the classification of costs necessary for the drawing up of a manufacturing account;
- explain what is meant by work in progress;
- explain what is meant by finished goods;
- understand their accounting treatment;
- produce final accounts for a manufacturing organisation.

26.2 Introduction

In Chapters 10 and 21 you saw how the final accounts of sole traders and limited companies include a statement called the ***trading, profit and loss account,*** a term which is now often abbreviated to the ***profit and loss account.*** You should revise these chapters now to ensure that you are completely familiar with their contents.

The profit and loss account may be made up of three sections:

- the ***trading section,*** which compares the sales and the cost of sales in order to obtain the ***gross profit*** for the period;
- the ***profit and loss section,*** which compares the gross profit with the expenses or overheads of the business in order to obtain the ***net profit*** for the period;
- the ***appropriation section,*** which is used in limited companies and partnerships in order to record what happens to the net profit. In a partnership it is shared between the partners, whereas in a limited company the appropriation section records what proportion of the profit is distributed as a dividend and what proportion is retained.

Notice that as the trading section compares the sales and cost of sales to obtain the gross profit, it assumes that the organisation is one which simply buys and sells products or commodities.

However, many organisations are involved in a manufacturing process where raw materials are worked on and converted into something else which is then sold. In this kind of organisation the trading, profit and loss account is inadequate, and for this reason the ***manufacturing account*** has been developed as an additional statement to those discussed above.

In building up a manufacturing account the costs are listed in the account according to the costs which are incurred when a product is manufactured. These product costs are ***classified*** according to costing principles.

26.3 Product direct costs

Product direct costs are costs which can be traced directly to the product or products which are being manufactured by the enterprise and comprise:

- direct materials
- direct wages
- direct expenses

Direct materials are those materials or parts and sub-assemblies which are used in the production of and feature in the final form of the products which are produced by the enterprise.

Example

Direct material	Product
Wood, screws, handles	Desk
Printed circuit boards, disk drives, cases	Computer
Steel, wheels, power train	Motor vehicle

Direct wages (direct labour) are those wages paid to the personnel who are directly involved in the production of each of the items produced. They include wages paid to operators of the machinery used to manufacture the products, wages paid to the workers who assemble the products and wages paid to those who finish them, such as painting, polishing and testing.

Direct expenses are those costs which can also be directly traced to the products which are being produced, but cannot be classified under direct materials or direct wages. For example, if in the manufacture of a machine the supply and installation of electronic controls is sub-contracted to an outside expert, the resultant cost is neither direct material nor direct wages. Nevertheless, this cost is clearly a product direct cost and would therefore be charged as a direct expense of manufacturing the product on which the technician worked.

26.4 Prime cost

The total of direct materials consumed, and direct wages and direct expenses incurred is known as the prime cost of a product, and is often shown as such in the manufacturing account.

26.5 Overheads

If a cost is not a product direct cost as described above, it is classified as a ***product indirect cost*** or ***overhead.*** Overheads are those items of revenue expenditure which, although incurred to enable business operations to take place, nevertheless cannot be traced directly to individual products where a range of products is manufactured. Overhead costs are often shared by the entire output.

Overheads can be classified as:

- production overheads
- administration overheads
- selling overheads
- distribution overheads

Only the production overheads are charged in the manufacturing account as part of the cost of production. Costs under the other overhead classifications are charged against the profit and loss account.

26.6 Production overheads

Production (manufacturing or ***factory) overheads*** are incurred as part of the cost of manufacture, but cannot be traced as direct costs to the products produced.

Example

Production overhead
Factory rent and business rates
Factory cleaning costs
(cleaners' wages and materials)
Depreciation of factory machinery
Power
Factory light and heat
Supervisors' salaries
Maintenance wages and expenses

26.7 Total production cost

The addition of prime cost and production overheads is known as ***total production cost*** or ***total manufacturing cost*** or ***total factory cost of finished goods***.

26.8 The manufacturing account – basic layout

The basic manufacturing account layout, which incorporates direct costs and production overheads, is as follows.

Example

Manufacturing account for the year ended (date)

	£	£
Direct costs		
Direct materials consumed	X	
Direct wages	X	
Direct expenses	X	
Prime cost		X
Production overheads		X
Total production cost of finished goods		X

Example

The following costs have been incurred by ***Manchester Manufacturers Ltd*** for the year ended 31st December 19X1:

	£'000
Office salaries	300
Depreciation of machinery	60
Machinery maintenance	82
Factory maintenance	105
Operators' wages	662
Factory rent	100
Factory insurance	30
Direct materials consumed	317
Office stationery	32
Factory canteen	204
Factory manager's salary	29
Accountancy and legal fees	49

	£
Depreciation of delivery vans	37
Telephone	18
Electricity	43
Power for factory machinery	102
Production sub-contract work	95
Business rates – office	32
– factory	65

Required

i) Identify from the list of costs those which should be included in a manufacturing account.

ii) Classify the costs you have identified as either direct costs or overheads.

iii) Arrange the production costs in the form of a manufacturing account showing prime cost and total production cost of finished goods.

Solution

Manchester Manufacturers Ltd.

Manufacturing account for the year ended 31 December 19X1

	£'000	£'000
Direct costs:		
Direct materials	317	
Direct wages (operators' wages)	662	
Direct expenses (subcontract)	95	
Prime cost		1,074
Production overheads:		
Depreciation of machinery	60	
Machinery maintenance	82	
Factory maintenance	105	
Factory rent	100	
Factory insurance	30	
Factory canteen	24	
Factory manager's salary	29	
Power for factory machinery	102	
Business rates – factory	65	
Total production overheads		597
Total production cost of finished goods		1,671

You should now be able to attempt Question 26.1 at the end of this chapter.

26.9 Changes to the trading account

The introduction of the manufacturing account into the final accounts of an organisation requires some minor changes to the *trading* section of the traditional profit and loss account as covered in Chapters 10 and 21.

You will recall that the trading account establishes the ***gross profit*** of the enterprise by comparing the sales income with the ***cost of goods sold*** or ***cost of sales.*** A typical layout is as follows.

Example

Trading, profit and loss account for the year ended (date) (Trading section only)

	£	£
Sales		X
Cost of goods sold:		
Opening stock	X	
Add purchases	X	
	X	
Less closing stock	X	
Cost of goods sold		X
Gross profit		X

The above trading section assumes that the items sold are obtained by purchasing them. If manufacturing takes place, the manufactured items are sold. Therefore the *purchases* in the trading section are replaced by a transfer of the *production cost of finished goods* from the manufacturing account. The trading section of the profit and loss account which accompanies the introduction of a manufacturing account becomes as follows.

Example

Trading, profit and loss account for the year ended (date) (Trading section only)

	£	£
Sales		X
Cost of goods sold:		
Opening stock	X	
Add production cost of finished goods	X	
	X	
Less closing stock	X	
Cost of goods sold		X
Gross profit		X

The opening and closing stocks included in this trading section refer to stocks of *finished goods*. These are goods which have completed the manufacturing process and have been transferred to a part of the business where completed products are held in a condition where they may be sent to the customer.

26.10 Direct material stocks

So far we have drawn up the basic manufacturing account on the basis of direct materials consumed forming part of the prime cost, making the assumption that the quantity of direct material ***purchased*** is the same as the quantity of direct material ***consumed***.

However, in practice this is rarely the case, as for a number of reasons it is considered to be beneficial for an organisation to maintain stocks of direct materials. As a result the difference in direct material stock levels at the beginning and the end of an accounting period must be taken into consideration in order to obtain a value of ***direct material stock consumed*** in the period.

This figure is obtained by including adjustments to the direct materials purchased figure in the manufacturing account. This is achieved by bringing in the values of opening and closing stock levels in the following manner.

Example

	£
Direct materials:	
Opening stock at the beginning of the period	X
Add purchases during the period	X
	X
Less closing stock at the end of the period	X
Cost of direct materials consumed during the period	X

26.11 The manufacturing account – revised layout incorporating the calculation of direct materials consumed

The revised ***manufacturing account*** layout which incorporates the calculation of ***direct materials consumed*** is as follows.

Example

Manufacturing account for the year ended (date)

	£	£	£
Direct costs:			
Direct materials:			
Opening stock	X		
Add purchases	X		
	X		
Less closing stock	X		
Direct materials consumed		X	
Direct wages		X	
Direct expenses		X	
Prime cost			X
Production overheads			X
Total production cost of finished goods			X

You should now be able to attempt Question 26.2 at the end of this chapter.

26.12 Carriage inwards on direct materials purchased

Occasionally the cost of ***carriage inwards on direct materials purchased*** is incurred. In this case, the carriage inwards cost is simply added to the cost of direct materials purchased, as carriage inwards is simply part of the cost of obtaining direct materials.

26.13 Work in progress

In practice it is not possible for the end of an accounting period to correspond to a circumstance where all the production is made up of completed or finished goods. It is inevitable that there will be some production which is only partially complete. This incomplete production is known as ***work in progress***. At the beginning of an accounting period there will be opening work in progress and at the end of the period, closing work in progress.

In assessing the production cost of finished goods for the accounting period, the impact of ***differences*** in opening and closing levels of work in progress must be considered when the manufacturing account is drawn up. The way this is done depends on how work in progress is valued. The alternative ways in which work in progress may be valued are outside the scope of this chapter, but it is quite normal to value work in progress at total production cost up to the stage of production reached.

We have already seen that total production cost is made up of prime cost plus production overhead, and the point at which the adjustment for the difference between opening and closing work in progress is incorporated into the manufacturing account is based on this valuation principle.

The adjustment for opening and closing stocks of ***direct materials*** is incorporated by adding the opening stocks and deducting the closing stocks from the costs which feature in the manufacturing account.

Similarly, the adjustment for the opening and closing stocks of ***finished goods*** is incorporated by adding the opening stocks and deducting the closing stocks from the costs which feature in the trading section of the profit and loss account.

The adjustment for ***work in progress*** is similarly treated in the manufacturing account by adding the value of the opening stocks of work in progress and deducting the value of closing stocks of work in progress. Because work in progress is normally valued at total production cost up to the stage of production reached, the work in progress adjustment is recorded in the manufacturing account by adjusting the total production cost for the period.

26.14 The manufacturing account – revised layout incorporating the work in progress adjustment

The revised ***manufacturing account*** layout which incorporates the valuation of ***work in progress*** is as follows.

Example

Manufacturing account for the year ended (date)

	£	£	£
Direct costs:			
Direct materials:			
Opening stock	X		
Add purchases	X		
Add carriage inwards	X		
	X		
Less closing stock	X		
Direct materials consumed		X	
Direct wages		X	
Direct expenses		X	
Prime cost			X
Production overheads			X
Total production costs			X
Work in progress adjustment:			
Add opening work in progress		X	
Less closing work in progress		(X)	
			X
Total production cost of finished goods			X

The total production cost of finished goods is then transferred to the trading section of the trading, profit and loss account as described in section 26.9.

You should now be able to attempt Question 26.3 at the end of this chapter.

26.15 Manufacturing profit

We have seen that the sales income of an organisation is usually shown in the trading section of the trading, profit and loss account. This figure refers to the sales to third parties which have been made during the accounting period to which the final accounts relate.

In some circumstances an organisation sets up an accounting system which records ***internal sales*** from one part of the business to another. For example, an internal price may be set at which the finished goods are transferred or sold by the manufacturing part of the business to the selling part of the business. This price is recorded in the accounts to show the ***sales*** by the manufacturing account which become the ***purchases*** by the trading account. There are a number of reasons why firms adopt this practice:

- Where a fixed price per unit is set for the transfer of finished goods from the manufacturing facility into the finished goods warehouse, a profit or loss on manufacturing can be established.
- The manufacturing facility is motivated to control costs so that the production of the finished goods is achieved within a fixed price, otherwise a loss on manufacturing would result.
- The selling function receives the goods from manufacturing already including a profit element. This is similar to them purchasing the goods for resale from an outside source.
- Different managers may be responsible for each part of the business. This can provide a measure of profits or losses for each part of the business which may be used to measure managers' individual performances.

26.16 The manufacturing account – revised layout incorporating manufacturing profit

The effect of creating an internal selling price for goods transferred from manufacturing is to bring a sales figure into the manufacturing account. This figure is normally described as ***sales value of finished goods produced.*** The result of bringing this additional element into the manufacturing account is to create an internal profit on manufacture known as ***profit on finished goods produced.***

The layout of the revised manufacturing account which incorporates these changes is as follows:

Example

Manufacturing account for the year ended (date)

	£	£	£
Sales value of finished goods produced			X
Direct costs:			
Direct materials:			
Opening stock	X		
Add purchases	X		
Add carriage inwards	X		
	X		
Less closing stock	X		
Direct materials consumed		X	
Direct wages		X	
Direct expenses		X	
Prime cost		X	
Production overheads		X	
Total production costs		X	
Work in progress adjustment:			
Add opening work in progress		X	
Less closing work in progress		(X)	
Total production cost of finished goods			X
Profit of loss on finished goods produced			X

26.17 Other changes to the final accounts

When a ***profit*** or ***loss on finished goods produced*** is recorded in the manufacturing account, other changes to the trading, profit and loss account are necessary. In this case the ***sales value of finished goods*** figure is transferred to the trading section of the trading, profit and loss account as referred to earlier.

The ***profit*** or ***loss on finished goods produced*** in the manufacturing account is transferred to the profit and loss section of the trading, profit and loss account and is added to (or subtracted from, if a loss) the ***gross profit*** from trading. From the total of these two profits the non-manufacturing expenses or overheads of the business are deducted to give the net profit for the period.

Example

Refer to the example in section 26.8 of ***Manchester Manufacturing Ltd.*** The list of balances on the accounts for the year ended 31st December 19X1 have been expanded below to include those which are entered in the trading, profit and loss accounts as well as those for the manufacturing account. Opening and closing work in progress have also been introduced.

The company has decided to transfer finished goods from the factory to the finished goods warehouse at £15 per unit and during the year 120,000 units were transferred.

	£'000
Office salaries	300
Depreciation of machinery	60
Machinery maintenance	82
Factory maintenance	105
Operators' wages	662
Factory rent	100
Factory insurance	30
Direct materials purchased	336
Factory canteen	204
Office stationery	32
Factory manager's salary	29
Accountancy and legal fees	49
Depreciation of delivery vans	37
Telephone	18
Electricity	43
Power for factory machinery	102
Production sub-contract work	95
Business rates– office	32
– factory	65
Sales	2,466
Stocks as at 1 January 19X1:	
Direct materials	127
Finished goods	61
Work in progress	43
Stocks as at 31 December 19X1:	
Direct materials	146
Finished goods	76
Work in progress	59

Required

i) Draw up a manufacturing account and trading, profit and loss account for the year ended 31 December 19X1.

ii) Clearly show the following in the respective accounts:

- ❑ sales value of finished goods produced;
- ❑ profit or loss on finished goods produced;
- ❑ gross or trading profit;
- ❑ total gross profit;
- ❑ net profit.

Solution

Manchester Manufacturing Ltd

Manufacturing account for the year ended 31st December 19X1

	£'000	£'000	£'000
Sales value of finished goods produced:			
120,000 units at £15 per unit			
(to trading section of trading, profit and loss account)			1,800
Direct costs:			
Direct materials:			
Opening stock	127		
Add purchases	336		
	463		
Less closing stock	146		
Direct materials consumed	317		
Direct wages (operators' wages)	662		
Direct expenses (sub-contract)	95		
Prime cost		1,074	
Production overheads:			
Depreciation of machinery	60		
Machinery maintenance	82		
Factory maintenance	105		
Factory rent	100		
Factory insurance	30		
Factory canteen	24		
Factory manager's salary	29		
Power for factory machinery	102		
Business rates – factory	65		
Total production overheads		597	
Total cost of production		1,671	
Work in progress adjustment:			
Opening work in progress	43		
Less closing work in progress	(59)		
Increase in work in progress		(16)	
Production cost of finished goods			1,655
Profit of loss on finished goods produced or manufacturing profit			145
(to profit and loss section of trading, profit and loss account)			

Trading, profit and loss account for the year ended 31 December 19X1

	£'000	£'000
Sales		2,466
Cost of sales:		
Opening stock	61	
Sales value of finished goods produced	1,800	
	1,861	
Less closing stock	76	
Cost of goods sold		1,785
Gross or trading profit		681
Profit on finished goods produced or manufacturing profit (from manufacturing account)		145
Total gross profit		826
Expenses or overheads:		
Office salaries	300	
Office stationery	32	
Accountancy and legal fees	49	
Depreciation of delivery vans	37	
Telephone	18	
Electricity	43	
Business rates – office	32	
		511
Net profit		315

26.18 Accruals and prepayments

Like profit and loss accounts, manufacturing accounts are prepared on an ***accruals*** basis. This means that the expenses charged in the manufacturing account for the accounting period are not restricted to those which have actually been paid for. Adjustments must be made for those expenses which have been ***incurred*** by adding to the amounts paid any amounts ***accrued,*** that is amounts due at the end of the period.

For example, wages which are paid a week in arrears would involve the final week's pay being paid in the first week of the new year. The amount of that payment would be added to the old year's wages as an ***accrual*** to ensure that the wages figure ***incurred,*** rather than the wages figure ***paid,*** is included in the accounts for the old year.

Similarly, if an amount has been paid in the period which includes an element that refers to the succeeding period, an adjustment to account for the ***prepayment*** element is made.

For example, a proportion of rent paid in the old year may refer to the new year. In this case the amount of rent which refers to the new year must be deducted from the charge for the old year as a ***prepayment*** so that the charge for the old year is restricted to the amount properly chargeable to that period. See Chapter 16 which goes into this aspect in more detail.

26.19 Apportionment of overhead costs

Manufacturing organisations often incur some overhead expenses which are shared between the factory and the office. Business rates are an example of this. They can be paid as a single invoice, but require apportioning between the manufacturing account and the profit and loss account on an equitable basis. The share of the business rates chargeable to production appears in the manufacturing account as an overhead; the proportion chargeable to the office premises is charged in the profit and loss account.

It is normal for students to be given the basis of apportionment of such shared overheads in examination questions, often as percentages or fractions. If such information is not available, then an equitable basis must be chosen. The following are examples of the ways in which some overhead costs can be apportioned between the manufacturing account and the profit and loss account.

Example

Cost	Basis of apportionment
Business rates	Floor areas of office and factory
Rents	Floor areas of office and factory
National insurance	Number of personnel in office and factory
Insurance – buildings	Floor areas of office and factory
– plant	Capital values of plant in office and factory

You should now be able to attempt Tasks 26.1, 26.2 and 26.3 and Questions 26.4 and 26.5 at the end of this chapter.

26.20 Summary

The use of the trading, profit and loss account to record the financial results of an organisation becomes inadequate when the organisation is one which manufactures the products. The ***trading section*** of the trading, profit and loss account is based on the assumption that the cost of sales or cost of goods sold are ***purchased***. In a manufacturing organisation this is clearly not the case.

The ***manufacturing*** account is drawn up before the trading, profit and loss account, and records the cost of converting the raw materials into the finished goods which are ultimately sold. It ***classifies*** the costs of production into the direct costs of direct materials consumed, direct wages and direct expenses, and indirect costs, which are otherwise known as production overheads. The figure for direct or raw materials consumed is obtained by adjusting the direct materials purchased by the opening and closing stocks of raw materials.

Unfinished production at any time is known as ***work in progress***. In order to obtain the production cost of finished goods, the total cost of production must be adjusted by the opening and closing work in progress of the period.

In some circumstances a ***manufacturing profit*** is calculated by arranging for an internal price to be set for the transfer of finished goods transferred from the factory to the warehouse or sales function. In these circumstances the manufacturing account records a profit or loss on finished goods produced by bringing in a ***sales value of finished goods manufactured***. This profit or loss is transferred to the profit and loss account to be added to (or subtracted from, if a loss) the normal gross or trading profit.

As there is no legal requirement under partnership or company legislation for a manufacturing account to be included in the published accounts of an organisation, it is generally used for internal purposes only. Consequently, the manufacturing account is never seen as part of the published report and final accounts, even though the organisation may be one involved in the manufacture of products.

You should now be able to attempt the Objective Test at the end of this chapter.

Student activities

Task 26.1 You have been asked by a local manufacturing company to advise them of the advantages and disadvantages of sharing the profits between manufacturing and trading activities. Write a report to the managing director of the company setting out how this might be achieved, the alternative transfer pricing methods which might be considered, the merits of such a system, and any other points which they should bear in mind before making such a change.

Task 26.2 Construct a diagram to illustrate the relationships between the figures in the manufacturing account, the trading, profit and loss account, and the balance sheet.

Task 26.3 A local businessman has been operating a successful manufacturing company for a number of years, but has only prepared a trading and profit and loss account at the year end. Make a list of the benefits he could gain by preparing a manufacturing account.

Question 26.1 ***Barnstaple Bolts Ltd*** manufactures nuts, bolts and other fasteners. The following financial information was taken from the books for the year ended 31 March 19X1.

	£
Raw materials consumed	100,235
Factory indirect wages	60,277
Factory manager's salary	25,616
Factory business rates	6,211
Factory rent	14,118
Depreciation of machinery	5,200
Direct wages	126,306
Insurance of machinery	2,198
Maintenance of machinery	14,205
Maintenance of factory	7,236
Factory power	2,876
Consumable materials	274
Factory heating	3,206

Required

Prepare a manufacturing account for Barnstaple Bolts Ltd for the year ended 31 March 19X1 showing clearly:

i) prime cost;

ii) production cost of finished goods.

Question 26.2 ***Kidderminster Kitchens Ltd*** produces flat-pack kitchen units from the basic raw materials. The following information was extracted from the books of the company for the year ended 30 June 19X5.

	£
Purchases of raw materials	105,200
Manufacturing wages:	
Direct	177,211
Indirect	116,300
Factory rent	40,000
Business rates	35,290
Insurance	7,302
Building maintenance	14,603
Depreciation of machinery	4,800
Stocks of raw materials:	
1 July 19X4	8,457
30 June 19X5	9,666
Maintenance of machinery	16,934
Consumable materials	3,298
Factory manager's salary	27,300
Factory power	45,874
Heat and light	12,875
General expenses	7,216
Depreciation of factory fixtures and fittings	5,400

Required

Prepare a manufacturing account for Kidderminster Kitchens Ltd showing clearly:

i) cost of raw materials consumed;

ii) prime cost;

iii) production cost of finished goods.

Question 26.3 The following financial information was taken from the books of *Wolverhampton Wagonwheels Ltd* at the 31 December 19X7 in respect of the year ended on that date.

	£
Stock of raw materials on 1 January 19X7	82,000
Stock of raw materials on 31 December 19X7	62,000
Work in progress on 1 January 19X7	25,000
Work in progress on 31 December 19X7	55,000
Purchases of raw materials	258,000
Fuel and power	37,800
Heat and light	4,800
Wages: Direct	202,000
Indirect	24,500
Direct expenses (sub-contractors' charges)	7,200
Carriage inwards on raw materials	3,900
Depreciation: Plant and machinery	61,000
Tools	4,700
Machine lubricants	6,300
Factory insurance	2,100
Factory general expenses	32,100

Required

Prepare a manufacturing account for Wolverhampton Wagonwheels Ltd for the year ended 31 December 19X7 in good form.

Question 26.4 *J. Colwyn* owns a small manufacturing business. The following financial information was extracted from his books for the year ended 31 December 19X6.

	£
Sales	625,500
Sales returns	1,250
Purchases of raw materials	132,200
Purchase returns	2,350
Plant and machinery (cost £350,000)	230,000
Office furniture (cost £15,000)	10,000
Factory power	30,000
Heat and light (factory 80%, office 20%)	10,000
Creditors	165,000
Debtors	110,000
Cash at bank	108,000
Stock of raw materials: 1 January	42,500
Stock of finished goods: 1 January	53,200
Manufacturing wages	160,000
General expenses (factory 2/3, office 1/3)	30,000
Insurance (factory 6/7, office 1/7)	9,800
Freehold factory at cost	200,000
Business rates (factory 6/7, office 1/7)	63,000
Motor vehicles (cost £220,000)	82,000
Office salaries	62,000
Work in progress: 1 January	25,000
Drawings	55,000
Carriage inwards	2,650

The following information is also available:

Stocks at 31 December 19X6	£
Raw materials	31,000
Finished goods	56,350
Work in progress	23,450

Depreciation is to be provided on the following fixed assets using the reducing balance method:

Plant and machinery	10%
Office furniture	15%
Motor vehicles	20%

Required

i) Prepare a manufacturing account and trading, profit and loss account for the year ended 31 December 19X6, and a balance sheet as at that date.

ii) Calculate J. Colwyn's capital as at 1 January 19X6.

Question 26.5 *Portsmouth Printers Ltd* prints repair manuals for the car trade, and the details extracted from the financial books of the company for the year ended 31 August 19X4 are as follows.

	£
Stocks as at 1 September 19X3:	
Direct materials	13,550
Work in progress	6,720
Finished books	12,490
Purchases and expenses incurred for the year:	
Direct materials	290,720
Indirect materials	3,700
Direct wages	106,500
Factory power	9,200
Light and heat (office 40%, factory 60%)	6,120
Direct expenses	1,121
Postage	1,210
Carriage inwards	3,120
Telephone	2,100
Factory salaries	22,720
Office salaries	21,210
Factory insurances	2,410
Other insurances	920
Depreciation – factory plant and machinery	10,000
– office equipment	1,300
Office expenses	3,200
Advertising	1,960
Business rates (office 20%, factory 80%)	10,200
Rent (office 30%, factory 70%)	9,000
Sales of finished goods for the year	752,390

The following additional information is relevant to the above accounting period:

Finished books printed during the accounting period are transferred from the factory at a manufacturing price of £5 per book. 113,000 books were completed during the year.

Stocks at 31 August 19X4	
	£
Direct materials	18,211
Work in progress	9,300
Finished goods	16,100
Expenses prepaid at 31 August 19X4	
	£
Factory insurances	110
Other insurances	140
Rent	1,000
Expenses accrued due at 31 August 19X4	
	£
Direct wages	4,200
Factory power	700
Light and heat	880

Required

Prepare the manufacturing account and trading, profit and loss account for the year ended 31 August 19X4.

Objective test *(tick the appropriate box)*

i) The total of the direct material consumed, direct labour and direct expenses is known as:

a) total production cost ☐

b) prime cost ☐

c) total factory cost ☐

d) overheads ☐

ii) The materials cost which is ultimately charged against profits is made up of:

a) opening stock plus purchases plus closing stock ☐

b) purchases less closing stock ☐

c) purchases plus carriage inwards ☐

d) opening stock plus purchases plus carriage inwards minus closing stock ☐

iii) Stocks of finished goods appear as adjustments in:

a) the manufacturing account ☐

b) the trading section of the profit and loss account ☐

c) the profit and loss section of the profit and loss account ☐

d) the balance sheet ☐

iv) The work in progress adjustment appears in:

a) the manufacturing account ☐

b) the trading section of the profit and loss account ☐

c) the profit and loss section of the profit and loss account ☐

d) the balance sheet ☐

v) When a manufacturing profit is shown in the manufacturing account, the value of finished goods transferred to the trading account section of the profit and loss account is made up of:

a) total cost of goods produced ☐

b) total production cost of finished goods ☐

c) profit on finished goods produced ☐

d) prime cost ☐

Assignment F

Jones, Morgan and Thomas

Context

Jones, Morgan and Thomas have been in partnership as garage proprietors for a number of years, but they are seriously considering dissolving the partnership, selling the assets, paying all the bills and going their own separate ways. Although they have employed a book-keeper who has maintained proper records, their accountant became fed up with the uncertainty of not knowing whether he had a future with the partnership or not, so he left to join Henleys. The partners have approached you for advice, and initially you decide to establish the state of the business at the end of 19X5, and the level of profit for that year. The list of balances at the end of 19X5 is as follows:

List of balances at 31 December 19X5

		£	£
Capital accounts:	Jones		25,000
	Morgan		25,000
	Thomas		20,000
Current Accounts:	Jones		9,000
	Morgan		12,000
	Thomas		5,000
Drawings:	Jones	9,000	
	Morgan	9,500	
	Thomas	4,000	
Premises and car showrooms		50,000	
Workshop equipment at cost		10,000	
Depreciation on workshop equipment to 31/12/X4			4,000
Petrol pumps at cost		2,000	
Depreciation on petrol pumps to 31/12/X4			800
Opening stock		23,485	
Debtors and creditors		33,040	19,400
Bank overdraft			1,650
Cash in hand		125	
Purchases and sales		236,890	306,990
Wages		40,660	
Workshop rent received to 30/6/X5			160
Rent, insurance and electricity		5,850	
Telephone		800	
Advertising		1,000	
Sundry office expenses		650	
Sundry materials		1,250	
Repairs and maintenance		750	
		429,000	429,000

After further investigation you ascertain the following additional information:

- Accrued expenses at 31 December 19X5 were electricity £150 and sundry office expenses £400.
- Depreciation on fixed assets other than premises and showrooms is charged at 10% per annum using the straight line method.
- The workshop is let at an annual rent of £320.
- Interest at 10% is allowed on the partners' capital accounts.
- The partners' profit sharing ratio is Jones 50%, Morgan 30% and Thomas 20%.
- Closing stock at 31 December 19X5 was valued at £30,135.

There is some argument between the partners as to whether they have a well-run business, and whether the business is in a sound state at the end of 19X5. They feel that the answers to these questions will influence their decision whether or not to dissolve the business.

You ascertain that the ratios for a comparative firm for the same year are:

Credit period taken by debtors: 75 days
Stock turnover (based on cost of sales): 6 times per annum
Current ratio: 2.4 : 1
Return on capital employed (based on closing capital): 23%
Gross Profit Margin: 22%
Net Profit Margin: 10%

Another consideration which will influence their decision whether to dissolve the partnership or not is the return which could be obtained if each partner invested the amounts due to him in an alternative investment outside the business. Assume that the partners' returns from the business this year are typical of past and future performances.

Student activities

i) Prepare the partnership trading, profit and loss account, including an appropriation section, for the year ended 31st December 19X5, together with a balance sheet as at that date.

ii) Draw up the detailed current account for each partner for the year.

iii) Calculate appropriate ratios to enable you to advise the partners of the performance of the firm compared to the typical firm for which you have the results. Write a brief note about each ratio you have calculated, explaining what it measures, whether it indicates strength or weakness and what actions might be pursued in order to improve it in this case.

iv) Assume that on dissolution of the partnership the balance sheet values would be realised. How much would each partner receive? Investigate other alternative investments into which each partner could place the funds released by the partnership dissolution, and provide a list of them, together with their characteristics such as risk level, minimum amounts invested, the period of time the money is tied up, brokerage and investment fees, and any other relevant points. You should restrict your list to investments rather than businesses.

v) Advise each partner whether he should be in favour of the dissolution, and where, if it takes place, his funds should be invested. To assist you to advise each partner, prepare a questionnaire for completion by each partner, which covers the information which it is necessary to know before it is possible to advise on the alternative investment to be pursued. Ask a fellow course-member to complete your questionnaire as a stand-in for the partner.

Format

A set of accounts, the calculation of, and a report on, the ratios revealed by the accounts, a list of alternative investment types, a questionnaire, and a report to each partner advising him/her of the action to be taken.

Objectives

The student should show an understanding and appreciation of:

- partnership accounts
- ratio analysis
- investment alternatives
- questionnaire design
- how investment alternatives are influenced by personal circumstances and attitudes

References

Chapters 4, 21-23

Part 3

Management accounting

Using costs for planning and control

This section (Chapters 27 – 30) considers how costs can be used to help in forming business plans and then helping to ensure that those plans are achieved by controlling the expenditure incurred during the period.

Chapter 27 explains a number of ways in which costs are grouped or classified according to common characteristics. This helps us to treat costs in groups, with particular emphasis on how costs are incurred in relation to the parts, products, or services which may be produced by the business.

In Chapter 28 we look at how costs are grouped according to the way in which they change as production or sales activity changes, known as cost behaviour.

Chapter 29 examines budgets, which are plans expressed in financial terms, and how they are formulated and applied in a manufacturing business. It also explains what is meant by budgetary control when the plan is compared with actual performance.

It is possible to construct a budget for a particular level of production or sales, but as we learned in Chapter 28, some costs change as activity changes. This concept makes a budget prepared for one level of activity less useful for control if a different level of activity is actually achieved. For this reason flexible budgets are formulated, and these are discussed in Chapter 30.

As budgets are used to control the costs of functions, standard costs are used to control the costs of products or manufacturing processes. As the principles of standard costing are similar to those used in flexible budgets, standard costing for product direct costs is also covered in Chapter 30.

Chapter 27

Principles of cost classification

27.1 Objectives

At the end of this chapter you should be able to:

- understand what costs are;
- classify costs in a number of ways;
- draw up a simple product cost statement;
- calculate a simple product selling price based on cost.

27.2 Introduction

It is easier to understand and deal with things in everyday life if we identify items with common characteristics, group them together, and treat all of them in the group in a similar way. For example, children in school are grouped according to age and/or ability, and therefore it is convenient to teach them in classes. This is not to say that all members of a class are treated in exactly the same way, as there will be some variations within a group. However, these variations are not regarded as major, otherwise the children with these different characteristics would be put into a different group.

Businesses are also classified, sometimes according to size, sometimes according to business type. Thus we have some differences in legislation for sole traders, partnerships, private limited companies and public limited companies.

Accountants group expenditure and revenue according to common characteristics in order to ease their understanding, processing and presentation to both internal managers and the outside users of annual reports and accounts. This is known as ***cost classification.***

27.3 Fixed assets and current assets

We saw in Chapter 11 that any business needs ***resources*** to enable it to operate. These ***resources*** may be classified as ***fixed assets*** or ***current assets. Fixed assets*** are those resources which the business owns and means to keep in the longer term, usually for longer than a year, out of which the business derives a benefit in being able to use them in operating the business for that period of time. Examples include:

- ***premises*** which the business owns and from which it operates. These might include ***factories, offices,*** and ***stores.***
- ***plant*** and ***machinery*** which the business owns and operates to enable production to take place.
- ***furniture*** and ***office equipment*** used by the administration, selling and distribution departments of the business.
- ***motor vehicles*** such as trucks to collect ***raw materials*** and deliver the ***finished goods*** and cars used by the salesmen to collect orders.

Current assets are those ***resources*** which the business owns and which are used up in the day-to-day activities of the business and which are part of the trading cycle of purchasing and converting the ***raw materials*** into ***finished goods.*** Examples include:

- ***stocks of raw materials*** which are purchased either for ***cash*** or on ***credit,*** for conversion into ***finished goods.***
- ***stocks of finished goods*** which have been manufactured or alternatively purchased for sale to customers.

- *stocks of work in progress* occur in a manufacturing business where, at any point in time, partly finished goods exist which require further work on them to convert them into *finished goods* for sale to the customer.
- *debtors* are the balances owing to the business by those customers who have purchased *finished goods* on credit.
- *bank balances* are those balances of cash held at a bank.
- *cash balances* are balances of cash held at the office either as *petty cash,* or as *cash* waiting to be banked.

You should now be able to attempt Question 27.1 at the end of this chapter.

27.4 Capital and revenue expenditure

The *resources* known as *current assets* can be converted into other *current assets.* For example, *cash in hand* or *bank balances* can be used to purchase *raw material stocks,* or *debtors* are converted into *cash* or *bank balances* when they pay the amounts which they owe.

Similarly, *current assets* can be used to create *fixed assets.* For example, *cash* or *bank balances* can be used to purchase land and buildings. Expenditure on *fixed assets* is known as *capital expenditure.*

In addition to *capital expenditure,* any business also incurs day-to-day expenditure on other items which are necessary to carry out the purchasing, production, administration, selling and distribution activities of the organisation. These other items of expenditure are known as *revenue expenditure* and share the characteristic that the benefit derived from the expenditure arises in the same period as the costs are incurred. Examples include:

- *raw materials consumed,* otherwise known as *direct materials,* are those materials which are used in the product or products manufactured by the organisation. Although most businesses purchase raw materials to be kept in store until needed, they do not represent a charge against profits, and therefore become a cost, until they are consumed.
- *production department wages* are wages paid to machine operators and other personnel engaged in the production process.
- *other wages and salaries* are wages and salaries paid to personnel in the stores, administration, sales, distribution and other departments of the business.
- *electricity* which may be the expenditure on *power* for operating the machines, *lighting* for the factory, stores and offices, and *heating* .
- *sub-contract work,* sometimes called *outwork,* is work which is carried out by another business which is engaged in providing a service or expertise in the production of the product. This may be in the form of a *sub-assembly* or partly finished part of the main product, or in extreme cases the production of the whole product may be sub-contracted in order, for example, to enable the business to satisfy a level of demand for the product which cannot be met from its own capacity.
- *lubricating oil* used for the production machinery.
- *running expenses* of the salesmen's motor cars such as *oil, petrol, tyres, repairs and maintenance,* and *licences.*
- although the expenditure on *fixed assets* of the business is classified as *capital expenditure,* the action of *writing off* or *amortising* the cost of the *fixed assets* against the profits of the business over their effective lives is known as *depreciation* and is classified as *revenue expenditure.*

Some items which by all normal definitions should be classified as *capital expenditure,* nevertheless are treated as *revenue expenditure* if they are of low value. For example, an office calculator which cost only £5 would be treated as *revenue expenditure* even though it possesses all the characteristics of an item of *capital expenditure* in that it has an extended life and would be used by the business for a period exceeding a year.

The definition of a ***small value item*** is a decision which would be made by each individual business and may be dependent on its size. It is quite common for a business to decide not to treat as ***capital expenditure*** any item which costs less than £50, but the precise limit will vary between businesses.

You should now be able to attempt Question 27.2 at the end of this chapter.

27.5 Cost classifications

Items of ***revenue expenditure*** are known as ***costs.*** Some ***costs*** are not charged against profits as soon as they are incurred, but are held in abeyance until they are actually used up in the manufacture of a product. An example of these costs is ***raw material*** which goes into a store when purchased and is used to manufacture a product at a later stage. When it is subsequently issued to production is the time when the raw material becomes a cost for accounting purposes. Other costs are charged against profits as soon as they are incurred. Examples are wages, salaries, insurances, light and heat, telephone and depreciation.

In order to help us deal with costs in a logical way, we group costs under a number of different headings relating to how costs are incurred in the manufacture or production of a product or service. This process of grouping costs is known as ***cost classification.***

Costs incurred in the manufacture of a product, known as ***product costs,*** can be classified either as ***direct costs*** or ***indirect costs. Indirect costs*** may also be described as ***overhead costs*** or ***overheads,*** and if a particular product cost cannot be described as a ***direct cost*** it is automatically classified as an ***overhead.***

A ***direct cost*** is a cost which can be traced or identified relatively easily to the product or products which are being produced, and is a cost which is incurred specifically for the production of those products.

An ***overhead cost*** is a cost which is incurred to enable the organisation to carry out its operations of purchasing, manufacturing, selling and distribution, but nevertheless such costs cannot be easily traced to or identified with particular products.

27.6 Product direct costs

Direct costs can be classified as ***direct materials, direct wages*** and ***direct expenses.***

- ***Direct materials***

  Direct materials are those materials which are used in the production of, and feature in the final form of, the products which are produced by the enterprise. Although for ease of expression and description they are described as materials, they are not restricted to ***raw materials,*** as they may also include ***parts*** and ***partly finished sub-assemblies*** which are purchased from an outside supplier and form part of the final products.

Example

Product	Direct material
Desks	Wood, screws, handles,
Books	Paper, glue, ink
Shoes	Leather, glue, rubber/plastics, laces
Motor vehicles	Steel, tyres, glass
China	Clay, transfers

An allowance is made for the normal levels of wastage incurred in the production process, such waste also being treated as direct material.

It should be noted that some materials which are used in the manufacture of the products do not come under the classification of ***direct materials.*** For example, lubrication and cooling oil for the production machinery, cleaning materials used by the factory cleaners, and maintenance and repair materials used for maintaining the production machinery, are all treated as ***indirect materials*** or ***overheads***, as none of these items feature in the final products which are being produced.

Even some small-value items which are really ***direct materials*** are often treated as ***overheads*** because their cost is difficult to measure when costing individual products. An example is sewing cotton when making clothing and glue in making boxes.

- ***Direct wages*** (or ***direct labour***)

  Direct wages are those wages paid to the personnel who are directly involved in the production of each of the items produced. This will include wages paid to operators of the machinery used to manufacture the products, wages paid to personnel who assemble the products, and wages paid to those personnel who finish them, such as painting, polishing and testing.

- ***Direct expenses***

  Direct expenses are those costs which can also be directly traced to the products which are being manufactured, but cannot be classified under the headings of ***direct materials*** or ***direct wages***. For example, in the manufacture of furniture, if the operation of french polishing is sub-contracted to an expert, the resultant cost is neither direct material, the french polish is never owned by the manufacturer, nor direct wages, as the expert is not on the payroll of the manufacturer. Nevertheless, the cost is clearly a product direct cost and would therefore be charged to direct expenses of the product on which the french polisher worked.

You should now be able to attempt Question 27.3 at the end of this chapter.

27.7 Product indirect costs or overheads

If a cost is not a ***product direct cost***, that is one that can be treated as ***direct material, direct wages*** or ***direct expenses***, it is classified as a ***product indirect cost*** or an ***overhead***. ***Overheads*** are those items of ***revenue expenditure*** which cannot be traced directly to the production of particular products where a range of products is manufactured, these costs often having the characteristic of being shared by all the output. Overheads can be classified as follows:

- ***Production overheads*** (or ***manufacturing*** or ***factory overheads***) are incurred as part of the cost of manufacture, but cannot be traced to the products produced as direct costs. Examples are factory rent and rates, factory cleaning costs (cleaners' wages and cleaning materials used), depreciation of machinery, power, light and heat, and salaries and wages paid to supervisory personnel.
- ***Administration overheads*** are those costs which are incurred by the administrative function which is necessary for the running of any business. These overheads mainly involve office costs and examples are office salaries, postage, stationery, rent & rates and light & heat of the offices, and secretarial expenses. The accounting department is often treated as an administration overhead.
- ***Selling overheads*** are those costs incurred by the selling function of the business. Examples are advertising, salesmen's salaries and commission, and salesmen's travel costs such as car depreciation, petrol, oil and maintenance costs.
- ***Distribution overheads*** are those costs incurred in getting the finished product into the hands of the customer. Examples are final packing costs, transportation and/or postage depending on the mode of distribution, and all the costs of operating a fleet of distribution vehicles such as trucks and vans would be classified under this heading.
- ***Research and development overheads*** are experienced by some organisations where costs are incurred in the researching and development of new products and processes. The costs of carrying out these activities often have to be borne by the income from the existing product range, as some time will elapse before income will be generated by the products or processes under development.

Example

Product cost classification

	Product cost
Direct costs:	**£**
Direct materials	X
Direct wages	X
Direct expenses	X
Prime cost	X
Indirect costs or overheads:	
Production	X
Production cost	X
Administration	X
Selling	X
Distribution	X
Research and development	X
Total cost	X

Notes

The term ***prime cost*** is applied to the total of the ***product direct costs***. The term ***production cost*** is applied to the ***prime cost*** plus ***production overhead***. ***Production costs*** exclude all non-production expenses such as ***administration, selling, distribution*** and ***research overheads***. This is particularly important when a valuation of ***work in progress*** or ***finished goods*** is required as, in general, these are valued at ***production cost***.

You should now be able to attempt Tasks 27.1, 27.2 and 27.3 and Question 27.4 at the end of this chapter.

27.8 Problems of cost classification

Each organisation needs to make its own decisions about how particular items of revenue expenditure should be classified according to product cost classification. There are no hard and fast rules, but there are general guidelines which help to define approaches. For example, one organisation may treat the wages paid to the supervisors of operators as a direct product cost in the same way as the operators' costs are treated. A similar organisation, however, may classify the wages of all supervisors as an indirect cost and thus treat them as a production overhead. Both approaches may be regarded as acceptable.

You will appreciate that as production becomes more automated and production personnel become more remote from the product itself, then the more difficult it becomes to classify such costs as direct wages. An example of this is the highly automated chemical process industry where, by its very nature, few operators actually handle the products which are being produced. In these cases the wages may be treated as ***production overhead***.

You should now be able to attempt Questions 27.5 and 27.6 at the end of this chapter.

27.9 Summary

The expenditure or costs of a business can be classified as either ***capital expenditure*** or ***revenue expenditure***. Capital expenditure is made up of costs, usually of a substantial nature, incurred for the procurement of assets which the business intends to keep in the longer-term and from which it derives the benefit from being able to use them over a period of time. These assets are known as ***fixed assets*** and may be further classified into such categories as ***land and buildings, plant and machinery, fixtures and fittings*** and ***motor vehicles.***

Revenue expenditure represents the costs of operating the business on a day-to-day basis where the benefit derived from the expenditure arises within the same period as the costs are incurred. Revenue expenditure is usually classified according to ***product costs.***

You should now be able to attempt Objective Test at the end of this chapter.

Student activities

Task 27.1 Select an everyday manufactured product of your choice. List as many costs which are incurred in the production, sale and distribution of that product as possible. Now classify the costs you have listed according to the normal way in which product costs are classified for costing purposes.

Task 27.2 Using your own organisation, whether it is the college where you are studying or your place of work, make a list of all the capital expenditure items you consider may be treated as revenue expenditure because they are of low value.

Task 27.3 See how many cost classifications you can apply to your personal expenditure for the last three months.

Question 27.1 Complete the columns below to analyse the ***assets*** into ***fixed assets*** and ***current assets*** respectively. Tick the appropriate column.

Asset	Current assets	Fixed assets
Office furniture		
Factory building		
Work in progress		
Cash in Building Society		
Trade debtors		
Fork-lift truck		
Goods awaiting delivery to customers		
Land		

Question 27.2 Complete the columns below to analyse the items of ***expenditure*** into ***capital*** and ***revenue expenditure*** respectively. Tick the appropriate column.

Expenditure	Capital expenditure	Revenue expenditure
Purchase of land		
Payment of pensions premiums		
Payment of storeman's wages		
Payment of sales manager's salary		
Payment for sales manager's car		
Repairs to factory roof		
Cost of factory extension		
Paint for product's finish		
Paint for factory windows		
Factory rent and rates		
Stationery for office use		

Question 27.3 i) List *two* direct materials appropriate to each of the following products.

Product	Direct materials
Desks	
Books	
Shoes	
Motor vehicles	
China	

ii) For the following products give *three* examples of direct materials used in their production:

Product	Direct materials
Canned beans	
Boxes of Corn Flakes	
Computers	
Diesel locomotives	
Men's suits	

Question 27.4 *P. Poole* manufactures desks and chairs. Indicate the correct cost classification of the following revenue expenditure items using the code below. The first one has been done for you.

Revenue expenditure item	Cost classification code
Direct wages	1
Direct materials	2
Direct expenses	3
Production overheads	4
Administration overheads	5
Selling overheads	6
Distribution overheads	7

Cost	Classification
Pre-formed chair legs purchased from B. Bournmouth	2
Factory rent	
Office rates	
Depreciation on salemen's cars	
Maintenance wages	
Power	
Factory lighting	
Lubrication oil for sawing machine	
Maintenance of truck used to send finished goods to customers	
Factory cleaners' wages	
Foreman's wages	
Factory manager's salary	
Canteen costs	
Consignment of timber	
Consignment of nails, screws and hinges	
Cleaning materials	
Depreciation of factory machinery	
Packing materials	
French polisher's wages	
Depreciation of office computer	

Question 27.5 ***B. Brixham*** **manufactures garden gnomes, and plans to produce 2,000 units over the next month. Each variety takes about the same amount of materials and time to produce, and B. Brixham is keen to determine the following.**

i) prime cost
ii) production cost
iii) administration overheads
iv) selling overheads
v) distribution overheads
vi) total cost

B. Brixham's costs for the month are:

Rent	
factory:	£500
office:	£100
Rates	
factory:	£300
office:	£100
Sand:	£1,000
Power:	£700
Light & heat	
factory:	£2,000
office:	£1,300
Wages	
operators:	£10,000
maintenance:	£1,500
canteen:	£2,500
Cement:	£5,000
Depreciation	
office equipment:	£500
moulds:	£2,200
fixtures & fittings:	£800
Salesmen's salary & commission:	£2,200
Delivery expenses:	£500
Office salaries:	£1,800
Cement mixer repairs:	£900
Salesmen's car expenses:	£1,100
Finishing paint:	£200
Packing:	£800

vii) If B. Brixham wishes to add 50% to his total costs as a mark-up, what should his selling price be, per gnome?

viii) Calculate his profit margin as a percentage of his sales.

Question 27.6 Classify the items of expenditure for ***Oman Engineering Ltd*** into revenue and capital expenditure using sub-categories for revenue expenditure and tick the appropriate columns.

DM = Direct materials
DL = Direct labour
DE = Direct expenses
P = Production overhead
A = Administration overhead
S = Selling overhead
D = Distribution overhead

Oman Engineering Ltd

Expenditure item	Revenue							Capital
	DM	DL	DE	P	A	S	D	
Factory rates								
Machinery depreciation								
Cleaners' wages								
Sheet steel for product								
Machinists' wages								
Canteen costs								
Fabrication wages								
Factory paint								
Salesmen's salaries								
Maintenance wages								
Electric motors (product)								
Power								
Gatehouse wages								
Heating								
Packing materials								
Delivery costs								
Insurance (factory)								
Stationery								
Office machinery								
Telephone								
Postage								
Sub-contract work (product)								
Chucks								
Paint (product)								
Electric motors (machinery)								
Pensions premiums								
Welding equipment								
Plant & machinery								
Salesmen's car depreciation								
Office desks								
Factory extension								
National insurance								
Welding gas or rods								
Rent of equipment								
Grinding discs								
Jigs and tools								
Nuts and bolts								

Objective test *(tick the appropriate box)*

i) In a business which trades in buying and selling motor vehicles, an example of a fixed asset would be:

a) A hand drill ☐

b) A motor car ☐

c) A computer ☐

d) None of these ☐

ii) Day-to-day expenditure on items necessary to carry out the functions of purchasing, production, administration, selling and distribution are known as:

a) Current assets ☐

b) Payments ☐

c) Income expenditure ☐

d) Revenue expenditure ☐

iii) An example of capital expenditure would be:

a) Repairs to office windows ☐

b) Repairs to factory windows ☐

c) A new Jaguar car for the managing director ☐

d) None of these. ☐

iv) An example of a direct cost would be:

a) Sub-contract work ☐

b) Factory foreman's wages ☐

c) Electricity to power a grinding machine ☐

d) None of these ☐

v) An example of a production overhead would be:

a) Sub-contract work ☐

b) Outwork ☐

c) Depreciation of managing director's Jaguar ☐

d) Factory cleaning costs ☐

The following costs apply to a product called Severn Blocks referred to in (vi)-(ix):

Direct materials: £654
Direct wages: £456
Direct expenses: £123
Factory indirect costs: £321
Administration costs: £789
Selling & distribution costs: £987
The profit margin on selling price: 10%

vi) Product prime cost of Severn Blocks is:

a) £1,431 ☐

b) £1,554 ☐

c) £1,110 ☐

d) £1,233 ☐

vii) Product production cost of Severn Blocks is:

a) £1,431 ☐

b) £1,554 ☐

c) £1,110 ☐

d) £1,233 ☐

viii) Product selling price of Severn Blocks is:

a) £2,587 ☐

b) £3,663 ☐

c) £4,033 ☐

d) £3,700 ☐

ix) The total overhead costs of Severn Blocks are:

a) £2,097 ☐

b) £1,110 ☐

c) £1,776 ☐

d) None of these ☐

x) Which, as far as direct or indirect cost classification is concerned, is the odd one out:

a) Paper to wrap the product to protect it during production ☐

b) Paper for office typewriter ☐

c) Paper for cleaning machinery ☐

d) Paper serviettes for works canteen ☐

Chapter 28

Cost behaviour

28.1 Objectives

At the end of this chapter you should be able to:

- understand why costs are classified according to cost behaviour;
- understand what fixed costs are;
- understand what variable and semi-variable costs are;
- understand how cost behaviour is shown graphically.

28.2 Introduction

In Chapter 27 we gave an an explanation of two ways in which expenditure may be classified. It is first possible to classify expenditure into ***capital*** and ***revenue*** (revise Question 27.2), and thereafter revenue expenditure or costs may be classified according to ***direct*** and ***indirect product costs*** (revise Question 27.4). A further method of classifying costs is according to the way in which they ***behave*** as production or sales increase or decrease.

28.3 Cost behaviour

This method of classifying costs, according to ***cost behaviour,*** is a very important one in management accounting, in that, as we shall see in later chapters, it has implications in the areas of budgeting, decision making and pricing.

Example

Tom Torquay rents a workshop in which he assembles buckets for children for use on the beach. Each bucket consists of a moulded plastic shape to which a metal handle is attached, and finished off with colourful transfers stuck around the outside. All three parts are bought in from outside. Tom's expected costs are as follows:

Bucket mouldings: 35p per bucket
Bucket handles: 15p per bucket
Bucket transfers: 5p per bucket
Rent: £200 per month
Rates: £50 per month
Insurance: £50 per month
Packaging: £10 per 1,000 buckets

The buckets are assembled by Tom and his wife, as Tom reasons that this enables him to avoid the cost of wages as he and his wife are rewarded by the profits of the business created when they sell the buckets at £1 each. In a poor month they can assemble and sell 500 buckets, but at the peak of the season they manage 2,000 buckets. What are his respective profits in a poor and a good month?

Solution

First it is necessary to determine how the costs behave according to the different levels of production. Some of the costs which are incurred move up and down in total as production changes. These are the costs which are expressed as a rate per unit, of which an example is bucket mouldings: produce one bucket and the moulding cost incurred is 35p; produce two buckets and it is 70p, and so on. This relationship applies also to bucket handles, bucket transfers and also packaging. Although packaging costs are expressed as a rate per 1,000 buckets, its total cost will also rise and fall according to the total number produced and sold.

Having identified all the costs which behave in this way, it is possible to determine what their total would be for each level of production:

		Poor month		Good month
Monthly production (buckets)		500		2,000
Total costs:		£		£
Mouldings	500 × 35p	175	2,000 × 35p	700
Handles	500 × 15p	75	2,000 × 15p	300
Transfers	500 × 5p	25	2,000 × 5p	100
Packing	500 × 1p / 1,000	5	2,000 × 1p / 1,000	20
Total		280		1,120

Because each of these costs varies in total with the level of production they are known as ***variable costs.*** Notice that the production in a good month is four times that in a poor month, and the variable costs also increase in sympathy (4 × £280 = £1,120).

There are also other costs which behave in a different way. Tom is required to pay rent of £200 per month irrespective of the number of buckets produced and sold. Even if he produces no buckets at all, he would be obliged to pay this monthly rent charge. Other costs which also behave in the same way are rates and insurance, and if these costs are grouped together for the two levels of production they would be as follows:

	Poor month	Good month
Monthly production (buckets)	500	2,000
Total costs:	£	£
Rent	200	200
Rates	50	50
Insurance	50	50
Total	300	300

Because each of these costs remains constant in total irrespective of the level of production they are known as ***fixed costs.*** Notice that each of these costs in total is uninfluenced by production levels and, unlike the variable costs above, does not increase as production rises.

It is now possible to determine T. Torquay's profits for each of the monthly production levels by comparing total costs with total sales revenue generated by sales at £1 per bucket. His income (profit & loss) statements become:

T Torquay

Profit and loss statements

		Poor month		Good month
Production and sales (buckets)		500		2,000
		£		£
Sales revenue	500 × £1	500	2,000 × £1	2,000
Total variable costs		280		1,120
Total fixed costs		300		300
Total costs		580		1,420
Profit or (loss)		(80)		580

T. Torquay makes a loss when the production and sales are as low as 500 buckets mainly due to the fact that costs which he has to bear whatever the activity level, the fixed costs, become a high cost per unit due to the lower volumes. Thus when sales are 500 units, the fixed costs per unit are:

$$\frac{£300}{500} = 60\text{p per unit}$$

which, when added to the variable costs of

$$\frac{£280}{500} = 56\text{p per unit}$$

gives a total unit cost of £1.16, which exceeds the selling price of £1 per unit by 16 pence. Hence the total loss of 500 units × 16p per unit = £80 at that level of production.

When 2,000 buckets are produced, however, the fixed costs of £300 are spread over 2,000 units to give a fixed cost per unit of:

$$\frac{£300}{2{,}000} = 15\text{p per unit}$$

which, when added to the variable costs of

$$\frac{£1{,}120}{2{,}000} = 56\text{p per unit}$$

gives a total unit cost of 71p, which, when compared to the selling price of £1, gives a profit of 29p per unit. Hence the total profit of

2,000 units × 29p per unit = £580

at that level of production.

Notice that the total variable costs per unit remain constant irrespective of the level of production, ie 56p per unit, whereas total variable costs change according to activity levels, ie £280 when 500 buckets are produced and £1,120 when 2,000 buckets are produced. Conversely, total fixed costs per unit change according to the number of units produced, ie 60p per unit when 500 buckets are produced, and falls to 15p per unit when production is 2,000 buckets. However, the fixed costs in total remain constant at £300 irrespective of the production levels.

28.4 Definitions

From the solution to ***T. Torquay*** we can draw some general definitions as follows:

A ***variable cost*** is a cost which, in total, increases or decreases in direct proportion to the volume of production or sales. Thus, an increase in production and sales of 20% would also be accompanied by a 20% increase in variable costs. Examples are direct materials and direct wages paid as a rate per item produced (known as piecework), both of which vary with production levels, and salesmen's commission and packing materials, both of which tend to vary with sales revenue and sales volume respectively. Variable costs behave like this:

Production (units)	1	5	10	15	25	38
Variable cost per unit	£1	£1	£1	£1	£1	£1
Total variable costs	£1	£5	£10	£15	£25	£38

Notice that this definition narrowly defines a variable cost as one which varies with activity, ie production or sales. However, this does not exclude the possibility that other factors may cause costs to vary such as inflation, management decisions to spend more money on advertising, and the negotiation of volume discounts on material purchases. These other cost changes, however, do ***not*** come under this definition of variable costs.

A ***fixed cost*** is a cost which, in total, remains constant and is uninfluenced by changes in the volume of production and/or sales in the short term. Examples are rent, rates, insurances, factory manager's salary and many administration overheads. Fixed costs behave like this:

Production (units)	1	5	10	15	25	38
Total fixed costs	£50	£50	£50	£50	£50	£50

Notice that this definition also narrowly defines fixed costs in relation to production or sales, but total fixed costs may change due to other factors such as a management policy to increase expenditure on, for example, research and development.

In the longer-term no cost is entirely fixed as considerable changes in activity levels would necessarily be accompanied by changes to total fixed costs. For example, to increase production beyond the capacity of the present plant and machinery would necessitate further investment which would increase fixed costs such as depreciation and maintenance as a consequence.

You should now be able to attempt Question 28.1 at the end of this chapter.

28.5 Graphical presentation of cost behaviour

In presenting the way in which variable and fixed costs behave in a ***graphical*** manner, three conventions are normally adopted.

1. The total fixed and variable costs respectively are plotted as opposed to the fixed and variable costs per unit of production.
2. Total fixed and/or variable costs in financial terms (eg £s) are shown on the vertical or y axis of the graph.
3. Because our definitions of fixed and variable costs are based on how they behave in relation to production or sales, activity is shown on the horizontal or x axis of the graph. Activity is usually expressed in units or sales value (£s), but may also be expressed as a percentage of total capacity of the business. Sales and production are regarded as equal.

Variable costs are shown as a straight line graph, commencing at zero cost and production to illustrate that no variable costs are incurred at zero activity. To construct a variable cost graph, we calculate the total variable costs for a particular level of production and plot that point on the graph. Because it is a straight line graph, we can draw the line from the point which represents the costs when production is zero, the origin, through the point, and all the points which are along this line represent the variable costs at each production level.

Taking the example of variable costs above in Section 28.4, where the variable cost for 25 units is £25, the variable cost graph would look like this:

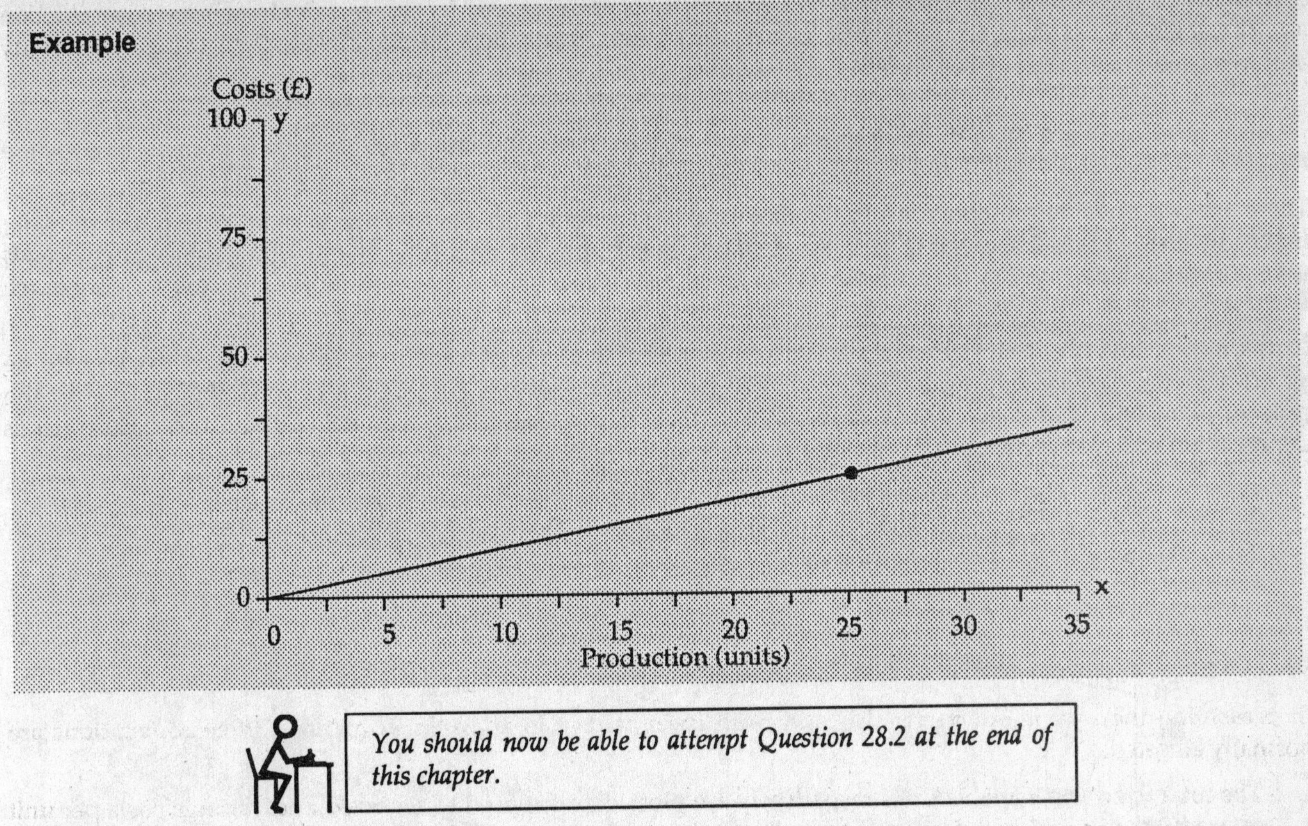

You should now be able to attempt Question 28.2 at the end of this chapter.

Fixed costs may be shown as a horizontal straight line which demonstrates that a given level of fixed costs are incurred whatever the activity level. This representation of fixed costs also shows that even at zero production level such costs will be incurred and cannot be avoided.

Taking the example above in Section 28.4 where fixed costs are £50 in total for all levels of activity, the fixed cost graph would look like this:

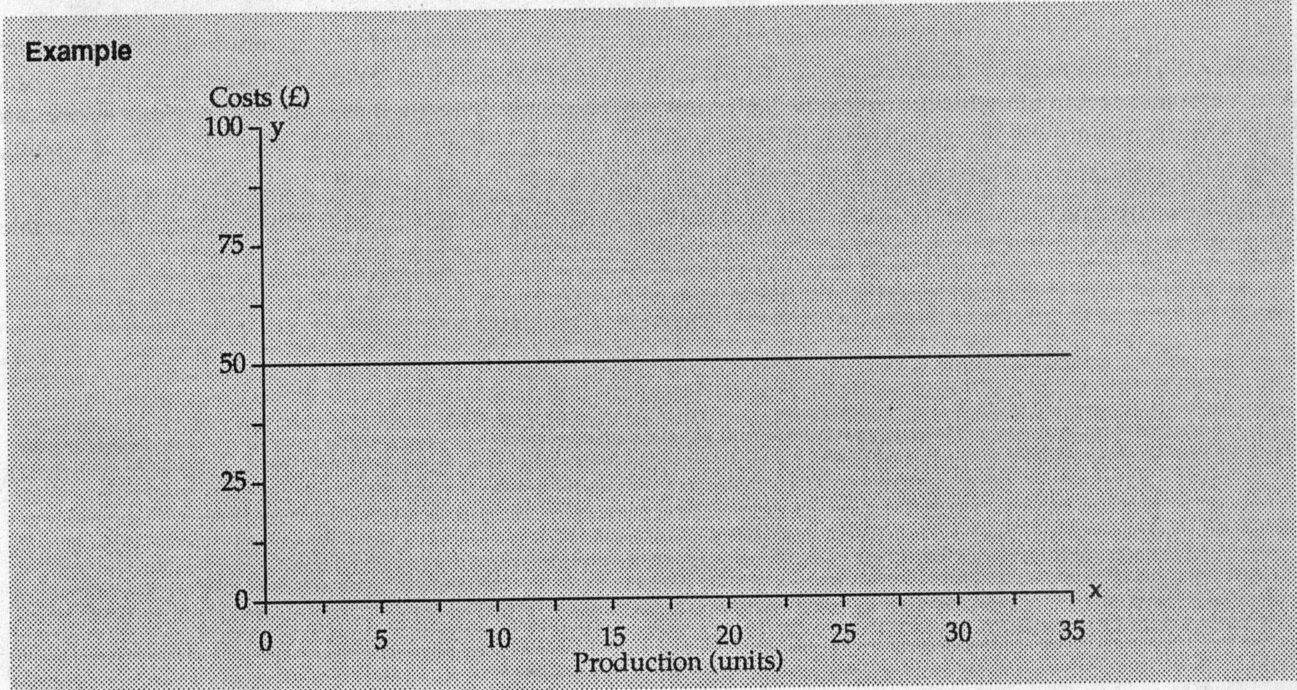

You should now be able to attempt Question 28.3 at the end of this chapter.

Because ***total costs*** are equal to the addition of total variable costs and total fixed costs, it is possible to combine the effects of the total variable and total fixed cost lines onto a single graph, to produce a total cost line.

There are two possible presentations. In the first example the total variable cost line is plotted first, and the total fixed cost line is plotted above it to give the total cost line. Using the data from the previous example the graph would look like this:

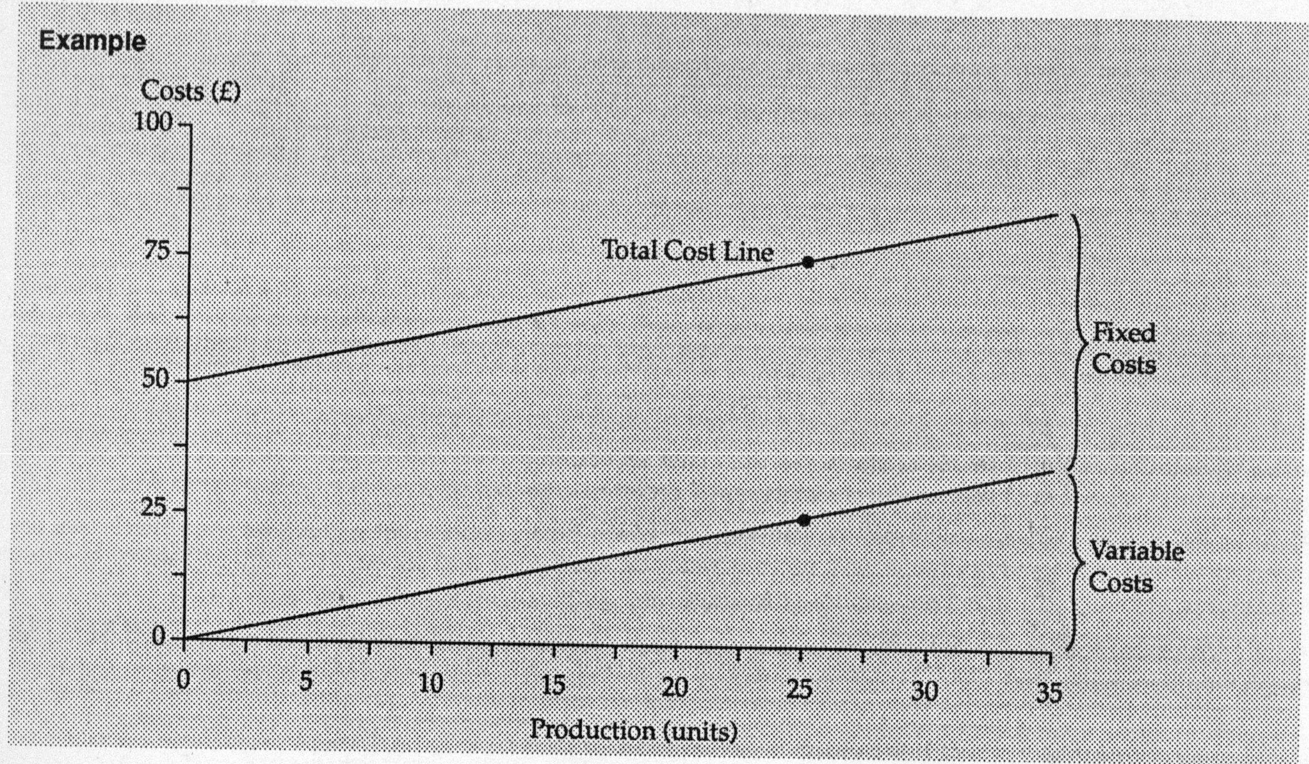

Notice that this presentation results in the total cost line being parallel to the total variable cost line due to the fact that the fixed costs are the same at all levels of activity.

In the second example the total fixed cost line is plotted first and the total variable cost line is plotted above it to give the total cost line.

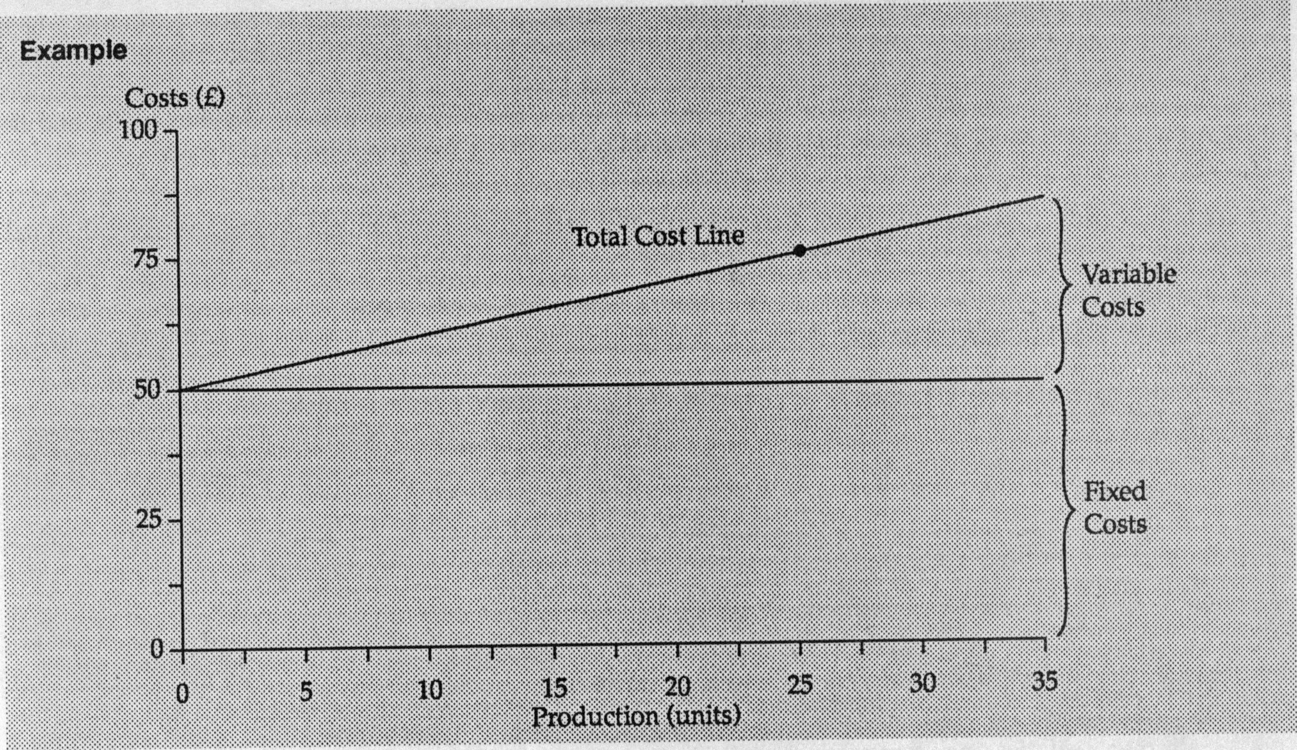

Both presentations should result in the same total cost line from a given set of data, therefore the choice of presentation to obtain total cost is simply a matter of preference at this stage in your studies. Example 1 does, however, enjoy an advantage which will be explained later in Chapter 33.

You should now be able to attempt Question 28.4 at the end of this chapter.

28.6 Some problems of cost behaviour

In identifying costs according to their cost behaviour characteristics and treating them as either fixed or variable, although a useful approach, tends to be an over-simplification, and some costs do not lend themselves easily to this treatment. Two particular problems which are met are those of classifying direct wages and semi-variable costs.

Direct wages costs

There is little doubt that both ***direct materials*** and ***direct expenses*** may be regarded as true ***variable costs***, a test being that both these costs are avoidable if production ceases. Although ***direct wages*** are regarded as a variable cost, present labour laws and agreements with trade unions do not allow employers to dismiss labour easily. It is difficult, therefore, to reduce direct labour cost in line with falling production, and in these circumstances, particularly in the short-term, labour behaves more like a fixed cost.

In costing the products manufactured, however, only the time actually spent on producing the output is regarded as a direct wages cost, and where operators are idle but remain employed because they cannot be dismissed in the short-term, then their idle time is charged to production overheads rather than as direct wages. In this way, direct wages assume the characteristic of being a variable cost, any fixed unavoidable element being treated as an overhead. For this reason, unless there are clear indications to the contrary, all ***product direct costs*** making up the ***prime cost*** should be regarded and treated as ***variable*** in terms of cost behaviour.

Semi-variable costs

Some items of cost are a mixture of fixed and variable costs, and this causes such costs to behave in a special way. The total cost changes as activity changes, but not in strict proportion as would happen if they were straightforward variable only costs.

An example of such a cost is power from electricity. Many businesses pay for electricity on a two-part tariff which is made up of a standing charge and a rate per unit or kilowatt-hour. The standing charge has all the characteristics of a fixed cost as it is payable whether production takes place or not, and furthermore the same amount is payable whatever the production level. The unit charge, however, tends to vary with production levels, and no unit charge would be payable where zero production causes no electricity consumption to take place.

Example

The following is a list of total costs for ***A. Auckland*** at two different levels of activity. The first three costs have already been classified into variable (V), fixed (F) and semi-variable (SV). The explanations in the part solution show how this has been done.

Production/sales levels (units)	2,000	5,000	Cost behaviour
	Total costs		
	£	£	
Supervision	20,000	20,000	F
Direct materials	100,000	250,000	V
Storage & handling	10,000	17,500	SV
Maintenance	30,000	60,000	
Direct wages	90,000	225,000	
Electricity	10,000	19,000	
Rent	26,000	26,000	
Insurance	8,000	8,000	
Salesmen's salaries (incl. commission)	50,000	65,000	
Packaging	27,500	68,750	
Staff salaries	80,000	80,000	
Distribution	30,000	52,500	
Rates	20,000	20,000	
Depreciation	40,000	40,000	

Solution

Supervision

The total cost of supervision remains constant at £20,000 for both levels of activity which is characteristic behaviour for a fixed cost.

Direct materials

The total cost of direct materials increases with output which is characteristic behaviour for a variable cost. Furthermore, the total direct material cost increases proportionately with activity - a production increase from 2,000 units to 5,000 units, an increase of 2.5 times, is accompanied by an increase in direct material costs also of 2.5 times, thus confirming that total direct material costs are variable.

An alternative approach is to calculate the direct material cost per unit at each level of production. At 2,000 units, the direct material cost per unit is:

$$\frac{£100{,}000}{2{,}000} = £50 \text{ per unit}$$

At 5,000 units the direct material cost per unit is:

$$\frac{£250{,}000}{5{,}000} = £50 \text{ per unit}$$

Where there is a constant cost per unit at both activity levels, this is an indication of a variable cost. (see the explanation of variable costs in section 28.4).

Storage and Handling

Clearly this cost is not a fixed cost as it increases in total as activity rises. At first sight, therefore, this cost appears to behave in a way similar to a variable cost. However, as production increases by 2.5 times if it were a variable cost it would also increase by 2.5 times, ie from £10,000 when 2,000 units are produced to £25,000 at the 5,000 unit level. The actual increase has been somewhat less than this due to a fixed cost element in total storage & handling costs. Therefore storage & handling in this case is a semi-variable cost.

You should now be able to attempt Question 28.5 at the end of this chapter.

28.7 Analysis of semi-variable costs into their fixed and variable elements

In addition to recognising a cost as a semi-variable one, it is also necessary to determine the fixed and variable elements of cost which make up a semi-variable cost. To achieve this analysis there are five basic steps:

1. Establish the total cost levels of a particular item at two levels of activity. In the example in Section 28.6 storage and handling costs have already been established for production levels of 2,000 units and 5,000 units as £10,000 and £17,500 respectively.

2. Calculate the change in cost which arises due to the change in production, sometimes known as the *differential cost*. For storage and handling this may be set out as follows:

Example

	Production units		Cost £
	5,000		17,500
	2,000		10,000
Change in production	3,000 units	Change in cost	7,500

3. Calculate the cost per unit arising from the change in cost and the change in production. For storage and handling this becomes:

$$\frac{\text{change in cost (£)}}{\text{change in production (units)}} = \frac{£7{,}500}{3{,}000} = £2.50 \text{ per unit}$$

Because the change in total cost arising from the change in production is brought about by changes in the total variable cost element only (remember, the total fixed cost element will not change as a result of increasing or decreasing activity), then the £2.50 represents the variable cost per unit of production.

4. Calculate the total variable costs for each level of production. For storage & handling this becomes:

Example

Production units	×	Variable cost per unit £	=	Total variable costs £
5,000		2.50		12,500
2,000		2.50		5,000

5. Subtract the total variable costs from the total costs at each production level to obtain the total fixed costs at each production level. This becomes:

Example

Production units	Total costs	–	Total variable costs	=	Total fixed costs
	£		£		£
5,000	17,500		12,500		5,000
2,000	10,000		5,000		5,000

Notice that for any truly semi-variable cost this procedure should give the same total fixed costs for each level of activity, which agrees with the characteristics associated with fixed costs described earlier.

You should now be able to attempt Question 28.6 at the end of this chapter.

28.8 Reason for analysis of semi-variable costs

The analysis of semi-variable costs into their fixed and variable elements enables all costs to be treated as either fixed or variable for the purposes of the graphical presentation referred to earlier. The fixed and variable elements of the semi-variable costs being added to the other fixed or variable costs of the organisation as appropriate.

The analysis of costs into fixed and variable according to their cost behaviour enables us to determine the way in which total costs change as activity changes. Nevertheless, some costs do not behave in these simple ways, and when shown graphically depict a more complex form of cost behaviour.

Example

N. Newlyn has graphed the behaviour of some of his costs. The descriptions of each cost behaviour have become detached from the original graphs. Match each description to the graph which depicts its behaviour. As usual, cost is depicted on the 'y' axis and activity on the 'x' axis.

i) Gas

The invoice from British Gas is made up of a fixed, so-called service charge, plus a rate per unit of gas consumed. Gas consumption varies with production levels.

ii) Consultancy Fee

I have to pay a fixed sum as a consultancy fee irrespective of the level of production up to a certain production level. Thereafter, if the consultants succeed in achieving higher production levels, the fee is paid as a rate per unit produced in order to reflect the success of the consultancy assignment.

iii) Supervision

I need one supervisor on a fixed salary irrespective of whether production takes place or not. However, as production rises to a certain level I require a second supervisor, and as production rises yet further I require a third.

Solution

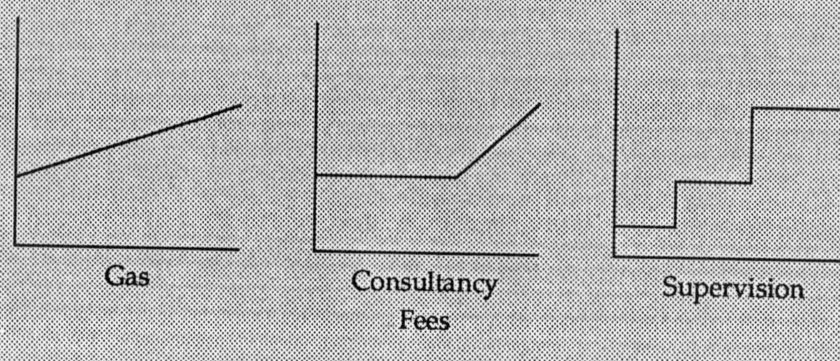

You should now be able to attempt Question 28.7 and Tasks 28.2 and 28.3 at the end of this chapter.

28.9 Summary

In addition to the way in which costs may be classified as set out in Chapter 27, costs can also be classified according to the way in which they ***behave*** in total relative to activity levels, ie production or sales. A cost is described as a ***variable cost*** if it increases or decreases, in total, in proportion to changes in the level of activity. Examples are direct materials, direct wages and power. A cost is described as a ***fixed cost*** if, in total, it remains constant irrespective of the level of activity. Examples are rent, rates and insurances.

In general, variable costs are avoidable if activity does not take place, and fixed costs are unavoidable in that they are incurred whether or not production is carried out. Some items of expenditure are ***semi-variable*** costs as they have both a fixed and a variable element in their makeup. Examples of these may be gas, electricity and salesmen's remuneration where a commission based on sales is added to a basic salary. An analysis of semi-variable costs into their fixed and variable elements enables all costs to be classified as either fixed or variable.

The method of classifying costs according to ***cost behaviour*** is a very useful one which helps in providing management information for planning, decision making, pricing and control. Some costs, however, behave in a more complex way than the comparatively straightforward manner of either fixed, variable or semi-variable costs based on activity levels.

You should now be able to attempt the Objective Test at the end of this chapter.

Student activities

Task 28.1 Cost behaviour may be portrayed in graphical form, a technique which is very often used in business as "a single picture is worth a thousand words". Review a number of quality newspapers and business magazines for a period, and prepare a collection of the different types of graphs used by the publication to present to their readers changes in various items such as share prices, production or costs over time.

Task 28.2 Working individually, draw up a list of industries where you consider the distinction between fixed and variable costs is important and a list of industries where it is not important. Compare your lists and explain any differences.

Task 28.3 A friend who is a member of a trade union has asked you to help her with a problem. During wage negotiations with her company she was told that in times of recession the management cannot regard labour as a fixed cost. She does not know what the implications of this statement are. Write her a letter of explanation.

Question 28.1 ***B. Brixham*** operates a factory which produces kits for self-assembly kitchen cupboards. Determine which of his costs are variable or fixed:

Cost	Variable	Fixed
Door hinges		
Chipboard panels		
Depreciation of cutting machine (straight line)		
Screws		
Depreciation of factory building (straight line)		
Factory manager's salary		
Salesmen's salary		
Salesmen's commission		
Boxes for final product		
Advertising		
Office salaries		
Stationery and printing		
Factory heating		
Wages of operators		
Factory insurance		

Question 28.2 ***N. Newquay*** operates a business producing ball-point pens. His variable costs per pen, i.e. the metal, plastic and assembly costs, amount to 55 pence. His maximum capacity is 100,000 pens per annum.

Required

i) Plot N. Newquay's variable cost graph to cover all possible levels of production.

ii) Read off from the graph the total variable costs which Newquay will incur at the 60% activity level.

Question 28.3 In addition to the variable costs per pen of 55p set out in Question 28.2 above, N. Newquay expects to incur some fixed costs. These will be, per annum:

	£
Rent	4,000
Rates	3,000
Depreciation	6,000
Administration	5,000
Light & heat	2,000
Salaries	10,000
	30,000

Required

Plot N. Newquay's fixed cost line to cover all possible levels of activity.

Question 28.4 Using the data already given concerning N. Newquay's cost levels set out in Questions 28.2 and 28.3, draw up graphs using the two alternative presentations discussed in the chapter, showing on each graph:

- ❒ the total cost line
- ❒ total variable costs
- ❒ total fixed costs
- ❒ total costs at 60% activity level

Question 28.5 The following is a list of total costs for ***A. Auckland*** at two different levels of activity. The first three costs have already been classified into variable (V), fixed (F) and semi-variable (SV), with explanations in the solution in Section 28.6 how this has been done. Read the notes again carefully and classify the other costs in the same way:

Production/sales levels (units)	**2,000**	**5,000**	**Cost behaviour**
	Total costs		
	£	**£**	
Supervision	20,000	20,000	F
Direct materials	100,000	250,000	V
Storage & handling	10,000	17,500	SV
Maintenance	30,000	60,000	
Direct wages	90,000	225,000	
Electricity	10,000	19,000	
Rent	26,000	26,000	
Insurance	8,000	8,000	
Salesmen's salaries (incl. Commission)	50,000	65,000	
Packaging	27,500	68,750	
Staff salaries	80,000	80,000	
Distribution	30,000	52,500	
Rates	20,000	20,000	
Depreciation	40,000	40,000	

Question 28.6 Analyse the other costs which you have identified for ***A. Auckland*** as semi-variable in Question 28.5 above into their fixed and variable elements using the five steps discussed in the chapter.

Question 28.7 ***N. Newlyn*** has charted the behaviour of some of his costs. The descriptions of each cost behaviour have become detached from the original graphs. Match each description to the graph which depicts its behaviour. As usual, cost is depicted on the y axis and activity on the x axis. The first three costs have already been identified in the Section 28.8.

iv) Direct material

I have an agreement for the purchase of direct material under which I have to pay a certain rate per unit until my production reaches a certain level, after which I am given a discount per unit. A further discount per unit is earned when a yet higher production level is attained.

v) Direct wages

I simply pay my operators a rate per item produced (piecework). There is no guaranteed minimum payment when production is low or zero.

vi) Water rates

I have an arrangement with the water authority whereby I pay a rate per litre consumed up to a maximum charge after which level I pay the same total sum irrespective of my consumption levels. Water consumption is based on activity levels.

vii) Other rates

I pay a certain sum completely unrelated to my production levels.

viii) Salesmen's salaries

The salesmen, who are entitled to a fixed basic salary plus a variable commission based on sales levels, are increased in number as sales rise.

ix) Royalty

I have a royalty agreement whereby I pay a rate per unit produced, up to a certain production level, when a maximum royalty is paid which remains constant for a further rise in production. At a yet higher production level, the royalty again becomes payable as a rate per unit produced.

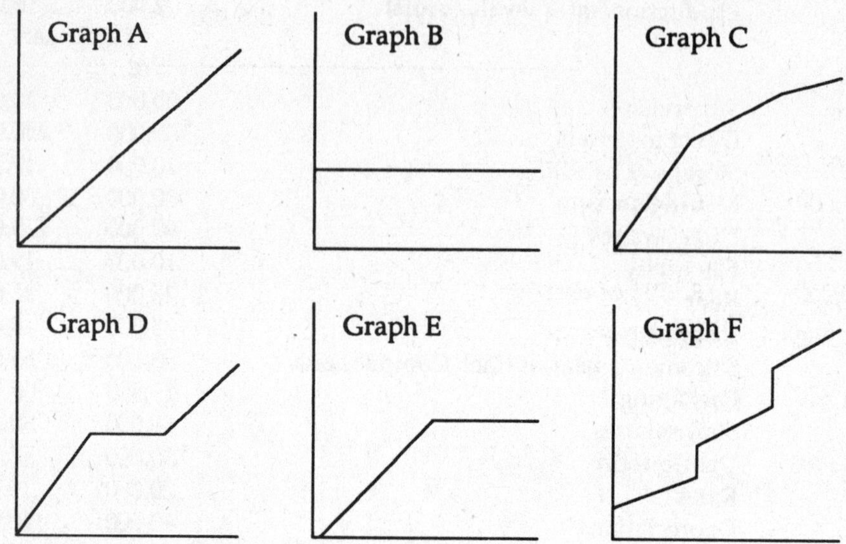

Objective test *(tick the appropriate box)*

i) Whether a cost is fixed, variable or semi-variable depends on its behaviour in relation to the volume of:

a) production ☐

b) sales ☐

c) both ☐

d) either ☐

ii) If a cost is described as fixed, when activity doubles its cost per unit:

a) remains constant ☐

b) doubles ☐

c) halves ☐

d) neither ☐

iii) If a cost is described as variable, when activity doubles its cost per unit:

a) remains constant ☐

b) doubles ☐

c) halves ☐

d) neither ☐

iv) If a cost is described as semi-variable, when activity doubles its total cost:

a) doubles ☐

b) less than doubles ☐

c) more than doubles ☐

d) remains constant ☐

v) Analysing the following semi-variable costs into fixed and variable elements,

Production (units)	Semi-variable costs
4,000	£14,000
10,000	£29,000

results in:

	Fixed costs	Variable costs
a)	£19,000	£1.00 per unit
b)	£6,000	£2.00 per unit
c)	£10,000	£2.50 per unit
d)	£4,000	£2.50 per unit

Chapter 29

Budgetary control

29.1 Objectives

At the end of this chapter you should be able to:

- ❐ understand how budgets are formulated;
- ❐ understand how budgetary control helps to run businesses;
- ❐ draw up budget statements;
- ❐ understand the advantages and problems of budgetary control systems.

29.2 Introduction

Small businesses are relatively easily controlled and directed by one person, usually the owner. He or she may have a very good idea:

- ❐ where the business is going (the business plan);
- ❐ what cost levels are acceptable (cost control);
- ❐ what income levels are required (pricing);
- ❐ what volumes of sales should be obtained (motivation);
- ❐ what profit levels are adequate (profit planning).

Many of these goals may not be explicitly expressed on paper in a small business, but implicitly pursued as ***business objectives***. This is possible and acceptable because most decisions which affect the achievement of these objectives in a business of this size are made by the owner. As the business expands, however, there is a tendency to split the organisation into different parts and employ a specialist manager to run each. These parts are known as ***functions***. The following example of a ***functional organisation chart*** is for a limited company engaged in manufacturing.

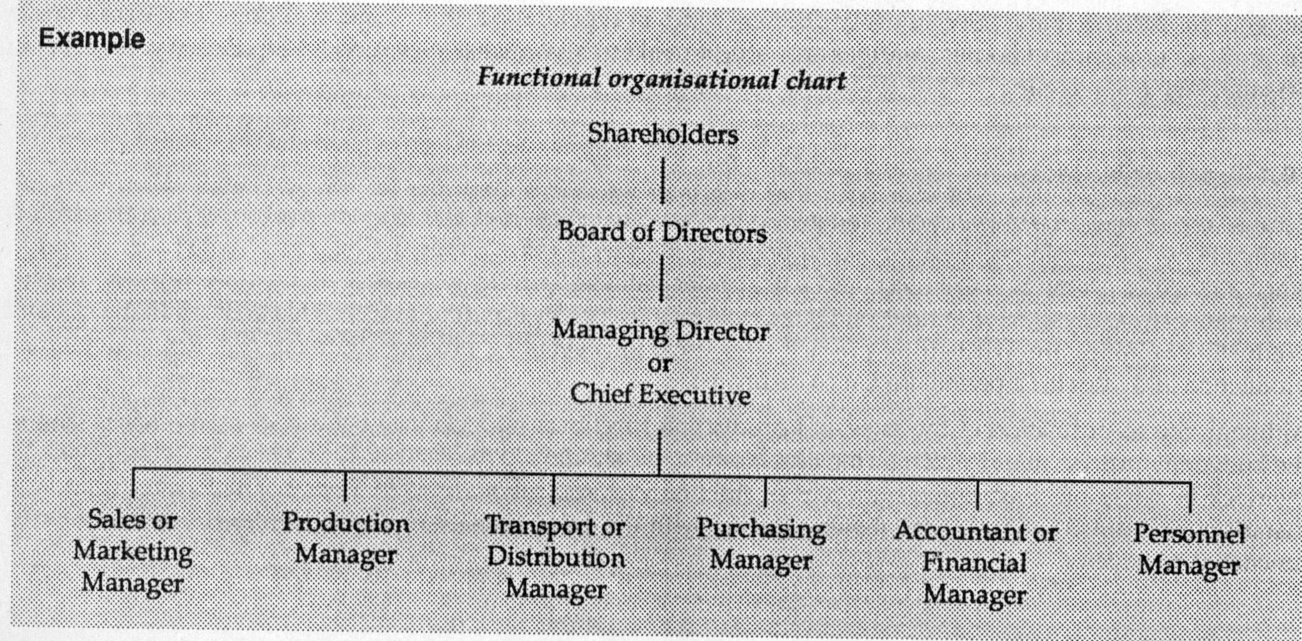

The ***shareholders*** own the business and appoint a ***board of directors*** to run it on their behalf. The ***managing director*** or ***chief executive*** is responsible to the board of directors for the day-to-day operation of the business, and he or she has a number of specialist ***functional or line managers*** who are responsible for the operation of their own particular functions. Their titles may vary from one organisation to another.

In such a complex organisation the regular decisions to achieve particular objectives are no longer made by the owner(s). Indeed, there is now no single owner because the company is likely to have many shareholders. Many of the daily decisions are made by the line managers. It is important that these decisions are made within an overall plan which will ensure that the business as a whole will achieve its agreed objectives. This is the ***business plan***.

Therefore, it is essential that the business develops a formal planning and control system which will state clearly the ***objectives*** for both the business as a whole and for each functional manager, The business also needs a ***reporting system*** which will inform the manager and the chief executive when any function is not operating according to the predetermined ***plan***, and allow corrective action to be taken. Such a planning, controlling and reporting system is known as ***budgetary control***.

29.3 Budgets

A ***budget*** is a quantitative and/or financial statement. It is prepared prior to the start of a trading or operating period and sets out the objectives, activities and policies to be carried out during that period by each functional area of the business (***functional budgets***) and for the business as a whole. Budgets are prepared for a specified time period known as the ***budget period***. This may be for any length of time, usually a year, in which case it is commonly broken down into shorter control periods of quarters, months, or in some cases, weeks. The longer the period taken for planning purposes, the greater the difficulty in predicting future performance.

Budgets are not only expressed in financial terms, but also in non-monetary measures wherever possible. Thus some budgets are expressed in units of sales or production, direct labour hours, or machine hours to be worked. Some functional financial budgets are expressed in income terms (a ***revenue budget***); others in expenditure terms (a ***cost budget***) or a combination of the two. For example, a sales income budget is a revenue budget, and the sales cost budget is a cost budget. Both are combined as being the responsibility of the sales or marketing manager.

Budgets are prepared for any part of the business which can be identified as being the responsibility of an individual manager, and therefore a breakdown of the functional budgets into sections is often carried out. For example, the marketing manager may analyse the overall sales revenue budget into sales budgets which would be the responsibility of each area sales manager. Each part of the business for which a budget is prepared is known as a ***budget centre***.

Budgets are produced and used in many different types of organisation, from manufacturing companies trading for profit, to government bodies, charities and educational establishments. They can also be used to good effect in personal financial planning.

29.4 Types of budgets

Because one of the aims of producing budgets is to co-ordinate activities and to produce an overall plan which is attainable by the whole organisation, some detailed analysis is often required from each budget. For example, when a range of products is produced and sold, co-ordination of production and sales functions is made easier if both managers analyse their annual budgeted volumes by product and by month. This ensures that sales and production volumes are matched by product over time, thus avoiding product shortages or overstocking when production and sales for a period are not co-ordinated.

Although the co-ordination of the sales and production functional budgets may be said to represent the core of the budgeting process in a manufacturing organisation, we should not overlook the concept that all budgets must interlock in a feasible way. Some examples of the financial and quantitative budgets normally produced by a manufacturing organisation are as follows, together with the detailed analysis which might be expected from the functional manager.

Example

Functional manager	*Financial budgets*	*Quantitative budgets*
Sales/ Marketing manager	Sales revenue budget Analysed by: Product Market Budget control period Salesman Outlet	Sales volume budget Analysed by: Product Market Budget control period Salesman Outlet
	Sales cost budget	Personnel budget Sales vehicles budget
	Advertising and promotion budget	Television time budget Column centimetres budget Display sites budget
Production manager	Direct material cost budget	Material quantities budget
	Direct wages cost budget	Manpower/Personnel direct labour hours budget
	Direct expenses cost budget	Quantities budget
	Production overheads budget	Direct labour hours budget Machine hours budget
	Total production cost budget Analysed by: Product Budget control period Factory, department or budget centre	Production quantities budget Analysed by: Product Budget control period Factory, department or budget centre

Some budgets do not fall under the responsibility of a specific manager, but may require a contribution from a number of managers with the accountant summarising the data or pulling together information from a number of sources. Some examples of other budgets found in organisations are set out below.

Example

Capital expenditure budget	Details of all projected expenditure on capital projects or assets Analysed by: Asset Project Functional responsibility Budget period
Budgeted profit and loss account (income statement) and budgeted balance sheet	
Master budget	The combination, co-ordination and integration of all the budgets to produce the master plan for the business as a whole for the budget period.

> *You should now be able to attempt Question 29.1 at the end of this chapter.*

29.5 Budget co-ordination

Co-ordination of the production and sales budgets enables the ***finished goods stocks budget*** to be produced. Future policy decisions may be required when budgeted production falls short of budgeted sales for any prolonged period such that stocks are exhausted. Capital expenditure may need to be planned to increase production capacity. Alternatively, sub- contracting of production may be planned.

In the event of budgeted sales falling short of budgeted production, the decisions to mitigate the effect of this by layoffs, holiday shutdown or increased advertising expenditure all have the effect of influencing other budgets.

The following examples illustrate the responsibilities of certain managers for budgets and identify how these must be *co-ordinated* with the activities of other managers.

Example

Transport/distribution manager

Financial budgets	**Quantitative budgets**
Distribution cost budget	Units budget
	Miles budget
	Tonne/miles budget

Co-ordination must be achieved with the sales quantities budget to determine the distribution cost by market and product.

Example

Purchasing manager

Financial budgets	**Quantitative budgets**
Purchases cost budget	Quantities budget
Purchasing department cost budget	Manpower or personnel budget
	Tonne/miles budget
Analysed by:	Analysed by:
Product	Product
Factory	Factory
Budget period	Budget period

Co-ordination must be achieved with the production and direct material cost budgets to produce the ***raw materials stocks budget***.

Example

Accountant/financial manager

Financial budgets	**Quantitative budgets**
Administration cost budget	Personnel budget
Cash flow budget	

Example

Personnel manager

Financial budgets	**Quantitative budgets**
Personnel department cost budget	Personnel budget
	Manpower budget
Analysed by:	Analysed by:
Grade	Grade
Skill	Skill
Gender	Gender

Co-ordination must be achieved with all other functional budgets to provide personnel or manpower content.

29.6 Cash flow budget

The ***cash flow budget*** (see Chapter 5) is a very important budget which co-ordinates with all the other budgets. All functional budgets are produced on an accruals basis. This means that they record expenditure and income when it is incurred or generated, rather than when the cash is paid or received. (See Chapter 12). The cash flow budget is created by converting all the budgeted amounts from the functional budgets into monthly cash flow terms, and including other items not included in the functional budgets such as capital expenditure, dividend and tax payments, and investment income. The cash flow budget helps predict when further cash resources are needed, or alternatively when surplus cash is available in the budget year. A typical layout is as follows:

Example

Limited company
Monthly cash flow budget

Month	1	2	3	4	etc
	£	£	£	£	
Cash inflows					
Cash sales					
Payment by debtors					
Investment income					
Sundry cash receipts					
(a) Total cash inflows	—	—	—	—	
Cash outflows					
Payments to creditors					
Cash purchases					
Wages					
Salaries					
Interest payments					
Capital expenditure					
Dividends payments					
Corporation tax payments					
Other taxation payments eg VAT					
Sundry cash payments					
(b) Total cash outflows	—	—	—	—	
(c) Net cash flows (a) – (b)	—	—	—	—	
(d) Opening cash balance					
Closing Cash Balance (c) + (d)	—	—	—	—	

> *You should now be able to attempt Task 29.1 and Question 29.1 at the end of this chapter.*

29.7 The budget setting process

The process of setting the functional and other budgets and drawing up the master budget can take a number of months, so preparation commences some time before the start of the period to which the budget refers. It is usual to form a ***budget committee*** made up of the functional heads chaired by the chief executive. The management accountant usually occupies the role of committee secretary, co-ordinating and assisting in the preparation of the budget data provided by each of the functional heads of the business.

Functional and other budgets are received by the budget committee and it is the committee's responsibility to ensure that all budgets have the following characteristics:

- The budgets conform to the organisation's policies and goals as established and communicated by the board of directors.
- The individual budgets are reasonable and achievable.
- The budgets are well co-ordinated so that no particular budget is out of phase with the other budgets which make up the master budget.
- The budgets take into consideration the conditions and constraints which are expected to apply during the budget period.

Budgets that do not conform to these requirements are returned for revision to the managers responsible . The final master budget is submitted to the board of directors for approval prior to the commencement of the budget period. After acceptance, the budget becomes the plan adopted by the business as a whole until such time as further amendments are made and approved perhaps later in the year when circumstances change.

In an organisation which trades for profit, it is essential that the final budgeted profit is acceptable before the budget is approved by the budget committee and ultimately the board of directors. Therefore the following questions must be answered satisfactorily:

- What is the level of profitability revealed by the budget? This could be established by the use of such measures as return on capital employed (prime ratio), or profit as a percentage of sales revenue (margins). See Chapter 22 for an explanation of these ratios.
- What are the returns achieved by competitors or from alternative investments?
- What is the increase or decrease in budgeted profit compared to last year or to previous years? The shareholders might expect to see a trend of rising profits over time.
- Is the budgeted profit adequate? The profit before taxation is appropriated in three ways: Corporation Tax is paid to the government, dividends are paid to the shareholders, and the balance of profit is retained in the business to finance future expansion. The adequacy of the profits, therefore, will be determined by the board of directors' policies with regard to the growth of dividends, and also what proportion of future expansion plans should be financed from retained profits.
- Is the level of profit attainable? Consideration should be given to the changes in the market and competitors' and suppliers' actions which might make the budgeted profit unattainable.

Once the master budget is formally accepted and approved by the board of directors it becomes the policy plan for the organisation for the budget period. The relevant budgets are then communicated to all budget centre managers, who are encouraged to operate within the approved budgetary framework of costs, sales and performance.

You should appreciate that the foregoing budgets and budget-setting process are based on what might happen in a typical manufacturing company. The approaches vary considerably from organisation to organisation.

> *You should now be able to attempt Question 29.3 at the end of this chapter.*

29.8 Budgetary control

Budgetary control is the process of financial control whereby the actual expenditure and income for a period is compared to an appropriate budget allowance for each item for the same period, and the variances established. Control is exercised by taking action to eliminate those variances which are adverse to an unacceptable degree.

An ***adverse variance*** reduces the budgeted profits and arises where the actual performance is worse than that budgeted for the period. That is, where costs are higher or income is lower than the budget allowance. A ***favourable variance*** increases the budgeted profits and arises where the actual performance is better than that budgeted. No action is generally required if the variance is either favourable or zero. Budgetary control conforms to the ***exception principle of management***, which suggests that action need only be taken when a predetermined plan is not achieved.

Advantages

Budgetary control is a very useful control device and the following advantages may arise from its introduction:

- The manager of each budget centre knows in financial and quantitative terms what is expected of him/her for the budget period and therefore is ***motivated*** to achieve this performance.
- Managers are usually given the opportunity to contribute to the setting of their budgets which encourages an attitude of ***responsibility***.
- The ***co-ordination*** of all the functions of the business is encouraged at the budget preparation stage.
- By considering the adverse variances only, management is able to determine those functions of the business which are contributing to its failure to achieve the budgeted profit, and also the extent to which they are contributing to that shortfall in financial and quantitative terms. ***Control*** is facilitated.
- The process of formulating budgets encourages managers to anticipate likely future events well in advance and to consider the options available for the resolution of those future problems well before they occur. In this way ***decision-making*** is facilitated.
- Producing budgets helps managers to ***plan*** the development of their activity or function in a progressive way, but at the same time conforming to the overall goals and policies of the organisation. ***Planning*** is encouraged and formalised.
- Any business must be aware to what extent its future income is likely to cover its future costs. The drafting of a budget will assist the business in determining when and to what extent price adjustments to its product range are likely to be necessary. ***Pricing*** is therefore facilitated.
- As co-ordination of all budgets must be achieved at the budget preparation stage, if each manager achieves budgeted performance he/she will have made his/her contribution to the overall business moving in the direction which was planned at the budgeting stage and accepted by the board of directors. A sense of ***direction*** is given to the organisation.
- The setting of a budget for each budget centre allows decisions to be made at budget centre level provided they are within the prescribed budget. This avoids every decision being made at the top of the organisation, but at the same time provides some constraint on the decisions being made at budget centre level. ***Decentralisation*** is facilitated.
- In any organisation the goals or aims of functional heads may not be the same as those of the organisation as a whole. For example, the sales manager may wish to achieve maximum sales volume, irrespective of the costs involved, whereas the organisation as a whole may only wish for additional sales at an acceptable cost. Preparation of budgets helps to resolve these differences by making personal goals subordinate to organisational ones, except where they coincide. ***Goal congruency*** is encouraged.

Disadvantages

In spite of the many advantages of operating a system of budgetary control, there are a number of problems associated with its introduction and operation:

- Some managers will understandably try to ensure that a budget is approved for their particular function of the business which will be very easy for them to achieve in practice. If they are responsible for an expenditure budget, for example, they will try to obtain approval for as high a budget allowance as possible. Conversely, if they are responsible for a revenue budget they will try to ensure that their income budgets are approved at as low a level as possible. This is known as ***budgetary slack***, and the budget committee must do all it can to detect and discourage such approaches to budget setting.
- There is a tendency in many organisations to create a budget by taking the current year's expected actual expenditure and adding a notional percentage for, say, expected increased price levels in the budget period. This approach called ***incremental budgeting*** should be discouraged as it is unlikely to create a budget which is relevant to the particular conditions likely to be experienced in the budget period. Furthermore, items of non-recurring expenditure or income unique to the current year will tend to be included in the budget for the succeeding year, and no effort is made to consider items peculiar to the budget period.
- Some chief executives fail to adopt a participative approach to preparing budgets by not involving their line managers in the budgeting process. The managers then feel that targets are set which are not achievable, and a ***lack of motivation*** to achieve the budgeted performance results.
- Some managers feel that the budget allowance for the budget period represents the total which must be spent. This results in their ***spending up to the budget allowance*** even though they could comfortably achieve savings. This action particularly applies to overhead and capital expenditure budgets, and tends to be pursued by the manager for two reasons:
  - i) Because an incremental approach to budgeting is often adopted, high current expenditure means that a high budget allowance is easily obtained in subsequent years.
  - ii) There is a fear that any failure to take advantage of approved high expenditure levels will be accompanied by a reluctance on the part of top management to allow underspending to be carried forward to a subsequent budget period.
- Although a variance may arise under a particular budget heading, ***the variance may not have been caused by the manager for that budget centre.*** For example, an overspending on direct material costs due to excess wastage which appears under the production budget may not be controllable by the production manager as it may be due to the purchasing manager buying inferior quality material.
- The establishment of a single ***fixed budget*** for a budget period does not satisfactorily provide a yardstick for control where a different level of production or sales is achieved from that predicted in formulating the budget. Some of the costs will change, therefore, not due to under or overspending arising from good or poor cost control, but due to differences which arise by virtue of the fact that the actual activity level differs from that budgeted.

You should now be able to attempt Tasks 29.2 and 29.3 at the end of this chapter.

29.9 Summary

Budgetary control is the process of control whereby financial and quantitative budgets are produced for a budget period, and actual expenditure and income are compared with the budget allowance throughout that period.

Any difference arising between the budgeted performance and the actual performance is known as a ***variance***. Variances can be ***favourable***, where actual performance is better than that budgeted (income is greater and/or expenditure is less) or they can be ***adverse*** (actual expenditure is higher than budgeted and/or actual income is lower).

Control is exercised by ensuring that budgets are produced for each manager in charge of a definable area of the business (***function managers***). They are required to take action to eliminate any variances where they are adverse to an unacceptable degree.

Whilst budgetary control is a very useful device for achieving motivation, responsibility, co-ordination, control and effective decision-making within an organisation, it also suffers from a number of problems which must be guarded against when operating such a system.

You should now be able to attempt the Objective Test at the end of this chapter.

Student activities

Task 29.1 You are working in a local company and the production manager has agreed that there is no need for him to co-ordinate his budget with other managers. Send him a memo giving examples of where problems can arise if there is no co-ordination of budgets.

Task 29.2 You are required to write an article for a business journal. The title is: Why budgetary control does not work. Your theme should be the problems of budgetary control and how they can be resolved.

Task 29.3 Draw up a personal cash flow budget for the next six months. You should plan your cash income and expenditure, together with a balance at the end of each month. Monitor your actual income and expenditure against the budgeted figures. Develop the cash flow budget into a rolling budget by adding another month's budget as each month passes so that at any time you have a plan for the succeeding six months. Does the process get easier or more difficult?

Hint: Revise Chapter 5.

Question 29.1 The planned or budgeted direct labour hours for ***Victoria Fabrications Ltd*** is made up of the following working practices in each of the three departments machining, fabrication and finishing:

Machining

15 operators are classified as direct labour. During the year (of 52 weeks), one week is taken up with bank holidays and the company employees are entitled to 3 weeks' holiday per annum. On average, the operators are sick for one week each year.

A 40 hour basic week is worked, with overtime which is expected to average at 4 hours per week per operator. 'Natural breaks' average 2.5 hours per week per operator, waiting time 3.5 hours, and other lost time amounts to an hour.

Fabrication

The conditions of employment are largely the same in the fabrication department as those in the machine department. However, only 5 operators are employed and virtually no overtime is worked.

Finishing

The conditions of employment are largely the same in the finishing department as those in the machine department. However, only 5 operators are employed and an average of 2 hours overtime is worked per employee.

Required

Calculate the budgeted annual productive or chargeable hours for each of the departments of the factory.

Question 29.2 ***Sonron plc*** produces two types of electric drill, the basic and the super. The budgeted production data for the year 19x1 for each product is as follows, each drill passing through the production departments of manufacturing, assembly, and finishing:

Production time

			Hours per unit	
			Basic	Super
Manufacturing dept	–	machine hours	0.2	0.2
Assembly dept	–	labour hours	0.1	0.15
Finishing dept	–	labour hours	0.1	0.1

Direct materials

	Costs per unit	
	Basic	Super
Motors	1@ £3	1@ £4
Parts	20@£0.25	25@ £0.30
Cases	1@ £2	1@£2.50

Sales and finished goods stocks

	Units	
	Basic	Super
Sales	132,000	72,000
Opening stocks	20,000	14,000
Desired closing stocks	8,000	2,000
Selling prices	£30	£40

Direct labour hourly rates

	£ per hour
Manufacturing dept	£6.00
Assembly dept	£5.00
Finishing dept	£4.00

It is the company's production planning policy for one operator in the manufacturing department to supervise two machines.

Other stocks

	Basic			Super		
	Motors	Parts	Cases	Motors	Parts	Cases
Opening stocks	750	15,000	1,000	350	5,000	400
Desired closing stocks	2,000	10,000	1,000	500	4,000	1,000

Production overheads

	£ per annum
Indirect wages	124,000
Wages on cost (Holiday pay, etc)	120,400
Supervision	33,360
Machine maintenance wages	28,000
Supplies	5,200
Power	8,400
Tooling	26,600
Insurance – Buildings	3,200
– Machinery	5,040
Depreciation – Machinery	21,000
Rent & rates	24,800
	400,000

Assume all production overheads accrue evenly throughout the year irrespective of production levels. Sales and production levels vary quarterly, but are constant per month during each quarter. The spread of production and sales is as follows:

Quarter	Sales % of Annual sales		Production % of Annual production	
	Basic	Super	Basic	Super
1	25	15	30	20
2	25	30	25	30
3	35	30	35	35
4	15	25	10	15

Required

Prepare monthly budgets for the year commencing January 19X1 suitable for presentation to the budget committee of Sonron plc. Your budgets should include:

i) Production quantities budget (monthly)

ii) Sales quantities and sales revenue budgets (monthly)

iii) Finished goods closing stock budget (monthly)

iv) Direct materials cost budget (monthly)

v) Direct materials purchases budget (annual)

vi) Direct labour cost budget (annual)

Question 29.3 ***Pan-European Tours Ltd*** operate tours of the Rhine Valley. During the year, they operate twenty of these tours, using fifty-seater coaches, on which the load factor is 80% over the whole season.

In 19X1 they operated these tours with a profit of £20,000, made up as follows:

	£	£
Tour price: £175 per person		140,000
Costs:		
Hire of coach: £480 per week	9,600	
Fuel: 1,200 miles per tour at 10 mpg at £2 per gallon	4,800	
Driver: £120 per week	2,400	
Courier: £80 per week	1,600	
Ferries:	4,000	
Hotels: 6 nights including meals @ £15 per person per night	72,000	
Excursions to gasthofs: two excursions per person per tour	9,600	
Head Office Administration:		
Share of HO costs to these 20 Rhine Valley tours	16,000	120,000
		20,000

For next season, 19X2, the following changes in costs are expected:

Coach hire:	increase by 5%
Fuel:	increase of 10p per gallon
Driver:	wage increase of £6 per week
Courier:	wage increase of £4 per week
Ferries:	increase of 10%
Hotels:	increase of 4%
Excursions:	increase of £1 per excursion
HO charge:	increase of 5%
Selling price:	reduced to £155 per person to maintain demand.

No change is expected in the number of tours or the average load factor.

Required

i) Produce the budget for 19X2 for the Rhine Valley tours.

ii) Calculate the increase in the load factor necessary to maintain the same profit as in 19X1.

Objective test *(tick the appropriate box)*

i) Budgetary control is used in the following types of organisation:
   a) limited companies ☐
   b) charities ☐
   c) sole trader ☐
   d) any organisation ☐

ii) In a limited company, budgets are usually produced for:
   a) individuals ☐
   b) functions ☐
   c) costs and revenues ☐
   d) all of these ☐

iii) Budget periods may be for:
   a) a year ☐
   b) a month ☐
   c) a week ☐
   d) any period ☐

iv) Budgetary control is exercised by:
   a) building up budgets ☐
   b) meeting in budget committees ☐
   c) comparing budgeted and actual expenditure ☐
   d) taking action on adverse variances ☐

v) Budgets are used for:
   a) motivation ☐
   b) planning ☐
   c) control ☐
   d) all of these ☐

Chapter 30

Flexible budgets and standard costs

30.1 Objectives

At the end of this chapter you should be able to:

- define fixed and flexible budgets;
- understand the differences between fixed and flexible budgets;
- understand how cost behaviour affects the use of budgets;
- understand how standard costs are set and are used in cost control;
- be able to carry out simple variance analysis on direct labour and materials.

30.2 Introduction

In Chapter 29 we considered how budgets are drawn up and used. Budgets are essentially planning and control techniques, but possess a number of other advantages. Comparison is made for each item between the actual performance and that budgeted, and control is exercised by taking corrective action where a variance is adverse to an unacceptable degree.

The budgeting approach so far described is of taking a single fixed budget. However, this suffers from a major drawback when applied to a manufacturing environment. This drawback is that the budget for a particular budget period may be drawn up for a level of production or sales which is different from the level of activity actually achieved in that period. Consequently the variances which are calculated may not give a true indication of the success or failure to achieve budgeted performance. Variances may arise, particularly in variable costs, which are due to these different activity levels affecting the variable costs incurred.

30.3 Fixed budgets

A *fixed budget* is one which is prepared for a single level of activity, either production or sales as appropriate, which it is planned to achieve during a budget period. The problem which arises from the use of a fixed budget can be illustrated by the following example of a variable cost, direct materials.

Example

Fixed budget	Budgeted	Actual	Variance
Production units	1,000	1,500	
Direct material costs	£20,000	£28,750	£8,750 (A)*

*A = Adverse variance or over-spending

This comparison suggests an adverse variance or overspending of £8,750 in direct material costs. However it does not take into consideration the fact that direct material costs are variable costs, and therefore could be expected to increase in proportion to production increases. Here the actual level of activity differs from the budgeted level of activity, and therefore some proportion of the variance shown is due to the higher activity level.

Based on the budget, the manager is expected to incur direct material cost at a rate of £20 per unit of production. In producing 1,500 units the manager could be expected to incur 1,500 × £20 = £30,000 which is more than the actual expenditure, and yet this approach shows an overspending of £8,750.

The variance shown by a fixed budget comparison fails to provide a useful variance for variable costs where budgeted and actual activity levels differ.

30.4 Flexible budgets

A ***flexible budget*** is one which separates costs according to their different behavioural characteristics. It recognises that some costs are variable and others fixed. For the variable costs it provides a budget allowance based on the actual level of activity achieved during a budget control period, e.g. a month.This approach then enables useful variances to be calculated which are restricted to those controllable by the manager concerned.

Applying a flexible budgeting approach to the example above, a budget allowance column would be introduced so as to flex the budget for the variable items to accommodate an actual production level of 1,500 units.

Example

Flexible budget	Budgeted	Budget allowance	Actual	Variance
Production units	1,000	1,500	1,500	
Direct material costs	£20,000	£30,000	£28,750	£1,250 (F)*

*F = Favourable variance or over-spending

Because direct material costs are variable, the budget allowance column adjusts or flexes the original budget figure to allow for the higher level of production achieved. This is obtained by calculating a budgeted rate per unit, and multiplying by the actual number of units produced:

$$\text{Budgeted rate per unit} = \frac{£20{,}000}{1{,}000 \text{ units}} = £20$$

$$\text{Budget allowance} = £20 \times 1{,}500 \text{ units} = £30{,}000$$

Notice that in flexible budgeting the variance is always calculated by comparing the actual performance with the budget allowance.

30.5 The two approaches compared

Using the ***fixed*** budget basis, the overspending or adverse variance is £8,750. This would suggest that the manager in charge of direct materials is required to take some remedial action to bring material costs into line with budgeted levels. Such a conclusion would be wrong. This is because no account has been taken of differing budgeted and actual production levels and their effect on variable costs.

Where the budget allowance is calculated to take into consideration the ***variable*** nature of direct material costs and the higher level of actual output compared to that budgeted, a favourable variance of £1,250 results. This indicates that instead of corrective action being required, there has been a saving on the expenditure on direct materials after adjusting for higher production levels achieved.

Clearly the variance which arises as a result of the use of a flexible budget is much more useful for control purposes than that shown by a fixed budget because:

- ❒ the variance shown by the flexible budget is adjusted for different budgeted and actual activity levels, whereas the variance shown by the use of the fixed budget hides the truly adverse or favourable result;
- ❒ the variance shown by the flexible budget shows the variance which may be regarded as controllable by the manager responsible for that item of expenditure.

30.6 Other cost behaviour

The example of the operation of a flexible budgeting system shown above covers direct material costs which are clearly variable in behaviour.

The process of setting up a flexible budget is to consider each cost item individually and determine how it is likely to behave in practice as a result of changes in activity levels. This approach then determines the budget allowance for various activity levels which are likely to be met during the budget period.

Fixed costs

A fixed cost is one which, in the short term, remains unchanged in total irrespective of the level of activity, that is production or sales.

We saw from Chapter 28 that fixed costs behave in two main ways:

i) They remain unchanged over the whole range of output. For example, working at 50% capacity, the rent payable by a company is £40,000 per annum. At all levels of activity up to 100% the rent will remain at £40,000 and it is only when additional property is rented in order to increase capacity that the rent will increase.

ii) They change in steps as output changes. For example working at 50% capacity, a company requires one supervisor at £10,000 per annum. If activity increases to 70%, then an additional supervisor is needed at the same rate, and with output at 90% capacity one more supervisor needs to be recruited.

Semi-variable costs

A semi-variable cost is an item of cost which has both a variable and a fixed element in its make-up. For example, each salesman's remuneration is made up of a fixed basic salary of £15,000, plus a variable element, being commission, which is calculated at 2% of total sales value.

Example

E. Exmouth operates a system of flexible budgetary control. He has investigated each cost item and wishes to classify it as either fixed (F), variable (V), or semi-variable (SV) from the following costs incurred at two levels of activity, 50,000 units and 80,000 units respectively:

Budget for the year 19X1

Activity level		50%	80%	
Production units		50,000	80,000	
		£	£	
Direct costs:	Material	140,000	224,000	V
Overheads:	Rent	40,000	40,000	F
	Royalties	6,000	8,400	SV

Solution

If direct materials cost £140,000 for 50,000 units of production then, if behaving in a manner typical of variable costs, their cost for 80,000 units would be:

$$\frac{£140,000}{50,000} \times 80,000 = £224,000, \text{ thus confirming their variable nature.}$$

Rent is budgeted at the same level for both levels of activity, thus confirming rent as a fixed cost.

Royalties are clearly not a fixed cost as its total changes as activity changes. If it were a variable cost the cost for production of 80,000 units would be:

$$\frac{£6,000}{50,000} \times 80,000 = £9,600$$

As the royalty cost for 80,000 units is less than £9,600, this cost has a semi-variable characteristic.

You should now be able to attempt Question 30.1 and Task 30.1 at the end of this chapter.

Example

Assume that the actual level of activity achieved by *E. Exmouth* was 60,000 units of production or 60% of capacity and calculate a flexible budget allowance for that activity level for each cost item.

Solution

As direct materials is a variable cost, the budget allowance for 60,000 units would be:

$$\frac{£140,000}{50,000} \times 60,000 = £168,000$$

or

$$\frac{£224,000}{80,000} \times 60,000 = £168,000$$

As rent is a fixed cost over the whole range of output, the budget allowance would be £40,000 for any activity level.

As under these circumstances royalties are a semi-variable cost, it is necessary to analyse the cost into its fixed and variable elements (see Chapter 28). Thus:

1. The total cost of Royalties for each of the two activity levels is shown.
2. The change in cost which arises due to the change in production:

	Production (units)	Total royalties (£)
	80,000	8,400
	50,000	6,000
Change	30,000	2,400

3. Variable cost per unit = $\frac{£2,400}{30,000} = £0.08$

4. The total variable element for each level of production becomes:

Production units	Total variables
80,000 × £0.08 =	£6,400
50,000 × £0.08 =	£4,000

5. Fixed cost element becomes:

Production units	Total royalties	–	Total variables	=	Total fixed
	£		£		£
80,000	8,400		6,400		2,000
50,000	6,000		4,000		2,000

The budget allowance for royalties at the 60,000 units level of output would be therefore:

Fixed cost element	£2,000
Variable cost element:	
60,000 units × £0.08 =	£4,800
Budget allowance	£6,800

> *You should now be able to attempt Question 30.2 at the end of this chapter.*

30.7 Standard costing

Standard costing, like ***budgetary control,*** is a management reporting and control system where levels of expenditure and income are set in advance and the difference between those levels and what is actually achieved is reported to management for action. Standard costing is linked to ***budgetary control*** in a manufacturing company because the figures which make up the budgets may also be used in standard costing and vice-versa. The major difference between standard costing and budgetary control is that standard costing tends to be applied to individual products and processes whereas budgetary control is applied to departments, ***budget centres*** and the business as a whole.

30.8 Direct cost variances

As we have seen the product ***direct costs*** of a manufacturing organisation are normally direct materials and direct wages. The reasons for over- or under-spending on either of these costs is based on the simple concept that:

Total cost of material or wages = quantity used × unit price

Differences between standard and actual total cost must be due to variations in either quantity used or unit price, or a combination of both.

30.9 Direct materials variances

Predetermined standards are set both for the level of ***direct material*** consumption for a given volume of production, and also for the price allowed per unit of direct material. The price standards are based on the price per unit expected to be paid or budgeted, for the level of purchases projected, over the period for which the standard is to be applied.

In general, any variations in price is regarded as the responsibility of the purchasing manager or buyer and any variations in the volume or quantity of materials consumed is regarded as the responsibility of the production manager. However, due to the interdependence of price and usage, responsibilities may be difficult to assign to specific functional heads. The calculation of the variances is as follows:

Direct materials price variance

This is calculated by the formula:

(SP – AP)AQ

where SP = standard price per unit of direct material

AP = actual price per unit of direct material

AQ = actual quantity of direct material consumed or purchased

The price variance may be calculated at the stage when the materials are purchased or when the materials are issued to production.

The formula may be expanded to:

(SP × AQ) – (AP × AQ)

where AP × AQ equals the actual cost of direct materials consumed or purchased as appropriate.

Direct materials usage variance

This is calculated by the formula:

(SQ – AQ)SP

where SQ = standard quantity of direct material allowed for the actual level of production achieved

AQ = actual quantity of direct material consumed

SP = standard price per unit of direct material

Direct wages variances

The same principles apply to the calculation of direct wages variances as are applied to the direct material variances. Standards are established for the rate of pay to be paid for the production of particular products and the labour time taken for their production. The standard time taken is expressed in ***standard hours***, which then becomes a measure of output. For example, if the standard direct labour hours allowed to produce a table is, say, 10 hours, then each time a table is produced 10 standard hours work will have been produced, irrespective of the actual time taken. By the comparison of standard hours allowed (or standard hours produced) and actual time taken, labour efficiency can be assessed. In practice, standard times are established by work, time and method study techniques.

Direct wages rate of pay variance

This is calculated by the formula:

(SR – AR)AH

where SR = standard rate per hour of direct labour

AR = actual rate per hour of direct labour

AH = actual number of direct labour hours worked

The formula may be expanded to:

(SR × AH) – (AR × AH)

where AR × AH equals the actual direct wages cost incurred.

Direct wages efficiency variance

This is calculated by the formula:

(SH – AH)SR

Where SH = standard direct labour hours allowed for the actual level of output achieved

AH = actual direct labour hours worked

SR = standard rate per hour for direct labour

Total cost variances

In the cases of both direct materials and direct wages the total cost variance is obtained from the formula:

SC – AC

where SC = the standard cost of the actual production, and

AC = the actual cost of the actual production

Note that as direct materials and direct wages costs are both treated as variable costs, under the rules of flexible budgeting described earlier in this chapter the standards are based on the actual level of activity or production achieved rather than that budgeted.

Example

Motorway Signs Ltd budgets to produce 10,000 standard signs each quarter. It operates a system of standard costing and flexible budgets for labour and materials, and its standard costs per sign are:

	£
Materials: 16 square metres @ £2 per square metre	32
Labour: 12 hours @ £4 per hour	48
Standard prime cost	80

For the first quarter of the year 7,500 standard signs were produced, and the actual costs incurred were:

		£
Materials:	125,000 square metres of material	252,000
Labour:	91,000 hours	313,500
Total actual prime cost		565,500

Required

Calculate the direct material and labour variances for the quarter, and reconcile standard and actual costs.

Solution

		£	£
Standard cost of the actual output: 7,500 signs at £80 per sign			600,000
Direct material price variance: (SP × AQ) – (AP × AQ) = (£2 × 125,000) – £252,000	=	2,000 (A)	
Direct material usage variance: (SQ – AQ)SP = [(7,500 × 16) – 125,000] £2	=	10,000 (A)	
Total direct material cost variance: SC – AC = (7,500 × £32) – £252,000	=	12,000 (A)	
Direct labour rate of pay variance: (SR × AH) – (AR × AH) = (£4 × 91,000) – £313,500	=	50,500 (F)	
Direct labour efficiency variance: (SH – AH)SR = [(7,500 × 12) – 91,000] £4	=	4,000 (A)	
Total direct labour cost variance: SC– AC = (7,500 × £48) – £313,500	=	46,500 (F)	
Total prime cost variance: SC – AC = (7,500 × £80) – £565,000	=		34,500 (F)
Actual cost of the actual output			565,500

Notice that at no point of the answer is the budgeted level of production (10,000 units) used. The budget allowance for the variable items is always flexed to take into consideration the actual level of activity.

You should now be able to attempt Task 30.2 and Questions 30.3 and 30.4 at the end of this chapter.

30.10 Summary

Fixed budgets suffer from the drawback that they are produced for a single level of activity, whereas the level of activity actually achieved will almost certainly differ from that budgeted. As a consequence, the variances revealed by fixed budgets are less useful for control purposes.

Flexible budgets overcome this problem by calculating a budget allowance for each cost item for the actual level of activity achieved. This is carried out by classifying each budget item according to its cost behavioural characteristics and determining whether it is a ***fixed, variable,*** or ***semi-variable cost*** over the possible levels of output.

The actual expenditure is then compared with a budget cost allowance appropriate to actual output levels, and differences between the two established. These ***variances*** are more useful for control purposes than those shown under a fixed budget as they take account of variations which almost inevitably arise between budgeted and actual levels of activity.

Standard costs are used for the control of costs and the measurement of performance in the production of products and the operation of processes. They are used in a way which is similar to the way in which flexible budgets are used, in that they are flexed to take into consideration actual levels of production achieved.

You should now be able to attempt Task 30.3 and the Objective Test at the end of this chapter.

Student activities

Task 30.1 You are employed in a small company where fixed budgets are used. Write a report to the managing director explaining why flexible budgets might be better.

Task 30.2 Keep a record of the number and price of any one particular item you consume in a month. This could be a favourite chocolate bar or your usual drink. By multiplying the number by the cost per item you will arrive at the total cost. Imagine that the price has been increased by 25%, but the number you consume decreases by 10% per month. Calculate the direct materials price and usage variances.

Task 30.3 Your friend is a highly paid marketing consultant and has been asked by a local company to investigate their financial controls. Her accounting knowledge is weak and she has told you that she does not know whether to recommend a standard costing system. Make a list of the questions you would required answered before you could advise her.

Question 30.1 *E. Exmouth* operates a system of flexible budgetary control. He has investigated each cost item and wishes to classify it as either fixed (F), variable (V), or semi-variable (SV) from the following costs incurred at two levels of activity, 50,000 units and 80,000 units respectively:

Budget for the year 19X1

		50%	80%	Classification
Activity level				
Production units		**50,000**	**80,000**	
		£	**£**	
Direct costs	Labour	210,000	336,000	
	Expenses	20,000	32,000	
Overheads	Rates	20,000	20,000	
	Depreciation	14,000	16,400	
	Supervision*	10,000 *	20,000	
	Insurances	4,000	4,000	
	Indirect wages	21,000	29,400	
	Maintenance	42,000	60,000	
	Cleaning	10,000	10,000	
	Canteen	30,000	42,000	
	Consumables	5,000	8,000	
	Power	5,000	7,400	
	Administration	35,000	35,000	

* Represents 1 supervisor. An additional supervisor at the same rate required when activity level reaches 60%.

Question 30.2 Using the data for *E. Exmouth* in Question 30.1 above, and the same approaches as those used in the chapter, determine the budget allowance for 60,000 units of output.

Question 30.3 *Perth Transport Company* has set standards for the distribution of a client's products. The standard for a round trip is:

Driver's wages: £5 per hour
Time allowed: 9 hours
Fuel consumption: 74 litres
Fuel cost: 35 pence per litre

In the month of June the actual wage costs for making 21 round trips was £912, and the fuel consumed cost £702. In June, there had been a wage increase of 20% per hour, and the price of fuel had been increased to 40 pence per litre.

Required

Calculate the fuel price and usage variances, and the wages rate of pay and efficiency variances for the month of June.

Question 30.4 *Amsterdam Silver Products* manufacture silver miniature coats-of-arms for which the standard prime cost is:

	£
Labour: 10 hours @ £8 per hour	80
Silver: 10 grams at £5 per gram	50
Total standard prime cost	130

The budgeted production is 1,000 units per month, but in the month of December, due to holidays, the production only reached 900 units and the actual costs were:

	£
Labour: 9,250 hours	72,150
Silver: 8,650 grams	41,520

Required

Calculate the possible variances, and give possible reasons for them.

Question 30.5 *Wooden Toys Ltd*, who manufacture a range of toys, operate a standard costing system for the product direct costs. The standard costs of a toy house are as follows:

	£
Materials (9 square metres @ £2)	18
Wages (6 hours @ £3.50)	21
Prime cost per unit	39

The company budgeted to produce 1,200 units in the last quarter, but the actual production was 1,345 units, and the actual costs incurred amounted to:

	£
Materials (11,900 square metres)	25,320
Wages (8,200 hours)	46,200
	71,520

Required

Calculate the cost variances and draw up a statement reconciling the standard and actual costs of production for the quarter.

Objective test *(tick the appropriate box)*

i) When fixed budgets are used, the variance is calculated by determining the difference between:

   a) the budget allowance and the original budget ☐

   b) the actual expenditure and the budget allowance ☐

   c) the actual expenditure and the original budget ☐

   d) none of these ☐

ii) When flexible budgets are used, the variance is calculated by determining the difference between:

   a) the budget allowance and the original budget ☐

   b) the actual expenditure and the budget allowance ☐

   c) the actual expenditure and the original budget ☐

   d) none of these ☐

iii) The major drawback with fixed budgets is that:

   a) they are drawn up for a single level of activity only ☐

   b) they cannot show the differences between budgeted and actual cost ☐

   c) they can never be used for cost control purposes ☐

   d) they are drawn up for the short term only ☐

iv) Flexible budgets can only be used where:

   a) the actual level of activity is uncertain ☐

   b) production and sales are equal ☐

   c) costs are classified according to cost behaviour ☐

   d) a fixed budget is impossible to construct ☐

v) In standard costing, the materials usage variance is:

   a) the budgeted consumption less actual consumption ☐

   b) the budgeted consumption for the actual production levels less actual consumption, both at actual cost ☐

   c) the budgeted consumption for the budgeted production levels less the actual consumption, both at actual cost ☐

   d) the budgeted consumption for the actual production levels less the actual consumption, both at standard cost ☐

Assignment G

Westbank Foods Ltd

Context

Westbank Foods Ltd is a manufacturer and canner of foods and drinks. One of the company's lines is cartons of pure orange juice which is packed into boxes and sold through wholesalers.

The company has a system of budgetary control and standard costing, and you, as the assistant in the cost office, have been asked to explain the cost differences which arose during a particular day's production. The oranges are processed and packed by automatic machinery which needs only one operator at any time to set it up, feed it with oranges, and supervise the production. The budgeted production is 1,200 boxes per day, and the standard cost of one box is as follows:

		£
Oranges:	50kg @ 6p per kg	3.00
Labour:	0.5 minute per box @ £4.80 per hour	0.04
Fixed overhead:	(based on direct labour hours)	
	0.5 minute @ £24 per hour	0.20
		3.24

The overhead charge of £24 per hour was calculated originally by dividing the budgeted overhead of £240 per day by 10 hours, which is the budgeted time for producing 1,200 boxes at ½ minute per box.

On the day in question, only 1,000 boxes were produced, and the actual cost was as follows:

		£
Oranges:	45,000kg @ 7p per kg	3,150
Labour:	10 hours @ £5.40 per hour	54
Fixed overhead:	(based on latest cost levels)	225
		3,429

Student activities

Write a memorandum to the general manager explaining the differences between the planned and actual costs. Your memorandum should include calculations of the following variances:

Oranges: price
usage or consumption
Labour: rate of pay
efficiency
Overhead: expenditure
volume

Write a brief note on each variance of the possible reasons for the variance arising. You may make any relevant assumptions you wish about what troubles arose that day at the packing plant.

Format

A memorandum to the general manager, with tables of data with supporting calculations.

Objectives

The student should show an understanding and appreciation of:

- budgets
- standard costing
- flexible budgets
- variance analysis

References

Chapters 27, 28, 29, 30 and (for overhead variances) 32.

Using costs for total costing

This section (Chapters 31 and 32) considers how costs are built up into a total cost of each part, product or service produced by the organisation. Some assessment of the total cost of producing a product is necessary to help management fix product prices which will enable all the costs of the business to be met and a profit made. Some indication of profitability by product is also useful in determining whether the cost of resources used in the production of each product is recovered in the prices charged.

Chapter 31 covers the first stage in building up a production cost to products by looking at the allocation of product direct costs to products called cost units, and overheads which are departmental or section direct costs to cost centres. Any other overheads are apportioned to cost centres by using bases of apportionment.

The overhead costs which are charged to production cost centres are subsequently charged to products by a number of alternative methods. These techniques are considered in Chapter 32.

Chapter 31

Cost allocation and apportionment

31.1 Objectives

At the end of this chapter you should be able to:

- understand the principles of cost allocation and apportionment;
- understand how cost allocation and apportionment enables total product costing to take place;
- define terms such as cost unit and cost centre;
- appreciate some of the drawbacks which accompany any system of cost allocation and apportionment.

31.2 Introduction

Where a range of different products is produced in a single factory, a cost and management accounting system is required in order to provide answers to a number of important questions, such as:

- What is the cost of operating each section or department of the business?
- How can individual managers in the organisation be made responsible for particular costs?
- What is the cost of producing each of the products manufactured?
- What prices should be charged for each product in order to give an adequate profit margin, both for the particular product and overall?
- How can costs be estimated so that each of the above questions can be considered in advance?

Cost allocation and apportionment are the first steps in answering these questions. The ultimate aim of the costing system may be to build up a cost of production of each of the products produced.

31.3 Cost units

A ***cost unit*** is any item, product, sub-assembly, part or service produced by the organisation for which it is desired to provide a cost per unit. Cost units are often the final products which are manufactured by the organisation.

Example

Industry	Cost unit
Vehicle manufacture	Vehicle
Aerospace	Aircraft
Shipbuilding	Vessel
General engineering	Job

The cost unit is not necessarily restricted to the final product of the organisation, however. If the final cost unit is either big or complex, the costing system may be organised so that the costing of intermediate parts or sub-assemblies takes place. In these cases, each part costed is treated as a cost unit. For example, in manufacturing a motor vehicle, a final cost unit, the engine, the gearbox, the body and the electrical parts may be treated as separate cost units if manufactured by the same organisation.

Where small units of output are produced, it is usual to combine the output into batches so that the cost unit does not have a cost which is so small as to be immeasurable.

Example

Industry	Cost unit
Pen manufacture	1,000 pens
Brick making	Batch
Newsprint production	Tonne
Paper bag manufacture	1,000 bags

You should now be able to attempt Question 31.1 at the end of this chapter.

31.4 Cost classification by product cost

In Chapter 27 it was demonstrated that where costs are classified according to ***product*** or ***cost unit***, the cost of production is made up as follows:

		£
Direct Costs:	Materials	X
	Wages	X
	Expenses	X
Prime cost:		X
Indirect costs or Overheads:		
	Production	X
Production Cost:		X

In building up a total cost there is also the addition of other overheads which are administration, selling, distribution and, in some cases, research. However the process of allocation and apportionment is primarily concerned with production costs and therefore is more often applied to production overheads rather than any of the other overhead categories.

31.5 Cost centres

As well as collecting costs by ***cost unit***, a manufacturer may also wish to build up the cost of particular sections or departments of the business. These sections or departments are known as ***cost centres***. A ***cost centre*** is any part of the business for which costs are collected. It may be a single factory, a department or section, a single machine or group of machines, an individual or a group of individuals.

In a business producing model cars, for example, the production processes may be organised into moulding, machining, and assembly departments. The management may wish to know the cost of running each of these for the purpose of making managers responsible for their own costs (***cost control***) and to identify expensive processes where savings might be made. There are two types of cost centre: ***production cost centres*** and ***service cost centres***.

Production cost centres are those cost centres in which part of the production process is carried out.

Example

Product	**Production cost centre**
Model cars	Moulding, machining, assembly
Furniture - wooden	Preparation, shaping, assembly, finishing
- metal	Moulding, welding, assembly, finishing
Yachts	Hull, spars, fitting out, finishing
Books	Typesetting, printing, binding, cutting

You should now be able to attempt Task 31.1 and Question 31.2 at the end of this chapter.

Service cost centres are those cost centres which are incidental to the production processes, although necessary for it to take place. For example, a canteen, stores, boiler house, maintenance department. Notice that the service cost centres are incidental to production in the sense that the products or cost units are not produced by them. However, service cost centres are often just as important and necessary to the carrying out of production as the production cost centres themselves.

Any costs which are incurred or charged to service cost centres must be apportioned subsequently to production cost centres to be incorporated in the cost of the product produced.

31.6 Cost allocation

Cost allocation is carried out where a cost can easily be identified with, and charged to, a particular ***cost unit*** or ***cost centre***. Therefore it is not necessary to analyse the cost on an arbitrary basis in order to reflect the use of that cost item by the cost unit or cost centre.

Direct costs

In costing the cost unit, direct costs are usually ***allocated*** to the cost unit because they can easily be identified with it. In any costing system, costs are established by analysing documentation which the business either receives from outside or generates internally. The documents which enable the business to allocate the costs to cost units are as follows:

Cost	**Documentation**
Direct wages	Time sheets, clock cards, computer time records, job cards, work tickets
Direct materials	Invoices received, material requisitions, stores issue notes, stores transfer notes, stores returns notes, direct charge vouchers, goods received notes
Direct expenses	Invoices received, direct charge vouchers, time sheets, work tickets

Production overheads

In charging production overheads to cost units it is not possible to use the same analysis as that used for direct costs. For example, where a general purpose machine is producing a range of different products it is not possible to determine directly how much rent or rates or insurances should be borne by product A as opposed to product B. This is because, in general, production overhead costs, unlike product direct costs, are not incurred by product. Production overheads, therefore, cannot be ***allocated*** to products, but must go through a more roundabout system to charge them to the cost units.

31.7 Allocation of production overheads

Although it is not usually possible to ***allocate*** production overheads to products or ***cost units***, it is often possible to ***allocate*** some of these costs to ***cost centres***. This may be done where the costs are directly attributable to a cost centre. For example, where a maintenance facility exists for the sole use of the machine shop, then this cost could be described as a ***cost centre direct cost***. This is because its cost is incurred on behalf of, and therefore can be traced to, the machine shop. Therefore it is ***allocated*** to the machine shop even though maintenance is classified as an overhead. Similarly any depreciation of machine shop plant and machinery can be ***allocated*** to the machine shop cost centre as a cost centre direct cost. This is because such depreciation is easily traceable to each individual piece of equipment in the machine shop.

Some overhead costs, however, cannot be treated as cost centre direct costs as they are shared by a number of cost centres. These costs are ***cost centre indirect costs***, and they require ***cost apportionment*** to enable them to be charged to cost centres.

31.8 Apportionment of production overheads

Cost apportionment is the charging of proportions of each indirect or overhead cost item to ***cost centres*** using an appropriate ***basis of apportionment*** so as to reflect the relative use of that cost item by each cost centre.

Example

Overhead cost item	Basis of apportionment to cost centres
Rates	Area or volume occupied
Rent	Area or volume occupied
Insurance of machinery	Capital values of machinery
Insurance of buildings	Area or volume occupied
Supervision	Number of personnel employed
Depreciation of buildings	Area or volume occupied
Indirect wages	Number of personnel employed
Power	Machine hours, horse power, or horsepower/hours
Cleaning	Area occupied
Light and heat	Area or volume occupied
Canteen	Number of personnel

Notice that with a number of overhead costs there is a choice of the basis of apportionment. In each case the most appropriate one should be chosen, and the most appropriate basis of apportionment should have the following characteristics:

- It should be related in some way to the manner in which the cost is incurred by each of the cost centres benefiting from its use.
- It should reflect the use by the cost centre of the resources represented by the overhead cost.
- It should be a basis which is relatively easily obtainable from the records of the organisation.
- It should apportion the costs which are shared by the cost centres in a way which could be described as fair, reasonable or equitable. Notice that because the methods of apportionment are arbitrary, and alternative methods can be used for the same cost, then they cannot necessarily be described as 'accurate' or 'correct'.

Example

L. Lord operates a small business manufacturing cricket bats and tennis raquets. There are three production cost centres, namely machining, assembly and finishing departments. The overheads budget for next year is set out below, together with the cost centre details, and L. Lord asks you to determine the annual cost of running each production cost centre.

Annual overheads budget

	£
Rent	20,000
Rates	40,000
Consumables	10,000
Power	4,750
Cleaning	6,000
Light and heat	2,120
Maintenance	10,200
Depreciation – Machinery	8,000
– Buildings	15,900
Indirect Wages	19,600
Canteen	23,800
Insurance – Machinery	4,250
– Buildings	5,300
Supervision	42,000
Total	211,920

Cost centre details

Basis	Machining	Assembly	Finishing	Total
Area (square metres)	5,000	2,000	3,000	10,000
Volume (cubic metres)	25,000	10,000	18,000	53,000
Capital values (£'000)	70,000	10,000	5,000	85,000
Number of employees	10	20	5	35
Machinery (hp/hours)	8,750	350	400	9,500
Maintenance (£)	9,500	500	200	10,200
Depreciation of machinery (£)	6,500	1,000	500	8,000
Consumables (£)	8,000	1,000	1,000	10,000

Solution

The total overhead cost of each cost centre can be obtained by constructing an overhead cost analysis statement, sometimes also referred to as an overhead cost distribution summary. This statement allocates costs to each cost centre if they are cost centre direct costs. If they are cost centre indirect costs then they are apportioned or shared between the cost centres using a suitable basis of apportionment.

L. Lord
Overhead cost analysis statement

Item	£	Basis	Cost centres Machining	Assembly	Finishing
			£	£	£
Rent	20,000	Area	10,000	4,000	6,000
Rates	40,000	Area	20,000	8,000	12,000
Consumables	10,000	Actual	8,000	1,000	1,000
Power	4,750	Hp/hours	4,375	175	200
Cleaning	6,000	Area	3,000	1,200	1,800
Light and heat	2,120	Volume	1,000	400	720
Maintenance	10,200	Actual	9,500	500	200
Depreciation – Machinery	8,000	Actual	6,500	1,000	500
– Building	15,900	Volume	7,500	3,000	5,400
Indirect wages	19,600	Number of employees	5,600	11,200	2,800

		£		£	£	£
Canteen		23,800	Number of employees	6,800	13,600	3,400
Insurance	– Machinery	4,250	Capital values	3,500	500	250
	– Building	5,300	volume	2,500	1,000	1,800
Supervision		42,000	personnel	12,000	24,000	6,000
Total		211,920		100,275	69,575	42,070

The items which have been marked actual have been ***allocated*** to cost centres as the overhead is directly attributable to those cost centres without apportionment being necessary. All other items have been charged proportionately to cost centres using a suitable ***basis of apportionment***. For example, rent has been apportioned using floor area occupied as a basis.

Example

$$\text{Total cost to be apportioned} \times \frac{\text{Each cost centre's share of the basis}}{\text{Total apportionment basis}}$$

$$\text{Machining} = £20{,}000 \times \frac{5{,}000 \text{ square metres}}{10{,}000 \text{ square metres}} = £10{,}000$$

$$\text{Assembly} = £20{,}000 \times \frac{2{,}000 \text{ square metres}}{10{,}000 \text{ square metres}} = £4{,}000$$

$$\text{Finishing} = £20{,}000 \times \frac{3{,}000 \text{ square metres}}{10{,}000 \text{ square metres}} = £6{,}000$$

Alternative appropriate bases of apportionment may be used which will give different results from those obtained above. For example, building volume may be just as appropriate for the apportionment of rent, rates and cleaning, whereas building area could have been used for light and heat, building depreciation and building insurance. It is important to find and use a basis of apportionment most appropriate for the cost being apportioned.

You should now be able to attempt Task 31.2 and Questions 31.3 and 31.4 at the end of this chapter.

31.9 Summary

The use of the techniques of ***allocation*** and ***apportionment*** are important steps in charging the production overhead costs to departments or ***cost centres*** of the business. This is done:

- to determine the cost of operating each cost centre;
- to determine how much production overhead should be borne by each product or cost unit worked on by each production cost centre. (This aspect will be covered later in Chapter 32.)

Product direct costs of wages, material and (occasionally) expenses can be ***allocated*** to ***cost units*** as they can be traced relatively easily to products by the analysis of documentation such as invoices, stores issue notes and time sheets.

Indirect product costs or ***production overheads*** cannot be charged directly to cost units as they are generally not incurred on a product basis.

However, some production overheads can be allocated to cost centres as cost centre direct costs where they can be related to cost centres as costs solely incurred by them. Otherwise, where overhead costs are shared by cost centres, they need to be ***apportioned***. This is achieved by using a basis of apportionment which reflects the use by the cost centres of the resources represented by the overhead cost.

Alternative appropriate bases of apportionment may be used, which will necessarily give a different total overhead cost for each cost centre when compared with the result achieved by the use of other bases.

You should now be able to attempt the Objective Test at the end of this chapter.

Student activities

Task 31.1 Draw up a list of the cost centres that you consider are appropriate for the organisation where you work or study.

Task 31.2 The manager of the company where you work has always allocated the factory rent on the basis of the number of employees occupying the various departments. Write him a memo explaining the limitations of this basis and propose alternatives.

Question 31.1 Suggest suitable cost units for the following industries:

i) Shirt manufacturer

ii) Dairy

iii) Oil refinery

iv) Box manufacturer

v) Pencil manufacturer

vi) Housebuilder

vii) Bridgebuilder

viii) Television manufacturer

ix) Zinc smelter

x) Paint producer

Question 31.2 Refer to Question 31.1. Suggest possible production cost centres which might exist in the industries for which you have already identified the cost units. Assume that some of the production for the housebuilder and the bridgebuilder is in prefabricated sections manufactured in a factory.

Question 31.3 Redraft the Overhead Cost Analysis Statement shown in Section 31.8 of the chapter using building volume as a basis of apportionment for rent, rates and cleaning, and building area as a basis of apportionment for light & heat, building depreciation and building insurance. Round all figures to the nearest £.

What difference does it make to the total costs of each cost centre?

In what way are the differences important to the managers in charge of each cost centre?

Are the totals of each of the costs which have caused the differences to arise controllable by the cost centre managers?

If the answer to the previous question is 'yes', explain how.

If the answer to the previous question is 'no', who is capable of controlling these costs?

Question 31.4 ***Durban Production Ltd***'s factory has three cost centres, machining, fabrication and finishing, and the company's budgets for next year include the following total production overheads:

	£
Cleaning	10,000
Rent and rates	40,000
Building insurance	1,000
Indirect labour	12,000
Machinery depreciation	11,000
Supervision	50,000
Material handling	22,000
Power	50,500
Canteen	50,000
	246,500

The three cost centres have the following characteristics:

	Machining	Fabrication	Finishing
Machine horsepower	100	5	–
Machine hours	5,000	1,000	–
Number of personnel	15	5	5
Area (square metres)	1,600	1,000	1,400
Value of materials (£)	1,000,000	50,000	50,000
Indirect labour hours	3,000	1,500	1,500
Capital values of machinery (£)	100,000	5,000	5,000

Required

Draw up the overheads budget for each cost centre for the year.

Question 31.5 *Multiproducts Ltd* produces three products, basic, extra and deluxe. The profit and loss account for the year is as follows:

Multiproducts Ltd
Profit and loss account for the year ending 31st December 19X2

	£	£
Sales		400,000
Production cost of sales		275,000
Gross profit		125,000
Selling and distribution:		
Advertising	20,000	
Salesmen's costs	5,275	
Sales office expenses	3,150	
Delivery	15,750	
Packing	3,150	
Storage	1,575	
Administration	10,000	
Credit control	1,050	
		59,950
Net profit		65,050

The following bases are used for the apportionment of revenue and costs between products:

	Basic	Extra	Deluxe
Sales (£)	50,000	150,000	200,000
Production cost (% of sales value)	70%	60%	75%
Advertising (proportion per product)	25%	25%	50%
Salesmen's costs	as a percentage of sales value		
Sales office expenses	as a percentage of sales value		
Credit control (orders received)	100	120	200
Delivery, packaging, storage (packages delivered)	5,000	6,000	10,000
Administration	as a percentage of sales value		

Required

Prepare a statement to show the net profit made by each product based on the apportionments shown.

Objective test *(tick the appropriate box)*

i) A cost centre may be:

a) a product ☐

b) a sub-assembly ☐

c) a service ☐

d) none of these ☐

ii) Costs must be allocated to a cost centre or cost unit if:

a) they are indirect costs ☐

b) they are direct costs ☐

c) they are production overheads ☐

d) they are other overheads ☐

iii) Costs must be apportioned to a cost centre if:

a) they are indirect costs ☐

b) they are direct costs ☐

c) they are shared costs ☐

d) they cannot be allocated ☐

iv) The reasons for charging costs to cost centres are:

a) to determine the costs of operating a cost centre ☐

b) to enable overheads to be charged to products ☐

c) neither of these ☐

d) both of these ☐

v) A cost unit may be:

a) a department ☐

b) a factory ☐

c) neither of these ☐

d) both of these ☐

Chapter 32

Overhead cost absorption

32.1 Objectives

At the end of this chapter you should be able to:

- ❒ understand what is meant by overhead cost absorption;
- ❒ understand how total production costs are charged to products;
- ❒ use alternative absorption methods;
- ❒ appreciate the advantages and disadvantages of each method;
- ❒ understand simple production overhead variance analysis.

32.2 Introduction

In Chapter 31 we saw how direct costs (prime costs) are allocated to products or cost units. However, this is not possible with production overheads because overheads are not generally incurred per product. For example, it is not possible to calculate how much factory rent should be charged a product in quite the same way as direct materials can be, so we charge production overheads to the product in a more roundabout way.

As already explained, the first stage in this process is to either ***allocate*** or ***apportion*** the overheads to cost centres. You should make sure that you thoroughly understand the contents of Chapter 31 before proceeding. In this chapter we are going to look at how the overhead costs are now transferred from the production cost centres to the products or cost units which are made in those cost centres. The method which is used to carry out this process is known as ***overhead cost absorption.***

32.3 Cost absorption

Cost absorption is a costing technique in which the production overheads, having been charged to production cost centres by the techniques of allocation or apportionment, are transferred to (***absorbed*** by) the cost units or products produced by those cost centres.

In order to charge the total costs of the production cost centre to the cost units, we need to calculate a rate for each cost centre known as the ***overhead cost absorption rate*** (or ***overhead cost recovery rate***). These rates are always calculated before the accounting period starts and therefore must be based on budgeted figures. The general formula for the calculation of an overhead cost absorption rate is:

$$\frac{\text{Total budgeted production cost centre overheads}}{\text{Total budgeted production}}$$

Although it is usual to calculate cost absorption rates in advance for a year, and therefore both budgeted costs and production will be for that period, shorter period rates are used in some organisations.

The ***total budgeted production cost centre overheads*** can be obtained by budgeting these overheads in total for the period, and then applying the techniques of ***allocation*** and ***apportionment*** used in Chapter 31 to get budgeted totals for each production cost centre.

In absorption costing there are a number of ways of measuring production. This is because a single measure would not be appropriate to all the cost centres in a factory, because not only do the production methods vary but also the types of products being produced. For example, a common way of measuring production is to express it in numbers of units manufactured. This is acceptable if a cost centre is always producing a standard product. But if a production cost centre for half the period makes, say, 100 window frames, and the other half 55 door frames, we cannot say that the production has been 155 units. This is because window frames and door frames are so different in terms of size, time taken to produce and value, that they cannot reasonably be added together.

Another common way of measuring production is in direct labour hours worked. The use of this measure is certainly acceptable where a cost centre's production is carried out primarily by direct labour. This we would call a labour intensive cost centre. However, some cost centres are machine intensive and to measure production in direct labour hours would be less appropriate than using machine hours.

There are six ways in which production can be measured in order to calculate an overhead cost absorption rate. A different way of measuring production may be used (although not necessarily) for each production cost centre in the factory. If the total overhead costs are charged to cost centres by allocation and apportionment, then a separate rate for each cost centre will almost certainly be calculated.

32.4 Rate per unit of production

In some cost centres the production may be expressed as the number of units of production. This is an appropriate means of measuring output if all the items produced by the cost centre are similar in terms of size, time spent being worked on by the cost centre and other characteristics.

Example

In ***Barry's Furniture Company*** the assembly department assembles one type of standard chair. Next year's budgeted production overhead for the department is £162,500, and the total number of chairs budgeted to be produced is 100 per day over a year of 250 working days.

Required

Calculate the overhead absorption cost rate per chair necessary to absorb into the output the budgeted cost centre production overheads of the assembly department for the year.

Solution

Overhead absorption cost rate per chair

$$= \frac{\text{Total budgeted cost centre production overheads}}{\text{Total budgeted units}}$$

$$= \frac{£162{,}500}{100 \text{ chairs} \times 250 \text{ working days}}$$

$$= £6.50$$

This means that each chair produced by the assembly department must have £6.50 added to it in order to ensure that each unit bears a fair share of assembly department overheads.

32.5 Rate per direct labour hour

In the previous example the use of a rate per unit would not be possible if the assembly department produced both chairs and tables. A single unit of production cannot be applied as a measure to both tables and chairs because of their obviously different characteristics. For this reason, a method of measuring production must be found which can be applied to both chairs and tables, and at the same time reflect the method of production used in the assembly department.

Because the assembly department carries out a labour intensive activity, the use of ***direct labour hours*** is both a useful and appropriate method of measuring output.

Example

Barry's Furniture Company has decided to extend their product range and the assembly department produces both chairs and tables. The budgeted production overhead for the department is still £162,500, but the budgeted production is expected to be 10,000 chairs and 10,000 tables, each taking five and eight direct labour hours respectively.

Required

i) Calculate the overhead cost absorption rate per direct labour hour necessary to absorb the budgeted cost centre overheads of the assembly department into the output.

ii) Calculate the amount of assembly department production overheads which will be borne or absorbed by a chair and a table if the budgeted times are actually achieved.

Solution

i) Rate per direct labour hour

$$\frac{\text{Total budgeted cost centre production overheads}}{\text{Total budgeted direct labour hours}}$$

$$= \frac{£162{,}500}{(10{,}000 \times 5) + (10{,}000 \times 8)}$$

$$= \frac{£162{,}500}{130{,}000 \text{ direct labour hours}}$$

$$= £1.25 \text{ per direct labour hour}$$

ii) This means that each chair produced by the assembly department must have 5 hours x £1.25 = £6.25 added to it to ensure that each unit bears a fair share of assembly department overheads. A table would require 8 hours × £1.25 = £10 added to it for the same reason.

This approach charges more overhead to tables than to chairs, as the former tend to take longer to assemble. This illustrates the fairness of using the rate per direct labour hour. The longer a product is worked on in a department, the greater should be the share of overhead borne by that product.

The overhead charged to a chair using this method is £6.25, whereas using the rate per unit of production in the example in section 32.4 it was £6.50. This shows that the system of cost absorption is not intended to be an accurate system, but rather one that ensures that all the overhead is accounted for in the costing of the product in a fair way. Thus, the use of a different absorption technique may cause different levels of costs to be borne by the cost unit.

32.6 Rate per machine hour

In the previous example a rate per direct labour hour was advocated for the assembly department where a range of dissimilar products are produced and the method of production is labour intensive. Where a range of different products is produced or worked on in a cost centre, but the method of production is machine intensive, a more appropriate method of measuring production is in machine hours, and a production overhead cost absorption rate per machine hour is calculated.

You should now be able to attempt Question 32.1 at the end of this chapter.

32.7 Percentage on direct labour cost

If the rate per direct labour hour method is used for overhead absorption it is necessary to maintain a record of the direct labour hours spent on each job, product or cost unit. This is necessary in order to determine the share of overhead it should bear. As the direct costs are normally allocated to cost units (see Chapter 31) and direct costs include direct labour cost, an alternative absorption method is to use a ***percentage on direct labour cost.*** In this case, the production is being measured in terms of the direct labour cost incurred.

Example

Barry's Furniture Company is considering using a percentage on direct labour cost for the absorption of production overhead cost in the assembly department as an alternative to using the rate per direct labour hour shown in the example in section 32.5. The wages rates payable to the operators are £6 per hour when producing chairs and £7 per hour when producing tables.

Required

i) Calculate an overhead absorption rate for the assembly department using the percentage on direct labour cost method of overhead absorption.

ii) Calculate the amount of assembly department production overheads which would be borne or absorbed by a chair and a table if the budgeted times are actually achieved.

Solution

i) The budgeted production overhead for the assembly department is £162,500. The budgeted direct labour costs are:

	£
Chairs 50,000 hours × £6 per hour =	300,000
Tables 80,000 hours × £7 per hour =	560,000
	860,000

The overhead absorption rate:

$$= \frac{\text{Total budgeted cost centre production overheads} \times 100}{\text{Total budgeted direct labour hours}}$$

$$= \frac{£162{,}500 \times 100}{£860{,}000}$$

$$= 18.9\%$$

This means that whatever direct labour is charged to a product, 18.9% of direct labour cost will be added to the product cost in order to ensure that the product bears a share of the production overheads.

ii) Each product would bear production overhead of:

Chair: 5 hours × £6 × 18.9% = £5.67

Table: 8 hours × £7 × 18.9% = £10.58

The value of overhead charged to chairs and tables is based on the direct labour cost of each product. If the same labour hour rate is paid for the production of both products, then the overhead borne by each product would be identical to that shown in the solution in section 32.5 where a rate per direct labour hour was used. Prove this by recalculating the solution above, assuming that a labour rate of £6 per hour is paid for the production of both tables and chairs.

You should now be able to attempt Question 32.2 at the end of this chapter.

32.8 Percentage on direct material cost

As the prime costs are allocated to the cost units, it follows that direct material costs are also allocated as part of the prime costs. It is possible to use a ***percentage on direct material cost*** as a basis for absorbing production overhead costs into the product or cost unit.

The other methods discussed so far, with the exception of the rate per unit method, charge overheads to production on the basis of time taken. This ensures that those products which take a longer time to produce are charged with a greater share of overhead cost. This may be regarded as a fair and equitable basis of overhead absorption as production overheads also tend to be incurred on a time basis. However, the use of the percentage on direct material cost basis does not relate overheads charged to time taken, and this may be regarded as a major drawback in the use of this method. It may be used where material costs are a substantial element of total production cost.

You should now be able to attempt Question 32.3 at the end of this chapter.

32.9 Percentage on prime cost

Percentage on prime cost can also be used as a basis for absorbing production overheads, but may be criticised, as can the percentage on direct material cost method, since it is not entirely time based.

You should now be able to attempt Question 32.4 at the end of this chapter.

32.10 Cost absorbed

Having calculated the overhead cost absorption rate, the cost charged to production, known as the ***cost absorbed*** or ***cost recovered,*** is determined for each cost centre by using the formula:

Actual cost centre production × Cost centre overhead cost absorption rate

where the actual production is expressed in the same terms as the absorption rate is calculated. Thus, if an absorption rate is expressed as a rate per unit, then actual production is also expressed in units; if the rate is expressed as a percentage on direct labour cost, then production must also be expressed in labour cost terms.

Example

Beach Ltd's machine department overhead cost was budgeted at £264,000 for the year and the budgeted machine hours at 105,600. By the end of the year the actual production totalled 110,260 machine hours.

Required

Calculate the total overhead cost absorbed by the production for the year.

Solution

Absorption rate:

$$= \frac{£264{,}000}{105{,}600 \text{ machine hours}}$$

= £2.50 per machine hour

Cost absorbed for the year:

= 110,260 machine hours × £2.50

= £275,650

Beach Ltd absorbed more cost than was budgeted for the department, £275,650 compared to £264,000. This difference of £11,650 represents a gain which arose because the production expressed in machine hours was greater than budgeted. The extra 4,660 machine hours worked at the absorption rate of £2.50 per hour created the gain of £11,650. This gain is known as a ***cost over-absorption*** or ***cost over-recovery*** and represents an addition to the profits of the business.

Example

Ogmore Ltd's finishing department's production is measured in units and was budgeted to produce 120,000 units in the year just ended. The budgeted production overhead was £762,000 and actual production fell short of that budgeted by 18,000 units.

Required

Calculate Ogmore Ltd's overhead absorbed by the output of the finishing department for the year.

Solution

Finishing department overhead absorption rate:

$$= \frac{£762{,}000}{120{,}000 \text{ units}}$$

= £6.35 per unit

Finishing department overhead cost absorbed:

= (120,000 – 18,000) × £6.35

= £647,700

Ogmore Ltd's cost absorbed falls short of that budgeted by £114,300 (£762,000 – £647,700). This is made up of the 18,000 fewer units produced at £6.35 per unit (£114,300). This is known as an ***under-absorption*** or ***under-recovery*** of overhead cost and represents a reduction in the profits of the business.

You should now be able to attempt Questions 32.5 and 32.6 at the end of this chapter.

32.11 Stock valuation

Absorption costing is often used in manufacturing organisations to value at the end of an accounting period both the work in progress up to the stage of production reached and finished goods for inclusion in manufacturing accounts and profits and loss accounts.

You may recall in chapter 12 that SSAP 9 requires to be valued at the lower of cost or net realisable value. In valuing stocks of work in progress and finished goods, cost is normally regarded as total production cost. Total production cost is made up of the product direct costs of materials, labour and expenses plus the production overheads.

You can see that the overhead cost absorption system described in this chapter enables production overhead to be charged to products so that stock valuations at total production cost may be calculated at the end of an accounting period for inclusion in the organisation's accounts.

32.12 Simple overhead variance analysis

We have seen how a department's overhead cost budgeted is not necessarily the same as that absorbed, the difference arising because a different level of actual production is achieved compared with that budgeted. For instance, in the example of Beach Ltd in section 32.10 the overhead budgeted was £264,000 and that absorbed was £275,650, resulting in a gain of £11,650. Because this ***difference*** or ***variance*** is due to the actual production in machine hours exceeding the budgeted production in machine hours, it could be described as an ***activity*** or ***volume variance.***

There is yet another difference which could arise in Beach Ltd's machine department. Assume that at the end of the year the ***actual expenditure*** on production overheads was £270,000, which was £6,000 more than planned or budgeted.

We now have three items for the machine department or cost centre:

- Production overhead ***absorbed***: £275,650 (actual production × budgeted absorption rate)
- Production overhead ***budgeted***: £264,000 (budgeted production × budgeted absorption rate)
- Production overhead ***incurred***: £270,000 (actual overhead paid and accrued)

The difference between the overhead absorbed and overhead budgeted we have described already as an activity or ***volume variance*** of £11,650, being a gain or ***favourable variance***. The difference between the overhead budgeted and overhead incurred arises because there is an overspending of £6,000, therefore this is described as an ***unfavourable*** or ***adverse expenditure variance.***

We now have a ***total variance*** made up of the difference between the production overhead cost absorbed of £275,650 and the production overhead cost incurred of £270,000, namely £5,650 favourable. This can be analysed into a favourable activity or volume variance of £11,650 and an adverse expenditure variance of £6,000. This is shown in the following table.

Production overhead absorbed:	£275,650		
		Volume variance:	£11,650 (F)
Production overhead budgeted:	£264,000		
		Expenditure variance:	£6,000 (A)
Production overhead incurred:	£270,000		
Total variance:	(£275,650 – £270,000)		£5,650 (F)

These overhead variances are important to management because they show the financial results of different performance. If production is different from that budgeted this causes the activity or volume variance, and the expenditure variance occurs if actual expenditure is different from that planned.

You should now be able to attempt Tasks 32.1 and 32.2 and Questions 32.7-32.11 at the end of this chapter.

32.13 Summary

The process of ***cost absorption*** is the transfer of the department or cost centre production overheads to the product or cost unit by using cost absorption or recovery rates. The rates used are based on budgeted or predetermined figures and are calculated using the general formula:

$$\frac{\text{Total budgeted cost centre production overheads}}{\text{Total budgeted production}}$$

Alternative time based methods are:

- Rate per direct labour hour
- Rate per machine hour
- Percentage on direct labour cost

Other methods are:

- Rate per unit
- Percentage on direct material cost
- Percentage on prime cost

A single rate is calculated for each ***cost centre,*** but different methods may be used for each cost centre of the business depending on the characteristics of that cost centre; for example, whether it is machine or labour intensive. The cost centre costs are then absorbed into ***cost units*** by the general formula:

Actual cost centre production × Cost absorption rate

The actual production must be expressed in the same terms as the absorption rate is calculated:

- Number of direct labour hours worked
- Number of machine hours operated
- Direct labour cost incurred
- Number of units produced
- Direct material cost incurred
- Prime cost incurred

By comparing the departmental overhead absorbed with that budgeted, it is possible to establish a ***volume*** or ***activity variance.*** By comparing the departmental overhead budgeted with that actually incurred, it is possible to establish an ***expenditure variance.*** By comparing the departmental overhead absorbed with that incurred, it is possible to establish a ***total variance.***

The main difficulties experienced by students are:

- Confusing cost allocation, cost apportionment and cost absorption. Remember costs are allocated if they can be directly charged to a cost unit or a cost centre. Direct costs are usually allocated to cost units; production overheads are allocated to cost centres if they can be solely identified with it. Otherwise shared costs are apportioned between cost centres using a basis of apportionment. Total cost centre production overheads are then absorbed using one of the alternatives for each cost centre.
- Forgetting that the overhead cost absorption rates are based on budgeted figures and calculated in advance.
- Forgetting that actual costs absorbed are based on actual production x overhead cost absorption rates.
- Failing to express production in the correct way. E.g. in direct labour hours worked if a direct labour hour rate is used, in units if a rate per unit is used.
- Forgetting that a total variance is the difference between overhead absorbed and overhead incurred, and not the difference between the overhead budgeted and the actual overhead incurred.

You should now be able to attempt the Objective Test at the end of this chapter.

Student activities

Task 32.1 Draft a plan of the cost collection procedures necessary to determine the manufacturing cost of any product of your choice. The plan should include:

- a list of the costs incurred in the manufacture of the product;
- an appropriate classification of those costs;
- a list of the prime documents from which those costs are collected;
- details of how the costs are to be charged to the product, particularly where the product is one of a product range;
- consideration of alternative methods of treating some costs, where appropriate.

Task 32.2 A friend has opened a mountain bike repair shop. He is competent to undertake all types of repair work from mending a puncture to a complete overhaul. He has calculated that his total overheads will be £8,000 per annum and he intends to charge them to each job on the basis of the number of repairs he estimates he will do in a year. Write him a letter explaining the problems with his proposal and suggest an alternative.

Question 32.1 *Barry's Furniture Company* machining department is machine intensive and produces dining chairs, tables and rocking chairs. The budgeted production overheads for the department next year are £192,500 and the number of machine hours are budgeted at 55,000.

Required

i) Calculate the absorption rate to be applied per machine hour to charge production overheads to the output.

ii) If a dining chair normally takes 2 hours to machine, a dining table 5 hours and a rocking chair 6 hours, calculate the production overhead cost to be charged to each unit of product for the machine department.

Question 32.2 *Barry's Furniture Company* finishing department is labour intensive, and a percentage on direct labour cost is to be used to absorb the finishing department production overheads to cost units. The budgeted finishing department overheads are £219,350 for next year and the budgeted departmental direct labour costs are £107,000 for the same period.

Required

i) Calculate the production overhead cost absorption rate for the year for the finishing department.

ii) The finishing department handles the dining chairs and tables and rocking chairs. The normal direct labour cost incurred in the department by each product is as follows:

	Direct labour cost per unit
	£
Dining chair	6
Dining table	14
Rocking chair	20

Calculate the production overhead cost to be charged to each product using a percentage on direct labour cost as a method of cost absorption.

Hint: This method differs from the others previously considered so far because a percentage rate is used. In these cases the calculation is:

$$\frac{\text{Total budgeted cost centre production overheads} \times 100}{\text{Total budgeted direct labour costs}}$$

Question 32.3 *Barry's Furniture Company* is considering using a production overhead cost absorption rate for the finishing department using a percentage on direct material cost as a basis. The budgeted production overheads for the department are £219,350 and the budgeted total direct material costs are £109,675.

Required

i) Calculate the finishing department overhead cost absorption rate based on a percentage on direct material cost.

ii) The normal direct material costs for each of the three products is as follows:

	Direct material cost per unit
	£
Dining chair	4
Dining table	26
Rocking chair	10

Calculate the production overhead cost to be charged to each unit of product using a percentage on direct material cost absorption rate.

Question 32.4 Using the information for *Barry's Furniture Company* in Questions 32.2 and 32.3 above, calculate the production overhead cost rate for the finishing department based on a percentage on prime cost rate for absorbing overheads and determine the overhead to be absorbed by each product. There are no direct expenses. Work to the nearest £.

Question 32.5 *Nelson Machinery Ltd's* annual budget contains the following information:

Direct labour:		
Machine Shop	6,000 hours @ £5 per hour	
Paint Shop	9,000 hours @ £4 per hour	
Production overheads:		
Indirect labour	£5,000	
Salaries	£10,000	
Depreciation	£15,000	
Maintenance	£11,000	
Rent, rates etc	£21,000	
Cost centre information:		
	Machine shop	Paint shop
Plant valuation	£45,000	£30,000
Maintenance	£7,000	£4,000
Floor area	7,000 sq m	3,500 sq m
Number of employees	6	9

Required

i) Calculate an overhead absorption rate for each cost centre based on a rate per direct labour hour.

ii) From the following information, calculate the total production cost of jobs 42 and 99:

	Job 42	Job 99
Direct materials	£76	£124
Sub-contract work	£115	–
Direct wages:		
Machine shop	9 hours	11 hours
Paint shop	–	7 hours

Question 32.6 The assembly department at ***Tenby Ltd*** has budgeted overheads for the year at £210,000 and has chosen a percentage on direct labour cost as a method of overhead absorption, budgeting direct labour at £84,000 for the period. The assembly department's actual direct labour cost incurred was £75,000.

Required

i) Calculate the overhead absorbed for the year.

ii) Calculate the amount of over or under-recovery.

Question 32.7 If the finishing department at ***Ogmore Ltd's*** actual overhead expenditure was £792,000 (see section 32.10), calculate the volume, expenditure and total variances for the year.

Question 32.8 If ***Tenby Ltd's*** assembly department had incurred actual overhead expenditure of £185,000 (see Question 32.6), calculate the volume, expenditure and total variances for the year.

Question 32.9 ***Machine Parts Ltd*** has two production cost centres (machine and assembly) and one service cost centre (maintenance). The company calculates absorption rates monthly, based on the budgeted results for that month. Maintenance costs are apportioned to production cost centres in proportion to the total costs which are incurred by those cost centres. The actual results for January were as follows:

	Machine	Assembly	Maintenance
Overheads incurred:	£	£	£
Indirect materials	550	450	230
Indirect labour	1,280	975	840
Rent and rates	240	180	80
Supervision	800	560	200
Depreciation of machinery	700	100	150
Light and heat	100	80	30
Other expenses	20	25	40
	Machine	**Assembly**	
Operating time:			
Machine hours	300 hours		
Direct labour hours		4,800 hours	
Budgeted results:			
Overheads	£4,200	£2,800	
Machine hours	280 hours		
Direct labour hours		4,200 hours	

Required

i) Calculate the overhead absorption rate for January.

ii) Prepare a statement to show how the total overhead for the month is borne by each of the cost centres.

iii) Calculate the over or under-recovery of overhead for the month for each production department.

Question 32.10 *Princetown Products Ltd* has calculated the overhead rates for the current year ending next 31st December 19X2 for two of its departments A and B from the following budgets:

	Dept A	Dept B
	£	£
Indirect materials	9,000	15,000
Indirect labour	50,000	4,000
Supervisors' salaries	15,000	3,000
Canteen costs	5,000	1,000
Depreciation		
Factory buildings	4,000	12,000
Factory equipment	3,000	33,000
Repairs and maintenance	2,000	10,000
Power and light	1,000	3,000
Maintenance	1,000	4,000
Total overheads	90,000	85,000

Budgets for direct labour costs, direct labour hours and machine hours for the current year are as follows:

	Dept A	Dept B
Direct labour costs	£45,000	£8,500
Direct labour hours	15,000 hours	2,125 hours
Machine hours	3,000 hours	42,500 hours

During January the firm completed three orders which used the facilities of Departments A and B only. Details of the relevant data and costs are as follows:

	Job 1	Job 2	Job 3
Direct material costs	£550	£750	£950
Direct labour costs:			
Department A	£350	£620	£960
Department B	£100	£120	£200
Direct labour hours:			
Department A	120 hours	200 hours	300 hours
Department B	24 hours	26 hours	55 hours
Machine hours:			
Department A	25 hours	45 hours	55 hours
Department B	400 hours	500 hours	1,000 hours

Required

i) Calculate the possible overhead recovery rates for the two departments, using the following bases:

a) direct labour costs

b) direct labour hours

c) machine hours

ii) Examine the data carefully and recommend which of the three methods of overhead recovery in (i) above should be used by each department. Give reasons for your choice.

iii) Calculate the total production costs of each of the three jobs using your chosen method of overhead cost absorption.

Question 32.11 *Marine Motors Ltd* manufactures two models of engine. The company has two production departments, a machine shop and an assembly department, as well as a canteen which serves all the employees. The budgeted sales and costs for the next year are as follows:

	Albatross	Buzzard
Selling price per unit	£600	£700
Sales/production volume	2,000 units	2,500 units
Material costs per unit	£80	£50
Direct labour		
Machine shop (£3 per hour)	50 hours/unit	60 hours/unit
Assembly department (£2 per hour)	40 hours/unit	40 hours/unit
Machine hours		
Machine shop	30 hours/unit	80 hours/unit
Assembly department	10 hours/unit	-

	Machine shop	Assembly dept	Canteen	Total
Production overhead				
Variable	£260,000	£90,000	-	£350,000
Fixed	£420,000	£300,000	£160,000	£880,000
Total	£680,000	£390,000	£160,000	£1,230,000
Number of employees	150	90	10	
Floor area (sq m)	40,000	10,000	10,000	

Required

i) Advise the company on the method of overhead absorption which should be used for each department. Give reasons for your choice.

ii) Calculate an appropriate overhead absorption rate for each production department.

iii) Calculate the total budgeted cost per unit of each model of engine.

iv) Assuming that the company operates a full absorption costing system, calculate the effect on budgeted profit for next year if the actual unit costs are as predicted, except that sales and production of the Albatross engine are 300 units more than budget. (You may need to refer to the behaviour of fixed and variable costs when production levels change given in Chapter 33.)

Objective Test *(tick the appropriate box)*

i) The total cost absorbed is obtained from the formula:

a) actual production × actual absorption rate ☐

b) budgeted production × actual absorption rate ☐

c) actual production × budgeted absorption rate ☐

d) budgeted production × budgeted absorption rate ☐

ii) Production can be measured as:

a) direct labour costs ☐

b) direct material costs ☐

c) prime costs ☐

d) none of these ☐

iii) The best overhead absorption cost rates are based on:

a) actual cost ☐

b) budgeted cost ☐

c) time ☐

d) none of these ☐

iv) The volume variance is the difference between:

a) total cost recovered and total cost incurred ☐

b) total cost recovered and total cost budgeted ☐

c) total cost budgeted and total cost incurred ☐

d) none of these ☐

v) The total variance is the difference between:

a) total cost recovered and total cost incurred ☐

b) total cost recovered and total cost budgeted ☐

c) total cost budgeted and total cost incurred ☐

d) none of these ☐

vi) The expenditure variance is the difference between:

a) total cost recovered and total cost incurred ☐

b) total cost recovered and total cost budgeted ☐

c) total cost budgeted and total cost incurred ☐

d) none of these ☐

Assignment H

Brisbane Briefcases Ltd

Context

You are the assistant to the chief accountant of ***Brisbane Briefcases Ltd*** who has gone home ill with suspected 'flu. The managing director bursts into your office with the news that he has arranged a meeting with Sydney Suitcases Ltd tomorrow with a view to discussing the possibilty of setting up a jointly owned plant to produce a new range of leather briefcases. He already has some projected data previously supplied by the chief accountant, but asks you to present the data in a more easily understandable form for tomorrow's meeting.

Four types of briefcases are planned and the planned monthly data are as follows:

Type	Selling price £ per unit	Production units	Sales units
Deluxe	100	400	200
Excel	75	400	100
Swish	50	300	200
Flash	50	200	100

Direct costs per unit :

Type		Direct Wages Costs		
	Materials	Cutting	Making	Finishing
	£	£	£	£
Deluxe	11.00	3.00	4.50	6.00
Excel	9.50	2.00	3.00	4.00
Swish	8.00	1.00	1.50	2.00
Flash	8.00	1.00	1.50	2.00

The total figures per month:

		£	£
Material purchases			14,400
Production overheads:			
Allocated :	Cutting	1,000	
	Making	2,250	
	Finishing	1,000	
			4,250
Apportioned:			5,625
Administration overheads			8,480
Selling and distribution overheads			9,334

It is company practice

- to value finished goods stock at full production cost (prime cost plus production overheads);
- to apportion production overheads on the basis of departmental direct wages;

- ❒ to charge other overheads to products using the basis of the full production cost of goods sold;
- ❒ to ignore work in progress.

Student activities

Re-arrange the data for the managing director's meeting showing:

i) Material cost of production, per product

ii) Direct wages, per product and per department

iii) Departmental overhead absorption rates

iv) Total production costs, per product

v) Overhead absorption, per product

vi) Value of closing stock of raw materials

vii) Value of closing stock of finished goods, by product

viii) Sales, by product

ix) Production cost of goods sold, by product

x) Profit & Loss account, analysed by product

Format

Tables of data, with calculations and comments where considered necessary.

Objectives

The student should show an appreciation and understanding of:

- ❒ cost classification
- ❒ cost allocation
- ❒ cost apportionment
- ❒ cost absorption
- ❒ budgeting
- ❒ stock valuations

References

Chapters 27, 28, 29, 31 and 32.

Using costs for decision-making

This section (Chapters 33 – 35) considers the costs which are required for making important decisions affecting the future of the business.

Chapter 33 looks at the way costs behave in relation to changes in activity or sales levels and incorporates this cost behaviour with levels of income. This approach to costs and revenue is known as cost-volume-profit analysis and is useful for answering questions which are commonly posed by management when making decisions.

Some decisions are made against a background of scarce resources. Chapter 34 identifies these as limiting factors and shows how they might be brought into the decision-making process.

Consideration must be given to the different circumstances and factors applicable to each individual decision. As a result, different cost information may be required for each decision made. Chapter 35 looks at the different costs which may be required for a variety of decisions. It considers the importance of fixed, variable, differential and opportunity costs and incremental revenue in the decision-making process.

Chapter 33

Cost – Volume – Profit analysis

33.1 Objectives

At the end of this chapter you should be able to:

- explain what is meant by marginal costing;
- define such terms as fixed and variable costs;
- understand what is meant by contribution;
- construct a marginal costing statement;
- calculate a breakeven point;
- constuct a breakeven chart or graph.

33.2 Introduction

The first section of this chapter is concerned with the way in which costs behave in relation to levels of output or sales. It would be useful, therefore, to revise your understanding of this topic by reviewing Chapter 28.

The calculation of profit, particularly for one unit, can be misleading if there are changes in the level of activity. This is because:

- some costs are ***fixed*** and ***do not*** change in total in relation to levels of activity;
- some costs are ***variable*** and ***do*** change in total in relation to levels of activity.

Cost-volume-profit analysis (CVP) considers how changes in ***costs*** resulting from different ***volumes*** of production and sales affect the levels of ***profits*** which are made by a business.

33.3 Marginal costing

In ***marginal costing***, only the ***variable costs*** are charged to the cost units. The profit per unit and total cost per unit are not calculated. By deducting the variable costs from the sales, we arrive at a figure of ***contribution***. Thus, marginal costing is different from ***total absorption costing*** which charges all production costs, both fixed and variable, to the products or cost units (see Chapters 31 and 32). In marginal costing, profit for a period is calculated by deducting the fixed costs for the period from the total contribution for the period.

A statement which shows variable and fixed costs separately with a calculation of contribution is known as a ***marginal costing statement***.

Example

Marginal costing statement

		Per unit	×	Production: 2,000 units		=	Total
		£				£	£
Sales Price		10		Sales revenue			20,000
Less Marginal costs:				*Less* Variable costs:			
Materials	4			Materials		8,000	
Labour	2			Labour		4,000	
Variable overheads	1			Variable overheads		2,000	
		7					14,000
Unit contribution		3		Total contribution			6,000

Notice that when variable costs are expressed as a rate per unit they are known as ***marginal costs***, ie the additional cost incurred in producing the extra or marginal unit of production, hence the title marginal costing.

To provide management with useful information about CVP, it is often necessary to construct a marginal costing statement.

Example

Percy Perth manufactures 1,000 plastic penholders per month. The costs are 25 pence for the plastic, and 25 pence for wages in respect of each penholder manufactured. The monthly costs (overheads) of the factory are £1,000, which in this case are incurred whatever the level of activity. The penholders are sold for £2 each. What is Percy's profit for the month, and the profit per penholder?

Solution

Profit statement for the month

Production: 1,000 penholders

	£	£
Sales (1,000 × £2)		2,000
Less Cost of sales:		
Direct materials (1,000 × £0.25)	250	
Direct labour (1,000 × £0.25)	250	
Factory overheads	1,000	
		1,500
Total profit		500

$$\text{Profit per penholder} = \frac{£500}{1,000} = 50 \text{ pence each}$$

On these figures, Percy might calculate that his profit for 500 penholders in one month should be 500 × 50p = £250. This would be wrong, however, and a profit and loss statement shows why.

Percy Perth
Profit and loss statement for the month

Production: 500 penholders

	£	£
Sales (500 × £2)		1,000
Less Cost of sales:		
Direct materials (500 × £0.25)	125	
Direct labour (500 × £0.25)	125	
Factory overheads	1,000	
		1,250
Total loss		(250)

If you calculate the costs per penholder at the different levels of activity, the reason for the loss is easy to appreciate:

Level of activity	Total costs	Cost per penholder
1,000 penholders	£1,500	£1.50
500 penholders	£1,250	£2.50

The average cost per penholder increases because the factory overheads of £1,000 must be paid no matter what the level of activity. Costs of this type are known as ***fixed costs***.

33.4 Fixed and variable costs

Fixed costs are those costs which, in total, stay the same regardless of changes in the level of activity (usually measured in terms of production or sales). The term *fixed* is directly related to ***activity***. However, these fixed costs ***may*** change or fluctuate for other reasons. For example, the local authority may increase the business rates. This has nothing to do with activity levels, and the cost is therefore still regarded as ***fixed***.

Variable costs are those costs which, in total, change in relation to changes in the level of activity. For example, if a worker is paid 25p for every penholder he makes, the total wages cost will increase as the worker makes more penholders.

Fixed costs, in total, stay the same as activity changes, but the fixed cost per unit changes as activity changes.

Example

	100 penholders	500 penholders	1,000 penholders
Total fixed costs	£1,000	£1,000	£1,000
Fixed costs per unit	£10	£2	£1

Variable costs, in total, increase or decrease in line with activity, but stay the same per unit.

Example

	100 penholders	500 penholders	1,000 penholders
Total Variable costs	£50	£250	£500
Variable costs per unit	£0.50	£0.50	£0.50

You should now be able to attempt Questions 33.1 and 33.2 at the end of this chapter.

33.5 Contribution

The ***contribution*** is calculated by deducting the variable costs from the sales. It is known as the contribution because it represents the amount which initially contributes towards the fixed costs of the business, and when these have been covered, contributes to the profit. Contribution is not profit, because no allowance has been made for the fixed costs of the business.

Sales – Variable costs = Contribution

The ***contribution per unit*** is calculated by deducting the variable cost per unit from the selling price per unit. The ***total contribution*** from a specified level of activity is calculated by deducting the total variable costs incurred from the total sales figure.

Example

	1 penholder	1,000 penholders
	£	£
Sales	2.00	2,000
Variable costs	.50	500
Contribution	1.50	1,500

You should now be able to attempt Questions 33.3 and 33.4 at the end of this chapter.

33.6 Break-even point

The level of activity at which a company makes neither a profit nor a loss is known as the ***break-even point***. It can be calculated as follows:

Break-even point in units

$$\text{Break-even point (units)} = \frac{\text{Total fixed costs}}{\text{Contribution per unit}}$$

Example

Using the *Percy Perth* data:

$$\text{Number of penholders to break even} = \frac{£1{,}000}{£1.50} = 667 \text{ approx.}$$

This can be proved as follows:

				£
Sales:	667 units	@	£2.00	1,333
Less Variable costs	667 units	@	£0.50	333
= Contribution	667 units	@	£1.50	1,000
Less Fixed costs				1,000
Profit/Loss (Break-even)				nil

Break-even point in £s of sales or turnover

$$\text{Break-even point (£s sales)} = \frac{\text{Total fixed costs}}{\text{Contribution*}} \times \text{Sales*}$$

* These can be per unit or totals at any particular level of activity.

Example

Using the Percy Perth data:

Sales value required to break-even:

$$\frac{£1{,}000}{£1.50} \times £2 \text{ or } \frac{£1{,}000}{£1{,}500} \times £2{,}000 = £1{,}333$$

An alternative calculation would be simply to calculate the break-even point in units, and multiply by the selling price per unit:

e.g. 667 units at £2 = £1,333

Break-even point expressed as a percentage of capacity

If ***Percy Perth's*** total capacity is 1,000 units, then the break-even point could be expressed as:

$$\frac{667 \text{ units}}{1{,}000 \text{ units}} \times 100 = 66.7\% \text{ of capacity}$$

or, using sales levels:

$$\frac{£1{,}333}{1{,}000 \times £2} = \frac{£1{,}000}{£1{,}500} \times 100 = 66.7\% \text{ of capacity}$$

33.7 Graphical presentation of break-even point

In Chapter 28 where the graphical presentation of cost behaviour was discussed, it was explained that there were two possible graphical presentations of total cost, either being acceptable. The two presentations are:

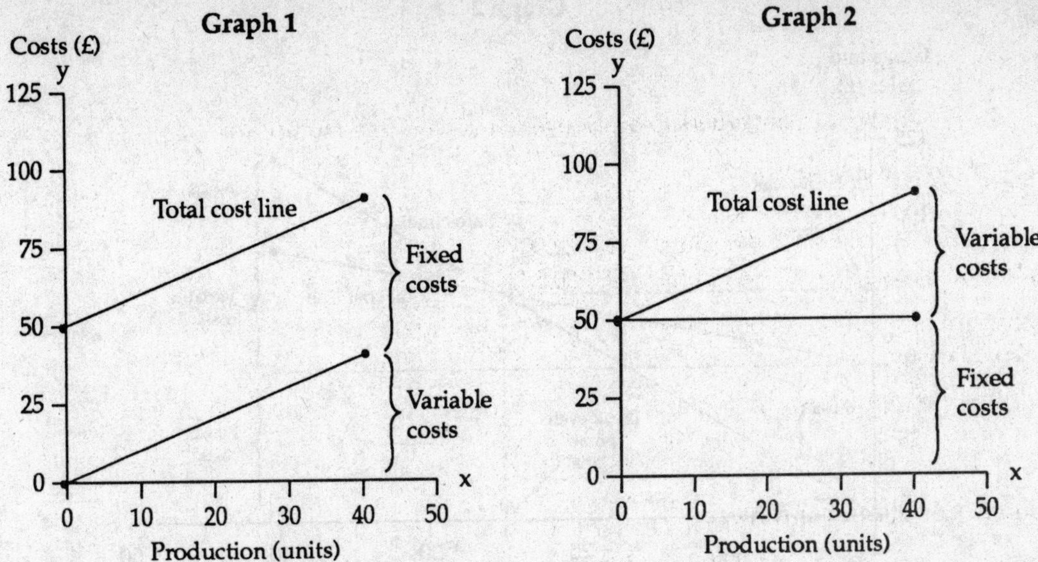

To establish the break-even point all that is now required is to plot a total sales line on either of the two graphs. The total sales line will rise from zero as production rises (here sales and production are always regarded as equal) and where total sales revenue equals total cost, i.e. no profit or loss is made, the break-even point can be read off on the 'x' and 'y' axes. The cost information has been taken from Section 28.4 in Chapter 28, and the selling price is assumed to be £3 per unit produced. The two forms of break-even graph are as follows:

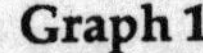

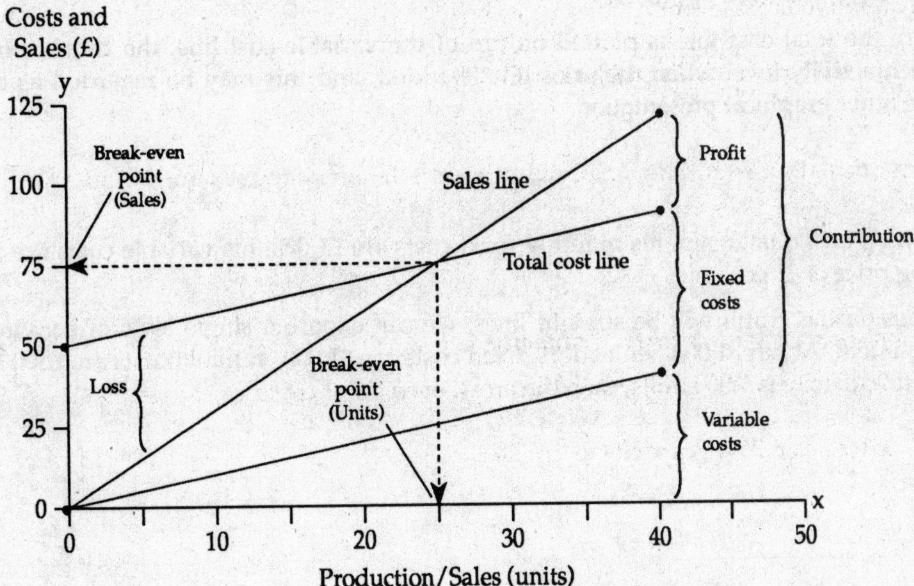

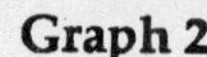

Graph 2

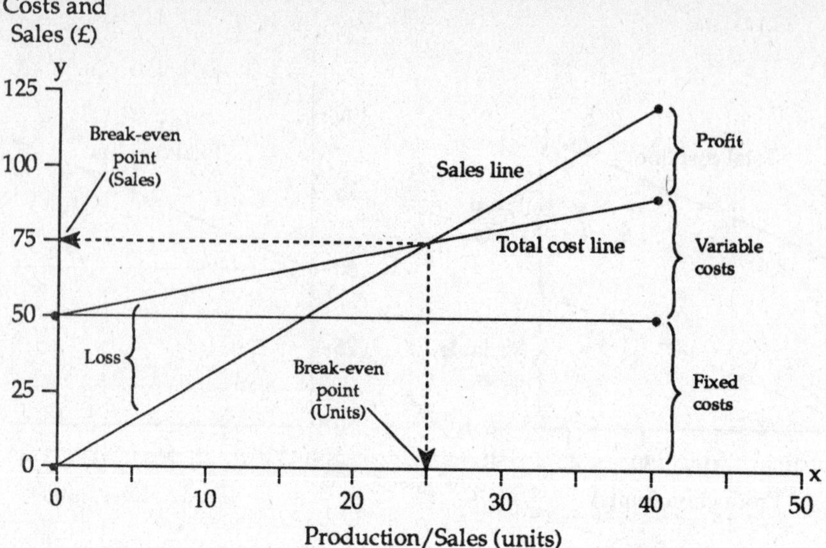

Notice that both charts show the same break-even point, which can be read off both 'x' and 'y' axes depending whether it is desired that the break-even point should be expressed in sales value (y axis), or units or % capacity (x axis).

Although we stated earlier in Chapter 28 that the choice of the two graphical approaches depicting costs was a matter of opinion, and either was acceptable, when adding a sales line to the graph so that a break-even point can be determined there is a preferred approach.

In Graph 1, where the total cost line is plotted on top of the variable cost line, the ***total contribution*** may be determined at each activity level when the sales line is added, and this may be regarded as an advantage not available from the other graphical presentation.

Example

Using the ***Percy Perth*** data again, his monthly fixed costs are £1,000, his variable costs are 50p per unit, and his selling price is £2 per unit.

As all the lines on the graph will be straight lines, we can choose a single level of activity to plot the points for each item. At, say, 1,000 penholders, fixed costs are £1,000, variable costs are £500 and sales are £2,000.

Solution

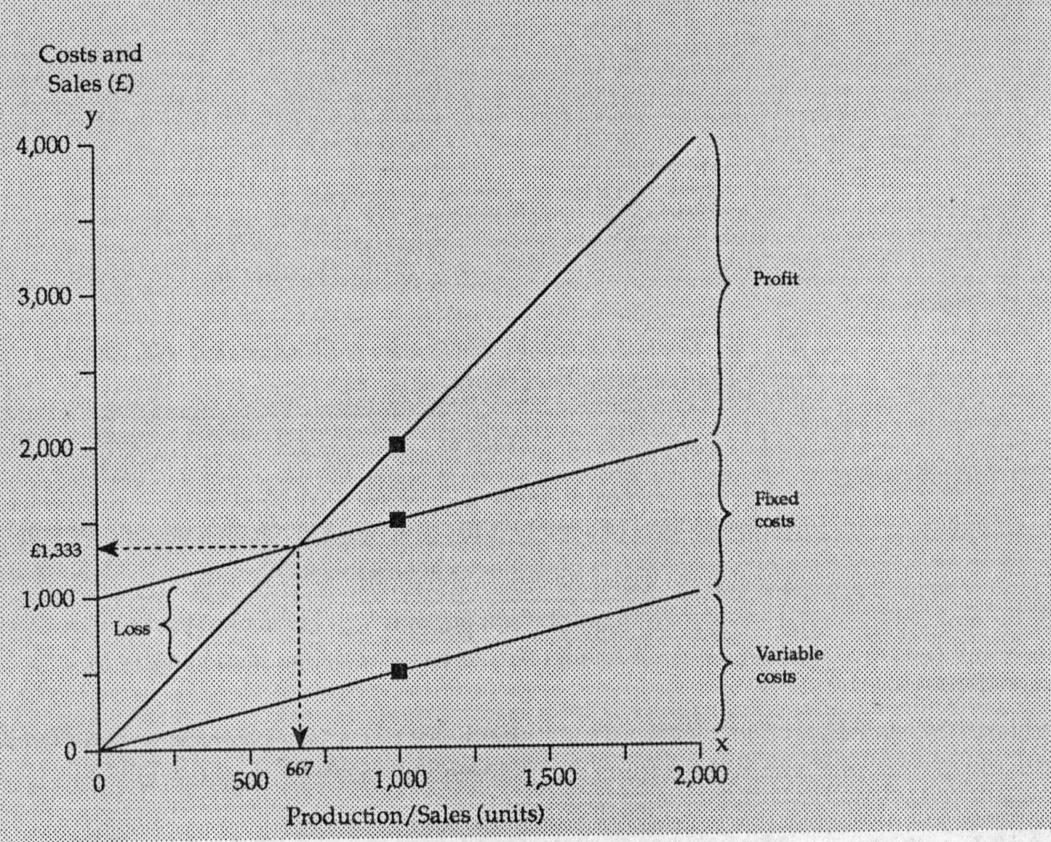

Using this layout enables the total contribution to be read off at any level of activity, a benefit which is not available from the alternative graph.

Notice that although the graph is called a break-even chart because it shows the break-even point, it also shows the costs and profits at various levels of activity, and it is also possible to determine the level of activity required to achieve a particular level of profit.

33.8 Margin of safety

The ***margin of safety*** is the difference between a given level of sales at which the firm is operating, or planning to operate, and the level of sales at which the firm breaks even. It may be expressed in units of production or sales, sales value (turnover), or it may be expressed as a percentage of the sales value. The margin of safety represents the fall in sales which must take place before the company hits break-even point and losses are incurred if sales continue to fall. The expression of the margin of safety as a percentage of sales value enables organisations of different sizes to be compared.

Example

Paphos Pillars Ltd breaks even at 10,000 units which are sold for £20 each. It is planning to produce 12,500 pillars next year. Calculate the company's margin of safety if the planned level of production and sales is achieved.

Solution

	Units	£
Planned sales	12,500	250,000
Break-even sales	10,000	200,000
Margin of safety	2,500	50,000

$$\frac{2,500}{12,500} \qquad \frac{50,000}{250,000} \times 100 = 20\%$$

You should now be able to attempt Question 33.5 and Task 33.2 at the end of this chapter.

33.9 Target profit

If a company wishes to know the level of activity it has to achieve to obtain a target profit, the formula is:

$$\text{Required activity (Units)} = \frac{\text{Fixed costs + Target profit}}{\text{Contribution per unit}}$$

Example

Using the data in the ***Percy Perth*** example above, Percy Perth wishes to make a profit of £500. How many units must he manufacture and sell to achieve this level of profit?

Solution

The calculation is:

$$\frac{\text{Fixed costs + desired profit}}{\text{Contribution per unit}} = \frac{£1,000 + £500}{£1.50} = 1,000 \text{ units}$$

This can be proved as follows:

		£
Sales	1,000 units @ £2.00	2,000
Less Variable costs	1,000 units @ £0.50	500
Contribution	1,000 units @ £5.50	1,500
Less Fixed costs		1,000
Target profit		£500

Example

Fixed costs: £1,000

Contribution per unit: £5

What is the break-even point in units?

Solution

$$\frac{£1,000}{£5} = 200 \text{ units}$$

Example

Fixed costs: £4,000

Sales: £10,000

Variable costs: £8,000

What level of turnover is required to break even?

Solution

Sales:	£10,000
Less Variable costs	£ 8,000
Contribution	£ 2,000

$$\frac{£4{,}000}{£2{,}000} \times £10{,}000 = £20{,}000$$

Example

Fixed costs: £10,000

Contribution per unit: £2

Target profit: £5,000

How many units are required to be produced to achieve the target profit?

Solution

$$\frac{£10{,}000 + £5{,}000}{£2} = 7{,}500 \text{ units}$$

You should now be able to attempt Questions 33.6 and 33.7 at the end of this chapter.

Example

The ***Stirling Bicycle Company*** is preparing budgets for next year. They plan to produce and sell four models, ranging from the Aberdeen racing bicycle to the Dundee popular tourer.

The sales director provides the following:

Model	Estimated sales demand Number of bicycles	Wholesale selling price per bicycle
Aberdeen	200	£400
Berwick	300	£300
Cairngorm	400	£200
Dundee	600	£100

The budgeted variable costs of production are as follows:

Model	Parts and materials per bicycle	Labour cost per bicycle
Aberdeen	£190	£60
Berwick	£140	£40
Cairngorm	£90	£30
Dundee	£40	£20

Fixed costs are budgeted at £100,000 for the year.

It is expected that all models produced will be sold immediately.

Required

As assistant to the managing director, you are asked to prepare a marginal costing statement for him showing the contribution from each model, and the total budgeted profit for next year.

Solution

Marginal cost statement
showing contribution from each model and the total budgeted profit for next year

Model	Sales price	Variable costs per unit Material	Labour	Total	Contribution per unit	Prod/ Sales (units)	Total contribution
	£	£	£	£	£		£
Aberdeen	400	190	60	250	150	200	30,000
Berwick	300	140	40	180	120	300	36,000
Cairngorm	200	90	30	120	80	400	32,000
Dundee	100	40	20	60	40	600	24,000
					Total contribution		122,000
					Less fixed costs		100,000
					Budgeted profit		22,000

You should now be able to attempt Question 33.8 at the end of this chapter.

33.10 Summary

Adding a sales line to the graphical presentation of variable, fixed and total costs considered in Chapter 28 enables a ***break-even chart*** or graph to be constructed. The ***break-even point*** is the level of activity where sales and total costs are equal. Total profit or loss may also be read off the graph at various levels of production or sales. The break-even point in units or sales values may also be obtained by calculation. The general formula is:

Break-even points:

$$\text{In units} = \frac{\text{Total fixed costs}}{\text{Contribution per unit}}$$

$$\text{In sales value} = \frac{\text{Total fixed costs}}{\text{Total contribution}} \times \text{Total sales}$$

The level of activity required to achieve a desired or target profit is obtained from the formula:

$$\text{Level of activity} = \frac{\text{Total fixed costs} + \text{Desired or target profit}}{\text{Contribution per unit}}$$

The main difficulties encountered by students are:

- Deciding whether a cost is variable or fixed. Remember that the decision is based on whether or not the cost varies with the level of activity.
- Failing to calculate the contribution. Contribution is a most valuable concept, the uses for which will be explained more fully in subsequent chapters.
- Forgetting the layout of a marginal costing statement.

- ❒ Insisting on calculating the ***total*** cost per unit, and profit per unit. These figures can be misleading if there are changes in levels of activity.
- ❒ Forgetting the formulae for calculating the break-even point.
- ❒ Forgetting the principles for constructing the break-even chart or graph.

You should now be able to attempt Objective Test at the end of this chapter.

Student activities

Task 33.1 A recent report by a motoring organisation suggested that the average cost per mile to run an average family car is 28.7 pence per mile. Carry out your own calculations, either for your own car or for what you would regard as the average family saloon. What do you need to carefully define before you collect your data and complete your calculations?

Task 33.2 Assuming that you are paid expenses of 35p per mile, construct a break-even chart based on the information you have collected for Task 33.1.

Question 33.1 Decide whether the following costs are ***fixed*** or ***variable***:

	Fixed	Variable
Rent of factory		
Materials used in products		
Managing director's salary		
Depreciation of office equipment		
Wages for employees working on the product		
Supervisors' salaries		
Light and heat in the factory		
Metered power to machines in the factory		
Salesmen's commissions		
Rates		
Routine repainting of the factory		
Royalties paid for each item manufactured		

Question 33.2 Decide whether the following costs are fixed or variable and compute the total cost for 500 penholders. The first two have been completed for you.

Cost	Total cost for 1,000 penholders	Type of cost (fixed or variable)	Total cost for 500 penholders
	£		£
Rent	5,000	F	5,000
Direct materials	250	V	125
Managing director's salary	1,500		
Depreciation	400		
Rates	1,000		
Operatives' wages	250		
Storekeeper's salary	250		

Question 33.3 If we know two of the three figures from the formula: Sales – Variable costs = Contribution, it is always possible to calculate the third figure.

Fill in the missing figures in the following table. The first example has been calculated for you, where the answer is in square brackets.

Example	A	B	C	D	E	F
Sales	[6]	3	5	84	?	64
Variable costs	4	?	2	27	12	?
Contribution	2	1	?	?	15	16

Question 33.4 *Mr Arbroath* owns a hotel on the promenade at the seaside. He has rooms for 30 guests, and his annual fixed costs are estimated as follows:

	£
Depreciation of furniture	1,000
Rates	1,200
Repairs and redecorations	1,400
Other annual costs	400
Staff (permanent)	6,000
	10,000

His variable costs, per guest, per week, are estimated as follows:

	£
Food, consumables	20
Domestic staff (part-time, occasional)	20
Heating, lighting, laundry etc.	20
	60

His charge, per guest, per week, is £110, and his normal season lasts for 20 weeks of the year.

He regards his profit (excess of income over all costs shown above) as being his return on capital (his investment in the hotel) as well as his remuneration.

Required

i) Calculate Mr Arbroath's annual profit if all rooms are occupied.

ii) In marginal costing terms, what is his contribution per guest-week?

Question 33.5 Draw up a break-even chart or graph on graph paper using the data on *Percy Perth's* business in the example in Section 33.3. Read off from your graph the break-even point in units and sales value, the approximate level of profit or loss at 500 units of output or sales, and the level of activity to achieve a profit of £500.

Question 33.6 i) From the following data, calculate the break-even point in units:

Selling price per unit: £7

Variable costs per unit: £5

Fixed costs: £10,000

ii) From the following data, calculate the break-even point in terms of turnover:

Selling price per unit: £25

Variable costs per unit: £18

Fixed costs: £7,000

iii) From the following data, calculate what turnover (£s of sales) is necessary to achieve the target profit?

A company aims for £20,000 profit next year.

Its fixed costs are budgeted at £40,000.

Selling price per unit: £100

Variable costs per unit: £75

Question 33.7 Using the data from Question 33.4:

i) How many guest-weeks has Mr Arbroath to rely on in order to break even?

ii) How else could this break-even point be expressed, other than in terms of "guest-weeks"?

iii) Draw a break-even chart or graph to represent Mr Arbroath's costs and sales, and indicate the break-even point.

iv) What is Mr Arbroath's margin of safety?

Question 33.8 *Montrose Ltd* manufactures high-quality soft toys, and has three products: rabbits, dogs and bears. Each of the products goes through the same process and uses the same quality of materials; the only difference arises from the different sizes of the products.

The manufacturing standards and selling prices set for the products for next year are as follows:

	Rabbits	Dogs	Bears
Budgeted production/sales (units)	4,000	3,000	2,000
Material costs per unit	£11.50	£17.50	£25.00
Labour hours per unit:			
Cutting department	2 hrs	2.5 hrs	3 hrs
Finishing department	2 hrs	1.5 hrs	1 hr
Selling price per unit	£32.50	£40.00	£49.00

Employees in the cutting department will be paid £4 per hour, and in the finishing department £3 per hour. Budgeted fixed overheads are £40,000 for next year.

Required

You are trainee production manager for Montrose Ltd, and you have been asked by the production director to produce a statement for him which will show the contribution from each product, and the total budgeted profit for next year.

i) Prepare this statement for him

ii) Calculate the turnover to achieve break-even next year

iii) Explain what happens to the break-even point if sales take place in different proportions from those budgeted.

Question 33.9 *Reigate Restaurant* has been serving a standard meal for £10 to its customers for many years. The meal consists of steak, chips and peas, suitably garnished. During the past three months the restaurant has suffered the effects of competition. Previously the restaurant had been running at full capacity serving 3,000 meals per month, but customers have been attracted to a new restaurant nearby and trade has fallen.

Details of revenues and costs for the last three months show the effect of the competition:

	September	October	November
	£	£	£
Revenues	24,600	21,900	19,500
Costs:			
Provisions and garnishes	7,380	6,570	5,850
Labour	6,920	6,380	5,900
Overheads	5,500	5,230	4,990
Total costs	19,800	18,180	16,740

The current month, December, looks even worse and the manager estimates that the restaurant is only working at 58% capacity. However, he is aware that the competition is about to close down because of problems with the lease and he expects Reigate Restaurant will return to full capacity in January and remain trading at that level for the rest of the year.

All costs are likely to rise by 5% from 1st January. To compensate for this, the price of the standard meal will be raised from £10.00 to £10.50.

Required

i) Calculate the anticipated profit for the month of December.

ii) Calculate the likely profit for the whole of next year.

iii) Calculate the break-even point of the restaurant for next year expressed as a percentage of full capacity.

Question 33.10 *Gloucester Grofits Ltd* has developed a new, improved, fluorescent plastic grofit which will be sold to the car industry where they are fixed to widgets by means of spiflicator pins. The company has a present production capacity for 4,500 grofits per annum, after which level of production additional investment in space, personnel and production facilities will be required which will cause higher fixed costs to be incurred. Yet more investment will be required at 8,500 units if higher production levels are required. Although the unit price of grofits tends to fall in order to achieve the higher levels of sales, no savings on unit variable costs are achieved from the higher levels of production.

The following information on sales, costs and profits for next year has been prepared for the managing director of Gloucester Grofits Ltd by the accountant:

Number of grofits Units	Fixed costs £	Variable costs £	Total costs £	Sales revenue £	Profit £	Loss £
0	5,000	0	5,000	0	–	5,000
1,000	5,000	2,000	7,000	4,500	–	2,500
2,000	5,000	4,000	9,000	9,000	0	0
3,000	5,000	6,000	11,000	13,000	2,000	–
4,000	5,000	8,000	13,000	17,000	4,000	–
5,000	9,000	10,000	19,000	20,000	1,000	–
6,000	9,000	12,000	21,000	23,000	2,000	–
7,000	9,000	14,000	23,000	26,000	3,000	–
8,000	9,000	16,000	25,000	29,000	4,000	–
9,000	13,000	18,000	31,000	31,000	0	0
10,000	13,000	20,000	33,000	33,000	0	0

Required

i) Construct a break-even graph from the above budgeted figures.

ii) Assuming that the best estimate of the demand for grofits next year is likely to be around 7,000 or 8,000 grofits, advise Gloucester Grofits Ltd of the production and sales strategy to be adopted.

Objective test *(tick the appropriate box)*

i) When activity is increasing, the total variable costs:

a) Increase ☐
b) Decrease ☐
c) Stay the same ☐
d) Sometimes increase, sometimes decrease ☐

ii) When activity is decreasing, the variable cost per unit:

a) Increases ☐
b) Decreases ☐
c) Stays the same ☐
d) Sometimes increases, sometimes decreases ☐

iii) When activity is increasing, the fixed cost per unit:

a) Increases ☐
b) Decreases ☐
c) Stays the same ☐
d) Sometimes increases, sometimes decreases ☐

iv) When activity is decreasing, the total fixed cost:

a) Increases ☐
b) Decreases ☐
c) Stays the same ☐
d) Sometimes increases, sometimes decreases ☐

v) If the selling price per unit is £27.00 and the variable costs per unit are £13.00, the contribution per unit is:

a) £40.00 ☐

b) £14.00 ☐

c) £13.00 ☐

d) None of these ☐

vi) If the total sales figure is £5,000, and the total variable costs are £3,000 for 1,000 units, the contribution per unit is:

a) £5.00 ☐

b) £2.00 ☐

c) £3,000 ☐

d) £2,000 ☐

vii) If the variable costs per unit are £6.00, and 500 units have been sold for £5,000, the total contribution is:

a) £4,000 ☐

b) £2,000 ☐

c) £3,000 ☐

d) £8,000 ☐

viii) If the contribution per unit is £2.00, and the total variable costs for 100 units is £300, the total sales figure for those 100 units is:

a) £200 ☐

b) £500 ☐

c) £700 ☐

d) £100 ☐

ix) If the total fixed costs are £12,000, the selling price per unit is £12, and the variable costs per unit are £8.00, the break-even point is:

a) 12,000 units ☐

b) 3,000 units ☐

c) 1,500 units ☐

d) 4,500 units ☐

x) If the break-even point is 3,000 units, and the contribution per unit is £3, total fixed costs must be:

a) £1,000 ☐

b) £9,000 ☐

c) £6,000 ☐

d) None of these ☐

xi) If fixed costs are £16,000, sales are £50,000, and variable costs are £30,000, the turnover required to break-even is:

a) £40,000 ☐

b) £26,667 ☐

c) £9,600 ☐

d) None of these ☐

xii) If fixed costs are £80,000, and contribution per unit is 50 pence, units to be sold to achieve a target profit of £50,000 are:

a) 60,000 ☐

b) 260,000 ☐

c) 600,000 ☐

d) 200,000 ☐

Chapter 34

Limiting factors

34.1 Objectives

At the end of this chapter you should be able to:

- understand what limiting factors are;
- explain the importance of limiting factors in budgeting;
- explain the importance of limiting factors in decision-making;
- calculate how to rank products using limiting factors in marginal costing;
- calculate how to maximise profits using limiting factors.

34.2 Introduction

Many factors must combine to enable a business to operate. Land and buildings, plant and machinery and other assets are necessary to form the fixed assets which the business uses; materials, labour and overhead resources are also necessary in order to carry out the buying, manufacturing and selling processes.

At any particular point in time it is possible to identify at least one factor, which if lacking prevents the business from achieving higher levels of activity and profitability. This factor is known as the ***limiting factor***.

Examples include are:

- shortage of skilled labour;
- shortage of production capacity, such as machinery;
- lack of customer demand for particular products;
- shortage of raw materials;
- shortage of factory space.

34.3 Reducing the effects of limiting factors

Having identified the limiting factor, the business must take action to reduce the effect of this particular constraint in order to improve the levels of activity and profitability. Each time the effect of a limiting factor is reduced, a new limiting factor comes into effect, constraining the operations of the business. In this way a limiting factor or constraint always exists, even if it is ultimately represented by a shortage of capital. In the examples of limiting factors given in the introduction, the business may pursue the following strategies in order to mitigate their effects:

- Shortage of skilled labour: Recruit skilled labour by giving incentives for skilled labour to move to the company. For example, increase rates of pay or encourage personnel to move from elsewhere by advertising vacancies there and perhaps paying removal costs.
- Shortage of production capacity, such as machinery: Purchase additional production machinery or sub-contract some work to outside companies.
- Lack of customer demand for particular products: Increase sales levels by price changes, advertising campaigns or giving sales incentives to staff and/or customers.
- Shortage of raw materials: Search for additional sources of raw materials or reduce dependency on a particular raw material by changing the product design and therefore raw material requirements.

- ❐ Shortage of factory space: Increase factory space by building an extension, purchasing an additional factory, or sub-contracting work to outside companies.

You should now be able to attempt Task 34.1 at the end of this chapter.

34.4 Principal budget factor

The concept of the limiting factor is particularly important in the budgeting process and the operation of the system of budgetary control. The identification of the limiting factor enables both the planning of higher levels of profitability and the co-ordination of the factors of production and sales, once its effect has been minimised. In budgeting this factor is known also as the ***principal budget factor*** as there is essentially no difference between this and the limiting factor.

Example

N. Neath (Compact Discs) Ltd

The sales manager has budgeted sales for the next year at 200,000 units, but the manpower budget allows a maximum of 400,000 labour hours for skilled labour, the limiting factor. It takes 2.5 hours of skilled labour to manufacture a disc.

Required:
Calculate the maximum number of discs which may be produced by the company.

Solution

The limit on the number of skilled labour hours available means that a maximum of 160,000 units of production may be achieved, thus:

$$\frac{\text{Skilled labour hours available}}{\text{Skilled labour hours per unit}} = \frac{400.000}{2.5} = 160{,}000 \text{ units}$$

Among the solutions which may be considered by N. Neath are:

- ❐ increase the skilled labour hours available by 40,000 units × 2.5 hours = 100,000 labour hours;
- ❐ sub-contract the work;
- ❐ change the product design or production processes in order to obviate the need for skilled labour.

Each solution may have a different time scale attached to it, but any decision which affects the availability of this resource will affect other parts of the master budget.

34.5 Product ranking

When a number of different products are produced, it is common for each product to use different amounts of the resources of material, labour and plant and machinery. In order to maximise profits, it is necessary to select the most profitable products and concentrate on the production and sale of these: first of all producing as many units as possible of the most profitable product, then the next most profitable and so on, until the scarcity of the limiting factor makes it impossible to produce further output. Each product must therefore be ***ranked*** in order of profitability.

In Chapter 33 we saw that the contributions which each product makes initially towards the general fixed costs of the business, and when these are covered, to the profits of the business, are used to determine product profitability. However there are four ways, or levels, in which the ***contribution*** can be used to rank products in terms of their contributions to profitability.

34.6 Ranking according to the size of the unit contribution

Level 1 uses the basic approach that the product with the largest contribution from each unit sold is the most profitable product on which the company should concentrate production.

Example

N. Neath (Compact Discs) Ltd

Neath produces two discs, Longplay and Shortplay. The selling prices and marginal costs per unit are as follows. Fixed costs are £45,000 per annum.

	Longplay	Shortplay
	£	£
Selling prices	10	6
Marginal costs	6	3
Unit contribution	4	3

Required

Determine the product on which Neath should concentrate production.

Solution

In selling a unit of Longplay a contribution of £4 is made towards the general fixed costs of the business, whereas selling a unit of Shortplay contributes £3 to those same overheads. Therefore, if it is as easy to sell a unit of Longplay as a unit of Shortplay, notwithstanding the higher selling price of the former, then Longplay is to be preferred because of its higher unit contribution. The fixed costs need not be used in determining the most profitable product because they remain unchanged irrespective of the volumes of Longplay or Shortplay produced.

You should now be able to attempt Question 34.1 at the end of this chapter.

34.7 Ranking according to the size of the profit-volume ratio

Level 2 recognises that ranking by the size of the unit contribution which was adopted by the level 1 ranking method does not take into consideration the size of the contribution in relation to the revenue per unit of sales. Some products may have a very small contribution relative to the selling price, and this should be an important factor when ranking products.

This approach expresses the contribution as a percentage of the selling price and is known as the ***profit-volume ratio (PV ratio)***. An alternative name for the profit-volume ratio is the ***contribution-margin ratio*** or the ***profit-to-sales ratio***. It is obtained by applying the formula:

$$\text{PV ratio} = \frac{\text{Contribution} \times 100}{\text{Sales}}$$

Notice that the PV ratio is the same percentage whether it is calculated per unit or in total. Thus if N. Neath (see the example in section 34.6) sells 100,000 units of Longplay, the PV ratios are:

$$\text{Per unit} = \frac{£4 \times 100}{£10} = 40\%$$

$$\text{In total} = \frac{£4 \times 100{,}000}{£10 \times 100{,}000} = 40\%$$

Example

N. Neath (Compact Discs) Ltd

Refer to the example in section 34.6 and calculate the PV ratios for the two products and determine the preferred product using this method.

Solution

	Longplay	Shortplay
Profit-volume ratios	$\frac{£4}{£10} \times 100 = 40\%$	$\frac{£3}{£6} \times 100 = 50\%$

The PV ratio of Shortplay is greater than that for Longplay. Therefore, if it is as easy to sell £1's worth of Shortplay as it is to sell £1's worth of Longplay, then Shortplay is to be preferred because of its higher profit-volume ratio.

One useful way of considering the PV ratio is to regard the percentage as representing the number of pence contribution obtained from selling £1's worth of each product. Thus Longplay contributes 40 pence per £1 of sales achieved, whereas Shortplay contributes 50 pence per £1 of sales achieved. In these circumstances Shortplay is preferred.

34.8 Ranking according to the size of the total contribution

The example in section 34.6, using a level 1 ranking according to the size of the unit contribution, ignores the fact that different sales volumes may be achievable for each product, so the total contributions may also vary in size. Level 3 ranks according to the size of the total contribution.

Example

N. Neath (Compact Discs) Ltd

Refer to the data in section 34.6, but assume that 20,000 units of Longplay and 100,000 units of Shortplay can be sold.

Required

Calculate the total contribution for each product.

Solution

The total contributions of each product become:

Longplay	= £4 × 20,000
	= £80,000
Shortplay	= £3 × 100,000
	= £300,000

Although the unit contribution of Longplay is greater than that of Shortplay (see the example in Section 34.6), the total contribution of Shortplay is greater than Longplay. Therefore Shortplay is preferred as the most profitable.

34.9 Ranking according to the effect of limiting factors

If a shortage of a particular resource is identified as the ***limiting factor***, the strategy the business should adopt is to use the scarce resource as effectively as possible so as to maximise profits. The general rule in ranking products according to the use of a limiting factor is to express the contribution per unit of product as a rate per unit of limiting factor used in producing that product.

Example

N. Neath (Compact Discs) Ltd

Refer to the data in section 34.6, but assume that the limiting factor is a shortage of skilled labour. In producing a unit of Longplay, 1 hour of skilled labour is used, whereas the production of a unit of Shortplay uses half an hour of skilled labour.

Required

Determine which is the most profitable product on which production should be concentrated.

Solution

The contribution per unit of each product expressed as a rate per unit of limiting factor is as follows:

$$\frac{\text{Unit contribution}}{\text{Limiting factor per unit}}$$

$$\text{Longplay} = \frac{£4}{1\text{ hour}}$$

= £4 per skilled labour hour

$$\text{Shortplay} = \frac{£3}{0.5\text{ hour}}$$

= £6 per skilled labour hour

Shortplay is preferred because its production represents a more effective use of the scarce resource of skilled labour. Production of Shortplay gives a contribution of £6 per hour of skilled labour used, whereas Longplay produces a contribution of only £4 per hour of skilled labour used in in its production.

34.10 Other measures of limiting factors

In the example in section 34.9 the quantity of skilled labour used, expressed in hours, is available and it was possible to express the contribution as a rate per skilled labour hour. However, in some circumstances only the cost of the limiting factor per unit of product is available. In such cases the contribution per £1 of limiting factor per unit of product is used to rank products.

Example

N. Neath (Compact Discs) Ltd

Refer to the data in section 34.6 again, but assume that the limiting factor is a shortage of direct material. Longplay uses £3 worth of direct material per unit, and Shortplay uses £1.50 of the same material per unit.

Required

Determine which is the most profitable product on which production should be concentrated.

Solution

The unit contribution per £1 of limiting factor for each product is as follows:

Longplay $= \frac{£4}{£3}$

= £1.33 per £1 of direct material

Shortplay $= \frac{£3}{£1.50}$

= £2.00 per £1 of direct material

Shortplay is preferred as its contribution per £1 of scarce resource (direct material) is higher than Longplay.

34.11 Two constraints

It is possible to use this ranking technique where ***two constraints*** exist, in circumstances where one of the constraints is a general constraint on the level of production or sales of a particular product.

Example

Channel Seven Ltd

Channel Seven Ltd manufactures three perfumes: Silk, Musk and Opia. The selling prices and the marginal costs of each product are as follows:

	Silk	Musk	Opia
	£	£	£
Selling price	15	20	30
Marginal cost	10	14	20
Contribution	5	6	10

The firm's fixed costs are £150,000 per annum. There is a shortage of the raw material called essence which is used in all three products. Silk uses 2 kilos, Musk uses 1 kilo, and Opia uses 3 kilos per unit of output. Only 120,000 kilos of essence will be available for the year. In addition, market constraints are expected to restrict the production and sales of each product to:

	Units
Silk	40,000
Musk	8,000
Opia	15,000

Required

Calculate the mix of sales which would enable Channel Seven Ltd to maximise profits, and calculate the profit which is achievable at that sales mix.

Solution

To rank the products according to their desirability having regard to the effect of the direct material constraint, calculate the contribution per kilo of essence:

	Silk	Musk	Opia
$\frac{\text{Contribution}}{\text{Kilos per unit}}$	$\frac{£5}{2\text{ kilos}} = £2.5$	$\frac{£6}{1\text{ kilo}} = £6$	$\frac{£10}{3\text{ kilos}} = £3.33$
Ranking:	3rd	1st	2nd

Because Musk produces the largest contribution per kilo of essence (the scarce resource), in the absence of any other constraints, profit would be maximised by using all the available essence to produce Musk. The number of units of Musk which would be produced under those circumstances would be:

$$\frac{\text{Number of kilos of essence available}}{\text{Number of kilos of essence per unit of Musk}}$$

$$= \frac{120{,}000}{1}$$

$$= 120{,}000 \text{ units}$$

However, the market constraint restricts the production of Musk to 8,000 units only, the production of which would not use all the available quantity of essence. It would only use:

8,000 units × 1 kilo per unit = 8,000 kilos of essence

Moving to the next most attractive product, Opia, the production of the maximum possible level of this product according to the market constraint at 15,000 units would use:

15,000 units × 3 kilos per unit = 45,000 kilos of essence

The production of the maximum possible number of units each of Musk and Opia have so far used 53,000 (8,000 + 45,000) kilos of essence, leaving 67,000 kilos available for the production of Silk. Because Silk uses 2 kilos of essence per unit, its production will be restricted to:

$$\frac{\text{67,000 kilos of essence}}{\text{2 kilos per unit of Silk}} = \text{33,500 units of Silk}$$

A summary of the production, use of constraint and maximum profit achieved is as follows:

Ranking	Overriding constraint	Essence kilos	Production units ×	Contribution per unit =	Total contribution
				£	£
1 Musk	Market	8,000	8,000	6	48,000
2 Opia	Market	45,000	15,000	10	150,000
3 Silk	Material	67,000	33,500	5	167,500
		120,000		Total contribution	365,500
				Less Fixed costs	150,000
				Maximum profit	215,500

You should now be able to attempt Question 34.2 and Task 34.2 at the end of this chapter.

34.12 Summary

A ***limiting factor*** is any factor of production and/or sales, the shortage or lack of which restricts the level of activity or profits achievable by a business. The identification and elimination of the limiting effects of any such factor allows higher levels of activity and profitability to be obtained. However, the limiting effects of other factors will come into play so that a limiting factor always exists.

If a range of products is produced it is important to ***rank*** them according to their relative profitability so that the business can use any scarce resources most effectively and concentrate on the most profitable products in order to maximise profits.

There are four levels of ranking products, each one superseding the previous one. These rank products according to the size of:

1. Unit contribution
2. Profit-volume ratio (or contribution-margin or profit-sales ratio)
3. Total contribution
4. Contribution per limiting factor

If ranking of products according to a limiting factor is used, the general rule is to express the unit contribution of each alternative product as a rate per unit or per £1 of scarce resource or limiting factor. The maximum production of the most profitable product is then carried out until another constraint applies.

You should now be able to attempt the Objective Test at the end of this chapter.

Student activities

Task 34.1 What do you think is the current limiting factor in your own organisation and how could its effect be minimised?

Task 34.2 A local manufacturer has found that his raw material supply has been reduced by 25% because of an industrial dispute. Write a report explaining the techniques which can be applied to ensure that the most profitable products are produced.

Question 34.1 Refer to the example in section 34.6. If ***N. Neath*** is able to produce either Longplay or Shortplay, but not both, calculate the break-even point in units and sales value when either Longplay or Shortplay are produced.

Notice that if Longplay has a larger unit contribution than Shortplay, then its break-even point should be met when fewer units are produced and sold.

Question 34.2 The management of ***Tours Bicycles Ltd*** is planning next year's production schedules and is considering what its production and sales strategy should be for its range of four models. The following information is available:

Model	Sales demand Units	Selling price £ per unit	Parts & materials £ per unit	Labour cost £ per unit
Super	200	400	190	60
Excel	300	300	140	40
GT	400	200	90	30
BMX	600	100	40	20

The labour hour rate will be £5, and the variable overheads will be absorbed at 10% on direct labour cost. Fixed costs are budgeted at £100,000 for the year, and will also be absorbed as a percentage on direct labour cost.

The sales director is of the opinion that, even if extra production capacity were to be made available, the volume of sales of any model could only be increased by a maximum of 25%, and then only at an additional advertising cost of £500 for any one model.

In addition to this limit on sales volume, the other constraint is direct labour.

Required

i) Draw up a schedule showing the budgeted profits for next year based on the planned levels of production shown above.

ii) Advise the management of the company which model(s) and how many units of each model should be produced in order to satisfy the existing demands and to maximise profits if the following total direct labour hours are made available:

a) 10,000 hours

b) 10,500 hours

iii) Calculate the profits which would be made by the company in each case.

Question 34.3 *Montrose Ltd* manufactures high quality soft toys and has three products: Rabbits, Dogs and Bears. Each product goes through the same process and uses the same quality of materials; the only difference arises from the different sizes of the products. The manufacturing standards set for the products and the selling prices for next year are as follows:

	Rabbits	Dogs	Bears
Budgeted production/Sales	4,000 units	3,000 units	2,000 units
Material costs per unit	£11.50	£17.50	£25.00
Labour hours per unit:			
Cutting department	2 hours	2.5 hours	3 hours
Finishing department	2 hours	1.5 hours	1 hour
Selling price per unit	£52.50	£61.00	£70.00

Employees in the cutting department will be paid £4 per hour and in the finishing department £3 per hour.

The total budgeted departmental overheads are split equally between fixed and variable at the budgeted levels of production.

The overhead absorption rates based on budgeted production are as follows:

Cutting department	£6 per direct labour hour
Finishing department	£4 per direct labour hour

Required

You are trainee production manager for Montrose Ltd and you have been asked by the production director to:

i) Produce a statement for him which will show the contribution from each product and the total budgeted profit for next year.

ii) Show calculations to indicate which product should be subject to reduced production in the event of material shortages.

iii) Show calculations to indicate which product should be subject to reduced production in the event of labour shortages in the finishing department.

iv) Write a brief explanation of the principles upon which your recommendations are based.

Question 34.4 *Radio Products Ltd* produces a range of radios known as the intercontinental range. The power rating of each radio is based on the number of wave bands, so they are called the Seven, Eight and Eleven. The costs and selling prices for each model are as follows:

	Seven	Eight	Eleven
	£	£	£
Selling price	85	100	120
Marginal costs	65	70	80

Budgeted fixed costs for the year are £600,000.

There is a shortage of skilled labour and therefore the total direct labour hours will be restricted to 200,000 for the year. In addition there is likely to be a limit on the total sales levels for each product. The direct labour hours and anticipated maximum sales levels are as follows:

	Seven	Eight	Eleven
Direct labour hours per unit	3	3	5
Maximum achievable sales	40,000 units	20,000 units	10,000 units

Required

i) Calculate the volume of sales of each model which should be produced and sold in order to maximise profits and state the level of profits which would be achieved.

ii) Calculate the value of total sales at which the company would break even, and the margin of safety. Assume the mix of sales is as put forward in your answer to (i).

iii) If an additional 20,000 hours of direct labour could be made available, how would that affect your answers in (i) and (ii).

Question 34.5 *National Business Computers* produce three desk models. In budgeting next year's production the management is attempting to make sure that the most profitable mix of sales is produced, assuming that one of each of the following constraints is experienced:

i) a restriction on the sales value achievable;

ii) a shortage of direct material;

iii) a shortage of direct labour.

The costs and sales prices per product are as follows:

	256K	512K	1024K
	£	£	£
Sales value	500	600	1,200
Direct materials	150	160	250
Direct labour	150	200	600
Other direct costs	50	100	120

Required

Rank each of the models in order of profitability for each constraint which is likely to be experienced in the budget year.

Question 34.6 *BMX Racing Ltd* is a company set up by some students who feel that there is a market for specialised cycling accessories. They have produced the following information on their initial range of products and asked your advice on the production and sales policy which they should pursue.

The students intend to make the products themselves and have calculated that, after allowing for administrative time, holidays etc, there will be an average of 150 hours per week throughout the year of 52 weeks spent on manufacture. They plan to pay themselves a small sum of £2 per hour for time spent on manufacturing. The estimated data per unit of each product are as follows:

	Knee pads	Elbow protectors	Gloves
	£	£	£
Selling price	15.00	18.00	23.00
Direct materials			
Covers	3.00	4.00	5.00
Padding	2.00	2.00	1.00
Agency commission	1.00	1.70	2.10
Production time	2 hours	2.5 hours	3 hours
Potential sales	2,000 units	2,000 units	1,000 units

Variable manufacturing overheads are estimated at 10% of selling price and fixed manufacturing overheads £5,000 per annum.

Required

Write a report to the students advising them of the production policy to be pursued. Your report should include:

i) the contribution per unit for each of the products;

ii) the contribution per unit of limiting factor for each of the products, assuming that direct labour hours is the main constraint;

iii) the quantities of each product to be manufactured bearing in mind the limits of the market and the restriction on direct labour hours available;

iv) the profit or loss which may be achieved if the most profitable product mix is manufactured.

Objective Test *(tick the appropriate box)*

i) In ranking products, we are mostly concerned with:

a) the gross profit ☐

b) the net profit ☐

c) the total absorption cost ☐

d) the contribution ☐

ii) The most important way in which to rank products is according to:

a) some constraint or limiting factor ☐

b) the size of the unit contribution ☐

c) the size of the total contribution ☐

d) the size of the profit-volume ratio ☐

iii) The least important way in which to rank products is according to:

a) some constraint or limiting factor ☐

b) the size of the unit contribution ☐

c) the size of the total contribution ☐

d) the size of the profit-volume ratio ☐

iv) The formula for the profit-volume ratio is:

a) profit/sales ☐

b) profit /fixed costs ☐

c) fixed costs/contribution ☐

d) contribution/sales ☐

v) Another name for the profit-volume ratio is:

a) contribution-margin ratio ☐

b) contribution-sales ratio ☐

c) neither of these ☐

d) both of these ☐

Chapter 35

Deciding the relevant costs

35.1 Objectives

At the end of this chapter you should be able to:

- understand why different costs are necessary for different decisions;
- understand and define what differential and incremental costs and revenue are, and how they are used;
- understand what opportunity costs are and how they are used;
- determine which costs are relevant to different decisions in business.

35.2 Introduction

In Chapters 33 and 34 we looked at the ways in which marginal or variable costs and limiting factors are used in making some decisions in business. The relationships between sales revenue and fixed and variable costs were used to work out answers to such questions as what level of production or sales are necessary for the the business to break-even or to make alternative levels of profit. Before you continue with this chapter you may find it beneficial to revise your understanding of the concepts and techniques which were covered in Chapters 33 and 34.

Besides the decision about what levels of production and sales should be achieved, there are many other decisions required in business. Managers require information which will enable them to answer such questions as:

- At what prices should output be sold?
- Should an order be accepted at less than full cost?
- Should we manufacture or buy a part which we use in the final product?
- What alternative manufacturing methods should we use?
- Should we close down or suspend production for a while in a particular factory?
- Which branch should we close down when there is a choice?
- Should changes be made to the design of a product and the materials used in its manufacture?

In order to obtain the correct answers to these and other questions and to make the most profitable decisions, financial information is required about how income and costs are likely to change as a result of making the alternative decisions which are available. The financial information must be relevant to the problem being considered.

35.3 General principles

In deciding which particular costs or revenues should be included in the financial information provided to managers to help them make the correct decision, the basic questions which must always be asked are:

- Which costs and revenues are changed by any of the alternative decisions which could be made?
- By how much are they changed by each decision?

The answers to these questions identify the costs and revenues which should be included when choosing alternative courses of action. These costs and revenues are known as the ***relevant costs and revenues***. In other words they are ***relevant*** to the proposals being considered.

When a manager makes a decision there are usually several alternative actions which he or she can take. There are always at least two alternatives, that is, either make a decision to change or make a decision to continue with the existing way of doing things.

35.4 Relevant costs

Relevant costs can be costs which behave in a number of different ways. Sometimes the relevant costs are variable costs, sometimes fixed costs or opportunity costs. In some circumstances the relevant costs are combinations of all three types.

35.5 Marginal costs and variable costs

You may remember from Chapter 33 that variable costs are those costs which, in total, change in relation to changes in the level of activity, and marginal costs are the variable costs expressed as a rate per unit of production or sales. For example, total material costs will increase or decrease in direct proportion to changes in production levels because the material costs per unit, which are part of the marginal costs, remain constant.

Example

M. Melbourne produces books. The marginal costs (for example, material, labour, power) amount to £2 per book. His total variable costs for various production levels are as follows:

Number of books	1,000	5,000	20,000	30,000
Marginal cost per book	£2	£2	£2	£2
Total variable costs	£2,000	£10,000	£40,000	£60,000

M. Melbourne's present level of production is 20,000 books per month. He is considering whether to increase his production by 50%, and wishes to know what effect this will have on total costs. The increase in production can be achieved without increasing any of the fixed costs of the factory. What are the relevant costs to this decision to increase production?

Solution

As the total fixed cost will not change, the only part of total cost which will alter will be the variable costs. As the variable costs will increase by:

50% x 20,000 units × £2 = £20,000

then these variable costs are the costs which are relevant to the decision.

35.6 Relevant revenue

In many cases a particular action or decision will also result in a change in sales revenue, either as a consequence of a price adjustment or as a result of an increase or decrease in the volume of sales, or both. The decision which M. Melbourne is considering could also result in an increase in sales revenue, and therefore the extra sales revenue could also be relevant to the decision.

Example

Using the example in Section 35.5 again, *M. Melbourne* expects that the additional 10,000 books (50% of 20,000 units of normal production) will be sold for £6 per book. What is the relevant revenue?

Solution

The resultant change in revenue is:

50% × 20,000 units × £6 = £60,000

This represents the relevant revenue of this decision.

35.7 Contribution

We have already met the contribution in Chapter 33, and you will remember that the contribution per unit is selling price per unit – the marginal cost per unit.

The total contribution is either contribution per unit × sales volume in units or total sales revenue – total variable costs.

In many decisions where the both the revenue and the variable costs are relevant factors, the difference between the two, the ***contribution***, may be used instead.

Example

Using the examples in Sections 35.5 and 35.6, calculate ***M. Melbourne's*** increased unit and total contribution which would result from the proposed 50% increase in production and sales.

Solution

M. Melbourne's unit and total contributions would be:

	Contributions		
	Unit		Total
	£		£
Selling price	6	× 10,000 =	60,000
Marginal cost	2	× 10,000 =	20,000
Contribution	4	× 10,000 =	40,000

The financial data relevant to the question of whether to increase production by 50% is summarised in the table above. Both the changes in total costs and revenue which arise because of the increase in activity are relevant. The costs are expected to increase by £20,000, which is less than the increase in the sales revenue of £60,000. Therefore the net increase in contribution and profit of £40,000 means that the proposed change to increase the sales and production should take place.

35.8 Differential costs and revenue

In each case it is always the changes in cost and revenue which arise from a proposed action which are relevant to that action. These changes are sometimes known as ***differential costs*** and ***differential revenue*** because we are concerned with the difference which would arise in each of the costs and revenue as a direct result of a particular decision, such as the one to increase production and sales levels.

Sometimes an alternative decision may cause costs and/or revenue to fall, in which case the amounts by which they fall are also called differential costs and differential revenue. Differential costs and revenues which increase are sometimes called ***incremental costs*** and ***incremental revenue***.

In M. Melbourne's examples the total costs and revenues increase by £20,000 and £60,000 respectively as a result of increasing production and sales. In this case, because increases are involved, these changes are known as incremental costs and incremental revenue. His proposal to increase production and sales is recommended because, as a result, his incremental revenue is greater than his incremental costs. His incremental contribution is therefore £40,000.

Many alternatives are looked at in this way. They should be pursued if incremental revenue exceeds incremental costs, but rejected if incremental costs exceed incremental revenue.

35.9 Fixed costs

So far we have considered M. Melbourne's decision to increase production and sales by 50%, and this decision has affected total revenue and variable costs only. As far as the costs are concerned, the ***incremental*** or ***differential costs*** are made up of changes to the ***variable costs*** only.

When some proposals are considered, however, the incremental or differential costs include also changes in the *fixed costs* of the business. You will remember from Chapter 33 that fixed costs are those costs which, in total, stay the same regardless of changes in the level of activity.

You will appreciate that it is not possible to increase production indefinitely without increasing fixed costs at some stage. In increasing production to a substantially higher level there comes a point where additional factory space is required, and this alone will cause fixed costs such as rent, rates, insurance, cleaning, depreciation and other fixed costs to rise.

The normal definition of fixed costs, therefore, only holds good for certain limited increases in activity, usually described as in the short-term, or between two levels of activity known as the ***relevant range***.

Example

Using the example in Sections 35.5, 35.6 and 35.7, *M. Melbourne* wishes to double output from the normal level of 20,000 books per month. The marginal costs will remain at £2 per book, but in order to obtain this level of production an investment in capacity is required which will increase the monthly fixed costs by £45,000.

Required

Calculate the relevant costs and revenue and advise M. Melbourne on whether the increase in production and sales is justified.

Solution

The relevant costs and revenue are those which change as a direct result of obtaining the increase in production and sales. In this case they are incremental because they increase:

	£
Incremental sales : 20,000 units × £6	120,000
Incremental variable costs : 20,000 units × £2	40,000
Incremental fixed costs	45,000
Total incremental costs	85,000
Incremental profit	35,000

The increase in production and sales is justified as there is a net increase in profits of £35,000. The incremental revenue exceeds the incremental costs.

Example

Now *M. Melbourne* plans to double capacity, with the consequent increase in fixed costs, but he is only able to increase production and sales by 50%.

Required

Calculate the relevant costs and revenue, and advise M. Melbourne on whether the planned increase in capacity is justified.

Solution

	£
Incremental sales : 10,000 units × £6	60,000
Incremental variable costs : 10,000 units × £2	20,000
Incremental fixed costs	45,000
	65,000
	(5,000)

In this case the increase in production capacity is not justified if this lower level of sales is achieved, as the incremental revenue is less than the incremental costs.

You should now be able to attempt Question 35.1 at the end of this chapter.

35.10 Opportunity costs

An ***opportunity cost*** is a way of measuring the cost of doing something in terms of the income that has been sacrificed by not being able to do something else at the same time. An opportunity cost arises because many resources are in limited supply and if used to carry out one course of action cannot be used for another. One factor or resource that is in short supply both in business and in personal life is time.

The fact that you are studying this subject at the moment itself has an opportunity cost. Instead of studying you might have been able to carry out a part-time paid job, possibly decorating a room or working behind a bar for which you could be paid £20. In this case the opportunity cost of studying is the income you would otherwise have earned and have therefore forgone by not working in the part-time job, the studying and the job not both being possible due to the scarcity of time. The opportunity cost of studying for a day is, therefore, £20.

In deciding alternative courses of action in business opportunity costs are particularly important where there are scarce resources featured in the decision.

Example

P. Perth runs a transport business with five trucks. His present net income from truck operations in which the trucks are fully employed throughout the year is £85,000. Mr Perth has been approached by a manufacturer with the proposal that the trucks should be leased to him at a rate of £20,000 per annum per truck. All costs would be born by the manufacturer.

Required

Assess Mr Perth's opportunity cost of continuing to operate the trucks himself.

Solution

The trucks are a scarce resource, and they cannot be both operated by Mr Perth and leased to the third party. If he continues to operate the trucks himself then he forgoes or sacrifices the income he would have earned from leasing. The opportunity cost of operating the trucks is therefore the leasing income forgone:

5 trucks × £20,000 per truck = £100,000 per annum.

Notice also that there is an opportunity cost relevant to leasing. If Mr Perth leases the trucks to the manufacturer he cannot operate them. Operating them creates an income of £85,000 per annum, which is therefore the opportunity cost of leasing the trucks, because this would be the income forgone if Mr Perth changed to leasing.

As the opportunity cost of operating the trucks (£100,000) is greater than the opportunity cost of leasing them (£85,000), then it is preferable to lease the trucks to the manufacturer.

You should now be able to attempt Task 35.2 at the end of this chapter.

35.11 Mutually exclusive decisions

The use of opportunity cost is particularly important where the alternative actions available are ***mutually exclusive***. These actions are where carrying out one action eliminates the possibility of another action taking place. For example, the availability of a plot of land will enable either an office block or a factory to be built to occupy the site, but not both. If a mixture of a factory and an office is built, then that becomes a third alternative, all three alternatives being mutually exclusive.

35.12 Opportunity costs and other costs

As we have seen earlier in this chapter and in Chapter 33, the costs that are most often relevant to decision-making in the short-term are the incremental variable or marginal costs. In the longer-term when further investment in capital expenditure such as plant and machinery, land and buildings, and fixtures and fittings may be necessary, then incremental fixed costs may also be relevant.

Example

S. Sidney has to decide whether to manufacture a part which is incorporated in the final product, or sub-contract its manufacture. The parts cost £1.50 per unit if manufactured outside, or a marginal cost of £1.00 if made internally. The fixed costs amount to £50,000 per annum, and 400 units are required per month. There is adequate spare capacity available for its internal manufacture.

Required

Advise S. Sidney on whether to purchase or manufacture.

Solution

This is a typical make or buy problem which is often faced in a manufacturing business. The fixed costs of £50,000 per annum are not relevant to this decision because they continue to be incurred whether the parts are purchased or manufactured. The decision must be based on the variable cost of manufacture compared to the cost if purchased:

	£ per month
Cost of purchase from outside supplier:	
400 units × £1.50	600
Variable cost of internal manufacture:	
400 units × £1.00	400
Advantage of internal manufacture assuming spare capacity	200

If there is no spare capacity available to manufacture the spare part internally, then it can only be made internally by ceasing to manufacture some other product in order to release enough capacity to manufacture the part.

In this case, not only are the variable costs relevant to the decision of whether to make or buy, but also the income which is foregone or sacrificed by not being able to manufacture and sell some of the final product. As explained earlier, this income forgone is the opportunity cost of making the part.

Example

Using the above example again of ***S. Sidney***, but in order to produce the parts internally assume that there is a shortage of manufacturing capacity. In order to manufacture 400 parts, S. Sydney would have to cease manufacturing some of the final product which takes 30 machine hours per month and makes a contribution, on average, of £10 per machine hour to the fixed costs of the business.

Required

Advise S. Sydney on whether to purchase or manufacture the part.

Solution

In this case both variable costs and opportunity costs are relevant to the decision because of the existence of scarce resources, ie production capacity. The alternatives now become:

	£ per month
Variable cost of internal manufacture:	
400 units × £1	400
Add	
Income forgone (opportunity cost of manufacturing the part internally) :	
30 hours × £10	300
	700
Cost of purchase from outside supplier: 400 units × £1.50	600
Advantage of purchase assuming no spare capacity	£100

There is an advantage in purchasing the part because the production of the part can only be achieved by transferring some capacity to its production. Its cost, therefore, is the addition of the actual cost of production, in this case the variable costs, and the income forgone by not being able to produce the product which was previously manufactured by the 30 hours of machine time. As this is greater than the purchase price, it is better to buy.

Notice that the effect of the scarce resource may be calculated by expressing the income forgone, usually the contribution, as a rate per unit of scarce resource. In the above example this amounts to £10 per machine hour. The opportunity cost is then the number of units of the scarce resource transferred to the production of the alternative product, (30 hours of machine time) at the rate per unit of scarce resource.

You should now be able to attempt Question 35.2 at the end of this chapter.

35.13 Accounting Information

In most cases ***financial information*** used in decision-making is available from the accounting system. For example, fixed costs and variable costs, differential and incremental costs and revenue may all be recorded in the books of the accounting system because they are accompanied by an actual payment or receipt. Opportunity costs, however, represent income forgone and are not recorded in the accounts.

For this reason, opportunity cost is often disregarded by some accountants and managers when considering alternative courses of action. You will now appreciate that the correct decisions cannot be made unless opportunity cost is taken into consideration, particularly where there are scarce resources.

You should now be able to attempt Questions 35.3 and 35.4 at the end of this chapter.

35.14 Aspects of relevant and non-relevant costs

Because it is the changes in costs which determine whether they are relevant to a particular decision, it is sometimes described that only cost changes which cause an additional ***cash outflow*** for the business should be considered in decision-making.

This definition therefore would describe a cost as relevant based not on whether it is fixed or variable for accounting purposes, but whether it causes additional outflow of cash, either immediately or in the future. Such cash outflows are sometimes known as ***out of pocket costs.***

Depreciation is not usually a relevant cost in decision-making. You will remember that depreciation is simply the accountant's way of charging a proportion of fixed assets against profits over their estimated useful lives. As no cash movements take place when depreciation is charged, and as it is a policy cost which can vary according to the method of depreciation used and the estimated lives of the assets, it cannot be treated as a cost which is relevant to decision-making.

When fixed assets are purchased, we have seen that they are capitalised in the balance sheet and written off by depreciating them against profits over their estimated useful lives. At any point in time, therefore, the firm's balance sheet will show each class of asset, for example, plant and machinery, at cost less the accumulated depreciation to date on that class of asset. This net figure is known as the ***net book value (NBV)***. These ***NBVs*** are not relevant to decision-making unless they are equal to the realisable or sales value of the asset at the time of the decision.

Example

A. Adelaide Ltd is considering whether to cease the production of widgets. If it continues to manufacture its annual net cash inflow will be £200,000, whereas it could sell the assets used for widget production for £1 million and invest the proceeds to generate 25% per annum interest. The company is unsure what to do as the assets have a book value of £2.5 million, and any sale would cause a £1.5 million loss.

Required

Advise A. Adelaide Ltd of the correct decision on purely financial grounds.

Solution

The book value of the plant is irrelevant. Today's true value is £1 million, its realisable value at the time the decision needs to be made. The potential £1.5 million loss on sale is a book loss, and although it may be important to the accountants and the Stock Exchange because it has to be recorded in the accounts, it really represents the result of a bad ***past*** decision, and should not affect the current decision. The alternatives are:

	£
Net annual cash flow from investing proceeds from sales of assets	250,000
Net cash flow from continuing the production of widgets	200,000
Advantage from selling assets and investing funds	50,000

Sunk costs are past costs which are irrecoverable at their book values and therefore are also irrelevant for decision-making. It is always the ***current realisable values*** which are relevant, whether they are greater or less than the net book values shown in the balance sheet.

35.15 Summary

In business, managers are concerned with making decisions and they need the type of financial information which will help them choose the most profitable course of action where alternatives are available. For this reason we must make sure that the information provided to managers is relevant to the alternative proposals which they are considering. ***Relevant costs and revenues*** are identified by recognising those costs and revenues which in total may change as a result of a particular course of action being taken. Those that do not change are usually not relevant to the decision.

When there is a possible change in costs or revenue as a result of a proposal then this change is known as ***differential cost or differential revenue.*** Sometimes costs or revenues may increase as the result of a proposal, and the general term for any increase in such items is ***incremental cost or incremental revenue.***

Differential or incremental costs are often variable costs, but they may also be fixed costs or semi-variable costs, particularly where additional capital expenditure is involved in a decision alternative. For this reason relevant costs can be identified as additional cash outflows which arise from a decision. They are often referred to as ***out of pocket costs.***

Opportunity costs must also be taken into consideration, in addition to the usual fixed and variable costs, where a scarce resource is concerned. This is because alternative A can only be carried out by not doing alternative B, and therefore the net income which alternative B would have generated is forgone or sacrificed. This is known as the opportunity cost of alternative A. Likewise, the opportunity cost of alternative B is the income forgone by not pursuing alternative A.

Other costs which are seldom relevant in decision-making are ***sunk costs, book values and depreciation charges.*** They must always be replaced by ***current realisable values.***

You should now be able to attempt the Objective Test at the end of this chapter.

Student activities

Task 35. 1 The following is an extract from a letter to a railway magazine:

> 'I am surprised that you published without questioning the absurd figure quoted by the minister in the House of Commons as the operating cost of a train from Berwick to Edinburgh. I suggest that the true cost of running the train of light weight for the 60 miles would be simply fuel and crew wages (assuming this to be the only revenue-earning work of the day). All the other things like rolling stock and station staff are there anyway.'

A response by another correspondent a month later said:

> 'May I suggest that the statement....was ridiculous? The idea that a train has to pay the cost of fuel, plus crew wages, with a little thrown in for maintenance is stupid. How much rolling stock or how many staff would be there if there were no trains? None! The train in question must help to pay for these and other costs.'

What revenue and costs are relevant to the decision whether to run a particular train or not? Write a memorandum to British Rail's local area manager advising him on how to go about solving this problem.

Task 35. 2 You have been asked by your local school to set an examination question which would test pupils' understanding of opportunity costs. A question that would require them to carry out calculations and solve a specific problem rather than repeating a definition is preferred. Set the question and the model answer.

Question 35.1 *Bendigo Tours Ltd* sells special packaged holidays to Europe at £600 each, and they expect to sell 1,000 holidays this year. The variable costs per holiday amount to £400, and the fixed costs of the operation total £100,000. As the holidays are very labour intensive, the company proposes to change to a self-catering holiday next year, which would reduce the variable costs of each holiday to £200 but would have the effect of increasing the fixed costs of the operation to £325,000. A selling price reduction of 5% is planned which is expected to increase the number of holidays by 10%.

Required

Identify the costs and revenues which are relevant to this proposal, and draw up a statement to indicate the financial effects of the proposed changes. Advise Bendigo Tours Ltd whether to make the change.

Question 35.2 *Darwin Gates Ltd* manufactures a standard line in garden gates for which there is already a heavy demand which the company cannot meet because there is a shortage of skilled labour able to weld the metal gates at the assembly stage. The selling price is £180 each. The variable costs are made up of material costs of £80 and direct labour costs. The skilled workers included in the latter take 10 hours per gate, and are paid £6 per hour.

Darwin Gates Ltd has received an enquiry from a large garden centre for some special gates to their own design. The value of the order amounts to £50,000, and the company calculates that the material cost would be £15,000 and the skilled labour would take 4,000 hours to complete the order.

Required

Advise Darwin Gates Ltd on whether it should accept the order and show the financial advantage of following your advice.

Question 35.3 *St. Kilda Model Cars Ltd* make model cars at a rate of 1,000 cars per week and their latest model of a Super Holden is experiencing heavy demand which cannot be met in full because of a shortage of skilled labour.

Details of a typical week's profit statement are as follows:

	£	£
Sales		3,800
Bought in materials	1,300	
Direct labour:		
100 hours @ £5 per hour	500	
Variable costs:		
80% of direct labour cost	400	
Fixed costs	1,000	3,200
Weekly profit		600

The company has received an enquiry from Geelong Stores Ltd to supply a batch of model trucks. The value of the order would be £2,200, and St Kilda estimates that the variable costs of the order would be:

Materials: £800

Included in the material costs is a special part which could be purchased for £60 or, alternatively, manufactured by St Kildas for £32 materials and 2 hours of skilled labour.

Direct labour: 50 hours

Variable overheads: Based on direct labour hours at normal rates

Required

Prepare calculations and advise the company on whether it should accept an order from Geelong Stores Ltd.

Question 35.4 *Heidelberg Golf Club* employs Bruce, a skilled craftsman, who makes hand-made sets of golf clubs for the members. The club pays Bruce £120 per week, which is based on a working week of 30 hours at £4 per hour during which time Bruce makes one set of clubs. The club sells the sets at £200 per set. The materials cost £20 per set and Bruce works in a room which has £24 of fixed overheads charged to it by the Club accountant. In addition, the accountant regards the £200 of holiday pay paid to Bruce yearly is also a fixed overhead.

Bruce doesn't work very hard. Having finished his set of clubs for the week he usually lights his pipe, picks up the paper and completes the crossword, in spite of the fact that there is a waiting list for the sets of clubs.

The Club secretary has been asked by a rich American member whether Bruce could make 5 special putters as Christmas presents for his business contacts. These putters would have special engraved brass plates attached, which Bruce says that he could make himself, or could be purchased for £22 each. If Bruce does make them, each plate would take 1.5 hours to make, engrave and fix, and the brass blank would cost £8. The putters themselves would also take 1.5 hours to make. All other materials required would cost £24 per putter and the American is prepared to pay up to £65 each for the putters. Surprisingly, Bruce indicates that he might be able to make the putters and the plates within his normal working week.

The Club secretary does not want to upset the American member, or the other members who are waiting for Bruce to make their orders for complete sets. He therefore tells everyone involved that he will ask Bruce to make whatever the Club's accounting assistant decides gives the Club the highest profit.

Required

If you were the accounting assistant at Heidelberg Golf Club, what would you recommend, assuming that either:

i) Bruce is able to make the American's order within the normal working week, that is, without affecting the making of one of the complete sets for the other members.

or

ii) Bruce has to work overtime to complete the order for the American.

or

iii) Bruce refuses to work overtime, and the American's order can only be completed by not producing one of the complete sets for the other members.

Provide figures for each alternative.

Question 35.5 *Angloflug plc* operates a twice-daily air service between London and Frankfurt on 350 days of each year. Three aircraft are allocated to this service from the company fleet. Two are in use each day whilst the third undergoes maintenance and is kept in reserve as a backup 'plane.

There are four flights a day, all of them at a meal-time. One 'plane leaves London at 12 noon and makes the return trip at 6pm the same day. Each trip takes approximately 2 hours. The other 'plane travels in the opposite direction at the same timings.

Market research has indicated that half of the passengers travelling on each flight would be prepared to purchase a meal during the flight and the company is considering satisfying this demand. The relevant data are as follows:

Number of seats per 'plane:	80
Normal occupancy rate:	75% average for the year
Cost of equipping the kitchens:	£21,000 per aircraft
Depreciation of kitchens:	3 years straight line basis (no residual value)
Staffing:	6 additional staff, 2 staff per aircraft
Staff salaries:	£4,200 each per annum
Cost per meal:	80p per meal, including packaging
Additional costs:	10p for disposables (plates, cutlery, cups)

Annual profit required on this service should be allowed for at a rate of 20% return on capital employed, which includes the capital cost of equipping the planes, and also an additional estimated £21,000 to cover increased working capital (stocks less creditors). No appreciable increase in other costs will be caused by the introduction of the service.

Required

i) Calculate the total cost of each meal to be served.

ii) Calculate a menu price to be charged for each meal which will satisfy the company's profit requirements.

iii) Calculate the total budgeted profit on this operation for next year, using your calculations in (i) and (ii) above. Show total sales, contribution and profit.

iv) Using the budgeted level of activity assumed above, calculate the number of passengers requiring meals per trip necessary to make the planned service break even.

Question 35.6 *Zed-Plan Furniture Company* manufactures a standard dining room chair for which there is heavy demand. However, the company cannot meet the demand, mainly because of a shortage of skilled labour. The selling price is £90 per chair. Material costs are £40 and the only other variable cost is direct labour, where a skilled worker takes 10 standard hours to make a chair and is paid £3 per hour.

The chair department has received an enquiry from a large furniture store for some special chairs. The total value of the order is £2,500. Zed-Plan's estimator calculates that the materials would cost £700 and the skilled labour would take 500 hours to complete the order.

Required

Advise Zed-Plan on whether it should accept the order, giving calculations to support your advice.

Objective test *(tick the appropriate box)*

i) In deciding the costs which are relevant to a decision, they tend to be:

a) those costs which remain unchanged by each proposal ☐

b) those costs which are changed by each proposal ☐

c) both ☐

d) neither ☐

ii) Differential costs are:

a) always variable costs ☐

b) always fixed costs ☐

c) sometimes both of these ☐

d) never either of these ☐

iii) Incremental costs are:

a) always variable costs ☐

b) always fixed costs ☐

c) sometimes both of these ☐

d) never either of these ☐

iv) Opportunity costs are:

a) the costs of not doing something ☐

b) the costs of doing something ☐

c) the income lost by doing something else ☐

d) the income generated by doing something else ☐

v) To get the total relevant costs, opportunity costs should be:

a) added to other relevant costs ☐

b) subtracted from other relevant costs ☐

c) sometimes considered ☐

d) always considered ☐

Assignment I

Aussie Woollen Products Ltd

Context

You are an assistant in the marketing department of ***Aussie Woollen Products Ltd***, and the company is considering the production and marketing of a new range of woollen products which uses a new type of wool. Because of their specialised nature, it is intended to market them through an agency which charges a fee per garment. There are three products in the range, a pullover,a sweater and a smoking jacket. The projected figures for each product are as follows:

	Pullover	**Sweater**	**Smoking jacket**
	£	**£**	**£**
Selling price	150	180	230
Direct materials	50	60	60
Agency fee	10	17	21
Direct labour time	[10 hours]	[12.5 hours]	[15 hours]
The market potential - maximum units per month	[2,000 units]	[2,000 units]	[1,000 units]

Other information is:

Rate of pay per hour £4

Variable production overheads are 50% of direct labour costs.

Fixed overheads are expected to be £50,000 per month.

A special curing process requires skilled labour which is in short supply and the number of direct labour hours required for this process, per garment, is:

Pullover	2 hours
Sweater	2.5 hours
Smoking jacket	4 hours

The company wishes to know whether the introduction of the new range is financially feasible, and if so, what product mix would give the highest profit.

Student activities

i) Prepare a report to the marketing director of the company, and advise him what strategy should be adopted by the company with regard to production and product mix if:

the market constraint applies;

and either

skilled labour in the curing process is limited to 9,250 hours per month

or

the direct material is in short supply, limited to £250,000 worth per month.

ii) calculate the break-even point expressed in sales value for each optimal mix of sales you have advised and explain why they differ. How do the margins of safety differ?

Format

A report, with tables of data and supporting calculations. A logically reasoned conclusion should be clearly stated.

Objectives

The student should show an appreciation and understanding of:

- ❒ marginal costing techniques
- ❒ relevant costs
- ❒ limiting factors
- ❒ break-even analysis

References

Chapters 28, 33, 34 and 35.

Project appraisal

This section (Chapters 36 – 39) is concerned with techniques used to examine the financial implications of business projects. Various techniques are available. None of them is completely satisfactory, but some tend to be more satisfactory than others. If you continue your studies further than can be covered by this book, you will become acquainted with some quite sophisticated techniques which are available for project appraisal.

In Chapter 36 we look at the techniques known as the payback period and accounting rate of return.

Chapter 37 describes the mathematics necessary for the techniques explained in Chapters 38 and 39.

In Chapter 38 the net present values are explained and in the final chapter, Chapter 39, we look at the internal rate of return.

Chapter 36

Payback and accounting rate of return

36.1 Objectives

At the end of this chapter you should be able to:

- calculate the payback period for projects;
- calculate the accounting rate of return;
- appreciate the advantages and limitations of these two techniques of project appraisal.

36.2 Introduction

In this chapter we shall consider two of the techniques of appraisal ***payback period*** and ***accounting rate of return***. Payback period is, put simply, the time it takes a business to get its money back. Accounting rate of return is a rather crude method of measuring the return (profit) on an investment (outlay), expressed as a percentage. We shall now consider both these techniques in detail.

36.3 Payback period

Payback period is a simple and easily understood technique of appraising the acceptability of projects - hence its popularity with the non-accountant businessman. The project is considered purely from the point of view of its *cash flows*, both in and out, over the life of the project. Our objective is to recover the cash outlay we have had to make in the shortest possible time.

Example

We are considering buying an ice cream van and employing someone to operate it. Cash spent on buying the van would be £12,000. For each year the cash flows are estimated as follows:

	£	£
Cash in		
Cash received from sale of icecream		20,000
Cash out		
Cash paid for:		
Ice cream ingredients, cones, wafers, flake chocolate etc.	5,000	
Wages for driver/salesperson	9,000	
Other expenses: petrol, tax and insurance, repairs, maintenance etc.	2,000	
Total cash out:		16,000
Net cash flow:		4,000

Note that *depreciation* of the van itself is *not* included. This is because depreciation is *not* a cash flow. The cash flow relative to the van is the cash paid for van when we buy it. This was explained in Chapter 5.

Solution

Year	Yearly net cash flows	Cumulative net cash flows
	£	£
0	(12,000)	(12,000)
1	4,000	(8,000)
2	4,000	(4,000)
3	4,000	NIL
4	4,000	4,000
5	4,000	8,000

There are several things in this table which need explanation:

- Year 0 is a conventional way of saying start of year 1. Year 1, 2, 3 etc. means end of year 1, 2, 3 etc.
- It is customary to assume that cash flows during a year will be received at the end of that year. This is, of course, not true, but it simplifies the calculation and errs on the side of conservatism, giving a slightly pessimistic rather than optimistic view if the cash flows are positive. It is possible to produce cash flows on a quarterly or monthly basis, but this is seldom done in payback calculations, because forecasting to this degree of refinement is rarely possible.
- Negative cash flows (cash going out) are shown in brackets, whereas positive ones (i.e. cash coming in) are not.

You will see that the cumulative cash flows are shown as ***nil*** at the end of year 3. This means that at the end of year 3 the cash flowing in from the project has reached the figure of £12,000, which is same as the initial cash outflow in payment for the van at the start of year 1. We therefore say that the ***payback period*** for the project is 3 years.

Example

What is the ***payback period*** for a project, the net cash flows for which have been budgeted as follows?

Year	Annual net cash flows
	£
0	(18,000)
1	8,000
2	8,000
3	8,000
4	8,000
5	8,000

Solution

Year	Annual net cash flows	Cumulative net cash flows
	£	£
0	(18,000)	(18,000)
1	8,000	(10,000)
2	8,000	(2,000)
3	8,000	6,000
4	8,000	14,000
5	8,000	22,000

The answer lies somewhere between 2 and 3 years. Assuming the cash flow is regular throughout the year, it should be easy to see that the answer is 2.25 or 2 years and 3 months. If the figures are not so simple, the way to calculate the part year is:

Year	Cumulative cash flows
	£
0	(18,000)
2	(2,000)
3	6,000

Add the two cumulative cash flows *ignoring* the fact that the first figure is negative (in brackets):

$$2{,}000 + 6{,}000 = 8{,}000$$

Then divide the earlier figure (2,000) by the total:

$$\frac{2{,}000}{8{,}000} = \frac{1}{4} = 0.25 \text{ of a year}$$

Therefore the payback period is 2 + 0.25 = 2.25 years.

An alternative method is to start adding from year 1 until you get to the total outlay you made in year 0,

	£	£		
Year 1	8,000	8,000		
Year 2	+8,000	= 16,000		2.00 years
Year 3	+2,000	= 18,000	$\frac{2{,}000}{8{,}000}$	= 0.25 years

You should now be able to attempt Question 36.1 at the end of this chapter.

Advantages

- It is very simple to calculate and is understood by managers who are not very numerate.
- Payback produces results which are useful for risky projects, where the prediction of cash flows for more than the first few years is difficult, due to possible changes in the market. Perhaps changes in technology have made a product obsolete in a year or so, although the current market for it seems assured.
- Some businesses may need to consider short-term cash flows more important than long-term cash flows, perhaps due to lack of capital adequate to sustain long-term objectives. It is not much use aiming for long-term profitability if the business fails in six months' time from lack of cash. (The importance of cash planning is illustrated in Chapter 5.)

Disadvantages

- Net cash inflows in year 5 are given the same degree of importance as those for year 1. Cash now or soon is worth more than the same amount of cash in 5 years' time. This is known as the ***time value of money.***
- Payback ignores cash flows ***after*** the payback period. In Question 36.1 (at the end of this chapter), project A's cash flows are increasing steadily, whereas those for project B are steadily decreasing.

Despite its disadvantages Payback is widely used in industry for evaluating projects.

36.4 Accounting rate of return

Payback is concerned with ***cash flow. Accounting rate of return*** is concerned with ***profit*** and ***average capital employed.*** The concept of profit has already been discussed in earlier chapters of this book.

The other figure used to calculate the accounting rate of return (ARR) is ***average capital employed. Capital employed*** means the money that is tied up in the business (all the assets owned by the business, less any money which the business owes) or, in other words, what the business is worth. Average capital employed means that if the business is worth £18,000 at the beginning of next year and £22,000 at the end of next year, then the ***average*** capital employed for next year is £20,000.

£
£18,000
£22,000
£40,000 ÷ 2(years) = £20,000

ARR is calculated as ***profit*** (before tax) as a percentage of ***average capital employed***:.

$$\frac{\text{Profit (before tax)}}{\text{Average capital employed}} \times 100$$

Example

Clive Camborne is contemplating a new project, and there is a choice of two. Details of the forecasts for these projects are:

	Project A	Project B
	£	£
Sales	100,000	210,000
Cost of sales including expense	60,000	130,000
Capital required to start the project	190,000	450,000
Extra capital which will need to be introduced during the year	20,000	100,000

What are the respective accounting rates of return for the two projects, and which project do you consider is the better one?

Solution

	Project A	Project B
	£	£
Pre-tax profit:		
Sales less cost of sales	40,000	80,000
Average capital employed:		
Start of year 1	190,000	450,000
End of year 1	210,000	550,000
	400,000	1,000,000
Divide by 2 = average capital employed	200,000	500,000
Pre-tax profit	40,000	80,000
Average capital employed	200,000	500,000
× 100 = ARR	20%	16%

If we rank these projects by their ARR, then project A has the higher ARR of 20%.

However, Mr. Camborne would be well advised not to base his decision purely on this method of project appraisal. For example, it would be interesting to know what the payback periods would be. (We cannot calculate them because the information given is inadequate.) Also, you will note that project B requires more capital, but makes more profit (£80,000 compared with £40,000) than project A in absolute terms.

Assuming that the capital required for project B (£450,000 increasing to £550,000) is available for investment, then, since project A requires less than half this amount, what is Mr. Camborne to do with the difference? He could put it in a building society, but the return would be likely to be much less than the 16% for project B.

How about investing in two projects of the A type? It could be considered, but it may not be possible. In other words, ARR is too poor a technique to be a satisfactory basis for a decision. It leaves too many questions unanswered.

You should now be able to attempt Question 36.2 at the end of this chapter.

Advantages

- ❐ Calculations are very simple.
- ❐ The entire life of the project is taken into account.

Disadvantages

- ❐ The timing of cash movements is completely ignored.
- ❐ There are a number of different definitions of accounting rate of return and various ways of calculating it which can lead to confusion.
- ❐ The crucial factor in investment decisions is cash flow and the accounting rate of return uses profits.
- ❐ It takes no account of the ***time value of money*** (a topic discussed in the next chapter).
- ❐ It takes no account of the incidence of profits; averages can be misleading. This is demonstrated in Question 36.2 at the end of this chapter.

36.5 Summary

Two techniques of project appraisal are ***payback period*** and ***accounting rate of return***. The payback period technique is concerned with cash flows and calculates the time it will take to recover the cash invested in the project. The accounting rate of return is concerned with profit and expresses this as a percentage of the average capital employed in the project.

Both techniques have the advantage of simplicity, but their disadvantages are significant. Therefore, more sophisticated techniques are required for effective decision-making. These are explained in the next chapter.

You should now be able to attempt Tasks 36.1, 36.2 and 36.3, Question 36.3 and the Objective Test at the end of this chapter.

Student activities

Task 36.1 A friend of yours has just started a new business, and is considering purchasing some new machinery. This machinery is the most advanced of its kind, and it will replace his existing machinery. Your friend intends to use the accounting rate of return method of project appraisal in order to evaluate this investment. Write a letter to him, stating why you think the payback method of project appraisal is preferable.

Task 36.2 The publisher of a new textbook on project appraisal wishes to include a diagram which clearly shows how the payback method of project appraisal operates. Draw such a diagram.

Task 36.3 Using any of your possessions, such as a bicycle, car, surf board or stereo system, calculate the monthly rental you would have to charge to give a payback period of 30 months.

Question 36.1 *Trevor Truro* wishes to decide between two alternative projects, the cash flows for which have been projected as follows:

Year	Project A	Project B
	£	£
0	(24,500)	(25,500)
1	8,000	12,000
2	9,000	11,000
3	10,000	10,000
4	11,000	9,000
5	12,000	8,000

Calculate the respective payback periods for Projects A and B, and comment on the figures.

Question 36.2 *Betty Bude* has the choice of buying one of two guest-houses as going concerns. Details of forecasts provided by her accountant are as follows:

	Guest-house A	Guest-house B
	£	£
Capital required (likely to be static over the next three years)	200,000	200,000
Pre-tax profits for the next three years:		
Year 1	30,000	50,000
Year 2	40,000	40,000
Year 3	50,000	30,000

Guesthouse A is in an area where holidays are increasing in popularity, whereas the area where guest-house B is situated is apparently decreasing in popularity.

Required

Calculate the average annual pre-tax profits and the respective accounting rates of return, and comment briefly on your figures.

Question 36.3 *Tina Tintagel* has some money that she wishes to invest in buying a business in Cornwall. There are two businesses available. The purchase prices for each are the same, £50,000.

Business A is a newsagency and sweet shop which is in a very good commercial position. Cash flows are expected to start at £8,000 per annum and increase steadily thereafter.

Business B is a gift shop which has done well in the past, but due to redevelopment and competition in the area is expected to go downhill and reach a level of cash flow of £8,000 per annum.

Details of the anticipated cash flows for the two businesses for the first ten years are given below:

	Business A	Business B
	£	£
Year 1	8,000	12,000
Year 2	9,000	11,000
Year 3	10,000	10,000
Year 4	11,000	9,000
Year 5	12,000	8,000
Year 6	13,000	8,000
Year 7	14,000	8,000
Year 8	15,000	8,000
Year 9	16,000	8,000
Year 10	17,000	8,000

It can be assumed that in both businesses the investment of £50,000 covers the purchase price of the business, both assets and stock, and that the value of the assets and stock will remain constant at about £50,000 throughout the ten years.

Required

Calculate the respective payback periods for businesses A and B, and also the accounting rates of return. Use the results of your calculations (if you consider they are relevant) to advise Tina Tintagel on which of the two businesses she should invest her £50,000.

Objective test *(tick the appropriate box)*

i) Payback period is the time, in years, which it takes for cash inflows of a project to equal:

a) the average capital employed ☐

b) the cost of capital employed ☐

c) the cash overdraft limit agreed with the bank ☐

d) the cash outflows ☐

ii) The cash flow figures used for payback calculations should not include:

a) sales receipts ☐

b) payments for wages ☐

c) depreciation ☐

d) interest on bank overdraft ☐

iii) A project has a cash outflow in year 0 of £17,100, and cash inflows for the first and subsequent years of £3,600 per annum. The payback period is:

a) 4 years 3 months ☐

b) 4 years 9 months ☐

c) 4 years 6 months ☐

d) 4 years 7.5 months ☐

iv) A project has a payback period of 2.5 years. The cash inflows for years 1, 2, 3 and 4 are budgeted £5,000, £5,500, £6,000 and £7,000 respectively. The cash outflow at the start of year 1 is expected to be:

a) £13,500 ☐

b) £16,500 ☐

c) £23,500 ☐

d) none of these ☐

v) Which one of the following four projects is to be preferred (using payback as the method of appraisal), the cash flows for which are as follows:

Project	Outflow	Year 1 inflow	Year 2 inflow	Year 3 inflow	
	£	£	£	£	
a)	18,000	8,000	9,000	10,000	☐
b)	18,000	10,000	10,000	9,000	☐
c)	18,000	9,000	10,000	10,000	☐
d)	18,000	12,000	8,000	9,000	☐

vi) Payback may be usefully employed as a first screening method in project appraisal because it is a rough measure of:

a) viability ☐

b) profitability ☐

c) liquidity ☐

d) none of these ☐

vii) Accounting rate of return on investment is a measure of:

a) liquidity ☐

b) profitability ☐

c) risk ☐

d) certainty ☐

viii) For project X, the average profit, before tax, for the next three years is budgeted at £8,500 per annum. The average capital employed over the three years is budgeted at £50,000. The accounting rate of return is:

a) 17% ☐

b) 58% ☐

c) 51% ☐

d) 19.33% ☐

ix) In calculating the profit figure for use in the accounting rate of return calculation, the following is necessary:

a) Tax on profit should be deducted from that profit ☐

b) Depreciation should be excluded from costs ☐

c) Depreciation should be included as a cost ☐

d) None of these ☐

x) Which of the following statements is true:

a) Payback takes account of the time value of money ☐

b) Payback is a reasonable indicator of profitability ☐

c) ARR at least gives an indication of liquidity ☐

d) ARR takes no account of the timing of profits ☐

Chapter 37

Principles of discounted cash flow

37.1 Objectives

At the end of this chapter you should be able to:

- understand what is meant by present value;
- understand what is meant by discounted cash flow;
- calculate the present values of future cash flows;
- look up and use discounted cash flow tables;
- be fluent in the mathematics necessary for Chapters 38 and 39.

37.2 Introducton

In Chapter 36, we said that the project appraisal techniques of ***payback*** and ***accounting rate of return (ARR)*** took no account of the ***time value of money***. The basic principle is that £1 received now is worth more than £1 received at some time in the future. One reason for this is that money received now can be invested.

Example

If we received £100 now, we could invest it, say, at 10% in a building society (assuming we could find one that paid 10%!). In twelve month's time the value of the £100 would have risen to £110, since interest of 10% would have been added to the original capital sum.

If we continued to leave the £110 invested, assuming that compounding was annual (and not half-yearly or quarterly or monthly – see Chapter 1), then at the end of two years a further £11 interest (10% of £110) would be added to the sum invested, which would now be worth £121. In order to see what the investment would be worth at the end of years 3, 4 and 5, it is more convenient to draw up a table:

Year	Original sum invested		Factor		Cumulative value of investment
	£				£
0	100	×	1.00	=	100.00
1	100	×	1.10	=	110.00
2	100	×	1.10^2	=	121.00
3	100	×	1.10^3	=	133.10
4	100	×	1.10^4	=	146.41
5	100	×	1.10^5	=	161.05

The factors in the above table are for compound interest. If you want to calculate them, try the following on your calculator:

Year 1	100 × 1.1	= 110
Year 2	100 × 1.1 × 1.1	= 121
Year 3	100 × 1.1 × 1.1 × 1.1	= 133.1

and so on.

The formula for this is:

$$A = P(1 + r)^t$$

where:

A = final amount or compounded sum
P = principal or amount invested
r = annual interest rate, expressed as a decimal (e.g. 10% = 0.10)
t = time, in number of years

37.3 Present value

From the above illustration we can see that £100 received now and invested at 10% will be worth £161.05 in 5 years' time. We could also say that £161.05, to be received in 5 years' time, is worth, at the ***present*** time, much less than £161.05. Assuming an annual compound interest rate of 10%, we could say, more precisely, that £161.05, to be received in 5 years' time, is the same as £100 now, or has a ***present value*** of £100.

Example

Suppose that we want to know what £100 to be received in five years' time is worth now, assuming a compound interest rate of 10%. We can calculate this as follows:

$$£100 \times \frac{£100}{£161.05} = £62.09$$

We can check this using compound interest by taking £62.09 as the present value and calculating its growth at 10% per annum interest, as follows:

Year	Original sum invested		Factor		Cumulative value of investment
	£				£
0	62.09	×	1.00	=	62.09
1	62.09	×	1.10	=	68.30
2	62.09	×	1.10^2	=	75.13
3	62.09	×	1.10^3	=	82.64
4	62.09	×	1.10^4	=	90.91
5	62.09	×	1.10^5	=	100.00

Example

Assuming a 10% annual rate of interest and using the above table:

i) What will £62.09 invested now be worth in 5 years' time?
ii) What will £68.30 invested now be worth in 4 years' time?
iii) What will £82.64 invested now be worth in 1 year's time?
iv) What will £62.09 invested now be worth in 3 years' time?
v) What is the present value of £100 received in 5 years' time?
vi) What is the present value of £ 90.91 received in 4 years' time?
vii) What is the present value of £ 82.64 received in 2 years' time?
viii) What is the present value of £ 90.91 received in 2 years' time?

Solution

i) £100	ii) £100	iii) £90.91	iv) £82.64
v) £62.09	vi) £62.09	vii) £68.30	viii) £75.13

You should now be able to attempt Question 37.1 at the end of this chapter.

37.4 Present value tables

If you have understood the above, you will see that we can produce another, more convenient, table which shows the present value of £100 received at the end of individual years. This table is simply the previous table with the last column reversed.

Year	Present value of £100 £
0	100.00
1	90.91
2	82.64
3	75.13
4	68.30
5	62.09

Obviously, the present value of £100 received now (i.e. year 0) must be £100. Reading from this table, we can see that, for example, the present value of £100 received in 5 years' time is £62.09.

Present value tables usually express values as a factor of £1 or simply 1 unit (thereby serving for dollars, francs etc.). For an interest rate of 10%, the table would look like this:

Year	Present value
0	1.000
1	0.909
2	0.826
3	0.751
4	0.683
5	0.621

You will notice that this table is rounded off to the third decimal place, which for most purposes is accurate enough.

Table 1, in Appendix I at the end of this book, is such a three-figure table and gives the present values of £1 at various percentages up to 50% for all the years up to 20 years.

You should now be able to attempt Task 37.1 at the end of this chapter.

37.5 Discounting

The process of finding the present value is called ***discounting*** and the calculations could be described as compound interest going backwards. If you are interested in formulae, the formula for present value is:

$$P = \frac{A}{(1+r)^t}$$

This formula is obtained from the compound interest formula given in the introduction to this chapter:

$$A = P(1 + r)^t$$

If we make P the subject, the formula becomes as shown above.

Where P = principal or present value

A = final amount received

r = annual interest rate, expressed as a decimal

t = time in number of years

Example

If we wanted the present value of £1 received in 5 years' time, using an interest rate of 10%, then

A = £1

r = 0.10

t = 5

Therefore:

$$P = \frac{£1}{(1+0.10)^5}$$

$$= \frac{£1}{1.1 \times 1.1 \times 1.1 \times 1.1 \times 1.1}$$

$$= \frac{£1}{1.61} = 0.621$$

Another example: A = £900, r = 0.12 (12%), t = 3 years.

Therefore:

$$P = \frac{900}{1.12 \times 1.12 \times 1.12} = \frac{900}{1.4049} = £640.60$$

You will get slightly different answers if you use Table 1, due to the fact that Table 1 rounds off to the third decimal place.

$$900 \times 0.712 = £640.80$$

A more exact figure in Table 1 for 0.712 could be calculated:

$$P = \frac{1}{1.12 \times 1.12 \times 1.12} = \frac{1}{1.404928} = 0.71178024 \times 900 = £640.60221$$

Example

Work out the present values from the data below, using the above formula. Calculate your answers to the nearest penny.

	(A) Final amount received £	(r) Rate of interest %	(t) Time in number of years
i)	1	12	5
ii)	1,000	12	5
iii)	500	15	3
iv)	600	20	4
v)	1	8	10
vi)	750	8	10

Solution

i) £0.57 ii) £567.43 iii) £328.76 iv) £289.35 v) £0.46 vi) £347.40

The purpose of the above example is to help you understand the principles of discounting calculations as applied to cash flows – known as ***discounted cash flow*** calculations. However, for Chapters 38 and 39, all you need do is refer to Table 1 or Table 2 in Appendix I at the end of this book. In most examinations, tables or extracts from tables are provided, but you can calculate the figures for yourself if they are not provided.

37.6 Cumulative present value tables

Table 2 in Appendix I at the end of this book gives ***cumulative present values***. These are not, strictly speaking, necessary, but are often very convenient and time-saving. Note that Table 2 is just the sum of the individual year present values from Table 1 added together.

Example

The following demonstrates how this table works, using a 10% rate:

Year	Table 1 Present values	Table 2 Cumulative present values
1	0.909	0.909
2	0.826	1.736
3	0.751	2.487
4	0.683	3.170
5	0.621	3.791

Note that the small discrepancy in the third decimal place for year 2 (0.909 + 0.826 = 1.735) is due to rounding off in the tables.

Table 2 is useful when cash flows are ***constant*** annual sums.

Example

What is the present value of £500 received annually at the end of each of the next 5 years, using a 10% discount rate?

Solution

We could use Table 1:

Year	£		Discount factor		Present value (£)
1	500	×	0.909	=	454.50
2	500	×	0.826	=	413.00
3	500	×	0.751	=	375.50
4	500	×	0.683	=	341.50
5	500	×	0.621	=	310.50
				Present value	1,895.00

However, using Table 2 we look up the cumulative factor at 10% for year 5, which is 3.791, and calculate:

Year	£		Discount factor		Present value (£)
1-5	500	×	3.791	=	1,895.50

The small discrepancy is due to rounding off in the tables. Note also that using Table 2 requires that only *one* year's cash flows be multiplied by the factor.

You should now be able to attempt Question 37.2 at the end of this chapter.

37.7 Applying cumulative present value tables

Example

What are the present values of the following amounts, received at the end of each year, using a 12% discount factor?

Years 1, 2 and 3	£ 2,000 per annum
Years 4, 5 and 6	£ 3,000 per annum

Solution

Table 2:

	£		Cumulative factor		Present value (£)
Years 1, 2 and 3	2,000	×	2.402	=	4,804
Years 4, 5 and 6	3,000	×	1.709 *	=	5,127
					9,931

* 1.709 is arrived at as follows:

	Cumulative factor for year 6	= 4.111
Less	Cumulative factor for year 3	= 2.402
		= 1.709

This is same as adding the individual factors (see Table 1) for years 4, 5 and 6:

	Annual factor
Year 4	0.636
Year 5	0.567
Year 6	0.507
	1.710

Again, the slight discrepancy is due to rounding-off in the tables.

An ***alternative*** short-cut method is as follows:

	£		Cumulative factor		Present value (£)
Years 1-6	2,000	×	4.111	=	8,222
Years 4-6 (extra)	1,000	×	1.709 *	=	1,709
					9,931

You should now be able to attempt Task 37.2 and Question 37.3 at the end of this chapter.

37.8 Summary

Present value is the cash equivalent now of a sum of money receivable or payable at a stated future date at a specified rate.

The formula is $P = \dfrac{A}{(1+r)^t}$

Present values of £1 can be found in Table 1 of Appendix I, by looking up the factor for the appropriate year and discount rate.

Where cash flows are ***constant*** annual sums, the amount of calculation can be reduced by using Table 2 (cumulative present values) in Appendix I. One year's cash flow is multiplied by the factor for the last year of the constant cash flow. If the ***constant*** cash flow does ***not*** start in year 1, the factor for the last year should be reduced by the factor for the year before the year in which the constant cash flow commences.

Discounted cash flow is the process of evaluating future net cash flows generated by a project by discounting them to their present-day values.

You should now be able to attempt the Objective Test at the end of this chapter.

Student activities

Task 37.1 i) Find the figures at the end of paragraph 37.4 (for 10%) in Table 1.

ii) Work out a table for 12% for 5 years, and check your figures with those in Table 1.

Task 37.2 Conduct a survey with fellow students or friends to find out how much (hypothetically) they would lend you now for the promise of a payment of £100 in four years' time. Calculate the discount rates they are using and present them either in the form of a bar chart or a line graph.

Question 37.1 Assuming a 10% annual rate of interest:

i) What will £68.30 invested now be worth in 2 years' time?

ii) What will £82.64 invested now be worth in 2 years' time?

iii) What will £62.09 invested now be worth in 4 years' time?

iv) What will £62.09 invested now be worth in 6 years' time?

v) What is the present value of £100 received in 4 years' time?

vi) What is the present value of £ 75.13 received in 1 year's time?

vii) What is the present value of £ 90.91 received in 3 years' time?

viii) What is the present value of £121 received in 6 years' time?

Question 37.2 What are the present values for the amounts indicated, received annually, for the stated number of years and discount rates? Answer to the nearest £1.

	Amounts received annually (£)	Years	Discount rate %
i)	140	5	12
ii)	200	4	8
iii)	300	10	15
iv)	590	3	20
v)	999	9	9

Question 37.3 What are the present values of the following cash inflows:

	Years	£ per annum	Discount rate
i)	1, 2 and 3	1,000	8%
	4 and 5	1,500	
ii)	1 and 2	5,000	10%
	3, 4, 5 and 6	7,500	
iii)	1, 2 and 3	8,000	16%
	4, 5 and 6	10,000	
	7, 8 and 9	12,000	

Objective test *(tick the appropriate box)*

i) The value of £100 invested at 12% per annum, compounded annually, after 5 years is:

a) £176.23 ☐
b) £161.05 ☐
c) £157.35 ☐
d) £160.00 ☐

ii) The present value of £1 to be received in 5 years' time, using a 17% rate of discount, is:

a) £0.654 ☐
b) £3.199 ☐
c) £0.456 ☐
d) £0.436 ☐

iii) The present value of £753 to be received in 10 years' time, using a 15% rate of discount, is:

a) £185.99 ☐
b) £247.00 ☐
c) £179.97 ☐
d) £179.96 ☐

iv) The present value of £1,000 to be received in 20 years' time, using an 18% rate of discount, is:

a) £ 38.00 ☐
b) £380.00 ☐
c) £ 37.00 ☐
d) £ 3.70 ☐

v) The present value of £100 to be received at the end of each year for the next 5 years, discounted at 12% is:

a) £360.50 ☐
b) £886.30 ☐
c) £ 56.70 ☐
d) £ 55.70 ☐

vi) The present value of £42 to be received at the end of each year for the next 10 years, discounted at 8% is:

a) £533.50 ☐

b) £671.00 ☐

c) £224.07 ☐

d) £281.82 ☐

vii) The present value of £1,000 to be received at the end of each year for the next 3 years, and of £1,500 to be received at the end of the following 3 years, discounted at 10% is:

a) £2,487.00 ☐

b) £5,598.50 ☐

c) £4,355.00 ☐

d) £5,289.00 ☐

viii) The present value of £1,500 to be received at the end of each year for the next 3 years, and of £1,000 to be received at the end of the following 3 years, discounted at 10% is:

a) £5,289.00 ☐

b) £5,598.50 ☐

c) £4,355.00 ☐

d) £2,487.00 ☐

ix) What is the total present value of the following amounts:

Amount to be received at end of year:	
£15,000	1
£16,000	2
£17,000	3

discounted at 14%?

a) £17,692 ☐

b) £36,934 ☐

c) £36,912 ☐

d) £12,311 ☐

x) What is the total present value of the following amounts:

Amount to be received at end of year:	
£10,000	0
£11,000	1
£12,000	2
£13,000	3
£14,000	4
£15,000	5

discounted at 11%?

a) £53,972 ☐

b) £57,279 ☐

c) £51,608 ☐

d) £55,743 ☐

Chapter 38

Net present value

38.1 Objectives

At the end of this chapter you should be able to:

- calculate the net present value of a simple project;
- calculate the net present value of a project taking working capital into account;
- calculate and compare the net present values of several projects;
- understand what is meant by the profitability index;
- appreciate the basic principles behind the choice of discount rate;
- calculate weighted average cost of capital.

38.2 Introduction

In Chapter 37, we looked at the mathematics necessary to calculate the present values of future cash flows. We can now apply this to examples which illustrate the uses of ***net present value (NPV)*** calculations. These are:

- simple examples which calculate the ***NPV*** of a single project;
- examples which include the cash flows arising from ***working capital***;
- comparisons of projects where we have to choose between two or more projects.

38.3 Single projects without working capital

Many problems, both in real life and in the examination room, are concerned with investing in only one project. For example, to buy or not to buy a new machine. The following example, demonstrates such a problem.

Example

Bobby Bodmin is considering buying a machine which will improve his cash flows by £30,000 per annum for the next five years, at the end of which the machine will be worn out and of no value. The machine will cost £75,000, and will be bought for cash. The discount rate which Mr Bodmin thinks is suitable is 15%. (Choice of a suitable discount rate is discussed later in this chapter).

Required

Calculate the ***net present value*** of this project.

Solution

Year	Detail	Cash flows	Discount factor 15%	Present value
		£		£
0	Purchase of machine	(75,000)	1.000	(75,000)
1	Net cash inflow	30,000		
2	Net cash inflow	30,000		
3	Net cash inflow	30,000		
4	Net cash inflow	30,000		
5	Net cash inflow	30,000	3.352	100,560
			Net present value	25,560

Notes

Purchase of machine is a negative cash flow (a cash *outflow*) and is shown in brackets. The discount factor is 1.000 because the cash outflow is at year 0.

The discount factor of 3.352 can be found in Table 2 (cumulative present values), and is used to save the effort of multiplying £30,000 in turn by the individual figures from Table 1 for years 1 to 5 inclusive. (See Chapter 37.)

The ***net present value*** of the project is ***positive*** £25,560. (It is called ***net*** because the initial outlay on the machine has been deducted from the total of the discounted inflows.)

Since the project has a ***positive NPV***, this means that Mr Bodmin will be getting a return on his investment of more than 15%.

If the *NPV* had been ***nil***, his return would be 15%.

If the project had shown a ***negative NPV***, the return would be less than 15%, and it would not therefore be worth undertaking.

The positive *NPV* of £25,560 could be said to represent the estimated current or immediate change in the value of Mr Bodmin's business if the project is undertaken.

You should now be able to attempt Question 38.1 at the end of this chapter.

38.4 Single projects with working capital

One of the consequences of any new project, apart from the initial outlays and the annual cash inflows which arise from it, is that ***working capital*** is often increased. Increased sales means that debtors increase, as do stocks of raw materials, work-in-progress, and stocks of finished goods. (On the other hand creditors also tend to increase, but not usually to the same extent.)

Example

Bobby Bodmin may find that, in addition to the figures in the previous example, the following increases are likely to occur for the whole 5 years of the project:

	£
Debtors: up by	35,000
Add Stocks: up by	20,000
	55,000
Less Creditors: up by	15,000
Therefore working capital up by	40,000

This increase of working capital is almost immediate as far as the project is concerned, it lasts for the life of the project although it may fluctuate during this time, and it is only released at the end of the project (when the debtors pay up and the stocks return to nil).

All we have to do is to introduce the increase in working capital as:

- a cash outflow at year 0 (start of year 1);
- a cash inflow at the end of year 5.

In order to see how this operates, we will re-work the example in Section 38.3.

Example

Bobby Bodmin has forgotten to allow for working capital in the figures he gave you for his project. He estimates that, on average, an extra £40,000 of working capital will be required, all of which will be released when the machine is worn out at the end of year 5.

Required

Rework the NPV for this project, taking working capital into account.

Solution

Year	Detail	Cash flows £	Discount factor 15%	Present value £
0	Purchase of machine	(75,000)	1.000	(75,000)
0	Increase in working capital	(40,000)	1.000	(40,000)
1	Cash inflow	30,000		
2	Cash inflow	30,000		
3	Cash inflow	30,000		
4	Cash inflow	30,000		
5	Cash inflow	30,000	3.352	100,560
5	Release of working capital	40,000	0.497	19,880
			Net present value	5,440

The ***net present value*** in the example in Section 38.3 (before the introduction of working capital into the data) was £25,560, whereas now it is reduced to £5,440. The project can therefore be said to be less attractive, but it is still acceptable, since it is superior to the discount rate of 15%.

Calculations which take working capital into account are more realistic, since if working capital is a factor, it should not be ignored. It has to be financed, a fact which sometimes comes as an unpleasant surprise to businessmen who have overlooked it.

> *You should now be able to attempt Question 38.2 at the end of this chapter.*

38.5 Comparison of two or more projects

We can now work through an example to illustrate how NPV can be used when we are asked to compare (and perhaps choose between) two mutually exclusive projects, i.e. two projects, only one of which can be pursued.

Example

Redruth and Company makes bricks. The owners are considering whether to undertake one of two mutually exclusive projects, each of which would require an initial asset cost of £100,000, which would have a zero value at the end of four years. Cost of capital is estimated at 15%. The cash flows associated with the two projects are as follows:

		Project X	Project Y
		£	£
Initial investment		100,000	100,000
Net cash inflows:	Year 1	40,000	80,000
	Year 2	60,000	40,000
	Year 3	40,000	40,000
	Year 4	80,000	40,000

Required:

i) Calculate the net present value for each project.

ii) Calculate the (non-discounted) payback period for each project.

iii) Calculate the accounting rate of return for each project.

iv) Compare the two projects and comment.

Solution

i) Net present value:

Year	Discount factor @ 15%	Project X Cash flow	Project X Present value	Project Y Cash flow	Project Y Present value
		£	£	£	£
0	1.000	(100,000)	(100,000)	(100,000)	(100,000)
1	0.870	40,000	34,800	80,000	69,600
2	0.756	60,000	45,360	40,000	30,240
3	0.658	40,000	26,320	40,000	26,320
4	0.572	80,000	45,760	40,000	22,880
		Net present values:	52,240		49,040

ii) Payback period (non-discounted):

Initial Investment: £100,000 (both projects).

		Project X	Project Y
		£	£
Cumulative cash inflows:	Year 1	40,000	80,000
	Year 2	100,000	120,000

For Project X, the payback period is 2 years.

For Project Y, the payback period is:

$$1 + \frac{(100{,}000 - 80{,}000)}{(120{,}000 - 80{,}000)} = 1 + \frac{20{,}000}{40{,}000} = 1\tfrac{1}{2} \text{ years}$$

iii) Accounting rate of return (ARR):

	Project X £	Project Y £
Calculate the profits of each project: Cash inflows (profit *before* depreciation):		
(X = £40,000 + £60,000 + £40,000 + £80,000)	220,000	
(Y = £80,000 + £40,000 + £40,000 + £40,000) =		200,000
Less Cost of project (depreciation for 4 years)	100,000	100,000
	120,000	100,000
Therefore average profit per annum (divide by 4 years)	30,000	25,000
Average capital employed for both projects: (£100,000 divided by 2)	50,000	50,000
Therefore ARR is	$\frac{30{,}000}{50{,}000}$	$\frac{25{,}000}{50{,}000}$
	[60%]	[50%]

iv) Comments

	Project X	Project Y
NPV	£52,240	£49,040
Payback period (non-discounted)	2years	1.5 years
ARR	60%	50%

In ranking these projects, ARR is not a recommended measure.

NPV for X is higher than for Y, but not much higher.

Project Y does seem to have an edge over X in that its payback period is 6 months less, which is quite a consideration if the venture is considered at all risky. Also Project Y has a projected cash inflow in year 1 of £80,000 compared with only £40,000 from Project X.

Other factors may influence the final decision. For example, the supplier of the equipment for Project X may have a better reputation for reliability of after-sales service than the supplier of the equipment for Project Y.

You should now be able to attempt Question 38.3 at the end of this chapter.

38.6 Profitability index

The ***profitability index (PI)*** is a ratio which compares the absolute value of the discounted cash inflows with the original investment. Like all ratios, care should be exercised in interpretation. For example, a high PI may be due to a low cost of the original investment, which, unless revealed, could mean that some available capital was unutilised. (This is an area of investment appraisal known as capital rationing, which is beyond the scope of this book.)

The calculation required is:

$$\frac{\text{PV of Cash inflows (Exclude original cost/outflow)}}{\text{Original cost/outflow}}$$

Example

Looking again at the example of Bobby Bodmin in Section 38.3, the PI would be:

$$\frac{100{,}560}{75{,}000} = 1.34$$

In the case of the example of Bobby Bodmin in Section 38.4 (including working capital), the PI would be:

$$\frac{100{,}560+19{,}880}{115{,}000} = 1.05$$

In the case of Redruth & Company, the example in section 38.5, the PIs would be:

Project X: $\frac{152{,}240}{100{,}000} = 1.52$

Project Y: $\frac{149{,}040}{100{,}000} = 1.49$

38.7 Choice of discount rate

So far, we have used discount rates without having discussed what an appropriate rate might be, although we have used the term ***cost of capital***. This is rather a complicated matter and in this book we discuss the basics only.

The most common basis is known as ***weighted average cost of capital*** (*WACC*). Here is an example of a typical calculation.

Example

The ***Penzance Company*** has a capital employed of £180,000. This comprises:

- loan (or debt) capital of £60,000, on which it has to pay interest at a rate of 13%;
- own capital of £120,000, on which Penzance Company already earns (or hopes to earn) a return of 16%.

Required

Calculate the WACC.

Solution

The WACC can be calculated in two ways:

i)

	£		£
Loan capital	60,000	× 13% =	7,800
Own capital	120,000	× 16% =	19,200
	180,000		27,000

$$\text{WACC} = \frac{27{,}000}{180{,}000} \times 100 = 15\%$$

ii)

	Rate	Weight	WACC %
Loan capital	13% ×	60/180 (33.3%) =	4.33
Own capital	16% ×	120/180 (66.7%) =	10.67
			15.00

This WACC is *guide* to choice of a discount rate for a particular project. For example, the Penzance Company may use a discount rate of 15% for a new project which is similar to projects of a type which it is used to carrying out, (on which it already receives a 16% return on its own capital).

However, if a proposed project holds more risk than usual, the company might add a risk premium of, say, 5% to the WACC, making a discount rate of 20% to be used in calculating the NPV for appraising the project.

38.8 Summary

The ***net present value (NPV)*** of a project is calculated by discounting cash inflows and deducting original investment cost. If the NPV is positive, the return is more than the discount rate. If the NPV is ***nil***, the return is the same as the discount rate. If the NPV is negative, the return is less than the discount rate.

It is more realistic if working capital is introduced into the calculation. For two mutually exclusive projects, the project with the higher NPV can be ranked as more acceptable than the other.

Other techniques, such as payback period may give different rankings and other factors may influence the final choice of project.

The choice of discount rate can cause difficulties in practice. A common basis is ***weighted average cost of capital (WACC)*** which takes account of the rate of interest on borrowed money, and the return (opportunity cost) already obtained or desired on own capital.

You should now be able to attempt Tasks 38.1, 38.2 and the Objective Test at the end of this chapter.

Student activities

Task 38.1 You are a trainee accountant in an engineering company. The assistant production manager has asked you for your help. He is contemplating buying a new machine, and does not know which one to select from the three machines which are available. Write him a memorandum specifying the types of information you require so that you can calculate and compare the net present values of the three machines.

Task 38.2 Make a list of what you consider to be the main rules to be applied when working out the net present value of any project.

Question 38.1 ***Liz Liskeard*** owns a secretarial agency, and is thinking of buying a computer mainly as a database for her records. Her accountant has produced a five-year budget for her, which shows that her cash flows are likely to diminish in the first two years (due to setting-up costs etc.), but will show positive results thereafter. The figures are as follows:

		£
Year 0:	Purchase of computer and software	(10,000)
Net cash flows:	Year 1	(4,000)
	Year 2	(1,000)
	Year 3	3,000
	Year 4	8,000
	Year 5	10,000

Required

Calculate the NPV of this project, using a discount rate of 12%. Comment on whether you think Liz Liskeard would be advised to go ahead with this project.

Question 38.2 ***Peter Polperro***, currently employed as a part-time waiter, is considering setting up a small pottery to produce, in his spare time, souvenirs for the tourist trade. He estimates that a kiln and other equipment will cost £6,000 at the start of this enterprise, and that working capital of £3,000 will be required for the life of the project. He is hesitant to budget the life of the project beyond a five-year period, at the end of which he assumes that the working capital will be released and that he could sell his kiln and other equipment for £2,000.

He also estimates that net cash inflows arising each year from the project will be £3,000, and has been advised by his bank manager, who is willing to finance the project, to use a discount rate of 16% for the purpose of project appraisal.

Required

Calculate the NPV of this project and state whether you think it is worthwhile.

Question 38.3 The owners of ***Redruth & Company*** have forgotten to allow for the effect which additional working capital will have on the projects considered in the example in Section 38.5.

The additional working capital required for either project is £50,000, which will be needed for the full 4 years of either project and will be released at the end of year 4. In addition, they have reconsidered the cost of capital, and have re-estimated this at 17%.

Required

Re-work the example in Section 38.5, allowing for this additional working capital and the altered cost of capital.

Objective test *(tick the appropriate box)*

i) Project X has the following cash flows:

Year	Cash flows £
0	(20,000)
1	10,000
2	10,000
3	10,000

Using a 15% discount rate, the NPV is:

a) £22,830 ☐

b) £2,830 ☐

c) £283 ☐

d) (£2,830) ☐

ii) Project Y has the following cash flows:

Year	Cash flows £
0	(20,000)
1	8,000
2	10,000
3	12,000

Using a 15% discount rate, the NPV is:

a) £22,416 ☐

b) £2,416 ☐

c) £242 ☐

d) (£2,416) ☐

iii) Referring to (i) and (ii) above, it is correct to say:

a) Project X has a lower NPV than Project Y ☐

b) Project Y is to be preferred to Project X ☐

c) Project X is to be preferred to Project Y ☐

d) Both projects have the same net present values ☐

iv) If £5,000 of working capital is needed for Project X (Question (i) above), for the life of the project, the NPV of Project X alters to:

a) £1,120 ☐

b) (£2,170) ☐

c) £6,120 ☐

d) (£4,717) ☐

v) If £5,000 of working capital is needed for Project Y (Question (ii) above), for the life of the project, the NPV of Project Y alters to:

a) £ 706 ☐

b) £5,706 ☐

c) (£2,584) ☐

d) £2,584 ☐

vi) Taking working capital into account, the following is true:

a) The NPV of Project Y exceeds that of Project X by £414 ☐

b) The NPV of Project X exceeds that of Project Y by £414 ☐

c) The introduction of working capital into the calculations has decreased the NPV of both projects by £414 ☐

d) None of the above is true ☐

vii) Ignoring working capital, the payback period of:

a) Project X is 3 years ☐

b) Project Y is 2 years and 2 months ☐

c) Project Y is 2 years and 3 months ☐

d) Project Y is 2 years and 4 months ☐

viii) The profitability index of Project X (ignoring working capital) is:

a) 1.11415 ☐

b) 1.415 ☐

c) 1.1415 ☐

d) None of these ☐

ix) The profitability index of Project X (including working capital) is:

a) 1.1448 ☐

b) 1.448 ☐

c) 1.0448 ☐

d) None of these ☐

x) Company Z has loan capital of £20,000 with an interest rate of 18%, and own capital of £40,000 on which at present it receives a return of 15%. The WACC is:

a) 16% ☐

b) 17% ☐

c) 16.5% ☐

d) 33% ☐

Chapter 39

Internal rate of return

39.1 Objectives

At the end of this chapter you should be able to:

- calculate the internal rate of return of a project;
- understand the difference between net present value and internal rate of return;
- have some confidence in applying and assessing the various investment appraisal techniques covered in this section.

39.2 Introduction

Internal rate of return (IRR) is a technique of investment appraisal which is related to the NPV method discussed in Chapter 38. In simple terms it is the discount rate which results in an NPV of nil or the discount rate which applies when the PV of outflows and the PV of inflows are equal.

Computers and some pocket calculators can be programmed to calculate the IRR of a project. Unfortunately, manual calculation of IRR requires some trial and error, but it is not too difficult. An understanding the calculations necessary to produce the IRR will help you understand what IRR is and appreciate its value and limitations.

39.3 Calculating the internal rate of return

An illustration is sometimes worth a thousand words, so we shall look again at the example in Section 38.3, where Mr Bodmin was considering buying a machine. The calculations were as follows:

Example

Bobby Bodmin

Year	Detail	Cash flows £	Discount factor 15%	Present value £
0	Purchase of machine	(75,000)	1.000	(75,000)
1–5	Net cash flows	30,000	3.352	100,560
			Net present value	25,560

Using a 15% discount rate, the NPV is £25,560 ***positive***, and we concluded that the investment would be worthwhile.

Now we shall recalculate the NPV, using discount rates of 20%, 25% and 30%.

Year	Cash flow	Discount rate 20% Discount factor	Present value	Discount rate 25% Discount factor	Present value	Discount rate 30% Discount factor	Present value
	£		£		£		£
0	(75,000)	1.000	(75,000)	1.000	(75,000)	1.000	(75,000)
1-5	30,000	2.991	89,730	2.689	80,670	2.436	73,080
			14,730		5,670		(1,920)

At a discount rate of 15%, the NPV is £25,560

At a discount rate of 20%, the NPV is £14,730

At a discount rate of 25%, the NPV is £5,760

At a discount rate of 30%, the NPV is (£1,920)

The higher the discount rate, the smaller the NPV becomes, until it eventually becomes negative somewhere between 25% and 30%. At the point where the NPV changes from positive to negative, (that is, where it is *nil*), lies the *internal rate of return.*

It may help if we now plot the NPVs calculated on the previous page on a graph, against the appropriate discount rates. Discount rates are marked on the x (horizontal) axis, and NPVs on the y (vertical) axis.

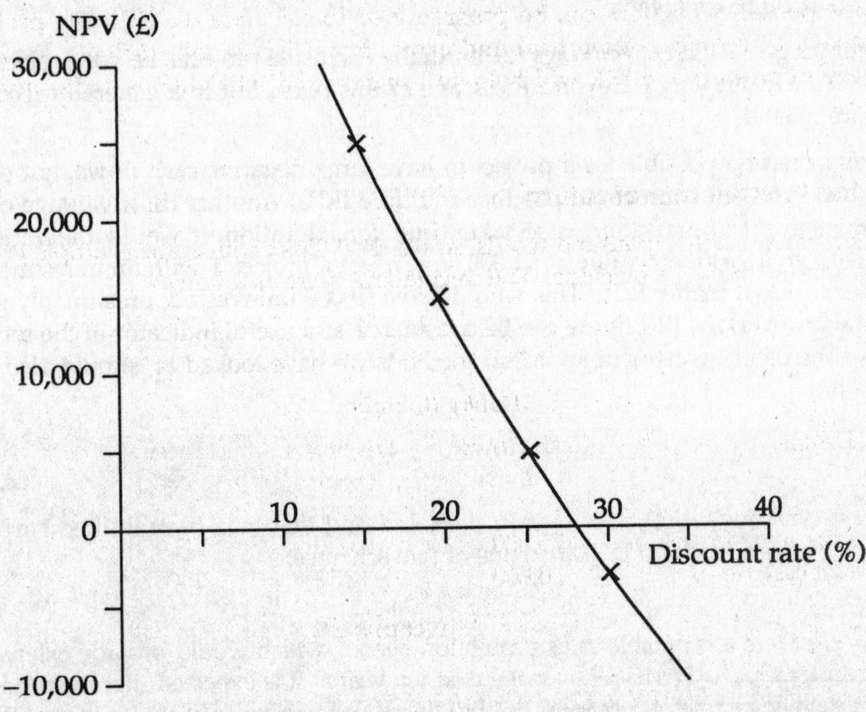

You will see that the line joining the four points is a slight curve, but for all practical purposes we can assume that it is a straight line provided that the points are not too far apart. We shall use the data at 25% and 30% discount rates.

The discount rate at which the line crosses the horizontal axis (where *NPV* is *nil*) is somewhere between 25% and 30%, i.e. 25 + a number between 0 and 5 (30 – 25). The calculation involves *linear interpolation (linear* because it assumes a straight line), and is as follows:

$$25 + 5 \times \left[\frac{5{,}670}{5{,}670 + 1{,}920} \right] = 28.7$$

The figures in square brackets represent the ***proportion*** of 5 that we require to be added to 25:

$$\frac{\text{NPV of 25\% rate}}{\text{NPV of 25\% rate } \textit{plus} \text{ NPV of 30\% rate}}$$

Note particularly that we ignore the fact that the NPV of the 30% rate (£1,920) is negative, i.e the difference (or distance) between 5,670 and (1,920) is the total of the two figures, ignoring the brackets on the second figure. Some students find this difficult to understand. The following explanations may help:

- If yesterday you had £100 in the bank (***positive*** figure), and today find you have an overdraft of £50 (***negative*** figure), how much money have you drawn out of the bank since yesterday?

  Answer: £100 ***plus*** £50 = £150!

- The denominator (lower part of the fraction) is the range which is $x - y$. When y is negative, the range is $x - (-y)$ or $x + y$.

You should now be able to attempt Question 39.1 at the end of this chapter.

39.4 Observations concerning the internal rate of return

The important point is that if a target figure of, say, 15% is set for a project, then a project which produces a return of approximately 22% could be acceptable.

IRR and NPV sometimes give ***different rankings*** for mutually exclusive projects, i.e. for projects of which only one will be undertaken. To explain why is beyond the scope of this book, but it is generally recognised that NPV is considered to be more reliable.

It is sometimes (though rarely) possible for a project to have large negative cash flows, not only at the start, but also ***during*** its lifetime. This situation could produce multiple IRRs. Another disadvantage of IRR is that unless other methods of investment appraisal are also taken into consideration, it would theoretically be possible to choose a project X with an investment value of £1,000, and reject a project Y with an investment value of £10,000, purely because project X has a higher IRR. This would leave £9,000 uninvested, presumably giving a return only of the cost of capital. However, the IRR figure can be considered as a useful indicator of the return of a project, but caution is necessary. The other investment appraisal methods we have looked at should also be worked out and taken into consideration.

Example

In preparing their cash budget for next year ***Porlock Ltd*** find that they have limited surplus funds. The managing director wishes to spend £7,000 on one of two schemes:

Alternative A

Pay immediately £7,000 to a reputable sales promotion agency which would provide extensive advertising and planned "maintenance" advertising over the next ten years. It is expected that the result of this would be an increase in cash flows from operations, through increased volume, of £2,000 per annum for the first 5 years, and, as the impact of the advertising decreases, £1,000 per annum for the following 5 years. There would be no effect after the lapse of the ten years.

Alternative B

Buy immediately new labour-saving equipment at a cost of £7,000 which will reduce the operating cash outflows by £1,500 per annum for each of the next ten years, at the end of which time the equipment would be worn out and of no value.

Required

i) Calculate the average accounting rates of return per annum on the average investment (over 10 years) for each alternative.

ii) Calculate the pay-back periods for each alternative.

iii) Calculate the net present value of each alternative, using the discounted cash flow technique, and assuming the minimum desired return is 18%.

iv) Calculate the internal rate of return (also known as the discounted cash flow yield rate) for each alternative.

v) State which alternative you would advise the managing director to adopt and briefly explain why.

Solution

i) **Accounting rates of return**

	A	B
	£	£
Investment	7,000	7,000
Average capital employed (divide by 2)	3,500	3,500
Increase in net cash flows for 10 years	15,000	15,000
Average increase in net cash flows per annum (divide by 10)	1,500	1,500
less depreciation / amortisation per annum	700	700
Average annual net income	800	800
Average annual rate of return on average investment:		
$\frac{800}{3,500}$ × 100 (both A & B) = 22.86, say	23%	23%

ii) **Payback**

		A	B
		£	£
Investment	year 0	(7,000)	(7,000)
Cash flows	year 1	2,000	1,500
	2	2,000	1,500
	3	2,000	1,500
	4	2,000	1,500
	5		1,500
Payback period		3.5 years	4.67 years

iii) **Net present values**

	A			B		
	Discount factor (18%)	Cash flow £	Present value £	Discount factor (18%)	Cash flow £	Present value £
Year 0	1.000	(7,000)	(7,000)	1.000	(7,000)	(7,000)
Years 1 – 10	4.494	1,000	4,494	4.494	1,500	6,741
Years 1 – 5	3.127	1,000	3,127			
			621			(259)

iv) **Internal rate of return**

	A			B		
	Discount factor (22%)	**Cash flow £**	**Present value £**	**Discount factor (16%)**	**Cash flow £**	**Present value £**
Year 0	1.000	(7,000)	(7,000)	1.000	(7,000)	(7,000)
Years 1 – 10	3.923	1,000	3,923	4.833	1,500	7,249
Years 1 – 5	2.864	1,000	2,864			
			(213)			249

$$18 + \left[\frac{621}{621 + 213} \times 4\right]$$

= 20.98, say 21%

$$16 + \left[\frac{249}{249 + 259} \times 2\right]$$

= 16.98, say 17%

Comments

Accounting rates of return are the same for both alternatives.

Alternative A has the shorter payback period, produces a higher discounted yield (NPV of £621) and also shows a higher internal rate of return which at 21% exceeds the minimum desired rate of return (18%).

Unless there are other factors which should be taken into consideration, it would appear that Alternative A is the more attractive proposal.

39.5 Summary

The ***internal rate of return (IRR)*** is related to ***net present value (NPV)*** and is the discount rate which results in a NPV of nil. The technique of ***linear interpolation*** must be used to calculate the IRR.

IRR and NPV may sometimes give different rankings for mutually exclusive projects. Generally it is accepted that the rankings produced by using NPV are more reliable. IRR does not show where widely differing investment amounts are required for alternative projects. If IRR alone is used to select a project in such circumstances, investment capital could remain underutilised.

IRR is a useful technique of investment appraisal, but should be applied with caution to investment decisions. Other capital appraisal techniques should always be used in conjunction with IRR to ensure that the best decision is made.

You should now be able to attempt Tasks 39.1 and 39.2, Questions 39.2 and 39.3 and the Objective Test at the end of this chapter.

Student activities

Task 39.1 You have been asked to give a presentation at a management meeting on Linear Interpolation. Draft notes for your talk and construct the diagrams you will need to illustrate the points you will make.

Task 39.2 The following letter appeared in the *Financial Times*:

> *From Mr Isambard Kingdom Brunel*
>
> Sir, I am not surprised that British Industry is in the state that it is when we use such poor methods for appraising the investments we make. Many businesses are still in the dark ages, and use the Payback Period method with all its shortcomings. The only method to use is the Internal Rate of Return. This provides unambiguous results, with no confusion. Using this method there is no need to take into account any other method, since it utilises the modern principle of discounting future cash flows.
>
> Isambard Brunel,
> *Engineer*

Write a reply to this letter, stating clearly whether you agree or disagree, and why.

Question 39.1 ***Terry Tavistock*** is considering buying a taxi for £20,000, which will, he hopes, last for 5 years before it becomes scrap (assume nil value).

Net cash flows (cash receipts less all costs , including a driver but excluding depreciation) are estimated at £7,000 per annum.

Required

Calculate the NPVs of this project using discount rates of 15% and 25%, and calculate the IRR to the nearest whole number %.

Question 39.2 We met ***Tina Tintagel*** in Question 36.3 in Chapter 36, where she had some money which she wished to invest in buying a business in Cornwall. If you attempted that question, you may remember that you were required to advise her concerning which of the two businesses (Business A, a newsagent and sweet shop, or Business B, a gift shop) she should buy with her money. The techniques of appraisal available to you at that time were payback period and accounting rate of return.

At present Tina favours Business A, the newsagents and sweet shop. She tells you that she currently has the £50,000 invested in an account which is producing a return of 16%, and wishes to know whether, on the basis of the anticipated cash flows for the next ten years, Business A will show any improvement on that return.

It can be assumed that the investment of £50,000 covers the purchase price of the business, both assets and stock, and that the value of the assets and level of stock will remain constant at about £50,000 throughout the ten years. Details of the anticipated cash flows for the first ten years are given below:

	Business A £
Year 1	8,000
Year 2	9,000
Year 3	10,000
Year 4	11,000
Year 5	12,000
Year 6	13,000
Year 7	14,000
Year 8	15,000
Year 9	16,000
Year 10	17,000

Required

Calculate the net present value of Business A, using a discount factor of 16%, and also calculate the internal rate of return. (Tip: Interpolate, using a discount factor of 20%.)

Question 39.3 This question follows on from Question 39.2. ***Tina Tintagel***, though impressed with your calculations concerning Business A, is not convinced that the newsagents and sweet shop is the right kind of business for her to acquire, since a newsagency necessitates early mornings and long hours of work. The gift shop, on the other hand, could be open at more congenial hours, and could close for long periods off-season. She requests you to perform for the gift shop calculations similar to those which you prepared for the newsagents and sweet shop.

It can be assumed that the investment of £50,000 covers the purchase price of the business, both assets and stock, and that the value of the assets and level of stock will remain constant at about £50,000 throughout the ten years.

Details of the anticipated cash flows for the first ten years are given below. Tina says that these cash flow figures (for both businesses A and B) assume that reasonable allowance has been made for managerial remuneration. Hence, it would be up to Tina whether she employed a manager (in which case Tina's involvement would be purely supervisory) or whether she acted as manager herself (in which case her return on the investment would be as shown by the figures provided, and, in addition, she herself would receive the allowance for managerial remuneration). Tina wishes to keep her options open in this respect.

	Business B
	£
Year 1	12,000
Year 2	11,000
Year 3	10,000
Year 4	9,000
Year 5	8,000
Year 6	8,000
Year 7	8,000
Year 8	8,000
Year 9	8,000
Year 10	8,000

Required

i) Calculate the net present value of Business B, using a discount factor of 16% (which is the present rate of return which is available to Tina on her £50,000), and also calculate the internal rate of return for Business B, using a suitable second discount rate for interpolation.

ii) Advise Tina on the advisability of investing her £50,000 in the gift shop, using your calculations as you consider appropriate, and making any assumptions concerning Tina's circumstances you feel are necessary to enable you to provide realistic advice.

Objective test *(tick the appropriate box)*

i) Internal rate of return is:

a) the method used to calculate the cost of capital ☐

b) the discount rate which results in an NPV of nil ☐

c) the mean of positive and negative NPVs ☐

d) a sophisticated development of the ARR technique ☐

ii) IRR can be calculated by:

a) taking the mean of positive and negative NPVs ☐

b) plotting the cash flows on a graph ☐

c) trial and error, using interpolation ☐

d) reading the co-ordinates in an IRR table ☐

iii) Project X has the following cash flows:

Year	Cash flows £
0	(2,000)
1	1,000
2	1,000
3	1,000

The IRR of this project is:

a) 21% ☐

b) 22% ☐

c) 23% ☐

d) 24% ☐

iv) The quickest way to solve the previous question would be:

a) calculate the NPV at 20% and 25%, and interpolate ☐

b) look up Table 2 and look along the line for year 3 for the nearest factor to 2.000 ☐

c) plot two NPVs on a graph, draw a line between the two points and read off where the line crosses the x (discount rate) axis. ☐

d) learn how to use a computer program which calculates IRR ☐

v) The most reliable method of investment appraisal is:

a) payback period ☐

b) NPV ☐

c) IRR ☐

d) a combination of these ☐

Assignment J

Wight Mineral Water Co Ltd

Context

You are assistant to Vic Ventnor, managing director of the ***Wight Mineral Water Co Ltd***, a company which has recently experienced a flat-spot in sales. Vic has thought of two alternative courses of action to remedy this situation:

Alternative A

Improved technology which will improve the quality and taste of the product. Investment of £30,000 (payable immediately) in new equipment is expected to improve the cash flows by £9,600 per annum. At the end of five years, it is conjectured that the technology and equipment will be obsolete.

Alternative B

Improved marketing: A reputable agency claims that for £30,000 (payable immediately) and £2,000 per annum (payable at the end of each of the next five years), it will provide extensive advertising and "maintenance" advertising over the next five years. This is expected to improve the annual net cash inflows (over present levels, and not taking into account the payments of £2,000 per annum to the agency), through increased volume of sales of the existing product, by £14,000 per annum for the next three years, dropping, as the impact of the campaign decreases, to an improvement of £8,000 per annum for the following two years.

Vic wishes to prepare a report which he can present to the next meeting of senior managers. He asks you for a memorandum concerning these alternatives, which will help him prepare his report.

Student activities

Write a memorandum to Vic Ventnor, which will help him write his report, and, hopefully, help you in your career.

Your memorandum should include:

i) In respect of each alternative, calculation of:
   - ❐ the payback period;
   - ❐ the accounting rate of return;
   - ❐ the net present value, assuming a minimum desired rate of return of 20%;
   - ❐ the internal rate of return.

ii) A clear explanation of what each of the four sets of calculations mean.

iii) Your advice on which alternative you consider to be of greater advantage to the Wight Mineral Water Company.

Ignore taxation, inflation and treat all cash flows as occurring at the end of complete years, except for the initial outlays at the start of year 1.

Format

A memorandum to Vic Ventnor, with tables of calculations and comments suitably appended.

Objectives

In this assignment the student should show an appreciation and understanding of the use of specific financial techniques for decision-making.

References

Chapters 36-39.

Chapter 40

Management accounting – current developments

40.1 Objectives

At the end of this chapter you should be able to:

- understand the reasons for the current developments in management accounting;
- understand just-in-time management;
- understand activity based costing;
- understand throughput accounting;
- understand backflush accounting.

40.2 Introduction

We have seen in earlier chapters how absorption costing is concerned with the collection of costs by product or cost unit and how production overhead costs are absorbed by those products by the establishment of overhead absorption rates. If you do not remember the way an absorption costing system operates you should revise chapters 31 and 32.

The absorption rates which are commonly used in manufacturing organisations include those which are based on direct labour. These rates are a rate per direct labour hour and a percentage on direct labour cost.

The changes which have taken place in recent years in the manufacturing sector in many cases now preclude the use of direct labour as a basis for overhead cost absorption and other methods of cost collection are now being developed.

40.3 Manufacturing Developments

The changes which have recently taken place in manufacturing may be summarised as follows:

- *Greater Mechanisation*

The introduction of high technology methods of production has accelerated and even higher levels of productivity have been achieved with the introduction of robot technology. This change has caused the overhead costs associated with the operation of machinery such as power, depreciation and maintenance to increase relative to the other costs of production.

- *Changes in the Incidence of Direct Labour*

As that proportion of total product cost defined as production overhead has increased, so the proportion of direct labour cost has declined. Robots and advanced production techniques have replaced direct labour on the production line, and the reduction of labour cost as a proportion of total cost, in some cases to a level of less than 12%, has made it increasingly more difficult to justify direct labour as a basis for absorbing overheads to products.

In many organisations the distinction between manual and staff status has also become less well defined. Production personnel in many cases now enjoy the same benefits and conditions of employment as those formerly given only to staff employees. In many cases production personnel are no longer paid on an hourly basis but are remunerated by an annual salary. Under these circumstances direct labour costs are difficult to define, and furthermore no longer behave as a variable cost related to production levels.

❒ ***Just-in-Time Developments***

There is an increasing tendency in manufacturing to produce using Just-in-Time (JIT) techniques. JIT is concerned with the organisation of production in such a way as to minimise the levels of raw material and finished goods stocks and work in progress. If stocks are reduced, then where profitability levels need to be determined the valuation of such stocks becomes less important. You will remember from earlier chapters that valuations of opening and closing stocks are necessary in order to measure the profit made in an accounting period.

❒ ***A Value-Added Approach to Production***

Managements are increasingly adopting a value-added approach to the operations which take place in converting raw materials into finished product. This means managements are attempting to eliminate operations which do not add value to the product. For example, moving parts and materials within the organisation, quality control checks, inspection and testing are all regarded as non-value added activities to be eliminated provided the final product quality is not impaired.

40.4 The Drawbacks of Absorption Costing

Absorption costing techniques have long been used in manufacturing industry to establish product costs for both stock valuation purposes and for profit measurement. However it is recognised that traditional absorption costing techniques suffer from a number of drawbacks, the major ones being:

❒ ***The encouragement of production for finished stock***

Because overhead absorption rates are based on budgeted projections then, provided actual costs do not exceed budgeted levels, when actual production exceeds budgeted production levels an over-recovery of fixed production overheads results. An over-recovery of overheads is normally treated as an addition to profits, and thus profits may be increased where additional production is achieved even though it is not sold. It should be appreciated that this approach may only be effective in increasing profits in the short term as the increased closing stock of one period becomes the opening stock of the succeeding period. Nevertheless, there exists in absorption costing an inherent encouragement to produce for stock.

❒ ***Valuation of Stocks is essentially for Financial Accounting purposes***

Stock valuation is a necessary requirement for the production of the published financial accounts of an enterprise to ensure that the costs incurred in the creation of those stocks are charged against the sales only when those stocks are sold. You will recall that there are a number of alternatives applied to stock valuation,including first-in-first-out (FIFO), last-in-first-out (LIFO) and average cost (AVCO), applicable both to marginal and absorption costing. Each method will result in different measures of profit for a period, and it is argued that these alternative approaches to stock valuation have little impact on the true performance of an organisation, but are mechanisms to enable financial accounts to be produced in conformity with certain rules. In general, however, absorption costing values stocks and work in progress at total production cost in conformity with Statement of Standard Accounting Practice No. 9.

❒ ***Costs are not incurred solely on a direct labour basis:***

Absorption costing often uses direct labour as a basis for absorbing production overhead costs by the product in spite of the fact that many of the overhead costs are fixed and not incurred on the same basis as, or are driven by, direct labour. It is recognised that other cost drivers exist, and that a multitude of activities throughout the organisation may cause costs to be incurred. For example, it may not be appropriate to charge material handling costs to products based on the direct labour incurred. In producing those products such costs may be more likely to be driven by the number of issues to production based on batch size or, alternatively, the units of raw material used by each product produced.

❒ ***Fixed Costs tend to be independent of production levels:***

Absorption costing often charges fixed costs to products based on production volumes, a basis which fails to recognise that fixed costs tend to be incurred independent of production levels. This approach fails to recognise the activities or cost drivers which cause such fixed costs to be incurred.

❒ ***Changes in the incidence of costs:***

Changes in manufacturing techniques have caused the incidence of fixed costs to increase, and absorption costing techniques have found it difficult to accommodate these higher fixed costs on a rational basis. Absorption costing continues to use direct labour-based approaches for overhead cost absorption even though there has been an increase in the proportions of fixed overheads incurred compared to direct labour cost.

❒ ***Absorption costing and variance analysis:***

The usual variance analysis associated with absorption costing and standard costing is often meaningless. For example, a favourable variance on maintenance overheads may not indicate a favourable situation when the saving has been brought about by lower maintenance activity. This may well cause greater machine downtime in the future, with all the consequences of lost production and profitability which this may cause. Similarly, favourable variances, or over-recoveries as described earlier, which might arise from over-activity may be misleading if it would have been more beneficial not to have produced the additional production anyway because of lack of sales demand.

Absorption Costing Example:

Essen PLC produces a range of three products, Alpha, Beta and Gamma, by means of a single process. It currently operates an absorption costing system, and the budgeted costs and production for the year to 31st December 19XX were as follows:

	Alpha	Beta	Gamma
Production quantity (units)	4,000	3,000	1,600
Resources per unit:			
Direct materials (kilos)	4	6	3
Direct labour (minutes)	30	45	60

The budgeted direct labour rate of pay was £5 per hour, and the budgeted material cost was £2 per kilo. Production overheads in total were budgeted at £99,450 and were absorbed to products as a rate per direct labour hour.

Required

Prepare a statement for management showing the unit costs and total costs for each product for the year ended 31st December 19XX using the absorption costing technique.

Solution

	Alpha	Beta	Gamma	Total
(a) Quantity (units)	4,000	3,000	1,600	-
(b) Direct labour (minutes)	30	45	60	-
(c) Direct labour hours (axb)	2,000	2,250	1,600	5,850

Overhead rate per direct labour hour = Total budgeted overheads ÷ Total budgeted DL hours

= £99,450 ÷ 5,850 hours

= £17 per DL hour.

Unit costs

	Alpha £		Beta £		Gamma £
Direct costs:					
Direct labour (£5x30/60)	2.50	(£5x45/60)	3.75	(£5x1)	5.00
Direct materials (£2x4)	8.00	(£2x6)	12.00	(£2x3)	6.00
Production overhead:					
(£17x30/60)	8.50				
(£17x45/60)			12.75		
(£17x60/60)					17.00
Total unit costs	19.00		28.50		28.00
Number of units	4,000		3,000		1,600
Total costs	£76,000		£85,000		£44,800

40.5 Activity Based Costing

Activity Based Costing, or ABC as it is more generally known, is a costing method which recognises that costs are incurred by the *activities* which take place within the organisation, and for each activity a cost driver may be identified. Those costs which are incurred or driven by the same *cost drivers* are grouped together into cost pools and the cost drivers are then used as a basis for charging the costs of each activity to the product.

40.6 Definitions

❒ ***Cost Pool***

A cost pool is a collection of costs which may be charged to products by the use of a common cost driver.

❒ ***Cost Driver***

A cost driver is any activity or series of activities which take place within an organisation which cause costs to be incurred. Cost drivers are not restricted to departments or sections, as more than one activity may be identified within a department.

Examples of cost pools and cost drivers are:

cost pool	*cost driver*
power	number of machine operations, machine hours
material handling	quantity or weight of material handled
material receipt	number of batches of material received
production planning	number of jobs planned
sales administration	number of customer orders received
set-up costs	number of jobs run
buying	number of orders placed

You should now be able to attempt Task 40.1 at the end of this chapter.

Example of ABC

Refer to the previous example of absorption costing. Essen PLC is now considering adopting a system of activity based costing, and before it develops the complete system the directors are keen to determine the impact which such a system would have on the existing product costs set out in the previous example. Use the existing budgets for the year ended 31st December 19XX together with the additional information set out below:

The budgeted overheads were analysed into

	£
Material handling	29,100
Storage costs	31,200
Electricity	39,150

The cost drivers were defined as:

Material handling	weight of materials handled
Storage costs	number of batches of material
Electricity	number of machine operations

Data on the cost drivers were:

	Alpha	Beta	Gamma
For complete production:			
Batches of material	10	5	15
Per unit of production:			
Number of machine operations	6	3	2

Required:

Prepare a statement for the management to show the product costs for the year ended 31st December 19XX using the principles of activity based costing. Compare your result with the previous example which used absorption costing as a basis.

Solution:

	Alpha	Beta	Gamma	Total
Quantity	4,000	3,000	1,600	-
Weight per unit (kilos)	4	6	3	
Total weight (kilos)	16,000	18,000	4,800	38,800
Machine operations per unit	6	3	2	-
Total operations	24,000	9,000	3,200	36,200
Total batches of material	10	5	15	30

Material handling - rate per kilo = £29,100 ÷ 38,800 kilos = £0.75 per kilo

Electricity - rate per machine operation = £39,150 ÷ 36,200 operations = £1.082 per machine operation

Storage - rate per batch = £31,200 ÷ 30 batches = £1,040 per batch

Unit costs

	Alpha		Beta		Gamma
	£		£		£
Direct costs:					
Direct labour (£5x30/60)	2.50	(£5x45/60)	3.75	(£5x1)	5.00
Direct materials (£2x4)	8.00	(£2x6)	12.00	(£2x3)	6.00
Production overheads:					
Material handling (£0.75x4)	3.00	(£0.75x6)	4.50	(£0.75x3)	2.25
Electricity (£1.082x6)	6.49	(£1.082x3)	3.25	(£1.082x2)	2.16
Storage					
(10x£1040/4000)	2.60				
(5x£1040/3000)			1.73		
(15x£1040/1600)					9.75
Total unit costs	22.59		25.23		25.16
Number of units	4,000		3,000		1,600
Total costs	£90,360		£75,690		£40,256

The difference in the total costs under the absorption and ABC approaches is due solely to the difference in the overhead borne by each of the products. The ABC system recognises the greater proportion of the activities engaged in producing Alpha, and ensures that Alpha should also bear commensurately more overhead as a consequence.

You should now be able to attempt Question 40.1 at the end of this chapter.

40.7 Benefits of Activity Based Costing

❐ *A more equitable method of charging costs to products:*

The products which use the activities which cause the costs to be incurred bear those costs associated with those activities in a more equitable manner. This overcomes the drawback in absorption costing where general overheads are spread over the product range using methods largely unrelated to the way costs are generated.

❐ *Takes into consideration product complexity:*

The costs charged to products relate to the production circumstances in which those products are produced. Under ABC, short runs and complex products might attract consequently higher levels of unit cost compared to long runs and simple products. This aspect would have considerable impact, therefore, in the measurement of relative product profitability compared to the absorption costing approach.

❐ *Costs are more closely related to activity levels:*

Those costs which under absorption and marginal costing approaches are traditionally regarded as fixed in total may be treated as variable in the longer term under ABC. As a consequence ABC encourages the measurement of efficiency levels of administrative functions. For example if the cost driver for the Planning & Progress Section is regarded as the number of jobs planned, then reductions in the number of jobs could be expected to be accompanied by a commensurate reduction in the cost of the activity in the longer term.

❐ *Encourages a more realistic approach to stock policy:*

ABC does not encourage the build up of finished goods stock in the same way as absorption costing tends to do as described earlier. In activity based costing the over-recoveries which encourage stock build-up in absorption costing do not arise to the same extent because a greater proportion of the costs are treated as variable rather than fixed.

❐ *Improves cost control:*

ABC reflects more closely what is happening in the production environment and identifies those elements which should be subject to managerial control. It recognises that cost management can best be achieved through the management of those activities which cause costs to be incurred.

40.8 Drawbacks of Activity Based Costing

❐ *More detailed analysis required:*

A more detailed analysis of cost pools and cost drivers than necessary for absorption costing is usually required for an effective ABC system, with the consequent increase in the cost of administration of the accounting system.

❐ *Some simplification required:*

The identification of cost pools and cost drivers is not always a straightforward exercise and it is sometimes necessary to rationalise the number of cost pools and cost drivers in the interests of reducing the complexity and cost of ABC. This may be regarded as a compromise to the ABC system.

❐ *Does not always conform to SSAP 9:*

The ABC system encourages all costs, including selling and distribution costs, to be charged to work in progress and finished goods as product costs. This cuts across the normal basis for valuing stocks for financial accounting purposes. Statement of Standard Accounting Practice No. 9 requires stocks and work in progress to be valued at total production cost up to the stage of production reached, which would normally exclude selling and distribution costs.

❐ *A more complex system of absorption costing:*

ABC is regarded by some as not so very different from absorption costing in that absorption rates as rates for each cost driver are still required, and furthermore a greater number of individual cost rates are required to be computed under ABC in order to recover the costs for each cost pool.

You should now be able to attempt Task 40.2 and Questions 40.2 and 40.3 at the end of this chapter.

40.9 Throughput accounting

Throughput accounting has developed as a result of the same changes in manufacturing which have encouraged the introduction of ABC approaches. Direct labour has reduced as a proportion of total cost, whilst fixed costs have increased. At the same time JIT and Value Added management philosophies have reduced stocks, which has reduced the importance of stock valuation in accounting systems.

Throughput accounting is concerned with providing short term decisions, and regards all the conversion costs of an enterprise as fixed in the short term, only material is regarded as a variable cost. Conversion costs are those costs incurred by the organisation which are incurred in order to change the raw materials into finished goods. Conversion costs exclude material costs.

In throughput accounting the existence of stocks is regarded as evidence of failure to respond to customer demand in the short term. Theoretically, no stocks would exist if the organisation were able to respond immediately to customer requirements directly from production, and Just-in-Time manufacturing and Value Added approaches are movements towards this situation where stock levels are minimised.

Throughput accounting uses the same approach to decision making as that used in marginal costing where the contribution per unit of limiting factor determines the ranking of the products to be produced. See Chapter 34 for a further explanation of the use of this approach in marginal costing.

In throughput accounting such decisions are made through the use of the throughput accounting ratio (TAR). The TAR is as follows:

$$\text{TAR} = \frac{\text{Return per factory hour}}{\text{Cost per factory hour}}$$

where: $$\text{the Return per factory hour} = \frac{\text{Sales price} - \text{material cost}}{\text{Hours on scarce resource}}$$

and: $$\text{the Cost per factory hour} = \frac{\text{Total factory cost}}{\text{Total hours available on scarce resource}}$$

The cost per factory hour is common to all products produced by the same production facility, and the return per factory hour is essentially the value added per unit of scarce resource. The TAR for each product therefore is a ranking measure, and the products should be ranked according to the size of the TAR.

You should now be able to attempt Task 40.3 at the end of this chapter.

40.10 Backflush accounting

Backflush accounting is another approach to costing which has grown as a result of the recent changes in management philosophies and technologies described earlier in this chapter.

Backflush accounting assumes that, with the minimisation of stock levels, valuation of stocks is immaterial in establishing an organisation's profitability, and the charging of overheads to products no longer requires the complex absorption and ABC techniques. Backflush accounting adopts a simpler approach by working backwards to allocate costs to stock and cost of sales to establish profitability.

Absorption costing constantly charges costs to production or work in progress over the production cycle whereas backflush accounting charges costs to production at a limited number of 'trigger points' during the production cycle. In the simplest system these trigger points would be when materials are issued to production and when the goods are completed, hence the term 'backflush accounting'. Standard costs are often used as the rates at which the charges are made to production.

40.11 Summary

There have been substantial changes to manufacturing systems in recent years which have been brought about by improvements in production technology and developments in management philosophies. These changes have concentrated on Just-in-Time and Value Added manufacturing systems which in turn have had an impact on the accounting systems in use within manufacturing organisations.

It is recognised that absorption costing systems suffer from a number of serious drawbacks, particularly when applied to modern manufacturing systems. The development of the activity based costing approaches in both the manufacturing and service sectors have gone some way to overcoming the drawbacks associated with absorption costing. In addition, throughput accounting and backflush accounting have also been developed as a means of responding to current manufacturing developments.

Student Activities

Task 40.1 Draw up a list of activities which take place in the departments or sections where you work or study. Determine the most appropriate cost drivers for each activity, and the ways in which each cost driver should be measured.

Task 40.2 The company where you work has always used a system of absorption costing in establishing product costs. You feel, however, that the company would benefit from the introduction of activity based costing (ABC) in determining product costs. Write a report to the managing director of the company setting out, inter alia,

i) the drawbacks of the current absorption costing system
ii) the benefits which might arise from the introduction of ABC
iii) the measures which are required to be taken in order to establish a successful ABC system.

Task 40.3 A local company which produces a range of products is anxious to ensure that it uses its production facilities in a manner which will optimise profitability. Write a memorandum to the chief executive explaining how the use of throughput accounting and throughput accounting ratios can help with this problem. Draw up an example to illustrate your argument.

Question 40.1 *Junior Ltd* has produced the following monthly fixed overhead budget:

	£
Machine running costs	51,000
Production planning	42,000
Job set-up costs	27,000
Quality control	24,600
Material receipts	32,400
Packaging	18,000
	195,000

Planned production for the month is as follows:

	Product 1	Product 2	Product 3
Production/sales (units)	6,000	8,000	4,000
Direct labour hours per unit	1 hour	1.5 hours	1 hour
Machine hours per unit	0.5 hours	1 hour	1.5 hours
Selling price per unit	£25	£35	£30
Variable costs per unit:			
Material	£8	£12	£10
Labour	£4	£6	£4

From an analysis of purchasing, stores and sales office records the following further information is available:

per month	Product 1	Product 2	Product 3
Number of customer orders	6	20	10
Number of production runs	6	16	8
Number of component receipts	18	80	64
Number of components per unit	3	5	8

Junior Ltd currently uses absorption costing and it is concerned about the variation in gross profit per unit from the two separate absorption bases which could be used. The company is now considering the alternatives of a contribution approach which, it feels, may be more useful as it has to make product market/price decisions, or an activity based costing approach.

Required:

i) Calculate the gross profit per unit using the two possible separate absorption rates.

ii) Prepare a contribution statement for the budgeted demand.

iii) Prepare a statement showing the cost per unit in which the fixed costs are treated using an activity based costing approach.

Question 40.2 *Hightec PLC* manufactures and sells two products. The following statement of profitability by product was produced for the year ended 31st March 19XX:

	Product A	%	Product B	%	Total
			£000s		
Sales	1,760	100	1,040	100	2,800
Variable production costs	440		290		730
Fixed production costs	920		490		1,410
Total costs	1,360		780		2,140
Gross Profit	400	22.7	260	25.0	660
Other costs:					
General administration					140
Marketing and distribution					250
Research and development					110
					500
Net Profit					160

The costs and revenues per unit for each of the products is as follows based on planned volumes which were actually achieved:

			Product A			Product B
Planned volumes (units)			20,000			10,000
			£			£
Selling price			88			104
Direct materials		10			12	
Direct labour:	Dept 1 (1hr)	6		(0.5hr)	9	
	Dept 2 (0.5hr)	2		(0.75hr)	3	
Variable Overhead:						
	Dept 1 (1 DLH)	2		(1.5DLH)	3	
	Dept 2 (1 MH)	2		(1MH)	2	
Fixed overhead:	Dept 1 (1DLH)	6		(1.5DLH)	9	
	Dept 2 (1MH)	40	68	(1MH)	40	78
Gross Profit			20			26

In an attempt to more closely relate overhead expenditure to particular products, a cost investigation was undertaken. Hightec PLC's budgeted and actual fixed production overheads were analysed to provide the bases upon which the overhead absorption rates were calculated:

	£000s	
Cost Pool	Department 1	Department 2
Staff	60	400
Productive (power, depreciation, maintenance)	80	700
Materials procurement	30	60
Information technology	40	40
	210	1200

Each cost pool was found to have one major cost driver whose impact and analysis was found to be as follows:

Cost Pool	Cost Driver	Dept 1 total	Dept 1 product A	Dept 1 product B	Dept 2 total	Dept 2 product A	Dept 2 product B
Staff	Numbers	5	2	3	40	15	25
Productive	Productive assets (£)	0.5m	0.2m	0.3m	2.0	1.2	0.8
Materials procurement	Orders placed	1200	300	900	800	400	400
Information technology	Computing hours	1250	350	900	2500	1250	1250

A similar investigation into other overheads revealed the following analysis:

		£000s		
		Product A	Product B	Total
General Administration	attributable equally	70	70	140
Marketing & Distribution	variable	40	60	100
	fixed	50	100	150
Research & Development		40	70	110

Required:

Prepare product profitability statements using activity based costing approaches to cost allotment.

Question 40.3 *BAC plc* produces printed circuit boards for computers. The business began with a large contract for a standard board for a home computer which was produced in large volumes. After two years a new customer asked for a new non-standard board which became known as the Special. The Special used some components of the Standard board and some unique to that product, but the labour time taken was the same, 2 hours per unit, and additional design and tooling costs were incurred.

As the expansion of the home computer business tailed off, BAC plc was able to fill the capacity with the production of Special boards for which a slightly higher price was obtained and although the Special was produced in smaller batches, its production levels in total were approaching those of the Standard. Data from last year's accounts (Fig. 1) showed that 15,000 Standards and 10,000 Specials were produced.

The marketing department reports further pressure on the price of the Standard, and demand for the Special continues to increase, and as the net profit as a % of sales is already lower for Standards there is pressure to go for more Specials and fewer Standards.

There is concern, however, over what is being revealed about product profitability by the existing absorption accounting system. As a result it was decided to examine the four production cost centres and produce a list of activities, cost drivers and costs. These are shown in figure 3, and the production overhead analysis is shown in figure 2. It has also been established that marketing, research and development and administration overheads were all fixed, and that of the production overhead, software and support group, depreciation group and general group were also fixed for the activity levels achieved. Other production overhead is considered to vary with direct labour, the cost of which is £6 per hour.

Required:

Produce an alternative income statement for 19XX based on activity based costing approaches.

Fig. 1

Income Statement by product - 19XX

	Standard	Special	Total
	£	£	£
Sales	2,700,000	2,000,000	4,700,000
Direct Costs:			
Materials	1,110,000	790,000	1,900,000
Labour	180,000	120,000	300,000
Production overhead	600,000	400,000	1,000,000
Total production costs	1,890,000	1,310,000	3,200,000
Gross Profit	810,000	690,000	1,500,000
*Marketing, R & D and Administration	344,681	255,319	600,000
Net Profit	465,319	434,681	900,000
Net profit as % Sales	17.23%	21.73%	19.15%

* apportioned on the basis of sales value.

Fig. 2

Production Overhead Analysis - Budget 19XX

	Product'n	Engineer'g	Material Control	Inspection
	£	£	£	£
Indirect labour group	180,000	120,000	120,000	80,000
Indirect material group	15,000	10,000	-	-
Energy group	43,000	1,000	1,000	5,000
Software & support group	30,000	40,000	180,000	-
Depreciation group	70,000	5,000	15,000	5,000
General group	25,000	20,000	20,000	15,000
	363,000	196,000	336,000	105,000
Reapportioned service department costs	637,000	(196,000)	(336,000)	(105,000)
	1,000,000	-	-	-

Budgeted Direct Labour Hours	50,000
Overhead absorption rate	£20 per hour

Note. There are no reciprocal service department charges.

Fig. 3

Investigation into support service activities - findings

Support service	Cost driver/ activity	£	Units of activity occurrence per 50 week year Standard	Special	Total
Production	Set-up	125,000	250	1,000	1,250
	Prod. Orders	238,000	60	100	160
		363,000			
Engineering Dept	New and re-designs (CAD)	120,000	7	23	30
	Production delays	76,000	5	40	45
		196,000			
Material Control	Placing & receiving supply orders	168,000	48	132	180
	Issuing materials	168,000	200	250	450
		336,000			
Inspection	No. of units inspected	105,000	3,000	20,000	23,000
Marketing, R & D and Admin General	Marketing	80,000	(50:50)		
	No. of promotions	64,000	14	66	80
	No. of R&D projects	120,000	6	9	15
	General R&D	120,000	(50:50)		
	Customer Liaison	80,000	40	360	400
	Other Admin.	136,000	(50:50)		

Objective Tests *(tick the appropriate box)*

i) Absorption costing techniques suffer from:

a) too much complexity ☐

b) an inability to enable product unit costs to be computed ☐

c) an inherent encouragement to produce for stock ☐

d) a lack of the use of cost rates ☐

ii) Modern approaches to manufacturing have a tendency to:

a) Use Just-in-Time techniques ☐

b) Encourage production for stock ☐

c) Maximise work in progress ☐

d) Increase the proportion of direct labour cost ☐

iii) The basic assumption behind ABC is that costs are generated by:

a) Products ☐

b) Activities ☐

c) Personnel ☐

d) Production ☐

iv) The characteristics of ABC are said to be that it:

a) takes into consideration production complexity ☐

b) ignores production complexity ☐

c) gives the same product costs as absorption costing ☐

d) encourages production for stock ☐

v) Throughput accounting assumes that in the short term:

a) all costs are variable ☐

b) material costs are fixed ☐

c) conversion costs are fixed ☐

d) no costs are variable ☐

Appendix I
Discounted cash flow tables

Table 1 – Present Value Factors

Rate of discount

Future years	1%	2%	3%	4%	5%	6%	7%	8%	9%	10%	11%	12%	13%	14%	15%	16%
1	0.990	0.980	0.971	0.962	0.952	0.943	0.935	0.926	0.917	0.909	0.901	0.893	0.885	0.877	0.870	0.862
2	0.980	0.961	0.943	0.925	0.907	0.890	0.873	0.857	0.842	0.826	0.812	0.797	0.783	0.770	0.756	0.743
3	0.971	0.942	0.915	0.889	0.864	0.840	0.816	0.794	0.772	0.751	0.731	0.712	0.693	0.675	0.658	0.641
4	0.961	0.924	0.889	0.855	0.823	0.792	0.763	0.735	0.708	0.683	0.659	0.636	0.613	0.592	0.572	0.552
5	0.952	0.906	0.863	0.822	0.784	0.747	0.713	0.681	0.650	0.621	0.594	0.567	0.543	0.519	0.497	0.476
6	0.942	0.888	0.838	0.790	0.746	0.705	0.666	0.630	0.596	0.565	0.535	0.507	0.480	0.456	0.432	0.410
7	0.933	0.871	0.813	0.760	0.711	0.665	0.623	0.584	0.547	0.513	0.482	0.452	0.425	0.400	0.376	0.354
8	0.924	0.854	0.789	0.731	0.677	0.627	0.582	0.540	0.502	0.467	0.434	0.404	0.376	0.351	0.327	0.305
9	0.914	0.837	0.766	0.703	0.645	0.592	0.544	0.500	0.460	0.424	0.391	0.361	0.333	0.308	0.284	0.263
10	0.905	0.820	0.744	0.676	0.614	0.558	0.508	0.463	0.422	0.386	0.352	0.322	0.295	0.270	0.247	0.227
11	0.896	0.804	0.722	0.650	0.585	0.527	0.475	0.429	0.388	0.350	0.317	0.287	0.261	0.237	0.215	0.195
12	0.887	0.789	0.701	0.625	0.557	0.497	0.444	0.397	0.356	0.319	0.286	0.257	0.231	0.208	0.187	0.168
13	0.879	0.773	0.681	0.601	0.530	0.469	0.415	0.368	0.326	0.286	0.258	0.229	0.204	0.182	0.163	0.145
14	0.870	0.758	0.661	0.578	0.505	0.442	0.388	0.341	0.299	0.263	0.232	0.205	0.181	0.160	0.141	0.125
15	0.861	0.743	0.642	0.555	0.481	0.417	0.362	0.315	0.275	0.239	0.209	0.183	0.160	0.140	0.123	0.108
16	0.853	0.728	0.623	0.534	0.458	0.394	0.339	0.292	0.252	0.218	0.188	0.163	0.142	0.123	0.107	0.093
17	0.844	0.714	0.605	0.513	0.436	0.371	0.317	0.270	0.231	0.198	0.170	0.146	0.125	0.108	0.093	0.080
18	0.836	0.700	0.587	0.494	0.416	0.350	0.296	0.250	0.212	0.180	0.153	0.130	0.111	0.095	0.081	0.069
19	0.828	0.686	0.570	0.475	0.396	0.331	0.277	0.232	0.195	0.164	0.138	0.116	0.098	0.083	0.070	0.060
20	0.820	0.673	0.554	0.456	0.377	0.312	0.258	0.215	0.178	0.149	0.124	0.104	0.087	0.073	0.061	0.051

Rate of discount

Future years	17%	18%	19%	20%	21%	22%	23%	24%	25%	26%	28%	30%	35%	40%	45%	50%
1	0.855	0.847	0.840	0.833	0.826	0.820	0.813	0.807	0.800	0.794	0.781	0.769	0.741	0.714	0.690	0.667
2	0.731	0.718	0.706	0.694	0.683	0.672	0.661	0.650	0.640	0.630	0.610	0.592	0.549	0.510	0.476	0.444
3	0.624	0.609	0.593	0.579	0.565	0.551	0.537	0.525	0.512	0.500	0.477	0.455	0.406	0.364	0.328	0.296
4	0.534	0.516	0.499	0.482	0.467	0.451	0.437	0.423	0.410	0.397	0.373	0.350	0.301	0.260	0.226	0.198
5	0.456	0.437	0.419	0.402	0.386	0.370	0.355	0.341	0.328	0.315	0.291	0.269	0.223	0.186	0.156	0.132
6	0.390	0.370	0.352	0.335	0.319	0.303	0.289	0.275	0.262	0.250	0.227	0.207	0.165	0.133	0.108	0.088
7	0.333	0.314	0.296	0.279	0.263	0.249	0.235	0.222	0.210	0.198	0.178	0.159	0.122	0.095	0.074	0.059
8	0.285	0.266	0.249	0.233	0.218	0.204	0.191	0.179	0.168	0.157	0.139	0.123	0.091	0.068	0.051	0.039
9	0.243	0.226	0.209	0.194	0.180	0.167	0.155	0.144	0.134	0.125	0.108	0.094	0.067	0.048	0.035	0.026
10	0.208	0.191	0.176	0.162	0.149	0.137	0.126	0.116	0.107	0.099	0.085	0.073	0.050	0.035	0.024	0.017
11	0.178	0.162	0.148	0.135	0.123	0.112	0.103	0.094	0.086	0.079	0.066	0.056	0.037	0.025	0.017	0.012
12	0.152	0.137	0.124	0.112	0.102	0.092	0.083	0.076	0.069	0.063	0.052	0.043	0.027	0.018	0.012	0.008
13	0.130	0.116	0.104	0.094	0.084	0.075	0.068	0.061	0.055	0.050	0.040	0.033	0.020	0.013	0.008	0.005
14	0.111	0.099	0.088	0.078	0.069	0.062	0.055	0.049	0.044	0.039	0.032	0.025	0.015	0.009	0.006	0.003
15	0.095	0.084	0.074	0.065	0.057	0.051	0.045	0.040	0.035	0.031	0.025	0.020	0.011	0.006	0.004	0.002
16	0.081	0.071	0.062	0.054	0.047	0.042	0.036	0.032	0.028	0.025	0.019	0.015	0.008	0.005	0.003	0.002
17	0.069	0.060	0.052	0.045	0.039	0.034	0.030	0.026	0.023	0.020	0.015	0.012	0.006	0.003	0.002	0.001
18	0.059	0.051	0.044	0.038	0.032	0.028	0.024	0.021	0.018	0.016	0.012	0.009	0.005	0.002	0.001	0.001
19	0.051	0.043	0.037	0.031	0.027	0.023	0.020	0.017	0.014	0.012	0.009	0.007	0.003	0.002	0.001	0.000
20	0.043	0.037	0.031	0.026	0.022	0.019	0.016	0.014	0.012	0.010	0.007	0.005	0.002	0.001	0.001	0.000

Table 2 – Cumulative Present Value Factors

Rate of discount

Future years	1%	2%	3%	4%	5%	6%	7%	8%	9%	10%	11%	12%	13%	14%	15%	16%
1	0.990	0.980	0.971	0.962	0.952	0.943	0.935	0.926	0.917	0.909	0.901	0.893	0.885	0.877	0.870	0.862
2	1.970	1.942	1.913	1.886	1.859	1.833	1.808	1.783	1.759	1.736	1.713	1.690	1.668	1.647	1.626	1.605
3	2.941	2.884	2.829	2.775	2.723	2.673	2.624	2.577	2.531	2.487	2.444	2.402	2.361	2.322	2.283	2.246
4	3.902	3.808	3.717	3.630	3.546	3.465	3.387	3.312	3.240	3.170	3.102	3.037	2.974	2.914	2.855	2.798
5	4.853	4.713	4.580	4.452	4.329	4.212	4.100	3.993	3.890	3.791	3.696	3.605	3.517	3.433	3.352	3.274
6	5.795	5.601	5.417	5.242	5.076	4.917	4.767	4.623	4.486	4.355	4.231	4.111	3.998	3.889	3.784	3.685
7	6.728	6.472	6.230	6.002	5.786	5.582	5.389	5.206	5.033	4.868	4.712	4.564	4.423	4.288	4.160	4.039
8	7.652	7.325	7.020	6.733	6.463	6.210	5.971	5.747	5.535	5.335	5.146	4.968	4.799	4.639	4.487	4.344
9	8.566	8.162	7.786	7.435	7.108	6.802	6.515	6.247	5.995	5.759	5.537	5.328	5.132	4.946	4.772	4.607
10	9.471	8.983	8.530	8.111	7.722	7.360	7.024	6.710	6.418	6.145	5.889	5.650	5.426	5.216	5.019	4.833
11	10.368	9.787	9.253	8.760	8.306	7.887	7.499	7.139	6.805	6.495	6.207	5.938	5.687	5.453	5.234	5.029
12	11.255	10.575	9.954	9.385	8.863	8.384	7.943	7.536	7.161	6.814	6.492	6.194	5.918	5.660	5.421	5.197
13	12.134	11.348	10.635	9.986	9.394	8.853	8.358	7.904	7.487	7.103	6.750	6.424	6.122	5.842	5.583	5.342
14	13.004	12.106	11.296	10.563	9.899	9.295	8.745	8.244	7.786	7.367	6.982	6.628	6.302	6.002	5.724	5.468
15	13.865	12.849	11.938	11.118	10.380	9.712	9.108	8.559	8.061	7.606	7.191	6.811	6.462	6.142	5.847	5.575
16	14.718	13.578	12.561	11.652	10.838	10.106	9.447	8.851	8.313	7.824	7.379	6.974	6.604	6.265	5.954	5.668
17	15.562	14.292	13.166	12.166	11.274	10.477	9.763	9.122	8.544	8.022	7.549	7.120	6.729	6.373	6.047	5.749
18	16.398	14.992	13.754	12.659	11.690	10.828	10.059	9.372	8.756	8.201	7.702	7.250	6.840	6.467	6.128	5.818
19	17.226	15.678	14.324	13.134	12.085	11.158	10.336	9.604	8.950	8.365	7.839	7.366	6.938	6.550	6.198	5.877
20	18.046	16.351	14.877	13.590	12.462	11.470	10.594	9.818	9.129	8.514	7.963	7.469	7.025	6.623	6.259	5.929

Rate of discount

Future years	17%	18%	19%	20%	21%	22%	23%	24%	25%	26%	28%	30%	35%	40%	45%	50%
1	0.855	0.847	0.840	0.833	0.826	0.820	0.813	0.806	0.800	0.794	0.781	0.769	0.741	0.714	0.690	0.667
2	1.585	1.566	1.547	1.528	1.509	1.492	1.474	1.457	1.440	1.424	1.392	1.361	1.289	1.224	1.165	1.111
3	2.210	2.174	2.140	2.106	2.074	2.042	2.011	1.981	1.952	1.923	1.868	1.816	1.696	1.589	1.493	1.407
4	2.743	2.690	2.639	2.589	2.540	2.494	2.448	2.404	2.362	2.320	2.241	2.166	1.997	1.849	1.720	1.605
5	3.199	3.127	3.058	2.991	2.926	2.864	2.803	2.745	2.689	2.635	2.532	2.436	2.220	2.035	1.876	1.737
6	3.589	3.498	3.410	3.326	3.245	3.167	3.092	3.020	2.951	2.885	2.759	2.643	2.385	2.168	1.983	1.824
7	3.922	3.812	3.706	3.605	3.508	3.416	3.327	3.242	3.161	3.083	2.937	2.802	2.508	2.263	2.057	1.883
8	4.207	4.078	3.954	3.837	3.726	3.619	3.518	3.421	3.329	3.241	3.076	2.925	2.598	2.331	2.109	1.922
9	4.451	4.303	4.163	4.031	3.905	3.786	3.673	3.566	3.463	3.366	3.184	3.019	2.665	2.379	2.144	1.948
10	4.659	4.494	4.339	4.192	4.054	3.923	3.799	3.682	3.571	3.465	3.269	3.092	2.715	2.414	2.168	1.965
11	4.836	4.656	4.486	4.327	4.177	4.035	3.902	3.776	3.656	3.543	3.335	3.147	2.752	2.438	2.185	1.977
12	4.988	4.793	4.611	4.439	4.278	4.127	3.985	3.851	3.725	3.606	3.387	3.190	2.779	2.456	2.196	1.985
13	5.118	4.910	4.715	4.533	4.362	4.203	4.053	3.912	3.780	3.656	3.427	3.223	2.799	2.469	2.204	1.990
14	5.229	5.008	4.802	4.611	4.432	4.265	4.108	3.962	3.824	3.695	3.459	3.249	2.814	2.478	2.210	1.993
15	5.324	5.092	4.876	4.675	4.489	4.315	4.153	4.001	3.859	3.726	3.483	3.268	2.825	2.484	2.214	1.995
16	5.405	5.162	4.938	4.730	4.536	4.357	4.189	4.033	3.887	3.751	3.503	3.283	2.834	2.489	2.216	1.997
17	5.475	5.222	4.990	4.775	4.576	4.391	4.219	4.059	3.910	3.771	3.518	3.295	2.840	2.492	2.218	1.998
18	5.534	5.273	5.033	4.812	4.608	4.419	4.243	4.080	3.928	3.786	3.529	3.304	2.844	2.494	2.219	1.999
19	5.584	5.316	5.070	4.843	4.635	4.442	4.263	4.097	3.942	3.799	3.539	3.311	2.848	2.496	2.220	1.999
20	5.628	5.353	5.101	4.870	4.657	4.460	4.279	4.110	3.954	3.808	3.546	3.316	2.850	2.497	2.221	1.999

Appendix II
Additional Assignments

Assignment K

The Passenger Transport Executive

Context

The Passenger Transport Executive (PTE) is responsible for running the bus services in Newtown and the surrounding area. The present accounting system is poorly developed and simply provides a quarterly analysis of the income by bus route, expenditure and type of expenditure, so that a profit or loss is determined for each quarter and the year to date.

The chief executive is anxious to improve the costing and accounting control information available to the management of the PTE. He has recently been to a seminar on management accounting where there was much discussion amongst the industrialists attending about total absorption costing and how it is used in a manufacturing environment. He feels sure that there must be a way of applying this system of costing to the PTE operations.

'After all,' he reasons, 'the PTE produces something which can be measured, perhaps in passengers carried, kilometres run or a combination of both, and we use machinery to produce it, namely buses!'

The PTE operates 25 routes of varying lengths throughout the city, and each route is served by a range of vehicle types and sizes, according to passenger demand and time of day. There is a single combined head office and central garage.

Student activities

The chief executive has asked you, his chief accountant, to provide a brief but comprehensive report of not more than 2,000 words for the next board meeting setting out how a form of absorption costing might be applied to PTE activities. Amongst the aspects he particularly wants you to address are:

i) What costs are incurred by vehicles or group of vehicles, their behavioural characteristics and how they might be collected in the costing system by vehicle type?

ii) How might the principles of absorption costing be adapted to enable route costs to be determined?

iii) What information might be presented to management for control purposes?

You can make any relevant and appropriate assumptions regarding the PTE and its operations, but they must fit in with the scenario set out above and they must be clearly stated. Quote any references used.

Care should be taken to choose appropriate cost centres and cost units. Remember, cost centres are those parts of the business to which level costs are collected, and cost units represent a measurement of those activities to which costs are recovered by the use of absorption costing.

Avoid using inappropriate terminology in your report. The terms and classification of costs into direct materials, direct labour and overheads do not have the same meaning in a transport business as those used in a manufacturing organisation. In addition, the bases of apportionment used in a manufacturing organisation may not be appropriate to a transport business.

Format

Your answer should take the form of a report addressed to the board of the PTE. This is not an essay and marks will be given for a good layout with paragraph headings and a clear, progressive structure. Document and cost flow diagrams will gain additional marks.

Objectives

This assignment is a sound test of the student's ability to recognise the characteristics of absorption costing and apply the system to a non-manufacturing environment. The student should therefore show an understanding and appreciation of:

- cost classification;
- cost allocation;
- cost apportionment;
- cost absorption;
- budgeting;
- variance analysis;
- documentation.

References

Chapters 17 and 27 – 33.

Assignment L

Wheeler & Company Limited

Context

At the beginning of October 19X1 Henry Wheeler started a small manufacturing business to produce bicycle components and accessories. The business specialises in security and safety products for which there has been increasing demand. Since Mr Wheeler commenced trading, demand has made it necessary for the company to buy in finished goods (such as crash helmets) to complement the firm's range.

Mr Wheeler's bookkeeper has extracted a list of balances from the books of accounts at the end of the first year's trading, together with other financial data, as follows:

List of balances as at 30th September 19X2

	£
Sales	51,750
Sales returns	125
Purchases:	
Raw materials	13,220
Finished accessories	7,900
Purchase returns:	
Raw materials	235
Plant and machinery (cost)	23,000
Office furniture (cost)	840
Factory power	3,125
Heat and light	950
Creditors	6,500
Debtors	11,000
Cash in hand and at bank	10,800
Manufacturing wages	16,000
General expenses	2,200
Insurances	980
Freehold factory at cost	85,000
Business rates	6,300
Motor vans (cost)	15,000
Office salaries	6,200
Drawings	5,500

The results of stocktaking on 30th September 19X2

	£
Raw materials	3,100
Work in progress	12,345
Finished goods manufactured	15,635
Finished goods purchased	3,250

Mr Wheeler has asked you to produce the accounts for the first year of trading. He has also asked you to provide some financial guidance on various issues. During your discussions with him, you explain the need to depreciate fixed assets and you agree that it should be provided as follows using the reducing balance method:

Plant and machinery	10%
Motor vans	40%
Office furniture	15%

As some of the costs were common to both the factory and the office, you agree with Mr Wheeler that a fair apportionment of these costs would be as follows:

	Factory	Office
Heat and light	$\frac{4}{5}$	$\frac{1}{5}$
Business rates	$\frac{6}{7}$	$\frac{1}{7}$
Insurances	$\frac{6}{7}$	$\frac{1}{7}$
General expenses	$\frac{4}{6}$	$\frac{2}{6}$

Student activities

i) Prepare a manufacturing, trading and profit account for the year ended 30th September 19X2.

ii) Prepare a report which addresses the following questions, each of which should be covered separately and in detail, in simple language which bears in mind that Mr Wheeler has little grasp of accounting.

a) Mr Wheeler tries to make his factory manager accountable for the results of his production by allowing him a transfer price of £1 per item produced. A total of 28,000 items have been produced during the year. How has the factory manager fared?

b) Calculate how much capital Mr Wheeler had tied up in the business at the end of September 19X2.

c) Explain the results for the first year and the state of the business at the end of it by calculating some useful ratios from the accounts. Give clear explanations for each ratio.

d) Mr Wheeler does not understand why achieving a profit does not necessarily increase the balance in his business bank account. Explain this apparent anomaly.

e) Mr Wheeler wants to know whether providing depreciation on his fixed assets makes funds available to replace his factory machinery and other assets when this becomes necessary. Explain where the money is at the end of the year and whether the depreciation provision for one asset, plant and machinery for example, could be used to finance another, say motor vans, when the latter requires replacement.

Format

Your answer should take the form of a report of not more than 2,000 words addressed to Mr Wheeler. Diagrams may be used to illustrate particular points. The accounts should be prepared in vertical form. Relevant and appropriate assumptions may be made, but they must be clearly stated.

Objectives

The assignment is intended to test th the student's ability to classify and construct financial statements for a manufacturing business and analyse and interpret the results. Knowledge of some of the accounting conventions and the treatment of depreciation is also required.

References

Chapters 10, 11, 13, 19, 22 and 26.

Assignment M

Gower Enterprises Limited

Context

Gower Enterprises Limited is a company which has already established itself in the holiday camp business. You have recently joined the company as a management trainee and have been asked to provide some figures and advice on a problem over which a decision is to be taken soon.

The company has found two sites, both of which have good potential as future sites for the next season. Each will require initial financing of £500,000. The problem is that due to difficulties beyond the control of the management, only £500,000 is easily available and at a 17% cost of capital rate; this is the maximum rate at which the company is prepared to borrow.

The two sites have different projected profitability patterns. Site A is in a position which has not yet been accepted by the public as a holiday location, but the management at Gower Enterprises considers the location to be attractive and one which could increase in popularity of the next four years. One drawback is that in the third year the camp would have to be closed, except during the height of the season, because the council has scheduled repairs to the sea defences which would close access to the site while the work was being carried out.

Site B, on the other hand, is in a well established tourism area and would be popular immediately; the only drawback being that existing competition is likely to continue increasing.

The accounts project manager and managing director of Gower Enterprises have agreed that likely cash flows for the next four years will be as follows:

	Site A	Site B
	£'000	£'000
Year 1	200	400
Year 2	300	200
Year 3	200	200
Year 4	400	200

The managing director considers that any analysis of the figures should be restricted to the first four years. He admits that either site would be likely to continue in use and profitability beyond the four years, but feels that the uncertainties of the industry would make projections beyond four years irrelevant to the decision now required. However, he is prepared to admit that if there is nothing much to choose between the two sites as a result of the four-year financial analysis, then the apparent better long-term future potential of site A might be relevant.

Student activities

Prepare a report for the management of Gower Enterprises Ltd which analyses and compares the figures for the two sites. You could use the payback period technique, the accounting rate of return, the net present value and the internal rate of return as you think appropriate.

Assume that not all the members of the management team are acquainted with these techniques and include explanations of the calculations and the significance of each technique for decision-making. Your report should end with a summary of your findings, a brief discussion of the value of your analysis and your recommendations.

Assume that the initial investment will occur immediately and that cash inflows will occur at the end of each year. Ignore taxation and depreciation and the realisation of assets at the end of year four. Assume that each site will continue in operation after the end of the fourth year and that in any case realisable value would be the same for each site and represent no significant change from the original investment value.

Format

Your answer should take the form of a report addressed to the managing director of Gower Enterprises Ltd.

Objectives

The student should show an appreciation and understanding of the use of specific financial techniques for decision-making.

References

Chapters 36 – 39.

Assignment N

Stonehouse Limited

Context

Stonehouse Limited owns a factory and, among other products, manufactures three different models of greenhouse:

Model	Code
Prince	P
Queen	Q
Regent	R

The budget for next year is given below.

Stonehouse Ltd
Budget for the 12 months to 30th June 19X3

Greenhouse model	P	Q	R
Budgeted production and sales	200 units	300 units	600 units
Selling price per unit	£897	£675	£567
Direct materials cost per unit	£234	£180	£154
Direct labour hours per unit	13 hours	9 hours	7 hours
Direct labour cost per direct labour hour	£5	£5	£5
Machine hours per unit	26 hours	18 hours	14 hours
Total indirect production costs:			£285,000
Total administration, selling and distribution costs:			£110,000
Allocation of administration, selling and distribution costs	£20,000	£30,000	£60,000
Buildings, at cost:			£200,000
Net current assets (average figure for the year):			£50,000

Of the total indirect production costs of £285,000, £150,000 is accounted for by depreciation of machines which are being written off on a straight line basis over five years. Because of this high proportion of cost, all indirect production costs are recovered using a machine hour rate which is calculated on the above budget figures.

Direct materials and direct labour can both be regarded as variable costs. Indirect production costs, and administration, selling and distribution costs can all be regarded as fixed costs. Buildings are not depreciated in the accounts.

Student activities

The company secretary of Stonehouse Ltd has asked you to answer the following questions:

i) Calculate the machine hour rate to be used for recovery of indirect production costs for next year's budget.

ii) Produce a profit statement for next year based on the above budget figures using absorption costing, analysing revenues, costs and profits for each model of greenhouse separately and in total.

iii) Calculate the return on capital employed (ROCE) produced by your budgeted profit statement. For the purposes of calculating the capital employed, machinery should be included at original cost value, before any depreciation.

iv) If the ROCE produced by next year's budget is less than 12%, by what percentage would the company have to increase its selling prices in order to achieve a ROCE of 12%?

v) a) Using a marginal costing approach, produce a statement for next year's budget showing the following:

- ❒ contribution per unit for each model of greenhouse
- ❒ total contribution
- ❒ total profit

b) Which model of greenhouse gives the best contribution per unit?

vi) Draw a break-even graph for next year's total budget (ignoring individual models) for the company showing the contribution obtained at all levels of activity up to the budgeted level of 1,100 units. Calculate and show the break-even point and margin of safety, both in terms of units and sales revenue, on the graph.

vii) a) The principal budget factor or limiting factor for production is machine hours. In view of this, how do the three models rank from the point of view of profitability? Show your calculations.

b) If more machine hours than are required for next year's budget become available, which model of greenhouse should the company produce more of to maximise profit?

c) If fewer machine hours become available, which model of greenhouse should the company reduce production of to maximise profit?

viii) a) By rationalising production methods and schedule, it may be possible to make another 1,200 machine hours available. The sales manager thinks it unlikely that more than 10% more of any one model over the budgeted sales and production levels can be sold. Produce a revised budget which utilises these 1,200 extra machine hours in such a way that profit is maximised. Use an abbreviated contribution format showing the revised production levels for each model of greenhouse and the resulting total maximum profit possible.

b) Set out in not more than 100 words any conclusion which may be drawn from your calculations.

ix) Produce a simple spreadsheet based on your answer to (viii) above which shows the following for each model separately and in total:

- ❒ revised production units;
- ❒ contribution per unit;
- ❒ total contribution;
- ❒ fixed costs and profit (totals only).

The spreadsheet should be designed so that production units, contribution per unit and the fixed cost figures can be altered and the resulting total contributions and profit calculated automatically. Print out the spreadsheet twice, once showing the figures as in your answer to (viii) above and once showing the formulae.

x) In no more than 200 words, list the ways in which you think Stonehouse Ltd could increase its profit next year.

Format

Your answer should take the form of a word-processed or typewritten memo, or a handwritten draft ready for typing by your secretary.

Objectives

The student should show an understanding and appreciation of:

- the management accounting techniques of break-even analysis, contribution costing with limiting factors and absorption costing, together with their employment in appropriate situations such as profit maximisation;
- the concept of return on capital employed;
- the basic principles of budgets;
- the basics of spreadsheet preparation and design.

References

Chapters 22, 27 and 32.

Assignment O

An investigation for a trade union

Context

A friend of yours is a shop steward with a major company. He has decided to give a 30-minute presentation to his local branch members on the finances of his company and asks if you will look at the accounts. He believes that the members have a sound knowledge of the business operations but not of the financial activities. The three topics he wants to cover in his presentation are:

- what the last set of published accounts show;
- what has been happening to the share price over the last three months;
- what the financial press have to say about the company.

He expects a number of questions to be asked following his presentation and has identified the following as possibilities:

1. Have here been any major redundancies recently or are any due in the near future?
2. What are our chances if we put in for a big wage increase?
3. What does *extraordinary profits/losses* mean and has our company had any over the last three years?
4. Would you buy shares in the company if you had the opportunity?
5. Who are the company's auditors and how much did we pay them?
6. What plans does the company have for new products or any major investments?

Your friend has asked you to help him by preparing some table of figures he can show the branch members, with notes explaining their meaning. He would also like answers to the above six potential questions.

Student activities

Select a major company of your choice to represent the company in this assignment and obtain a copy of its annual report and accounts.

i) Prepare a handout to be distributed to the union members. It should be approximately one side of A4 paper and give simplified information on the three topics of the presentation.

ii) Prepare graphs that your friend can adopt for overhead transparencies or flip charts during his presentation. You should also prepare accompanying notes so that he can explain the meaning of the graphs and highlight any significant points.

iii) Prepare answers to the six potential questions.

You should bear in mind the level of knowledge of the audience and their possible interests.

Format

Your answer should take the form of a word-processed handout, together with graphs and presentation notes for your friend and the answers to the six potential questions.

Objectives

The student should show an understanding and appreciation of:

- the use of accounting ratios to interpret financial statements;
- the structure and information content of a company's annual report and accounts;
- different sources of information on company's activities;
- the information needs of specific user groups;
- the presentation of financial information.

References

Chapters 9, 20 – 22.

Assignment P

Granny Smith's Stores

Context

Peter Smith is a sole trader and has owned Granny Smith's Stores for some years. The shop is basically a food shop but also sells newspapers, a variety of stationery goods and confectionery. Recently two other local sole traders have been declared bankrupt as a result of intensive competition from a new supermarket which opened in the area six months ago. Although his own business is solvent and trade is reasonable, Peter is considering turning it into a limited company which would safeguard his personal assets.

Peter has an accountant to prepare his accounts for tax purposes, but he finds it very difficult to understand his explanations of accounting matters. For this reason he turns to you, as a friend, and asks if you would be interested in drafting him a report for a modest fee.

Student activities

i) Prepare a written report for Peter Smith using simple clear language which will help him make a decision on whether or not to form a limited liability company. Your report should cover the following points:

   a) the advantages and disadvantages of forming a limited liability company;

   b) an outline of the main legal requirements affecting limited liability companies;

   c) the main differences between the profit and loss account and balance sheet of a sole trader and those of a limited liability company.

ii) Provide Peter with an example of the type of accounts any company he forms would be required to produce under the Companies Act 1985 (give illustrative figures).

Format

Your report should not exceed 3,000 words. The accounts should be prepared in vertical format and should be used to illustrate aspects of the report.

Objectives

The student should show an understanding and appreciation of:

- ❒ the advantages and disadvantages of different organisational structures;
- ❒ the regulatory framework affecting the reports of limited liability companies;
- ❒ the significant differences between the profit and loss account and balance sheet of a sole trader and that of a limited liability company.

References

Chapters 6, 10, 11, 20 and 21.

Index

Essential Elements

covering the **core** of **modular** courses

Essential Elements of
Management Accounting *Jill & Roger Hussey*

Contents The role of management accounting; Cost classification and control; Total costing; Marginal costing; Capital investment and appraisal; Budgetary control; Standard costing; Appendices.

ISBN 1 85805 103 7

Essential Elements of
Financial Accounting *Jill & Roger Hussey*

Contents The accounting framework; Users and uses of financial information; The cash flow forecast; The profit and loss account for a sole trader; The balance sheet for a sole trader; The financial statements of a limited company; Interpretation of financial statements.

ISBN 1 85805 091 X

Essential Elements of
Business Economics *Mark Sutcliffe*

Contents: The UK economy – an overview; Resource allocation; Business costs; The structure of business and its conduct; Small firms and multinationals; Wages and the labour market; Investment, R & D and training; National economic change and business activity; Money, banking and inflation; Economic policy and the business environment; The international dimension; Europe and business.

ISBN 1 85805 095 2

Essential Elements of
Business Planning and Policy *Jim Jones*

Contents The nature and importance of policy and planning; Organisation philosophy and objectives; Policy and levels of planning; Analysis for strategic planning; Choosing the strategy; Implementation of strategy; Evaluation of strategy; Framework of project planning; Project planning and control; Annual plans; Information systems for planning; Contingency planning.

ISBN 1 85805 100 2

Essential Elements of
Business Statistics *Les Oakshott*

Contents Survey Methods, Presentation of data, Summarising data, Probability and decision making, The Normal Distribution, Analysis and interpretation of sample data, Testing a hypothesis, Correlation and regression.

ISBN 1 85805 103 7

Essential Elements of
Quantitative Methods *Les Oakshott*

Contents: Index numbers, Investment appraisal, Time series analysis, Linear programming, Critical path analysis, Stock control methods, Simulation.

ISBN 1 85805 098 7

All titles in this series are approximately 128 pages long, and measure 275 x 215mm.

Cost and Management Accounting

An Active-Learning Approach

T Lucey

This book provides a complete teaching course in cost and management accounting. For details on the Promoting Active Learning series approach see page 4.

It is known to be used on the following courses: BTEC National Business and Finance; DMS; RSA; LCCI; AAT; CIPFA; Management and Supervisory Studies; Business Studies and Marketing courses; Access courses; Purchasing and Supply and other courses requiring a broad, non-specialist treatment of cost and management accounting.

Review comments

'The book lends itself well to students working on their own with limited class contact.'

'Plenty of examples, 'real-life' situations, opportunity for students to think and respond.'

'Very useful for A Level groups.'

Lecturers

2nd edition • 304 pp • 275 x 215 mm • August 1995 • ISBN 1 85805 127 4

Excel for Business Students

Using Excel for Windows versions 3 & 4

J Muir

This book is aimed at students who need to learn Excel 3 or 4 to acquire spreadsheet skills. Both Excel and its business applications are explained in simple terms, and the author has deliberately avoided biasing the examples towards areas where specialised knowledge of accountancy is required.

It is known to be used on the following courses: BA Business, Accounting Foundation courses, DMS, HND Computing, BTEC National Travel and Tourism, MSc Business IT, BTEC HND Business Studies, GNVQ Intermediate and Advanced Business.

Review comments

'Excellent – the only authoritative text on the market.'

'Well explained and illustrated, with good examples.'

'Excellent course book that will be used extensively.'

Lecturers

1st edition • 192 pp • 245 x 190 mm • 1993 • ISBN 1 85805 029 4

Finance for Non-Financial Managers

An Active-Learning Approach

A H Millichamp

This book provides a complete course of study in the areas of accounting and finance that students on many professional, vocational and degree courses are required to cover. For details on the Promoting Active Learning series app-roach see page 4.

It is known to be used on the following courses: BTEC Higher National, NEBS, BA Business Studies, DMS, professional courses (e.g. ACCA Certified Diploma in Accounting and Finance, IPS, IAM,

IM), and all courses (e.g. engineering, personnel, sales, purchasing, catering, tourism, etc.) on which students need an understanding of accountancy in order to communicate with accountants and implement necessary financial controls and plans as part of their management role.

Review comments

'Well structured, attractive layout and excellent value for money.'

'Excellent for use in a variety of modular courses.'

'Lends itself to use on student centred learning.'

Lecturers

2nd edition • 384 pp • 275 x 215 mm • September 1995 • ISBN 1 85805 123 1

Spreadsheets for Business Students

An Active-Learning Approach

C West

The aim of this book is to provide a 'user friendly' guide for students on the innumerable courses where acquaintance with the basics of spreadsheets is required. All examples have a business emphasis. For details on the Promoting Active Learning series approach see page 4.

The book can be used with any machine/system with Lotus 1-2-3 release 2.0 (or higher) and compatible spreadsheets. Specific instructions for As-Easy-As, VP-Planner and VP-Planner Plus are provided where commands in these programs vary from those in Lotus 1-2-3. The book can also be used with Lotus 1-2-3 for Windows (releases 1, 1.1 and 4) using the 1-2-3 Classic window (which provides the 1-2-3 release 3.1 command menu).

The book is known to be used on the following courses: BTEC Higher National Business and Finance, and Computing, BA Business Studies, ACCA, AAT, IPM, DMS, CLAIT III, NEBSM, CIS.

The lecturers' supplement is a copyright-free 51/4" (340K) PC-compatible disk, incorporating files in .WKS format for the models in the book, for checking students' activities.

Contents: Models include: VAT calculations, Cash flow forecast, Integrated cash flow forecast/profit and loss account/balance sheet, Accounting ratios, Cost behaviour, Cost allocation and apportionment, Cost-volume-profit analysis.

Each session contains: Objectives, Active learning, Sum-mary, Activities, Objective (multiple choice) test.

Review comments

'Excellent self-learning package.'

'Very good value for money. Just the right level.'

'Ideal for new modularised units – all activity based.'

Lecturers

1st edition • 192 pp • 245 x 190 mm • 1991 • ISBN 1 873981 83 7

Spreadsheets for Accountancy Students

An Active-Learning Approach

C West

The aim of this book is to provide a 'user friendly' guide to spreadsheets for accountancy students. The book is in two parts:

Part A Apart from minor amendments, this part is the complete content of Spreadsheets for

Business Students, as accountancy students starting from scratch need a foundation of these more basic techniques before concentrating on those aspects specific to accountants.

Part B This consists of a series of 21 models, some interrelated, covering financial accounting, management accounting, and financial management. Basic skills will be learned through applying spreadsheet principles to solve accountancy problems.

For details on the Promoting Active Learning series approach see page 4.

The book is known to be used on the following courses: BA Business Studies/Accounting, ACCA, AAT, CIMA, BTEC HND, DMS, MBA, many professional accountancy courses and accountancy degree courses, and accounting options on business courses.

The lecturers' supplement is a copyright-free 31/2" (720K) PC-compatible disk, incorporating files mainly in .WKS format for the models in the book, for checking students' activities.

Understanding Business and Finance

Edited by Jill Hussey

The aim of this book is to provide a course text covering the whole of the core subjects of HNC/D Business and Finance. It will also be of considerable value to business and finance students on other courses.

The opportunity has been taken in the second edition to update the chapters to take account of changes in legislation and economic conditions. Information technology has been given prominence in a new stand-alone chapter. This reflects its increasingly important role in business and its inclusion as a separate topic in a wide range of courses.

The book is known to be used on the following courses: BTEC National and Higher National Business and Finance, Certificate in Business Administration, ISM Diploma, CMS, HNC Business Information Technology, HND Business and Finance, BA Business Studies.

Contents: Accounting and Finance, Business Environment, Business Law, Business Policy, Employee Relations, Marketing, Operations Management, People and Organisations, Quantitative Methods, Information Technology.

Review comments

'Comprehensive, well explained and good value for money. Integrated assignments are very useful.'

'Excellent exercises and case studies'

Lecturers

2nd edition • 384 pp (approx) • 275 x 215 mm • April 1994 • ISBN 1 85805 079 0